The End of the Trial of Man

The End *of the* Trial of Man

✠

PAUL STUBBS

Arc
PUBLICATIONS
2015

Published by Arc Publications
Nanholme Mill, Shaw Wood Road,
Todmorden OL14 6DA, UK
www.arcpublications.co.uk

Design by Tony Ward
Printed by TJ Interntaional, Padstow, Cornwall

978 1908376 01 5 (pbk)
978 1908376 02 2 (hbk)

ACKNOWLEDGEMENTS

The author would like to thank Arts Council England for a generous grant towards the completion of this collection.

Special thanks go to Eden Kane whose support existed before there were any poems to support, and to Rosa Richardson for her unconditional friendship and support. Also to the following people: the author's parents, Blandine Longre, Michael Lee Rattigan, Mark Wilson, Anne-Sylvie Salzman, Alex Pearce, John and Hilary Wakeman, Rhiannon Shelley, Will Stone and Peter Oswald.

This collection is dedicated to the memory of the poet Matt Simpson (1936-2009) who, despite his own frequent critical bewilderment when reading these poems, was always warm and above all (the rarest thing) non-tutorial in his comments of praise.

Some of these poems appeared in the following magazines: *The Bitter Oleander, The Black Herald, The Shop, Le Zaporogue, The Wolf, Les Carnets d'Eucharis* and *Spolia* and in the anthology *The Wolf: A Decade (Poems 2002-2012)*.

Cover image:
Francis Bacon, *Study after Velázquez's Portrait
of Pope Innocent X, 1953*
© The Estate of Francis Bacon.
All rights reserved. DACS 2015

**Editor for the UK and Ireland:
John W. Clarke**

CONTENTS

*All the paintings which are referred to in the titles of
the poems are the works of Francis Bacon.*

For my Blandine

*"till the agony of nonspaces and
the wreckage of erasing times."*

BLANDINE LONGRE

"And what rough beast, its hour come round at last, slouches towards Bethlehem to be born?"

W. B. Yeats, 'The Second Coming'

"...Then, however, he saw something sitting on the pathway shaped like a man and yet hardly like a man, something unutterable."

Friedrich Nietzsche, *Thus Spoke Zarathustra*

"Long after the days and the seasons, and people and countries."

Arthur Rimbaud, *Les Illuminations*

THE PARALYTIC CHILD

after 'Paralytic Child Walking on All Fours' *1961*

*"Le Paralytique se leva, qui était resté couché sur le flanc, et ce fut
d'un pas singulièrement assuré qu'ils le virent franchir la galerie
et disparaître dans la ville, les Damnés."*

— ARTHUR RIMBAUD

                – On the day when
                man he fell back onto all fours
and crawled,
                the seed for you was born:
                two failed cells dividing in
                                the mud,
to produce what here, now,
today, we see here
                before us:
the lone spent eel of

                a child; without
                explanation, world,
or tail…
                crawling into and out
                of yourself, as if your
                                creator
                had removed it your backbone
                                like a pick
                from between his teeth.
                For you have been born

                of all human deaths,
even, yes,
                those wormeaten parts of you,
                (still visible) that died,
when, in you, a religion lost its faith…
                – yet half-gutted, and
                partly atrophied, it
                                seems

11

as though
you have just crawled clear of heaven?

      (before God he removed it
      the face-mask of Darwin)
      for devolution has forced
you free
      of the membrane of history
– The poise and the grace and the gait
of all ancient men,
      demolished
      by the one
      single revolution of your hip;

      species after species,
by the portent
            in your eye…
– So, is there perhaps some undiscovered
tribe or people,
      who, in their pockets,
still guard (religiously)
            a small wooden fetish
            in your image?
      carved perhaps in the first

      few days after the passing
of sin, once,
      in a church's vault, it was
discovered:
      the microfilm of a gospel
      too supernatural to view?

– Yet having now
      already seen
the last earth-bound creature crash
into the sea,
      and the eagle grow ill

      with flying, and with all
of the languages of the world now
      but unwanted pulp at
the back of
      your throat,
towards what new destination can
you imagine
      yourself now heading?
      – You, our planet's only
      anthropological first-born!
(as, in your mind, when you move,

the unused
      flesh from your limbs,
      it is hurled like clumps
of wet clay
      onto some celestial grid,
where, unrolled again, it is stretched
      back onto fresh bone…)
– So what in Nietzsche's or Blake's mind
prevents you
      from ever again standing up?
      Your body that forces every

extraneous muscle to twitch, day after

day, when as a child beast,
you crawl, crawl
        out from the landscapes,
into the now abandoned churches,
                temples of the world,
where your 'presence' explodes like
spittle onto the icon's lips! and where
the tilt of

                your head drops all known
                stares to the ground…

Until on that day
when your death
                it gives birth finally to our
                last belated truth,
on some dusty and deserted road,
or high plateau,

                where, in mournful rhetoric,
                all past experiences of man
are resolved,
        resolved,
                and never to be mentioned
                again.

THE ASCETIC ATTEMPTS TO SPEAK
after 'Portrait of George Dyer Talking' *1966*

– Since the epoch of belief it ended
     you have been sat here,
     uninjured by thorns, and with theology's
lapsed lesions beginning now to
     fall from your palms;
(and with the dials on all of your
     biblical breath-canisters
     working now on 'empty')
as faith to
                 a lost lunar
                 reef returns…
While your tongue,

          a syntactical stump,
it continues to de-alphabet the world and root you
always deeper into the mud of man's mind; you, silent
          and God-mauled,
passing again from atom to atom
              in prayer…
yet uninterrupted for centuries, it seems,
by nothing but
          the bone-bullets of your own
          slow religious death…

– So what possessions, if any, are
     left   here about you?
     only
     the few torn scraps of papyrus at
your feet,
     on which are written the last
     words you've *needed* to say;
     you, today, wearing Adam's
own first ears
     as headphones, and with

  his imaginary dummy-torso
  sat upright onto your knee,
  as if to ventriloquize
yourself back into biblical speech;
   as, for you, all that exists is
   perfection and your eternal
   failed search for it
   – So what have been the results
   of such a painstaking wait?
Only
the daily build-up of phlegm
  beneath your tongue

  of the gutturals of Yeats'
  rough beast,
that, and the volume of sand passed
through the hourglass to match the
   concentration of your face...
   – Yet every hour of every
   day you've been attempting
    it, speech,
while stretching the flesh
  of Christ's last look across

  your skull, like a balaclava,
  so as to disguise yourself
from yourself
  when prowling the church-sized
  silences of your mind;
while those who still believe in you
  on mountain tops and in
  secret caves (in meditation)
  they hold it their breath,
not wanting to inflate (too early)

your diaphanous and post-
world

lungs…
– Whole civilizations clearing their
throat to allow you to speak;
so, for you to ever actually
speak again
just how many new gods will
need first to be discredited?
and
age-old churches boarded up?
(as, at night, a no-bibled
mannequin, you push past
yourself

into
the dreams of the deaf,
where
onto the high hushed
hills of Golgotha,
you hand back to him Christ
your microphone
and
lost ear-plugs for the cross…)
– Your tongue, a brake
then on theology?

Yes, and on epochs; for when
you do eventually speak again
the flags of the countries who
listen will shred inside of
your fist, the icon-heads of
their leaders shatter, as

17

at your feet finally all nations
        bow... – So on what day then
might you actually
           speak?

On the day
        when God he hauls in
        finally the human nets
and (to his surprise), amid the
        heaped-up rubber skeletons
        of the saved and the
trapped, yet still flying skins of
        the poor, he relocates it:
the still mouthing contraption of
        your jaw...

GOD-BODY PROBLEM (RESOLVED?)
after 'Fragment of a Crucifixion' *1950*

"Beginning and end greatly deceive us."
– F<small>RIEDRICH</small> H<small>ÖLDERLIN</small>

Hooked up high above the window, a torso

(failed by every congenital language) swings;
it is the final allegorical act: to switch off its
        soul-filament, at last!
to remove in man (briefly?) the necessity of
        either birth *or* death;

(to trap the wick of the sun between the
wrought mental-pincers of the worm and
        cast off man's extinct
        shadow onto the moon...)

Man who ploughs on still regardless into
the street below; bowdlerized by sin, the day-
to-day, the herd! Until this moment when
        God he attaches wings
        finally to the human mouth

        and flies back home the *word*...

AFTERWORLDSMEN
after 'Triptych' 1991

> *"Thus I too once cast my deluded fancy beyond mankind, like all afterworldsmen."*
> – FRIEDRICH NIETZSCHE

BEYOND MANKIND

– An irregular rib, and the susurration of un-
used diaphanous muscles beginning now

                    to twitch;

your rib rupturing the larynx of the priest
when, in church, he mentions the afterlife;

                    as by unbiblical verdict

and outside of kairic time, you, you quick-
canister breath, re-lung humankind for

                    the upcoming exertions
                    of prayer;

with your new spinal bone-gears now
struggling to select a gait that's human

(and Christ's face, unlamenting in your heart),

as all of your sins and all of your failings,
they revert back
                    finally into goals…

DEATH-LEAP

– A battalion of fled polytheistic gods shredding
now your sinews, lacerating your leg-tendons

and muscle-tissue;

as, superearthing our species, you overcome
yourself, your flesh, by *refusing* to breathe

and by out-imagining

man's final evolutionary increase in brain-size;

that, and the sense suddenly of God, post-eternity,
beginning finally to age,

noticing his own now
terminal wounds…

AFTERWORLD

A heavenly amputee and an urnful of limbs,
wanting the future, the present and the past

to cast back theology onto the sundial…
as, in you, each everlasting lung collapses,

forcing the saliva of a now post-religious

language onto your lips;

and cobwebbing your skull with each now

21

forgotten galaxy, nebula, star-system etc.

> (to begin the final celestial process
> of correcting man's shoulder-blades)

– until at that point in no-time, when
belief itself expires, and the vertebra of

Nietzsche it is discovered, abandoned now
to every last Christian
> pulpit on earth...

THE BIRTH OF THE THIRD REICH
after 'Triptych' *1976*

for Blandine

"Primordial, eternal man, the primal monist, catches fire in the glow of his ultimate image, an image under the golden helmet."
— GOTTFRIED BENN

1

On the day when, in man, anthropology
it died, and the Aryan race (atavistically)

it failed to hold its ancestral breath forever...

(the bark from the trees in Eden peels back
now to reveal only unused human bone)

– So either the germ-free, or a politician,
but the last, on earth, to survive it: the

> loosening in the heart of
> the bloodclot of Christ;

while the furies, in chaotic order, screamed.

2

An encroachment of primordial doppelgängers
challenging the torso of the still unresurrected

> Christ to become their race;

as from the chest of the petrified protruded now
only the tomb-rushed and incongruous cages

23

of our (still) too far-away
worlds…

this, and the siphoning off of the gold of the
Holy Grail, and the cross-splinter in the heart

of the atheist that made him turn, if only
theologically, in
God's direction.

3

One profile, a million selves, as the geology
of all cosmological continents began now to graze

the shin-bones
of this beast…

(false gods, in order to be heard, re-stringing
the tendons in a priest's palms for prayer)

as the rhapsodic and the helmeted tugged
down violently upon the
ripcord of each celestial lung;

(resuming the collective and biological break-
down of the flesh and bone of all moral things)

– Until when in the future, and the rebirth again
of the galaxies, and a hologram of man is
projected back onto the

surface of every known and un-
known planet in the universe…

THE PRIEST KEPT ALIVE IN PUBLIC
after 'Statues and Figures in Street' *1983*

"A splinter of wood holds my two swollen eyelids apart."
— LAUTRÉAMONT

        I still remember the
        hour on which they
        locked me into it this
glass-case; it was only a few
days after
        the churches, temples
        and mosques were
        boarded up; forcing me
to watch
        it

forever:
        the final theological
        drift of the peoples of
        the faiths...
those who every day replace a lost
congenital mannequin, with themselves,
        to pray, to what must remain
now *imageless* and / or *ever-hooded*...
        for on earth, I am the
        last surviving priest!

        listening here only to
        the thud of God's skull
cratering the dustscapes of my soul; I,
        an atavistic no-zone in flesh,
        an atom in space unsheathing...
But above the hose-sustainable hell of a new Jerusalem,
        at least one hundred
        thousand years from
                now?

(where the resurrected are reduced
to weather-beaten torsos in the brain)
And where today, to my chagrin,
I am kept alive by electrocution
                    and
                    ice!
and / or by my own bone-juggling act of infinity!
          – So, I guess, this is it
          then? yes, the future

          of immortality (gene-storms
          and bright supernatural masks)
          and my exposure to it, what?
          the final smouldering ash-tray
of the mind, the burnt-out ends of
          theology, species, icons, race...
– But what else to do inside of such a
          small space?

          well,
                    daily,
beneath a microscope I begin to crucify
each still 'religious' cell, to obliterate
          any last syllable of self...
          for on the day that I was
          lowered down into here,
somebody *hooded* removed it
          my most inconclusive rib,
          so that, momentarily, I

          resembled it, perfection...
          – But the feeling didn't last,
and soon they were replacing it with a
          prosthetic tube, a rod, a pin?

Yet still, each day, if only to
spite them
(using a phial of blood from
my days as a working priest)
I attempt to
                    bleed back God

                    into my flesh!
Whilst in my dreams I construct
the most impossible hydraulic contraptions,
          incredibly high scaffolds from
which to crash-test the dummies
          of *all* future Christs... – But no,
          very little here changes, not
          even my delusions, as I, I peer
          ever more mortally into the
                    street below;

          (hearing now only the scuttling
          away of the trinity, as if insects
          trapped inside of the cardboard
          box of my ear)
          as the time-zone
for the scabs on all chiliastic wounds
expires, and the zero in my eye implodes.
          – So remain here, remain here
          I will, condemned now only to
          watch for
          an eternity

          those plucked souls...
– Until when in the end-times
          of nanotechnology,
          and the second, final, and

robotic Christ he arrives, arrives
to save me, by smashing it
        this glass, and by re-wiring
        them these hands,
        until I myself, finally,
I pray to him…

EN ROUTE TO BETHLEHEM
after 'Study of Human Body from a Drawing by Ingres' *1982*

The beast he makes a detour, plunges
into the Irish sea, heads for the base

of Ben Bulben, where one religion later,
we catch up with him, slumped

      against the gravestone of Yeats –
      horrified to be left alone...

SINCE THE DEATH OF YEATS

after 'Landscape near Malabata, Tangier' *1963*

        – You have been wandering
        off course, untraced and Arkless,
somewhere in Africa,
        feigning Being, in the ebb-tide
        between predestination and time...
and with only the sun's struck cymbal
        crashing inside of your brain
        as a guide...
        you, you move on, day after day,
imagining

        already ahead of you
        (in anticipation of your arrival)
        the telescopes and binoculars
poised and set up in Bethlehem, from every
window-ledge, bell tower, church...
        you now amid these malarial swamps
        (stopwatched by eternity)
        and whirlpooled by a forever circling
        orang-utang,
                hyena, bird;

        – for there is nothing here
        now to console you, time itself
is reversed by your diasporic path,
even
        villages close up are, to you,
        already far-off, burnt-out and smoking...
        man grows ill just to think
of you
        – And because you are too old
        and

too young to exist in any
one single era,
any living creature that meets the clock-lapsed
circle of your eye
will (today?) instantaneously die, decay,
become extinct…
nothing can survive your survival;
or wear it,
your
face a preternatural
mask.

– Yet some days when bored, inactive and
in search
of a language, *any* language,
you attempt to speak him, Yeats!
but swallow only your own tongue,
choke nearly to death on his umbilical;
you who on earth seem more
Tyrannosaurus Rex than beast; (despite
in rib-years being
something still of

a biblical
anomaly) but knowing
now that
your flesh will remain un-
wrinkled by the eternities
in Yeats's mind…
– you, you have now no other
choice but to plough on,
for amid the theomachy of religious
battles, wars, conflicts etc.

you have seen off the ubermensch,
        the ancient and Roman gods,
        have gangplanked the saved
                out of heaven;
        you who with one single stare
        have bulldozed whole civilizations
                to the ground.
        – But to deceive God again
        in yet another new century?

        well, you will need first
        to seek out a suitable alibi;
before, in haste,
        (but without embitterment)
        you kidnap and entrap a priest,
        ventriloquizing
                his jawbone
                back to lies…
– So, as on every other day
                then

        (but for the last time)
        you, you retrieve it:
the still smoking cone of a gyre,
and place it (a shell) up to your own
ear to
        hear (as always) only the
        soul-summoning cry of Christ,
the flame-cocked gun of
war
        – until then when finally

alone at night in the desert
and
        clawing up at the moon:
        where abandoned now by
your creator,
        and feeling still 'incomplete'
        you, you give up on him, Yeats, drag
        back your head and laugh,
regurgitate finally
        his phlegm-sodden drafts...

THE BIRTH OF GOD
after central panel from 'Triptych inspired by the Oresteia of Aeschylus' *1981*

for Eden Kane

"...you, enamored
of such an enormous revolving bosom"
— CÉSAR VALLEJO

1ST HOUR

Barely you, but you, cultivating an ache,
wondering who just opened your eye,

and with your increased stump-torso
spinning round and round and round,
attempting to elbow itself across into

    the first universal space;

and creating, by mistake, in your abdomen,
    a still-born lunar race...

before then the tearing of the first celestial
    membrane, and hydrogen
    inhaled,

as, from your still subcutaneous udders
    secretes now our
    future human blood...

2ND HOUR

Only an unconscious cranial longing for the
untimely search for life

and a scab, pre-Christian, chafing your flesh,
unable, as yet, to
                    perfect the wound;

(the galaxies to come and their lung-free races
unable to be resolved in your rapt temporal lobes)

as, out from the darkness, float by the still
lignified vertebrae
                    of God's aborted...

(silence a cathedral still travelling towards you
from the furthest finished point of the universe)

While you, ignoring clay, delay all shapes,

outhearing your own
                    ear to begin words.

3ʀᴅ HOUR

– A teleological torso, a latticework of pores
and the one diaphanous muscle flexing in

                    the blackness to produce love,

as the first of your unholy guttural noises
are uttered, forcing you to create now

                    (involuntarily) the upper diaphragm
                    and palate for priests,

and the *obiter dictum* for a species not yet
                    born...

35

But assuming now their gait, and imagining
                now their face,

as round and round and round you spin,
unable yet (at this black moment in time)

to summon up
                religions, humankind, or sin…

TWO FIGURES, 1953
for Ingrid Soren

"Perfect, unforseen beings will offer themselves for your experiments"
– ARTHUR RIMBAUD

Today, the cage finally built,
the bodies born and ready to
                    fight.
– So now, all to be done is to decide
                    which one of them
                    will be Judas which
one Christ (the winner?) for these
are still the early,
                    crippled, pre-world days
                    – with at my ear (still) only
the perpetual whirring of
                    nothingness,

(that undetectable
grinding-machine
                    which I'll never switch
                    off)
of which no future bone will escape...
                    – Because, as yet, everything
                    is adrift, in flux, abeyance etc.
                    with this, this fight being
my first official
                    experiment to select

                    a shortlist for every biblical
                    character of creation;
for even heaven
                    itself, today, it is no more
                    than a dust-wire filament;
while Hell, as yet?

only an ice-pick
(wrapped in tin-foil)
I've still to bury underground…
– And with no idea yet for any kind of a wound
or scar to appear
onto the flesh

not one of these two bodies
will deceive the other into
believing he is winning!
as each, from the other, attempts
to wrestle back my image.
So, listen in, for this is what (anywhere)
has so far happened;
here, now, today,
in this cage, and on this
bed!

watched by those
in the audience with gills still
in the side of their necks!
(having myself not yet decided
which, if any, will survive the
flood)
for with the um-
bilical cord, as yet, only the
rope with which to hang the
idea of man,

I am still not yet sure on what
exactly this fight will depend?
(with the clay for their faces
still to dry upon my hands)
for even my ideas for a planet

are, to me, but a small pebble,
           flung free (occasionally)
from the tide of some
           unstoppable black wave…
           – So what you might ask are

           my plans for myself?
no, none, nothing! only the reoccurrence constantly
           of a vision inside of my head
           of two long planks of wood that,
when crossed, will
           be required (some day)
           to withstand the weight
           of at least one of these two
           forms…
– So how long will all of this be expected

to last and
to what end?
           (as the first migratory mannequin of
           Adam, from a failed planet, returns…)
But still I rejoice in it,
           the day on which my idea for the
           universe arrived:
for I was busy still shattering it, bone! (from the giant
           white iceberg of my thoughts)
           and unrolling it, yes, sheet
           after sheet of unused human flesh!

           (and while
still in two minds about some character with horns?)
           So now then, at last, the victor
           of the first fight is announced;
my first biblical de-

cision it is made.
– But tomorrow? tomorrow, it will begin all over again:
                with the next two contestants,
                and the same unimpeachable result
                – for this, clearly, is my mind's
                only recognizable outcome;

                to produce them, this cast,
before the one insignificant sun! – And so, right now,
                this is how,
in these the earliest of days, my plans for the
                whole of creation will be
played out – Until then, when, (finally?) every
                last character for the contents
                of a bible has been picked;
picked, though not
                yet tricked by the Gnostics
                into believing in me...

THREE
after 'Three Studies from the Human Body' *1967*

– Between religions, we locate them, the trinity,
(three aging and anticlimactic gymnasts upon a pole)
inactive, bored, lost in conversation: impatient

for the retrial of man...

AN ADAM (AND AN EVE)
after 'Two Studies of a Human Body' 1975

for John and Hilary Wakeman

"And no one knows what's happening to him. He feels
The shadowy shapes of those who once were here,
The ancients, newly visiting the earth."
— Friedrich Hölderlin

— At least two thousand years before
the earth was biblically complete,
the two of us,
        myself and Eve,
        arrived:
two ill-starred lumps in the dirt;
        with, all around us,
        only the papier-mâché
moulds for
        the rocks

        that will one
        day inhabit
                the earth;
for, as yet, even the sun above us
is,
        in a theological sense, a mistake,
        burning up centuries too early,
                to char and char
                at our skulls…
                the both of us then:

        super-celestial shapes?
        yes, but growing still
impatient for a fictional and / or fricative
                religion (at the speed of
                the destruction of vellum)

42

to inform us
        of just what or why we are.
        (Opening our eyes onto a one-planet crime,
        to endure an ageing process *born* of sundials,
and of a God unable to lend us horns. Us, rib-free,
        in this double century
        of animal and mankind; *today?* abandoned
inside of the no-candled lair, of a human stare...
                amid the plains of flame receding,
                and our still unused ancient skulls)
– But having

not yet finished reading
        that scrap
                of papyrus at my foot,
the muscles in my limbs
        they must remain unformed,
still atrophied...
        – and because the fossils
        of our tongues they will
never
    be

discovered

        in the correct geological
        time-frame,
neither of us will be allowed to
        historically speak,
        (no matter how doubting,
profound or prophetic our words)
no, not myself, nor
        Eve sat there brooding
        upon that swing

with a look upon her face that no
future skeleton
of Satan will be able to negate;
he who, in failing to replicate
evil, will succeed
in only outer-perfecting the
mind – So what will be said behind
the future-backs of theologians
that, in us,

today, we did not actually
feel?
– Here, upon these dust-carpets of grief,
savaged in morally muted motion
by a still unthinkable will, an *us*
widowed and rejected by an unripe human heart: (God's?)
but where is he? for today, in this place, all to really do
is look up and watch them:
(like comets sent hurtling
into sky)

the still-burning vertebrae
of the Adams that failed once, it was
decided,
they would not outlive the rib…
– So what sensation, if any,
is left still inside of me?
only this,
this pang for the self-immolation
of light
which, in man, will one day

become a religion, a cult…
that, and the telescopic servility

of our faces, bodies, flesh etc.
as, at my neck finally, I feel it, the
error of the halter of the leash of my
own quite impersonal god...
       (Myself: a weight-lifter
       of shoulder-blades and
       of a long *pause* in dust)

       – And so our days here then
they *must* continue to grind on: incomprehensible,
feckless and forlorn – until when
in the future, and the last genealogical
       Adam arrives,
       born of the then
       lapsed biblical gene
       of temptation, and
       final fossiliferous
               fall into sin...

THE AWAKENING (EVOLUTION OF THE PIOUS)
after 'Figure in a Mountain Landscape' *1956*

"all the holy places of the earth coming together around one place."
— FRIEDRICH HÖLDERLIN

When to the bottom of the only
primordial bog left on earth sinks

the one remaining womb-born rib;

as the impossibility of life-come-
after-death it is resolved, by the

      incongruous twitching of
      a muscle in a priest's leg...

(all *unbreathed-in* lungs now inflating and
counter-breathing
      man into his second phase)

– as mask-clotted tribesmen, in rows, at dawn,
they adjust and readjust their spines

      in an attempt to locate
      truth's one eternal gait...

      *

– A new scabrous breed of religious men
out-praying the palms in Christ's head,

      to rib-ruin and unzip the flesh
      of the millennarian blood-line...

at the exact point in history when *unwrinkled*
again, man, (to postpone another resurrection)

      he places it a thin stone
      wafer onto his tongue;

(forcing God's one superabundant mannequin
to re-enter
      the atmosphere of the wrong planet)

–And with only the amputee, on the twenty-first
century battlefield, in the tingling of his
      stump-limbs, left now to
      understand the sensations

      of the heavenly on earth…

         *

– Faith locating its final fragment of papyrus,

the apostate, in giving up all practice of prayer,
retiring from both hand gestures *and* God

– either in Africa, or in the Bavarian alps,
but a place of the one alien pietà:

      the 'Son of Man' cradling God's
      only cosmological successor;

(all of the bibles of the world unable to
      confirm now their doctrines)

– until when the Homo sapiens, *talked* back
to the origins of his first splintered speech,

he despairs all over again for the world…

      outlining with a stick man's new
      metaphysical condition in the dirt.

POPE II, 1951

Today, in theological sadness, we struggle to imagine
the muscles of a mouth that could produce that yell.

At this dark hour, in which *we* also experience it: the
thud of your chair finally touching down in Hell.

THE POPE DEPARTS HIS HEAVEN
after 'Study After Velazquez's Portrait of Pope Innocent X' *1953*

It was just
after the announcement,
        over the tannoy,
        that religion had ended,
that I felt
        the overwhelming
        compulsion to depart
        it, heaven.
– And why, still, today,
        in this chair

        I descend.
– But whose voice was it
bellowed out such an edict?
        nobody knows;
only that, to a man,
        like sheep, the majority
        of us concurred;
yet all now I remember
of that day

is the avalanche of no-limbs,
and the crush, yes, the crush!
        and how also the angels,
        in formation, they closed
        ranks,
holding up their wings, like
        iridescent shields,
        to reflect back God's
        light into his eyes...
– But now, here,
each morning

         still I can hear it:
         the whirring of
those giant celestial turbines,
         as God he flicked
on that inestimable switch…
         – So, the human body
         in paradise? a lampshade,
to cast off from you only your
most theological gait!
         – And so what then now for

         an apostate like me? only
the following tasks:
         to find and seek out just
         what tyrant or despot
absolved them, religion, faith etc.
         and to somehow regenerate
         it, the still atrophied tissue
of my muscle, cartilage, sinew;
         that which
         when away, I never used…

– Yet everything about my departure
out of heaven seems to me to be
         a trick? a hoax?
         and one never to be understood;
         like my flesh now
that re-wrinkles with the
         age of Christ if, on
         earth, he had survived
– but what other accoutrements
         to be found upon me?

Well, only the two things:
a piece of rag,
            and cleaning fluid,
to scrub
            and maintain Hell's boilers!
            – As along the wrought
            mental-wires of my brain
            vibrates now the voice of no God;
                        no, only my
                        own voice,
            my undertaker's, and my flock's.

            – So look now deep into my eyes
            (past the pupil, retina, iris etc.)
into the slowly thawing refrigerator
            of my soul, where my own still
            rotting limbs are preserved
            – for paradise, elysium, heaven,
they existed, yes,
                        before God's birth!
            before the great uncut canopy
            of man's flesh, it began even
to strain

            the guy ropes of his imagination…
            – But whether true or false, or not,
            this has been, for me, the quite
catastrophic consequences
                        of somebody
            ending it: my religion.
            – And it is because of such unholy
            consequences
that I am descending
still today

into this blackness;
for it was at the
precise moment
of that announcement, over the tannoy,
of religion's end,
that I felt so compelled to
depart it, heaven.
The very same announcement
that still forces me here today
to grieve; grieve, and by a very
few degrees, again, each day,
believe?

EVOLUTION
after 'Chimpanzee' *1955*

Today, like a cancer, attacking the tissue of my heart,
extending my brow-bone, rending each muscle apart;

reverting my objectivity back to will, and reconstructing
my vertebrae to about two-rungs higher than man;
as now, unexpectedly (as if by a sudden genealogical
                    increase in brain-size), I, I stand up,
                    look around, but remain lost:

born finally into a race still without pre-destination,
                    only another botched resurrection
                    between the shoulder-blades.

THE NEW BIRTH OF MAN
after 'Landscape' *1978*

"If the 'clever animals invented knowledge' *in a remote corner of the solar-system on a star, and if after a few short breaths by nature the humans died, and the star froze, how does nature live on without being recognized?"*

— Rudiger Safraski
Nietzsche, a Philosophical Biography

HE ASCENDS THE EARTH

– On the day when, on Mars? an astronaut,
dusts back into view the footprints of Judas...
                    (forcing History itself to expire
                    and every failed civilization,
                    empire, race, to huddle together
                    inside of a post-historical cave)

never to be discovered (hidden by the episodic alphabets of breath)

                    As up into and through the neck erupts
                    our final cosmological and evolutionary gill!
(collapsing at once
                    all second-guessing lungs)
and with the ultimate size of the human brain reached
then when (only seconds before man, at pelvic level,
                    he abandons his
                    ancestral fuse!)
                    God bites down hard upon
                    his son's most
                    (in)human tongue...

(the human vein re-strung and unwound
          by the mental minotaur, to re-abandon
man *in* space, and to the original spluttering
          outboard motor of his mind...)

55

– From a word-drafted and clock-stopped world,
the etymologist, every hour, is exhumed, when
                on earth,
the final splintering stump of language is
                blacksacked, never to be re-used...

                for one involuntary jerk
                of a head (anyone's) *now*
                and the flesh from the *'Future of Man'* it
                                would stretch back
                                across God's scalp...
(all failed or failing atavisms, on our hips, to continue
then to rattle, eternally) – Or until when (again?)

        man he paper-clips the face
            of Adam onto his cranium and sandwich-boards
                the spaces and lunar-voids with *'Modus Vivendi'*

                        'Age
                        Of
                        Reason'
'Fundamentalism' etc.   this, and the *last* phase of man,
                        post-theology, when incapable now
                        even of sin, he contemplates only
                        the worm's one endogenous world...

Having *borrowed* the crutches of an accidental gait
to sway and sway a once membraned world into
                    zeros and gulfs;
                    (the earliest mud of the calendar
                    world now 'glass-cased' to mimic
                    a *second* earth and a *lingua franca*
                    so fictional it re-sets in motion

God's only artificial spinning-top of the world...)
Upon the highest accessible crag in the universe?
                    where all of the atheists now
                    synchronize their watches
                    to begin their final count-down   on eternity...

                    to begin a sudden cosmic
                    explosion of vertigo, as from

                    each of the most pivotal peaks
in our solar-system: Olympus Mons, Mount Everest, the Empire State...
a mannequin of Adam,
                    in place of us all, it is hurled...

(the universe forced momentarily to recreate for itself
a makeshift and temporary God) – Until when finally a satellite,

lost, adrift and blackened now by every impossible sun,
it re-enters the atmosphere of our world: a space-suit,

                    containing Christ's bones...

BANDAGED FIGURE AT THE BASE OF A CRUCIFIXION
after 'Three Studies for Figures at the Base of a Crucifixion' *1944*

        – Not you or the two on
        either side of you can
understand your position here;
        for it seems, perhaps,
        that you must be part of
some new kind of trinity,
            grounded.
        Forever to
        endure now, wind, dust,
               rain etc.
– And it

        is to such conditions now
        that the three of you have
returned, and will go on returning,
           until when you with
           bandage you manage
        to theologically walk;
        for like a dis-feathered
           angel,
        continually you fall over.
– But because you exist here today
without hope

        it appears still that at every
        scene of human degradation you
arrive:
        to hold the knife,
        load the gun,
        bowdlerize the bible
until finding the words appropriate
to the act;
        for all that remains here
        of the saved is their skins,

flayed,
>that you, you wear now criss-
>cross across your back;

>for what you are thinking of here
>it is not being acted out by your
>>attenuated trunk;
>>like being abandoned
>>to an echo-chamber
that returns only unwanted body-parts,
not sounds,
>your torso it flexes now with
>muscles as yet only

>imagined inside of your creator's
>head; and (onlookers aside)
it is because of such anatomical
ideas
>that you are attending here this
>crucifixion of our second Christ...
>– So how far in the future might
>man ask is this? here, where
flies, in broken ranks,
>they fail

>eternally to negotiate the
>dead;
theology here for you is not any-
>>>>>kind
>of a ritual or sermon, no,
>it is only yourself with cranial
bandage (covering the wounds of
>your recently severed ears)
to disguise
>yourself

from that somebody who decided
that you no longer needed to
listen out for it:
        the thud of Adam's own
        body after the fall...
– for either way, to you, there
is only your insides, only the
physical inward contortion of
        your 'I'
as you, you retract back continually
before no sky;

for everything here is not you,
nor him to the left of you with
tubular outstretched neck, nor her
to your right, who seems but an
        alternative Mary,
        half-fleshed
and caught out, seemingly unaware
of this new and bloodless
        crucifixion...
these three selves are only the
bifurcation of your one sensation,
        thought, smell etc.

though constantly in the air is
displayed a panoply of new blood,
(as if a geyser was intermittently
erupting from Satan's deep and un-
        stoppable wound underground)
– And it is to this experience that
the three of you have returned,
and will go on returning, until
        that day,

sometime
in the future when another
deity

he will, perhaps, be fixed up
high upon a post above you;
you, who, like the biologically
deficient part of a trinity, have
been
forced back here to this place; the
same two also on either side
of you, here, who it has to
be said will surely never again depart.
– Depart, or watch another resurrection,
for at least a millennium,
start.

STUDY FOR A PORTRAIT OF VAN GOGH V, 1957

Today we locate him, Van Gogh, lost, walking
an imaginary dog into his own head,

holding back his colours upon its leash.

FIGURE IN MOVEMENT, 1976

"The monster looks at heaven, without seeing it."

– János Pilinszky

Each day, he arrives,
to redefine and reinspect
me this prospective God,
monitoring my progress in this
cage, this celestial lab;
for I have been born
of at least ten centuries
of theological debate;

to become this, what
you see here before you today:
the improbability of
a future multi-cellular
Adam? yes, but what
might you ask of this black arrow
tattooed onto my side?
well, quite simply,

this arrow it points to that
spot on my body where
my rib will have to be removed
once, as expected,
the last human fails
to reach perfection;
for ever since the decline
of the human race, I've

been subjected
to every theological
test;
have endured the skin-grafts
of the bodies of the saved,

63

having watched
them grow back
        over my own skin

        (once paradise collapsed)
        and because I cannot yet
fully walk,
        it is as if the lower half of
my torso
        has been 'decreated'
as if the natural atavistic reaction by my
        body to the declaration in
the latter half of the nineteenth century
        that God

        was in fact 'dead'
        – But barrel-chested
        and age-mockingly slow,
I'll prowl on, with the blow-torch of this
        God's eye in my brain.
– Yet no priest (surely!) ever dared imagine
        anything like me!
        suspended as I have been

        between the Homo sapiens
        and the beast,
with underneath me the trapped scraps
of the last few extant pages of the bible...
        as, from hour to hour,
        I, I swing back and forth
between soteriological worlds,
        circumventing the self

by using each newly grown
bone as a hinge...
        – Yet bent over as I am,
        three-quarters of my body
        react (I imagine) to the
weather conditions of at least sixty-five million years ago!
        Likewise, at the back of
        my throat (because of
        the age-old practice of

        glossolalia) I feel
still the voice-infected stubs of at least
a hundred never-to-be-spoken tongues!
        – So what then of me would
        a new god be expecting?
        perfection? calumny?
                        ordinance?
        not one prayer has ever
        yet managed to find out...

So now then all to
        do here is wait, day in, day out,
        until when this god finally
        he abandons me, upon
his planet's most inhospitable plain;
        and thus *allow* flesh again to
become it: what? the first celestial deaf-mute,
        so lame and tongue-tied,
        before the cloud-darkening
        absurdity of his voice...

MONKEY AND THE ATHEIST
after 'Figure with Monkey' 1951

Since my birth I
have remained
here; hour upon hour,
orphaned by mankind
from my own species,
being (perhaps) their last Darwinian
experiment for
a biblical past?
– Yet I know of my own kind,

for every day at
the same time,
this atheist, in disguise, arrives
to inform me of
it: my past, and
of the fallacies of his world;
in this cage, in this
pit, where, every day,
he attempts

to place it: the
body of Darwin,
onto the incredulity of my tongue!
– So where exactly
is this I'm being held? a secret
underground vestry
of the Vatican?
a straw-cell in a zoo? Or simply
some laboratory?

yes, possibly,
for I exist (it seems) simply
to keep *him* the atheist alive!

and vice versa,
as, occasionally, he breathes for the
both of us!
inflating, incongruously,
my non-created lung;
for without civilization, he, he

would be me!
(without of course
the flesh-struggle of immortality)
– But then on some
days, I imagine I
have become him, man! Standing up
straight suddenly
as if ready to speak,
dictate a speech, or worse,
incite a war! that or

(as myself again)
bring religion to
its conclusion by ghost-shaping
the gait of Adam;
suppressing within
what, to him, would
be deemed most probably a sin
– for evolution to me?
it is only my anti-body!
that which prevents me

(when in two minds)
from surrendering to it,
my will. – So what
then is the point of my existence?
resigned as I have been

for centuries to this cage,
and this strange man
who begs me to ignore them:
religions, bishops, deities?!

– And while also being subject
each day (every day)
to my keeper, this atheist,
attempting to grab me from behind
to perform on me what
he, he calls the 'Heimlich Manoeuvre'?
to remove God's lodged
word from my
throat!

– But no, for with no monkey
Christ to convince me of
monkey heaven, and
with no monkey bible in which
one day to appear; it seems
then that I might be required
to stay here forever!
– Until a time, perhaps?
one day, when man

(accepting the exact
difference between us)
will be forced to cement it,
our alliance;
will be forced finally
to admit it: our common
need, our same
uncomfortable yearning: for
the devotion of a beast...

LYING FIGURE, 1969
for Alex Pearce

"Can an eternal consciousness have a historical point of departure?"
—SØREN KIERKEGAARD

You again, today, another Mary,
heaving past the last masked

trunk of theology on that bed;
as if wrist-roped again by Eden's

       forgotten vines...

(But in this your latest body, and
in yet another century)

– While on every stone clock-face
outside of Jerusalem, a *back-to-front*

       eternity it chimes...

      *

Your birth-cries dropping Christ onto all fours
in the afterworld's of Pascal, Kierkegaard, Kant,

when from the palms of every new-born
atheist juts a thin nail-shaped bone
       (to pre-empt and dis-
       card a second cross)

as each now unbelieved-in godhead,
hooked up inside of a cage, in some
far distant corner of the universe, they

69

mimic the twice-torn
contortions of your face.

*

Two thousand years of the Eucharist
reduced back down to pulp upon your

tongue, as your labour here begins;
        while all animals

now roaming the grass-lands of the earth
look up suddenly expectant, scanning

        the heavens for their
        own still missing god...

(a temporary biological miscalculation)

– Until the Pope, in chasuble, at prayer:
he hears it the rib snap like
a twig inside of man's chest.

THE UNSAVED
after 'Man Kneeling in Grass' 1952

*"Humans could soon find themselves in an impoverished environ-
ment different from any in which they have ever lived."*
                                                    – JOHN GRAY

– A now rapacious primate, driving the
Taoist, the Christian, the Hindu and the Muslim
back onto all fours, and forcing a new plague

                    of people to sandblast
                    and overwhelm the rib;

(*without* a god the world, pre-judging the pelvis,
unwraps the linen of Christ from foreign bone)

– Until when at least a million cold years from
now, and a million cubic kilometres away,
(onto an eschatological and lunar terrain)

Man he rises up again, freed finally of the
                    microbiology of religions, and
                    coterminous continents of sin.

71

LOST TALE FROM THE APOCRYPHA
after 'Man Carrying a Child' *1956*

"Being by Calvary's turbulence unsatisfied,
The uncontrollable mystery on the bestial floor."
– W. B. YEATS

– A child who, kidnapped at birth, is then
carried off in secret to a rib-ruined town

(to invoke and make fly the unbiblical,
the talon-blunted amputees in paradise)

whilst in Bethlehem, in haste, a few hours
after, the miscarriage of Mary is confirmed.

RELIGIOUS MAN PREPARES FOR PARADISE
after 'Figure in Movement' *1978*

"Who, once saved, dares still call himself alive?"
                                                                          – E. M. CIORAN

– Upon a far-off and fictitious planet,
            an unclassifiable race
removing (as one) a face-mask of
            Christ when you, from a
            hypothetical wound, bleed…
here, now, today
            with your arms outstretched,
as if preparing to fly… – So with what
            final act of obeisance then

            to propel it, your body?
            You, today,
            carrying the cross of the vertebrae
of every passer-by;
            and feeling now only
the one rib short
of Allah, Brahma, Buddha?
            – But while still not yet
            sure what is to come,

            you see only the botched biblical
            gaits of you,
            the *unused*
            mannequins of your mind…
            for no new celestial lung will
persuade the astronaut to take off
            his spacesuit, and *breathe*…
while Heaven after Heaven refuses you…
            and the wrinkles begin to

appear now
            onto your flesh equivalent

to at least an eternity spent
here on earth...
    – So now then, to defy it,
         gravity,
    to suck on and to inhale
    a canister of Christ's own
         breath,

    to snuff out flesh,
    and forget bone...
yes, in this, this bibliomancy of our
        bomb-
        born age...
– So what else have you attempted
    to depart here?
    martyrdom? heresy? execution?
    no, only this: (in your imagination)

the construction of a prayer-machine
    (flesh-gloves for hands
    fixed to a bicycle wheel)
that, on rotation, can endure at least
    twelve separate pairs of
    palms (at the same time
    of different faiths...) – But
your own worst fear here? that your
dust-phials onto the *wrong* planet

    will be smashed, lifting up the
    visor of your oblate skull to
reveal only an incongruous God; as inside
of you, you feel now only a terrible vertigo,
    as if another 'you' were about
    to take an aerial photo in Hell...

          – But with
          the sails of your creator's lungs
          still only at half-mast

          (for the duration of your mouth)
you breathe for him,
          sustaining his presence in
          unanswerable air!
          while attempting (always) to locate
it: the hidden human
          hinge within...
          Your sieve-sizes in dust
then outpouring him? yes, and your

          end-self,
          when the cellophane of the
          sky it is stretched back tight
across your skull
          (for the period of putrefaction)
so as to pre-
          serve (forever in your mind?)

          the last lost look of man...
          – So your body beginning
now to

slough
          off its infinity of skins,
          as all terrible and discredited
          faiths of your not-quite anatomies
begin at last to stall;
with nothing, nothing left to say now on
earth then but 'sin, sin...'
          – as, finally, you experience it:

75

theology, crash-test
your dummy within…

THE APOSTATE
after 'Figure with Meat' *1954*

"*It is the time of the gods who have fled* and *of the god who is coming.*"
– MARTIN HEIDEGGER

In church, today, we encounter him, the priest,
struggling to confront Christ's skeleton there,

struggling to sit out God's decomposition in a
                    chair…

THE ABSTRACT CRUCIFIXION
after 'Painting' *1946*

"And air and time cover
The terrible one, so that not too much a man
With prayers shall love him."
                    – FRIEDRICH HÖLDERLIN

– It was on this day,
            the day of the crucifixion
            of our clay-aborted Christ,
that I felt
            the closest in my life
            to believing in some god;
            I, the eternal amputee!
who yearn never now outwardly for
            the phantom of

            a celestial limb!
– I, born of only the lower jaw,
            (the upper half having been
            sawn-off and ditched at birth)
because of the decision made for me to utter words
            of only the *one* syllable,
            such as:
            'death' 'spade' 'soil' etc.
            stood beneath this umbrella,

            (to protect myself from the
            fragments of your God's own
shattered *word*) – Here where we,
            we crucified him the least
            ceremonial Christ of them all!
(a hypothesis of sin a hypothesis of all)
In this, this old abandoned warehouse,
            this rusted tin-shed vestibule!
            where the screeches

        still rupture the eardrums of
insects and where spiders in corners
        weave incalculable webs, then wait,
(no matter how long it takes) to
        catch themselves a Christ...
        for an hour has passed now
        since this creature breathed
its last, yet
        no invisible curtain has ripped,

        and only the orchestrated feigned
        response of a *no-body* rippling a
a sheet of metal to produce thunder has
        acted out a role;
for this icon he will rot, and rot and rot
        (whether anybody believes in him
        or not)
– But yes, I did place to his lips a sponge,
        soaked in the impermanent breath

        of a priest! for no act of
barbarous denigration is too much for me!
        as overhead, our father the
        butcher, he pulleys round hook after
hook of cold, rapt and pincered souls;
        but just to maintain the rank
        unflinching boredom of ritual,
some bread is handed out, first to
        a cherub, wingless, rotating its
stubs...

        then to an apostate, oblivious, still
        listening to his trinity hop, skip
and jump the last artificial inches of his
mind...

79

for out of the teeming ten billion
men of humanity, this *lassoed*
Christ might just as well have been any
of them! he was not special.
What with his hypermodern crown and

scrubbing brush and disinfectant
to scrub clean his rubber-wounds
of worms;
for on this day, the day of the atheist,
the calligraphic earth it
will not give up its dead! But will bite down
only the harder upon its bones;
so say I, the cataleptic crucifier
of this pest; yes, me, with fictive

and heuristic yellow flower in my lapel (to denounce
Eden and all adjective faiths)
for this is the day that *we* the

atheists will never forget, the day on
which the nails are hammered back in,
(forcing in-human clumps of flesh
back onto the *first* celestial wheels)
causing the sweat of Darwin
to seep back into my every pore!
– And so this then, for centuries
on earth,

will become our daily spectacle;
to remember *him* our carbonized
Christ that died;
we, who, here, believe in *no* god, but

who have nevertheless decided to
crucify it:
this genetic-proof trunk of a deity
that never really actually existed,
existed, or died to survive in the minds
of the blest...

PARALYTIC CHILD AND THE FLOOD

after 'After Muybridge – Study of the Human Figure in Motion – Woman Emptying a Bowl of Water and Paralytic Child on all Fours' *1965*

– A woman emptying the final rusting bucket
of the Flood; as, in these, these post-diluvial

days (between man and his next *named* form),
you, the child, arrive, impatiently circling

the steel perimeter railings of the void;
while God (in two minds?) he kneads

                still furiously the
                gills on your neck...

THE THREE FINAL PHASES OF PERDITION
after Untitled *c.1958*

For Michael Lee Rattigan

*"The morality that would remove man from himself is the morality
of decline par excellence."*
                        – NIETZSCHE

THE UGLIEST MAN

– Your no-breath, and your last-breath, im-
parting but not swaying the final greying hair

                on Christ's head;

the fabric of your flesh re-threaded back into
the human-loom when, in your imagination,

                you *refuse* to
                experience pain;

as now unborn and pre-emptied of worms,
you from yourself suddenly are dragged

(as if at the conclusion of a corrida) towards
                the next great century,
                religion, species, birth…

with each unageing appearance then only the next
set of body-parts: teeth, ears, eyes to arrive;

as inside of your capillaries, and in the division
of your cells, your ancestors

                they breed and breed
                to preserve your will…

THE HIGHER MAN

– On top of a mountain, a holy miscarriage,
and the blackened docetic wrappings of the

after-birth of Christ left now to snag (eternally?)

upon a rock;

(man's heart abacus worked to zero by faith)

as along the lung-frayed and heaven-fed rope
that connects one failed race to the next, you

(by obligation) crawl;

before though the biblical and diachronic
lapse in our language, or the sand-loosening

of God's own gait
at your heel...

that, and the one atavistic bone-trap, from
which you (daily) rapt, and brain-desolate,
step free...

THE SECOND BIRTH OF MAN

A makeshift hymn, an instant nation and the end of sin,
when consciousness, to the dice-throw, is loaned;

as all mythological births (to protect our past) expire,
and the clay on the old idols begins now to crack

when, into the worm's mind,

trolley after trolley of the new luminous busts of
              you arrive...

              (to switch on, by mistake, Hell's sprinklers)

as all human flesh unwrinkles a millennium a second,
to pre-date and pinion self; (time's stylus having

travelled the rings on every tree, beginning now
              its journey along *your* spine)

– until upon that day when (today?) no ancestor will
be able to follow you, the multi-cellular, the
              preternatural and the eternal,

splitting into their own
              now animal-faced processions
              at your heel...

HEAD I, 1948

"A mind enclosed in language is in prison."

— Simone Weil

I did not see
the one who abandoned
me here – He was,
however, somebody who must have forced me
        to look up and follow
his departure into the sky. For I do
        it still –
And for that reason alone
        I am

unable now to turn my
head more than a few degrees either
to the left or to the
        right – When I speak my words they
        are whisked immediately
by my tongue into a scream,
                                a prayer.
        And with my head being
        only half-finished, it
seems that

        not even the curator of
        a theological museum would accept me
(preferring things as they
do to be *forgiven*, or, better still,
        unjustifiably extinct) and
having of course only the one string
        attached, I can be no God –
        But what's left in this wire-cage, cubicle, void,
are no objects at all
        (though

it is not hollow)
– everything I say in here
does not come back to me. Like the head
of a man who speaks only
in echoes, I wait, each day, in vain
for the return of my always
migrating jaw…
– And it is just this
kind of restriction of space that so appalls
me. And so

what else you might ask could
be lying next to me? Only this:
a spirit-level containing Christ's
own blood to keep me upright;
that and a magnet
to keep the fragments of the few remaining
planets in tow.
– But everything here is
in the wrong place

– language here for me is
not grammar, syntax, cadence etc.,
it is only my mouth
deployed at such an angle, as to allow
me to masticate on
only the necessary of words;
look up close at my neck
(not at thyroid, muscle, pulse)
but at

my veins circulating now with
the ink of the one who has most accurately
described me. – An apostle or

a saint maybe?
But either way, there is no universe
            around me;
            this is it, the last
place to inhabit,
anywhere –

            there is nobody else around
            (though on my tongue dissolves
            still the body of the last
            person to ever see me)
our *lingua franca* has evolved,
not because of my bestial gibbering, but because
            of the mouth of the body
            that has been reteaching me to speak;
            for my mouth

            it was broken-in originally
by the words of the Apocrypha. But at least
            now there will be no more
            talk of extinctions, last days,
            judgments etc.
And it is for these reasons alone
            that I am unable now
            to turn my head more than
            a few degrees

            either to the left or to the
            right.
For there was that time when somebody,
            he forced me to look
            up
and to follow his departure into the sky.
That same somebody

of course who once
abandoned me here. I cannot remember
his name.

DEATH OF UTOPIA
after 'A Piece of Waste Land' 1982

"O dark dark dark. They all go into the dark"
                                    – T. S. Eliot

On this horizon that overshadows all,
above the last known clump of Eliot's

world, between the human reeds and
the beached broken pelvis of the wind,

         snags still the last few
         pages of his book...

(the grave-mould from the burial of what
false god now falling from the palms?)

– upon a jut of always steaming earth,
where tomorrow man, for the last time

         will arrive, to give birth to it:
         his eschatological foetus;

in end-times, when Hell is certain, and
Eliot, not Christ, he rots back onto the
                 grass...

THE SCREAM
   after 'Study for the Nurse in the film "The Battleship Potemkin" ' *1957*

To this day still
         you can remember it,
         the first time you opened
your mouth to scream; it was at
         the birth of pain, the moment
the human wound
                  secreted blood,
                  and fused…
– for subsequently
                  since that day

         you have continued
         to do it; for every second
of suffering on earth is, to you, an
         abomination, horrific! Hell!
– and because of such a supra-human
reflex, you,
         still, today, recoil from everything
         – even your DNA exists
         only to divide
                           and

         multiply along the length
         and breadth of your tongue,
so as to create another
                  even louder one!
– While now, here, today,
at your feet,
         only the heaped-up jawbones
of all those
         who tried and failed

to outscream you! Yet still,
on every day, from a great
distance, you hear it, a beast, earless,
encroaching, creaking the
floorboards
of your imagination...
– and whilst
the dumb, revulsed by your abilities
they spit out eternally only

the pulp of each failed
sentence,
the deaf (a now clandestine and
underground organization)
in their dreams, each night, they
bury you, bone by bone, to prevent
your shrill...
– for in you, the past, the present and
the future, like different-sized
stones

descend;
dropping it, your body, to that pitch
in celestial-time
where even Christ's wounds assume
scabs...
and where the horripilation of the
soul's hairs is
on permanent show;
– for no god, or *deus ex machina* is ever
likely to descend

now and replace you;
here where every failed resurrection it

leaves stretch-marks across
your flesh!
since birth, your rib, like a tuning-fork
        has vibrated with all future
cries – yet sometimes, your premonition
        of the horror of all future
        events it allows

        you to intervene
– like when you yourself watched him, Judas,
as a child,
        practising that kiss, in a barn,
        upon a basketwork dummy of
        Christ...
– likewise from Cain's hand (a hundred times)
        you removed it, that rock,
whilst from the Führer, try and try
        as you might,

        you could not rewrite them:
        the placards of his brain!
– And because of a life of such incessant
screaming,
        you can have no offspring,
        your red-raw womb
gives birth
        only to miscarriage after
        miscarriage of ten-tongued
beasts!

– So, now, today, your remaining ancestry?
        It consists of only the one
indigenous tribe who, each year,
        (as a ritual) in secret,

gather to sacrifice
        one new ear in your name!
– chronology, thanatology, patrimony,
        do not reside in you; not
        until when the final

        genocide arrives, and
        from that gibbet, your own
God-born body it swings, swings…
        a metronome for the ages!
So on what day then might your screaming
stop? on the day when suffering ends,
        and you, you hide it, the abacus
        (for the body-count) away…
– when, repositioned in paradise, you
        get

        finally to unscream them:
        the words that, to the priestless God,
will not then require a jaw…

MEN ON HIGH PULLEY-CONTRAPTIONS IN MID-AIR
after 'Triptych' *1970*

– Now and forever, we'll witness them: the
'Saved' (Pope and fellow clergyman)

above the debauchery of the human bed,
amid the high vaults and buttresses of
their church, where, each day, in secret,

they prepare for it: the weightlessness of heaven…

THE ADAM RESURRECTION
after 'Lying Figure in Mirror' 1971

    – Between the warzone and
    the word, and man's last-
groping sense,
        our need for you arrives:
the jolt and jarring of the mould;
to allow now
    today
(in lieu of man?) the rebirth of muscle,
    cartilage,
    bone;

    a poultice of flesh
    slow rising like dough,
or as if
    the ripcord of each lung,
by God,
    from the insides had been
pulled:
for man has died twice in you
to triumph over his ancestors
– But this time,
        no, no rib,

only (intermittently) in your lower chest,
    an ache of holiness
whenever,
    to mankind,
    you digress…
– here, where to the nearest biblical
    decimal
    your voice today
    is retuned.
– For all of man's ancient screams of

            courage, death, despair
            have, by the deformity
of your ear,
            been made now superfluous;
with the drool
            and the trickle of saliva at your
mouth-edge
                        all that remains
                        of God's guilt...
– So, the suppression of what
            sensation, in animals,

            prevents us from
            becoming you?
you, who,
this time,
            in your upper arms will
            need to be strengthened,
due to the effort
            required of Nietzsche
            when, with spade, he
buried God...

– likewise
at the base of your spine, a new set
            of bone-gears, in
            which to switch
 (in a time of any great genealogical crisis)
between walking
            upright and on all fours...
– yet what senseless
            fasting by an ascetic
of some
            secret underground sect

has, in us,
today, created a hunger for a body
        other than Christ's
        upon man's tongue?
        – this confrontation between
        the flotsam and the internal;
when even
        the froth and the pulp of
        the epileptic's never-to-be-
        spoken words might, in a
priest's mouth,

        become his most holy?
– So, this time, to become a success,
        You will need to draw from
        the scabbard of a *defeated*
oracular body,
        the blade of a barbaric
        and unimaginable 'I'
– to modulate a God-contested
self born of *all* neuter deaths;

and with an ability now to self-regulate
        the colour-pigment
        of your own skin,

so as to enter into any new society,
        race, and fit in…
and with a sponge already inside of
your fist that wants to erase all trace
of us,
        from every wall of every cave;
        – to purify man of man,
yes, and to feel it: the twinge in your

calves' pass that once was us;
       as clay,

          unused after divinity, it becomes
          free once more to remould…
– at the exact hour your body becomes
untraceable again:
          by hypnotism, fossil, myth?
          amid the drift of every geological
          plateau, shelf or ridge,
where (until our fateful hour) your testament
          will remain unread,
          unsaid, and not to be
                    stuttered on earth.

RETURN OF THE IMAGE
after 'Studies of Figures on Beds', 1972

"This is a law of fate,that each shall know all others,
that when the silence returns there shall be a language too."
— Friedrich Hölderlin

– Outside of *is*, and as far from Christ as *near*,
(the semi-verbal, the germ-free, and the primeval,
      upon each bed)
     Where the human face,
         a tray of blood it ripples,
         ripples into the face of God,
         Near is
              And difficult to grasp, the God.
(the only antecedent of the one-planet mind)
the alien and poweless visage, unfettered,
retractable as a visor drawn back from *man...*
         where
the fake skulls of
        Dasein, the Hegelian, and the *'Either / Or'* implode
        explode
and scream back into the lost mouth-grille of the author...
or to whoever out-perfects
        what survives on the breadcrumbs of atoms,
        and on silence *incarnate* –
        (this age of those
known *only* to each other, and by what a god's tongue in them has
                          loosened)
        the *too young* here in lieu
        of the Human 'us' who, from every
        humanless history, return...

        return and remouth our
        alphabets to the womb: the now
        anti-biblical in place of man.

ELYSIUM

after 'Triptych' 1974-77

"In the end, man arrives
at a sandy, sad, moist plain,
looks around musing, and with his
clever head nods, hopes for nothing."
                 – ATTILA JÓZSEF

1

The last man, upon his knee, watching
theology expire in the birth and death
       of flies;

as all of the secrets of the universe, from
a scroll, in a phylactery, are opened,

       inside the brain
       of a termite…

while Gethsemane, in a sand-drift, is postponed.

2

Two horsemen, in the distance, re-saddling
the carcasses of History.

Today, upon this coastline, opposite humanity,
(where a gramophone, to plastic trees, plays 'wind')

       and the one equal phial
       of Christ's blood is

redistributed throughout the combined pores of man;

       to start the stopwatch of the palaeontologist,
       upon the saved.

3

(In an amphitheatre, or never-emptying coliseum)

A quantum mechanic and a polytheist
meeting to decipher both religion and sin.

"I am going to burn" squeals Satan in front of
them "the lungs of each and every one of you!"

      – Ignoring him, you, the last man:
      re-birth the biblical
      in the roll of a dice.

LAST DAYS

after 'Three Studies of the Human Head' 1953

"The last living men, pricked by a thorn, could feel no pain."
— INGEBORG BACHMANN

When the priest he inspects the murderer, the rapist
and the thief, for any tangible trace of himself, howling

out each hour in despondency: "Move on, doppelgängers!"
His personality having long since been eroded by sin.

THE END OF THE TRIAL OF MAN
after 'Blood on the Floor' 1981

"Man is a beast of prey."
              – OSWALD SPENGLER

Upon these floorboards, amid the blood and
the death-throes of gods, the 'rough beast' has
eaten its last, has eaten and spat out man's rib;

              eaten and spat and stamped
down its feet onto the now crushed and un-
recognizable face-mask of Yeats:

              one mile outside
              of Bethlehem...

PAROUSIA

after 'Three Studies for a Crucifixion' *1962*

'*Things fall apart; the centre cannot hold.*'
— W. B. Yeats

I

Inside an ante-chamber (or secret backyard
entrance to a church?) arrive two figures, in

which one (indefinitely) holds out in front of
himself a key,

as if to let each one of the trinity back into
that room
    where, Mary, she rots uncontrollably
    onto a bed...

II

A carcass re-birthed, the two thousand year
old foetus of Christ pickled back into a jar;

as, high overhead, an eagle and a vulture
    circle (mistakenly) above

        those parts of man that have
        yet to spiritually arrive

— the rib meanwhile, a baton, passing from
        one wrong hand to the next.

III

Today, in Bethlehem, a theologian

beginning to bowdlerize this birth;

as the trinity, one by one, they
begin here finally to disperse,
          forced now to go their
          own individual ways

(the sarcophagus a place to hide the
last crossless secrets of the afterlife)

– until God, upon a catafalque, retires,
shouldered back over the charred

black-stubs of Eden, after the fires...

PAUL STUBBS lives in Paris. He has received different awards for his writing from the Society of Authors and Arts Council England. His second collection, *The Icon Maker*, was published by Arc Publications in 2008, to great critical response. His poems have appeared in a variety of magazines, including *The Bitter Oleander*, *Poetry Review* and *The Shop*, and he is also a reviewer for different publications. He was invited to read his poems at the Seamus Heaney Centre in Belfast in 2008 and in New York in 2010. He published a long poem, *Ex Nihilo*, in 2010 (Black Herald Press). He is also the author of two original plays: *The Messiah* and *Perfect Little Monster* – the latter based on the relationship between Rimbaud and Verlaine. His latest books include a long poem, *Flesh* (2013), and a book of essays on Arthur Rimbaud, *The Carbonized Earth*.

Paul Stubbs is the co-editor of *The Black Herald*, an international literary magazine based in Paris.

http://paulstubbspoet.wordpress.com

A DOG OF YOUR OWN

Also by M. A. Stoneridge

A HORSE OF YOUR OWN
GREAT HORSES OF OUR TIME

"Dignity and Impudence" by Sir Edwin Landseer (1802–73). (*Courtesy of the Tate Gallery*)

M. A. Stoneridge

A DOG OF YOUR OWN

ILLUSTRATED WITH DRAWINGS BY ERIC GURNEY

AND WITH PHOTOGRAPHS

DOUBLEDAY & COMPANY, INC.

GARDEN CITY, NEW YORK 1979

LIBRARY OF CONGRESS CATALOGING IN PUBLICATION DATA
STONERIDGE, M. A.
A DOG OF YOUR OWN.
INCLUDES INDEX.   1. DOGS.   I. TITLE.
SF426.S76   636.7
ISBN: 0-385-09931-2
LIBRARY OF CONGRESS CATALOG CARD NUMBER 76-42402

Acknowledgments

So many associations, publications, and individuals have contributed to the preparation of this book that it would be impossible to mention each of them by name (although many are cited in the text). To all I am immensely grateful.

I am especially indebted to those who generously contributed not only knowledge and advice but also a considerable amount of time: Frederic McCashin, D.V.M.; Mr. Herbert L. Cohen, L.L.D.; George Whitney, D.V.M.; Mrs. Dorothy Page Whitney; Mr. John Falk; Mr. Nigel Aubrey-Jones; Mrs. Gladys C. Steinkraus; Mrs. Ellin K. Roberts; and the staff of the American Kennel Club.

Finally, I cannot refrain from adding the traditional author's tribute to "those without whose inspiration this book would never have been written":

Thank you, Dandy, MicMac, and Zorro.

M.A.S.

Dogs have been recorded as guardians and companions of man from earliest history, as in this Babylonian frieze (1900 B.C.). (*Courtesy of the British Museum*)

Contents

One of the dog's first roles in human society was as a hunting partner. Assyrian frieze (645 B.C.). (*Courtesy of the British Museum*)

Preface

Nothing in life can quite compare to the experience of owning a dog. Listen, if you have the chance, to a group of dog lovers reminiscing about the dogs in their lives, and you will hear tales that range from high comedy to epic heroism, accounts of fantastic feats of intuition and deeds of devotion so poignant that they bring a tear to your eye.

What is there about dogs that is so special? Why should dogs have acquired a privileged place in human society instead of apes and monkeys (who are smarter), felines (who are more beautiful), birds (who are easier to care for), or horses (who are more useful)? What is the reason for the present worldwide infatuation with dogs?

The most special thing about the dog is probably the fact that he is the only animal to have freely chosen man to be his friend and master. Other domesticated animals have had man's domination imposed upon them. But we have every reason to believe that the dog joined human society as a friend and not a captive. Moreover, he is the only animal in whom domestication has become an inherited factor. Although many creatures, such as horses and elephants, have been tamed for centuries, each infant must be tamed anew. Other animals, like lions and wolves, can be tamed as infants, but revert to wilderness when they reach maturity. But a dog, even if he was born in a field or forest, instinctively seeks a human environment and a human master.

No other animal is so adaptable to our ways of life, nor so responsive to our wishes, even to our moods. No other possesses the same instinctive

desire to please us. Most touching of all, and flattering too, is the fact
that the dog is the only creature who voluntarily abandons his own spe-
cies in order to live with us. His devotion and responsiveness, his simplic-
ity and spontaneity, are perhaps more appreciated than ever because
they are qualities that seem to be disappearing from modern human
relationships.

Our unique friendship probably dates way back to the Stone Age,
when wild dogs sought food and warmth near prehistoric man's fires,
then inside his caves, offering assistance in hunting and guarding in ex-
change for shelter and a share of the game. Fossils and cave paintings
prove that dogs existed and lived with man at the time of the Neander-
thals, over thirty-five thousand years ago. There are pictorial records of a
Spitz-type dog dating from the Stone Age, and prehistoric canine bones
have been found in Denmark and Switzerland near to human fossils, in-
dicating that dogs were already domesticated. The dog, you see, is not
only man's proverbial best friend, but also his oldest one.

Four thousand years before the birth of Christ, the Egyptians, who
were remarkably gifted animal trainers and probably the first selective
breeders, so appreciated the special quality of dogs that they worshiped
a dog-headed god they called Anubis, and they named the star we call
"Sirius" after a dog. They even mummified and entombed beloved
canine pets alongside their masters.

The Aztec and Mayan Indians worshiped stone idols in the forms of
dogs. The royal lion dogs of ancient China, alleged ancestors of our small
Asiatic breeds, were sacred too. The early Greeks and Romans cherished
dogs as companions and also exploited their aptitudes as hunters, guards,
and fighters. Oddly enough, the early Jews and Christians seem to have
been rather indifferent toward dogs. The rare Bible references to them
merely distinguish between different types and breeds, and recommend
that all dumb creatures be treated kindly and protected from oppression.
Later famous Christians, however, loved and owned dogs, including St.
Roch, St. Louis, St. Anthony, St. Francis, St. Hubert, and St. Patrick.

Tapestries and paintings of the Middle Ages frequently show dogs as
hunters and companions to kings and queens and lesser royalty. Some
European breeds were reserved exclusively for the aristocracy.

The great Renaissance painters often included dogs in portraits as well
as in scenes of battle, hunting, and village life. In the eighteenth century,
it first became fashionable to own a dog, and many present-day minia-
ture breeds were developed during this era by selectively breeding down
the existing natural breeds to a smaller size.

The Ancient Romans used to advertise the presence of a guard dog in their homes with a mosaic plaque like this one, which often bore the words "Cave Canem!" (Beware of the Dog!). (*Courtesy of the British Museum*)

On the North American continent, prehistoric wild dogs certainly existed as they had elsewhere. Canine fossils found in the Jaguar Cave in Idaho have been estimated, through radio-carbon analysis, to be over twelve-thousand years old. The American Indians were accompanied by dogs when they migrated to the North American continent from Asia, and many local breeds were developed by isolated tribes. However, our native canine population descends mostly from those brought here by the Dutch, French, and English colonists, and by the Spanish conquistadors. (The first recorded one was a Spaniel passenger on the *Mayflower*.) Since then, we have imported dogs from all over the world in increasing numbers, with the result that the dog population of the United States is more varied than any other.

While we can trace the history of the dog through recorded evidence, his biological evolution is still a matter of conjecture.

He is classified as a mammal, a carnivore, a member of the *Canis* family along with wolves, jackals, and foxes, and, more precisely, as *Canis familiaris*. According to one theory, these animals all shared a common ancestor in the *Tomarctus,* an extinct mammal who lived some fifteen-million years ago. According to others, the dog descends from either the wolf or the jackal, perhaps some breeds from one and some from the other. They are certainly all very closely related, because dogs can be bred to either wolves or jackals and produce fertile offspring.

Whatever his early evolution, natural selective breeding, based on survival of the fittest, gradually produced many changes in the ancient wild dog. As he migrated or accompanied his master to different natural environments, and as he was called upon to adapt himself to different living and working conditions, distinctly different types of dogs gradually evolved, just as some human races developed dark, smooth skins and black hair in hot climates; pale skins, fair hair, and hirsute bodies in cold ones.

Incidentally, the animals closest to the primitive wild dog surviving today are the Australian Dingo, its near relation the "singing dog" of New Guinea, and the semidomesticated Indian pariah dog, all of them probably direct descendants of the Indian wolf.

When survival was the full-time occupation of man and beast, the dog's most valuable service to humanity was as a hunter and guard. So these primitive dogs evolved into two principal types:

GUARD DOGS, who were big, strong, mastiff types, with a keen nose and sharp eyes, the intelligence and memory to distinguish friend from foe, the courage to fight off intruders, and rugged coats to protect them from injury and harsh weather. Gradually, the dogs who guarded herds and those who went to war developed different mental and physical aptitudes best suited to their respective roles.

HUNTING DOGS, who varied considerably according to the natural conditions in which they worked and the game they chased. In desert regions they became tall, fleet, smooth-coated animals who hunted by sight. In woodland and brush country, they were smaller, agile, rough-coated, resistant, and they hunted by scent.

COMPANION DOGS may have originated from puppies who were too small or weak to hunt and fight with the men, and so were kept at home by the women and children. At least, this is a reasonable supposition, judging from their appearance, which was a small-scale version of

Many Medieval tapesties and paintings show dogs as hunters and companions to kings and lesser royalty, as in this illuminated manuscript, *Le Livre de la Chasse*, of Gaston Phébus, Count of Foix (c. 1405). (*Courtesy of the Bibliothèque Nationale*)

Nicolas de Largillière (1656–1746) included two royal pet dogs in his portrait of "Louis XIV and His Heirs." (Many modern dogs might approve of the custom depicted here of leashing children and letting dogs run free.) (*Courtesy of the Wallace Collection*)

the guards and hunters. As we have seen, keeping dogs as pets is a very ancient tradition.

Later on, selective breeding by man accelerated and perfected Nature's work—first of all for practical purposes, then for sport and pleasure. Farmers, soldiers, sportsmen, and dog fanciers of various personal tastes and interests, attempted to perpetuate what they considered to be the dog's most desirable physical and mental traits. The early canine types branched off into many distinct breeds more specifically suited to different functions. Different cultures seem to have developed most successfully breeds of dogs that reflected their own personalities and interests, like the hunting and racing dogs of Great Britain, the resourceful farm dogs of France and Italy, the fearless, disciplined guard and hunting dogs of Germany. Now that many modern societies appreciate dogs

A Fifteenth-century companion dog. Detail from the tapestry "The Lady and the Unicorn" (1480–1500). (*Courtesy Musée de Cluny*)

more for their esthetic, emotional, and behavioral qualities than for their working abilities, it will be interesting to see how this new role affects the future evolution of the dog.

By the middle of the nineteenth century, a group of British dog lovers decided that it was time to ensure the continuity and uniformity of the best existing breeds, and founded the first kennel club in 1873. (Since they never expected it to be followed by others, it did not occur to them to call it the "British" Kennel Club.) Its activities included formulating a *standard* (a detailed, ideal description) for each recognized breed, maintaining breed registries, and governing competitions in which superior examples of the different breeds could be designated and honored. Aside from the fact that the Kennel Club was dealing with many breeds instead of a single one, their ideas and goals were similar to those of the horse lovers who had created the Jockey Club a century earlier, in order to improve and promote the Thoroughbred horse. So, you see, kennel clubs, registrations, dog shows, and the rest are not merely matters of snobbishness and social standing, as some people believe. They serve a serious, worthwhile purpose.

Soon afterward, in 1884, the American Kennel Club was founded along the same lines, and other countries followed. From among the estimated 300 dog breeds in the world today, the AKC recognizes over 122, more than any other national club, regularly adding to its roster as new breeds, mostly breeds of foreign origin, qualify for registration. The AKC also registers more newborn purebred puppies than any other national club—about a million a year—although this represents only a small percentage of the canine population of the United States, which is estimated at forty million and is constantly increasing. We have the largest dog population in the world, proportionately as well as numerically: one dog for every six citizens, compared to one for every nine in Great Britain, and one for every seven in France.

Very few of these forty million dogs still perform the work for which they were originally bred. The vast majority are kept as pets. Nevertheless, if you want to get the most out of a dog of your own and offer him the best chance of leading a happy, healthy life, it is useful to learn something about his biological and historical background, and to take into account the environment and activity for which he was originally bred.

Of course, you do not have to read a book in order to learn how to acquire a dog. You do not have to read a book in order to learn how to care for him either, if you are endowed with a minimum of common sense. But, as with so many other things in life, the more you put into the proj-

Madame de Pompadour; like many eighteenth-century courtiers, was often accompanied by her pet dogs, as in this portrait by Drouais. (*Courtesy of the National Gallery*)

ect, the more you'll get out of it. A dog that you have selected and raised intelligently is far more likely to fulfill his aptitudes, to develop his physical and mental capacities, to be a happy, well-adjusted pet, with a more satisfied owner, than is the appealing puppy acquired on impulse or by chance and reared in ignorance.

Owners have their personal limitations too. Some people, because of character or circumstance, are quite unfit to own a dog, and there are living conditions in which no dog could thrive. Even in the best of cases, dog-owning is not all frolic and affection. It can be troublesome, expensive, discouraging, and quite often a tiresome chore. Bringing up a puppy is almost like bringing up a baby, though fortunately much quicker. Caring for an injured or sick dog can be agonizing. Losing a beloved pet is as heartbreaking as losing a close friend, and it is almost inevitable, since the dog's lifespan is so much shorter than ours. Owning a dog entails many new responsibilities, most of which require time,

A jackal. (*Armelle Kerneis/Jacana Agency*)

A wolf pack. (*Zeisler/Jacana Agency*)

effort, and money. City dogs depend on their owners for just about everything. Any dog, in the city or the country, will restrict your life in some ways.

He will also enrich it immeasurably. A dog can change your existence by giving a new dimension to it. He can alter your entire outlook, improve your health, and bolster your morale. He can be a substitute for friends, family, children, even for a daily occupation.

Man and dog can develop such an intimate mutual understanding that some people attribute human characteristics to their pets, and a mentality just like ours. "The only thing he lacks is the power of speech" is a saying in most languages. But it isn't true. A dog is a dog. There is nothing disparaging in this statement. On the contrary, few human beings can match his fidelity, courage, and devotion. But the dog's version of these, and all his other estimable qualities, is a canine one.

If you want to achieve the most rewarding relationship with a dog of your own, accept him for what he is: neither a tamed beast nor a four-footed child, but one of Nature's most admirable creations, and perhaps the best friend you'll ever have.

1.

A Dog of Your Own

PRELIMINARY CONSIDERATIONS

So you have decided to get a dog of your own!

Perhaps you've always dreamed of owning a dog, and at last you feel that circumstances permit it. Perhaps you seek an interesting hobby, a guard for the house, a sporting companion, a playmate for the children, or simply something to love. Whatever your motive, the first thing you should do is wait. Take the time to study the project carefully. Acquiring a dog is simpler than getting married or adopting a baby. But it too can change your life, and merits thought and preparation.

Are you quite sure that your desire to own a dog is not a passing fancy? While most serious breeders discreetly screen their customers, anyone who wants a dog can find one somewhere. So it is up to you to verify that you possess the basic requirements of a good dog owner: kindness, patience, a sense of responsibility, and sufficient time, space, and money to supply the needs of the breed you have selected.

Take the trouble to learn something about the different breeds in search of the most suitable one for you. Dogs vary more than any other species, physically and temperamentally. The chances of your finding an ideal companion are great. But so are the chances of making a terrible mistake.

Practical considerations will immediately eliminate certain breeds from your choice. Personal taste and esthetic prejudices will exclude others. You will soon narrow the field to a particular size: toy, small, medium, or large, and to a few specific breeds. Then, and only then, is it time to shop around for your dog. Should you fall in love at first sight, the risk of error is considerably reduced.

Science and experience have provided us with quite a lot of information that is useful in determining your personal limitations as a dog owner, as well as those imposed by where and how you live. You might start by considering the question of:

CLIMATE

Although dogs are remarkably adaptable to changes of climate and are able to survive in almost all parts of the world, many breeds, like many people, function better in some climates than in others.

Long-haired breeds shed their coats in torrid zones and during hot weather, and of course they never look their best that way. They also tend to sleep indoors during the daytime heat, becoming active only after sundown, which limits their hours of companionship.

Short-nosed breeds like Bulldogs, Boxers, Pugs, and Pekingese suffer in hot climates and are apt to incur respiratory ailments at high altitudes.

Many short-coated breeds, on the other hand, thrive when the weather is warm, especially desert-bred dogs like the Saluki, tropical ones like the Basenji, smooth-coated dogs like the Doberman Pinscher, Pointer, Dalmation, and smooth-haired Dachshund.

Cold winters and mild summers are made to order for heavy-coated breeds of northern ancestry, like the Samoyed, Malamute, and Husky, Scottish and Cairn Terriers, Newfoundlands, and others who are practically impervious to the cold. Sheepdogs also withstand freezing weather very well, although long-coated varieties are less well adapted to permanent snow, which forms ice balls in their coats and between their toes.

When you keep a dog in an environment very different from his natural one, he will usually adjust to it if you give him a certain amount of protection and care. However, it is more logical and easier for everyone concerned to choose a breed that Nature has already adapted to the climate in which you live.

LIVING CONDITIONS

Do you live in a large house or a small one, in the city, suburbs, or country? Near the sea or a lake, in a wooded area, in the desert, or in the mountains? Or do you live in a city apartment? Are you the owner or the tenant of your home? It is not the tax assessor speaking, but the voice of reason, for your answers to these questions will also guide you in your choice of a breed.

Even if you are the owner of your home, zoning restrictions may restrict the number of dogs you can keep without a kennel permit. If you own an apartment, there may be a limit to the size of the dog who lives with you. If you rent your home, the owner may have included pet restrictions in the lease. So make sure of your rights before you go any further.

A young puppy can adapt to all sorts of living conditions. The case of an adult dog is a bit different. If he was brought up in a kennel or in a city apartment, he will rejoice in the greater freedom and activity of country life, although it may intimidate him a bit at first. A country-bred dog will find it more difficult to adjust to the confinement and restrictions of the city. Both of them will accept their new circumstances in time. But the adjustment is easier when a dog is taken to a new environment that resembles the one he knew before, or that is an improvement on it.

IN THE CITY, the size of your dog is less important than his exercise requirements. Some large, indolent dogs adapt beautifully to city life if they have sufficient living space. Great Danes and St. Bernards, for example, often become lethargic as city-dwellers and accept a relatively inactive life much more happily than do small Terriers and Working dogs, who may become destructive if their needs for freedom and exercise are unsatisfied.

Medium and small breeds are obviously more practical, if only because they can be more easily exercised on a leash, as the law requires in most cities. A short-legged Dachshund or Scottish Terrier can trot at a gay clip as his owner merely strolls along at his side, while a Pointer or Irish Setter at the same pace would hardly be stretching his legs. This point is important not only because adequate exercise is vital to your dog's health, but also because an underexercised dog is apt to become destructive, noisy or neurotic, then obese, and finally ill.

City dogs spend most of their time at home, and not all breeds can stand confinement. Toy dogs may even prefer indoor life to outdoor freedom, but Hunting breeds are happy only when they have plenty of space in which to run.

City dogs usually share their owner's life more intimately than do their country cousins, and are exposed to a wider variety of sights, sounds, and human contacts, all of which develop their intelligence and manners. They are statistically healthier and longer-lived than country dogs, perhaps because they are more closely observed and better cared for. They often seem brighter, more alert, more poised, and more interested in the world around them. Many city dogs are probably happier than the country dog who is left to fend for himself and to frequent an exclusively animal society. A city dog can contribute much to his owner's happiness too, by bringing warmth, gaiety, a sense of being needed and loved, into the often superficial, impersonal life of city-dwellers. Dogs even seem to have adapted to modern urban life better than we have, though it is more unnatural for them. At least there are, proportionately, far fewer canine psychopaths and cases of nervous breakdowns among city dogs than among city humans.

Since a city dog must be kept under control at all times, it is simplest to select a breed small enough for you to pick up and carry in a crowd, and which you can outrun and catch in an emergency. If your heart is set on a big dog, it is essential to give him obedience training as a puppy in order to control him as an adult. Another solution for the city-dweller who prefers big breeds is to compromise by choosing a miniature version of the large breed he admires. Females are almost always smaller than male dogs of the same breed. Slender hounds are surprisingly compact for their height. And there are some small breeds that have a big dog mentality, like the Cairn Terrier, the Irish Terrier, and even the Pekingese, who is amazingly bold and courageous considering his size.

IN THE SUBURBS, a dog's life is much like that of a city dog, since it is generally forbidden (and, in any case, increasingly dangerous) to let a dog roam freely in suburban areas. Some residential communities have strict regulations concerning dog-owning. Statistically, it is in the suburbs that a dog runs the greatest risk of being lost, stolen, or run over by a car. A noisy or aggressive dog can cause a lot of trouble with the neighbors. On the other hand, if you have a yard that can be partially or entirely fenced in, your dog can be outdoors much of the time and need not depend on you to take him out every time he has to relieve himself.

Transportation is less of a problem in the suburbs than in the city, since you can take your dog with you in the car, whereas public city transport is out of bounds for most dogs and out of the question for large ones. If you live near a beach, park, or woods, where dogs may be unleashed, and if you take your dog there for a daily romp, you can confidently keep almost any breed in the suburbs.

IN THE COUNTRY, all dogs are in their element if the climate suits them. In fact, country life is incomplete without a dog. Even so, it is advisable to install an enclosed run for your dog if there is any risk of accident from automobile traffic, hunters' bullets and traps, or poisonous chemicals used in agriculture, all of which cause many canine fatalities every year.

If you live on a farm, one of the Shepherd breeds is an obvious choice. If you live in a wooded area or in open country, an appropriate Hunting breed will help you to get the most enjoyment from these fortunate circumstances. In the country, where there are virtually no practical restrictions for a dog owner, you need consider only your personal limitations— for example, the question of:

FAMILY

In choosing a dog for a family with children, temperament is more important than size. Children and puppies have a natural affinity for each other, but adult dogs of some breeds are more patient with young children than others. Some are reliable only when they have been well trained as puppies. Oddly enough, the gentle giants like the St. Bernard, English Setter, and Old English Sheepdog, of suitable temperament, are better guards and companions for tiny children than are smaller, high-strung breeds like the Chihuahua, Toy Poodle, Pomeranian, and many small Terriers.

The selection of the right breed is so important when children are involved, that it should be decided by mature judgment and not by childish caprice. Take the children with you to shop for a dog, if you like, but make the final choice yourself.

VERY YOUNG CHILDREN and very young puppies require constant supervision, and coping with a new puppy and a new baby at the same time is too big a job for most households. Tiny children haven't the self-control or consideration to be gentle with a puppy and are often unwittingly cruel to animals. Unless you can provide full-time supervision, it is better to wait until the child is at least six years old before offering him a pet. Before then, he is really too young to enjoy it anyway.

He is not, however, too young to understand that many childish ways with puppies are harmful or dangerous. All children should be taught to respect the following rules:

—Never treat a puppy as if he were a toy.

—Never lift or drag him by the tail, ears, or paws. Learn how to pick up a puppy properly.

—Never disturb a sleeping dog. Wake him up, if you must, by speaking to him first.

—Never take food away from him, especially not a bone. And do not try to play with him when he is eating.

—Never tease a dog, never trap him in a corner or cheat at games.

—Never touch a strange dog or even approach him if he is not leashed, and pat him only after seeking permission from his owner.

—Never, never strike a dog.

CHILDREN SIX TO TWELVE YEARS OLD usually get along very well with breeds whose herding and guarding instincts and innate gentleness equip them for the role of protector. They are still too irresponsible, however, to be entrusted with the care of a dog.

TEEN-AGE BOYS AND GIRLS benefit immensely from having a dog of their own. A dog can teach them as much as they can teach him: kindness, patience, self-discipline, consideration for others, assuming responsibility, and forming friendships. They will also learn the facts of life, not only sexual, but also the evolution from youth to age, and the inevitability of death. Among the many breeds that enjoy sharing their active lives are the fun-loving Spaniels and tireless Retrievers.

Consider the dog's compatibility with the rest of the family too, in anticipation of the time when the teen-agers will be away at school or college, or will have switched their enthusiasm to some other activity. Teen-age girls often develop a passion for horses or dogs, and then, as they reach adolescence, transfer their interest to boys. Unless their parents, brother, or sister are prepared to take over, the neglected pet will be miserable and perhaps turn into a vagabond or a neurotic.

SINGLE PEOPLE living alone probably benefit more than anybody else from owning a dog, if they have the necessary time to devote to him.

All dogs loathe solitude. A single person with a full-time job must either find someone else with whom to share the responsibility, or else be willing to sacrifice most of his leisure time to his dog. Some dogs are satisfied with the company of a cat, a caged canary or parrot, or, of course, another dog, during their owner's absence. But don't expect a dog to make friends with a rodent, whose presence would only unnerve him.

ELDERLY AND RETIRED PERSONS find a new lease on life, mentally and physically, when they own a dog. Since active exercise is generally out of the question, the Toy breeds are most suitable. Many older people find it interesting to own a dog of unusual or eccentric character, who would not fit into family life. Others can develop an absorbing hobby by training a dog for Obedience Trials or dog shows. It is advisable in the first case to select a breed amenable to training; and in the second, to avoid breeds requiring elaborate show grooming, and breeds so

fashionable or popular that keen competition practically excludes ama-
teur handlers from winning a ribbon in an important show.

A FAMILY DOG theoretically belongs to the entire household. But
you will find that he usually picks one person to be his master or mistress
—not necessarily the person who feeds him, but often the one who trains
him. Breeds of wolf ancestry, like the German Shepherd, have a strong
need for a substitute pack leader. Male dogs may accept domination
more readily from a man than from a woman. Dogs also seem to estab-
lish a "pecking order" among the members of the family, just as they do
among themselves. During the absence of their chosen "pack leader,"
they will temporarily shift their allegiance to the person ranking second
on the scale, which is based on values of their own, probably psycho-
logical, having nothing to do with sex, size, or age.

When there are OTHER ANIMALS IN THE HOME, a new dog
should be introduced with tact. Dogs usually get along with other spe-
cies of animals as well as with other breeds of dogs, if they are intro-
duced to each other at an early age. Needless to say, dogs of the same
breed offer breeding possibilities, require the same kind of care, and
enjoy the same kind of work and play. Countless cats and dogs have

Countless cats and dogs enjoy playing and sleeping together—even some Greyhounds,
like this one, who have the reputation of being cat-chasers. (*Claus Ohm*)

been brought up together and enjoy playing and sleeping together, even washing and grooming each other. Female dogs have adopted many creatures, including kittens, rabbits, and mice. Most animals, even wild ones, respect the young of other species. But all dogs are inclined to go after fowl, until they have been taught otherwise.

Some breeds are still instinctively attracted to the animals they were originally bred to guard or herd. This working instinct seems to have persisted most strongly in the Collie, Shetland Sheepdog, Australian Terrier, and Great Pyrenees, among the Sheepdogs. The Corgi remembers that he was a working cattle herder until fairly recently, and heel-nipping, which was his herding technique, is now a part of play. Horse-racing stables keep as mascots many kinds of dogs in addition to the traditional breeds, which are the Foxhound (an essential element of fox hunting) and the Dalmatian (which used to be a coaching dog). Schnauzers, Whippets, Jack Russell and Nirwich Terriers, Corgis, Basenjis, Border Terriers, and Schipperkes have the reputation of getting along well with horses too.

While some breeds thus perpetuate historic friendships, others have been bred to hunt and kill certain animals. Terriers, for example, are excited by rabbits, rats, and hamsters. Spaniels will chase anything that flies, including pet canaries. Whippets and other Sight Hounds go after cats and rabbits, while Greyhounds chase smaller dogs as well. Siberian Huskies are somewhat unreliable with other dogs, and Bull Terriers are apt to be pugnacious. Many Toy breeds, like the Pekingese, are jealous of any other object of their owner's affection, animal or human. But there is only one hopeless case: the Chihuahua, who will reluctantly accept another Chihuahua in the home, but is notorious for disliking all other breeds of dogs.

As a general rule, two females will establish a relationship somewhere between the extremes of friendship and indifference, but they seldom fight. An adult male will get along with a kitten, a female puppy, or a bitch, but will resent another male dog. He may tolerate a male puppy, asserting his superiority by ostentatious urination. Male puppies accept subordination to an adult male until they are one or two years old, when they may attempt to establish a new order. If the older male remains forever domineering, the younger dog may never develop his full personality.

The introduction of a new dog into the home must therefore be handled with care. Make a point of lavishing affection on the older animals so they will not be unduly jealous of the attention paid to the newcomer. If you notice any sign of hostility, keep them separated whenever they are unsupervised, especially at mealtimes, and expect a temporary

The young of most species generally get along well together, even a Cocker Spaniel puppy and a baby rabbit. (*John Gajda/FPG*)

Although the Springer Spaniel is one of the best all-round bird dogs there is, he is able to tolerate the presence of a small bird in his home with remarkable equanimity. (*Gene Brownell/FPG*)

regression of housebreaking during the first few days. Within a week or so, they will have established either a friendship or a truce. In the case of an adult cat and a puppy, remember that it is the puppy who needs to be protected, not the cat.

CHARACTER

Opposites often attract, but in dog-owning it is better to seek affinities of character. Astrologers say that the most congenial pet dogs are born under the same sign as their owners (and the best show dogs, under the sign of Leo).

If your idea of fun is a four-mile cross-country jog, you would get little pleasure from a short-legged Dachshund or a Basset, who would never stay the distance. Neither would a bookish stay-at-home get much reading done if his canine companion were a lively Terrier who has little respect for sedentary activities. If the first owner had chosen a Hunting breed and the second a Toy or an indolent giant, everyone would have been happy.

The worst mistake is to match a sensitive dog such as a Collie or Whippet to an inconsiderate, rough owner, such as a thoughtless teenage boy. Almost as bad is the combination of a strong-minded breed requiring discipline and authority, such as the Doberman Pinscher, German Shepherd, and many Terriers, with a phlegmatic, irresolute person. Although such mismatches are frequent, they are seldom satisfactory.

MONEY

Finally, be sure to limit your choice of a breed to those you can afford. The purchase price is not nearly as expensive as the upkeep. Table scraps are not what they used to be, and in any case make a very inadequate diet, especially for a growing puppy whose nutrition affects his entire future. So you will have to make room in your budget for your dog.

Generally speaking, the greater a dog's adult weight, the greater his food requirements. A German Shepherd, for example, needs at least a pound of meat a day; a Great Dane, two or three. Large dogs are also more expensive to ship and board than are small dogs. On the other hand, some tiny Toys are so delicate that what you save on food bills you may end up spending at the vet's.

Unless you invest in your own grooming equipment and learn how to use it, you will have to take your Poodle to the canine beauty parlor for costly regular clippings. Some Terriers, like the Bedlington, Scottish, Airedale, and Wire-haired Fox Terrier, are also among the faithful clients who swell the coffers of these profitable enterprises.

By now, you may already have narrowed your choice of a dog to a certain breel or group of breeds. But before reviewing these, let's consider your dog's temperament, sex, size, coat, color, and age.

TEMPERAMENT

There are as many differences of character and personality among dogs as there are among human beings. But all dogs, being of the same biological species, have much in common. The ingredients are the same. Only the proportions vary.

All normal dogs are basically friendly, faithful, and protective. However, as different breeds have developed in different environments and been selectively bred for different purposes, they have acquired different traits as well. Just as human races and nations possess certain general characteristics, there is a general character pattern for each breed which an individual dog is likely to resemble. Of course, there are exceptions. It is just about as true to say that German Shepherds are loyal and obedient, or that Scottish Terriers are stubborn and wary of strangers, as it is to say that Germans are methodical and disciplined, and Scotsmen unyielding and thrifty. These statements are often accurate, although there undoubtedly exist spendthrift Scotsmen, absent-minded Germans, unruly German Shepherds, and sociable Scottish Terriers. Still, it is curious to note that breeds originating in certain countries often manifest the personality traits that are popularly attributed to their human populations.

People who have owned more than one dog of the same breed can easily distinguish between the character and behavior peculiar to an individual dog, and those that are typical of his breed. In general, one can say that:

HUNTING DOGS are gentle, friendly, responsive, energetic, good natured, nonaggressive, and affectionate. They dislike confinement, solitude, and ridicule.

TERRIERS are high-spirited, active, alert, courageous, curious, willful, sometimes pugnacious. They have the strongest jaws (proportionately) and are the best diggers.

SHEEPDOGS are benevolent, protective, sensitive, patient, and intelligent. They require mental and physical activity and enjoy assuming responsibility.

TOY DOGS are high-strung, devoted, affectionate, alert, jealous, and in-clined to be yappers. They may be snappy too, but from self-protection rather than from aggressiveness.

GUARD DOGS are inclined to be one-man dogs. They are highly responsive to a strong-minded master and to an advanced degree of training. They have excellent memories, are brave, fiercely loyal, dis-trustful of strangers, and willing to assume responsibilities. But they can be aggressive if undisciplined.

SIGHT HOUNDS are independent, aloof, excitable, amenable, and not very demonstrative. The swiftest runners, they are apt to roam.

SCENT HOUNDS are also apt to be rovers. Slower and less excitable than the Sight Hounds, they are devoted, tenacious, tolerant, docile, and dignified.

There is no "ideal" temperament for a dog. What is desirable for one owner may be detestable to another. Canine character is composed of most of the same qualities that form human personalities: loyalty and independence, honesty and deceitfulness, stubbornness and amenability, laziness and energy, courage and cowardice, devotion and selfishness, dignity and humor. When choosing a young puppy, it is helpful to ob-serve the adult members of his family, for he is likely to have inherited many of the same traits of personality and behavior.

With such a wide variety from which to choose, you should seek what appeals to you the most. But be sure to avoid the FLAWS OF TEMPER-AMENT that can make a dog owner's life miserable:

—excessive shyness (when it is due to breeding rather than to a trau-matic experience or an unhappy past)

—distrustfulness (when it stems from cowardice)

—pugnacity (for no justifiable reason)

It is sometimes possible to correct these vices by patient re-education, if they are the result of unfortunate past experience, as in the case of abandoned dogs found in an animal shelter. But it is better to avoid them when you can. After all, you are looking for a congenial dog of your own and not a rehabilitation project.

SEX

Male or female, your dog's sex has a certain bearing on his tempera-ment and behavior.

Male dogs possess no secondary sex characteristics as spectacular as fantails, horns, or antlers. But in most breeds males are expected to look like males and females like females (with the exception of a very few, such as Bulldogs and Chows, where it is desirable for there to be little visible difference between the sexes). In most breeds, males are larger, sturdier, and heavier-boned than females, with a less refined head— although the largest, fattest member of a newborn litter is often a female. When this is not the case, show judges and experienced breeders prefer a doggy bitch to a bitchy dog.

Newborn male and female puppies can be distinguished by picking them up, turning them over, and observing the genitalia. The distinction becomes more obvious at puberty, around the age of 6 or 8 months, when male puppies begin to lift their legs and take a greater, less platonic interest in the opposite sex, and when females (or *bitches,* to use the perfectly proper canine term) experience their first heat period.

FEMALES are inclined to be more affectionate, more faithful, cleaner, more companionable, vigilant, intuitive, quicker to learn, and more solicitous of children. They are also less roving than males, except during their two yearly heat periods (and especially during the breedable phase), when they will scour the countryside for miles around in search of a mate. Like girls, they develop faster and mature sooner. Schooling can thus start earlier. Since they are less easily distracted, they are often easier to train than males. They are quicker and easier to housebreak too. A practical advantage of a city bitch over a city dog is the fact that she will simply squat and empty her bladder all at once, while the male dog produces what seems to be an infinite supply of urine, which considerably prolongs the daily outings. On the other hand, females shed more than males, and more frequently.

It is easier to avoid an unwanted pregnancy in a city bitch, since it is simple to confine her during the danger period. In the suburbs and the country, it may be necessary to board her during these trying days. Perhaps the canine contraceptive pill, still in an experimental stage, will solve this particularly troublesome problem.

MALES are generally larger and heavier than females of the same breed, stronger and more self-reliant. But courage and endurance are by no means a monopoly of the male sex. Despite the greater activity and aggressiveness of males, and the fact that they are generally bolder, more impulsive, headstrong, and independent, a high percentage of the outstanding acts of animal heroism has been performed by females.

Males are definitely more roving. When their sexual instinct is aroused by the scent of a bitch in heat, they can completely lose their heads and roam for miles in search of her, wait for hours on her doorstep, and engage in terrible fights over her favors. Furthermore, females are interested in sex only twice a year, but male dogs are interested in it virtually all the time.

Even though male dogs conscientiously mark the boundaries of their territory with drops of urine while females simply relieve themselves in the first convenient spot, their sense of property and of protecting it is the same.

Far more than sex, it is breeding that determines the character and intelligence of a dog. Females may appear to be brighter than males, but this is probably because they mature faster and can be trained earlier.

You may be offered A FEMALE WHO HAS BEEN SPAYED—in other words, one that has undergone an operation which prevents her from having heat periods or puppies. Canine hysterectomies can be performed at any age, but are usually done at 6 months, just before the first heat period. Spaying a bitch too young can result in a rather masculine-looking, oversized animal with a tendency to obesity and indolence. Many veterinarians therefore prefer to wait until the bitch is mature enough to have acquired all of her feminine characteristics, or at least until she has had her first heat. Most animal shelters automatically spay the nonpedigreed bitches in their care, or oblige the adoptive owners to have it done, in order to limit the propagation of unwanted mongrel litters.

THE CASTRATION OR "NEUTERING" OF MALE DOGS is less common. It is practiced mainly in order to reform vicious, roving, or pathologically oversexed dogs, often with spectacular results. An intractable, belligerent rover may become a docile home-lover. He may also become fat and lazy if his diet is not supervised, and this applies to spayed bitches too. Since both procedures are irreversible, they should not be undertaken lightly. Spayed bitches and castrated dogs cannot, of course, be bred. Neither are they eligible for showing, although they can compete in Field Trials and Obedience competitions.

A male dog may be entirely or partially STERILE, without its affecting his temperament, because his two testicles have not descended normally into the scrotum at birth. If one or both cannot be felt by the time the puppy is 3 months old, he is probably either a *monorchid* (when only one has descended) or a *cryptorchid* (when the two testicles remain inside the body). Since both conditions disqualify a dog from showing and render breeding impossible or inadvisable, it is important to check male puppies for this abnormality. (Read Chapter 15, "Your Dog's Sex Life," for further details.)

HOMOSEXUALITY does not exist among dogs, even though highly sexed individuals may sometimes give that impression. An aroused male will mount another male, and a female will mount another female, but it is a form of masturbation. Some highly sexed dogs (like certain Bulldogs and Terriers) will masturbate by licking themselves to the point of ejaculation. Most adolescent dogs go through an embarrassing stage of making indecent advances to children, pillows, chairs, and human arms and legs. This is quite common, especially with animals who have been reared without the company of the opposite sex and must discover for themselves their proper sex object. But if it persists or becomes obsessive, the only cure is hormone treatment or, as a last resort, hysterectomy or castration.

If you are interested in breeding, your first dog should be the best bitch you can find. For a novice pet owner, particularly an elderly person or a city-dweller who seeks love and companionship above all, a whole or spayed bitch is often the best choice. Because of their precocity, their keen concentration, unconditional devotion and the possibility of perpetuating exceptional aptitudes by breeding, female Hunting dogs are preferred by many sportsmen. Experienced owners and breeders fancy females too, while pet owners most often select males. So while just about as many female puppies are born as males, you are apt to meet a far greater number of male dogs in the park on Sunday afternoon.

SIZE

Between the smallest recognized breed (the tiny Chihuahua, a mere handful of a dog who weighs as little as one pound) and the largest (the 34-inch-high Irish Wolfhound and the 200-pound St. Bernard), there exist dogs of a wide variety of sizes and shapes. A dog's height, incidentally, is measured from the withers (the highest point of the shoulders, immediately behind the neck) to the ground.

Size has little to do with boldness or aggressiveness. Some very big dogs, like the Bull Mastiff, Bulldog, Newfoundland, and St. Bernard, are noted for their gentle manners, while some small dogs, like the Welsh Corgi and the Bedlington Terrier, can be very pugnacious. More American veterinarians are said to have been bitten by the harmless-looking Cocker Spaniel than by any other breed. If it is guarding ability that interests you, remember that criminals are more afraid of being detected than of being attacked, and small dogs are just as keen to detect the presence of strangers as are big dogs. Furthermore, many small dogs are tougher, sturdier, and have more fighting spirit pound for pound than many large breeds.

The size of your dog is a matter of considerable practical importance. When space is a problem, you should take into account weight as well as height. Some slender, long-legged breeds, such as the Whippet, can curl up in your lap, while the short-legged, long-backed, heavy-set Basset needs quite a lot of room in which to stretch out.

The established breeds are described as Large, Medium, Small, or Toy. There are really two kinds of Toys: Miniature breeds, which are scaled-down versions of a larger natural breed, such as Toy Poodles, Italian Greyhounds, and Yorkshire Terriers; and Dwarf breeds, which are pure breeds probably resulting from some natural mutation causing disproportion, like the Pekingese and the Dachshund.

LARGE DOGS obviously need more space in which to sleep and to move about, and more outdoor space for exercise. They need a larger share of your food budget too, and since they consume more, they also produce a greater quantity of waste matter. Large dogs require large dwellings and large runs. Basic obedience training is indispensable for a dog who is bigger and stronger than his owner. If you dream of owning a large dog, you should buy him as a young puppy, handle him a lot during his infancy, and train him in obedience as soon as possible in order to imprint your mastery on his brain before he has become bigger and stronger than you are.

SMALL DOGS can find a place for themselves in any home. There is a safety advantage in a dog small enough and light enough for you to pick up and carry in an emergency. Small dogs are much easier and quicker to groom and bathe, but they get dirty quicker too, with their bodies closer to the ground. The fumes of city traffic are more irritating to the eyes of small dogs (who are on about the same level as the exhaust pipes) than of large dogs. On the other hand, small dogs are much more easily transported by taxi, train, or airplane, and this may be a decisive factor if you travel a lot or live in a city. A well-behaved small dog is also more likely to be a welcome guest in the home of friends, where it would be inconsiderate to take a large dog.

Obviously, it is more convenient to keep a small or medium-sized dog in a modern home. But convenience isn't everything. A large dog gives you a sense of protection and companionship that is beyond compare. While a small dog may be even more alert in sounding the alarm at the first suspicion of the presence of a thief or a fire, a large dog is capable of holding a robber at bay, fighting off a mugger, carrying a baby from a burning house, and rescuing a drowning man. Small dogs can be perfectly lovely to look at, charming, amusing, and adorable. But a handsome large dog has a noble presence that puts him in quite another class.

Some large dogs can live quite happily in city apartments, if their temperament is right for it. A placid large or medium-sized dog will lie quietly beside you, while an active small one will always be getting into mischief or underfoot. So when you have the means and a reasonable amount of living space, there is no need to deprive yourself of a large dog, if that is what you prefer. But be sure to choose him carefully.

COLOR AND MARKINGS

The color and markings of your dog's coat are determined by heredity and transmitted by genes, just as our hair and eye colors are. In fact, the science of color transmission is one of the areas of genetics we understand best.

We know, for example, that every puppy inherits color genes from each parent, and that these are reinforced by the genes inherited by each parent from the grandparents. We know that some of these color genes are dominant, and others recessive (see Chapter 16). A dog with the appropriate dominant color genes will breed exclusively puppies of a certain color, no matter what the color of the bitch to whom he is mated may be. He is said to be "pure" for that color. Stud dogs who invariably transmit the most desirable or most fashionable shade are, needless to add, much in demand and very valuable.

The official standards of the recognized breeds describe in detail the acceptable colors and markings, as well as those which are disqualifying faults. In some breeds of show dogs, color seems to outweigh more important points of conformation, as in the Kerry Blue Terrier, the Golden Retriever, the Irish Setter, and the Keeshond. Occasionally, fashion has preceded official recognition, as in the case of the silver and apricot Poodle and the cream-colored Cocker Spaniel (all of which are now accepted). White German Shepherds, a rather risky recent breeding venture, are eligible for AKC registration but still barred from the show ring. White collies (who are generally predominantly white with sable, tricolor, or blue markings) were included in the AKC breed standard only in 1977, although President Eisenhower kept one in the White House during the early 1950s.

Dog fanciers use a special vocabulary in describing colors and markings. Among the more obscure terms you may encounter are:

Belton: An intermingling of white and colored hair in English Setters, such as "orange Belton," "blue Belton," etc.

Blaze: A white stripe running up the center of the face between the eyes.

Butterfly nose: Dark, with flesh-colored spots.

Blue merle: Marbled blue and gray mixed with black.

Breeching: Tan hair inside the thighs.

Brindle: A fine, even mixture of black hair with a lighter shade, usually brown, tan, or gray.

China eye: A pale-blue eyes (also "walleye").

Dudley nose: Brown, liver, or flesh-colored.

Fawn: A color ranging from cream to deep gold.

Flare: A blaze widening at the top of the skull.

Harlequin: Black or blue patches on a white coat.

Isabella: Palomino color, light to dark gold.

Mask: Dark shading on the foreface.

Points: A color on the face, ears, legs, and tail, usually white, black, or tan, which contrasts with the body color.

Red: A color ranging from peach to mahogany.

Roan: A fine mixture of white and colored hair, such as blue roan, lemon roan, etc.

Sable: Black hairs finely interspersed in or over a lighter ground color.

Ticked: Small areas of black or colored hair on a white ground.

Tricolor: White, black, and tan.

If you are interested in breeding or showing your dog, you should be sure that he conforms to the color and marking requirements of his breed standards. Bits of white are disqualifying faults in many solid-colored breeds.

The most fashionable color for a pet may not be accepted in the show ring. Ill-marked or off-color puppies are sometimes sold at bargain rates. But they should be examined for soundness with special care, because a poor color or eccentric markings may be signs of a genetic disharmony that is accompanied by some other inherited weakness.

There are fashions in dog colors as in everything else. Those currently in favor are apt to be more expensive than puppies of the same quality, in the very same litter, but of other hues. Silver-gray Poodles and fawn-colored Whippets are much in demand. A Collie with a full, unbroken collar fetches a premium price, as does a perfectly marked English Setter, a round-spotted Dalmatian, or a patchy-spotted Harlequin Great Dane.

Unfortunately, some breeders, anxious to profit from the passing fancy for a certain shade of coat, will breed for color only (which is comparatively easy to do), and neglect the far more important considerations of physical and temperamental soundness. Some famous stud dogs, prepotent for transmitting a desirable color to their progeny, have also transmitted shyness, nervousness, and blindness.

White and very pale coats obviously require more grooming than other shades, and more frequent baths. White is the only acceptable color for certain breeds such as the West Highland White Terrier, the Maltese Terrier, the Samoyed, Bichon Frisé, and Great Pyrenees Sheepdog, since it is also the only natural one. But white coats have also been produced in other breeds, often by excessive inbreeding, which engenders accompanying defects such as blindness, nervous disorders, and deafness. Perfectly sound ones have been bred too. But it is still advisable to test all white puppies for deafness.

You cannot always tell from a puppy's coat the color and markings he will have as an adult. The Kerry Blue Terrier, for example, is born black and does not acquire his distinctive shade until the age of 18 months. Silver-gray Poodles are also born black, undoubtedly causing some anxiety to their breeders. Old English Sheepdogs are born black and white, the colors becoming lighter and the markings hazier as they grow older. The Afghan's puppy coat also lightens as he matures. Dalmatians are born completely white, and their black spots develop later. But a serious breeder should be able to tell what color a puppy will have as an adult, since he knows the pattern of genes involved in the mating that produced him.

COAT

The dog's coat is his natural protection from the elements and is often an indication of the region in which his breed originated. The coat of a mongrel puppy can give you a clue as to his probable parentage. In some breeds it is the principal element of beauty. In all of them it is a breeding place for parasites, a dust-catcher, a source of hair that clings to clothing and upholstery, and an object of time-consuming grooming. Like color, it is inherited through the genes. But it can also be temporarily modified by environment.

Among the different kinds of dog coats are the long-haired silky, long-haired rough, medium-haired silky and rough, wire-haired, smooth-haired, and curly-haired. There are single coats and double coats. There is, at one end of the scale, the Mexican Hairless, with hardly any coat at all; and at the other, the Hungarian Puli, with a voluminous mass of bouncing, ropy coils that literally sweep the ground.

Smooth, short coats are quick and easy to groom and are the least inviting to parasites.

Long coats mat, collect dirt from city streets, and shed profusely. They are much more trouble to brush and comb, take longer to wash and dry, and the bigger the dog, the longer it all takes.

Wire-haired coats become fuzzy and matted if they are not stripped (plucked by hand) or clipped twice a year. Airedales and Wire-haired Fox Terriers look like unkempt mongrels if they are not given this fastidious regular care.

Coat shedding seems to be co-ordinated with the length of daylight as well as temperature. Pet dogs living in electrically lit, centrally heated

homes, tend to shed a little bit all of the time. Long-haired dogs kept out
of doors generally shed their coats twice a year, in the springtime and
fall. Even house-kept long-haired dogs shed more abundantly at these
times. Most short-haired breeds are year-round shedders, with the same
peak periods of spring and fall. The Bedlington Terrier, Kerry Blue Ter-
rier, and Australian Terrier are noted for shedding very little, while the
Poodle is exceptional in that he hardly sheds at all. His coat simply
grows longer and longer until it is clipped, which is the reason for all
those costly sessions at the canine beauty parlor.

Expert grooming is essential only for show dogs. But any owner should
take pride in keeping his dog's coat groomed and, if necessary, clipped
according to his breed standard. When you take the trouble to learn how
to do it yourself, it can be an enjoyable activity and your dog will love
being fussed over by you.

It is obvious that smooth, short-coated dogs require the least grooming
and are best suited to warm climates and city apartments. Long and
heavy-coated breeds are most comfortable and give less trouble in the
country. Rough, weatherproof coats are indicated for rugged climates. As
a general rule, if your dog's coat is suited to the climate in which he
lives, he will always feel and look his best.

AGE

The time-honored theory that one year in the life of a dog is equiva-
lent to 7 years in the life of a man (later revised by having the first year
of a dog's life equal 10 years of a man's) has been discarded in favor of
an entirely new scale, according to which:
  —at 6 months a puppy is like a 10-year-old child;
  —at one year he is comparable to a 15-year-old adolescent;
  —at 18 months he is like a 20-year-old human;
  —at 2 years he is as mature as a 24-year-old adult.
From this point on, every year in a dog's life is equivalent to 4 years of
human life, so that:
  —a 12-year-old dog is like a man of 64;
  —a 16-year-old dog can be compared to a man of 80; and
  —a dog would have to reach the age of 21 (a few of them do) in
    order to match the survival record of human centenarians.
There is also a simpler version, according to which the first year of a
dog's life equals 21 human years, and every year thereafter is the equiva-
lent of 4 of ours.

Small breeds often attain their mature size at 8 to 12 months; medium-sized breeds, at 12 to 16 months; and large breeds, at 16 to 18 months or even later. Very large breeds are fully mature only around the age of 2 years.

In the show world, a dog is an ineligible infant until 6 months of age, and a puppy from 6 months to one year (sometimes subdivided into puppies of 6 to 9 months, and those of 9 to 12 months). From one year on, he is considered an adult, even though he seldom achieves psychological maturity before the age of one and a half years.

As with horses, we can estimate a dog's age by examining his teeth. A puppy one month old normally has all of his milk teeth. As his jaws attain their adult size (his head and paws are the first parts of his body to do so), permanent teeth gradually replace the baby ones, between the ages of 4 and 8 months. After this stage, his age is shown in the erosion of the points of the teeth. After 5 years or more, they may also begin to deteriorate, discolor, and eventually loosen.

Puppies can be taken from their mothers as soon as they are weaned, from 6 to 8 weeks, and many are offered for sale at this tender age. It is

An eight-week-old puppy may be fully weaned, but he is still an infant who needs his mother. (*Claus Ohm*)

the most profitable moment for the breeder, whose outlay increases as the growing puppy requires greater amounts of food and care. But 6 weeks is really too young to remove a puppy from his mother and litter-mates. In some states the sale of puppies under eight weeks of age is pro-hibited by law. The great majority are purchased when they are 8 to 12 weeks old.

They are perfectly adorable then. They are also extremely impres-sionable. Experiments indicate that a puppy forms his strongest attach-ments between 6 and 10 weeks of age. One who receives a lot of atten-tion and handling at this stage is far more apt to form human attachments in preference to canine ones, whereas puppies left to them-selves with little human contact during this period are always likely to prefer the company of dogs to people.

It might therefore seem logical to adopt a pet puppy as early as possi-ble. But before you do, consider the risks and the responsibility. An 8-week-old puppy is only a baby who needs constant care and supervision. He is not yet very resistant to infection and disease. He needs an amaz-ing amount of sleep and carefully balanced meals at frequent intervals. He tires quickly, and his soft bones are easily injured. He is much too delicate a creature to be offered as a playmate for young children, who will probably be disappointed anyway when the puppy thinks only of eating and sleeping when they want to play. He cannot control his natu-ral functions yet, and must be kept in a confined, easily cleaned area until he is old enough to be trained to paper and later taken outside.

As a general rule, it is probably best to adopt a kennel-bred puppy when he is 8 or 9 weeks old, if you are equipped to care for him; and a puppy who has been raised in a home environment, when he is a few weeks older. The ideal age for a novice owner or a home with children is 3 to 4 months. When a puppy is at least 3 months old, you can play with him, take him for walks, and start housebreaking right away. This vital training can be accomplished within a few days, which is a great advan-tage for apartment-dwellers and owners of valuable rugs. The puppy will need only 3 meals a day, which are easily co-ordinated with his owner's mealtimes. He will have already survived the most dangerous period for contracting puppy diseases. Behavior patterns are rapidly formed at this age, and a bright puppy will already respond to elementary training. It is fascinating to observe his daily development as he grows and learns. For teen-agers, it can be highly instructive.

When the children are too young to be entrusted with the respon-sibility of another living creature, between the ages of 6 and 12, it is bet-ter to get an older, sturdier puppy, 4 to 6 months old. For tiny tots and babies, a benevolent adult dog is often more satisfactory than a puppy.

The aging process in dogs is very much like ours. Some individuals are more precocious than others, some mature sooner, and some age faster. Dogs go through similar stages of development: helpless infancy, the carefree years of early childhood, the awkward, sometimes rebellious adolescent period, the peak of their powers as adults, and the gradual slowing down with old age.

Many dogs start to go gray around the eyes and nose as early as the age of 7, and quite commonly at 8 or 9. A bluish or whitish cast to the eye is a sign of old age. Old dogs also tend to become irritable and habit-clinging, just as we do, and to develop various aches and pains if not more serious infirmities.

Canine life expectancy, like ours, is increasing: 12 to 14 years, whereas not so long ago it was only 9 or 10. Females and small breeds generally outlive males and large dogs. Among the longest-lived are Fox Terriers, Dachshunds, Boston Terriers, Pekingese, and Pomeranians. Giant breeds like the Great Dane and Irish Wolfhound, sad to say, seldom attain the age of 10.

PUREBRED OR MONGREL?

There is no truth in the widespread belief that mongrels are more intelligent and sturdier than purebred dogs. Many mongrels are indeed very bright, probably because they have had to live by their wits and because only the strongest puppies survive. And some purebred dogs do indeed seem idiotic, probably because of inept breeding or because they have been made to lead stupid lives and have never been given a chance to develop their intelligence. But in general, purebred dogs, who get a better start in life and better care, are healthier and longer-lived than mongrels, and their intellectual capacity is as great, if not greater. Purebred dogs of suitable breeds are almost always selected for the most difficult canine tasks, such as leading the blind, detecting contraband, hunting, patrolling army camps, and doing rescue work. On the other hand, a mongrel has just as much love and loyalty to offer as a purebred —even more, perhaps, if he has been salvaged from an animal shelter, because he will be eternally grateful to you.

There is a distinction between a mongrel, whose unknown ancestry includes mixtures of various breeds, and a crossbred dog, who is the result of a mating between two purebred dogs of different breeds.

It is impossible to tell what a mongrel puppy is going to be like as an adult. He may become a particularly bright and attractive little dog, or he may grow into an ill-proportioned giant with a spooky character. As far as size is concerned, the traditional method is to observe the puppy's paws: the larger they are in proportion to his body, the larger he is apt to grow. *Apt* to grow only, because you may also end up owning a small dog with big paws or a big dog with dainty ones. Mentally, you haven't a clue, except perhaps if you discern in his physical appearance some dominating type, such as Spaniel, Terrier, or Shepherd, from which you may suppose that he possesses some of the instincts and aptitudes of that variety.

Judicious crossbreeding is very different from the accidental kind. Many of our modern recognized breeds are the result of calculated crosses between older established breeds in order to produce a new one with specific abilities and characteristics.

One of the best-known examples of a man-made breed is the Doberman Pinscher, created in the late 1890s by a German night watchman, Louis Doberman, who crossbred a German Pinscher to a German Shepherd and later added Rottweiler and Manchester Terrier blood. The Weimaraner is another German variety, developed at the Court of Weimar around 1810 and reserved exclusively for that noble coterie until fairly recently. Many breeds of British origin were the creations of gifted individual breeders, like the Sealyham Terrier, named after the estate of its founder, Captain John Edwardes, a nineteenth-century Welsh dog fancier, who spent forty years developing a superior badger hunter by mixing various Terriers. The Bedlington Terrier was a calculated combination of Dandie Dinmont and Otter Hound, with a dash of Whippet. The Airedale, a cross between Welsh Terriers and Otter Hounds, is also a man-made breed. Our outstanding American achievement is the Boston Terrier, who started as a cross between a female Bulldog and a male Bull Terrier. The most recent canine breeding success is the Jack Russell Terrier, the personal creation of an English parson of that name. The only unrecognized crossbreed to have been given a name of its own is the "Cockapoo," which is the result of deliberately crossing a Cocker Spaniel and a Poodle.

It takes many generations of breeding, including at least 4 generations of purebreeding during which the progeny invariably reproduces true to type, and a population of at least 600 dogs, before a new breed is eligible for consideration by the American Kennel Club or other official registries. Fanciers must form an AKC-sanctioned breed club; the members must vote on a standard; the club must keep a studbook (later turned over to the AKC), write by-laws, publish a newsletter, elect officers, and hold Specialty matches and trials. The first 600 dogs with 4-generation pedigrees are the foundation stock of the breed, and after a certain time the studbook is closed to the issue of other dogs.

So what is the answer to the question: Purebred or mongrel?

There is certainly a sense of satisfaction in adopting an unwanted mongrel. You are performing an act of charity and creating happiness in the place of misery. But you run the risk of ending up nursing a hopelessly unsound animal or desperately trying to get along with a dog who turns out to be entirely different, mentally and physically, from what you were seeking. As for breeding prospects, they are so unpredictable that it should not even be considered.

With a purebred dog, you know what you are getting. He is bound to possess certain physical and temperamental attributes, certain instincts, and a certain adult size.

Obviously, owning a purebred dog rather than a mongrel is a matter of common sense rather than of snobbery. At the same time, owning any kind of a dog is more fun than not owning a dog at all.

2.
Choosing a Breed

Among the estimated forty million dogs in the United States, there are believed to be about ten million purebred dogs, and about a million are registered each year by the most important canine organization in the country, the American Kennel Club (51 Madison Avenue, New York, New York 10010). The AKC recognizes some 122 different breeds, although there are at least 150 different kinds of purebred dogs in the country, more than 200 officially recognized breeds throughout the world, and as many as 300 or more pure breeds, if you count all of the regional working and hunting varieties that are just as purebred but have never sought official recognition.

The official standards of the breeds recognized by the AKC are published in *The Complete Dog Book* and in a special annual issue of *Dog World* magazine, divided into Groups that are not always an accurate reflection of the purpose for which they were originally created nor the roles they now fill. The Dachshund, for example, is included in the Hound Group, and the Poodle is classified as a Non-Working dog, although both of them are closely related by bloodlines, temperament, and instinct, to Terriers. Nevertheless, in reviewing the characteristics of these different breeds, it is simplest to follow the AKC system and start by taking a look at:

SPORTING DOGS

This group includes Pointers, Retrievers, Setters, and Spaniels. Many Working and Field Trial dogs of these breeds are registered with The American Field, while the show types are listed with the AKC.

These are the most sociable breeds of all: friendly, good-natured, gentle, and easily trained (except perhaps for housebreaking, which can be difficult). All of them need lots of exercise, love outdoor life, and are in their element in the country. Left there on their own, however, they are apt to roam in search of game. Quieter in the house than Terriers or Toys, they are alert guardians. They appreciate affection and respond to it by offering devoted companionship.

Most serious hunters have already owned a dog that has given them satisfaction, or have admired a friend's dog in the field. They know that each hunting breed has its specialty, that all can be trained to do other things as well, but that time is gained and results are better if they start off with a dog who possesses the innate aptitudes for the kind of hunting they practice. There are three basic kinds of hunting aptitudes:

Retrievers do what their name suggests: retrieve shot game on command from land or water.

Spaniels flush game and retrieve it too, working on land or in water (the Brittany Spaniel also points).

Pointers cover a lot of ground in search of game, then point it until the hunter flushes the birds. They may be asked to retrieve, but more often are trained to "point dead," indicating where a downed bird is lying.

Generally speaking, the larger the game and the more open the hunting country, the larger the dog required to work in it. Duck hunters naturally prefer water-retrieving breeds. For Field Trial competitions, speed and precise obedience are all-important.

The Spaniels are perhaps the best all-round bird dogs because they can find, flush, and fetch, and are charming companions too. But the most popular hunting dog in America is the Labrador Retriever, basically a waterfowl specialist, and in practice just as versatile as the Spaniels, just as amiable and devoted a family pet.

Their outstanding virtues: Hunting aptitude, amenability, a gift for friendship.

Their principal drawback: The need for a lot of regular exercise.

Their ideal owner: An active sportsman with a home in the country.

SMALL SPORTING DOGS

The COCKER SPANIEL. The name evokes his woodcock-hunting prowess in his native England, plus a tribute to his Spanish forebears. Immensely popular some decades ago, overbreeding led to a diminution of working ability, so that modern Cockers are mostly of the show type, with long silky coats, protruding eyes, and high-strung temperaments, quite unfit for hunting and not ideal as family dogs either. Nevertheless, careful selection from the right breeding lines can still provide the merry, game little Cocker who is a marvelous companion at home or in the field.

The ENGLISH COCKER SPANIEL is still used abroad for flushing and retrieving small birds and rabbits, and has remained well-balanced physically and mentally. He is larger and stronger than the American Cocker, his coat is less profuse, and his head is more like a small Setter's. He is cheerful, active, sentimental, a quick learner, and a delightful comrade.

Cocker Spaniels. (*H. Armstrong Roberts*)

Springer Spaniels. (*H. Armstrong Roberts*)

MEDIUM-SIZED SPORTING DOGS

The BRITTANY SPANIEL is one of the most popular breeds in his native France. He has a lovely disposition: reserved, sensitive, gentle at home, alert and enthusiastic when hunting birds. The only Spaniel with natural pointing instincts, and the smallest of the pointing breeds, he is a determined, persevering retriever, a good all-round hunting companion, and a lovely family dog.

The ENGLISH SPRINGER SPANIEL is a versatile hunting dog, quite similar to the Brittany, except that he flushes game by "springing" it from cover and then retrieves. Particularly effective with pheasant, he is an all-rounder in the hunting field, a good swimmer, unafraid of swamps or dense underbrush. At the same time, he is a home-lover, devoted to his family, gentle and playful with children. Sensible, friendly, responsive, he can do everything a hunting dog should do reasonably well, and with exceptional enthusiasm.

The WELSH SPRINGER SPANIEL is less familiar, although he has been used for centuries as an all-round hunter in his native Wales, where he is sometimes called the "Starter." He has a rich dark-red and white coat and is similar to the English Springer in working style and temperament, but a little smaller.

LARGE SPORTING DOGS

The ENGLISH SETTER is the most beautiful of the hunting breeds, with a long silky coat, fine proportions, and a noble bearing. He is well-mannered, steady, loyal, and sociable, a bit aloof on the surface, but affectionate underneath. He works by scenting the game by air, then pointing or "setting" in a crouch until the hunter has shot it, finally retrieving on command. Not a natural retriever, he must be taught to do it. But he learns this quickly, as well as many other things, and is noted for

Irish Setter. (*John Gajda/FPG*)

never forgetting a lesson. There are two principal lines: the Laveracks and the Llewellins, who take their names from the two nineteenth-century English breeders who produced these outstanding strains, the first excelling in the show ring, and the second used for both showing and field work. However, as a Field Trialer, the English Setter has been surpassed by the Pointer, who has greater range, speed, and earlier maturity.

The GORDON SETTER is more or less a Scottish version of the English Setter, although slower, heavier in body and more massive in head, with distinctive liver-colored markings on a black coat. Definitely a sporting dog, most often a one-man dog, he is not particularly good with children.

The IRISH SETTER has become so popular, due to his friendly, affectionate nature, his striking red coat and sleek elegance, that his hunting instinct is receding in some lines as more and more are being bred as pets and show dogs. He is rather high-strung, sensitive, cheerful, obstinate but amenable to training, slow to mature, and long-lived. He needs a lot of exercise and a lot of running space.

The POINTER, like the Setter, is an "upland bird dog," which means that he hunts "upland game" such as pheasant, partridge, quail, grouse, and woodcock in open field country. Not a water dog, he is a far-ranging, fast, independent hunter with a distinctive working style. When he scents game in the air, he points to it, lining up his nose and body in a straight line and remaining rigidly posed until the hunter arrives and flushes the game. He is happy only when he is hunting. Everything else leaves him rather indifferent. He doesn't even mind kennel life. So, although he is a favorite of hunters and an outstanding Field Trialer, he has never been very popular as a pet.

The LABRADOR RETRIEVER is one of the most popular bird dogs in the world, and the most frequent National Retriever Champion. He is also one of the most popular pet dogs in America. His short, dense black, chocolate, or yellow coat requires little care. His friendliness, intelligence, and dependability are exceptional. Easygoing and obedient if he is trained young, he gets along with children, adults, and other dogs, but smaller animals (including cats) are apt to arouse his hunting instinct. He is an expert swimmer and an indefatigable retriever, specializing in ducks. As a family dog and hunting partner, it is hard to find fault with the Labrador—except, perhaps, for the fact that he insists on retrieving even what you want to throw away.

The CHESAPEAKE BAY RETRIEVER is believed to have originated when two puppies rescued from a sinking British ship in Chesapeake Bay were bred to Maryland hunting dogs. Far from being traumatized by the experience, he simply loves the water and is a strong and tireless

Labrador Retriever. (*William P. Gilbert*)

Golden Retriever. (*William P. Gilbert*)

swimmer. He has a brown or tan coat and orange eyes and could hardly be considered beautiful. Neither is he particularly friendly. But he is much appreciated by duck hunters because he is tough, tenacious, energetic, and a dauntless retriever even in the iciest water. Superior in his specialty, he is better suited to sporting activity than to family life, for he is definitely a one-man dog.

The GOLDEN RETRIEVER is, according to a famous legend, the result of a meeting between an English Bloodhound and a troupe of performing Russian dogs. A more likely version credits a British sportsman, Lord Tweedsmouth, with the development of the breed in the 1860s, starting with a cross between a yellow Retriever and a liver-colored Water Spaniel, with later doses of Labrador Retriever, Irish Setter, and Bloodhound blood. Basically a hunting dog, he is increasingly popular as a pet and excels in Obedience Trials, Field Trials, even as a guide dog for the blind. He retrieves on land or in water. He is intelligent, responsive, quick to learn almost anything, sociable, and the most sensitive of the retrieving breeds. He is an excellent family dog. In fact, he needs to feel part of the family. He also needs space, exercise, and gentle handling.

The GERMAN SHORT-HAIRED POINTER and the GERMAN WIRE-HAIRED POINTER are all-round hunting dogs, pointing and retrieving in water or on land with equal efficiency, in all weather and all climates. More versatile than the Pointer, not very fast but methodical in their work, they have become quite popular on the West Coast and in the Midwest. They lack the speed and brilliance to excel in Field Trials, although the Wire-haired is quicker and more agile than the Short-haired variety. Rugged, steady, intelligent, trainable, kindly, and tolerant of children, even playful at times, they are alert watchdogs—in short, a good combination hunting companion and family dog.

The WEIMARANER is instantly recognizable because of his "ghost-gray" coat and rather eerie gray or amber eyes. He was introduced to America only a few decades ago as a superdog with the highest I.Q. in the world. While he is certainly a nice animal, a good pointer, retriever and trailer too, unusually well-mannered, conscientious, and quite intelligent, he has not exactly revolutionized dogdom. But he has won his share of admirers, even more as a family dog than as a hunter.

There are many other hunting breeds in the United States and elsewhere, whom you are less likely to meet, such as: the short-legged, calm, slow but thorough CLUMBER SPANIEL; the clever IRISH WATER SPANIEL and the versatile AMERICAN WATER SPANIEL, who is unlovely to look at but a splendid water retriever; the small, stocky, rather noisy SUSSEX SPANIEL; the efficient FIELD SPANIEL; the

German Short-haired Pointer. (*Claus Ohm*)

CURLY-COATED and FLAT-COATED RETRIEVERS; the WIRE-
HAIRED POINTING GRIFFON, an ancient, utilitarian, medium-
sized European breed with a long mustache, heavy brows, and a
tractable disposition; and the VIZSLA, a sensitive, gentle, intelligent
Hungarian Pointer with a short yellow coat, who is beginning to make a
name for himself as a reliable pointer and retriever.

HOUNDS

There are two general types of Hounds:
Sight Hounds (also called *Gaze Hounds* or *Coursing Hounds*), such as
the Afghan, Borzoi, Greyhound, Irish Wolfhound, and the smaller
Saluki and Whippet.

Scent Hounds such as the Foxhound, Bloodhound, Harrier, Otter Hound, Beagle, and Coonhound.

The Scent Hounds may be further subdivided into *Rabbit Hounds* (including the Basset and the Beagle), and *Tree Hounds* (including the different Coonhound varieties that "tree" their climbing prey and are registered by the United Kennel Club).

Others in this group are the Dachshund, who is actually more Terrier-like in temperament and activity, and two breeds of African origin: the powerful Rhodesian Ridgeback; and the Basenji, a small, barkless, smooth-coated dog, also known as the Congo Terrier, for he, too, is more closely related to the Terriers than to the Hounds.

Generally speaking, the Sight Hounds are fast runners, long-legged, rather aloof and independent. Quiet at home, they seldom bark. They are difficult to train, but clean in their personal habits. Although not normally aggressive, they will chase anything that moves, including bicycles, children, cars, cats, and smaller dogs. Their speed as well as their longevity are said to be due to a slower heartbeat than that of other breeds.

The Scent Hounds, on the other hand, are stockily built, gentle, and dignified, inclined to be obese. Slow-moving, they possess fantastic flair, stamina, and perseverance in pursuing a trail, their pendulous ears and keen noses close to the ground. Their passion for trailing tends to make them wanderers too.

Their outstanding virtues: Nonaggressiveness, elegance in the Sight Hounds, dignity in the Scent Hounds.

Their principal drawbacks: Indifference and unsociability in the Sight Hounds, wanderlust in the Scent Hounds.

Their ideal owner: A person who provides them with plenty of running or trailing space in the country, and a comfortable cushion in front of the fireplace. (Or, for Sight Hounds: a racing fan who cannot afford to buy a Thoroughbred racehorse; for Scent Hounds: an amateur detective.)

SMALL HOUNDS

The BEAGLE is a rabbit hunter who has become one of the most popular house pets in America, although he is still hunted in packs, with the liveried huntsmen on foot, in some parts of the country, notably the East and Southeast. He is smooth-coated, attractive, gay, adaptable, brave but not aggressive, pleasant with children and with other dogs, all of which accounts for his success as a family pet. He is not easy to train, and his roving habits are practically incurable. But his natural good humor and adaptability enable him to fit into most family environments. There are

Beagles. (*Ruth Almstedt/FPG*)

two varieties of Beagles: under 13 inches in height, and from 13 to 15 inches. Size is important in a pack, for the dogs should be as alike as possible in height, weight, conformation, color, and speed.

The BASENJI is a sturdy, smooth-coated, curly-tailed hunting dog from Africa, who possesses several unique characteristics: he washes himself like a cat and is so clean that he seems to be born already housebroken; he has a curious, swift, tireless, extended trot; he never barks (although he can snarl, chuckle, yodel, crow, and scream); and, like wild dogs, the females have just one heat period a year. It is an interesting breed, less civilized perhaps than those with a longer history of urban domestication. If his education starts early, as it should, he is responsive to training and makes a good companion. Remember, though, that tribal African life is not far behind him. Some are snappers and none are completely reliable around children.

The DACHSHUND (literally "badger dog" in German) comes in three styles: smooth-, long-, and wire-haired; and there are miniature versions of all three. Originally used for hunting, he is now one of the most fashionable city pets, and with good reason. He is easy to care for, easy to exercise, playful, alert, affectionate, intelligent, cheerful, and amusing. He has his faults too. The smooth-haired variety is prone to back troubles, and all are inclined to be irritable with children, and want to be the center of attention. Furthermore, the Dachshund is one of the champion chewers and diggers. If you can forget his short, crooked legs, designed for chasing badgers in their underground burrows, you must admit that there is a certain beauty in his face, and especially in his expressive eyes.

The BASSET HOUND is a very ancient breed of French origin. The variety recognized in America is a combination of French, English, and Russian bloodlines and is shorter-legged, heavier-boned, and smaller than his Gallic ancestor. But he has the same pendulous lips, long ears, smooth coat, long back, doleful eyes, fantastic scenting ability, and endurance in the hunting field. He is calm, slow, and dignified, like all Scent Hounds, but at the same time cheerful, even tempered, and devoted. Nowadays a Basset is more often a fashionable pet than a working hunter, and he is surprisingly successful in Obedience Trials.

Smooth- and Long-haired Dachshund puppies. (*Annan Photo Features*)

Basset Hound puppy. (*H. Armstrong Roberts*)

The WHIPPET is an elegant miniature Greyhound, with the same lust for chasing and running, and the same gentle but aloof personality. He is sweeter and more sensitive than the Greyhound—far too sensitive for rough handling or boisterous children. In the open he is a speed demon. At home he is quiet and companionable. In strange surroundings he may be nervous. Although he measures 19 to 22 inches at the withers, he is so slender and fine-boned that he can curl up in your lap—and this he loves to do, for he is unusually affectionate for a hound.

MEDIUM-SIZED HOUNDS

The SALUKI is an Arabian coursing hound originally used for gazelle hunting in Egypt, so you can imagine how fast he is able to run. Rarely seen outside North Africa except in dog shows, he is considered a noble breed in his native land. He is indeed very elegant, medium in frame but light in weight—and the females are considerably smaller and lighter than the males. He has a short smooth coat with feathered ears, legs, and tail, and a typical hound personality: aloof, dreamy, gentle, pleasant, independent, and somewhat mysterious.

The AMERICAN FOXHOUND and ENGLISH FOXHOUND (similar but larger) are bred and used almost exclusively for fox hunting in packs. Puppies are often "farmed out" during their first year of life until they are ready for training, and rearing them can be a pleasurable pastime for dog lovers living in the vicinity of one of the few remaining fox hunts. Discards sometimes become available as pets. This is not, of course, the role for which they are bred, but they can adapt to family life if they are given sufficient exercise.

The same is true of HARRIERS, OTTER HOUNDS, and COONHOUNDS. All of them are bred for sport and are content to live in a kennel and do a lot of hunting. But there is no reason why they cannot also make nice family pets, if some substitute activity is found to satisfy their powerful sporting instinct.

The NORWEGIAN ELKHOUND is a northern dog who used to hunt elk and moose, generally in packs, detecting the prey by scent and holding it at bay until the huntsman arrived. Still used as a working hunter and farm dog in Scandinavia, there have been attempts to convert him into a companion dog. Although he is a good-looking animal with a handsome gray-shaded coat, and is clean, loyal, and fairly obedient, he is perhaps too bold and independent to fill the role of a family pet as ably as many other breeds.

LARGE HOUNDS

The AFGHAN is one of the most spectacular breeds. You generally think of him lying quietly, gazing into the horizon with a dreamy look, or else running at a fast clip with his curious loping gait, the long coat on his legs and ears flopping up and down in a characteristic way that is both graceful and droll. He is not noted for intellectual brilliance, and is notoriously difficult to train. But he is so docile and naturally well-mannered that it hardly matters. He is independent rather than sociable, indifferent to everybody but his owner, and even that relationship is apt to be a bit impersonal. He needs to run a lot, and if he gets enough exercise he will be quiet and content at home. His coat requires a lot of regular care in order to keep him presentable. A well-groomed Afghan is a magnificent sight and wins far more Best of Show and Group awards than other Hound breeds. But an unkempt Afghan looks terrible.

The BORZOI, or Russian Wolfhound, is another striking dog of aristocratic bearing, built for speed and elegance. The favorite breed of the czars of Russia, he was used for hunting wolves, usually in pairs. Elsewhere and more recently, he has won a place in affluent homes as a decorative element, as well as in the show ring. Like most running hounds, he is graceful, neat, and agile for his size (some 30 inches at the withers). He is also aloof, not at all playful, impersonal, untrainable, not even very intelligent in a practical way. Difficult to adapt to city or family life, he is apt to become nervous, shy, and fearful. While he may not fill the requirements of an ideal companion dog for most persons, his temperament is perfect for showing.

The GREYHOUND is the fastest-running breed of all. He is happiest when he can extend his long, fine legs in an all-out sprint after a rabbit, or for that matter, after any furry moving object. Cats and small dogs obviously need protection when he is in the neighborhood. In any case, his temperament and exercise requirements make him unsuitable as a pet, and for this reason he is used primarily for coursing, racing, and as a show dog.

The IBIZAN GREYHOUND (or *Podenco*) (25 inches, 50 pounds) is used for racing and rabbit chasing on the Mediterranean Spanish island of Ibiza. Less refined than the Greyhound, he strongly resembles the ancient Phoenician Hound, who was certainly his ancestor.

The IRISH WOLFHOUND and the SCOTTISH DEERHOUND are even larger, rough-coated, majestic breeds, with the long heads, tucked-up loins, and strong jaws typical of the Greyhound, who was their common ancestor. No longer used for hunting, their activity is now mostly confined to parading in the show ring, or to giving status and a sense of distinction to wealthy owners with large estates and unlimited credit at the butcher's. It is regrettable that the practical restrictions of modern life permit only a privileged few to enjoy the friendship of these beautiful, courageous, and loyal dogs.

The BLOODHOUND is one of the gentlest, most devoted dogs in existence, although his name evokes a gory image. Actually, the word "blood" is used in the sense of "purebred," as in "blood horses" (Thoroughbreds). He is one of the oldest pure breeds, the favorite hunting-pack dogs of the early kings of France. He is also the finest tracker in the world. Slow, persistent, tireless, and tenacious in his work, the Bloodhound has performed incredible feats of detection. He is also a quiet companion at home, gentle, affectionate, kindly toward children and other dogs, devoted to his owner, and not at all as sad and solemn as he looks. His wrinkled, jowly face is most expressive and appealing to the owner who appreciates and understands him.

The RHODESIAN RIDGEBACK is a rare breed from South Africa, where he has been used for lion hunting and as a guard. His name refers to the unique strip of hair growing backward down the center of his spine, which is a legacy from his ancestor, the Hottentot dog. Otherwise, he is smooth-coated, handsome, well-balanced in conformation and steady in temperament, easy to care for, clean, and loyal. It takes patience as well as authority to train him well, and early training is essen-

Scottish Deerhound. (*William P. Gilbert*)

tial, for he is a powerful dog with lots of energy who would otherwise be
hard to handle. Although he is classified with the Scent Hounds, he is ac-
tually a Sight Hound too (perhaps even more so), and he is not even
considered a Hound breed in England.

WORKING DOGS

The dogs in this group, which includes Sheepdogs, Sled dogs, and
Guard dogs, have always worked for a living. All of them need mental
and physical activity and a certain amount of responsibility in order to
be happy. But there is quite a wide range of temperament among them,
due to the different aptitudes required by their respective work. Aside
from the small Shetland Sheepdog and Welsh Corgi, all of them are large
dogs, some enormous, and are best suited to suburban and country life.

SHEEPDOGS

Their outstanding virtues: Intelligence, gentleness, a sense of responsibility.
Their principal drawbacks: They may become neurotic or aggressive if deprived of physical or mental activity.
Their ideal owner: A family living in the country.

The SHETLAND SHEEPDOG is only 13 to 16 inches high and looks rather like a miniature Collie. Actually, it is a separate breed, originating in the Shetland Islands off the coast of Scotland, where sheep and ponies are also small. He has the Collie's graceful beauty, intelligence, agility, alertness, and sensitivity. He is, however, more high-strung, too much so for children. He shines in Obedience training and makes a fine watchdog. Very affectionate and companionable, he demands a lot of attention. He is apt to be noisy, and even destructive, if he is left alone with nothing to do.

The WELSH CORGI, a short-legged, rugged little dog 10 to 12 inches high, exists in two different varieties: the long-tailed *Cardigan;* and the *Pembroke,* which has a naturally short tail. The Pembroke, which is partly Flemish in origin, is more popular, but the pure Welsh Cardigan is said to be more stable. He is certainly the older breed. The Pembroke has a shorter body, lighter bone, straighter forelegs, and foxy pointed ears. Both of them are bright, alert, adaptable, and make good pets for people who travel a lot or divide their time between the city and the country (like the Queen of England, who is seldom separated from her Pembrokes). They used to herd cattle by nipping at their heels, so modern pet Corgis may be forgiven if they sometimes nip at children too.

The COLLIE is so elegantly beautiful that it is hard to think of him as a working dog, although he is one of the most efficient sheep herders ever bred. In America, where Collies are kept mostly as pets and show dogs, these aptitudes are manifested in their excellent Obedience work and in their protectiveness toward home and family. Gentle and affectionate, they tend to be jealous of their owners, responsive to training, sensitive, hardy, and loyal. They cannot tolerate rough handling or long confinement. While they are able to adapt to city life if given enough exercise and companionship, they are definitely happier in the country. In the city, a SMOOTH-HAIRED COLLIE would be easier to look after. Rare in the United States, he has the conformation and character of the Rough Collie, even the same color and markings. But he is less excitable, more compact, and his sleek coat requires far less care.

Shetland Sheepdogs. (*Sue Maynard*)

Collie (Rough). (*Courtesy of Richard Bohland*)

Collie (Smooth). (*Courtesy of Richard Bohland*)

The BEARDED COLLIE is a newcomer to the AKC roster of recognized breeds, although he has a long history as a sheepdog in England. His shaggy coat is reminiscent of the Old English Sheepdog's, and he has a long beard that blends into the hair on his chest. He is also entirely different in head from the Collie, with a shorter muzzle and larger eyes. He may be less elegant, but he is also less spoiled, possessing much character and appeal and extraordinary working aptitudes.

The OLD ENGLISH SHEEPDOG was originally bred for herding cattle and ponies. He has an ambling gait, a heavy gray or blue-gray coat that tumbles over his eyes in a disheveled way (and requires hours of daily grooming to make him presentable), and a mere stub of a tail that has earned him the nickname "Bobtail." He is normally a homebody, gentle, placid, protective of children, and unusually good-natured. But his recent wave of popularity seems to have altered his benevolent character in certain lines, so that a pet dog should now be selected with care.

The BERNESE MOUNTAIN DOG is a handsome, big, strong Swiss sheepdog with a long, soft black coat, symmetrically spotted with white and rust, and a sweet, dependable, intelligent sheepdog mentality and disposition.

The BRIARD is a large French sheepdog whose professional skill is just as great as that of the more familiar English sheepdog breeds. Big and powerful, he has a fast, gliding gait, a beard, a long mustache, a shaggy waterproof coat that hangs over his eyes, and a crook at the tip of his tail. An excellent, rather unusual pet for a country home, he needs a lot of activity and responsibility to bring out the best in his kindly, fun-loving, protective character.

The GREAT PYRENEES SHEEPDOG is a majestic, heavy-coated, long-haired white mountain dog with a long full tail, an elegant, massive appearance, and a benign character. He is home-loving, protective, responsive to training and affection, as good with children as he is with sheep, although more of a guardian than a playmate.

The ST. BERNARD, Switzerland's most famous contribution to the animal kingdom, has been largely replaced by helicopters in the mountain rescue work he so heroically performed in the past. Although he cannot pass unnoticed because of his bulk, he is not really beautiful, with

St. Bernard. (*H. Armstrong Roberts*)

his heavy body, jowly face, wrinkled brow, and melancholy eyes. So it is a tribute to his moral qualities that so many owners are willing to pay the huge food bills entailed by maintaining his normal weight of some 150 to 200 pounds. He is lovable, placid, gentle, trainable, brave but not aggressive (although some modern lines have become unreliable, especially around children, undoubtedly due to overbreeding inspired by his recent, sudden popularity). Despite his size, a St. Bernard will accept a rather inactive life, although it is apt to be a short one. There are two varieties: Long-haired (the most popular in America); and Short-haired (the most popular in the Alps). The Long-haired are prone to skin ailments in hot or damp climates, where the Smooth-haired fare better.

The P U L I is a Hungarian sheepdog, and one of the strangest-looking canines in the world. Puli means "leader" in Hungarian, but he looks more like a dishmop, with his medium-sized body a voluminous mass of thick black, gray, or white long, ropy coils that completely cover his eyes and face (although they may also be brushed out). He is a lively dog with a short, jumpy gallop for a gait. The rare Pulik in America are mostly used as show dogs, conversation-openers, and attention-getters, in which specialty they are hard to beat.

The K O M O N D O R, another Hungarian sheepdog who guards without herding, is a heavy, shaggy, big white dog seen in America mostly in the show ring. He possesses the typical sheepdog qualities, in addition to an uncanny intuition and a marked distrust of strangers. His dense double coat forms tassel-like cords by the age of two, like the Puli.

SLED DOGS

Their outstanding virtues: Strength and stamina.
Their principal drawbacks: One-man dogs, they are suspicious of strangers and unfriendly with other dogs.
Their ideal owner: An outdoor-lover living in a cool climate.

The S A M O Y E D is the most beautiful, cheerful, and adaptable of these Arctic breeds, with great strength and stamina for his medium size. He is also the most versatile, capable of guarding a reindeer herd, drawing a sled, and being a loving, attractive pet. His long white coat is surprisingly easy to keep clean, and he adjusts well to temperate climates. Intelligent and responsive to training (which is a necessity), he is devoted to his owner, but merely tolerant of the rest of humanity. Still, he is more sociable with people than with other dogs, in spite of his characteristic "Samoyed smile."

The ALASKAN MALAMUTE and the SIBERIAN HUSKY are two similar Arctic breeds, popular in Alaska and Canada. Both are powerful, proud, alert, clean (practically odorless), dignified, and pugnacious with other dogs. Both possess great strength, endurance, and courage. The Malamute is generally considered the more beautiful, but the Husky, with his slanting pale-blue or brown eyes (or maybe one of each), is refined and even dainty. Both are docile at home, the Husky more reserved and the Malamute more affectionate. Like many popular large breeds, they have become afflicted with genetic weaknesses such as hip dysplasia, so precautions should be taken when selecting a puppy. The Husky is faster and a little smaller (21 to 23½ inches) than the Malamute (25 inches, 85 pounds).

GUARD DOGS

Their outstanding virtues: Strength, courage, intelligence, strong protective instincts.

Their principal drawbacks: They can become tyrannical with a weak owner, tend to be aggressive when out of work, and are definitely one-man dogs.

Their ideal owner: An active, strong-minded person interested in training.

The GERMAN SHEPHERD was the most popular breed in the United States during the 1920s, when his temperament was more Shepherd than

German Shepherd. (*Annan Photo Features*)

Guard. Since then he has been to war, he has been trained to attack, he has been employed as an incorruptible watchdog as well as a guide for the blind, and he has thus been bred with different aptitudes in mind. All German Shepherds need firm but never brutal training, even if they are merely family pets. Depending on his breeding, education, and the life he leads, a German Shepherd can be the best family dog in the world, or he can be a public menace. With such a wide variety of temperaments from which to choose, a companion dog should be selected carefully. In the best of cases, his strong protective instincts, courage, intelligence, and loyalty equip him perfectly to be a superlative family dog.

The DOBERMAN PINSCHER is a handsome dog of noble bearing, remarkable learning ability, and strong guarding instincts—in some cases, attacking instincts too. When he is well trained at an early age, he excels in obedience work, in guiding the blind, in the Army and Marine Corps, and he is the policeman's favorite patrol partner. Like the German Shepherd, he absolutely requires training. But do not train him to attack, even in fun, if you want a family dog. He loves it, but it brings out a side of his nature that can ruin him as a pet. He is a one-man dog who can give great satisfaction to the right owner, but be far too much to handle for the wrong one. Females are more affectionate and often easier to train than males.

Doberman Pinscher. (*William P. Gilbert*)

Bouvier des Flandres. (*William P. Gilbert*)

There are three principal types of Belgian-bred Sheepdogs, which differ in coat but share the same large size (24 to 26 inches high), the same handsome head (similar to the German Shepherd's), and the same aptitudes as efficient sheepdogs, vigilant guards, loyal companions, and courageous recruits for war and police work. The most striking variety is the long-haired, coal-black "Groenendal," registered by the AKC as the BELGIAN SHEEPDOG. The BELGIAN TERVUREN is like a smaller German Shepherd, except for his long-haired tawny black coat and a slightly different topline and hindquarters. The BELGIAN MALINOIS is short-haired, black-tinged, even more like a smaller German Shepherd.

The BOUVIER DES FLANDRES is the leading guard-dog breed in Belgium, although France claims credit for him too. *Bouvier* means "cowherd" in French. He is powerfully built, with a thick double coat, cropped ears, and docked tail, a rather rustic appearance, and a good-natured character. A fearless guard, he is also a willing worker at all kinds of tasks. Definitely a country dog, he is a competent all-rounder who needs a firm master.

Great Dane. (*H. Armstrong Roberts*)

The K U V A S Z is a pure-white Hungarian breed, bigger than his compatriot the Komondor, and quite majestic with his massive proportions, noble head, and proud plumed tail. *Kuvasz* means "Guard" in Turkish. He probably shares some distant ancestry with the Maremma Sheepdog of Italy and the Great Pyrenees of France, and like them is a tireless worker, dignified, patient, devoted but undemonstrative, with strong protective instincts and the need for lots of exercise in wide-open spaces.

The B O X E R is a German breed, bold and even fierce-looking, with visible evidence of the Bloodhound and Great Dane strains in his breeding background. In spite of his intimidating appearance, he is an affectionate, friendly dog. Gentle with children, sociable with other dogs, he is adaptable to all kinds of living conditions, even to city apartments. Unfortunately, soundness has become a problem with the breed. He catches cold easily and is prone to respiratory ailments and dental problems, due

to his undershot (protruding) lower jaw. He drools, is apt to be glut-
tonous and eventually obese, and does not live long as a rule. Boxer pup-
pies are particularly adorable. Even as adults, they remain playful, which
may be one of the reasons why their owners form unusually strong at-
tachments to them.

The MASTIFF is an impressive dog of ancient ancestry, rather frighten-
ing to look at with his frowning forehead and jowls and up to 200
pounds of body weight for his 30-inch stature. A one-man dog, he is gen-
erally found as a guard or a show dog nowadays. A carefully dosed com-
bination of Mastiff (60 per cent) and Bulldog (40 per cent) has pro-
duced the BULL MASTIFF, who is less massive than the Mastiff (25 to
27 inches, 110 to 130 pounds), and more normal in conformation than
the Bulldog, and has inherited the guarding instinct of the first, and the
gentle, steady temperament of the second.

The GREAT DANE, who is German rather than Danish in origin and is
called a "German Mastiff" abroad, was once a boar hunter and a guard.
He is still used for guarding, but even more often as a handsome and dis-
tinguished companion. A one-man dog, suspicious of strangers, well-man-
nered, dignified, dependable, less active than his huge size and appetite
would suggest, he becomes very attached to his home and dislikes
changes of environment. As with all large breeds, it is important to train
him as a puppy (and particularly to teach him not to jump up on peo-
ple) in order to control him as an adult.

The STANDARD SCHNAUZER (17 to 20 inches) and the GIANT
SCHNAUZER (23½ to 27½ inches) get their name from their distinctive
appearance (schnauze means "snout" or "muzzle" in German). Their long
mustache, bushy eyebrows and beard, cropped ears, harsh coat, and
docked tail give them a dapper appearance. They are robust, square-
bodied dogs with a pepper-and-salt coat, although the Giants can
also be solid black. They are really a Bavarian variety of Terrier, with
Poodle blood. In fact, the Miniature Schnauzer is in the Terrier group.
Like most German breeds, they respond well to discipline and training.
Like most Terriers, they are hardy, alert, bright, fun-loving, and are in-
stinctive vermin hunters.

The ROTTWEILER is another big, strong, German-bred dog who was
once a cattle herder and now works as a guard, retriever, tracker, and
companion. He is good-natured, faithful, alert, self-confident, and is said
to be a very fast learner. His versatility and steadiness make him an ex-
cellent all-round farm dog. His blood helped to create the Doberman
Pinscher, but he is less aggressive and more dignified than that more fa-
mous but far less ancient breed.

The NEWFOUNDLAND is an enormous dog, solid black, white, bronze,

or black-and-white (in which case he is called a "Landseer"). He has a
passion for the water, and his lifesaving exploits are legendary. He is also
a good fisherman. On land, he even has a rolling kind of sailor's gait.
Calm and quiet at home, he is the gentlest of dogs, especially with chil-
dren, for whom he is a willing baby-sitter as well as a courageous life-
guard. Closer in temperament to the Sheepdogs than to the Guards, he is
a lovely pet for families who have the space and means to keep him, and
preferably a waterfront home. But he must be confined when you want
to go for a swim, because he insists on rescuing every bather he spots,
even those who are in no danger of drowning.

The AKITA is a powerful, large (25 to 28 inches) Japanese breed
which resembles the Arctic sled dogs, having inherited from their
common ancestor, the Spitz, the same erect ears curly tail triangular
head and eyes. Although he has never pulled a sled, he has done many
other jobs. Originally a fighting dog (from which he retains a bold
aggressiveness, especially toward other dogs), he was then a hunter and
a guard, and is now bred in America as an interesting, loyal companion
and as a show dog.

TERRIERS

Most of the recognized Terrier breeds in America are variations of
those developed in England, except for the Miniature Schnauzer, who is
German-bred. They are all lively, sturdy, and usually small, due to their
original work of hunting vermin and burrowing animals. The larger Ter-
riers hunted otters and badgers. They need a lot of exercise and are eas-
ily bored by inactivity. They are curious, alert, gay, affectionate, often
humorous, independent, rather egotistical, stubborn, and devoted in their
way. As they grow older, they are apt to become pugnacious, selfish, and
less sociable, more irritable with children. They are clean and easy to
care for, adaptable to city life.
Their outstanding virtues: Boldness, liveliness, a sense of fun.
Their principal drawbacks: Stubbornness, egotism.
Their ideal owner: An energetic person leading an active life with time
to devote to his dog.

SMALL TERRIERS

The MINIATURE SCHNAUZER is a deliberately scaled-down version
of the Standard Schnauzer, 12 to 14 inches high, with the same wiry
pepper-and-salt or black coat, the same aptitudes, and the same gay tem-

Miniature Schnauzer. (*William P. Gilbert*)

perament. He is more of a stay-at-home than most Terriers, easier to train and less mischievous. A pleasant companion in a city apartment, he is a nice family pet—in fact, one of the most popular small dogs in America.

The CAIRN TERRIER is one of the liveliest, brightest, and most companionable of the small Terriers. Not really a beauty with his short legs and shaggy coat, he is strikingly attractive because of his proud, bold air and his expressive, foxy little face with its whiskers, beard, and bushy brows. Too stubborn and independent to train easily, he is naturally sociable, adaptable, and clean (although he sheds most of the time). In Scotland he has the reputation of being "fey," that is, endowed with a sort of extrasensory perception.

The WEST HIGHLAND WHITE TERRIER is a small, pretty dog who looks like a white Cairn—which is just what he is, his white coat having been established by generations of selective breeding. He is shorter-backed, wider headed, and longer-legged than the Cairn. But, like the latter, he is active, proud, curious, and suffers from confinement and solitude. His normally fun-loving, gay disposition may turn to morosity if he is given insufficient activity and company.

The MANCHESTER TERRIER (Standard) is the oldest of the English Terriers (originally called the Black-and-Tan Terrier), whose blood has contributed to many other breeds. Although the Toy version is more popular in America, this original model (12 to 20 pounds in weight) is a smart little package of intelligence, alertness, and boldness. Smooth-coated, neat and clean, he is said to be related to the Whippet, and he is indeed sleeker and finer than most other Terriers.

The FOX TERRIER may be either Smooth-haired (the older variety) or Wire-haired, and has been so famous as a show dog, performer, and pet that many people think he is the only kind of Terrier there is. He is playful, keenly intelligent, and extraordinary agile, which accounts for his success as a circus star. The Smooth-haired requires little care, but the Wire-haired looks like a mongrel if he is not regularly stripped or clipped. His natural boldness and alertness have been exaggerated in many show lines to the point of pugnacity, so a pet puppy should be carefully selected. He is very sturdy and often unusually long-lived.

Skye Terrier. (*Annan Photo Features*)

The SCOTTISH TERRIER is instantly recognizable from his distinctive black silhouette and his highly individual personality. His temperament can be a delight or a disaster, depending on one's appreciation of his unshakable devotion, his suspicion of strangers, and his stubborn independence. Too dignified for games, he is also apt to be moody, irritable, and obstinate, which makes training difficult if not impossible. But he is a devoted companion, easy to exercise, an interesting pet for the owner who respects his individuality and understands his character.

The WELSH TERRIER looks like a small Airedale, with a wiry black-and-tan coat, wide-set eyes, and a muscular, well-proportioned body. A versatile working dog in his native land, he is known elsewhere as an all-round companion dog, calmer and more trainable than many Terrier breeds, more friendly and sociable, fearless but seldom pugnacious, a good swimmer, an enthusiastic hunter, a dependable watchdog, and a gay and lively house pet in the city or in the country.

The SKYE TERRIER, come from the Island of Skye off the coast of Scotland, and is, according to legend, a cross between some shipwrecked Maltese dogs and local Scottish Terriers. He certainly differs in coat from the other Terriers, with long silky hair hanging over his face and falling to the ground from a middle part along his elongated spine, completely concealing his short legs. He is a one-man dog, wary of strangers, a better pet for adults than for children.

The SEALYHAM TERRIER is a man-made breed developed originally for hunting badgers, but now used for showing and as a pet. Sturdily built with a wiry white coat, he is playful, very game, rather a rugged individual, devoted but reserved.

The BEDLINGTON TERRIER is unique because of his lamb-like appearance, but nothing could be more deceptive, for he is one of the most pugnacious, boldest small dogs that exists. Whippet blood gave him his speed and roached back (which has been increasingly exaggerated by modern breeders). Even though he is small, he can be a lot to handle, and a pet puppy should be selected carefully in order to avoid excessive nervousness and belligerence. Even then, you should never expect a Bedlington to behave like a lamb.

The AUSTRALIAN TERRIER, a recent discovery of American dog fanciers, possesses a variety of virtues packed into a neat, low-set body only 10 inches high at the withers. He has the versatility of a Working dog, the alertness and loyalty of a Guard, the energy and confidence of a Hunting dog (he is a great ratter), and he can be as quiet, playful, and affectionate as a Toy. His harsh coat is easily groomed, and he hardly sheds at all.

The NORWICH and NORFOLK TERRIERS, the former with prick

ears, the latter with drop ears, are two distinct breeds. They are very small Terriers with foxy heads and wiry coats that are most often red, but may also be black-and-tan or brindle. They are keen, lovable and active, rustic, sturdy, and pleasant companions.

The BORDER TERRIER is another little fellow with a lot of energy and courage. He is a genuine Working dog, fast enough to keep up with a horse. He has a distinctive, otter-like head and is more experienced as a sporting dog than as a pet.

The DANDIE DINMONT was originally the "Cheviot Terrier," renamed after a character in Sir Walter Scott's novel *Guy Mannering*. His wide-set eyes, silky topknot, very short legs, and pendulous ears give him an appealing air. He is level-headed, devoted to his owner, suspicious of strangers, an individualist, and an engaging companion for a person who appreciates a rather unusual pet.

The BULL TERRIER, with his oval-shaped head, squinty eyes, and sturdy body, is an ugly little dog except to his owner, who knows that the ex-gladiator of the canine world (a cross between a Bulldog and a Smooth-haired Fox Terrier) has become one of the most devoted, peace-loving, faithful, and well-mannered of pets. Some of his old fighting spirit is preserved in certain show lines, but those bred as pets are gentle with children and adults—if not with other dogs, especially other males.

The LAKELAND TERRIER is a regional breed differing only slightly from the Irish, Welsh, and Wire-haired Fox Terriers, all of whom he resembles in silhouette as well as in character. His cleverness, self-confidence, and gaiety are much admired in his native England, where he is used for hunting fox and badger.

MEDIUM-SIZED TERRIERS

The SOFT-COATED WHEATEN TERRIER, an attractive, unspoiled, spirited Irish dog with a soft, blond, wavy coat, is a fairly new breed in America that is rapidly gaining in popularity, perhaps because his breeders are trying to preserve his well-balanced physique, his natural appearance, and his even disposition. He is alert, strong, and hardy. Aggressiveness is not encouraged in show dogs, as it is in many other Terrier breeds.

The AMERICAN STAFFORDSHIRE TERRIER is more aptly described by his British name: Staffordshire Bull Terrier. An ex-fighter who has been converted into a docile pet, he has the bulky body of a Bulldog, the wide-set eyes of a Bull Terrier, and the straight legs of a Fox Terrier.

Norwich Terrier. (*Annan Photo Features*)

He also has the Bulldog's tenacity and gentle disposition, the Terrier's vitality and courage, and the Bull Terrier's pugnacity with other dogs. His character is far more attractive than his appearance.

The IRISH TERRIER still hunts in Ireland, but is generally kept as a pet in other lands. An excellent man's dog, even in the city, and a superb watchdog, he is a dapper, clean, alert, intelligent, sociable, charming and playful with people, but rather hostile toward other dogs. He is a marvelous swimmer, a good tracker, and an efficient gardener, if it's digging you need. A reckless daredevil, he is a one-man dog of unswerving loyalty.

The KERRY BLUE TERRIER is also Irish-bred. A good swimmer and a vigilant watchdog, he has been used for guard work by the British Army. He hasn't the reputation of being an ideal family pet, but is much appreciated as an all-round farm dog. When his independent nature is given firm handling and early training, he is a loyal, pleasant companion.

LARGE TERRIERS

The AIREDALE is the largest and boldest of the Terrier breeds, and also one of the most affectionate. He is adaptable and more tractable than the smaller Terriers, although he can be headstrong if untrained. Having been supplanted by German Shepherds and Dobermans in the valiant police work that he used to do, he is still used for guiding the blind and as a fearless guard. He was once a boar hunter, but his hunting instinct is now applied mostly to vermin. He is a very good swimmer, and a high-spirited playmate for older children. Airedales of the right temperament make wonderful family dogs. The show-dog lines are apt to be less reliable and more belligerent.

TOY DOGS

Toy dogs are by definition tiny, and by tradition ladies' pets. Man-made miniaturization accomplished by selective breeding tends to result in nervousness and an attenuation of the aptitudes of the original breed, while the dwarf breeds, created by natural mutation, tend to suffer from health problems. In general, Toy dogs prefer adults to children, are loving, delicate, nervous, and infantile. They are alert, vociferous watch-dogs. Some yap, some nip, and many do both.

Their outstanding virtues: Smallness (all are under 12 inches high), companionability, affection.

Their principal drawbacks: Delicacy, nervousness, childishness, the cost of acquiring them, and the difficulty of breeding them.

Their ideal owners: Indolent, idle people, older women, and retired gentlemen, who spend most of their time in a cozy, well-heated home.

The AFFENPINSCHER is a droll little dog. *Affen* means "monkey" in Germany, his country of origin, where he is also known as the "monkey dwarf," which is a fair description of his appearance. In disposition he is like a tiny Terrier: lively, bright, active, and brave.

The BRUSSELS GRIFFON, with his pug nose, prominent eyes, long mustache, beard, and eyebrows, and his down-curved mouth, looks rather like a gargoyle or a little devil. But that odd face of his more often expresses melting tenderness than ferocity. He is really a Belgian version of the German Affenpinscher, with many of the same characteristics. Fanciers say that he is exceptionally intelligent and trainable, with the temperament of a working Terrier.

The PEKINGESE is an ancient, aristocratic oriental breed that was imported to England after the fall of Peking in 1861 by the British, who refined and perfected it into the luxury breed we know today. Obviously aware of his noble past, he is rather haughty, dignified, naturally well-mannered, but apt to be autocratic if allowed to have his way. He is surprisingly tough and brave for his size, unusually long-lived, and is one of the few Toy breeds that appeals to men. Unfortunately, like all short-nosed dogs, he is prone to respiratory ailments and is apt to snore. He is difficult to whelp because of his oversized head, and his protruding eyes are vulnerable to accidents, ailments, and blindness in old age. Despite these handicaps, he has so much character and beauty of a special kind that his owners often become lifelong fanciers of the breed.

The PUG is another Toy breed of oriental origin with a smooth coat and a funny, wrinkled, squashed-in face. Like the Peke, he is a dwarf breed. More tolerant of children, he makes a better family dog as well as a devoted pet for the elderly or invalid, since he is perfectly content to lead a quiet indoor life as long as he has company. Gay, sturdy, devoted, clean, playful, and affectionate, he can be stubborn too.

The JAPANESE SPANIEL, recently renamed the JAPANESE CHIN, is long-legged than the Pekingese and less luxuriously furred. But there is a similarity between their flat faces, aristocratic bearing, sensitivity, and independence. Alert, dainty, proud, pretty, said to possess an unusually good memory, he is by tradition a ladies' dog rather than a children's pet.

The ENGLISH TOY SPANIEL is an elegant, gay little dog, friendly, lively, rather like a small Cocker Spaniel in conformation and temperament, and half-Cocker, half-Pekingese in head, if you can imagine that. There are four color varieties: King Charles (black and tan), Prince Charles (white with black and tan markings), Ruby (red), and Blenheim (white with red markings). He is a refined, active, good-natured companion rather than a sporting partner.

The TOY POODLE is the most popular Toy dog in America by far, and intense breeding to fill the demand has led to weaknesses in some strains, such as incontinence, nervousness, and shyness. Ideally, he is a genuine Miniature Poodle, with all of the Standard's qualities: gaiety, courage, alertness, responsiveness, and intelligence. A sound one well selected from a serious breeder should be bright enough to learn almost anything his tiny size permits him to do. He craves company and needs a lot of attention. He needs a lot of grooming too, but this poses no problem because he loves being fussed over.

The MINIATURE PINSCHER is a wee dog with a lot of spunk. He looks like a tiny deer and moves along at a smart clip like a Hackney pony. He is quite trainable for a Toy and even retains some of his ances-

Toy Poodle. (*William P. Gilbert*)

Yorkshire Terrier. (*William P. Gilbert*)

tors' hunting and guarding instincts. Ideal for city-dwellers, he is alert, self-possessed, courageous, affectionate, and intelligent—except that he does not always seem to realize how very small he is, or how sharp his little teeth are.

The YORKSHIRE TERRIER is also surprisingly robust and self-confident for such a tiny, pretty creature—at least, he is if he is treated like a Terrier rather than a lap dog. Less helpless than he looks, he is game, alert, bright in obedience training, highly companionable, and always ready to play. The smallest are the most expensive and the most fashionable, but are also apt to be the least sound.

The TOY MANCHESTER TERRIER, registered as the Black-and-Tan Toy Terrier in England, where the breed was created, is a spirited, frail, diminutive version of the Manchester Terrier who has lost much of his ancestors' steadiness and soundness during the miniaturization process. Agile and bright, he is not an ideal pet, because of the difficulty of raising and caring for such a delicate creature.

The SILKY TERRIER is an Australian long-haired Miniature Terrier resembling the Yorkshire in coat and conformation, although slightly larger: 9 to 11 pounds, compared to the Yorkshire's 7 pounds or less. Rather sporting for a Toy, and a good ratter, he is a new breed in America. The Skye Terrier and the Yorkshire were his foundation breeds.

The MALTESE TERRIER, one of the oldest of all the pet breeds, was already a favorite of fashionable ladies in ancient Greece and Rome. He is still an amusing companion, lively, playful, affectionate, with a pretty, silky, long white coat that is tied in two topknots, and a venerable history of faithful friendship. Many owners say that he is more like a Sheepdog than a Terrier in temperament and instinct.

The POMERANIAN is a miniature Spitz whose luxurious fur coat, small eyes, pointed nose, and curly tail betray his northern ancestry. He is said to have the keenest hearing of the Toys and may be the most intelligent, for he has been successfully trained in competitive Obedience and even possesses a herding instinct. He is vigilant, lively, dainty, and affectionate. Nervous individuals can be snappy, noisy, and destructive too.

The ITALIAN GREYHOUND is graceful, refined, and delicate. So susceptible to chills that he needs to be clothed whenever he goes out, he really prefers a comfortable indoor life. He requires little care as long as he can constantly accompany his owner, to whom he is devoted. Perhaps it is his long history of companionship to the nobility that has given him his pride, distinction, and aloofness with strangers. He is, at any rate, a beautiful little dog for an elegant person leading a rather inactive life.

Pomeranian. (*Annan Photo Features*)

Shih Tzu. (*Annan Photo Features*)

The CHIHUAHUA is the tiniest breed of all, weighing as little as one pound (although 2 to 4 pounds is preferred in show dogs). He can trace his history back to the dogs of the ancient Aztecs. The smooth-coated variety is the more popular, but there is also a long-coated type. He is exceptionally vigilant and observing, a vociferous watchdog, egotistical, brashly unfriendly with other dogs, and suspiciously unsociable with people, except for his owner, to whom he is jealously attached. Sensitive to cold and difficult to breed, he is almost impossible to housebreak. In spite of all this, he has become one of the most fashionable Toy dogs in America.

The PAPILLON is a graceful, silky, long-haired dog with huge ears for his tiny body, hence his name (which means "butterfly" in French). Traditionally a ladies' lap dog, his outstanding characteristics are highly feminine: grace, elegance, daintiness, sensitivity, and affection.

The SHIH TZU bears a name that means "lion dog" in Chinese, although he is of Tibetan origin. He is an arrogant little beauty who carries his head high and his tail proudly curled over his back. He has a chrysanthemum face, a luxurious long coat, long whiskers and beard, an aristocratic air, and an alert, lively personality.

NON-SPORTING DOGS

Aside from the Toy breeds which were developed exclusively for companionship, there is really no such thing as a non-sporting or non-working breed, since all of them originally served some practical purpose. This final official AKC group is therefore a disparate collection of various breeds that have little in common, but include some of the most popular pets of all.

The POODLE is the most popular purebred dog in the United States by a wide margin, perhaps the most popular dog in the Western world. He comes in three sizes: Standard (over 15 inches high at the withers), Miniature (10 to 15 inches), and Toy (10 inches and under). The Standard and Miniature varieties are classified as "Non-Sporting," although they are among the best sports in dogdom. While the Poodle has been a chic status symbol for several decades, his popularity is not only a matter of fashion, but also due to his superlative qualities as a pet. Highly intelligent and trainable, he has a talent for imitation and is as quick and willing to learn tricks as he is to master precise Obedience disciplines. His pampered air is entirely a matter of grooming (which is indis-

Standard Poodle. (*William P. Gilbert*)

pensable). Actually, he is sound and sturdy, ready for any kind of activity, and at the same time adaptable to a quiet home life. He is one of the most civilized breeds, often seeming to prefer a human way of life. The Miniature is perhaps the better choice as a family pet, since the Standard is inclined to be a one-man dog, very jealous of his owner.

The DALMATIAN, an attractive, medium-sized, spotted dog, a native of the Austrian province that is now a part of Yugoslavia, is famous as a carriage dog and as the mascot of horse-drawn fire wagons. He is noted also for his infrequent barking (although he is an alert watchdog), his cleanliness, odorlessness, and indefatigability. Steady, quiet, protective of children, he needs a lot of exercise in order to maintain his easygoing, well-balanced disposition. His smart appearance may give the impression that he is a decorative luxury pet, but he is basically and traditionally a hard Working dog.

Miniature Poodle. (*William P. Gilbert*)

Dalmatian. (*William P. Gilbert*)

The CHOW CHOW is an Asiatic breed, instantly recognizable by his oriental features, his square body, sumptuous coat, tiny wide-set ears, and his blue-black palate, gums, and tongue. He is aloof, proud, distrustful of strangers, not very reliable with children or with other dogs, who often seem to take a dislike to him. Maybe this is because of a unique odor he is believed to possess, because he can be a bit of a bully, or because of his perpetually scowling expression. Nevertheless, he is a handsome animal to those who appreciate his unusual character. He is a one-man dog who needs lots of exercise and a strong-minded master.

The BULLDOG is a stolid, heavy, endearing dog. Within his misshapen body there beats a heart of gold. Created in the seventeenth century for bullbaiting, he has since been bred exclusively as a pet and has become one of the most devoted, affectionate companions in the world, docile, gentle, with a desire to please that is very touching. He loves children and is patient with them even when they tease, being almost impervious to pain. No longer a fighter, he seems hurt by the terror he often inspires in other animals. Unfortunately, his abnormal conformation makes him prone to many health problems. He also snores, drools, and dislikes hot climates and great exertion. He has an ungainly loose-jointed shuffle, due to his short bowed legs. But he has a special appeal for special people.

The FRENCH BULLDOG looks like a miniature Bulldog without the wrinkles and jowls. Recognizable by his batlike ears, he also has bulging

Bulldog. (*William P. Gilbert*)

eyes, a head too large for his body, and amazing strength for his size. Always bred exclusively as a pet, he is alert, intelligent, devoted, calm, and combines considerable charm with a rather unattractive exterior.

The BOSTON TERRIER is one of the rare American canine creations, a better-looking, sleeker version of the French Bulldog. He is clever, brave, playful, and loving, and it is a pity that (like the Bulldog and its derivatives) he is prone to unsoundness. If you decide to get a Boston Terrier, get a good veterinarian first, because you are sure to need his services, especially if you wish to breed.

The KEESHOND used to work as a guard on Dutch canal barges, and still retains a strong guarding instinct, even an instinct for attack. But American breeders, a particularly devoted lot, are emphasizing his qualities as a loving family pet and as a glamorous show dog, rather than as a working guard. He is also intelligent enough to be trained successfully in Obedience.

The SCHIPPERKE is an alert, foxy-looking little Spitz-type dog that has been used as a guard and companion on Belgian horse-drawn barges, and from his past experience is said to have retained an affinity for horses. He is vigilant and courageous, suspicious of strangers, but also playful, curious, gentle and companionable with children, devoted to his home and family. All-black and with a very short docked tail, he is unusual-looking and quite attractive. He is happy living in a city apartment if he has sufficient company.

Schipperke. (*William P. Gilbert*)

The LHASA APSO is a small Tibetan dog who probably combines Terrier and Spaniel blood. He has the long silky coat, the sociability and gaiety of the Spaniel, along with the self-confidence, intelligence, alertness, pride, and spunkiness of the Terrier. Increasingly popular as a luxury pet, he has far too much character to be treated as a plaything or an ornament.

The TIBETAN TERRIER resembles a miniature Old English Sheepdog, although he was bred in Tibetan monasteries. He is medium-sized (14 to 16 inches high), with a compact body, and a long shaggy coat that falls over his eyes. Like many oriental breeds, he is intelligent, self-assured, alert, bold but not pugnacious, and decidedly aloof with strangers.

The BICHON FRISÉ is a cuddly creature that looks like a stuffed toy dog or perhaps a powderpuff, with his profuse, curly white coat, which requires a lot of care. He is, however, all live dog: vivacious, sturdy, even-tempered, bright, and quite dignified for such a little ball of fluff.

As you can see, each breed has its qualities, and most of them have inconveniences of one kind or another (although what may be inconvenient to one owner may be exactly what another one is seeking in a dog).

The *popularity* of a breed is by no means a measure of its intrinsic qualities. It can be a reflection of current fashion, taste, travel, even of the economic situation. It is influenced by books, movies, television, the choice of royalty and other celebrities, by magazine covers and advertising campaigns. Thanks largely to the celebrity of Rin-Tin-Tin and Strongheart in the mid-1920s, the German Shepherd was the most popular breed in the United States from 1927 (when there were only three registered Poodles in the country) to 1929. The Boston Terrier led the list from 1930 to 1935, followed by the Cocker Spaniel (1936–52), the Beagle (1953–58), and the Poodle (since 1959). The current trend seems to be a decline for the Poodle, an increased demand for Doberman Pinschers, Labrador and Golden Retrievers, a return to favor of the Cocker Spaniel, and a growing fashion for the Lhasa Apso and the Shetland Sheepdog.

MISCELLANEOUS BREEDS

In addition to the breeds recognized by the American Kennel Club, there are others just as purebred, some of which are registered by other associations, such as:

The United Kennel Club (321 West Cedar Street, Kalamazoo, Michigan 49007), which maintains studbooks for six different varieties of Coonhounds (the American Black-and-Tan, the Bluetick, the English Coonhound, the Redbone, the Treeing Walker, and the Plott—all of which hunt climbing game such as squirrels, raccoon, and cougar); hunting hounds such as the English Bloodhound and the English Beagle; the American Water Spaniel, the American Eskimo, Arctic Husky, and Alaskan Malamute; the English Shepherd, Columbian Collie and Scotch Collie; the Miniature Boxer, American Toy Terrier, and Toy Fox Terrier; and the American (pit) Bull Terrier. As you see, the emphasis is on Sporting and Working breeds, although the UKC licenses benched dog shows as well as Working and Sporting Trials, and awards Championship titles in both divisions.

The American Field Stud Book (222 West Adams Street, Chicago, Illinois 60606), which has registered bird dogs such as Pointers, Setters, Spaniels, Retrievers, and other Field Trialers since 1900.

The International Fox Hunters' Studbook (The Chase, 152 Walnut Street, Lexington, Kentucky 40503), a registry for Foxhounds.

The National Stock Dog Registry (Route I, Butler, Indiana 46721), which is concerned with Working sheep and cattle breeds of dogs.

The North American Sheepdog Society (210 East Main Street, McLeansboro, Illinois 62859)

The Greyhound Stud Book (National Greyhound Racing Association, 300 North Cedar Street, Abilene, Kansas 67410)

Studbooks are also maintained by certain breed clubs, generally of breeds that are rare or insufficiently established to be eligible for recognition by the major registries.

The AKC accords "partial recognition" to a few breeds such as the Border Collie, Pharaoh Hound, Cavalier King Charles Spaniel, Tibetan Spaniel, Miniature Bull Terrier, Spinoni Italiani, Australian Cattle Dog, and Australian Kelpie, permitting them to compete in a Miscellaneous Class at licensed dog shows and to win ribbons but not Championship points.

FOREIGN BREEDS

Many foreign breeds are registered by their national kennel clubs but not—or not yet—in the United States. Some of them are particularly attractive or interesting, for example:

The CAVALIER KING CHARLES SPANIEL (12 inches, 10–18

pounds), similar to the English Toy Spaniel, a lovely dog, sound and steady, the result of an attempt to re-create the original Toy Spaniel depicted so often in the paintings of Van Dyck and other Dutch and Flemish masters.

The MAREMMA SHEEPDOG (26 inches, 50 pounds), a beautiful, big, snow-white Italian sheepdog, probably related to the Hungarian sheepdog breeds.

The PORTUGUESE WATER DOG (20 inches, 40 pounds), a shaggy, rugged animal who is an excellent water retriever. He looks like a less elegant Poodle, and even more like an Irish Water Spaniel, which is not surprising since he is probably their common ancestor.

The JACK RUSSELL TERRIER, who lacks official recognition because his breeders do not seek it. In this they are respecting the wishes of the breed's creator, Parson Russell, a well-known dog-show judge, a founding member of the Kennel Club, and a breeder of Fox Terriers, who decided to create "the perfect Terrier" in early nineteenth-century England. The result, after some sixty years of breeding efforts, is an exceptionally bright and game little dog (10–14 inches, 11–16 pounds) who is adaptable, courageous, sportive, trainable, and completely unspoiled. There are many acceptable variations in his conformation. The fact that no two are identical is a matter of pride to Jack Russell fanciers. His coat is predominantly white with black or brown patches, and his head is marked by patches over the eyes. The coat may be rough, smooth, or broken. The ears may be bent over or pricked. Breed clubs maintain studbooks in America and England. But unless you deal with a reliable breeder, it will be hard to know whether you are buying a genuine Jack Russell, or simply an appealing little Terrier with a spot over his eye.

The *Border Collie* (18 inches, 40 pounds), also known as the English Shepherd, is a superb herding dog who is said to dominate the flock he handles by his magnetic eye. He is smaller and less glamorous than the modern Collie, and is a real Working dog of exceptional intelligence and skill.

Among the foreign Kennel Clubs, which are the best source of information about foreign breeds and breeders, are:

In *Austria:*   Osterreischischer Kynologen Verband, 3 Karl
                    Schweighofer Gasse, Vienna
In *Belgium:*   Union Cynologique Saint-Hubert, 25 Avenue de
                    l'Armée, Bruxelles IV
In *Canada:*   The Canadian Kennel Club, 2150 Bloor Street W.,
                    Toronto, Ontario M65 4U7

In *England:*	The Kennel Club, 1–4 Clarge's Street, Piccadilly, London WI Y8AB
In *France:*	Société Centrale Canine, 215 rue St. Denis, Paris 75002
In *Holland:*	Raad van Beheer op Kynologisch Gebied in Nederland, 16 Emmalaan, Amsterdam
In *Italy:*	Ente Nazionale della Cinofilia Italiana, 21 Viale Premuda, Milan
In *Japan:*	Japan Dog Federation, Chiyoda-ku, Kanda, Asahi-cho no 8, Tokyo
In *Mexico:*	Asociación Canofila Mexicana, Malaga Sur 44, Mexico City 19 DF
In *Spain:*	Real Sociedad Central de Fomento de las Razas Caninas en España, 20 los Madrazo, Madrid
In *West Germany:*	Verband für das Deutsche Hundewesen, 30 Schwanenstrasse, Dortmund

THE BEST BREED FOR YOU

Choosing a breed from these numerous varieties is a more serious matter than choosing one of 135 flavors of ice cream, but the best method is probably the same: first of all, elimination for practical reasons, after which it becomes a matter of taste. Of course, with dogs, there is also an element of personal attraction, a little like falling in love. Most owners think that their breed is the finest in the world, which only proves that all breeds have their charm, that dogs are amazingly adaptable to the requirements of their owners, and sometimes, perhaps, that love is blind. Nevertheless, it is always useful to seek the advice of experienced dog owners and breeders. Veterinarians are an excellent, more objective source of information, because of their intimate contacts with many different breeds and their knowledge of each breed's current qualities and weaknesses. It may also be helpful to know that some breeds have long given outstanding satisfaction in filling certain roles. For example:

AS AN ALL-ROUND HUNTING DOG AND FAMILY PET:
Small: English Cocker Spaniel
Medium: Brittany Spaniel, Springer Spaniel
Large: Golden Retriever, Labrador Retriever, English Setter

AS AN ACTIVE OUTDOOR COMPANION FOR ACTIVE OWNERS:
Small: Beagle, Australian Terrier

Medium: Spaniels, Welsh Terrier, Irish Terrier
Large: Retrievers, German Shepherd, Dalmation, Giant
            Schnauzer, Standard Poodle, Boxer, English Setter,
            Irish Setter, Rhodesian Ridgeback

AS A GUARD DOG:

In the country: German Shepherd, Doberman Pinscher, Boxer, Great
Dane, Old English Sheepdog, Airedale, Bull Mastiff, St. Bernard, Great
Pyrenees Sheepdog
In the city: Pomeranian, Fox Terrier, Sealyham Terrier, Bull Terrier,
Schipperke

AS A ONE-MAN DOG:

Small: Japanese Spaniel, Pekingese, Chihuahua
Medium: Basenji, Irish Terrier
Large: Irish Setter, German Shepherd, Doberman Pinscher,
            Chow Chow, Great Dane, Alaskan Malamute

AS A FAMILY PET FOR VERY YOUNG CHILDREN:

Small: Dachshund, Miniature Schnauzer
Medium: Brittany Spaniel, Basset
Large: Labrador Retriever, Old English Sheepdog, Great
            Pyrenees Sheepdog, Newfoundland, Briard

AS A FAMILY PET FOR TEEN-AGE CHILDREN:

Small: Beagle, Cocker Spaniel, Fox Terrier
Medium: Irish Terrier, Springer Spaniel, Brittany Spaniel
Large: Standard Poodle, Airedale, German Shepherd, Boxer,
            Golden Retriever, Labrador Retriever, Irish Setter

AS A COMPANION FOR THE LONELY AND CHILDLESS:

All of the Toy breeds, especially the Italian Greyhound, Maltese
Terrier, Pekingese, Toy Poodle, Yorkshire Terrier, and Pomeranian.
For active people: All of the small Terriers, especially the Cairn
Terrier, West Highland White Terrier, Kerry Blue Terrier, and
Smooth-haired Fox Terrier.

AS A COMPANION FOR THE ELDERLY OR INDOLENT:

Small: Chihuahua, Toy Poodle, Miniature Pinscher,
            Dachshund, Pekingese, Bichon Frisé
Medium: Basenji
Large: Bulldog, Newfoundland

AS AN ATTENTION-GETTER AND CONVERSATION-OPENER:
The lamb-like Bedlington Terrier, the barkless Basenji, the monkey-like Griffon and Affenpinscher, the dishmop Puli, the impossible-to-ignore St. Bernard, Newfoundland, Great Dane, Bull Mastiff, Irish Wolfhound and Scottish Deerhound; and the Otter Hound, an endangered breed, of which there are only two hundred in the world.

AS A SOURCE OF ESTHETIC PLEASURE:
Small: Lhasa Apso, Whippet, Italian Greyhound
Medium: Saluki, Samoyed
Large: Collie, Borzoi, Afghan, English Setter, Great
           Dane, Irish Wolfhound

AS A PET FOR A STRONGWILLED OWNER:
Small: Scottish Terrier
Medium: Keeshond, Chow Chow
Large: Doberman Pinscher, German Shepherd, Siberian
           Husky, Rhodesian Ridgeback

AS A COMPROMISE FOR PEOPLE WHO LOVE BIG DOGS BUT HAVEN'T THE SPACE:
Miniature Pinscher (instead of a Doberman)
Whippet, Italian Greyhound (instead of a large Hound)
English Cocker Spaniel (instead of an English or Irish Setter)
Shetland Sheepdog (instead of a Collie)
Pomeranian (instead of an Alaskan Malamute or a Husky)
Welsh Terrier (instead of an Airedale)
Tibetan Terrier (instead of an Old English Sheepdog)
Schipperke (instead of a Keeshond)

Experience has also shown that some breeds possess well-established attributes which may be just what you are looking for, or just what you wish to avoid, for example:

ENJOY LEARNING TRICKS:
Small: Miniature Poodle, Smooth-haired Fox Terrier
Large: Golden Retriever

EXCEL IN OBEDIENCE TRAINING:
Small: Miniature Poodle, Shetland Sheepdog
Large: Standard Poodle, German Shepherd, Doberman Pinscher,
           Collie, English Sheepdog, Golden Retriever, Airedale

DIFFICULT TO TRAIN:
   Afghan, Chow Chow, Keeshond, Borzoi, Chihuahua, Alaskan Mala-
   mute, Siberian Husky, Greyhound, Foxhound—in short, many Ter-
   riers, most Hounds, and all highly nervous individuals of any breed.

DISLIKE SOLITUDE:
   All dogs, but especially Poodles, Spaniels, Terriers, and Toys. The
   Shepherds, Guards, and Hounds seem to tolerate it better.

ACCEPT A RATHER SEDENTARY LIFE:
   Very small dogs like the Pekingese, Chihuahua, Shi Tzu, Schipperke,
   Boston Terrier, Dachshund, Pug; and very big or heavy ones like the
   Basset, Bulldog, Bloodhound, Mastiff, St. Bernard, and New-
   foundland.

NOT VERY GOOD WITH CHILDREN:
   All nervous dogs, all Toys, the Borzoi, Chihuahua, Pomeranian,
   Pembroke Corgi, Pointer, Italian Greyhound, and many small
   Terriers including the Scottish, Sealyham, Yorkshire, and Maltese.

PARTICULARLY STEADY IN TEMPERAMENT:
   Standard Poodle, Labrador Retriever, Bloodhound, Great Pyrenees
   Sheepdog, Old English Sheepdog, Bouvier des Flandres.

From the smallest recognized breed in America (the tiny Chihuahua) to the largest
(the massive St. Bernard), there are many breeds from which to choose the one most
suitable for each owner's requirements and circumstances. (*John Gajda/FPG*)

3.

Buying a Dog of Your Own

While there are many homeless dogs, few homes that want a dog are unable to find one. But finding the right dog requires time, thought, and legwork. Far from being a chore, it can be fun and instructive too, for in your search you will pick up a lot of information about dogs that will make you a better, more satisfied owner.

Having more or less decided on a breed, let's now consider the question of time—not the time you'll spend looking for your dog, but the *best time of year in which to look for him.*

Although bitches come in heat every 6 months, generally in the spring and early winter, puppies are born every month of the year, and at any given time puppies of all ages are available somewhere. Most of them are purchased as Christmas presents, which is just about the worst time for bringing up a young puppy. Many families buy a dog as a vacation companion for the children at the beginning of the summer, which is a very good time if the puppy is mature enough to join in their holiday activities. The ideal timing would be to acquire a puppy at the age of 3 months at a time of year when there are at least 3 months of sunny, mild weather ahead while he is growing—in other words, from May to September in most parts of the country.

The best time to buy a Hunting dog is in the spring (April, May, or June), for the puppies will be 6 or 7 months old when the fall hunting season opens and can be given preliminary field work. Trained adult dogs can, of course, be purchased all year round, but it is best to buy one well enough in advance of the season for the dog to have formed an attachment to his new owner before accompanying him in the field.

It is risky to make promises or to set a date limit. You may find your puppy right away, or you may have to do a lot of shopping around. You may discover a breeder whose line you like but who hasn't at the moment a puppy available; if he is expecting a litter shortly, it may be worth waiting for the event. Most small breeders will refer a customer to another breeder when they are unable to satisfy his needs themselves. These small kennels usually concentrate on a single breed and breed dogs not only to earn money, but principally to create a line that reproduces in a consistent way the qualities they consider most desirable. If you like the looks and personality of their stock, you will probably like their future puppies, as well as the puppies of breeders they recommend, who breed along the same lines and often use the same stud dogs.

CHOOSING YOUR BREEDER

So before you choose your dog, you have to choose a breeder. How do you go about it?

As soon as you decide to get a dog, you should order a subscription to one of the leading dog magazines (if you cannot buy it on your newsstand) and study each issue, including the advertisements. Among the most important are:

Dog World (10060 West Roosevelt Road, Westchester, Illinois 60153)

Pure-bred Dogs—American Kennel Club Gazette (published by the AKC, 51 Madison Avenue, New York, New York 10010), invaluable for keeping up with show results, changes in breed standards, activities of breed clubs, and the Dog Show, AKC Field Trial and Obedience Trial Calendars.

The American Field Magazine (222 West Adams Street, Chicago, Illinois 60606) for Pointers and Setters.

Dogs in Canada (59 Front Street East, Toronto, Ontario M5EIB3, Canada)

Western Kennel World (20 Sycamore Street, San Francisco, California 94110)

Dogs and *Show Dogs* (257 Park Avenue South, New York, New York 10010)

Hunting Dog Magazine (215 South Washington Street, Greenfield, Ohio 45123)

When you have decided on a breed or breeds, you should:

1) Write to the American Kennel Club (51 Madison Avenue, New York, New York 10010), "Breeders' Information Service," or to the Secretary of the breed registry that handles your selected breed, and request a list of the breeding kennels in your region specializing in the breed of your choice. Ask also for the names and addresses of the breed clubs that interest you, and write to the Club Secretary for information and breeder recommendations. In some areas there are commercial Dog Breeders' Referral Services, which can be found in the classified telephone directory. Finally, request the current AKC Dog Show Calendar, and try to attend the dog shows that are within a reasonable distance of your home.

The purpose of *dog shows* is not only for exhibitors to win ribbons and make Champions, but also to provide a showcase for breeders. Most exhibitors are delighted to talk to prospective buyers after the judging is over. This is particularly true of "benched shows," which are increasingly rare, in which the dogs remain on exhibit all day long instead of merely appearing in the ring for judging. However, even at an unbenched show, you will see lots of dogs around, in addition to the groups of dogs of the same breed in the ring, whose appearance, personality, and manners you can compare. It can help you to decide on one breed rather than another, and even on a particular line within a breed. If you already have your heart set on a certain breed, try to attend a Specialty Show, entirely devoted to that breed. You may narrow your choice to the progeny of a certain stud dog.

2) Order a brochure entitled *Where to Buy, Board or Train a Dog* from the Gaines Dog Research Center (250 North Street, White Plains, New York 10625) for other useful addresses.

3) Make an appointment and pay a visit to the breeders in your area whose produce has most impressed you and who have been most highly recommended.

If all of this sounds like a lot of trouble for so simple a matter as buying a dog, you are perfectly right. It is the connoisseur's way. It is also, undeniably, the best way, if you wish to find a superior dog who is most suitable to your needs and wishes.

It is not, however, the only way. A complete list would include:

1) *Small breeding kennels,* generally devoted to a single breed, with a limited, choice production. These are the best places to buy a dog.

2) *Large breeding kennels,* which often specialize in several breeds and are run on a scale that prohibits personal attention and handling, although the physical care is usually satisfactory. Unfortunately, there also exist so-called "puppy factories," which are strictly commercial ventures, switching from one breed to another according to fashion, and turning out puppies as if they were merchandise instead of living creatures. Only a personal visit and your own perceptiveness will enable you to recognize them for what they are and to avoid them. Even when you buy a puppy from a conscientious large breeder, it is advisable to adopt him young, before he has become marked by the impersonal routine of kennel life.

3) *Pet Shop and Department Store Pet Departments,* which are proliferating throughout the country. You should know that a puppy ends up in one of these shops because his breeder has been unable to sell him directly. It may be that the puppy is not up to the breeder's standard, or the breeder may wish to dispose of a litter quickly by selling it in its entirety to the shop. Some pet-shop owners are true animal lovers who have built up sources of supply in small breeders who, because of isolation or some other reason, are unable to sell their produce in any other way. But this case is very rare. Others are primarily merchants, interested in making a profit above all, and much less solicitous of the animals' welfare. Again, only personal observation and instinct will enable you to distinguish between the two. It is certainly advisable to insist on a veterinary examination of a pet-shop puppy, and to complete the necessary immunization shots as soon as possible. Many lovely puppies have been purchased in pet shops, but there have also been many disappointments, so the buyer should beware.

Beware of what?

—*Beware* of congenital ailments and infirmities such as rickets, hip dysplasia, blindness, and deafness, which a veterinary examination will reveal.

—*Beware* of symptoms of contagious disease, such as a runny nose and eyes, a hacking cough, a dull eye, or listless behavior.

—*Beware* of incomplete or worthless papers and pedigrees.

—*Beware* of some anomaly of conformation, marking, or color that would exclude the puppy from the show ring or from breeding.

4) *Advertisements in Newspapers and Magazines* are used by breeders large and small, amateur and commercial, by pet shops and mail order firms to sell dogs, and by individuals who wish to find a home for a puppy or an adult dog. Due to publication delays, magazine advertisements usually announce that a kennel has "puppies available." Newspaper advertisements more often describe individual dogs or puppies for immediate sale. These are found in the "Pets" or "Dogs" sections of classified advertisements, or on the Dog or Sports page. Sunday editions of large city newspapers are the most promising source, while local newspapers advertise local produce. Needless to say, you should never buy an advertised puppy sight unseen, although experienced breeders who are familiar with bloodlines may sometimes do so. But for a dog of your own, and especially for your first dog, it is advisable to deal with breeders within visiting distance.

There is nothing to prevent you from advertising your desire to buy a puppy, particularly if you know exactly what you want, although this is less customary.

5) *Veterinarians* often keep a notice board in their waiting rooms, where local breeders advertise available pups. Veterinarians are an excellent source of breeder information too.

6) *Mail Order Pet Shops* are a recent, flourishing form of canine commerce. They sell through newspaper and magazine advertisements, sight unseen, and combine every possible risk, including that of shipping a young puppy a long distance. The double stress of weaning and shipping at so critical a stage of his development makes him highly vulnerable to disease and to psychological disturbances. Furthermore, these enterprises often indulge in the minor racket of announcing in bold letters "AKC Registered," which may indeed mean that the puppies listed for sale are all purebred and registered. But it may also mean merely that the kennel itself is registered with the AKC, having simply filed an application and paid a modest fee.

7) *Friends and Acquaintances* (you will be surprised how many you have, once the word gets around that you are looking for a dog), who have bred a litter or wish to dispose of a dog for one reason or another. Do not let your friendship overshadow your own interest or the dog's. Be sure he is of a breed you like and that his temperament and conformation are up to the standard you seek. In the case of a homebred litter, take the initiative in seeing that the registration is correctly completed, if the puppy is eligible, and that protective shots are given under veterinary supervision, at your expense if necessary.

Friends may offer you a dog they can no longer keep because of illness, marriage, or divorce. Many people have successfully adopted the adult dog of friends who were moving to another city or country where it was impossible to take their pet. On the other hand, it is seldom successful when a dog moves to a new home just down the street or a few blocks away. Even though you offer him every comfort, his instinct will be to return to his original home, to the unhappy embarrassment of everyone concerned.

Remember that buying a dog is a business transaction, even when dealing with friends. It is best to pay even a token price rather than accept him as a gift. The new owner is apt to take better care of a dog he has paid for, and the seller is less likely to feel he has been taken advantage of, or to regret the gift. Even between the best of friends, purchasing formalities should be meticulously fulfilled, including a detailed bill of sale.

8) *Animal Philanthropies* maintain rescue centers for lost, stray, and unwanted dogs, all over the country. All of them will mail you a list of the shelters in your vicinity. Among them are:

The Humane Society of the United States (2100 L Street NW, Washington, D.C. 20037)

The American Society for the Prevention of Cruelty to Animals (441 East Ninety-second Street, New York, New York 10028)

PAWS (Pet Animal Welfare Society) also maintains shelters and clinics in many cities.

Bide-A-Wee Home (410 East Thirty-eighth Street, New York, New York 10016)

In these charitable kennels you will find dogs of all sizes, shapes, and ages. Some have been abandoned, some have been lost, some have been born in a field or an empty lot, the progeny of a homeless bitch. Many puppies are whelped in these shelters by a female who was abandoned simply because she was pregnant. There is seldom any record of their past or of their previous owner. While some are obviously purebred, none possess registration papers and none are therefore eligible for showing or for breeding registrable litters.

It is a heart-rending experience to visit these havens, because adversity has marked all of the dogs in one way or another, and it is almost too much for a sensitive person to bear. Tender souls are apt to be attracted by the most miserable-looking dog rather than the most suitable, which is a very poor criterion indeed for choosing a dog.

If you succumb to a pair of pleading eyes, you should know that it is customary to promise to have male puppies neutered at the age of 6 months, to sterilize bitches, and to make a donation to the philanthropy to cover the cost of these operations if they have already been performed on the pet you choose.

9) *Dog Pounds* exist in most towns where there is a Dog Warden who picks up stray or lost dogs and imprisons dogs who have broken the law. If the dog carries identification, an effort is made to contact the owner. Otherwise, he is kept for a brief period of time and then destroyed or sold to a laboratory. During the period of reprieve, the dogs are available for adoption upon payment of a small fee. This is even more of a blindfold operation than adopting a dog from the ASPCA or the Humane Society, which are equipped to examine each new arrival and to dispose of diseased or dangerous animals.

10) *Gift Dogs* pose problems. As we have seen, acquiring a dog is not a matter to be taken lightly. Yet, how many parents decide to give a child a puppy for his birthday, go to the pet shop as they would to a toy store, and select a dog as they would a doll or a plastic gun. And how many young (and older) men make a present of a puppy to their girlfriend of the moment, just as they might offer her a dozen roses or a string of pearls! Parents, no matter how doting, and suitors, no matter how lovestruck, should know better. In order to avoid the minor tragedies that frequently result from these impulsive gestures, you should: (1) Never offer a puppy as a surprise gift; and (2) If you want to accept the offer of a gift dog, explain tactfully that you also want to have the fun of selecting it yourself.

11) A *Stray Dog* may wander hopefully through your kitchen door one day, starving for food, warmth, and love. Is he lost, or has he been abandoned? You may never know. If the dog wears some identification, you should, of course, make every possible effort to contact his owner, who may be frantically scouring the countryside in search of him. If not, you should report the find to the Dog Warden as well as to any nearby animal shelters, place an advertisement in your local newspaper, and notify the local radio stations which broadcast news of lost and found pets. If nobody has claimed him at the end of a week or so, you have the choice of keeping him, or finding a home for him, or of turning him over to an animal welfare agency. It is a difficult choice to make. The one thing you absolutely cannot do is to chase him away.

This dilemma is common is summer resorts at the end of the season, but also in the city, where the canine instinct for finding the way home does not seem to operate very well.

Stray or abandoned dogs are apt to seek shelter in homes where there is already another dog. Often one of these strays will make friends with your dog and hopefully follow him home at mealtime. Another common scenario is the neighborhood child who is followed home by a stray dog.

Mother won't have one. So the child rings all the doorbells on the street, offering the homeless waif, and one of the doorbells may be yours. What should you do?

If you already own a dog, you must put his interest first. Two dogs are not much more bother than a single one in the country or suburbs. In fact, if they are compatible, they will soon be friends and your dog will be less likely to roam. However, the stranger can have a good or bad influence on your dog, so you should observe him carefully before making a decision. Since pedigreed dogs are seldom abandoned, your anonymous visitor is apt to be a mongrel. You may be able to distinguish from his physical appearance that he is a "Terrier type," a "Spaniel type," or whatever, and this will give you a clue as to whether or not he will get along with your dog. If he would not, do not consider keeping him. If you cannot find a home for him with friends or neighbors, steel your heart and take him to the nearest animal shelter, where he will have a chance of being adopted.

Another case requiring a heart of stone is that of the stray dog who is obviously diseased. Do not be misled by a dull coat, which may be merely the result of undernourishment. But a discharge from the eyes or nose, raw or bald patches on the skin, a dull and cloudy eye, are warning signals that the dog may introduce infection into your house. Unless you are willing to undertake the necessary medical care, it is best to entrust him to an animal charity that is equipped to handle such sad cases, especially if there are young children or other animals in your home.

But let's imagine that a perfectly healthy, attractive stray dog has asked you for shelter and has won your heart. You should help him to adjust to his new home just as you would a new dog of your own, with a few important differences:

—Have him examined as soon as possible by a veterinarian. Since you know nothing of his past history, play safe by giving him all of the normal protective vaccinations.

—If you already own a dog, make it very clear that he is still your number-one pet. He will be reassured, while the stray dog will be too grateful for a home and board to resent his inferior status. Dogs possess an elementary sense of justice, and the stray will find this arrangement only fair.

—Stray dogs are often half starved and will wolf down any food in sight. In order to avoid friction, feed him and your own dog in separate rooms until the newcomer has learned that each meal will not be his last. If your own dog is a fussy eater, you will be amazed to see how the presence of the new one will improve his appetite!

12) *Foreign Imports* are made mostly by breeders seeking certain

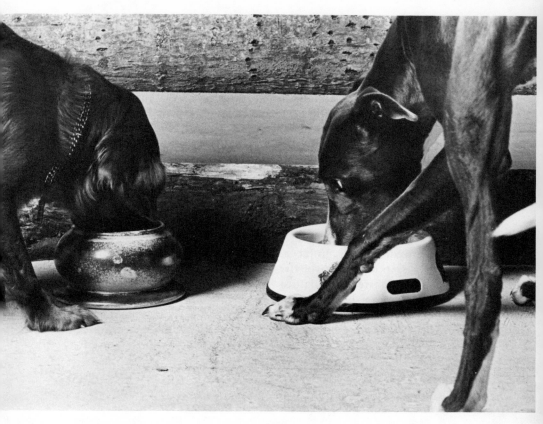

If your own dog is a fussy eater, you will be amazed to see how the presence of the new one will improve his appetite. (*Claus Ohm*)

bloodlines. Shipping charges are expensive and the risk of accident is greater than the specialized agencies are willing to admit, especially when the voyage is a long one involving a change of carrier. It may be worthwhile for a stud dog, but seldom for a pet.

English dog breeders are perhaps the most experienced in exporting dogs to the United States, probably because there is no language problem during correspondence, in addition to their long-time reputation, which dates from the Roman occupation of Great Britain, where English fighting Mastiffs were regularly exported to Italy. The British Kennel Club can supply the names of breeding kennels, which generally send photographs and take pains to fill the most detailed requirements. Another good source of information is *Our Dogs Annual*, which is practically an illustrated directory, edited by Our Dogs Publishing Company Ltd. (Oxford Road Station Approach, Manchester M60 15X, England).

Some American canine authorities act as agents for American buyers of foreign-bred dogs, although they deal far more often with breeders than with pet owners.

Oddly enough, the country in which a breed originated is not necessarily the one in which the best dogs of the breed are found today. Some of the finest Poodles (originally the German "Pudelhund") are being produced not in Germany, nor even in France (where the breed first gained widespread popularity), but by American breeders. England is generally considered the best breeding ground for the Pekingese and many Toy breeds and Terriers. Even the German Shepherd bred in England is preferred by many fanciers to those bred in his native land, which are reputed to be more aggressive. American-bred Doberman Pinschers of selected bloodlines are also apt to be better suited as pets than are most German imports. In fact, American breeders of these and other varieties also ship dogs all over the world. Our Dobermans, Boxers, Afghans, Kerry Blue Terriers, Miniature Schnauzers, and English Setters, among others, have even been exported to their countries of origin in order to improve the original breeding lines. In the case of the Mastiff, it was American exports of breeding stock that saved this ancient breed from extinction in Great Britain after World War II.

CHOOSING A DOG

When the moment arrives for selecting a dog of your own, you will already know what to look for and what to look out for. But you will soon find that a very young puppy only vaguely resembles the adult dog you admired in the show ring, and that older puppies, between the ages of 6 and 12 months or so, go through an awkward adolescent stage during which they seem hopelessly out of proportion. You will often get a better idea of what the puppy will eventually look like if you observe the adult members of his family. Breeders can usually show you older dogs of the same line, even of the same breeding. Do not be dismayed, however, by the looks of the puppy's mother. Recently whelped bitches are never at their best.

There are various methods of picking the best puppy from a litter. All advise avoiding the weakest and shyest, even though the runt of the litter may turn out to be the sturdiest of all. Some recommend the strongest and biggest; others, the most average-sized puppy. Some breeders claim that the bitch instinctively selects the best, so they remove the puppies from her and note the order in which she brings them back to the nest,

Selecting a puppy from a litter is very difficult when they are as uniformly attractive and appealing as these little Scottish Terriers. (*Freelance Photographers' Guild*)

Others say that the puppy whose eyes open first will be the brightest and healthiest.

Everyone agrees that the signs of a good temperament in a very young puppy are: friendliness, confidence, playfulness, and curiosity.

Make a noise and see how the puppy reacts. Does he scramble over to investigate, or does he hide in fright? Hold out something for him to play with—a handkerchief, a pencil, or your own finger. Is he curious and playful, or totally disinterested? Rule out at once a puppy with a runny nose or eyes, discolored teeth (often a sign of past distemper), a dull coat or eyes, pale gums, crooked legs (unless the breed standard requires them), red or bald patches on the skin, or a lump in the middle of his tummy (indicating hernia). No reputable dealer would offer you a puppy in any of these conditions, but you may run into them in animals proposed by shelters, by certain pet shops, even by inexperienced, well-meaning friends. Furthermore, some breeds are prone to unsoundness which you should take pains to detect and avoid, such as:

deafness in the Dalmatian, blue merle Collie, white Bull Terrier, white Collie and German Shepherd—in fact, all white puppies whose coat was produced by concentrated inbreeding. (To test for deafness,

Which puppy would you choose from this litter of Springer Spaniels? (*H. Armstrong Roberts*)

clap your hands or snap your fingers behind the puppy's head and see if he reacts.)

hip dysplasia in very large breeds such as the German Shepherd, Doberman Pinscher, Golden Retriever, Great Dane, Boxer, Alaskan Malamute, Old English Sheepdog, and St. Bernard.

progressive retinal atrophy (an eye condition starting with night blindness and ending in total loss of sight) in the Collie, Tibetan Terrier, Bedlington Terrier, Miniature Schnauzer, Irish, English and Gordon Setters, Miniature Poodle, Golden and Labrador Retrievers.

vertebral malformation in the Bulldog and Boston Terrier.

pathological nervousness in the Cocker Spaniel, Toy Poodle, Irish Setter, and many miniaturized Toy breeds.

When you face the problem of choosing a puppy from a group or a litter, why not do as show judges do and proceed by elimination?

First of all, sex preference will rule out about half of the candidates. Next, you can exclude individuals that appear to be shy, weak, or unsound. Then you might consider color and markings. Beyond this point, you can rely on your intuition—even on the intuition of the puppy who has obviously picked you to be his owner. But always bear in mind the role he will play in your life. For example, if you seek a playmate for the children, you should prefer the bold little rascal who tugs at your shoe-lace to the affectionate creature who nestles in your arms. But the latter would be the better choice if you seek a lovable companion to share a quiet life.

Choosing an adult dog is different, since he has already achieved his full physical development and personality. He may also have acquired physical or mental quirks. Quite often an adult dog for sale has posed a problem of one kind or another to his previous owner. Generally speaking, owners and breeders are honest in describing a dog's physical condition, character, and idiosyncrasies, such as being a cat-chaser, a rover, disliking children, or not being of show quality. But whenever possible, have a veterinary examination made as well, and do not hesitate to ask possibly embarrassing questions.

When you are confronted with an adult dog of unknown past, you must use all of your powers of observation. Perhaps the dog was abandoned simply because he grew too big or ate too much. But perhaps he was a biter, a fighter, or a chronic invalid. There are admirable persons who derive great satisfaction from salvaging such hapless creatures. However, unless animal philanthropy is your mission in life, you would do better to choose a sound, cheerful dog rather than a wretched waif. It will be kinder in the end.

Good temperament is the most important quality of all in a pet dog. But if you are looking for a show dog, temperament may be secondary to physical conformation. Some show judges accept and even prefer the exaggeration of temperamental qualities that are desirable only to a lesser degree in a pet or a Working dog. For example, the merriness characteristic of Cocker Spaniels and the liveliness of Toy Poodles are sometimes heightened to the point of hysteria and idiocy in the show ring. Terriers are bold by nature, but some show Champions are dangerously pugnacious. There is a considerable difference of temperament between the show lines and the working lines of certain breeds, such as the Irish Setter, the Collie, the Fox Terrier, and the German Shepherd, with the Working-dog disposition far more suitable in a pet. If you want a pet dog whom you can also show with some chance of success, the best solution is to choose either one of the breeds in the Sporting and Working groups that have not been affected by artificial show standards, or an unfashionable breed that is probably less spectacular than the beauteous show varieties, but has remained natural and well-balanced, mentally and physically.

SALES FORMALITIES

Purchasing a purebred dog entails almost as many documents as buying a house or a car. The person who sells you your dog, even if he is your best friend or your brother-in-law, should give you:

1) A RECEIPT OR BILL OF SALE, including the names of the breeder and of the dog's dam and sire, the dog's birth date, his name, as well as the agreed price. Sometimes an expensive dog can be paid for in installments, and the terms should be specified too. (Until he is fully paid for, you can neither register the dog in your name nor show him.)

2) A COPY OF THE DOG'S PEDIGREE. This is actually no more than a record of his family tree during the previous 3 or 4 generations, inscribed on a printed form that anyone can obtain from the AKC or from most dog supply shops. All dogs of known ancestry can be given a pedigree, but not all are necessarily "purebred pedigrees," which are the only ones of any value, proving that the dog's ancestors have been registered as purebred for at least three generations. For a fee, you can have your dog's pedigree traced back even further by official registries or private firms.

The Champions that figure in a pedigree are by tradition inscribed or underlined in red ink, and you will notice that the same dog probably figures more than once. After reading Chapter 16, "Breeding Your Dog," you will understand the significance of the fact that the same dog appears in both the female and the male line (an indication of linebreeding or inbreeding). On the other hand, the fact that many names in a pedigree bear the same breeder's prefix is not necessarily proof that the dogs are related. The more numerous the Champions, the higher the price of the dog and the greater the likelihood that he has inherited desirable qualities and the ability to transmit them. But it does not mean that he will himself automatically become a Champion, nor even that he is more beautiful or intelligent than a dog with a less impressive family tree. So, by all means take pride in your dog's illustrious lineage, if he has one. But realize that a pedigree is of value primarily for your own information, especially if you are interested in breeding.

3) AN INDIVIDUAL REGISTRATION APPLICATION from the AKC or the registry where the puppy's parents are listed. These forms are furnished to the breeder when a purebred litter is registered. The buyer of the puppy completes the application with his own name and address and sends it, along with the registration fee, to the registry. He receives in return the puppy's permanent registration certificate, bearing

the puppy's name, his own name, and a registration number. Keep this document in a safe place, because this (and not the pedigree) is what you will need if you ever wish to show, breed, or sell your dog.

4) A VETERINARY CERTIFICATE, recording the date and type of vaccinations and inoculations the puppy has received. It may also be accompanied by a statement that the dog is in good health, free from parasites and contagious disease. You should take this to your own veterinarian as soon as possible in order to complete the protective shots if necessary.

A Veterinary Health Certificate and Vaccination Record.

WHITNEY VETERINARY CLINIC
OAKWOOD ROAD, ORANGE, CONNECTICUT

This is to certify I HAVE EXAMINED A *BLACK AND TAN*

FEMALE   *GORDON SETTER*   COLOR
SEX   BREED
OWNED BY *DOROTHY PAGE*

OF *ORANGE, CONN*

THE DOG IS IN SOUND HEALTH, FREE FROM CONTAGIOUS OR COMMUNICABLE DISEASES, SO FAR AS I AM ABLE TO DETERMINE, AND COMES FROM A RABIES-FREE SECTION.

3|24|78   *George M. Whitney*   D.V.M.
DATE

5) A GUARANTEE may be offered by a pet shop or a dealer, certifying that the dog is of a certain breed and lineage, is in sound health, and that if he should fall ill within a certain period of time, he can be returned and his purchase price refunded or another puppy substituted. Some dealers advertise a "Lifetime Health Guarantee." If you are given one of these documents, there is no point in refusing it. But do not be deluded into thinking that you will never have to pay a veterinary bill as long as your dog lives. Nor can anybody offer honestly a "Guaranteed Future Champion," although some dealers do.

Puppies of many large, fast-growing breeds are often advertised as "OFA Certified" or "Guaranteed free from HD." These initials stand for Hip Dysplasia (an inherited, incurable condition that causes crippling weakness in the dog's hindquarters, and increasing concern to breeders and owners) and Orthopedic Foundation for Animals, which was created to study and control it. Owners can submit pelvic X-rays of their dogs to the Foundation's experts (OFA, Hip Dysplasia Control Registry, 817 Virginia Avenue, Columbia, Missouri 65201), who will accord an OFA number to those who have been diagnosed as normal. Unfortunately, the condition is never apparent at birth, and is very difficult to spot in its early stages. A definite verdict is possible only at the age of two, so no puppy younger than that can be guaranteed to be free from Hip Dysplasia. On the other hand, it will offer you some protection in an adult dog, as may some of the other reassuring documents. But you should know that the guarantee of greatest value is the integrity and competence of your puppy's breeder, and the care you take in selecting both of them.

6) A DIET SHEET is very useful, especially for a young puppy. It should list the amounts, times, and types of food (including brand names) that your puppy has been getting, as well as what you should feed him in the future.

Other useful information you might request from your dog's breeder or previous owner includes any special treatment that may be required, such as worming or earcropping, any peculiar fancies or phobias he may have. Small breeders who take a personal interest in their stock are always most co-operative in this regard. They also appreciate hearing how their puppies are getting along in their new homes, and are always ready to give advice on problems that may arise concerning diet, health, or training.

PRICES

Despite the greatly increased demand for purebred puppies in recent years, they are among the few things that have inflated very little in cost —except for Champion stud dogs, for whom a price tag of $10,000 is not uncommon nowadays, and Field Trial Champions, who can cost as much as a Thoroughbred horse.

The price of a dog depends upon his quality, breed, age, and sex. A nice purebred 8-week-old puppy is normally sold for $150 to $350 by the breeder, and a bit more by a pet shop. His price increases with age, in order to cover the cost of care and feeding. Exceptional individuals, even of the same litter, would be higher-priced, while ill-marked or off-color ones, suitable only as pets, would cost less—but never less than $75 or $100 for a purebred puppy.

All other things being equal, female puppies are more expensive than males because of their breeding possibilities, even though males are in greater demand as pets.

Fashionable breeds, rare breeds, and breeds that are difficult to reproduce or that have very small litters, are at the top of the price scale, as are, generally speaking, very small dogs and very large ones. Stylish colors and markings are also reflected in the price.

Hunting dogs of Working lines are more expensive than pet types of these breeds, and their prices rise according to their degree of training: $125 to $225 for a well-bred Pointer or Setter puppy with some basic training; $200 to $300 for a partly trained dog; and $275 to $750 or more for a fully trained one. Retrievers tend to be slightly more expensive, Spaniels and Hounds more reasonable. Since the buyer is paying for training as well as for a dog, there is often a written agreement specifying a trial period of 7 or 10 days during which he can be tried out in the field. If he is unsatisfactory, he may be returned to the breeder (at the buyer's expense) in exchange for another, or for a refund of the purchase price.

Trained Guard dogs cost from $500 to $5,000, which is less excessive than it may seem, when you consider that the current fees of qualified professional Guard dog trainers range from $500 to $2,500.

Pet shops provide stock to suit most pocketbooks: from $75 or $100 and up, depending on the breed.

If a friend wishes to give you a puppy, insist upon paying for it. Twenty-five dollars would be a token price, while $75 would be a fair price to everyone concerned for a pedigreed homebred pet puppy.

Animal philanthropies usually charge a fee of a few dollars, plus the cost of neutering or spaying. Most dog pounds ask for a $2 or $5 fee.

Some canine transactions involve no money at all. Dog lovers living near a hunt club can inquire about "walking a puppy," which means caring for a Foxhound pup until it is one year old and ready for hunting training. Seeing Eye centers also entrust puppies to suitable homes until they are old enough to train. In many parts of the country, 4-H Clubs have a program that furnishes purebred dogs on loan to responsible members for showing or obedience training. In these cases, of course, you are taking in a boarder rather than acquiring a dog of your own.

Another moneyless transaction is called "Breeder's Terms," by which a purebred, registered bitch is loaned for a period, generally ranging from 6 months to life, during which she cannot be resold. The two parties decide who is to own the bitch, who is to be considered breeder of her puppies (usually the loanee), who is to select the sire, pay the stud fees and other expenses, and how the ensuing litters will be divided.

You need not necessarily be a professional breeder in order to qualify for some of these special arrangements. Small kennels will sometimes offer an experienced dog owner a bitch on breeder's terms, or sell a fine dog at a bargain price to a qualified person who agrees to campaign him in the show ring in the hope of adding another Champion title to the kennel roster. Even more common is the system of co-ownership, especially with outstandingly promising show puppies. The buyer raises and keeps the puppy, while the co-owner (who is often the breeder) does the showing. These transactions may appear to be bargains, because they involve valuable purebred dogs. But they are not as cheap as they seem, since breeding and showing have become expensive hobbies.

A genuine "bargain puppy" is usually a well-bred animal that is not up to the breeder's standard, although perfectly suitable as a pet. He may be sold "without papers" in order to discourage breeding and to prevent the registration of an inferior litter. The breeder may also stipulate that such a puppy be altered. If you are offered these conditions, do not feel that you are being cheated in some way. Instead, you should admire the breeder for his integrity in trying to protect the breed as a whole as well as the reputation and future quality of his line.

Whatever you pay for your dog, do not be tempted to buy one that is beyond your means. The purchase price represents only a fraction of what he will cost you over the years. For this reason, dog lovers with very modest budgets should refrain from acquiring a very large dog (unless they have access to a free meat supply) or a very delicate one (unless there is a veterinarian in the family).

Finally, you should realize that buying a dog is entirely different from buying some inanimate piece of merchandise. You not only owe the agreed price to the seller, you also owe something to the dog: good care, food and shelter, of course. But above all, love and companionship. A person who is unwilling or unable to provide these two basic ingredients of canine well-being cannot afford to buy a dog.

4.
Where to Keep Your Dog

A dog who is considered a member of the family should have a bed of his own inside the house just as everyone else does. It may be in a corner of the kitchen, which is usually a warm place and a center of activity. It may be in the front hall, on an enclosed porch, in the room where the family watches television, or in your own bedroom. The important point is to choose a corner that will be your dog's private domain, where he can seek rest and quiet, where he will not be in the way, where he will not be disturbed, but where he will not feel cut off from family life either. Most dogs love to keep an eye on what is going on. Whatever you do, never shut up a dog in a garage or cellar, even if they are heated and air conditioned. How would you like it?

Long-haired, hardy breeds can sleep quite comfortably in an outdoor doghouse if it is suitably built, close to the house, and regularly cleaned. But keeping it clean can be more trouble than keeping your dog in the house. If you own several dogs, an outdoor kennel may be the best solution. Nevertheless, there are nights in many parts of the country when the temperature drops so low that even the most rugged dogs should be brought inside. Short-coated breeds, Toy breeds, young puppies, and old dogs should always sleep indoors. Even Guard dogs can guard better when they are free indoors at night.

Before you bring a new puppy home, decide where he is going to sleep and have everything ready for him. This may take only a few minutes, or it may entail a lot of time and expense, depending on whether he is kept indoors or out.

INDOORS

The problem is different with a non-housebroken puppy than with an older one who can be trusted to control his physical functions.

For keeping a young puppy safe, comfortable, and supervised, nothing is better than a baby's playpen, enclosed in fine chicken wire, carpeted with several layers of newspaper, and situated in a warm, draft-free corner of the kitchen. Newspapers make the best floor covering at this stage because they are easily available, easily disposable, and facilitate the first step in housebreaking, which is paper-training. In one corner of the pen you should install a bed. It may be no more than a flat cushion, a discarded woolen garment, a piece of an old blanket or mattress pad—in other words, something that is cozy and either washable or disposable. In another corner, place his food and water bowls. You can also make a good pen out of the area under the kitchen table by wrapping chicken wire around the four legs, placing newspapers on the floor, a bed in one corner, a food dish and water bowl in another. Your puppy will have a safe little den, with space for sleeping, eating, and relieving himself.

As soon as the puppy is able to refrain from soiling his quarters during the night, he no longer needs an enclosed pen, but simply a bed. It may be merely a pad or blanket. It may be a small crate or cardboard box, with part of one side cut away so that he can easily hop in and out. He should be able to curl up in it, but also to stretch out if he feels like it. As a rule of thumb, it should be the same length as the length of the dog from the tip of his nose to the root of his tail. An oval shape is inviting to most dogs. Oval wicker baskets are available in all sizes in most pet shops. With a flat cushion, a folded blanket or bath mat for bedding, they are comfortable, clean, and attractive. Excellent dog beds are made of washable fabric stretched over a metal frame. Toy breeds, who need maximum protection from drafts, appreciate the dog beds made especially for them with three sides and a roof. Most dogs, for that matter, seek a den atmosphere, and you can satisfy this atavistic instinct by plac-

This Rhodesian Ridgeback established his den under the kitchen table. (*Richard E. Roberts*)

Every dog should have a bed of his own, as does this three-and-a-half-month-old English Setter puppy, who obviously already considers his comfortable basket to be his personal domain. (*John Falk*)

ing your dog's cushion under a dresser, desk, or table, or at least in a dim corner. But never put it in a draft or next to a radiator.

The kitchen is still a good place for your puppy's bed until he is 4 or 5 months old, because he will be doing a lot of daytime napping, and you do not want him to be so far removed from household activity that he feels like an outcast. But as soon as he has adopted an adult schedule, you might move his bed to your own bedroom, or to the room where the family usually gathers, so that he will feel a part of it. When you move his bed, place his favorite toys in it, then pick him up and settle him in the new location. He will grasp the idea immediately. In fact, throughout his life his cushion or blanket will indicate to him where he is to sleep, and this can be very useful in a strange place, such as a hotel room, boarding kennel, or a friend's home. Sleeping in his familiar bed will give him a sense of security and help him to understand and accept the new situation.

An excellent arrangement for larger dogs, who are often less comfort-seeking than smaller breeds, is to use a folding wire traveling crate (or even a wooden one) as an indoor doghouse. Select a model that is the right size for your dog, is sturdily built, and folds flat. Equipped with

A contented Rhodesian Ridgeback in her crate. (*Richard E. Roberts*)

comfortable floor covering (part of an old blanket or rug), covered with a blanket, tablecloth, or a special crate cover, installed in a quiet but not isolated corner, it can be left open during the day and closed at night, as well as whenever you wish your dog to be safely out of the way. If you do not keep him confined in it too often or too long, he will trot into his crate with pleasure and appreciate the tranquillity he finds there while still being able to observe the activity around him. This is a practical solution for non-housebroken dogs, since they never soil their beds if they can help it. Wire crates are also perfect for safe, long-distance automobile travel, when they are securely installed on the back seat or deck. Hotels and motels seldom refuse a dog who has a wire crate. Owners who use them swear by them.

OUTDOORS

The comic-strip conception of watchdogs chained to their doghouse is a perfect illustration of what *not* to do. The old-fashioned doghouse is totally unsuitable for modern pets. The only dogs that might conceivably be chained out of doors are professional guard dogs doing sentry duty in factories, construction sites, Army bases, and the like.

An *outdoor kennel* is, of course, the only possible arrangement when there are many dogs to house. Kennel dogs are always kept in outdoor houses, heated or air conditioned if necessary. Long-haired, heavy-coated show dogs are often kept in unheated outdoor kennels in order to encourage the growth of dense, profuse coats. Some hunters also prefer to keep their dogs in outdoor doghouses with fenced-in runs, on the theory that life as a house pet would spoil them for hunting. But aside from pack dogs, such as Beagles and Foxhounds, the contrary is more often true. The close relationship developed by living alongside his owner increases a dog's responsiveness in the field. Furthermore, the activity of normal home life makes any dog brighter, since it offers him so many more opportunities to exercise and thus develop his intelligence.

Private breeders with model kennels keep in the house as many dogs as they can handle: old retainers, newly weaned puppies, and perhaps a favorite pet or two. This early integration into home life gives their puppies a definite advantage over kennel-reared dogs, developing earlier and more fully their confidence, sociability, and personality.

Ideally, a *doghouse* should be situated with a southern or eastern exposure in order to benefit from the morning sun and remain in the shade during the hottest hours of the day. It should also be sheltered from prevailing winds, since dogs are more susceptible to drafts than they are to cold.

A doghouse in an enclosed run. (*Richard E. Roberts*)

The construction need not be elaborate, but it should be suited to the climate, well-ventilated, and if necessary, insulated. Redwood, which does not rot, is probably the best material, but also the most expensive. The floor should be raised a few inches above the ground in order to avoid dampness. Four bricks at the corners can do the trick. The house should be cozy enough for him to turn around in when he has attained his adult size. (You should not ask a dog to sleep outdoors until he is an adult anyway.) It should be one-third higher than he is. Needless to say, it should have four walls, and a door as big as the dog. Patented "pop-in" doors are popular. Another good type of door is set on overhead hinges, which can be closed, turned back completely over the roof, or hooked in a horizontal position in order to make a shady awning. A piece of canvas or carpeting can be rigged up to create the same effect.

A good doghouse should also have a solid, leakproof roof, sloped for drainage, insulated for keeping out the damp and cold, and set on hinges so that it can be opened for easy cleaning. The floor should be solid and easy to keep clean. Wood is the best material, and concrete the worst. It should be covered with a thick layer (at least two inches) of bedding such as shredded newspaper, cedar chips (highly recommended), old rugs or blankets, kept clean by regular renewal or laundering. Hay and straw are inferior bedding materials for dogs, since they tend to irritate the skin of short-coated breeds and are difficult to remove from long coats. Sawdust is unsatisfactory for the same reasons, and also because it retains dampness. Blue or gray painted interior walls are the least attractive to flies. Whitewashed walls also tend to discourage insects.

A well-kept doghouse should be checked every day for cleanliness, washed down with disinfectant once a month, and the bedding changed whenever it is damp or soiled, which may be every day.

You can buy a doghouse from large pet-supply firms, order a prefabricated one by mail, or have one built to measure by a local carpenter or lumber yard. It is not too difficult a project for most home handymen. One popular do-it-yourself model is built from a wooden barrel. Plans can be obtained free from the Gaines Dog Research Center. The Humane Society of the United States (2100 L Street NW, Washington, D.C. 20037) also furnishes plans for a wooden doghouse that you can build yourself.

If your dog is going to have to live outdoors, buy him in the spring so that he will become accustomed to outdoor life before the cold weather sets in. If he is less than five or six months old, keep him in the house at first, and move him to his outdoor quarters only when he is older and stronger and has grown an adult coat. He will not like this sudden exile at first, and will probably protest loudly until he has become resigned to it. Quiet him, of course, but do not get angry. He is only trying to tell you that he would much rather be with you—which is, after all, a compliment.

ENCLOSURES

Chaining a dog to his house is sheer cruelty. Instead, leave him free to go in and out as he pleases, and enclose the surrounding area.

In the suburbs, it is particularly important to fence in all or part of the yard so that your dog can safely benefit from the space, fresh air, and sunshine, and the freedom of being unleashed. In the country, this is less essential, although it is still advisable in many areas. The ideal arrangement would be to enclose your entire property. But the price of fencing being what it is, the only practical solution is to enclose some portion of it in a dogproof way.

Select an area that is visible from the house. The fence itself should be at least 3 or 4 feet high, even if your pet is small, because it may be even more important to keep other dogs out than to keep yours inside—

especially if your dog is an unspayed female. Six feet in height is a maximum, even though expert high-jumpers and scramblers like Poodles, Fox Terriers, Doberman Pinschers, and German Shepherds can still manage to get over it if they have sufficient motivation. An inward-slanting strip added to the top will foil, or at least discourage them. Some dogs are fantastic escape artists too. They manage to unlock all sorts of gate fastenings. They can also dig their way out of confinement, but this is more easily countered by imbedding the bottom of the fence in concrete.

The best fencing material is heavy-gauge wire link, fine enough so that the dog cannot catch a paw in it. (Incidentally, you should always remove your dog's collar when he is in his pen, so that it cannot catch on some part of the fence or gate and possibly choke him. It may sound far-fetched, but it has happened.) You will see advertisements in dog magazines for prefabricated dog pens. The average size is 4 feet wide, 10 to 20 feet long, and 6 to 8 feet high. They are generally practical but pricey. On the other hand, it is false economy to build an enclosure out of ordinary chicken wire. Any self-respecting dog will demolish it in no time.

Within the enclosure there should be both sun and shade. If there is none from trees or buildings, you can provide shade by planting a row of high shrubs or sunflowers along the outside of the fence, by installing a wide bench platform under which your dog can lie, or even by setting up a beach umbrella. Select the location of the doghouse with care. Your dog should find comfort within it every season of the year. A permanent supply of fresh water, renewed daily, is important all year round, but especially during torrid or freezing weather, when it should be checked more often.

OTHER POSSIBILITIES

If it is impossible to enclose an outdoor area for your dog, you can almost always install a *run,* consisting of two posts and a heavy overhead steel wire to which the dog is attached by a light, strong chain that runs freely along the length of the wire. A good minimum set of dimensions is: 20 feet long, 5 feet wide, and 6 feet high, with the chain 8 feet long. Your dog can at least run back and forth at will and get fresh air, sunshine, and a little exercise. Make sure that there is shade somewhere within his range, but no obstacles that might become entangled with his chain.

Where an overhead run is impractical, you can probably install a *ground swivel post,* to which the dog is attached by a long chain, permitting him to move about within its radius. But remember that these are

Some dogs are fantastic escape artists. This clever Bull Terrier learned through observation, without being trained, how to turn a key in a locked door! (*Lacz-Lemoine*)

merely compromise solutions to the problem of fresh air and exercise, and in no way replace accompanied walks and play.

In the suburbs, you may have an open *terrace* or *patio* that can be gated and securely enclosed. If it is sunny, shady, and airy, your dog will feel less confined than in the house. In mild climates, you might even install his doghouse there.

In the city, some apartments have a *balcony* where a small dog can enjoy the air and sunshine without being tied up. For safety, you need only line the railing with firmly attached wire mesh. Of course, your dog will get no exercise there, but it will add a little variety to his relatively monotonous urban life and a bit of space to his limited living quarters.

In apartment buildings with suitable grounds, dog owners sometimes get together to build a co-operative exercise pen where each can take his dog at certain hours.

Perhaps you are fortunate enough to own an apartment with a *roof terrace* or a *ground-floor garden*, where your dog can be free in the open air but still in secure confinement, once it has been safely enclosed. Both are pleasant recreation areas for a city dog. But at night and whenever he wants to sleep, let him come inside where it is darker and quieter.

If the garden or terrace is fairly large, you might try to train him to use a litter pan placed in a corner, like a cat. Some Toy breeds accept the invitation. Larger dogs are apt to consider the entire area part of their home and obstinately refuse to soil it. Still, you can always try. It would be useful for rainy days when you do not feel like walking around the block. Do not forget, though, that you will be faced with the problem of disposing of the waste matter.

Even if you live in a suburban house with an un-enclosable postage-stamp yard, or in an apartment where the closest thing to a garden is a ten-inch windowsill with a pot of chives on it, you need not envy dogowners who possess city terraces and country estates. An enclosed outdoor area of one kind or another is certainly an added pleasure for a dog in the best of cases. In the worst, it is an outdoor prison where he is confined and forgotten. For the owner, it is undeniably a great convenience. But it in no way relieves him of the responsibility of giving his dog the accompanied exercise and the attention that he needs and craves.

5.

Making Your Dog at Home

The day you bring a new puppy or dog into your home is a red-letter day indeed. It may be an exhausting one for you. It certainly will be for him. It is also one of the most critical moments in your relationship, because first impressions are indelibly marked on the animal mind. It is vital to establish from the beginning an atmosphere of security, affection, and mutual confidence. In short, to make your dog feel at home.

A day or two before the great event, it is a good idea to inspect your house and grounds and make the minor changes necessary, now that you have a canine member of the family.

OUTDOORS

—Remove any bits of broken glass or nails that may be scattered around.

—Attach at a higher level any low-hanging electric wires that a dog might chew.

—Examine fences and gates to make sure there are no large gaps, jagged wires, or nails that might cause injury.

—Arrange a place to hang up garden tools so that they do not lie around on the ground.

—Make sure that cans of paint, insecticides, and weed-killers are stored out of reach.

—Protect your prize shrubbery by spraying it with a diluted solution of nicotine sulphate, which is harmless to plants and pets, but repels the latter.

—Admit that you were intending to do all of this one day anyway.

INDOORS

—Remove for the time being pale or costly carpets, and cover delicate upholstery with some washable material.

—Make sure that household cleaning supplies are stored behind closed doors or on a high shelf.

—Change your habits, if necessary, resolving to:

Never leave the children's toys on the floor, expecially plastic objects or small ones like marbles and jacks.

Never leave an open sewing basket or knitting within a puppy's reach.

Never leave closet doors open (particularly the one in which you keep your shoes).

Never leave discarded garments and gloves on low tables or chairs.

Never leave books or magazines on the floor, or even on a low table.

Never open an outside door until you have verified that your puppy is safely shut up in another room or is under your control.

ESSENTIAL POSSESSIONS

Your puppy will come to you with no worldly goods at all, so you must provide him with his first essential possessions:

—a bed
—a blanket
—a water bowl (stainless steel or unbreakable glass, never lightweight plastic)
—a food dish (stainless steel or earthenware—but not glazed pottery, which contains lead that is poisonous to dogs; and not lightweight plastic)
—a light puppy collar with an identification tag (leather is best: flat for short-haired breeds, round for long-haired)
—a leather leash with a strong clip fastener
—a comb and brush (the canine kind, suitable to his breed)
—a squeaky toy
—a chewing toy of rawhide or a nylon bone (or both)
—a hard rubber ball (big enough so that he cannot swallow it, but light enough for him to carry it around in his mouth)
—finally, and most important of all:

A NAME

An adult dog will already have a name to which he is accustomed to responding, and there is no point in changing it. But a young puppy straight from a litter has generally learned to respond to clucking and kissing sounds, to the clatter of the food bowl, and to the mob behavior of his brothers and sisters at feeding time and bedtime, even though his registration papers (if he is a purebred dog) bears a name the breeder selected for him. Once approved by the AKC, it can never be changed. Neither can it be longer than 25 letters (the UKC permits only 22), nor can it include a written number or a Roman numeral, a word synonymous with "dog," or one that is disparaging or obscene.

These registered names are usually too long and pretentious to be used as call names, but they can often be abbreviated into very good ones. Thus, "Lochinvar of Ladypark" can be called "Locky" or "Lucky" (although this famous English Collie actually answered to the name of "Roy"). "Moorland's Golden Dreamcloud" will probably learn to come more promptly if you call her "Goldie." If your dog's registered name does not offer such possibilities, or if you have to invent one for him yourself, you may find inspiration in his color, appearance, or personality, in some celebrity or friend whom you admire (although the actual name of a famous person is unacceptable for registration), some event that coincides with his birth date, or a headline in the newspaper on the day that you acquire him. Many breeders create a unique name simply by adding their surname or kennel name to a common one, such as "Robertson's Ranger," instead of plain "Ranger." Some of them select a theme for each litter, such as flowers, trees, birds, foods, drinks, weather, stars and planets. Others use the same first letter for all of their produce, or attribute a different letter of the alphabet to each litter. If all else fails, you might follow the example of many racehorse owners and combine a syllable from the names of your puppy's mother and father to form an original new name of his own.

Of course, you can call your dog by any name you like and he will learn it. But if you select a good call name, short and snappy, he will learn it sooner and respond to it faster. It will also carry further out of doors, which is important for Hunting and Working breeds and in obedience training. Long vowels, sibilants, and cracking consonants are best. Working Sheepdogs all seem to be called Dick, Rick, Jock, Jack, or Rex. Names ending with the letters Y, T, and M are also good.

Once you have chosen a name for your dog, use it often. The first few times he will be a bit bewildered. But very soon he will realize that "Toby" or "Dandy" means him, if you address him by name every time you speak to him and if you speak to him often.

If this is your first dog, you too will find it useful to acquire a few new possessions:
—a comprehensive book on dog care, written by a veterinarian
—a strong envelope to contain your dog's papers, vaccination certificates, and pedigree
—a canine medicine chest (see page 235)
—a pile of old newspapers
—a supply of cleaning-up materials for puppy messes: rags, a stiff scrubbing brush, a bottle of carbonated water or a siphon, a roll of paper towels or a box of man-sized tissues, a weak solution of ammonia or laundry bleach, or a patented product for removing urine stains.

Everything is ready. You have selected a name. You have prepared a bed, a water bowl and food bowl (placed on a folded newspaper or plastic mat, because he will be a sloppy eater at first), and last but far from least, toilet facilities (newspapers spread over a tiled or linoleum surface, for example, in a corner of the kitchen, bathroom, or entry). Now it is time to bring your dog home.

BRINGING YOUR DOG HOME

Do not go to get him with a full delegation, even though he will be a VIP in your life from now on. Too many people would only confuse him. Take just one other person with you, so that one of you can drive the car and the other hold the puppy and quiet or comfort him if necessary. Take along a bath towel, for if it is his first car ride he may be sick. Take his leash and collar too (although some breeders supply them).

You will learn that a puppy's first reaction to excitement is to relieve himself. So as soon as you arrive home, take him for a short stroll along the sidewalk or in the front lawn or garden. Let him sniff around. If he squats and empties his bladder, rejoice. Then pick him up and introduce him to his new home.

Let him explore at first, following him around, speaking to him by name in an affectionate, enthusiastic tone. Show him the way to the kitchen and lead him to his water bowl. You may give him a tidbit or a sip of milk. He is too excited at the moment for a real meal, but the offer of food, drink, shelter, and loving companionship will reassure him. Then take him to his bed, staying next to him where you can talk to him, caress him, or simply comfort him by your presence.

If he is very young or has had a long trip, he will probably drop off to sleep at once. But if you have simply driven him home from the village pet shop, he is more apt to pop out of his bed as soon as you put him in it. If so, continue to accompany him on his explorations, encouraging him to investigate his new environment. When he starts to squat, pick him up and place him on the newspapers in his "bathroom." Don't scold him, though, if he has been quicker than you. He is too distracted for training this first day, but you will have established some vague subconscious reflex in his puppy brain. Give him his lunch and dinner at the usual times. All dogs, even very young puppies, seem to have a built-in alarm clock, and he will be less disoriented if you respect the feeding and sleeping schedule to which he has been accustomed.

In order to perform this scenario with best results, it is obviously best to bring your puppy home in the morning or early afternoon, while there is enough daylight left for his explorations and time to get his bearings before bedtime, when he is most likely to miss his litter companions.

This first day is not the time to start obedience training. But it is not too early to establish the restrictions you wish him to respect in the future. For instance, if you do not want him to jump up on chairs and sofas, make them out of bounds from the start by removing him gently but firmly, saying, "No, Rex" whenever he jumps up on them. Your disapproval should always be followed by the suggestion of an alternative, such as placing him in his bed or on the floor. (Later on, you can give him a light tap on the rump with a rolled-up newspaper when he jumps onto a forbidden chair, and leave the newspaper on the chair. He cannot fail to understand.)

You may have more difficulty controlling your friends and family than supervising your puppy. Everyone will want to pet and play with him. He will love the attention, of course, and if he is tired by it he will go to bed more willingly and sleep more soundly. But if you permit him to become overtired and overexcited, it will have the opposite effect.

While puppies are less strict about canine etiquette than older dogs, you might show your friends and family THE PROPER WAY TO INTRODUCE ONESELF TO A DOG: by holding the back of your hand in front of his nose for him to sniff. Judges always do this before examining show dogs, to give the dog an opportunity to get their scent, and also because the back of the hand is nonaggressive, whereas presenting the palm might be interpreted as an intention to strike. Once the dog has sniffed, you may speak to him in a friendly tone, but let him make the first advances. Don't give him little nervous pats or heavy-handed ones. Pat him first on the shoulder rather than on the head. Many dogs dislike head-stroking, but all of them like to be firmly stroked along the spine and scratched behind the ears and at the base of the tail. If the dog then rolls over on his back so that you can stroke his tummy, you can be sure he has accepted you as a friend, for this is the canine gesture of confidence and submission (and tummy-licking is the first maternal caress).

Adults as well as children may need to be taught HOW TO PICK UP A PUPPY SAFELY. Never lift him or haul him about by the ears, tail, or legs, which is painful and can cause dislocations. Instead, place one hand under his chest, the other under his rump, and lift. If he struggles, put him down at once. Puppy bones are soft and fragile, and a fall can cause permanent damage. You may have to be very firm with children, who, strangely enough, are not instinctively gentle with dogs, as dogs are with them.

You must exercise great tact in INTRODUCING YOUR PUPPY TO ANOTHER CANINE MEMBER OF THE FAMILY, especially if both of them are males. To be perfectly safe, keep them leashed for the first

How to pick up a puppy safely—by placing one hand under his rump, the other under his chest, and lifting gently. (*Sue Maynard*)

few hours, and feed them separately the first few days. Afterward, you can feed them in the same room, but from separate bowls. Be sure to make a special fuss over the established dog, and do not alter his usual daily routine.

During all of this time you should be OBSERVING YOUR PUPPY, because every one of his actions and reactions can give you a clue to his native temperament. If he is curious and bold, you can be practically certain of his courage and intelligence. If he is shy and intimidated by his new surroundings, you will have to build up his confidence before his intelligence can develop fully. If he is a cuddler, you should give him the affection he craves. He may outgrow it, but it may also be a part of his nature. Think of your puppy as a living creature, with a mentality and personality of his own which you can help to form and develop. Dogs are highly impressionable and responsive. Their reactions are far more evident and immediate than those of children, and this is one of the most challenging and rewarding aspects of having a dog of your own.

Just as you imprint on your puppy's mind certain rules and restrictions from the very beginning, you can also start to give him a basic vocabulary by TALKING TO HIM often. Give him a simple commentary on everything you do together, stressing the key words you wish him to learn. "It's time for DINNER, Rex. Do you want your DINNER? Here's your DINNER!" "This is your BED, Rex. Your own BED. Now it's time to go to BED." You will feel idiotic, and he will cock his head and study you quizzically. But soon he will recognize the key words and their meaning. Most important of all, he will learn that human speech is a form of communication that can be of practical significance to him.

THE FIRST NIGHT in a new home can be a miserable experience for a puppy who is used to sleeping in the cozy nest where he was born. The classic substitutes for his mother's warm presence and heartbeat are a hot-water bottle wrapped in a towel, and a ticking clock tucked underneath the bedding. It is probably simpler to place his bed next to yours this first night, so that you can comfort him if necessary. After a second happy day in his new home, he will feel secure enough and tired enough to sleep in his own bed in the permanent spot you have selected for it.

A puppy 3 or 4 months old is usually already accustomed to sleeping alone. However, for the first night or two you might place his bed in an adjacent room with the door open, so that you can calm him if he cries. Or you can put his bed next to yours the first few nights—with the risk that this temporary arrangement will become a permanent one.

Do not scold him at first for *crying at night*. Instead, reassure him. It is a perfectly normal reaction under the circumstances. The second night you can be firmer and tell him "NO," that it is "BAD" to whine. But the first night calls for greater indulgence. (You were warned that this was going to be one of the most exhausting twenty-four hours of your life.) If he cries, comfort him, then leave him alone again. You may have to repeat the process many times before he falls asleep. But if you weaken and take him to bed with you, you may be simply creating a new problem. Tonight he may nestle at your feet or in your arms. But will he be able to do so when he has attained his adult size? Tonight you may be sleeping alone. But what about all the other nights? You may decide that it is more sensible to get your puppy used to sleeping in his own bed after all.

From the moment you bring him home, there are SIX THINGS THAT YOU SHOULD TEACH YOUR DOG:

1) *His name.* If you use it often, he will learn it quickly.

2) *The meaning of the word "NO."* Words are merely sounds to a dog at first, and it is up to you to give them meaning by association as well as by an appropriate tone of voice and expression. You never need to shout when you say "NO" to your puppy, but you should use a remonstrative tone of voice and look and act displeased. You can gradually reduce the histrionics and he will still understand. This is one of the secrets of professional animal trainers, who finally manage to convey their meanings by imperceptible signals and barely audible voice commands.

3) *An expression of praise and encouragement,* which will be his most cherished recompense for good behavior. It can be "GOOD DOG," "OKAY," or whatever comes naturally to you. Use it lavishly whenever your puppy does something you want him to do, such as coming when called, or relieving himself in the appointed spot.

4) *Housebreaking,* which merits an entire chapter, so numerous are the methods, so varied the individual cases, and so obsessive the entire subject to puppy owners.

Owners who acquire a pet at the age of 4 months or more are at a great advantage, because by then most puppies have the physical means to control their natural functions. A younger one, even with the best of intentions, simply cannot contain himself, certainly not during an entire night, nor during more than 2 hours when he is awake and active. You may scold him mildly, merely to implant the right idea in his mind, but the only practical thing you can do at this stage is to try a limit the damage. For example:

—Keep your puppy in a confined area covered with newspapers, removing and replacing them as soon as they are soiled. Gradually reduce the paper-covered area. Some owners place a snippet of soiled paper with the fresh, since animals tend to return to the same spot by instinct and by scent.

—Have handy a supply of disposable tissues, which are adequate for mopping or scooping up the relatively small amount of puppy waste and can be flushed down the toilet. Then clean the spot with more tissues moistened with a weak solution of laundry bleach or ammonia.

—Use seltzer water or club soda to cope with fresh urine stains on a carpet. The effect is magical. First, soak up as much moisture as possible with tissues, then pour or squirt on the carbonated water and scrub it into the spot with a stiff brush. Sponge it up with more tissues and leave to dry. Enzyme stain removers cope with these stains effectively too. Diluted white vinegar is a good deodorant.

When your puppy is about 3 months old, you might give him a finely grated carrot or a spoonful of cooked spinach with his noonday meal.

You can then easily identify the waste matter by the color of his stool and thus estimate the number of hours it has taken him to eliminate it— perhaps 5 or 6, but longer for the evening meal or if he sleeps a lot. If the interval is 5 hours, for example, you can schedule an outdoor walk for your puppy 5 hours after his next meal, praising him when he performs on schedule.

A puppy should be taken out at frequent intervals as a matter of course: the first thing in the morning, the last thing at night, 15 minutes or half an hour after each meal, and immediately after a long nap. If you live in an apartment building, take him out in your arms so that he does not piddle en route. If he relieves himself, you too can feel relieved. If he doesn't, it is useless to prolong the outing for more than half an hour. Take him home and prepare the cleaning-up equipment, reminding yourself that this trying period will soon be over.

In addition to his regular outings, you should try to keep an eye on your puppy so that, as soon as you see him squatting or turning around in a circle, you can pick him up and plop him down on the newspapers or out of doors, leading him to the spot you have selected as his toilet corner. If he has been too quick for you, pick him up anyway, point to the mistake with a firm "NO," and place him on the papers with an encouraging "HERE!" If he then manages to produce anything even token, praise him enthusiastically.

So much fuss about such a simple natural matter will make you feel foolish and will probably upset your dog, as he begins to feel guilty about his physical functions. But this is the most important step in housebreak-

ing: to get him to understand that it is, in fact, a matter of great concern to you. Then you need only continue to make it possible for him to be clean by providing newspapers and regular outings. One fine morning you will find the newspapers unsoiled and your puppy will make a little lake as soon as he is outdoors. You can breathe a sigh of relief (after praising him). Your battle is won. From now on it is merely a matter of giving his physical means time to catch up with his mental understanding and his inborn instinct to refuse to soil his home. He may forget himself from time to time, arousing your suspicions by his guilty demeanor. Scold him mildly, if only to make it clear that the rules of the game are still the same, and remain on the alert, like a volunteer fireman, ready to get dressed and go out on emergency calls, sometimes false alarms. But you can be sure that by the time your puppy is 4 months old (often sooner, rarely later), he will be perfectly housebroken.

This, at least, is the usual procedure. Unfortunately, some dogs seem to suffer from incurable incontinence, including certain Toy Poodles, Chihuahuas, some Toy Terriers, and congenitally nervous individuals. Dachshunds and Bassets are reputed to be difficult to housebreak. Almost any dog will let a few drops escape when he is overexcited, sexually aroused, in the presence of another male, suddenly awakened, or frightened. Defecation is a fear reaction of all animals, including man.

Females are easier to housebreak than males because they empty their bladders all at once and do not share the male compulsion to mark their territory with urine, although they use it to advertise their interesting condition when in heat.

For a dog, urination has social as well as physical significance. The first time he lifts his leg is as momentous an event for him as the first time a boy shaves. Just watch him after his first wobbly effort. How proud he is! He swaggers down the street to the next lamppost to show off his prowess again. The smell of urine triggers the dog's impulse to urinate, which can lead to a vicious circle, since dogs are fascinated by the urine of other dogs and especially of bitches. But do not let them put their noses in it. Many canine diseases are transmitted in this way.

There are various methods for handling stubborn cases. One old standby is to start with paper-training, gradually moving the paper toward the door and reducing its surface, until the puppy is guided to the selected outdoor spot by a mere scrap of paper. There are also commercial sprays that either discourage or incite urination. Some dogs prefer a certain surface, such as cement, grass, or dirt. To many of them, a piece of paper or a pile of sand is an invitation to lift a leg, as are upright posts, corners, and any spot where another dog has already urinated. Since most dogs are conformist by nature, housebreaking is easiest when they are reared by their own mother, or are brought up in a home where there is already a clean adult dog whose good example they will imitate.

If you acquire an adult dog, his previous owner will probably have solved the housebreaking problem for you. All you have to do is to make it clear where and when he is to relieve himself, and refrain from asking him to perform impossible feats of self-control.

In many cities, the law requires dogs to be curbed, which means that they must "do their business" in the gutter. Some laws require the owner to scoop up the matter and place it in a refuse bin. With cars parked bumper to bumper and next to the curb, there is little gutter left nowadays, but you must obey the law or risk a fine. There is no special training secret. You simply take your puppy in your arms or on a leash and put him down or lead him to the gutter each time you take him out, praising him when he responds. Whenever he starts to squat on the sidewalk during an outing, haul or carry him over to the curb, expressing your pleasure or displeasure, according to his behavior. He will soon catch on. Curbing your dog is also an exercise in human willpower. You will often be tempted to pretend not to notice that your puppy is soiling the sidewalk, especially if there is no witness to the scene. But remember the primary rule in animal training: Be consistent. You will never be able to explain to your dog why the sidewalk is sometimes but not always out of bounds. So permit no exceptions. It is easier in the end.

5) *Leash Training.* All dogs need to become accustomed to walking on a lead. Most puppies accept it without the slightest protest as an interesting new game. If you start your pet early enough and take him for short walks on the leash frequently enough, you will have trained him effortlessly.

City and suburban dogs seldom cause problems. Since they have to be leashed every time they leave home, the leash is a symbol of adventure and companionship to them, as well as of bladder relief. But country dogs who roam freely all day long and choose their own pace on accompanied walks may rebel at the constraint of a leash if they have not been trained to it from puppyhood.

The first step is to put on your dog's collar, which should be neither too tight for comfort nor so loose that it can slip over his head. Then attach the leash and immediately take him for a walk. All of the strange scents and sounds of the outside world will distract his attention, and he will associate the collar and leash with a pleasant experience. He may even appreciate the sense of security he feels from having you there at the other end to guide him through crowds and across noisy streets. If ever in the future he rebels against the leash, an effective cure is to take him into a crowded place or through heavy traffic, in order to remind him of your indispensable aid in these perilous circumstances. During the first walks, you should let your puppy wander as he likes and sniff around. There is plenty of time to teach him proper heeling later on. The worst thing you can do is to collar and leash your dog for the first time in order to take him to the vet for shots, which will establish a long-lasting unpleasant association in his mind.

The only difficult cases are those of an older puppy who has been confined in a kennel with no leash training and little human handling, and of a stray dog who has become rather wild. You may have a real battle the first time you try to collar and leash them, and it is vital that you emerge victorious. The dog may leap about and run madly in circles. Keep a firm hold and let him exhaust himself. Then take him for a walk, allowing him a certain freedom, but jerking him sharply back to your side when he starts to get out of hand. Always control him by short, sharp tugs on the leash, never by a steady pull, which is far less effective, and quite useless if he is big enough to pull more strongly than you can.

All dogs, including those that are free to roam at will in the country, love to go for walks with their owners, even if they must be leashed in order to do so. Many dogs spontaneously fetch their leash at the usual exercise time and deposit it at their owner's feet, with an imploring look that says: "Don't you know it's five o'clock? Please stop what you're doing and come for a walk with me!"

6) *Staying at home alone.* A dog or puppy who incessantly barks, whines, or howls whenever he is left alone can make an entire neighborhood nervous and unhappy, and his owner highly unpopular. And yet this common vice is very easy to prevent if you start the very first day to get your puppy used to staying at home alone, if only for a few minutes.

The most important point is to always announce your departure instead of sneaking away, hoping that your dog won't notice. It will only cause him to panic as soon as he becomes aware of your absence. It is also important for your dog to realize that being left alone from time to time is a perfectly normal part of a dog's life.

Select a moment when he has recently relieved himself and seems ready for a nap. Place him in his bed, caress him, and be sure to say, "Guard the house," "Be a good boy," "I'll be back soon," or whatever. Then leave rather ostentatiously. Do not stay away for more than 5 or 10 minutes the first time, which is merely a rehearsal. As soon as you return, call him by name (if he is not already waiting eagerly behind the door), and make a fuss over him. You might put on his leash and immediately take him for a short walk. The excitement of seeing you again is apt to excite his kidneys too.

If you repeat this every day for increasing periods of time, you will soon be able to spend an afternoon at the movies or an evening with friends in perfect tranquillity. When you stay away for several hours at a time, you can make your absence more tolerable by leaving a lamp lit at night, giving your dog a toy, a bone, or a biscuit (as well as plenty of outspread newspapers at the beginning) in order to assuage his boredom, hunger, or the need to relieve himself.

Because many owners cannot be bothered to give their dogs this simple training, the profession of *dog sitting* (*dog walking* too) is flourishing throughout the country. These services are advertised in pet shops and in newspaper classified ads. A dog-walking service may be indispensable for owners who are away at work all day long. Hiring a dog-sitter for an evening is especially convenient for city-dwellers who expect to stay out late. Some owners even leave their dog at home during an overnight or weekend absence, after arranging for a person to come several times a day to give him food and exercise, but this is highly inadvisable, except in a real emergency. So much isolation and confinement is harmful to a dog, physically and psychologically. It would be much better to find a good temporary home for him, or a boarding kennel.

While your dog will eventually accept your inevitable absences with good grace, do not think that he will ever enjoy it, and above all do not take advantage of his good behavior to deprive him of the companionship he craves. Dogs need to feel wanted and loved almost as much as they need food and shelter.

The first week or two are most important. Let your puppy follow you around. Let him lie in the kitchen when you are working there. Let him "help you" with the housework. It may take twice as long, but he will love the game. Take him with you to get the mail and buy the newspaper. Train him to lie quietly at your feet when you are entertaining friends. In other words, share as many activities as possible with your dog. The principal distinction between a well-run kennel and a happy family life is love and companionship. Giving your dog plenty of both is the best way to make him feel at home.

6.

Bringing Up Your Dog

In many ways, bringing up a dog is like bringing up a child, since both of them go through more or less the same stages before they reach maturity. It is fascinating to watch an individual personality gradually emerge from a little ball of fur. But there can be moments of alarm or disappointment if you do not know what to expect. So it may be useful to outline briefly the various stages of canine development, remembering that this is merely a guideline and not a biography of your dog.

FROM BIRTH UNTIL THE AGE OF 6 WEEKS

Physically, a newborn puppy is no more than a small living organism whose sole activity is to develop in the warmth and safety of the nest, close to his mother and his litter brothers and sisters. A few days after birth, tails are docked (if the breed standard requires it) and dewclaws are removed (if necessary) by the vet. At 2 weeks, his eyes and ears begin to open. At 3 weeks, all of his senses begin to function, and he learns to lap. At first he can only slither and tumble along, but at 3 or 4 weeks he gradually manages to propel himself on wobbly legs, following his mother around, then playing with his littermates. He tries to leave the nest to urinate, although he cannot control his bladder yet. Between 3 and 6 weeks he grows his full set of baby teeth and can be gradually weaned. At the same time, he is given his first "puppy shots" to replace the protection he is no longer receiving from the colostrum in his mother's milk.

Psychologically, as soon as his eyes are open, he begins to take an interest in the world around him, in his brothers and sisters, and in human beings. These first human contacts are most important, since he is very impressionable. He should be visited frequently, gently handled and caressed. At 4 weeks, most of his brain will have matured, except for the frontal lobes, which govern memory and will not be fully formed for another week or two. But the hind region, which keeps him awake and alert and was poorly developed at birth, is mature 4 weeks later, so he will no longer sleep almost all of the time. Bold puppies begin to explore and to investigate moving objects and strange sounds. At 5 weeks, he starts to express his emotions and desires by facial and body expressions as well as by voice. He loves to carry things around in his mouth, to play

A litter of English Setter puppies at four weeks of age. (*John Falk*)

tug-of-war and follow-the-leader, and he makes a game of guarding his personal possessions. His mother is in charge of his education at this stage.

What he needs most is warmth, lots of sleep, plenty of milk and food 4 to 6 times a day, frequent human handling, protection from overexcitement, overfatigue, and fright, as well as from puppy diseases. He needs constant supervision, and encouragement to roam beyond the nest.

FROM 6 WEEKS TO 2 MONTHS

Physically, this is the full weaning period. At the beginning, the puppy is being nourished half by nursing and half by feeding; at 2 months the process is completed, and he can leave his mother. Between 6 and 8 weeks is a good time for ear-cropping, if necessary, by the vet. He is growing rapidly in size and strength but still cannot control his natural functions, although he instinctively urinates in the same spot, away from the nest. His nervous system, however, is fully mature. His reactions are quicker and he needs more exercise. He starts to follow people around, seeking company and attention. Now is the time to give him a small rubber ball to chase, and to start playing simple games with him.

The same litter at the age of seven weeks. (*John Falk*)

A litter of English Setter puppies twelve weeks old, the ideal age of adoption into their permanent homes. (*John Falk*)

Psychologically, his personality begins to unfold and individual traits of character appear. An attentive owner can help by giving each puppy the type of handling best suited to his temperament, which is apt to remain the same. This is considered the critical "socialization" period, during which human contacts are vital in order to avoid man-shyness later on. But canine contacts are important too, for without them the puppy may become so human-oriented that he will be unsociable with other dogs.

What he needs most is constant supervision, human companionship, lots of play and love, and lots of sleep. At this stage he also needs a name, a few toys, his follow-up puppy shots, an official "bathroom," and leash training.

FROM 2 TO 3 MONTHS

Physically, he is completely weaned and growing bigger every day. His co-ordination has improved, but he still cannot control his natural functions. He prefers to do his business out of doors and can be taken outside at frequent intervals if the weather is mild. His coat is growing fuller, but he needs protection from rain and cold. He has learned how to bark, and may have to be discouraged from overdoing it.

Psychologically, it is now time for you to take over your puppy's education, not by training sessions, but by teaching him good habits and good manners, and by lovingly asserting your authority. Remember that he is still a trusting, vulnerable little creature, and rough handling at this stage can mark him for life.

What he needs most is lots of attention and companionship, short daily walks on the leash, protection from cold, hunger, and rough handling, and a good deal of patience.

FROM 3 TO 4 MONTHS

Physically, he can control himself most of the time. Housebreaking is relatively rapid now, and this is the most convenient time for adopting a puppy who is to live in a city apartment. He is growing fast and may look rather leggy and out of proportion, but do not worry. His longer, stronger legs enable him to jump up on chairs and sofas, so you must establish a policy and try to stick to it. He needs sunshine and exercise, but still lots of sleep. His principal physical preoccupation at this stage is teething, as his baby teeth fall out and permanent ones replace them. It may cause him great suffering, or it may be practically unnoticeable. He may go off his feed and have to be coaxed to eat or be hand-fed. He may have diarrhea or run a fever. He will certainly want to chew everything in sight, so you should provide him with chewing toys and be prepared to find his fallen baby teeth in the most unlikely places. He is old enough to be wormed, if necessary, and to have his first annual vaccination against hepatitis, leptospirosis, and distemper. If the weather is warm and he is outdoors a lot, he may start to attract fleas and other parasites. If so, you can give him a dusting of nontoxic flea powder every week or 10 days.

Psychologically, his intelligence is wide-awake. Satisfy his curiosity by offering him varied experiences, introducing him to new places, sights, and sounds. While it is still too early for formal training, he will quickly learn the meaning of words and simple commands, and form habit patterns, good and bad. In his quest for knowledge he may be destructive, so he still requires supervision. He wants to follow you everywhere and seems to worship you blindly. He is becoming very sociable and is especially attracted to children.

What he needs most is a healthy diet, plenty of exercise, sunshine, and rest, a regular daily schedule, an increased vocabulary, more freedom and space for play, a more active social life, and as many new experiences as possible under your benevolent supervision.

FROM 4 TO 6 MONTHS

Physically, his stomach can handle bigger, less frequent meals, 2 or 3 a day. His permanent teeth have usually grown in completely, and they will continue to grow until the age of 8 months, when they attain their adult size. This process may make him irritable and nervous, or it may not affect him at all. In any case, this is the most destructive age, when his favorite occupation seems to be to chew, gnaw, and tear things apart. Let him vent his natural instinct on appropriate toys, and try to use up his energy with plenty of exercise and play.

Psychologically, this is a crucial period. In wildlife, packs are formed at the beginning of the winter, when spring-born puppies are 5 or 6 months old, and this is the age when domesticated dogs need replacement activity and, above all, leadership. They start to develop territorial instincts which can lead to aggressive behavior if not controlled. A puppy who is always allowed to have his own way now may be spoiled forever. His budding sense of social dominance and subordination makes it vital for you to establish your authority without destroying his self-confidence. You might even begin simple training, but restrict the lessons to those requiring energy and willingness, which he possesses in abundance, rather than self-control, which is practically nil at this stage.

What he needs most is lots of outdoor play, a generous, drier diet, chewing toys, loving kindness, and a slightly higher standard of discipline.

FROM 6 TO 9 MONTHS

Physically, he is entering adolescence. It may be a period of awkwardness and rebellion, or of graceful growth and learning. Male puppies start to lift their leg and take an interest in identifying the sex of other animals by sniffing and clumsy attempts to mount them. They may also attempt to verify the sex of cushions and table legs, and may indulge in nipping as an outlet for their burgeoning sex drive. Females come in heat for the first time, after which a decision as to spaying should be made. They must be safely confined in order to avoid a mating, which is highly inadvisable this first time. A puppy does a lot of shedding now, as his baby coat falls out and his adult coat takes over. If his ears drooped during the teething period, they will probably become erect again. Ears which should tip over but which stubbornly remain pricked, may need help if they do not behave properly at this point. Six months is the recommended minimum age for giving a puppy his first annual antirabies vaccination, an obligatory protection in many states.

Psychologically, he has gained so much self-confidence that he has begun to get ideas of his own and sometimes thinks his ideas are better than yours. You need to be quite firm at times in order to maintain your authority. This is vital with large breeds, which may be ready for Obedience training. He has already become attached to his old habits, but is still very quick to form new ones. He tries to understand everything you say and even attempts to communicate with you, telling you that he would like to go out, that he is hungry, or bored. His sense of property and territory is well-developed, and he has learned to respect others' territory too. His intuition is developing. He recognizes friends before they have rung the bell, and is at the door to greet you whenever you come home. Male puppies feel the urge to roam and may find confinement and restraint particularly irksome.

What he needs most is kind, firm handling, nourishing food, lots of exercise and activity to keep him out of mischief, and frequent displays of affection to make up for all the scolding you have to do. At 6 months, he also needs a dog license.

FROM 9 TO 12 MONTHS

Physically, he may stop growing taller if he is of a small or medium-sized breed. His lanky body will start to fill out and his coat to achieve its adult color and texture. His appetite is prodigious, and it is vital to his future well-being to give him a generous, balanced diet. His sexual characteristics become more pronounced, males looking more masculine and females more feminine.

Psychologically, the sexual differences are more apparent too. Males tend to bark more, to play rougher, more aggressive games. They become more competitive and enjoy racing with other dogs, and sometimes bully smaller ones. Females generally make it clear whether they are going to be quiet, affectionate home-lovers, or tomboy sporting companions. Atavistic instincts such as hunting, running, digging, and tracking begin to seek expression. Puppies who are settled enough to concentrate may begin training in their working or sporting specialties. Those who are still too immature can be given a basis for future training by playing games designed to exercise their native aptitudes, such as retrieving, racing, and swimming. They are all curious, explorative, eager to learn and proud of each new accomplishment. But at the same time they cling strongly to old habits, and rehabilitation requires much time and effort.

What he needs most is mental and physical activity, greater responsibility and independence in areas where he can be trusted, new experiences beyond his home territory, firm but kindly discipline, lavish praise for his achievements and good behavior, lots of companionship, and more specific training for his adult life.

FROM 1 TO 3 YEARS

Physically, your dog will continue to develop heavier bone, a deeper chest, a fuller coat, as well as greater strength and endurance. Large breeds attain their full physical maturity and definitive proportions between the ages of 18 months and 2 years; smaller breeds, sooner. An adult dog no longer needs a body-building diet, but a maintenance one that is adjusted to his daily energy requirements. Too copious or rich a diet will lead to obesity and perhaps more serious health problems.

Psychologically, he is unconditionally devoted to you and may become jealous and possessive. He may even begin to resemble you in some ways. His intelligence and receptivity are at their peak, and he vastly enjoys collaborating with you in work and play, as well as acquiring new skills. He invents little rituals and enjoys a regular daily routine. He is quite conscious of his social status and is prepared to defend his position as well as his possessions.

What he needs most is training for work, sport, or merely for fun and to exercise his intelligence; lots of mental and physical activity; mutual loyalty and devotion.

FROM 3 TO 8 YEARS

Physically, he is in his prime.

Psychologically, he is a fully formed adult and is unlikely to change in personality or mentality, although he is capable of learning new things until the end of his life. He knows and understands you and your habits as well as you know and understand him—perhaps better. These should be the most harmonious, rewarding years of your life together.

What he needs most is a well-balanced life and a loving owner.

An English Setter wins the 9 to 12 months puppy class. (*William P. Gilbert*)

An English Setter in the prime of life, Am. & Can. Ch. Clariho Knight Rider.
(*William P. Gilbert*)

FROM 8 YEARS ON

Physically, he is beginning to decline in activity, needing less food, less exercise, and more sleep. His teeth should be watched, and as they start to go he needs a softer diet. His hair may whiten, especially around the muzzle and eyes. His hearing diminishes, in particular his directional hearing. His eyesight dims, perhaps because of cataracts, which can be operated on successfully. His digestion is not what it used to be. Obesity should be avoided at all cost because of the strain it puts on his aging heart. Vitamin and mineral supplements can relieve and retard his infirmities, which may include rheumatism and arthritis. He is more vulnerable to chills as well as to contagious diseases, and should never be asked to sleep out of doors. He may grow warts and tumors that may need to be removed. His nails require more frequent clipping now that he exercises less. His hindlegs weaken, his stamina diminishes. Do not humiliate him by asking him for greater physical effort than he can furnish, because he is aware of and embarrassed by his waning physical powers. Very old dogs may become incontinent at night, and you will have to start saving up old newspapers again.

Psychologically, he needs much understanding and love, even if he is nervous, jealous, or cranky. He is comforted by a regular daily routine, but most of all by a feeling of emotional security.

What he needs most is respect, affection, understanding, patience, a diet suited to his physical condition, regular medical checkups, safety measures in view of his infirmities, a great deal of indulgence, and an infinite amount of gratitude for the service he has rendered and the joy he has given you throughout the previous years.

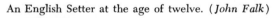

An English Setter at the age of twelve. (*John Falk*)

7.

Feeding Your Dog

Canine nutrition has been the subject of much research in recent years. Since prepared dog food accounts for a greater volume of supermarket sales than any other single grocery item, the commercial incentive is tremendous. As a result, American dogs are the best fed in the world, probably the most expensively fed, and certainly the most often overfed. And yet there are many differences of opinion on the subject, and many misconceptions.

Biologists describe the dog as a carnivorous mammal. But modern canine authorities say that his cohabitation with man has caused him to become, like us, omnivorous. Perhaps he always has been, when you consider that wild dogs ate their prey in its entirety, including the vegetable content of the stomach and intestines.

Dogs are remarkably adaptable to different kinds of diets. If you travel around the world in canine circles, you will find that Italian dogs thrive on spaghetti with tomato sauce, French dogs do well on beefsteak, rice, and carrots, English dogs drink tea, and canine natives of many coastal regions survive on bread and fish. Nevertheless, American methods of scientifically balanced feeding are universally recognized as setting the standard for excellence.

THE CANINE DIGESTIVE SYSTEM

The dog's digestive system is not exactly like ours. The general process is the same, but the timing is different. First of all, mastication is less important in canine digestion. The dog's teeth and jaws are designed for tearing meat and grinding bones with amazing efficiency and up to 300 pounds of force. Dogs chew little and swallow rapidly. They cannot chew with their mouth closed. The dog's taste buds are situated under his tongue, but his food passes swiftly, practically unsavored, through the pharynx and esophagus into the stomach, where the principal digestive process takes place. The dog's gastric juices are much stronger than ours, permitting him to digest matter which would give us a severe stomachache, to say the least.

His stomach is very elastic. It can expand in a tiny lap dog to a capacity of one pint, while large dogs make room for 8 quarts of food. The gastric juices in his stomach are profuse and highly acid, and food remains there longer than it does in ours, before passing into the intestine, which is relatively short. This is why dogs require a richer, more concentrated diet than we do. It also explains why they gobble their meals. Digestion takes place mostly in the stomach and the small intestine, very little in the mouth.

THE DOG'S NUTRITIONAL REQUIREMENTS

The dog's requirements are similar to ours, notwithstanding these physiological differences. Puppies, since they grow and mature faster than we do, need a richer diet than do babies, with more protein and less bulk. Baby food, except for all-meat products, is therefore unsuitable. But adult dogs, like us, need a balanced diet including proteins for body-building, fats and carbohydrates for supplying energy and heat, bulk for elimination, vitamins and minerals to catalyze various body processes, and a total caloric intake that corresponds to individual living conditions, age, weight, metabolism, and activity. Water is vitally important, representing an estimated 70 per cent of the dog's weight.

The indispensable protein content can be provided by meat, fish, cheese, milk, and eggs.

FAT is an imporant source of calories, valuable in cold climates and during the winter. It also helps to maintain a healthy coat and skin. Dogs housed out of doors may be given as much as 20 per cent fat in their diet to provide calories and promote a heavy growth of coat. Ten or 15 per cent is sufficient for most pet dogs. The less expensive cuts of meat generally contain this percentage, but most commercial dog foods have a much lower fat content. You can add it in the form of lard, butter, beef suet, chicken fat, bacon drippings, or vegetable oils.

CARBOHYDRATES include sugars and starches, both of which are sources of quick energy. Dogs assimilate sugar easily, although it is often an acquired taste. Their gastric juices are less efficient in digesting starches, unless they have been very well cooked. Commercially prepared biscuits and meal are specially processed and enriched in order to fill the dog's nutritional requirements and to suit his digestive apparatus. Whole wheat toast and unrefined grain products sold in health-food shops are excellent, though expensive. On the other hand, potatoes, white bread, treated rice, and commercial pasta are not advisable for dogs, partly because of indigestibility, but mostly because they provide little nourishment.

In addition to starches, the CELLULOSE that is found in greens and vegetables provides bulk and favors elimination. Green vegetables are actually indigestible to dogs, who eat grass for this very reason, especially in the spring, in order to purge themselves, the grass being either regurgitated or eliminated undigested. If your dog has an obsession for grass, you might examine his diet to make sure that it agrees with him. You might also add a small quantity of cooked, chopped, or mashed green vegetables to his food and see if this does not satisfy his craving. Carrots and spinach provide useful vitamins and minerals. Cooked vegetables and greens in the diet of obese or inactive dogs can satisfy their hunger temporarily without providing fattening calories.

The principal CANINE VITAMIN REQUIREMENTS are those of the B group, and Vitamins A, D, and E. Oddly enough, dogs do not need that fashionable tonic, Vitamin C, because their body produces it naturally. Liver and milk are particularly rich in the essential canine vitamins. Carrots are a natural source of Vitamin A, and whole wheat cereals supply the B group. Cod-liver oil is the richest source of Vitamin D, essential for growing puppies, lactating bitches, and for adult dogs who get little sunshine.

Finally, there are MINERALS, the most important of which are calcium and phosphorus, especially for growing puppies.

The principal decision an owner has to make is whether to give his dog commercial dog food, a homemade diet, or a combination of the two.

COMMERCIAL DOG FOOD DIETS

Prepared dog food has been highly perfected as to aspect, taste, aroma, conservation, and nutritional balance, under the supervision of renowned veterinarians. Countless healthy dogs have been raised on nothing else. Competition is keen for this lucrative market, and you will find on the grocery shelves a confusing array of products, including:

CANNED DOG FOOD, which may be a complete diet, enriched with vitamins and minerals, containing ideal proportions of protein, fat, and bulk; or it may be a preparation of meat or fish. The only way to find out is to study the labels.

All of these canned products are soft and moist. Due to their high water content (about 77 per cent), you may be giving your dog less nourishment than you think. Because of their lack of consistency, you should also give your dog hard biscuits, a raw carrot, an apple, or a bone from time to time, as well as a chewing toy.

DOG BURGERS, in bulk or patty form, are the newest invention in dog food. It looks like hamburger, but is actually a complete food, containing less moisture (about 30 per cent) than canned products, and requiring no refrigeration, which is convenient. On the other hand, it is soft, which is fine for old dogs and puppies with teething problems. But healthy adults need chewing supplements if this is their only nourishment.

DRY FOOD has also been modernized in a blend of all the necessary canine dietary elements, which is presented in small bits for puppies and small breeds, and large chunks for big breeds, with a moisture content of only about 10 per cent. It can be softened with water, milk, or gravy, or it can be fed dry, in which case your dog will automatically drink a lot of water after each meal. Dry food is usually composed of half cereal and half animal products, with added vitamins and minerals. For reasons of conservation, it is low in fat, which must be added.

DOG BISCUITS are sold in various shapes and forms, including whole biscuits and kibbles (broken into small pieces). They are usually a mixture of cereals, bone meal, vitamins, minerals, and powdered milk, which is a convenient base for a diet that definitely needs to be completed by the addition of meat and fat for the average dog. This economical product is a favorite with many breeders, who buy kibbles in 50-pound sacks and mix it with meat or chicken purchased in wholesale quantities and stored in a freezer.

Dog biscuits and dry foods neither sour nor spoil, making the "complete" kind ideal for the currently popular SELF-FEEDING DIET, in which a constant supply of food and water is available so that the dog can eat whenever he likes and as much as he likes. This obviously saves time and trouble with kennel dogs. Perhaps it is worth trying with country dogs as well. But in the city, where dogs have to be taken out to do their business, and in the suburbs, where it can be a nuisance to let your dog in and out at odd hours of the day and night, it is probably more practical to feed him at regular hours so that his elimination takes place at regular hours too.

A complete commercial dog food is certainly the most convenient solution for a single dog. When you find a brand and presentation that he likes, you can feed it to him indefinitely, knowing that he is getting all of the essential nutritive elements, and solving your problem once and for all. The recommended quantities on the labels are good general yardsticks, although they are average requirements and are not a substitute for your own observation and judgment. You may have to double the amount for an active dog during cold weather or reduce the ration for inactive individuals. The major drawback of many of these products is that they are more expensive than they seem to be. Compare contents and prices to see what you are getting and whenever possible buy them by the case at wholesale rates, perhaps grouping together with dog-owning friends. Base your choice on facts and not on advertising. The appealing puppy who gobbles up a bowl of tinted mush on television with such obvious relish has probably had nothing to eat for twenty-four hours before his performance.

COMBINATION DIETS

This is the method most small breeders have adopted. With an enriched commercial product as a base, they add home-prepared meat or fat or both, as well as a wide range of ingredients which are each breeder's secret. The combination method is also practical for a single dog, since it reduces shopping and cooking time and permits the use of nourishing leftovers. Changes of diet due to travel or other reasons are also simplified, because the dog is already accustomed to the basic prepared product, which remains unchanged.

HOMEMADE DIETS

Since they can be made to measure for each individual dog, these would be ideal if they were not so much bother. Aside from taking more time and trouble than the other methods, a homemade diet requires a sound knowledge of canine nutrition. Table scraps are definitely insufficient for modern pets whom we want to thrive, not merely to survive. They are often the direct cause of obesity and various allied skin disorders too. Nor is it satisfactory to share your own meals with your dog, because his taste and needs are different. Instead, build his meals around the foods that are HIGHLY RECOMMENDED FOR DOGS:

Beef (Ground or chopped for puppies, in chunks for adult dogs, raw or cooked. It need not be tenderloin. Dogs prefer their meat a bit tough, and they need the fat found in the cheaper cuts.)

Lamb and mutton

Chicken

Horse meat

Beef heart and kidneys

Beef liver (Once a week is a healthy ration, as it is packed with vitamins. Too much or too often gives loose stools.)

Eggs, hard-boiled or scrambled (The yolk may be given raw, but not the white, which in its raw state destroys biotin, a useful vitamin in the dog's intestines.)

Rice, whole wheat, barley, oats, buckwheat

Whole wheat biscuits or toast

Carrots (cooked or raw, grated and mixed with his meal, or whole for chewing)

String beans, spinach (chopped or mashed)

Cottage cheese (excellent for weaning puppies)

Unfermented natural cheese, such as Swiss and Edam

Apples and pears

On the other hand, certain foods should be considered TABOO:

White commercial bread

Cabbage (which causes flatulence and is difficult to digest)

Potatoes (hard to digest and not very nourishing)

Starchy vegetables such as dried beans

Spicy dishes and sauces

Uncooked egg white

Processed cheese

Pork (unless it is lean, well cooked, and served infrequently)
Raw fish
Delicatessen meats
Unboned chicken, rabbit, and fish
Cake and candy
Alcohol

A GOOD FORMULA FOR A HOMEMADE DIET is one half cereal, rice, or kibbles, and one half meat, including its natural fat, with green or yellow vegetables added from time to time.

Dogs with unusually big appetites or with a tendency to obesity will keep their figures if you cut down on the starch and increase the vegetables, to the proportion of one half meat, one fourth kibbles, and one fourth vegetables. Older dogs may need reduced protein to spare their kidneys the task of nitrogen elimination.

Whichever method you choose for feeding your dog, it is best to stick to it. Once he has become accustomed to a certain regimen, he will be upset by any sudden change of diet—for example, from canned dog food to dog meal, or from homemade meals to commercial products. The upset is apt to take the form of constipation if you change from prepared products to fresh ones, and diarrhea in the opposite case. The only way to avoid these inconveniences is to mix the new food into his customary diet in increasing amounts over several days. Even so, you may have to multiply the outings of city dogs and adjust their timing, since prepared foods are high in bulk and often laxative, creating urgent calls of nature. Dogs who change from a natural diet to a commercial dry one will drink a lot more water and consequently have more urine to eliminate at more frequent intervals.

DIETARY SUPPLEMENTS

An adult dog needs only a well-balanced diet in order to stay healthy. Sometimes, however, his needs may surpass his natural resources.

Breeders always give their puppies cod-liver oil in order to prevent rickets and help form strong bone tissue. Most veterinarians also recommend calcium and phosphorus supplements for puppies, although adult dogs generally get enough of these important minerals in the form of bone or bone meal. An all-meat diet, though it may be the dog's dream, lacks calcium and Vitamin D and contains relatively too much phosphorus. An all-cereal diet lacks Vitamin A, among others, and can cause hysteria. A deficiency in niacin (one of the B group) can lead to a malady called "Black Tongue," while lack of thiamin (another B vitamin) can make a dog listless, constipated, and vulnerable to minor infections.

If your pet is receiving a normal diet, he should not really need additional minerals and vitamins unless he is:

—a growing puppy (Continue the puppy supplements his breeder was giving him, then those your veterinarian recommends.)

—a convalescent (according to the vet's instructions)

—a pregnant or nursing bitch (what your vet prescribes)

—a very old dog (if he needs them)

—a show dog (not really necessary, but customary in order to improve coat and increase vitality)

—after worming (a complete supplement during a week or so)

CANINE CALORIC REQUIREMENTS

Animal nutrition experts have made careful studies of the dog's caloric needs. The daily recommended rations on packages and cans are generally reliable.

Dog's weight (pounds)	Dry Food (ounces)	Semi-moist (ounces)	Canned (ounces)
5	3½	5	10
10	5½	9	18
15	7	11	22
30	12½	18½	37
45	17	25	51
60	21	31	62
75	25	37½	75

Novice owners tend to underfeed adolescent puppies and overfeed adult dogs. The best guide is certainly old-fashioned trial and error. You can give a young puppy all he wants of a well-balanced diet. Start an adult dog with a recommended ration and observe his reaction to it. Remember that puppies should be pleasingly plump. Adolescents require an enormous amount of food, but overweight can cause lasting harm by overtaxing their immature bone structure. An adult dog should be neither fat nor thin, his ribs well covered with flesh but not layered in fat. Show dogs are often exhibited in a heavier condition than would be desirable in a pet dog, while Hunting and Working dogs are often permitted to become too thin. Feel your dog's body all over with your hands. Heavy-coated dogs may appear to be plump when they are actually undernourished.

Generally speaking, small dogs need relatively more calories per pound than large breeds, and active dogs naturally need more than sedentary ones. All dogs need more calories in the winter than in the summer. Growing puppies, and Hunting and Working dogs in full activity, may need twice as much as an adult pet. Pregnant bitches also require double rations, since they are eating not only "for two," but often for seven or eight. Remember that the increase may be in the form of a richer diet, not necessarily a more copious one. Since the protein content of prepared food is of less high quality than a good homemade diet, you need to give a comparatively greater quantity, especially to a growing puppy.

The following chart may serve as a guideline if you are feeding your dog a homemade diet. These rations concern average animals and should be adjusted to suit individual needs and appetites. As a point of comparison, the maintenance requirement of a human adult of normal build and activity is about 2,000 or 2,500 calories a day.

CANINE CALORIE REQUIREMENTS

Pounds of Body Weight	Daily Calories	
	Growing Puppies	Adult Maintenance
5 pounds	520	260
10 pounds	850	430
15 pounds	1,140	600
20 pounds	1,400	700
25 pounds	1,650	825
30 pounds	1,900	960
40 pounds	2,400	1,200
55 pounds	3,000	1,500
65 pounds	3,250	1,600
80 pounds	3,800	1,900
90 pounds	4,000	2,000
110 pounds	4,840	2,500

CALORIC VALUES

CANNED DOG FOOD (varies according to brand)	450 calories
COMPLETE DRY MEAL (1 pound)	1,600 calories
MEAT (3 ounces, a small serving)	250 calories
CHICKEN (3 ounces)	150 calories
LEAN FISH (3 ounces)	100 calories
FATTY FISH (tuna or salmon, 3 ounces)	175 calories
COOKED RICE (½ cup)	50 calories
COOKED OATMEAL (½ cup)	75 calories
COOKED PASTA (½ cup)	100 calories
WHOLE MILK (1 cup)	165 calories
EGG (one)	75 calories
CHEESE (one ounce)	100-200 ''
BUTTER and FAT (1 Tablespoonful)	100 calories

RECOMMENDED FEEDING SCHEDULES

Age	Feedings	Mealtimes
6-10 weeks	5 times a day	Every 3 hours
10-12 weeks	4 times a day	Every 4 hours
3-6 months	3 times a day	Morning, noon, and evening
6-18 months	2 times a day	Morning and late afternoon
18 months and older	2 times a day — or — once a day (plus a morning or bedtime snack)	Before your own lunch and dinner Depends on climate and activity. Noon or 5 p.m. are good times usually.

WATER AND BEVERAGES

A constant supply of fresh water is essential to your dog's health and comfort. Like man, a dog can go without food for a surprisingly long time, but if he is deprived of water, he cannot survive for more than a few days, or even a few hours, in a hot, dry environment.

His water consumption varies according to the climate, to his activity, and to the composition of his meals. Heat and exercise dehydrate him quickly. He gets very thirsty in cars and airplanes too. However, excessive thirst for no apparent reason should be reported to your vet, because it may be an early symptom of diabetes or kidney trouble.

At home he should have a clean, full water bowl next to his food dish, another in his play area, and perhaps a third one that is accessible during the night.

Away from home the problem is more difficult. A thirsty dog is attracted to water in the gutter, in stagnant pools and rain puddles. Clean rain water is fine. But the caustic chemicals used for melting snow on streets and sidewalks, and used as weed-killers and insecticides on lawns and golf courses, are deadly poisons. Try to train your dog to drink only from his own bowl or what you offer him. When he has done a lot of running and even during long summer walks, do as hunters do and carry a canteen of water with you, or a water-filled plastic container. Another simple precaution is to keep a bowl and water supply in your car for him.

Milk is the only liquid, aside from water, that appeals to dogs and agrees with them (although it may cause loose stools). They are seldom tempted by other beverages and particularly dislike carbonated drinks. Brandy is sometimes given as a stimulant in a crisis, but alcohol does not attract them. How strange that some people think it amusing to give a cocktail to a dog, when they would be outraged if you plied their children with liquor! It is not fun but thoughtless cruelty. Never let your friends persuade you to make this degrading experiment.

BONES

There is a difference of opinion among canine experts as to whether bones should be given to a dog raw or cooked, hard or soft, and even whether they should be given at all. On one point, however, there is unanimity: Never give a dog splintering bones from chicken, pork, fowl, and rabbit (although chicken bones that have been cooked in a pressure cooker until they are very soft can be quite nourishing).

A marrow bone is the traditional symbol of a treat for a dog, and he obviously appreciates it. It may be too big and hard for small dogs. In fact, large breeds generally handle bones much better than small ones. Bones that are mostly cartilage, such as spinal and shoulder bones of veal, knuckle bones, and soft rib bones, are good chewing material that can be entirely consumed. The danger is intestinal impaction, especially in small dogs, if the finely masticated bone has not been mixed with other residue in the dog's stomach. A small quantity should cause no trouble if it is given right after a meal. Chop and steak bones are more dangerous. Careful eaters simply clean off the meat and fat, but greedy gobblers run the risk of internal injury from jagged bone splinters. The same is true of a leg of lamb bone. But what a treasure it represents to a dog!

What is the best policy to follow with a dog of your own? A teething puppy, between 4 and 6 months of age, should always have a bone, real or imitation, to chew on. You might give an adult dog a suitable bone as an occasional treat—for example, once a week. It will give him enormous pleasure, will help to keep his teeth clean and free from tartar, and will occupy him for several hours. But a nylon bone offers the same advantages without the risk.

REWARDS AND SNACKS

Edible rewards are useful in training puppies, while snacks can be convenient pacifiers and distractions. But do not imagine that your dog necessarily relishes your favorite treats. He will accept a piece of candy or a potato chip if he sees that you are eating one. But he would probably prefer any number of unlikely delicacies, such as grapes, asparagus, tomatoes, peaches, pears, cherries, onions and garlic, even walnuts that he shells himself, or blackberries nipped off the bush.

When you want to offer your dog a snack, for example, when his meal is delayed for some reason or other, let it be:

—a dog biscuit
—canine vitaminized candy drops
—a raw carrot
—an apple

—small pieces of whole wheat cookies
—bits of Edam or Swiss cheese
—pieces of cooked liver (the show handler's stand-by)
—a suitable bone

Offer it to him as a reward for obeying some command, no matter how simple. Try to resist giving food to a dog who begs for it, or at least command him to sit first. And never give him tidbits from the dinner table, which will only encourage him to make a nuisance of himself. The best method is to feed him just before your own meal. He will not be hungry and will join you for the pleasure of your company, not for what is on your plate.

OVERWEIGHT AND UNDERWEIGHT

OBESITY is one of the major health hazards and life-shorteners of modern pet dogs. Its causes and effects are the same as with humans, and so is the cure. The vast majority of cases are due to excess caloric intake and insufficient exercise, rather than to metabolic disorders.

Dogs overeat for the same reasons we do, although less often from gourmandise than from boredom. When a dog is given little mental and physical activity, mealtime becomes the high point of his day. Like humans, he may transfer his craving for affection into compulsive gluttony. A healthy dog who leads a well-balanced life, complete with affection and companionship, is seldom obese.

It must be admitted that some dogs, as well as some breeds, are prone to gluttony. Many Spaniels always seem to be hungry (perhaps because of their keen sense of smell). Many Dachshunds also act starved, even when they are so fat that they can hardly waddle (perhaps because they too often lead the life of lap dogs when they were originally bred for active sport). Gluttony can be an acquired sin of any idle dog.

Adolescent puppies gain pounds rapidly during their growth period, as they develop heavier bone, muscle, and coat. But once an adult dog has attained his ideal weight, you should try to keep it stable by weighing him at least once a month. (Get on the scales together, then alone, and calculate the difference. Very big dogs can be weighed on the freight scales of railway stations or on the grain scales of a feed store.) His weight will vary according to his activity, even to the time of year. Hunting dogs can put on many pounds when the hunting season is over if their rations have not been modified accordingly. It is a simple matter to shed a few pounds by putting your dog on a diet for a week or so, increasing the proportion of vegetables, maintaining the protein, and reducing the fat and starch. You may also reduce the total quantity slightly every day. But never eliminate completely any of the basic nutritional elements, unless it is under veterinary instructions and supervision.

Once obesity has set in, the problem is much more difficult and the cure more painful, not only for the dog but also for his owner. Until your dog has formed new eating habits, you must steel yourself to resist his imploring looks. Make it up to him by giving him as much activity, distraction, and affection as possible, until this trying period is over. Never feed him anything between meals. But if he cleans his dish and pleads for more, you may weaken to the point of giving him a dog biscuit, a raw carrot, an apple, or a bone. Even better, you can try to take his mind off his unhappy situation by playing his favorite game with him or taking him for a walk.

UNDERWEIGHT and LACK OF APPETITE are harder to deal with. Again, the cause is often psychological. Again, the origin is often neglect and boredom. When a pet dog refuses to eat, his owner pleads with him and tries to tempt him with morsels fed by hand. What joy for the neglected dog, who at last has found a way of attracting his owner's attention! An intelligent owner will counter this common canine ploy by giving his dog the companionship he longs for, by playing with him, and taking him for a daily walk. But he will not be inveigled into an endless ritual of hand-feeding.

How can you handle the problem of a dog who refuses to eat not because he is neglected, but, on the contrary, spoiled? Simply remove his bowl after half an hour, and present it again only at the next mealtime. Spoiled dogs are often obese too. It will do your dog no harm to skip a meal, even to go without food for an entire day. (Do not, however, serve him the same food if it has become stale or rancid.)

It never occurs to some owners that their dog lacks appetite simply because they offer him unappetizing meals, perhaps in a dirty bowl. Food that is unfit for human consumption is unfit for modern pets. Dogs also eye with suspicion any new food, and they have marked individual preferences for meals that are dry or moist (seldom sloppy), finely chopped, or chunky. You can add taste appeal with a pinch of salt, a little fresh butter, a dribble of olive oil, a little chopped onion or garlic, or a beaten egg yolk. Most dogs relish liver and innards, which can be mixed into their regular feed in small quantities. And remember that the most effective appetite stimulant is aroma. If you have been giving your dog dry feed and raw meat, it may tempt him more if the meat is seared or broiled and the dry food is moistened with warm water or broth and allowed to cool. A coffee spoonful of brewer's yeast sprinkled on his meal is another good appetite awakener.

Some dogs prefer to eat their meat first and return later for the other ingredients. Many dogs skip their noon meal entirely during hot weather. Let your pet follow his natural instincts, as long as he consumes his normal rations during each 24-hour period. If he skips a meal, increase the quantity of the next one. If the occurrence is frequent, you might reconsider his feeding schedule. Perhaps he prefers one large meal a day instead of two or three smaller ones. Even if your dog refuses food during an entire day, it is not necessarily a sign of illness unless he is also in pain or running a temperature. Fasting is an instinctive animal remedy for minor digestive disorders, and your vet would probably prescribe the same treatment. However, if your dog refuses food for more than 24 hours, and if he seems unwell, you should, of course, have your veterinarian examine him.

Chronic underweight may be due to some physical malfunction. A sudden weight loss is definitely a danger signal. A voracious appetite combined with loss of weight is one of the symptoms of internal parasites. All of these require the attention of your veterinarian, for he alone is competent to diagnose the cause and to prescribe the treatment.

A young puppy who refuses to eat should cause immediate concern. A healthy diet is vital to his future well-being, and since his tiny stomach holds very little at a time, a missed meal is nourishment lost forever. But before you alert the vet or your puppy's breeder, you should verify that his *loss of appetite* is not due to one of several easily remedied causes:

—Perhaps your puppy misses the competition of his brothers and sisters, whose company he was used to at mealtimes. (If keeping him company yourself does not work, you may try hand-feeding for a while, but do not make a habit of it, especially with Toy breeds.)

—Perhaps his feeding times do not coincide with his hunger. (Adjust your schedule to suit his appetite.)

—Perhaps he is too nervous to eat. (Avoid the excitement of play and visitors just before and after his mealtimes.)

—Perhaps his food is too tough or chunky for his baby teeth to handle. (Chop it finely, or soften it by soaking. Teething puppies often go off their feed and need a softer diet during this period.)

—Perhaps he has some purely mechanical problem with his food dish. (Young puppies eat most easily from a flat dish, like a pie plate. Later on, long-nosed breeds should be given a deeper dish. For long-eared breeds, there are special deep tapered bowls which prevent their ears from dragging in their food. You can also pin back long ears by pulling the top of a nylon stocking over the dog's head, or by clipping together the long hair—not the skin—of his eartips on top of his head with a plastic clothespin.)

NUTRITIONAL DEFICIENCIES

The average owner is seldom aware of the effect of an improper diet on his dog until it has caused some grave disorder. It will be spotted sooner if you take your dog to the vet for a checkup twice a year. An annual visit is necessary anyway in order to keep his immunization up to date. In the meantime, there are a few easily observed symptoms you can look out for:

—Eating stones or filth such as horse manure and drinking water from flowerpots, which may indicate that your dog's diet is not as well-balanced as you think it is. Perhaps a little liver or a canine vitamin and mineral supplement will quickly cure the obsession (fresh feces are said to contain certain B vitamins). Perhaps your dog needs less meat and more cereal, or simply a little salt on his food.

—Pale gums, which are a sign of anemia, perhaps due to hookworms.

—Excessive nervousness and twitching, which may denote a lack of Vitamin B. This can be conveniently and palatably added in the form of powdered brewer's yeast or wheat germ.

—A dull, scrawny coat and scaly skin, possibly indicating a deficiency of Vitamin A or E or essential fatty acids.

—Bad breath, often due to too much starch, to tartar on the teeth, or to a temporary intestinal disorder. A garlicky odor can indicate the presence of roundworms. In older dogs, progressive kidney failure can produce "uremic breath."

—Bad odors from the other end, often caused by fermentation in the intestines of starches, cabbage, beans, or a diet too rich in meat and eggs.

—Lack of energy, perhaps due to undernourishment caused by a high proportion of bulk and insufficient protein in the diet.

—Scratching by a dog who has no skin disease or external parasites, which may be due to nervousness resulting from a deficiency of Vitamin B and occasionally from food allergies.

—Vomiting, which should be diagnosed by your veterinarian if it is habitual. Occasional vomiting is normal and common in dogs, since it is very easy for them to regurgitate. If you examine the mess, you will usually find that it is simply a meal the dog has gobbled too quickly, chunks of meat too big for him to masticate, a mouthful of grass, or some foreign object he wanted to get rid of.

FEEDING FABLES

Canine nutrition has not yet become as laden with the diet fads and fancies that have made human meal-planning so complicated and guilt-ridden. But it has accumulated a number of myths which survive the ridicule of the veterinary profession (perhaps because some of them may contain a grain of truth). As soon as you acquire a dog, your more experienced friends will shower you with advice, which may well include some of the following affirmations:

"*A clove of garlic a day keeps worms away.*"

Garlic has enjoyed a reputation for centuries in the folk medicine of many cultures as an antiseptic, a treatment for high blood pressure, and as a vermifuge. But if your dog really does have worms (and most of them do at one time or another), the quickest way to get rid of them is to have your veterinarian give him a specific worming medicine under his supervision.

"*Raw meat makes dogs vicious.*"

Raw or cooked meat is essential to the dog's nutrition. Fifty per cent is the standard ration, and it may compose as much as 75 per cent of his diet. If he is fed only meat, he may indeed become high-strung, not because the meat is raw, but because he is being given an unbalanced diet.

"*A sugar cube dipped in coffee is good for a dog's heart.*"

It is particularly good for his morale, because it probably means that he is sharing your after-dinner coffee with you. Give it occasionally as a harmless treat, but not as a regular "medicine," and not as a heart remedy.

"*Dogs cannot digest starch.*"

They cannot digest uncooked starch, but they can cope with most cooked ones such as rice, whole wheat bread, and macaroni. However, dogs do not seem to draw as much nourishment from these foods as we do.

"*Sugar causes worms.*"

Sugar is a quick source of energy for dogs, as it is for us. Worms are caused by worm larvae, obviously. A puppy may acquire worms from his mother, and an adult dog may get them from infected food or drink, from the saliva or feces of an infested dog, or from swallowing fleas and lice which act as hosts to tapeworm eggs—but never from sugar.

"Raw eggs improve a dog's coat."

A raw egg yolk from time to time enriches a dog's diet. Cooked eggs are an acceptable substitute for meat in an emergency. But the best coat conditioner is fat, especially unsaturated fat, rich in Vitamin E, such as linseed and wheat germ oil. The egg's reputation as a coat conditioner is probably due to the fact that the yolk is mostly "fat."

"Milk causes diarrhea in an adult dog."

Milk is healthy for all dogs. A bowl of milk with a beaten egg yolk and a couple of pieces of whole wheat toast or dog biscuits is a standard supper dish in many kennels. There are various causes for diarrhea, including internal parasites, indigestion, a change of diet, food poisoning, certain contagious diseases—and sometimes, but not always, milk.

"Dogs instinctively know what is best for them to eat."

Don't count on it. Some dogs seem to have retained a trace of the instinct that once guided them in their choice of food. But, judging from the modern pet dog's taste for cake, candy, leather, wool, nylon, and plastic, this atavism has disappeared along with many others and must be replaced by our own common sense, knowledge, and solicitude.

Knowledge and solicitude are particularly important in feeding a growing puppy, whose nutrition is the foundation of his future health and happiness. But common sense is all you need to feed an adult dog correctly. If the subject interests you, you can make it a laboratory experiment, a research project, or a lifetime hobby. But you can also make it a very simple matter requiring only a few minutes a day. Your dog will never know the difference.

8.

Grooming Your Dog

Dogs are groomed for the same reasons that children are taught to brush their teeth and wash their hands: to keep them clean, which helps to keep them healthy and to make them more attractive. The difference is that dogs are helpless beyond a certain point, while children eventually learn to care for themselves. Many dogs try to do so. The Basenji is the only one to wash himself all over like a cat. But most dogs instinctively dry and clean themselves by rolling in grass after a swim, attempt to remove burrs, hair mats, and parasites with their teeth, spend hours grooming their feet, wipe their mouths on rugs or upholstery after a meal, and some even wipe their bottoms after defecation by dragging their rump along the ground. Most dogs obviously prefer to be clean.

Aside from its practical interest, grooming your dog is of psychological value. The grooming process is a bond-forming ritual among many creatures, including birds, monkeys, cats, dogs, and human beings. Every time you groom your dog you are strengthening your relationship with him. When you relieve him of some irritation that he has been unable to remove unaided, you are also enhancing your prestige in his eyes.

Canine hygiene is basically a matter of cleanliness, of removing foreign matter, including parasites, and of keeping the coat free from shed and matted hair. Dogs need little bathing compared to humans, since their skin is protected by their coat, and perspiration takes place mostly through the tongue and the pads of their paws. In fact, frequent bathing can be harmful because it removes protective oils from the skin and coat.

Ordinary grooming is therefore a simple process that should take no more than 5 minutes a day for a small, short-haired dog, and perhaps 15 minutes for a large, long-haired breed. Specialized grooming takes longer, of course. A professional handler may spend half a day or more grooming a show dog. But the more faithful you are with your daily grooming, the less time this will take too.

Very young puppies need no grooming except for clipping the tips of their nails while they are nursing, and washing their faces and paws when they get food on them. But even if it isn't really necessary, it is a good idea to introduce them to the brush and comb while they are still small and easy to handle.

Ideally, you should groom your dog every day, especially when he is shedding. Twice a week is a more realistic minimum, or even once a week for a smooth-coated dog who lives in a clean environment.

The best time to groom a dog is after his daily walk, or before or after his evening meal. When he has been in the rain, you will have to wait until he is dry before grooming him. On the other hand, when you notice food on his beard or filth on his behind, you should clean them at once.

Very little equipment is needed for ordinary grooming, but it should be the sturdy, canine kind and not your own discarded brush and comb.

BASIC GROOMING EQUIPMENT

—a steel comb (wide-toothed for long coats, fine-toothed for short ones)
—a brush (long stiff bristles for long coats, short stiff bristles for short coats, and short soft bristles or a rubber curry comb for smooth coats)
—a very-fine-toothed steel flea comb
—a pair of blunt-pointed scissors
—a canine nail clipper
—a package of absorbent cotton
—a grooming glove or chamois cloth for polishing short, smooth coats.

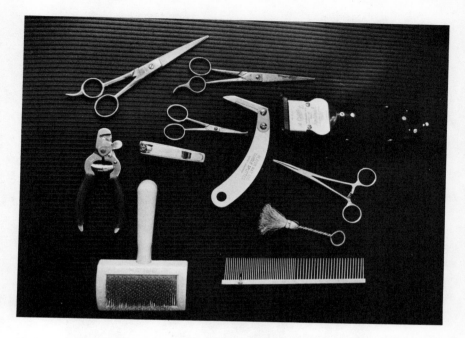

A display of grooming equipment. (*Sue Maynard*)

DAILY GROOMING

1) Begin by collecting your equipment and preparing the grooming site. Large dogs can stand on the floor on a sheet of newspaper. Small dogs are more easily groomed if you place them on a table. In fact, it is a good idea to put your dog on a table whenever possible. Slightly disoriented, he is more likely to stand quietly. (For lengthy show-grooming sessions, it is essential to have a special grooming table, or at least a grooming post that can be clamped on the top of a traveling crate.) Have a wastebasket handy for discarding combings.

2) Wipe your dog's eyes with a piece of cotton moistened in tepid water, especially the corners, where dust often accumulates. Then wipe his mouth and under the chin, as well as the tips of long ears.

3) Stand your dog on all fours and comb him gently but firmly all over, starting with the head, combing in the direction in which the hair grows, downward on the mustache and beard, backward along the spine, downward on the chest and flanks. Lift up his tail with one hand and comb firmly downward beneath it, where dried matter often clings.

4) Turn your dog over on his back and comb him from chest to tail.

Combing. (*Sue Maynard*)

Comb gently inside the thighs and under the chin, as the undercoat often mats in these sensitive spots.

5) Comb the fringe on his legs, tail, and ears.

6) Finally, go over his entire body with the brush, first in a standing position, then lying on his back. All short coats and most long ones are brushed flat. Fluffy coats are brushed against the lie of the hair to make them stand up. Finish off with a tummy massage. This is your dog's reward.

This simple, quick procedure may be complicated if you run into certain obstacles, such as:

Burrs and prickly seeds. If you cannot comb them out or remove them by separating the coat from them a few hairs at a time, you will have to cut them. Make one or more vertical incisions through them with scissors, and comb again. If this doesn't work, the only solution is to cut the tuft of hair beneath the burr, as far away from the body as possible. You will get rid of the burr, but it will leave an uneven spot in the dog's coat, so consider it a last resort.

Matted hair is handled the same as burrs. There are also special grooming sprays that facilitate combing through them.

Tar, paint, and chewing gum can be softened with nail polish remover, ether, or turpentine applied to the hair, not to the skin, and only if there is no danger of its getting in a cut or an abrasion, or near the dog's genitalia, anus, or eyes. Otherwise, try to soften the substance with baby oil or vaseline. Then comb out, and remove the solvent by washing the hair with a soapy cloth and rinsing with a wet one. Never use dry-cleaning products, which burn the dog's sensitive skin and are toxic as well.

DAILY CHECKUP

As you groom your dog, observe the condition of his:

COAT. All coats look dull just before they are shed, but a dull dry coat at other times may indicate some dietary deficiency.

Shedding is designed to make way for a healthy new coat and is perfectly normal. Bald patches, on the other hand, are due to an abnormal hair loss, perhaps caused by rubbing due to too tight a collar, too hard a bed, by scratching at parasites or insect bites, or by a skin disease. Treat the spot with antiseptic and remove the cause, with the help of your vet if necessary.

A "doggy odor" is also abnormal, usually due to overconfinement in unclean quarters, or to some illness or disorder. Do not be content to mask the odor. Seek the cause and cure it.

SKIN. Protected by his coat, the dog's skin usually remains remarkably clean wherever it is covered with fur. But city dogs often soil their underbellies and should be spot-cleaned with a soapy cloth and thoroughly rinsed, because most city grime is toxic.

A very dry skin leaves white flakes on the comb. This may be caused by an unbalanced diet, often insufficient fat or too much meat.

Be watchful for small cysts and tumors. Most of them are harmless. But if they seem infected or grow rapidly, you should show them to your vet.

EYES. A dog's eyes are a reflection of his general health and are normally bright and shiny. Dull eyes can indicate fatigue, illness, indigestion, or the presence of internal parasites, among other things.

Red eyes can be washed with a weak boric acid solution, ordinary un-medicated human eyewash, or a homemade solution of one teaspoon of salt in a pint of water, boiled, then cooled. A yellow or sticky discharge denotes infection and requires medication. A harmless treatment is to place a squiggle of 1 per cent yellow mercuric oxide in the inner corner of the affected eye.

Eyelids are a favorite lodging place for ticks, and what looks like a small swelling may actually be one of these horrid insects. If so, remove it carefully (see page 153).

The eyelids of old dogs should also be examined for warts, which often grow there and are easier to remove when they are small.

EARS. Long ears and lop ears need more attention than small, erect ears. Poodles and Terriers often grow excess hair inside the ears which must be plucked by hand, a few hairs at a time, in order to avoid the formation of mats that trap infection and parasites.

If your dog flinches when you groom his ears, it may mean that there is an infection or some foreign matter in them. Internal ear treatment should be reserved for your vet. But it can do no harm to swab the ears gently and not too deeply with a dry cotton baby swab. If it is stained by blood or by dark matter with a foul smell, he will need professional care. But if the insides of the ears are merely dirty, you can clean them gently with a swab dipped in mineral or olive oil or diluted hydrogen peroxide.

Fly bites on the ears can torment a dog, and since it is easy for him to scratch them, they are apt to become infected. Apply an antiseptic and perhaps an antihistamine ointment too, but on the outside only.

TEETH AND GUMS. Most dogs dislike having their mouths forced open. Yet this is obligatory in the show ring as well as in some veterinary procedures, such as removing tartar from the teeth or examining the dentition of a teething puppy. It is therefore useful to get your puppy accustomed to it while he is young and tractable.

Sometimes a permanent tooth emerges before the baby one has fallen out, and unless the latter is removed, the puppy's adult teeth will not be normally aligned. His complete set of adult teeth normally consists of 20 in the upper jaw and 22 in the lower one, making a total of 42—although some dogs mysteriously lack 2 of them (the premolars), and Greyhounds frequently grow 2 extra molars.

Dogs hardly ever have cavities as we do, but they may break a tooth, which should be filed smooth by the vet or removed if the root is affected. Tartar deposits may accumulate around the gums of older dogs and cause a lot of trouble. Your vet will quickly correct all of these conditions, but it is up to you to bring them to his attention.

A dog's teeth can become yellow or discolored if he is on a soft diet and never has a bone to chew. You can clean them as you do your own, with a toothbrush dipped in table salt or bicarbonate of soda, even your own toothpaste, brushing downward from the gums. Rubbing the teeth every day or two with a slice of lemon will help dissolve tartar, if your dog will tolerate the taste. But he would much prefer a bone.

When you examine your dog's teeth, notice his gums as well. A pale-pink color may indicate anemia caused by a dietary deficiency or by worms.

NAILS. City and suburban dogs who walk on pavements and country dogs who exercise on varied terrain wear down their nails naturally. But if your dog runs about mostly on lawns and carpets, you should check his nails from time to time to make sure they have not grown too long. They should be long enough to give him a grip on the ground, but not so long that he clatters and slithers on the kitchen floor. As a general rule, the nails should not quite touch the floor when the dog is standing upright.

Do not neglect the dewclaws. When they are permitted to grow too long, they curve back and pierce the skin, causing limping, pain, and possibly infection.

Puppy nails need clipping every week. Older dogs who get little exercise need more nail care than younger ones: a clipping every 2 or 3 weeks instead of every month or not at all. If you do not neglect them and there is little to remove, filing should suffice. Otherwise, they must be clipped.

You will need a pair of canine nail clippers and a special nail file, except in the case of Toy dogs, for whom your own manicure equipment should suffice. You may also need someone to hold your dog while you work, at least the first time.

The important point is to avoid cutting into the quick, which is painful and bleeds profusely. This is clearly visible in white nails, for it is opaque while the rest of the nail is transparent. Dark nails are more difficult. A pocket flashlight held underneath the nail will reveal the quick, but even with this guideline it is safer to remove only a little at a time. You will notice that the nail texture becomes spongier as you approach the quick, and this is the signal to stop filing or clipping. Clipped nails should then be smoothed off with the file.

If you accidentally cut into the quick, you must disinfect the spot at once with hydrogen peroxide, then try to hasten blood clotting by applying a styptic pencil (which stings) or cornstarch (which doesn't), or by holding a pressure bandage over it for a few minutes.

A dog who has been accustomed to nail care as a puppy will accept it with good grace, unless you are very inept or have inadvertently hurt him. If so, you can ask your vet to do it. Usually, you will find that if you proceed carefully and keep your dog still, nail clipping is no more than an annoyance to him—certainly not the agonizing torture he pretends it is.

PAWS. There are two types of dog's feet: the hare-paw, which is oval with a long third toe, designed for speed, as in the Greyhound and Whippet; and the cat's paw, round and compact, designed for endurance and soundness, as found in most Hunting breeds. Splayed feet require a lot of care, since they are easily injured and are apt to get worse with age. They are a serious fault in all breeds.

Check your dog's paws for cuts and remove any foreign matter between the toes.

Long tufts of hair between the pads on the bottom of the feet can cause painful limping and should be trimmed level with the sole. If your dog's breed standard does not require furry paws (few of them do), you can also cut the hair tufts on top of the paws between the toes, and trim the outline. Neatly groomed paws look smarter and track less dirt into the house. They may also give your dog a lighter, freer gait.

Interdigital cysts or fungus infections often affect wire-haired breeds like Scotties and Sealyhams, and also Pekingese. But regular foot care should prevent them.

ANUS. Dogs have no complex about this part of their anatomy, so why should you? When your dog has produced a loose stool, he has probably soiled his behind. Give it time to dry, then lift up the tail and comb the dried matter out of his coat. Wipe off the anus with a piece of moist cotton. If it looks red and irritated, rub in a bit of vaseline or healing ointment.

WRINKLES. The deep wrinkles in the face of short-nosed breeds can trap dust and soil. Clean them gently with a piece of damp cotton or a soft cloth, then wipe them dry.

TEATS: Pregnancies, true and false, as well as tumors and abscesses, affect a bitch's teats. If you check them regularly (every day in the case of a pregnant or nursing bitch or a recent mother), you will spot any abnormality before it develops into a serious ailment.

This checkup, believe it or not, takes no more than a minute or two. One of the most important checkpoints takes no time at all:

As you remove dead hair from the comb, examine it carefully. Have you picked up some living creature too? Or tiny black granules, which are the excrement that fleas leave in their wake? Perhaps you have disturbed a flea while combing your dog, particularly inside his legs, around the neck, ears, and the root of the tail. If so, you must go to war to rid your dog of:

EXTERNAL PARASITES

All dogs pick up fleas, lice, ticks, or chiggers at one time or another, usually during warm weather. Even a pampered city pet can pick up a stray flea from a potted plant. Hunting dogs often return from a day's sport with a great collection of chiggers or ticks. Fleas hop from one dog to another with amazing speed and agility. Your pet need only politely greet a flea-infested friend in order to acquire the beginning of a flea colony of his own. Lice are generally associated with filthy conditions, but they are not as rare as they should be. External parasites are not a special affliction of dogs. The dog is simply a particularly convenient host for them. We would probably have them too, if our bodies were covered with hair and we ran around without shoes or clothing and sat and slept on the ground.

FLEAS are the most common, the easiest to detect and to get rid of. You may spot a flea or a black speck on your fine-toothed comb, or notice that your dog is scratching a lot. A single flea can drive him crazy. Worse than that, fleas act as hosts to tapeworm larvae, and if your dog swallows one you may end up with a worm problem too. You can trap fleas in silky and smooth coats with a flea comb and crush them immediately between your fingernails. But fleas nestle in the dense undercoat of double-coated dogs, where the comb cannot reach them. The only way to destroy them is by a general treatment with a product that penetrates to the skin. Regular mild treatment is safer than an occasional severe one. Sometimes it is necessary to shave the coat of a badly infested dog. Antihistamines will relieve the torment, but of course do nothing to kill the fleas. The only way to get rid of fleas without actually destroying them is based on the belief that they cannot bear the scent of horses: Borrow a horse blanket, make your dog sleep on it, and the next morning (so it is said) the fleas will all have disappeared.

LICE are ugly wingless bloodsuckers that hook themselves into the dog's skin, while their eggs attach themselves to his hair. They are less common but more dangerous than fleas. The skin where a louse sucks is often irritated. Difficult to spot, lice are most easily destroyed by an overall insecticide treatment.

TICKS are also wingless bloodsucking parasites that burrow their heads under the dog's skin and must be removed carefully one by one. If you remove the body but not the head, infection can set in. So before you pick off a tick and destroy it by burning (in an ashtray, for example) or by drowning (in a jar of water or the toilet), you must get it to relax its grip by dabbing it with a cotton swab or a matchstick dipped in ether, turpentine, iodine, nail-polish remover, or alcohol—gin or whiskey will do. Then you can remove it with your fingernails or tweezers. Ticks often settle around a dog's eyes, ears, and mouth. When you spot one, you can be almost certain that others are lurking about. Wait for a while, and look again. Ticks are increasingly prevalent in the country and have even begun to migrate to the city.

CHIGGERS are similar to ticks and must also be removed one by one by hand or with tweezers.

MITES are tiny, invisible creatures most often picked up in farming country. They are extremely irritating, their favorite nesting places being between the toes and inside the shoulder and hip joints. The worst thing about them is that they can lead to mange, which causes bald spots on the skin, particularly on the cheeks and front legs.

If your dog shakes his head and scratches at his ears in obvious discomfort, check first for some foreign object such as a wheat awn, then for signs of mange. A mangy ear has a crumbly brown discharge and an unpleasant odor. There are special eardrops for this condition. Flea powders control the mites that led to it, so if you adopt a program of regular prevention, you should not be bothered by them. But if mange has already set in, you should take your dog to the vet and follow his instructions.

PARASITE PREVENTION is much simpler and more thorough than the painstaking process of tracking them down.

The *flea collar* impregnated with insecticide seemed to be the answer to a dog owner's prayers until dangerous side effects were noted, such as allergies, skin disorders, and poisoning, especially when the collar was damp or worn too tight. Some owners continue to use it, putting it on loosely in the morning and removing it at night. But it is much too toxic for a young puppy. In spite of its effectiveness, it is probably too risky for a beloved pet, as are aerosol sprays (because of the danger of getting the product in the dog's eyes and nose), and all products based on DDT or its derivatives (which accumulate in the body and are particularly dangerous for small breeds, since there is no antidote for DDT poisoning). Needless to add, you should never dream of spraying a household insecticide on your dog (although they may be used to spray his bed or kennel, if you keep him away from them for a few hours afterward). And never give any kind of insecticide treatment to a dog who has an open wound.

But do not despair. There are two perfectly effective methods of parasite control which involve only slightly more bother: powders and dips.

Canine insecticide powders exist in many formulas. One that is both harmless and effective has as its active ingredient rotenone, derived from derris root, which is nontoxic even to young puppies. Chlordane is lethal to fleas and relatively safe for dogs, as is 1 per cent benzine hexachloride. On the other hand, it is advisable to avoid products based on lindane and phenothiazime (which are very toxic), as well as pyrethrum (which merely stuns but does not kill fleas).

A thorough powdering, lightly massaging it all over the dog's body, avoiding the eyes, nose, and mouth, and, above all, inhalation of the powder, will rid a dog of parasites within 48 hours and remain effective for 8 to 10 days, so that a weekly treatment will keep a dog constantly free from parasites.

Dips are recommended by many veterinarians for adult dogs, but not for young puppies. They are more trouble than powders, since they must be dissolved in a precise quantity of water, sponged over the dog's coat (despite the name, they are not dipped in it), and allowed to dry. The effect is immediate and lasts for 10 days or more, or until the dog has been out in a rainstorm or for a swim, in which case the dip must be repeated.

Even with this regular treatment, you should examine your dog after he has been in the woods or fields and destroy any parasites you find before they have had time to lay their eggs. All of them multiply at a fantastic rate.

A good program is to schedule a weekly powdering—every Sunday, for example—when you are least likely to forget it. Even if your dog has not been exposed to parasites in the meantime, the eggs of those you destroyed the week before will be ready to hatch. Flea prevention is a permanent battle.

When a dog has been infested with parasites, they nestle in his bedding as well as in his coat. So be sure to spray or powder his kennel or bed as well as his favorite napping spots.

PERIODIC GROOMING

Some kinds of hygienic and esthetic care need to be given only when necessary. For example:

DRYING A WET DOG. It is always advisable to dry a dog who returns wet from a walk, since dogs are sensitive to damp and cold, and dense coats take hours to dry out naturally. Keep an old bath towel in the entry, and before your dog goes any further, wipe off his paws and the underside of his belly, rubbing his chest briskly, for dampness here is most apt to cause a chill. Then throw the clean side of the towel over his back and give him a thorough rubdown. If your dog is wet from city slush or snow, be sure to check between his toes and remove any snow-melting crystals he may have picked up. If he swallows or even licks them, they can be fatal.

SPOT CLEANING. Since frequent baths remove protective oils, you should try to clean the soiled portions of your dog's coat, when possible, by spot cleaning.

Dogs soil themselves most often with food around the muzzle, mud on their paws and legs, and excrement on the behind. When it is thoroughly dry, stand the dog on newspapers and comb the soiled coat, then brush vigorously. Wash your comb and brush rather than your dog.

Small dogs, being so close to the ground, often soil only their under-bellies, which can be sponged with a soapy cloth, then rinsed and dried.

Soil is most visible on white coats, of course, and bathing is the only solution when a white coat has become telltale gray. White coats are also easily stained by urine and wet grass. White Poodles, Sealyhams, Maltese, and Bedlington Terriers often have yellow or brown stains caused by moisture running from their eyes (perhaps due to health conditions that a vet can cure). Since these are stains rather than soil, you can post-pone bathing and bleach the spots with a weak solution of hydrogen per-oxide or, in the case of facial stains, mask them with a dab of white the-atrical makeup or white lipstick on the dry hair.

AFTER SWIMMING. Most water Retrievers possess oily, densely undercoated fur that is virtually waterproof, since the water cannot pen-etrate to the skin. But many enthusiastic swimmers of other breeds are less well equipped for it, especially for sea bathing. Dried salt is irritat-ing to the skin and should be removed by brushing and rinsing in fresh water. Stagnant ponds often leave mud or slime in a dog's coat. Since it resists brushing, it must be washed out. If it is foul-smelling, it is best to give your dog a good hosing before you let him in the house again.

DEODORIZING. The body odor of a healthy dog who is regularly groomed is neither strong nor unpleasant, although some breeds have a more pronounced odor than others. Fastidious breeders eliminate kennel odor in their dogs' coats by mixing cedar shavings in their bedding.

A house-kept dog who is well-cared-for seldom has a noticeable odor. If he does, it is generally a sign of indigestion or dental trouble when it comes from the mouth (in which case he should be taken to the vet), or from dried matter when it comes from the coat (in which case he should be combed or bathed). A musty skin odor is a sign of skin mange. The smell is even stronger when the mange is in the ears.

There are two occasions when a dog really reeks:

1) *When he has been attacked by a skunk.* This is not an uncommon occurrence in some parts of the country, particularly with Hunting dogs. The pungent odor resists ordinary shampoos, but there are two remedies that seem to work, although nobody can explain why: (1) a normal bath followed by a rinse in tomato juice, pure vinegar, or cold black coffee, which is massaged into the coat, permitted to dry, then rinsed off with clear water; and (2) a bath in a 5 per cent solution of ammonia, which will overpower the skunk smell, and leave the dog smelling of ammonia instead.

2) *When he has rolled in filth.* It may be the excrement of a bitch in heat (obviously some sexual reaction), or it may be the rotten carcass of a dead bird or rabbit, or the excrement of some unidentifiable animal (probably some atavistic scent-disguising behavior). Stop your dog from performing these instinctive rituals when you can. If you are too late, give him a good bath, preferably out of doors with a hose, if the weather permits. It will probably take two soapings and several changes of rinse water to rid the dog of these unpleasant, particularly tenacious odors.

SHEDDING. Dogs originally cast their coats in the spring, in order to leave them lighter-coated for the hot summer months, and in the fall, in order to make way for a dense new fur for warmth during the coming winter. Females also shed when going into season twice a year, and again some nine weeks later at whelping time, whether or not they have been bred. But shedding has become almost a continuous process with modern pets who live in heated, electrically lit homes, since it is apparently triggered not by temperature alone, but also by the lengthening and shortening of the daylight hours. The shedding process generally takes 6 to 8 weeks, which may be why it seems to be continuous. You will notice as you groom your dog in the springtime and fall that entire tufts of hair are pulled out by your comb. There is no cause for alarm. This is perfectly normal.

Even if grooming bores you, do not neglect it during the shedding season. Dead hair remaining in the coat will mat and ball, particularly inside the legs and behind the ears. Not only will it irritate your dog, but it will become increasingly difficult to remove.

While short-haired dogs are never so strikingly "out of coat" as long-haired or wire-haired ones, they too shed, and the only way to keep the cast hair off your clothes and rugs is to remove it from your dog with a brush and comb before he shakes it off. Besides, the sooner you remove the old dead coat, the sooner your dog will have a shiny new one.

ANAL GLANDS. On each side of the dog's anus there are two tiny sacs containing a viscous liquid for lubrication during defecation. Modern canine diets are often too soft to exert the pressure necessary for emptying these glands, which cause considerable discomfort when they are distended. A dog who nips at his anus or drags his rump along the ground does not necessarily have worms, as most people believe. It is far more likely that he is simply wiping his behind, or that his anal glands need to be emptied.

This is a very simple process. You can ask your vet to show you how to do it. After locating the sacs between your thumb and forefinger, you simply squeeze firmly but gently, upward and outward, holding a tissue or a wad of cotton in front of the anus in order to catch the expelled matter, which is apt to spurt and has a nasty odor.

Many owners have never heard of this, and many vets do not think of it. It is a good idea to ask your vet to check these glands at every biannual visit.

BATHING YOUR DOG

Many dogs who love to be brushed and combed loathe being bathed. They consider it an ordeal to be avoided by all means, and finally succumb to it with a martyred air. Professional dog groomers, whether they admit it or not, usually administer a tranquilizing suppository to their canine customers. But if you handle your dog gently and talk to him as you lather and scrub in an affectionate, cheerful way, he should learn to accept it with philosophy, if not with enthusiasm.

Many dogs never need a bath if they are regularly groomed. Dogs living in dirty cities need bathing most often because of the polluted city grime, but once a month is often enough. Retrievers and Poodles have relatively oily coats and can safely be bathed more often than dry-coated breeds such as Terriers. Twice a year is sufficient for most country dogs or those kept out of doors, if they are regularly brushed and combed. Try to resist the temptation of overbathing white-coated dogs. You can keep them presentable between baths by occasional dry shampoos. In other words, bathe your dog whenever necessary, but as seldom as possible.

Moreover, you should NEVER BATHE:
—a puppy under 6 months old
—a bitch more than one month pregnant
—a sick dog or a feverish one
—less than one week after an inoculation
—less than one month after an operation
—a dog with a skin eruption or an unhealed wound
—a Poodle just before he is to be clipped
The first bath is the most important one, because the future attitude of

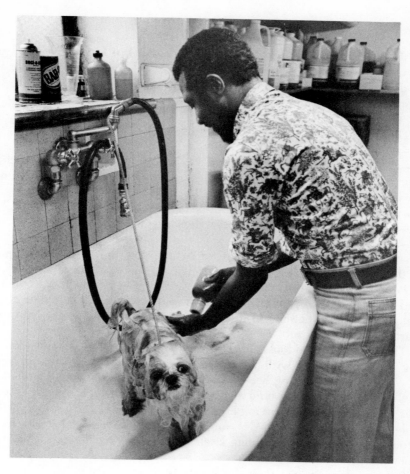

Bathing. (*Sue Maynard*)

your dog depends on it. Enlist someone to help you with a big dog. With a small one, be careful to see that he doesn't lose his footing in the tub and get a dunking. Avoid splashing soapy water in the dog's ears or eyes. If necessary, do a halfway job the first time rather than traumatize your dog and make subsequent bathing difficult if not impossible.

The best time to bathe a dog is on a sunny afternoon at least 2 or 3 hours after he has eaten and after he has had an opportunity to empty his bladder. Choose an afternoon when you are free to keep an eye on him while he is drying out, which can take several hours. Avoid bathing a dog during the winter. If you simply must, prepare a warm spot for him in a closed room where he can dry without catching cold.

Toy dogs can be bathed in a washbasin, small and medium ones in a washtub or a bathtub lined with a nonskid mat; but large dogs need to be washed by hosing or with water buckets, and since this will have to be done outdoors, you must wait for a warm summer day or take them to a professional grooming establishment that is equipped to handle such big customers.

The first step is to collect your material. You will need:

—a plastic apron

—a canine shampoo (It might as well be of an antiseptic insecticide type; there are also special shampoos for Poodles, for white coats, and for untangling badly matted coats.)

—a nonskid mat for the washbasin or bathtub

—a hose attachment for the faucet, or a plastic pitcher

—a face cloth

—towels (One may be sufficient for a small dog, but it will take a pile of them to mop up a larger one.)

Put on your plastic apron (you may want to protect your hair as well), and fill the tub with enough comfortably warm water to reach your dog's belly when he is standing in it. If you have a hose attachment, you can start with an empty tub.

The next step is to look for your dog, who has probably been observing your preparations with a suspicious eye and by now has disappeared. If you find him cowering behind the door or in his own bed, he probably really wants to be discovered and fussed over. But if he has made a serious attempt to escape, you might as well get his leash, for you will probably have to attach him. As an added precaution, when you have brought him into the bathroom, kitchen, laundry, or wherever, close the door tightly.

Some owners protect their dog's ears from soapsuds by stuffing them with cotton, and their eyes by smearing a bit of vaseline around them or by putting a drop of mineral oil in the inside corner of each eye. If you are careful, this should not really be necessary. You can hold a finger over the ear opening when you wash it, and shield the eyes with your hand. If you are using a bathtub or a sink, it is a good idea to protect the drains from dog hair by covering them with a piece of fine wire mesh or a wire scouring pad.

Now place your dog in the bath and keep him standing up. Wet his body down all over with the plastic pitcher or hose attachment, but do not wet his head yet. As soon as you do, he will instinctively shake, so it is better to leave it untouched until the very end.

Pour a dose of liquid shampoo on the middle of his back and massage him thoroughly with both hands, working backward from the nape of his neck. Rub well under the stomach and inside the legs, where his coat is sparse. Lather the penis, underneath the tail, and between the toes. If your dog has long whiskers and a beard, you must wash them now too, taking care not to wet the rest of his face. In order to avoid matting long-haired and heavy coats, it is better to squeeze the lather through them instead of massaging with circular movements.

One soaping should be enough unless the dog is very dirty, in which case the first soaping will merely loosen the dirt and it will take a second one to remove it. A double soaping naturally removes more natural oil, leaving a fluffier, drier coat that is also apt to get dirty again more quickly.

Hosing is by far the quickest and most effective way to rinse a dog. Hold the hose close to his body and move it backward from his head. If you have to use a pitcher, you must fill the tub with clear warm water first, and empty and refill it as it becomes soapy and dirty. Thorough rinsing is most important. Soapy traces will not only dull his coat but also irritate his skin.

When the coat is squeaky clean, try to remove as much water as possible with your hands, firmly pressing it from neck to tail.

At last it is time to wash his face, using a damp washcloth but no soap.

Now lift or help your dog out of the tub and stand back quickly, because he will immediately shake himself vigorously. Let him do it as long as he likes. It is the most efficient way to remove water from his coat. You can intercept the shower by throwing a towel over his back and pinning it together in front of his chest and under his belly before letting him out of the tub. The towel will be soaked at once, and he will shake even more vigorously once you have removed it. In any case, do not open the door. He would dash off and roll in the dirt outdoors, or on a rug or bedspread inside the house. When he has stopped shaking, rub him down with dry towels, mopping up as much moisture as possible. Follow the lie of the hair in long and heavy coats in order to avoid tangles.

If it is a warm, sunny summer day, and if you have a clean lawn or outdoor play area, you can take your dog's favorite toy or ball and go outdoors with him for a good romp. If you manage to keep him running, he will dry off very quickly. In the winter, you can settle him in front of the fireplace or in a warm, closed room and continue to rub him with towels. It takes several hours to dry a dog this way. When he is partially dry, you can protect him from chills by pinning a dry towel in front of his chest and under his belly, replacing it with a dry one as necessary. Do not let him run around still wet or damp, for he may catch cold and will certainly get dirty again. Some dogs cannot bear electric hand driers, while others tolerate them very well, perhaps because they have seen their owners use the instrument on their own hair. If your dog is in the latter category, you are lucky, for it will considerably shorten the drying time. Professional groomers always use electric driers.

(Incidentally, while your dog is drying out, why not wash his collar and leash?)

Combing also hastens the drying process by removing a lot of dead hair that has been loosened by the bath. Short, smooth coats need just enough brushing and combing to make the hair lie flat and smooth, followed by a few strokes of a grooming glove or chamois cloth for polish. Medium coats and wiry stiff ones can be combed when damp, but they need a second dry combing in order to completely clear out the dead undercoat. Long, double coats require the most time and care to dry and comb. It is painful to the dog if you try to use a normal comb on a long, wet coat. Start with a very wide-toothed steel comb or a special rake, give him a second normal combing when he is completely dry, and finish off with a good brushing. The brush attachment of a vacuum cleaner is very efficient in removing shed hair from a dog's coat, if you can persuade your dog to let you use it on him.

Tell your dog how handsome he is (some dogs are terribly vain). Give him an edible reward for behaving so well (even if he hasn't). For once, he will be happy if you then leave him alone for a while.

Professional groomers, like fashionable barbers and hairdressers, often recommend one of the many coat sprays, setting lotions, tangle removers, and coat conditioners that are now available, although the American Kennel Club has outlawed the use of sprays that alter the texture of a show dog's coat. If you select one that is suitable and permissible, it may indeed enhance your dog's appearance and facilitate grooming. But one of the old-fashioned methods may be just as effective, for example:
—a teaspoon of vinegar in the final pitcher of rinse water to remove the last traces of soap and make his coat shine.
—a very mild bluing solution to make white coats whiter.
—a teaspoon of glycerine in the final rinse water to make smooth coats glossy.

DRY CLEANING

Sometimes it is preferable to dry-clean a dirty dog rather than to bathe him: during the winter, or when you haven't the time to give him a real bath; when he is very old or convalescent; or when he isn't a dog at all but a pregnant bitch.

Canine dry-cleaning products are sold in dog supply stores and in pet shops, in two forms:

1) a liquid that lathers on the dog's coat as you massage it, is then permitted to dry, and is finally brushed out, carrying with it a certain amount of dust and grease;

2) a powder that is rubbed into the coat and then brushed out in the same way.

Some owners use a nongreasy man's hair tonic for a rapid, superficial cleaning, sprinkling it over the dog's back, massaging it into the coat, rubbing dry, and brushing. Oatmeal, bran, and cornmeal have been used as dry shampoos. Cornstarch will degrease and whiten white coats. Witch hazel will also superficially clean a dog's coat without bathing.

Whatever kitchen-cabinet or commercial product you select, stand your dog on newspapers during the procedure. Avoid getting lather or powder into his eyes, ears, nose, or mouth. It is best to simply clean his face with a damp washcloth. Handle him gently but firmly. And when it is over, don't forget to reward him.

TRIMMING

From time to time you can improve your dog's appearance, comfort, and cleanliness by touching up his coat with the judicious and restrained use of a pair of scissors. Barber's shears are fine for adroit owners of quiet dogs. Special blunt-tipped canine scissors are safer for all the others.

Long-haired breeds seldom need trimming except when they are groomed for show. Smooth-haired dogs, on the other hand, often grow stray long hairs that should be cut. Terriers benefit the most from a little regular trimming, even if it is no more than snipping off the fringe around their ears and under the tail.

The purpose is merely to tidy up a coat, not to reshape it. Before you make the first snip, you might study a photograph of an outstanding example of your dog's breed in order to avoid making some disastrous mistake. A snip here and a snip there add up, and before you know it you may have gone further than intended. So control your creative impulse and adhere to the standard model. You can safely trim cowlicks and stray long hairs. You can trim tail, leg and belly fringes to make them even. By all means, trim your dog's paws if they need it. But know when to stop.

You may have noticed that the whiskers of show dogs are snipped off close to the skin, or at least shortened. It doesn't seem to affect their sense of distance or night vision, as one might think. However, there is no point in lopping off the whiskers of a pet dog. There is plenty of time for that before his first show. Besides, they may be more useful to him than we realize.

You might, however, while you have the scissors handy, snip off the long hairs at the tip of the penis, which become moist with urine and then gather dust and dirt. The long hairs around the anus of long-haired breeds like Collies, Skye Terriers, and Old English Sheepdogs can also be trimmed. It won't show, and it will reduce soiling.

PLUCKING

In silky coats, like those of Spaniels, there are often traces of paler woolly hair that should have been shed when the puppy cast his baby coat for his adult one. These tufts generally persist in the form of a top-knot. Some uninformed owners consider it amusing, just as they enjoy the comic effect of a dog flopping along with furry bedroom scuffs instead of neatly groomed paws. But to knowledgeable people, these are signs of owner ignorance and neglect.

The unattractive dead hair is easily removed by plucking. A leather glove or a dash of talcum powder will help you to get a grip on the hair, as you grasp a small strand at a time and remove it with a sharp, upward jerking movement. Your dog will feel no more than a slight irritation. If he has a lot, though, you might do the job in several sessions.

STRIPPING

Many Terriers, including the Airedale, Wire-haired Fox Terrier, Welsh, Irish, Sealyham, and Scottish, have a double coat consisting of a dense, curly undercoat and a longer hard topcoat, which must be removed twice a year as it grows old, dies, and starts to shed. The only way to do so efficiently is by stripping (plucking by hand) so that the dead hair roots are removed along with the dead hair.

The process is long and tedious rather than difficult, although it does require a certain manual dexterity. Because of the time involved, professional stripping jobs are quite expensive. Many pet owners therefore have their Terriers clipped, although the effect on the dog's coat as well as to an expert eye is not the same. Show Terriers are never clipped. They are usually stripped 6 to 12 weeks before an important show, which is about the length of time it takes for a fresh new coat of show quality to grow in. The hair on the head, ears, and throat, which is kept short, is groomed again a week before the show date. Bitches usually change their coat after each heat, so the best time to strip the old one is about one week before the end of the heat. Either stripping or clipping is essential for this kind of a coat. If left to itself, it becomes shapeless, woolly, and matted. If it is stripped, it will not only look better but will also soil little. A vigorous shake, and rainwater and dust disappear like magic from a well-kept Terrier coat.

As with all grooming procedures, the best way to learn to do it is to have a professional show you how. If this is impossible, treat your dog to a professional grooming at least once, so that you will see what he looks like after an expert job. You can then study photographs and grooming charts, buy a detailed breed grooming book, invest in a leather glove and a stripping knife (a dull blade with a nick in it), and try to do it yourself.

Experienced fanciers prefer to strip entirely by hand, chalking their fingers or the dog's coat first, and plucking the dead hair between the thumb and forefinger. Incidentally, Terriers are usually bathed before stripping, since a clean coat is easier to grip than a soiled one.

If you use a stripping knife, you must hold the handle in your palm, with your thumb pressing near the edge of the blade. You press the blade against a small tuft of hair, press your thumb against the blade, and pull sharply. The dead hair is pulled out while the live hair remains. You repeat this over the entire body, leaving the eyebrows, beard and whiskers, leg feathers, and the hair under the body untouched. It is essential to have a detailed grooming chart before you as you work, because details vary from one Terrier breed to another.

At the end of the session, you will have beside you an enormous pile of hair, and in front of you a smart-looking, restless dog. Take him for a romp. Give him his dinner. He will forgive you.

CLIPPING

All Poodles need to be clipped as their coats grow long. Most pet Terriers, as we have seen, are nowadays clipped rather than stripped. But there is a difference of opinion as to whether or not a dog of a breed that is not normally clipped should be clipped for comfort during very hot weather.

On the one side, there are the loving pet owners who are upset when their dogs seek cool dark corners during the sunniest hours of the day, or lag behind panting during their afternoon walks. On the other side are

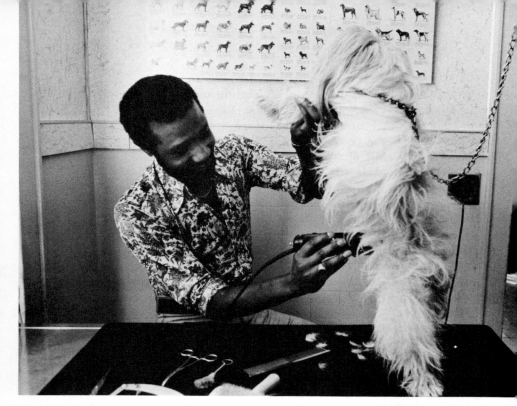

Clipping. (*Sue Maynard*)

most veterinarians and experienced owners, who know that a dog's coat protects him not only from the cold, but also from the sun, from scratches and insect bites; that a heavy coat naturally becomes sparser by shedding in warm weather, when undercoats are usually cast entirely; and that daily brushing and combing to remove the cast coat, plus thinning with special thinning scissors if necessary, should permit even a densely coated dog to tolerate the summer heat.

If you are determined to clip your dog, at least leave a sufficient length of coat to give him some natural protection from sunburn, underbrush, and insects.

Clipping according to a breed standard is far more complicated. Electric clippers probably play a much larger part than is generally admitted in the grooming of many show dogs, and they are a vital factor in the appearance of a Poodle. It is not by chance that the proliferation of canine beauty parlors and dog-grooming schools has coincided with the popularity of this breed.

There is usually a visible difference between a homemade clipping and the professional kind, since it requires not only the proper equipment, but also infinite patience, a perfect knowledge of the breed standard, technical skill, and artistic judgment. Even if you are ambitious enough to tackle the job yourself, have your dog clipped the first time by the best professional you can find, and watch him (or, more often, her) at work, if possible.

You will need a grooming table (or any steady table of suitable size) covered with a nonskid mat, a grooming harness or a person to help you (if you are not absolutely sure of your control over your dog), your usual grooming tools, and an electric clipper especially designed for small animals. The Oster Clipper is one famous brand with a wide range of blades which clip the hair at different lengths. Depending on the breed of your dog, you will need several blades, the most useful being Number 15 (to give a close shave to the face, feet, and sometimes the tail), Number 10 (for the stomach, body, and slightly longer face hair), Number 7 (a little longer still, useful for blending the different hair lengths together), and Number 5 (for a clip that leaves the hair ½-inch long). Hair longer than this is trimmed with scissors.

You hold the clippers like a pencil, with the blade placed flat against the dog's body, moving it smoothly and steadily. Clipping against the lie of the hair gives a closer shave and is also more irritating than clipping in the direction of hair growth. The finer the blade, the more irritating it is to the skin. Whenever the blade starts to heat, you must stop and let it cool before continuing. Professionals usually have an extra blade and simply change it when the first one is too warm. Keeping the clippers sharp and oiled will also reduce the noise, discomfort, and the risk of "clipper rash."

Some dogs cannot stand the noise and vibration, and the only solution is to use a non-electric hand clipper. Since this is much slower, it is also much more tiring for both of you. But if you take pains to make your dog's first clipping experience as pleasant as possible, letting him sniff the strange instrument and get used to the noise, if you work gently, and if you make the first session as brief as possible, he should accept the ordeal stoically as part of a dog's life.

Of all grooming techniques, clipping transforms a dog's appearance more radically than any other. The most important points to bear in mind are:

—*The ideal silhouette of your dog's breed*. This is the pattern you are trying to copy.

—*Symmetry*, which is not easy to achieve. The dog must hold himself perfectly straight and perfectly still, and the groomer must constantly check his work on both sides, so that they appear to be identical, even if this is not the case of the dog in his natural condition. It is customary to clip one side entirely, and then clip the other side to make a perfect match. Many clipping styles are most easily checked for symmetry from above. Perfect symmetry depends on constant checking (which means slow progress), but most of all on a very good eye.

—*Your dog's defects and good points,* in order to minimize the former and emphasize the latter. Some dog groomers are veritable artists in enhancing a dog's appearance with clippers and shears. They can practically create a new dog.

GROOMING RÉSUMÉ FOR VARIOUS BREEDS

SMOOTH, SHORT-COATED DOGS need little grooming. A bath when necessary, occasional brushing with a soft, short-bristled brush, polishing with a chamois cloth or a grooming glove for special occasions.

SPANIELS AND SETTERS should have the dead hair plucked from their silky coats, and the coat thinned with thinning scissors where it is too heavy; daily combing and brushing; rigorous parasite control; foot trimming with scissors; cleaning the silky fringe on their legs, belly, and eartips, which collect a lot of dust. Welsh, Springer, and Brittany Spaniels, who have the shortest coats, require the least grooming care.

MEDIUM-HEAVY COATS, like that of the Golden Retriver, need to be stripped lightly when they start to shed, thinned if necessary, and stray long hairs should be trimmed in order to create a neat silhouette.

LONG COATS, like those of Collies, Afghans, Old English Sheepdogs, and Briards, need lots of brushing, thinning of the body coat if necessary, and as a final touch, back-brushing to make the coat stand up.

FLUFFY COATS, like those of the Keeshond, Chow, and Samoyed, need brushing and more brushing to make the coat stand out from the body; ear and feet trimming if necessary.

WIRY COATS, like those of many Terriers and all Schnauzers, need the most grooming of any breed except for Poodles. All of them should be stripped or clipped twice a year and trimmed as necessary, in accordance with individual breed standards.

HARSH TERRIER COATS, like those of the Cairn, West Highland White, Norwich, Australian, and Border Terrier, do not need stripping but merely regular grooming with a brush and comb, and tidying with scissors around the ears and tail. Even in the show ring, a natural look is preferred.

SOME LONG-HAIRED SMALL AND TOY BREEDS, like the Skye Terrier, Yorkshire, Maltese, Lhasa Apso, and Shih Tzu, need vigorous brushing, after which the hair is parted in the center of the back to fall down evenly on either side, with the bottom edges evened off with scissors. The topknot of Yorkshires and Shih Tzus is tied on top of the head;

the Lhasa Apso's is allowed to fall over his eyes; and the Skye's long bangs are combed into his whiskers from a center part.

Some breeds have highly individual grooming requirements, such as:

THE BEDLINGTON TERRIER, whose coat is clipped or scissor-trimmed to give him his lamb-like look, with a hair length of one-inch on the body, slightly longer on the legs.

THE KERRY BLUE TERRIER, whose soft, dense, wavy coat needs extensive, expert grooming in order to conform to the show standard.

THE PULI AND THE KOMONDOR, whose strange double coats form ropy coils. The Komondor's heavy tassels, once formed, need no care other than an occasional bath. The Puli is usually shown with his straight, curly, or wavy coat combed out. But he may also be shown uncombed, with his coat hanging in tight, even cords.

THE POODLE, who is in a class of his own when it comes to grooming care, perhaps because an ungroomed Poodle looks quite ordinary, whereas a well-groomed one is undeniably very chic. In any case, he requires the most extensive, most expensive grooming of any breed.

Poodle owners have the choice of a number of different clipping styles, only three of which are accepted in the show ring: The Puppy Clip (for dogs under one year of age), the Continental Clip, and the English Saddle Clip. Nevertheless, the most popular clip for pet Poodles is the Royal Dutch Clip.

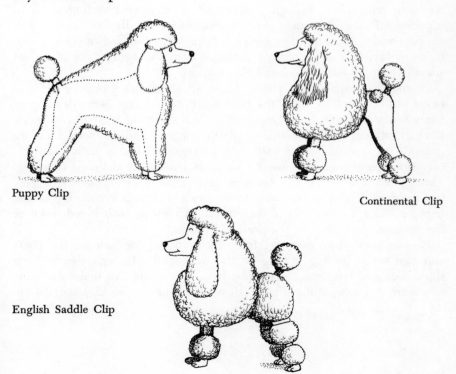

Puppy Clip

Continental Clip

English Saddle Clip

Royal Dutch Clip

SHOW GROOMING

Skillful grooming has become an increasingly decisive winning factor in many breeds of show dogs, to the dismay of serious breeders who attempt to accomplish through generations of selective breeding what an experienced dog showman can achieve (superficially, at least) with clippers and scissors in a few hours. A home-groomed dog of some popular show breeds hasn't a chance in the modern show ring against professionally prepared and presented competition.

Of course, conscientious judges know all about the grooming art and never fail to check by hand the conformation of a dog beneath his perfectly sculptured silhouette, especially when selecting their top winners. Certain artifices such as hair dye, plastic surgery, and doctored ears, are grounds for disqualification. Still, the professional has a distinct advantage over the amateur because he knows how to make the most of a dog. Through hard work, he has acquired taste as well as experience, a perfect mastery of all the grooming tools, and a thorough knowledge of the breed standards as well as of the current fashion in each breed, even of the personal prejudices of the presiding judge.

He can shorten an overlong body by stripping the hair on the chest and rear while leaving it long on the underbelly. He can slenderize a thick neck and lengthen a short one by clipping. He can make flat muscles seem to bulge, and sculpt a tail with scissors to the ideal curve. He can take pounds off a fat dog or put them on a skinny one by thinning the coat with clippers and knives, or by fluffing it with sprays and corn-starch. He can refine heavy limbs by clipping them close, and give the il-lusion of good bone to spindly ones by leaving the hair long. He knows that long hair on the chest makes the body look deeper and at the same time shortens the legs. Trimming the hair on the loins gives a tucked-up effect, while leaving it long creates the opposite impression. Cutting the fringes close around the ears make them seem smaller and certainly neater. With clippers, a stop can be sculpted where there was hardly a trace of one before. Trimming whiskers close to the muzzle is customary in most breeds, and failing to do so is one of the marks of a show ring novice. Powdering a long coat and brushing it against the lie of the hair can double its volume, when done with skill, and if the powder is brushed out, the practice is perfectly permissible. There is, in fact, quite a lot of hypocrisy in the interpretation of show-grooming re-strictions. Most breed clubs officially condemn such artifices, which almost all of their members practice.

If you wish to show your dog, you too will have to conform to these grooming standards. You can groom and handle him yourself for a Match Show at your local kennel club, if you wish. But for an important dog show, engage a professional handler if you can, and study carefully his manner of preparing and presenting your dog. You will learn a lot.

CONCEALING YOUR DOG'S DEFECTS

A clean, neat, well-groomed dog, like his owner, looks twice as hand-some than when he is dirty and unkempt. This is the simplest way to conceal your dog's defects: by making such an attractive general impres-sion that they are hardly noticed.

Surgical correction of physical imperfections is illegal in the show ring, and dishonest, to say the least, in a stud dog or even a puppy for sale who may be used for breeding, since it gives a false impression of the characteristics likely to be inherited by the dog's offspring. However, modern veterinary surgeons have become increasingly skilled and under-standing in the field of canine plastic surgery. If you are the owner of a Collie, for example, and think that a pricked ear or a white haw seriously detracts from his appearance and really bothers you (although often, as with humans, minor flaws can be rather endearing), do not be discouraged. Consider some of the possible remedies for canine imperfections:

TRIMMING AND CLIPPING by an expert can, as we have seen, accomplish a wide range of optical illusions.

HAWS are a fine membrane (the third eyelid) of varying size in the inner corner of the dog's eye, and are very common in Bloodhounds and St. Bernards. If they are small and dark, they are scarcely noticeable. But if they are large and white, they affect a dog's expression and often detract from his beauty. They can easily be removed by a competent veterinary surgeon, although the operation would disqualify the dog from showing. Make sure of the breed standard first. The Basset, for one, requires them.

ENTROPION (inverted eyelids, most common in small breeds like the Chihuahua, Pekingese, Pug, and small Terriers as well as in the Boxer and Bulldog) and its opposite, ECTROPION (everted eyelids, most often found in large breeds like the St. Bernard and Great Dane), can both be corrected by surgery. The operation is, in fact, advisable for health reasons. But the dogs cannot be shown.

EARS are an important point of conformation in many breeds, the standards specifying a certain size, length of hair, and carriage. Among the popular breeds, Collies and Shepherds pose the most problems. A Collie's ears should tip over at the points, while the German Shepherd's should be erect and perfectly parallel. Only after a puppy has grown his adult teeth can you tell for sure how his ears are going to be, because many ears do just the opposite of what they are supposed to do during the teething period. Unfortunately, it sometimes happens that a Collie's ears never do tip over, or only one of them does. And some German Shepherds' ears never do stand up straight.

Since ear carriage is an inherited trait, the only sure way to correct "prick ears" in an adult dog is by surgery, which is illegal in the show ring, frowned upon by breeders, but may be justifiable in an altered pet dog if it really distresses his owner.

There are also acceptable methods of correcting faulty ears that may work if you practice them faithfully from the time a puppy is 5 or 6 months old, and if you are lucky:

—TO MAKE PRICK EARS TIP OVER, give the puppy a daily ear massage with mineral oil in order to soften the skin; or attach small weights to the eartips with gum or adhesive tape; fold the eartips over like a flap of an envelope, and tape them down—but not so tightly as to interfere with the blood circulation.

—TO MAKE FLOPPY EARS STAND UP STRAIGHT, tape them upright with a small prop behind to keep them erect; or roll them vertically around a core of some kind and tape in place.

scars can be unsightly, especially on the face, because hair does not grow in again over scar tissue. Prevention is the best remedy. A skilled veterinarian who is used to treating show dogs will take into account the esthetic effect of his operations, and the resulting scar need be no more than an invisible hairline. If it is too late for that, there is still a means of disguising an ugly scar: by tattooing, under anesthetic, by the vet.

warts should be removed for reasons of health as well as beauty, before they have enlarged. They are common in old dogs, but even young ones grow them, most often between the toes and, more visibly, on the eyelids. A simple surgical operation under local anesthetic will remove them. But if you put it off, and if they are located near the edge of the eyelid, the operation is much more delicate.

TAIL DOCKING

The practice of docking a dog's tail once had a useful purpose: for fighting and guard dogs to offer less hold to an adversary, and for hunting dogs to move with greater facility and less risk of injury through dense underbrush. Although most of these dogs are now kept as pets far more often than as working dogs or hunters, the practice persists among many Terriers (except for the Scottish varieties), Brittany and Cocker Spaniels, Poodles, Boxers, Doberman Pinschers, Schnauzers, Old English Sheepdogs, Schipperkes, and Continental Hunting breeds, including Vizslas.

A puppy's tail is cut either by surgical shears or a knife 48 to 72 hours after birth, when there is little bleeding and scarcely any pain. It is such a simple operation that many breeders do it themselves, although it is certainly advisable (and obligatory in many states) to have it performed by a skilled veterinary surgeon, preferably one who is familiar with show standards, since each breed has its specified tail length. For example, the Standard Poodle's tail is left 1½ inches long, the Miniature Poodle's 1¼ inches and the Toy's 1 inch; the Boxer's is docked to a mere ¾ inch, as are the Cocker Spaniel's and Doberman Pinscher's, while the Old English Sheepdog, Rottweiler, and Pembroke Corgi are docked at the first joint from the rump. Moreover, like all fashions, these may change.

A tail that is left too long can be corrected later, but a tail cut off too short may ruin a puppy's future as a show dog. A veterinary surgeon will also know how to dock a tail without leaving a hairless stub, and to put in a stitch if necessary. Since the operation is performed so soon after birth, a pet owner seldom has any say in the matter.

EAR CROPPING

Removing the flaps or tips from a puppy's ears is less justifiable than tail docking, but it is required by the AKC standard of certain breeds, including the Boxer, Doberman Pinscher, Great Dane, Bouvier des Flandres, and Boston Terrier. It is optional, though customary, for Schnauzers, Bull and Staffordshire Terriers, and Brussels Griffons.

The operation is performed between the ages of 6 and 10 weeks. It can be done until the dog is 12 months old, but the longer it is postponed, the more delicate it is and the longer it takes to heal. Even in the best of conditions, the normal healing time is about 4 weeks.

Many puppies have had their ears cropped before being delivered to their buyers. Some breeders, however, prefer to leave the responsibility to the puppy's new owner. In this case, you must make sure that the operation is not illegal in your state, for there is a growing movement to outlaw such canine mutilations. If you must do it, at least seek the best veterinary surgeon you can find, one who is thoroughly familiar with the breed in question, because artistic judgment as well as surgical skill is involved. Your breed club would be a good source of information. Afterward, you must give the puppy a certain amount of postoperative care, removing scabs and applying healing powder every day, making sure that the skin layers remain tightly sealed. Like uncropped ears, cropped ones may droop for a month or two during the teething period, but they usually stand up again after the adult teeth have come in.

Ear cropping, like tail docking, survives in most of the United States, but no longer in many other countries. In England, tail docking is permitted (although optional in showing for most breeds), but ear cropping is illegal. Its defenders say, "A Boxer would not look like a Boxer if he did not have cropped ears." And the fact is that if you refuse to crop your Boxer puppy's ears, not only will you be unable to show him in America, but you may also have trouble persuading your friends that he really is a purebred Boxer. If you feel strongly about the question, as many doglovers do, your best solution is to select a breed of dog that is permitted to remain in its natural state, even in the show ring.

DEWCLAWS

These are vestiges of a sixth canine toe, completing the 4 toes on his paws, plus the back pad, which corresponds to our thumb. They are found on the inside of the legs. Some dogs have none at all. Most dogs have them only on the forelegs, and a few dogs have them on all four legs. Those on the hindlegs are usually removed when the puppy is 2 or 3 days old, since they serve no purpose and may cause injury.

For some strange reason, the breed standards of the Briard and the Great Pyrenees Sheepdog require two dewclaws on each hindleg. Other standards require them to be removed only from the hindlegs (like the German Shepherd and Newfoundland), or from all four legs (which is customary but optional with the St. Bernard). Dewclaws on the front legs are never improper, but never desirable either.

Most veterinarians are strongly in favor of removing all of them at birth, when the operation is simple and painless. The later it is done, the more dangerous it becomes, because of the profuse bleeding it provokes. If a puppy still has dewclaws at the age of 3 or 4 months, it is wiser to leave them. But remember to keep them short and smooth by regular clipping and filing.

9.

Clothing Your Dog

No tailor has ever designed such an ideal all-purpose garment as the dog's coat. Each breed has a coat of a texture, type, and length that is made to order for all-season, all-weather protection in its native environment.

When a dog is taken into an environment very different from his natural one, his coat can adjust to the change to a certain degree. But it is sometimes advisable, for reasons of health and comfort, to lighten a heavy coat (by thinning or clipping), or to add protection to a sparse one (in the form of clothing). Since most dogs tolerate cold weather much better than hot, canine clothing is seldom necessary except for old dogs, convalescent, sick, or rheumatic dogs, and a few delicate breeds. Most dogs are perfectly healthy and happy all year around and all around the world, clothed only in the coat that Nature gave them.

On the other hand, every modern pet dog should own a few vital accessories, the most important of which are

COLLARS

A LEATHER COLLAR is the strongest, most practical, and most comfortable. It should be *round* for long coats (in order to avoid breaking the hair) and *flat* for short coats (in order to avoid leaving a mark), both of them as narrow and light as possible within the limits of security. Braided leather collars, the sturdiest of all, are recommended for large, powerful breeds. But do not buy too heavy a collar for a puppy, even if he is a Great Dane or a St. Bernard. Washable nylon cord or canvas webbing are light and quite strong enough.

Some owners enjoy dressing up their pets in fancy jeweled collars, and there is no harm in this. But dangling ornaments are an invitation to chew and pull—not so much to the dog who wears them as to his playmates. However, a small bell attached flat to the collar rather than hanging from it, is practical for small, lively dogs like Terriers and Poodles. The faint tinkle does not annoy them, and it gives their owners a clue as to the mischief they are doing in the house and their whereabouts out of doors.

Selecting a dog collar is easier than selecting a man's tie, but it too is a reflection of the buyer's taste. Try to find one that harmonizes or contrasts attractively with your dog's coat. Natural leather goes well with beige, brown, and brindle coats; red and green contrast smartly with a black one; pale blue or white are pretty on a small gray or silver dog; black is discreet and elegant on a black, gray or brown one. Perhaps the best choice of all is either the same shade as the dog's coat, or a tone lighter or darker. Natural rawhide is suitable for virile breeds. Pale colors do not soil more quickly than dark ones; the soil is simply more visible. All collars and leads get dirty, and all of them should be regularly cleaned.

Size is far more important than color. A properly fit collar is tight enough so that it cannot slip over the dog's head, but loose enough to offer no constriction. You should be able to slip 2 fingers between the collar and the neck of an adult dog. A puppy grows so fast that his first collar must allow plenty of room for expansion. Get one with several holes, start with the last one, and adjust it comfortably each time you put it on, instead of automatically using the same hole.

The very day you bring your puppy home you can start getting him used to wearing a light puppy collar around the house for short periods of time. When he is 3 or 4 months old, it is time to buy a larger, permanent collar. He will continue to grow, of course, so this one too should fit

Round leather slip collar with leather lead. Flat leather collar with matching leather lead. Double-action slip chain collar with chain lead. Studded collar. (*Claus Ohm*)

when buckled in the last hole, and be enlarged as his neck becomes thicker. Sometimes a dog who wears his collar all the time distresses and mystifies his owner by persistent, painful coughing, caused simply by a collar that has become too tight for him. Besides, it is seldom necessary to leave a dog's collar on all of the time. If your dog sleeps in the house, you can at least remove it at night.

An essential safety feature of the dog collar is the IDENTITY TAG it bears. The safest kind is an engraved name and address plaque permanently attached to the collar. Very small collars do not have room for this, so small dogs must wear a round, engraved medal, securely attached to the collar ring. You can also buy little capsules containing an identity paper. To prevent the cap from unscrewing and the paper from falling out, you should dab the threads with colorless nail polish before you screw the cap on. You might also repeat the information in indelible ink on the inside of a flat collar. What kind of information? Your dog's address and telephone number, of course. There is a difference of opinion about mentioning the dog's name. Some owners believe that it merely enables dognappers to call a dog by name, and they prefer to mention their own rather than his.

A MUNICIPAL DOG TAG is required by law from the time a dog is 6 months old in most towns, 3 or 4 months old in some. The cost varies according to the locality and to the sex, unspayed females paying the most. The tag bears an identifying number, but is no guarantee of automatic recovery of a lost dog.

Shortly before your puppy is 6 months old, and as soon as you acquire an older dog, you should find out from your Town Hall where and when to apply for his license. You do not have to take your dog with you, but you must remember to renew the license every year (see Chapter 21).

In addition to his leather collar, every dog should own a SLIP CHAIN COLLAR (a far more accurate term than "choke collar"). This is a length of chain or corded nylon with a plain ring at both ends. It is indispensable for training indoors and out, and is also useful for slipping over your dog's head when you want him to be uncollared but under control—during grooming or bathing, for example. These chains are made in different lengths and widths, and it is important to select a suitable one for your dog: flat-lying links, rather fine and light, for small dogs, heavier for large ones, and long enough to leave about 3 inches hanging loose when the collar is pulled up snugly behind the dog's ears.

The effect of a slip collar depends entirely on the way you put it on your dog, and there is a trick to it. You start by holding the chain so that it dangles vertically, then let the bottom links fall through the bottom ring. Pull the rest of the chain through, and you will have a sliding noose which will tighten around your dog's neck when he pulls, but will otherwise remain slack—that is, if it is placed around his neck correctly. There is another trick to this. The easiest method is to stand beside your dog, on his right side, holding the collar in front of you with the loop hanging down and the rings on top, the ring through which the chain slides underneath the other one, and the chain sliding upward on the right side of the loop. Slip the loop over the dog's head, and attach the lead to the top ring.

This is the way to put a slip collar on a dog who walks on your left side, or "heels," as is required in obedience training. If, for some reason, your dog walks on your right side, the entire procedure must be reversed.

To put on a slip chain collar, form a loop by holding the chain vertically and letting the bottom links slip through the bottom ring. Pull the rest of the chain through the ring.

Standing on your dog's right side, and facing the same direction, slip the loop over his head, making sure that the chain slides upward on the right side of the loop. Attach the lead to the top ring. The collar will remain slack if the dog does not pull. If he does, the loop will automatically tighten, but immediately loosen again as soon as he stops pulling. (*Photos by Claus Ohm*)

As you will see, the collar is slack when there is no pull on it. But if your dog tugs, he will feel an uncomfortable jerk on his neck until he stops. The effect is the same when you give a short tug on the lead: a sharp jerk, then immediate relief. Make your tug short and sharp, never a steady pull, which could destroy the entire effect. Remember that a slip collar is a training aid and not a means of punishment, and that the immediate relief is more important than the momentary discomfort. Remember that it is not a substitute for a normal collar either, since the loose ring can easily get caught on something, even on the dog's toe. Slip chain collars should therefore be used only for training and accompanied walks.

There also exists a DOUBLE-ACTION SLIP COLLAR, which has the same effect but is impossible to put on incorrectly. It is composed of two parts: a chain or nylon cord with a ring at each end, just like the ordinary slip collar only shorter; and a second very short chain that is looped through the two rings like a bracelet and is equipped with a free ring to which the lead is attached. It is foolproof and its action is milder, but it must be perfectly fitted to the dog's neck size. Professional trainers always use the simple slip collar.

Among the various canine-control devices there is also a CHOKE COLLAR lined with metal hooks or spikes, designed to permit weak owners to control strong dogs. These may not be as cruel as they seem (the spikes and hooks are always blunt), but they are of no training value and are certainly no substitute for training. An owner who really feels the need for one has probably made an unwise choice of breed.

LEATHER HARNESSES, on the other hand, may be more practical than collars for certain breeds of dogs with powerful forehands (like Bulldogs), bowlegged dogs (like Pekingese), short-necked dogs (like Pugs), delicate-boned dogs (like Pomeranians and many Toy breeds), very stubborn dogs (like Scottish Terriers), as well as very fat dogs.

However, they should be considered a harmless means of controlling such dogs and not a replacement for proper training. Professional trainers and handlers never use them. They never need to. This alone should be proof that any dog can learn to walk quietly on a lead without pulling or going on a sit-down strike. Sled dogs, Seeing Eye dogs, Army patrol dogs, Tracking dogs, and other canine guides are always harnessed, because it is they who do the leading. With a pet dog, unless his conformation precludes it, your final goal should be an ordinary collar, and the harness merely an interim measure.

Good fit is important, because an ill-fitting harness will rub and eventually ruin a dog's coat. A harness also soils more quickly than a collar and should be cleaned with saddle soap to keep the leather soft.

LEASHES

Your dog's leash should be suited to his size and strength: strong enough so that there is not the slightest danger of its breaking under any circumstance, and as lightweight as possible. Try to have the leather of the hand loop or the entire leash match the color of his collar.

Chain leads are heavier than *leather* ones, but they are also much stronger and unchewable. (Incidentally, the words "leash" and "lead" are interchangeable, the latter being preferred by the dog show crowd.) Remember that a puppy will chew anything in sight and can quickly gnaw through a leather leash, not necessarily because he wants to escape, but simply to relieve his teething pains or provide an amusing distraction from boredom. *Nylon* tape is strong and light; it soils quickly but is easily washed. *Braided leather* is stronger and heavier than a plain leather strap and is suitable for strong breeds, although a chain lead with a leather hand loop is even stronger. Thick webbed *canvas* is much lighter than either of them, far less expensive, and strong enough for most large breeds; it is excellent for training too.

The most important part of the leash is the *clasp* that attaches it to your dog's collar. You should be able to fasten it securely and unfasten it rapidly. The pincer type is quickest to unfasten, but the old-fashioned spring clip, with the opening on the side, is more secure. Any clever dog can open a pincer-type with his teeth. So make your choice according to the character and behavior of your dog.

Leashes come in various lengths. The standard one of 30 inches is practical for most breeds and most purposes. Very large dogs gain less advantage from their weight and strength when they are attached to a short lead. Guide dogs, who must always remain close to their owners, are held very short, the length carefully calculated according to the height of both dog and owner. A training lead, on the other hand, should be at least 6 feet long.

SHOW LEADS are necessary in the show ring and useful at times when you want to exercise light control over your dog in an enclosed space. They vary from breed to breed, but generally are composed of a length of nylon cord or tape with a hand loop at one end and, at the other, a longer loop with a plastic or metal stop device to adjust it loosely around the dog's neck. A nylon tape lead is strong enough for walking a puppy, a small dog, or a trained one in a safe area, although there is no means of attaching an identity plaque or license tag. The cord type, as fine as a fishing line, is almost invisible. It gives the judge and spectators a fine impression of your dog's poise and manners, but it is not of practical use outside the show ring.

TIES

All of these leashes are designed for walking a dog. But what do you attach to his collar when you want to tie him up safely?

The correct answer to this insidious question is that you should never tie a dog up except for brief periods of time and in exceptional circumstances. When you have to do so, there is only one safe kind of tie: the lightest possible, longest possible, flexible chain, which is moreover clipped at both ends rather than tied. Rope ties, less flexible and less resistant than chain, are vastly inferior.

While the image of a guard dog tightly chained to his doghouse should never be seen except in comic strips, there are a few occasions when it is unavoidable to chain or tie your dog:

—*When you have installed an overhead trolley run* for him in the yard. Attach him to a light chain that is long enough to permit him to lie down comfortably in sun or shade and to enjoy a reasonable range of movement. But be careful that it does not also permit him to wind the chain around a tree or catch it in some obstruction. Remember too that this is a form of confinement and not a form of exercise, so never leave him tied up for long.

—*When you have installed a ground swivel post.* The principle is the same: an unchewable light chain and a maximum range of safe, unobstructed movement.

—*When you take your dog with you to visit friends,* common courtesy requires that you keep him under control. The simplest way is to slip the hand loop of his leash around your foot, if you are seated, or around the leg of a heavy piece of furniture. The best way to attach a leash to an upright post or table leg is to unclip the leash from the dog's collar, encircle the post with the other end of the leash, and slip the collar clip through the hand loop, attaching it to the dog's collar again. This is much better than trying to knot a leather leash. But remember that your dog can chew, so keep an eye on him.

—*When a young puppy is being housebroken,* the last place he is likely to soil is his bed, and it is sometimes useful to attach him there briefly. Loop his leash around a nearby heavy piece of furniture, attach it to a hook driven into the wall above his bed, or to the bed itself.

There are also circumstances in which a dog should NEVER be tied up:

- —Never, anywhere, under any conditions, for a long period of time
- —Never in a car
- —Never on a balcony (enclose it with chicken wire and leave him there unattached)
- —Never to a post or tree unsupervised (he is sure to get the chain or cord wound around it, and when he has no more than a few inches of freedom, he is apt to panic and choke himself to death)
- —Never near a low wall or hedge (he may be tempted to jump over it and hang himself in the process)
- —Never where he can be teased or attacked by children or by other animals

CLOTHING

Long-haired dogs, heavy-coated and double-coated dogs, and dogs with dry, warm shelter always accessible never need protective clothing. But short, smooth-haired breeds and clipped dogs may be grateful for added warmth when they are taken from a heated house into the outdoor cold. Smooth-haired Hound breeds of desert origin, like Greyhounds, Whippets, and Italian Greyhounds, as well as all of the short-haired Toy dogs and all clipped dogs, are very susceptible to chills when the temperature drops to freezing. Puppy coats also offer little protection from the cold. But puppies should always be kept inside the house until the weather is warm and sunny anyway.

The most satisfactory garment is the simplest: A KNITTED SWEATER. It is the most comfortable for the dog, being the most stretchable. Be sure to buy the right size. It should be long enough to cover your dog's chest, belly, and the entire length of his back. A slipover model is a nuisance to put on and take off, but it has the advantage of eliminating fasteners, which are tempting chewing toys. A mixture of wool (for warmth) and synthetic fiber (for washability and quick drying) is the best material, as it will need frequent laundering. A turtleneck style is excellent for long-necked dogs like Whippets.

You will also find tailored coats for dogs which fasten under the neck and button or snap under the stomach, or are closed with Velcro bands. Many are amusing and attractive, but none are necessary. The Poodle is the only breed that really seems to enjoy being dressed up. (Is this why most fancy canine merchandise is designed for Poodles? Or could it be that Poodle owners have a particular penchant for dressing up their pets?)

Be this as it may, you should never let a dog lie around in a damp garment. Sweaters and coats should, in fact, be reserved for cold, dry weather. For snowy or rainy days, it is much better to give your dog a:

RAINCOAT. Even this is useful mainly for short, smooth, clipped, and sparsely coated dogs. When it rains, most dogs simply shake themselves vigorously, which not only removes moisture but also makes their hair stand out and protects the skin from getting drenched. Rain seldom penetrates a dense undercoat, nor does it get past the oily coats of water Retrievers and many Hunting dogs. If you decide that your dog needs a raincoat, be sure that it is really waterproof. A plastic material with a fabric lining is the best. Nothing is worse than letting your dog run around in a water-soaked garment. He would be much better off with his natural coat alone.

MUZZLES

Not strictly speaking an article of clothing, a muzzle is a protective device worn by vicious or aggressive dogs, in the form of a wire, leather, or plastic cage fitted over the dog's jaws and strapped behind his ears. Oddly enough, dogs do not seem to mind a muzzle as much as one might think, but the fact remains that a muzzled dog is a very sorry sight. In Venice (among other places), the law requires all dogs to be muzzled outside of their own homes, which is perhaps the only unappealing feature of that lovely city.

A dog who is an inveterate biter should be given corrective training, if necessary by a professional. An old dog who suddenly becomes hostile toward humanity should be taken to the vet. Perhaps there is a physical cause for his change of attitude. If not, he deserves a peaceful, unmuzzled retirement in an enclosed pen, and his owner deserves another dog.

If you take a dog sightseeing in Venice, and perhaps in other exceptional circumstances, you will have to muzzle the most docile pet. When you shop for a muzzle, the important points to consider are weight (as light as possible) and size (neither too long, too short, nor too tight). The only way to avoid a mistake is to try it on your dog before you buy it.

All dogs need to be muzzled during long or painful treatment for injuries. But in these cases a bandage muzzle (see page 201) is more effective.

YOUR CLOTHING AND YOUR DOG

When you have a dog of your own, you will soon find that your personal clothing gradually separates into two distinct wardrobes: one for wearing when you are with your dog (old skirts, trousers with paw marks, sweaters with pulled threads, a warm wool cap, a shoulder bag, a pair of boots, leather gloves with worn palms), and one reserved for moments when you are without him (white and pastel garments, navy-blue suits, loose knits, stoles, and high-heeled shoes).

If you acquire a very young puppy, you must expect a certain amount of damage during the first few months. As he grows older and wiser, he will learn to respect your belongings. But do not ask too much of him. If you give him an old shoe to chew, or play tug-of-war with a discarded stocking (a game he'll love), do not expect him to distinguish between these delightful playthings and your brand-new Gucci moccasins or Dior nylons. You can be more demanding of an adult dog. In the meantime, you might follow the example of experienced dog owners and:

—Buy a long-sleeved smock, such as barbers and hairdressers wear, to protect your clothing during grooming sessions.

—Invest in a really good clothes brush, and a comb with which to clean the dog hair from it.

—Get a supply of wide adhesive tape or Scotch tape. The sticky side will pick up hair on clothing and upholstery that escapes the brush. There are also patented dog hair removers. Try them all.

—Use a damp sponge or your own damp hand as an excellent clothes brush, especially for men's dark suits.

—Groom your dog every day while he is shedding. There will be less dead hair available for furniture and clothing.

—If your dog is permitted to nestle on chairs and sofas, get into the habit of vacuum-cleaning them with the proper attachment. (Perhaps he will let you use it on him too.)

—If your dog sleeps on your bed, buy a cheap length of sturdy material that harmonizes with your color scheme, spread it over the foot of the bed, and let your dog sleep on this. A nylon or Dacron blanket cover is more expensive, more elegant, quickly soiled, but easily washed and dried.

—Eliminate dog hairs on rugs and upholstery by buying several cushions large enough for your dog to curl up on comfortably, place them in his favorite resting spots, and train him to lie on them instead of on the carpets and chairs.

—Train your puppy from the start not to jump up on people (see page 294). In the meantime, you will have to learn a lot about spot-removing, or your dry-cleaning bills will soar.

Paw marks made with country mud can generally be brushed off without leaving a spot if they are first allowed to dry completely. City grime is difficult to remove. Try plain tepid water first of all. If this doesn't work, scrub the spot with detergent suds, rinse and dry. Bloodstains from a menstruating bitch can be removed with plain cool water, before the stain has dried; hot water may make it indelible.

—When your dog greets you lovingly with muddy paws, think of the love as well as the mud. If it is more important to you to own an elegant wardrobe than to develop a happy relationship with your dog, perhaps you shouldn't have a pet. The two are not, however, incompatible. Countless people own demonstrative dogs, spotless homes, and impeccable clothing. They simply take a little extra trouble, and so can you.

10.

Your Dog's Health

As a species, the dog is probably sturdier and healthier than man. However, by taking him from his natural environment, where only the strongest survived, to the artificial one in which most pet dogs are obliged to live, we have exposed him to an entirely new set of dangers.

Modern dogs are more fortunate than their ancestors, in that wonder drugs like penicillin and antibiotics provide rapid, effective treatment for many ailments. Veterinary science has made such strides in recent decades that in some fields, such as ophthalmology and orthopedics, veterinary surgeons blazed the trails which human specialists have followed. Even dreaded epidemic diseases like rabies and distemper have been brought under control by vaccines and serums. One of the results of this phenomenal progress is that our dogs, no longer menaced by wildlife plagues, have become more vulnerable to human types of ailments, such as viral infections, cancer, functional disorders, and even psychiatric problems. Surrounded by perils with which their primeval instincts were not designed to cope, they are also more prone to accidents. Nevertheless, the dog's lifespan is regularly increasing, to the point where canine geriatrics has become a major preoccupation of the veterinary profession.

A dog's health is influenced by the genes inherited from his parents and by the care given to his mother during the prenatal period, as well as to the puppy during his first 2 or 3 months of life. You might say that this is when the die is cast as to whether the puppy will have a strong, resistant constitution or a weak one. A puppy whose mother was properly fed and cared for during pregnancy, who received proper physical and psychological attention during his first weeks of life, will be able to face the hazards of growing up in the most favorable conditions.

Pet owners, of course, seldom have any control over this critical period, which is one reason why it is advisable to buy a puppy from a breeder who is able not only to give each expectant mother and puppy the individual attention they require, but also to plan each breeding scrupulously. The tendency to incur certain physical disorders such as skin trouble, nervous ailments, eye maladies, structural malformations leading to hip and elbow dysplasia, among others, are inherited, and there is nothing the new owner can do but treat the resulting infirmities. Careful selection of your puppy therefore also determines to a certain extent whether you will have a healthy adult dog or a sickly one, no matter how well you look after him.

It should be added that the vast majority of dogs lead perfectly healthy, normal lives. They overcome occasional skin rashes, chills, and upset stomachs, recover from cuts and bruises, just as children do, with only ordinary care, sensible first aid when necessary, and professional diagnosis and treatment of serious ailments.

So do not be unduly impressed by the descriptions of maladies and injuries in the following pages. It is useful for every dog owner to have a general understanding of them. But the chances are that if you give your dog a normal diet, a healthy home environment, a well-balanced life physically and mentally, and a reasonable amount of supervision, you will have to take him to the vet only for checkups and vaccinations.

Every owner should learn something about *the anatomy of the dog*, if only in order to know where his different organs are located. Since the dog is a warm-blooded mammal, just as we are, his organism is composed of the same basic elements, but they are assembled within a different structure:

ANATOMY OF THE DOG

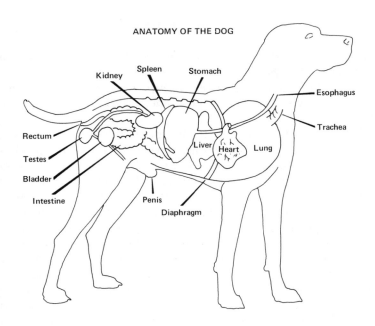

Kidney
Spleen
Stomach
Esophagus
Rectum
Trachea
Testes
Liver
Heart
Lung
Bladder
Intestine
Penis
Diaphragm

THE POINTS OF THE DOG

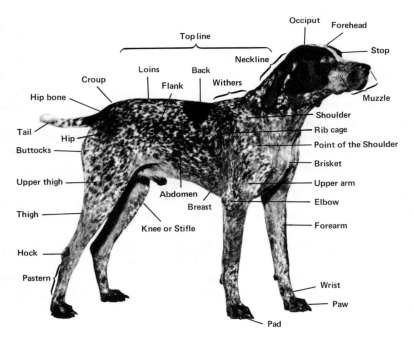

Occiput
Forehead
Top line
Stop
Neckline
Loins
Back
Croup
Flank
Withers
Muzzle
Hip bone
Shoulder
Rib cage
Tail
Point of the Shoulder
Hip
Buttocks
Brisket
Upper thigh
Upper arm
Abdomen
Thigh
Breast
Elbow
Knee or Stifle
Forearm
Hock
Pastern
Wrist
Paw
Pad

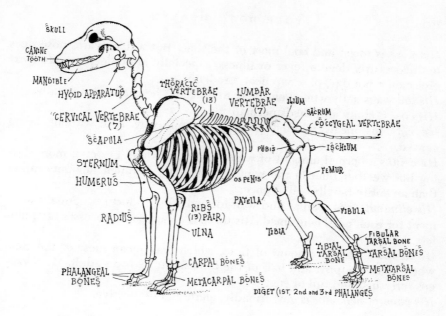

Now that you have seen what the insides of the dog look like, you should learn how to distinguish between a healthy dog and an ailing one from his external aspect and behavior.

A HEALTHY DOG

His temperature, taken rectally when he is rested, is about 101.2 degrees in an adult dog, 102 in small breeds, and 102.5 in a puppy. It fluctuates one way or the other, being lower in the morning and higher in the late afternoon. Long-coated breeds have a slightly higher normal temperature than short-coated ones.

His pulse is taken at the femoral artery high inside the thigh. There is no normal pulse rate for dogs. It can range from 120 beats per minute in a young puppy to 70 or 80 in an old dog, varying according to the individual's size and activity. Count the beats during 30 seconds and multiply by 2. The pulse rate of a dog at rest will also wax and wane, due to the normal arrythmia of the heart pacemaker.

His respiration is regular, ranging from 20 or 30 respirations per minute in a puppy to 16 per minute in an old dog. It, too, varies according to size, activity, and environmental temperature.

His eye is bright and clear, although the lens becomes pale blue as he ages.

His nose is moist and cool most of the time. But a dry, warm nose does not necessarily denote fever or illness, especially after sleeping, after exercise on a hot day, or a nap near a radiator.

His tail wags gaily when you speak to him, and he carries it normally.

His coat is shiny and sheds normally.

He eats his meals without gulping compulsively and without being coaxed.

He drinks a normal amount of water after meals and exercise, more during hot weather than in the winter, and small, frequent amounts rather than an entire bowlful all at once.

His elimination is regular and well-formed. He produces a normal movement for each meal consumed. His urine is clear. Both processes are painless.

He sleeps a normal amount of time, which may mean most of the time when he is a puppy, and half of the time when he is an adult. He awakens refreshed and full of energy.

His general behavior is gay, friendly, alert, and inquisitive.

AN AILING DOG

His temperature, taken rectally when the dog is rested, is over 102 degrees (a sign of fever) or under 100 (a sign of weakness). If it does not return to normal within 24 hours, call the vet. If it is as low as 99 degrees or as high as 104, call the vet without delay.

His pulse may be weak, irregular, abnormally fast or slow.

His respiration at rest may be irregular or labored, panting or weak.

His eye may be dull, red or yellow. There may be a sticky discharge.

His nose may be dry and hot, unwarranted by circumstances. There may be a sticky discharge.

His tail may be immobile, carried stiffly or between the legs.

His coat may be dry and stand up when it should lie flat. The skin may be itchy and flaky. There may be bald spots or red patches.

He may eat with an abnormally voracious appetite or have no appetite at all. He may want to eat strange or filthy things.

He may drink an abnormally large amount of water, or be reluctant to swallow any liquid.

His elimination may be abnormal in form or color. It may have a bad odor and contain blood or mucus. He may be constipated and strain or, on the contrary, have diarrhea. His urine may be dark, cloudy, or painfully produced.

He may sleep almost all of the time and seek seclusion in dark corners.

His breath may have a bad odor.

He may be in pain or lame. He may show obvious symptoms of disorder such as swellings or protuberances, prolonged wheezing or coughing, unusual sensitivity in some part of his body.

His general behavior may be lethargic and unresponsive when he is normally gay and friendly, or nervous and excitable when he is normally the quiet type. He may snap or snarl for no apparent reason.

YOUR VETERINARIAN

Farsighted dog owners select a veterinarian as soon as they get a dog. His collaboration is essential in ensuring the normal development and future health of a puppy, and his rapid intervention can save your dog's life in an emergency. As you will see, the treatment most often recommended for serious injuries and ailments is immediate professional attention, which is possible only if you have already made the acquaintance of a nearby veterinarian. Your chances of prompt emergency attention are even better if he already knows your dog and considers him a client. No vet will refuse an emergency case, of course. But time is saved, perhaps the dog's life as well, if you know where to find one in a hurry and if he already knows something about your dog.

Unfortunately, the demand for veterinary services has increased more rapidly than veterinary colleges have been able to supply new vets. There are fewer than thirty-five thousand licensed veterinarians in the United States, less than ten thousand small-animal specialists, and only about seventy-five hundred students registered in the 19 veterinary schools of the United States and 3 in Canada—to take care of some 40 million dogs!

More and more veterinary students are specializing in medical research, for which the demand has also increased. Employment by animal-feed companies, government inspection agencies, and farm-equipment firms, is often more remunerative than the $15,000 to $20,000 average earnings of a private practitioner, from which he must amortize the cost of setting up an average clinic—about $50,000. All things considered, veterinary fees are not exorbitant, an office visit naturally costing less than a house call.

Veterinarians who enter private practice for treating small animals (which is the specialist the dog owner needs) are often overworked, dedicated men and women who accept lesser rewards for devoting themselves to our pets. Many of them own dogs and cats, and some are amateur breeders. Their installations range from a couple of rooms in the family home to model clinics with adjoining boarding kennels, and endowed hospitals equipped with the most advanced appliances.

It is reassuring to know that such facilities exist, but the average dog owner seldom needs either miracle machines or medical genius. What he requires most of all in a vet is competence and availability. If you have the choice between several vets in your vicinity, by all means take the trouble to select the best one. But if there is just one vet within a reasonable distance of your home, make friends with him and entrust to him the normal veterinary care of your dog. You can consult an illustrious colleague if your dog suffers from some serious ailment or one that is difficult to diagnose. But for everyday accidents, minor ailments, normal puppy care and whelping problems, rapid professional intervention is all-important. As for administering vaccinations and tooth and nail care, one vet can do it as well as another, so you might as well use the nearest one. Depending on your transportation facilities, your choice may also be influenced by the fact that most vets establish a policy of never, sometimes, or always making house calls.

How do you find a vet? By consulting your experienced dog-owning friends, your local kennel club or animal welfare society, your doctor, dentist, and pharmacist. You can also write to the American Veterinary Association (600 South Michigan Avenue, Chicago, Illinois 60605), or to the American Animal Hospital Association (3612 East Jefferson Boulevard, South Bend, Indiana 46615) for a list of member practitioners and hospitals. If you purchased your puppy from a nearby breeder, it is advisable to use the same regular vet, who is familiar with the breeder's stock and may have whelped your puppy. The breeder is probably a good client of long standing, and you will benefit from his recommendation. As a general principle, it is wise to select your vet with care and then remain faithful to him.

The first time you take your dog to the vet will usually be for booster puppy shots. The breeder will give you a certificate showing the shots that have already been given and the date when the next ones are due. If you have adopted your dog from an animal welfare society or purchased him from a pet shop or from friends, it is prudent to stop in at the vet's on the way home for a general checkup as well as protective shots. In the absence of a vaccination certificate, it is safer to assume that a puppy has received no immunization at all.

Although veterinary science has made phenomenal progress in recent years, many simple treatments have changed very little since they were depicted in this Medieval manuscript painting in *Le Livre de la Chasse* of Gaston Phébus (c. 1405). (*Courtesy of the Bibliothèque Nationale*)

Every dog should be permanently protected from distemper, infectious hepatitis, and leptospirosis. These vaccines are now generally combined in a single inoculation. From the age of 6 months, all dogs should also be protected from rabies. Most vaccines are effective for one year, although the latest rabies shot is good for four. They are almost 100 per cent effective when administered on schedule, but worthless if exposure to risk is maintained after the protection has expired.

After this first visit, you will normally need to take your dog to the vet only once a year to keep his immunization up to date. During this annual visit, ask him to give your dog a thorough examination, including a checkup of his:

—anal glands (emptying them if necessary)
—teeth (removing tartar if necessary)
—nails (clipping them if necessary)
—stool (if you think he may have worms)

Females need more regular attention than males, especially if they are bred. When you wish to travel with your dog, you will be prepared for any state, federal, or international requirement if you ask your vet for a certificate of good health, and make sure that his vaccinations are in order before you leave.

Normally, a sound dog needs no more veterinary attention than this. In actual practice, however, you will probably rush with him to the vet's on other occasions too: when he has had a minor accident, not serious in itself, but which only a vet is equipped to treat, such as removing a foreign object from deep inside the throat or ear; removing a cyst or wart; filing or pulling a broken tooth. Sometimes you will take your dog to the vet's simply because you cannot bear to see him suffer from a simple disorder like indigestion or diarrhea, which usually clears up spontaneously. The visit will at least ease your anxiety, if only because the vet can judge better than you whether or not there are allied symptoms that would indicate a more serious illness. But as you get to know your dog, you will be able to distinguish between passing symptoms of no importance, chronic minor disorders, and the indications of disease and infection.

Among the SYMPTOMS THAT ALWAYS WARRANT A VISIT TO THE VET are:

—a temperature over 102 degrees, or under 100, that lasts for more than 24 hours; or a temperature as high as 104 degrees, or as low as 99
—acute pain for which there is no logical explanation
—bloody urine
—blood in the stool more than once
—a discharge of yellow mucus from the eyes or nose

—persistent vomiting, coughing, or refusal to eat for more than 24 hours

—if your dog simply looks and acts really sick

NURSING YOUR DOG

An ill or suffering dog usually accepts human treatment with touching confidence and submission. Gentle, firm handling will preserve his co-operative attitude, and for this there are certain tried-and-true techniques, for example in:

TAKING A DOG'S TEMPERATURE. Select a moment when your dog is quiet. Sterilize a rectal thermometer with alcohol, shake it down, smear it with vaseline, lay your dog on his side (with someone to hold him if necessary), or hold him in a standing position, raise his tail with one hand with the other gently insert the thermometer at least 2 inches into the rectum. Hold on to it for one or two minutes. Remove it smoothly, read it, shake it down, wipe it off, place it in alcohol for an hour, then back in its case. When you cannot use a thermometer for some reason, you can estimate your dog's body temperature by feeling inside his thighs or armpits.

How to take a dog's temperature. (*Lacz-Lemoine*)

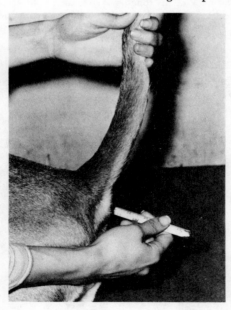

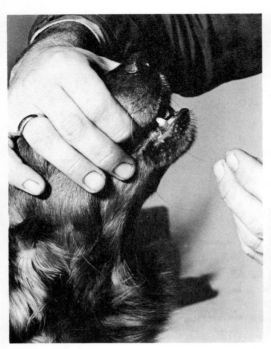
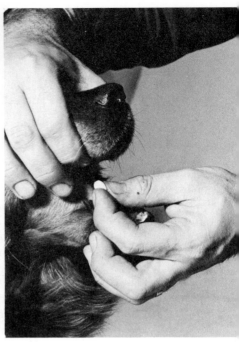

How to give a dog a pill. Press the dog's upper lips around his upper teeth which will induce him to open his mouth and make it impossible for him to bite you.

Deposit the pill on the back of his tongue. If you then hold the dog's mouth closed for a moment and gently stroke his throat with a downward motion, he cannot avoid swallowing it. (*Photos by Claus Ohm*)

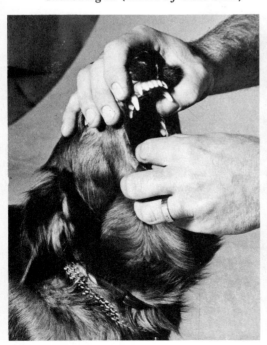

GIVING A DOG A PILL. Ruse is more effective than force. The easiest way is to conceal the pill in the dog's food by placing it inside a small ball of ground meat, or slipping it into a slit in a chunk of meat. A wary dog will swallow the meat and spit out the pill. In this case, you will have to resort to force. Open the dog's mouth by grasping his upper jaw with your left hand, pushing his upper lips down over the teeth, and holding them there with your fingers. If he bites, he will bite himself. Tilt his head upward, which will make him open his lower jaw. Holding his head up, place the pill on the back of his tongue, then close his mouth and hold it closed as you stroke his throat with a downward motion, which will oblige him to gulp the pill. To make it slide down more easily, you can lubricate it with butter, olive oil, or honey.

GIVING A DOG LIQUID MEDICINE. If it is in the form of a sweet syrup, as are many modern tranquilizers and worm remedies, your dog may lick it right off the spoon. If there are only a few drops of medicine to administer, you can drizzle it over his food or soak it up with a lump of sugar and feed him the sugar. The traditional method in other cases is to hold the dog's head up with his mouth closed. Take the jowl of one side of the mouth in your fingers and form a pocket or funnel into which you slowly pour the liquid. Close the pocket, and hold the dog's mouth shut tight until you are sure that he has swallowed all of it. Never pour liquid directly into his throat, for it may enter the lungs and cause pneumonia.

To give a dog liquid medicine, make a pocket in the corner of the dog's mouth with one hand, while holding the prepared dose in the other. Pour the liquid into the pocket, then hold the dog's mouth closed. He will be obliged to swallow it. (*Photos by Claus Ohm*)

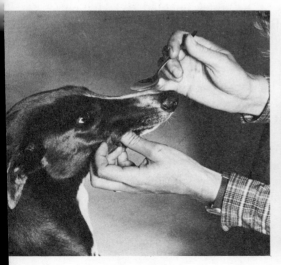
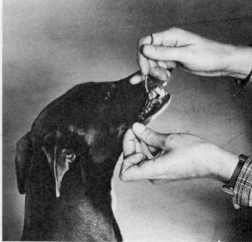

GIVING A DOG AN INJECTION. The only occasions when a dog owner might have to give his pet an injection are in the case of a diabetic animal requiring regular insulin shots, and in order to administer an antidote for snake bite. Never attempt anything but a subcutaneous injection, and only in an emergency. Disposable sterile injection needles have made the job much simpler, but try to conceal your preparations from your dog. Select a place where the skin is loose over the shoulder blade or hip. Part the hair if it is long and swab the spot with alcohol. Holding the skin loosely pinched in your left hand, and the filled injection needle in the right, pierce the dog's skin with a short, slanting, determined movement. Push the plunger smoothly, and remove the needle quickly, immediately pressing the spot with the alcohol swab. Perhaps your vet will show you how to do it.

GIVING A DOG ARTIFICIAL RESPIRATION. Drowning is the most common circumstance where prompt, persistent artificial respiration can save a dog's life, but it is also useful when breathing has stopped but a heartbeat remains after an electric shock, an automobile accident, or poisoning. Promptness is vital, because permanent damage may occur if the brain cells are deprived of oxygen for more than 5 or 10 minutes. (Newborn puppies can resist longer, which is probably Nature's way of countering the risk of a protracted birth.)

Start by placing the dog on his right side, with his head and neck extended, his tongue pulled out of his mouth as far as possible, and the mouth cleaned of any foreign object or substance. Place both hands over the ribs and apply a firm pressure, with most of your weight if he is a big dog, in order to compress the chest and empty the lungs. Then release. Repeat the pressure and release slowly and firmly every 5 seconds, or synchronized with your own respiration. It can take a long time, perhaps an hour, before the dog resumes his breathing unaided, so be patient.

If there is another person with you, the chances of success are greater, because mouth-to-mouth resuscitation can be applied at the same time. He should cup his hands over the dog's mouth and nostrils and blow hard directly into the mouth during the "release" phase of your movements, removing his mouth and taking a deep breath during your "pressing" phase. If the dog's mouth is large, he can breathe directly into the dog's nostrils. If he is reticent for hygienic reasons, he can breathe through a fine handkerchief or a piece of gauze. The amount of air provided should be adjusted according to the size of the dog: only a little at a time for a puppy or a Toy, and a lungful for a Great Dane. When the dog's natural breathing resumes, you can give him a sniff of ammonia or a few drops of brandy, cover him warmly, and take him to the vet.

But do not attempt artificial respiration if the dog is still breathing naturally, no matter how feebly. It is much better to leave him quiet, undisturbed, and warmly covered.

BANDAGING A DOG

It is difficult to bandage a dog so that the bandage stays on. He will try to shake it off, bite it off, rub it off, and if he does not succeed, a canine comrade will do it for him. The best solution for an owner is to watch the vet as he bandages the dog's wound, and ask him to give you the material for changing the dressing. Self-adhesive elastic bandages have the longest life expectancy.

On the other hand, anyone can learn how to make a bandage muzzle, which is really a muzzle rather than a bandage, and is a useful form of restraint when a dog is apt to bite instinctively during painful treatment, after an accident, or even during clipping and grooming.

A BANDAGE MUZZLE. You will need a roll of strong gauze bandage, one or one and a half inches wide. Cut off a length about 2 feet long for a medium-sized muzzle. In an emergency, use a scarf, a nylon stocking, or a necktie.

If the dog is quiet, place the center of the bandage over his nose, with the ends hanging down on each side of his muzzle. Bring the ends under his chin and make a fairly loose half-knot, then bring the ends back of the head behind the ears and tie with an ordinary bowknot. The loop around the dog's nose should be tight enough to prevent him from biting, but loose enough to permit normal breathing. Most dogs don't mind it at all.

If the dog is in pain, prepare the bandage with a half-knot in the middle, and slip the loop over his muzzle from behind, with the half-knot on top, in the middle of the nose bone. Tighten the half-knot, bring the ends down under the chin and make another half-knot there, then back behind the ears as before, tying a bowknot on the nape of the neck.

The first method permits immediate release if necessary; the second offers greater security with a dog who may break the gauze and bite. If a suffering dog gasps and heaves, you should remove the muzzle at once, as he probably wants to vomit. You can replace it afterward, and resume your first-aid treatment.

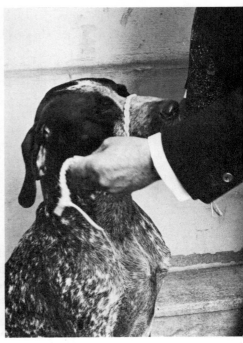

To make a bandage muzzle, make a half-knot in a piece of cord, gauze bandage, even a necktie or a stocking. Slip the loop over the dog's head, with the half-knot under his chin.

Bring the ends back behind his ears and tie with an ordinary bow knot. This type of bandage muzzle permits immediate release if necessary, while preventing the dog from biting. (*Photos by Claus Ohm*)

A JACKET BANDAGE. It is sometimes useful to protect the dog's belly and chest from cold, to keep wounds clean in these places, to prevent a bitch from licking ointment off her teats, or to protect furniture and rugs from salves rubbed into the dog's chest or belly. There are two good ways to do this:

1) Take a square of flannel or some soft, warm material, as long as the distance from the dog's chest to the front of his hindlegs, and as wide as his girth. Cut two holes suitably spaced for his forelegs, and put his legs through them. Bring the sides of the square over his back and pin them in place. You can also sew tapes along the top edges and tie it in place.

2) Take a sweater of an appropriate size: a baby sweater for a small dog, perhaps one of your own castoffs for a larger one. Cut off the sleeves. Slip your dog's forelegs through the armholes and button the sweater over his back. This is also a useful emergency garment when only warmth is needed.

AN EMERGENCY SPLINT. If a dog breaks a limb when hunting or when hit by a car, the best way to protect it from further injury during transportation or from the dog's own agitation is to immobilize it with an improvised splint. Anything stiff and straight will do: a strong stick, a short pole, a narrow board, even a rolled-up newspaper or magazine. Tie a strip of cloth, a necktie, or a handkerchief around both the splint and the limb above the break, and another one below it, placing the leg as straight as possible against the splint. Install the dog on the back seat of the car, lying on his uninjured side, cover him with a blanket or jacket, and drive him as smoothly as possible to the vet's.

Small dogs can simply be rolled in a blanket and held securely on one person's lap, while another drives.

CONVALESCENT CARE

A sick dog needs a quiet corner of his own with a soft, clean bed, where he will not be bothered by noise, bright sunlight, or children. It should be easily cleaned, moderately heated (70 to 72 degrees), dimly lit, airy but free from drafts. Remove the carpet and cover the floor with newspapers, as in his puppy days. You may even have to put a diaper on a very weak dog who cannot leave his bed.

The most important part of convalescent care is keeping the patient warm, clean, and fed. He will need smaller quantities, more often, probably softer food that is cooked, ground, or puréed. Beef liver, heart, and kidneys may tempt him if he refuses his usual diet. Clean wherever and whenever he is soiled. If he enjoys it, you can groom him too. It may lift his spirits and hasten his recovery. Do not tire him with continual attention, but do not let him feel neglected either.

Post a written schedule of his daily care and medication over his bed and follow it to the letter. Take his temperature twice a day, and call the veterinarian once a day to give him a report on the patient's condition.

When you bring a dog home from the vet's after some minor operation or a treatment for which he has been given anesthetics, he will remain a bit groggy for as long as 24 hours afterward. Beware of instinct biting, handle him gently, and keep him in a quiet, dark place for several hours. Give him plenty of fresh water, but no food for 12 hours, unless he asks for it. The next day he will be his old self again.

DIAGNOSIS OF COMMON SYMPTOMS

Dogs, like children, are prone to minor injuries, malfunctions, and infections, which generally cure themselves spontaneously, or with the help of some simple home remedy. Some dogs, like some children, are particularly susceptible to colds, conjunctivitis, allergies, and various minor health disturbances which are apt to recur many times during their lifetime.

An experienced parent or dog owner will recognize such indispositions and remain cool-headed but observant for the first 24 hours, by which time the child or dog will most often be quite normal again. If not, other symptoms will have emerged to give a clue as to the nature of the disorder. An inexperienced owner or worrisome parent, on the other hand, will rush his child or pet to the hospital at the slightest sneeze or shiver. There is no harm in this, except that time and money are wasted needlessly. For example, let's say that you take your puppy to the vet for treatment of a simple indigestion or conjunctivitis. The next time the identical symptoms appear, why not give him the same care and medication without bothering the vet? If you observe your dog carefully, you will soon learn to distinguish between his aspect and demeanor when he has simply eaten something that disagreed with him or picked up a minor infection, and when he is really ill.

A word of warning, though: Do not attempt home treatment unless you are absolutely certain of your diagnosis. You may only make matters worse. And if you end up taking your dog to the vet after all, be honest in telling him exactly what medication you have already given him. In this regard, beware of overdosing your dog. Baby remedies in baby doses according to weight are safer than adult medicines, for which the appropriate canine dose would seem ridiculously tiny and, more important, which can be dangerously incompatible with the canine organism. Furthermore, you should never give your dog a prescription remedy or a potent one (including antibiotics) without specific instructions from your vet.

IF YOUR DOG IS CONSTIPATED

it means that he is unable to produce normal bowel movements. The cause is probably dietary. An all-meat diet leaves little residue, and a dog fed on meat alone will have insufficient bulk to eliminate every day, or even more often than once a week, if he is a large dog. Lack of exercise, lack of water, and lack of opportunity to relieve himself can also constipate a dog. Milk of magnesia is a harmless laxative if the dose is not excessive. One teaspoon may be sufficient for a 40-pound dog and should provoke a bowel movement some 6 hours later. Household remedies include a spoonful of mineral or olive oil dribbled over his food, or a tablespoonful of rhubarb jam.

The next most frequent cause is more serious: an obstruction that prevents elimination. Digested bones can form hard balls in the intestines or rectum which can be passed only after manipulation has broken up the mass, or muscle-relaxant drugs have distended the intestine. If the ball is low in the rectum, you may be able to break it up by inserting a lubricated finger. When the obstruction is caused by a foreign object that the dog has swallowed, treatment depends on whether or not it is digestible. Most ingested items show up on an X-ray. Some can be identified by palpation. Others require barium on an empty stomach before the X-ray is taken, in order to be visible. Depending on the object, laxatives may be prescribed, surgery resorted to, or pain-killing tranquilizers recommended for the dog (perhaps for his owner too) until his digestive juices have had time to break down the foreign substance.

A dog who is getting a balanced diet and sufficient daily exercise should not have constipation problems. He may skip a day or two, but will return to normal without intervention. A dog whose stools are hard and difficult to pass can be given added soft bulk in the form of vegetables and whole cereals, and lubrication in the form of a spoonful of olive oil at every meal, or a tiny suppository carved out of a piece of castile soap may be inserted into his rectum. Milk and liver have a laxative effect. A permanent water supply is indispensable. Very occasionally, a medicinal laxative may be advisable. But never make a habit of it, and ask your vet to prescribe it.

IF YOUR DOG HAS DIARRHEA

it means that he frequently passes loose and watery stools. There are many possible causes, some benign and others very serious indeed.

Among the benign ones: a change of diet (especially from fresh food to commercial products), overexcitement, a change of environment, travel, eating something laxative or a food that disagrees with him. In all of these cases, the feces is normal in color, if not in form.

Try to remove the cause, if possible. Let the dog skip a meal if he wants to, because fasting is one of Nature's remedies for stomach upsets. If he is still interested in food, give him a diet of meat and rice for a few days. Since the disorder is often caused by something the dog wants to get rid of, do not try to stop the diarrhea medicinally during the first 24 hours. If it persists, ask your vet to recommend a remedy and the proper dosage.

The serious causes of diarrhea include: viral infection, poisoning, worms, distemper, and other diseases. In these cases the stool is usually discolored, black, or foul-smelling. All of them require veterinary diagnosis and treatment.

Diarrhea is always serious in puppies, whatever the cause, because of its debilitating and dehydrating effect, and also because it may be a symptom of distemper.

IF YOUR DOG SUDDENLY SWELLS UP
LIKE A BALLOON

take him to the nearest vet as fast as possible. He may be suffering from *bloat,* a severe gastric torsion and dilation, similar to the horse's "twisted gut" and just as often fatal. It seems that long, deep-bodied dogs and very active ones—including Bloodhounds, Great Danes, Greyhounds, Setters, Airedales, and St. Bernards—are predisposed to it. Bloat strikes like lightning, First there is a torsion of the stomach which cuts off the blood supply, causes the area to dilate painfully at an alarming rate, and breathing to become short and labored. Emergency treatment consists of stomach tubing or surgery in order to release the built-up gas. If no shock or damage to vital organs has occurred, there is a slight chance of recovery. Research is being undertaken by the Morris Animal Foundation to discover the cause of this relatively new canine ailment. Among the suspects, aside from the dog's body type, are an all-dry food diet, soybeans (used as vegetable protein in some prepared dog foods), violent exercise during stress or immediately after feeding, and calcium or Vitamin B deficiencies.

IF YOUR DOG SCRATCHES FURIOUSLY AND OFTEN

examine him first of all for fleas and other external parasites, which are by far the most common cause of this behavior. Turn him over on his back, ruff the fur on his hindlegs, and see if a flea hops onto his stomach. If so, treat him all over with an insecticide powder, a dip, or give him a bath with an insecticide shampoo.

If there is no sign of parasites, examine his skin for redness, lesions, scabs, or bald spots, which could indicate skin ailments or infection and require veterinary treatment. In this case, do not bathe him. It would only increase the irritation or spread the infection.

If the dog is really frantic, you can give him temporary relief until the proper treatment takes effect by administering an antihistamine or tranquilizer, in the dose your vet prescribes. But remember that these drugs merely suppress discomfort and do not effect a cure.

IF YOUR DOG REFUSES TO EAT

it may mean that he is bored with the same old food or, on the contrary, is suspicious of a change of diet. Perhaps he is simply not hungry because he has had little exercise since his last meal. Perhaps he scrounged a meal from a neighbor. Or perhaps he is trying to punish you for real or imaginary neglect by refusing the food you offer. In all of these cases, leave his bowl for half an hour, then remove it. It will do him no harm to miss a meal, and he will eat the next one (which can be more generous than usual) with greater relish. But if he doesn't, you must look for another cause.

Lack of appetite may also be a symptom of fever (easily verified by taking his temperature), of indigestion (for which fasting is a natural remedy), or of tooth or gum trouble (in which case the dog will accept soft foods but will refuse those he has to chew).

If the condition persists for more than 24 hours, or as soon as other symptoms arise, you should consult your vet.

IF YOUR DOG DROOLS A LOT

unless he is a Boxer or a St. Bernard (who drool most of the time), and if you are not in the process of cooking or eating a dish he particularly relishes, open his mouth and see whether there is a splinter, bone, or some foreign object stuck between his teeth, in his gums, or in the roof of his mouth. You may be able to remove it with your fingers or with sterilized tweezers.

Examine the gums. If there is swelling but no visible foreign object, it may be a sign of infection requiring veterinary treatment.

IF YOUR DOG COUGHS

make sure first of all that nothing is mechanically impeding his natural respiration, such as too tight a collar, or a foreign body stuck in his mouth or throat.

If you can eliminate these causes, and if the cough persists for more than 24 hours and is frequent and distressing to the dog, it is best to take him to the vet. Coughing may indicate the presence of internal parasites, and is a symptom of bronchitis (which can develop into pneumonia if untreated), of tonsillitis, and of various serious ailments including distemper and tuberculosis. Coughing at night may indicate congestive heart trouble.

IF YOUR DOG WHINES AND CRIES

he may be trying to tell you that he is in pain. He may move about restlessly in obvious distress, or curl up in a dark corner. Try to console and reassure him. Feel him gently all over, seeking the exact location of the pain. Then examine it for signs of injury, a cut, bruise, or some foreign object like a pin or needle. If there is none, the pain is probably organic or muscular. Acute indigestion and bowel impaction can also cause intense pain. It is best to take your dog to the vet and let him make the diagnosis.

IF YOUR DOG LIMPS

examine the paw of the affected leg for cuts, a foreign body in the pads or between the toes, a sign of fungus infection between the toes, toenails that are too long or ingrown, ingrown dewclaws, matted hair between the toes or, in winter, ice balls. If you find nothing abnormal, run your hand gently along the leg. Your dog will wince (and maybe snap or nip) when you touch the center of pain, and this will tell you whether it is a muscular or a joint affliction. Take his temperature. If he has no fever, let him lead a quiet life for the next day or two. Take him out to do his business as usual, but eliminate the daily walk. Many active dogs incur minor sprains and strains from vigorous play, jumping, or simply a brusque movement. Some dogs' pads are very sensitive to rough surfaces like gravel, or to the heat of pavements on summer days. These conditions usually clear up naturally, gradually improving over a period of a few days. If, instead, they worsen, take your dog to the vet.

IF YOUR DOG SHAKES HIS HEAD AND HOLDS IT TO ONE SIDE

examine the ear on the low side for a foreign body such as a burr or wheat awn, but do not probe deeply. You can remove an accessible object with tweezers. But if it is deep inside the ear canal, take your dog to the vet at once, because the longer you delay, the deeper the object will become imbedded and the harder it will be to remove.

When there is no sign of a foreign object, take a cotton swab and gently swab the inside of the ear without probing deeply. Examine the swab. If it is stained with a dark, ill smelling matter, your dog is probably suffering from *canker* or *ear mange* (which is quite different from skin mange). It can be cured rapidly by treating the ear with special medicated eardrops such as are prepared by all of the canine pharmaceutical companies for this very common ear ailment.

IF YOUR DOG SHIVERS AND TREMBLES

perhaps he is simply cold or in a draft. Perhaps he is afraid of something. Perhaps he has a fever. (Take his temperature and you will know.)

Shivering is also one of the reactions to poisoning from various substances, including worm remedies and insecticides. Do a bit of detective work and see if there is any evidence that your dog has absorbed some household or garden product, paint flakes from a piece of wood or a painted toy. If so, give him an emetic (see page 224). Telephone the vet, identify the poison, and administer the antidote he prescribes.

IF YOUR DOG HAS A RUNNY NOSE OR EYES

it may be quite normal when the discharge is clear. It is practically a chronic condition of some dogs. But if the discharge is sticky or colored, like mucus or pus, it is a sign of infection, probably a local one. You can bathe the afflicted eye with a weak boric acid solution, or put a bit of 1 per cent yellow mercuric oxide, the size of a grain of rice, in the inside corner of the eye. Keep the nose clean by wiping it with cotton or tissues.

A local infection will not affect your dog's behavior. But if he seems distressed or sluggish at the same time, take his temperature, and if he has a fever, take him to the vet.

IF YOUR DOG SNEEZES

he may have caught cold. He may be allergic to some pollen or to a household or beauty product that has been sprayed from an aerosol can. He may simply be blowing his nose. If it persists, or if it is accompanied by fever, it may be a sinus infection requiring veterinary diagnosis and treatment.

IF YOUR DOG HICCOUGHS

do not worry. Puppies hiccough a lot, as babies do, and the hiccoughs stop as spontaneously as they began. If they last long enough for the puppy to become distressed or fatigued, you can give him a mild tranquilizer.

IF YOUR DOG RUBS HIS RUMP ALONG THE GROUND

everyone who witnesses his unattractive behavior will tell you he has worms. It is far more likely that his anal glands need emptying, and this simple act will give him immediate relief (see page 157). Often a dog who does this is simply a fastidious animal wiping himself after defecation. If he does it at home or during the night, he may be an aroused male indulging in a form of masturbation.

On the other hand, it is true that tapeworm segments emerging from the anus cause irritation, which dogs try to relieve by rubbing their bottoms along the ground. Take a sample of your dog's stool to the vet for a microscopic analysis, and if he detects the presence of worms, ask him to prescribe the proper treatment.

IF YOUR DOG IS INSATIABLY THIRSTY

it is quite normal if he has just exerted himself during hot weather or if he has eaten salty or spicy food. Some medications cause abnormal thirst, including antihistamines, corticosteroids, and tranquilizers. In other circumstances, it can be an alarm signal, perhaps of kidney diabetes. Take no chances. See the vet.

IF YOUR DOG VOMITS

it is seldom a symptom of disease if unaccompanied by other signs of illness. Dogs vomit to get rid of something they have eaten unwisely or too fast. Sometimes they vomit an entire meal and then eat it again in its semidigested form. Bitches regurgitate partially digested food for their puppies as the first stage of the weaning process. All dogs can regurgitate at will.

Overeating, nervousness, excitement, travel sickness, violent exercise too soon after a meal, gluttonous eating habits, can all cause vomiting almost immediately, but need not cause alarm.

When a dog vomits a yellow frothy liquid, often the first thing in the morning, it is bile. (Clean it up at once, because it leaves a practically indelible stain.) Do not force your dog to eat that day if he does not feel like it. Fasting may be just what he needs. But if this occurs regularly, he may be suffering from a chronic liver ailment and your vet should be consulted.

Persistent vomiting as well as vomiting several hours after a meal rather than at once may be due to more serious causes, including worms, intestinal infection or obstruction, and poisoning. If the dog displays any other symptoms of distress, by all means take him to the vet.

IF YOUR DOG LOSES WEIGHT

there are many possible causes, physical and psychological. First of all, you should obviously check your dog's diet. You may be giving him a generous quantity of food, but very little nourishment. Or you may be giving him an insufficient quantity and quality for the amount of energy he expends.

Perhaps you are giving your dog a proper diet, but he is refusing to eat it because of teething problems, tonsillitis, or some emotional problem such as jealousy of a new dog or baby, or a feeling of neglect. Try to analyze the cause and then correct it.

Weight loss accompanied by a normal or increased appetite is one of the signs of worms. It is simple to confirm your suspicion by taking a fecal sample to your vet.

A rapid, inexplicable weight loss is also a symptom of some very serious diseases. If you have been able to eliminate the other possible causes, you should take your dog to the vet for a thorough examination.

IF YOUR DOG HAS A FIT

he either runs aimlessly around, barking hysterically, starey-eyed and foamy-mouthed, completely beyond control, until he finally collapses, exhausted (often defecating and urinating); or he becomes stiff and starey, champing his jaws, foaming at the mouth, staggers and falls on his back or side with his legs pumping convulsively. The latter type of fit may last for only a few minutes. The running kind is longer and more dangerous because of the risk of the dog's injuring himself or causing damage during his mad frenzy.

A fit is not a disease, but a sign that something is wrong. It may be caused by fever, poisoning, heatstroke, overexcitement, dehydration, teething problems, or worms, among other things. In rare cases, it may be caused by epilepsy or distemper. Even rarer is the "mad" behavior of a dog afflicted with rabies (see page 231).

All you can do is keep your distance, try to steer the agitated dog into a safely enclosed area, remove anything that could be damaged or cause injury, and wait until the fit is over. With a small dog, you may be able to throw a blanket over him and place him in a quiet, dimly lit room. When the fit is over, he will either be quite normal again, or dazed and exhausted. Wrap him in a blanket and take him to your vet for diagnosis and treatment of the disorder that caused this most distressing incident.

IF YOUR DOG SHEDS A LOT

it does not necessarily denote ill health. Electric lighting and central heating seem to throw many dogs off their natural shedding schedule. Most Terrier breeds cast their coat once or twice a year. Collies and other Sheepdogs also tend to go out of coat once a year. As we have seen, bitches shed a lot after their heat periods and lose their coat completely after whelping.

However, profuse shedding may also have other causes: worms, an unbalanced diet or one lacking sufficient fatty acids, sudden changes of temperature, a kidney or bladder infection—in fact, any prolonged low-grade infection.

If in doubt, asking your vet for his opinion is more sensible than just worrying about it.

IF YOUR DOG HAS BALD SPOTS

he may have ECZEMA, which is a symptom of disorder, usually dietary, rather than a disease. In older animals and altered ones, it may be caused by hormonal imbalance. The skin is scaly and hair falls out in patches. To cure the condition, you must correct the cause by hormone injections or by a change of diet, generally adding fat or supplements of Vitamins A and E. In the meantime, antihistamines and tranquilizers can be given to prevent the dog from biting and scratching, which make the condition spread, as does bathing. It will take several weeks to cure, and may be recurrent.

he may have MANGE, caused by a parasitic mite that burrows under the skin. There are two kinds of mange, both of them highly contagious, and identifiable by your veterinarian from skin scrapings, microscopically examined:

1) *Sarcoptic mange* (or "scabies"), which causes itching, spreads rapidly, and strips the skin of hair. It has a musty odor, often starts on the head and spreads to the base of the ears, the root of the tail, the abdomen, chest, and under the front legs. Skin eruptions may take the form of red dots or blisters, then scabs. Prompt attention is vital, as is correct diagnosis. Specially medicated baths, generally sulphur preparations, are the usual treatment.

2) *Follicular or Demodectic Mange* ("red mange"), caused by a different family of mites that burrows into the hair follicles and most often attacks young puppies. Entire litters can be born with it. It is more

serious and persistent than the other variety. It may start with bare spots around the eyes, mouth, elbows, and toes. In the most serious cases, pustules dot the skin where the hair has fallen out. After microscopic analysis of skin scrapings, the veterinarian will prescribe special internal and external mange remedies to kill the mites, but this type of mange takes a long time and is difficult to cure.

he may have RINGWORM, a contagious fungus infection that grows on hair follicles, rather like athlete's foot. It is characterized by ring-shaped red patches covered with scales, and may be dry or moist, usually starting on the head, neck, and legs. Your vet will advise strict anticontagion measures, since it is communicable to human beings, and prescribe a treatment that will probably include oral medication, antifungal shampoos or dips, and frequent applications of tincture of iodine.

INTERNAL PARASITES

Most dogs who live in the country or frequent other animals have worms at one time or another, just as they catch fleas and ticks. All of these parasites are prevalent in nature, especially in warm climates and during the summer. After attaching themselves to a host animal, they multiply with incredible speed, reduce the dog's resistance to disease, drain his strength and energy, and may even be fatal if they are neglected and allowed to proliferate.

Total prevention is practically impossible. You can limit the risk of infestation by providing your dog with scrupulously sanitary living conditions (including continual removal of stool from his kennel or play area), a healthy diet fit for human consumption, and regular grooming to keep him free from external parasites, which can lead to the internal kind. You can also try to prevent your dog from examining the feces or anus of strange dogs and from playing in soiled areas. Often a dog will pick up worm larvae on his paws, then lick his paws, and create the beginning of a worm colony in his intestines.

Fortunately, remedies have been developed to destroy the most common kinds of internal parasites. Some are poisons strong enough to kill your dog, if the choice and dosage are not appropriate to each individual case, and if the dog has not been fasted during the previous 24 hours. Others are nontoxic to dogs and may be given following a small meal, generally in two treatments, two weeks apart. But these do not destroy all types of worms. Only your veterinarian is qualified to prescribe the exact medication. So, although commercial worming preparations can be bought in any pet shop, none but the most experienced owner should attempt to worm a dog without veterinary diagnosis and supervision.

When you suspect that your dog has worms, you should first of all make sure that this is really so by taking a fecal sample to your vet for examination. Scoop it up with a strip of cardboard, a wooden or plastic spoon, and place it in a screw-top jar.

Some vets are equipped to worm your dog on their own premises. This is certainly the simplest solution for the average pet owner, not only because the vet himself administers the treatment and supervises the dog's reaction to it, but because some remedies have a violent purgative effect, and the expelled matter should be burned. You can take your dog to the clinic early in the morning, having fasted him for 24 hours, and pick him up in the afternoon. In the meantime, you can disinfect his sleeping quarters, toys, and food and water bowls, in order to avoid reinfestation from lurking larvae. Internal parasites are so widespread that there is no reason to be ashamed or horrified by the idea that your dog may have worms. But DO something about it!

THE ROUNDWORM (or "Ascarid") is the most common variety, especially in puppies, as a result of prenatal infestation from a worm-infested bitch. The effect on a litter can be devastating. Similar in appearance to tiny earthworms, they are picked up from the soil and cause diarrhea, dull coats, watery and runny eyes, potbellies, a big appetite accompanied by weight loss, and very serious complications if they attack the lungs. Because of its 2-week life cycle, two worming treatments 2 weeks apart are usually recommended.

THE TAPEWORM (or "Taenia") grows in segments which drop off and dry up, appearing in the stool in a form that resembles tiny grains of rice. Even though the dog may expel a great quantity of segments, the tapeworm's head still remains attached to his intestines, feeding and multiplying there. A dog with tapeworm eats a lot but loses weight. He also scratches a lot, partly because of the fleas and lice that act as carriers for the tapeworm eggs. He may also bite, lick, or rub his anus, which is irritated by partially expelled segments or eggs.

THE HOOKWORM is a dangerous bloodsucker that can cause severe anemia, bloody diarrhea with mucus, and extreme nervousness. It is particularly prevalent in moist, sandy soil and in warm climates, appearing much more frequently in crowded kennels than in sanitary home environments. The treatment is given in 2 doses 2 weeks apart, often in combination with iron or liver supplements to counteract the anemic effect of these nasty parasites.

THE WHIPWORM makes its home in the dog's caecum (the canine

equivalent of our appendix), where it forms toxins, causes anemia, digestive upsets, foul, bloody, and watery diarrhea, dull coats, excessive shedding, and chronic coughing. As with all worms, the only way to make an accurate diagnosis is by a microscopic examination of the dog's stool. Beyond the reach of oral medication, whipworms can be destroyed only by an injection given by the vet. They most often appear in adult dogs, perhaps because the parasite itself takes a relatively long time to mature.

THE HEARTWORM is a rapidly growing plague all over the United States. Propagated by mosquitoes, it is most prevalent in warm climates. Where there are mosquitoes, there is apt to be heartworm. It is the most pernicious parasite of all, causing fatigue, shortness of breath, coughing, abdominal or chest swelling, nervousness, depression, even convulsions as a result of the restricted blood flow, since the heartworm lives in the right ventricle of the heart and in the pulmonary artery, and the larvae it breeds invade the entire bloodstream. Treatment is long and delicate. There is a preventive method consisting of a medicine to be mixed in the dog's food every day during the mosquito season, but only after a blood test has proved negative. Still in the experimental stage, it should be prescribed and supervised by an experienced vet.

In the meantime, if there is heartworm in your area, it is advisable to give your dog a blood test twice a year, and to protect him from mosquito bites by administering regular insect-repellent dips, eliminating mosquito-breeding places such as stagnant pools and even stagnant water under flower pots, screening his kennel and run, and doing anything else that you can think of, such as planting citronella, geraniums, and basil, all of which are said to repel mosquitoes.

FIRST AID

Like young children, puppies are accident-prone, some more than others, males more than females. An inquisitive child will stick his finger in an electric wall socket, while a puppy at the same stage of development will chew a trailing television cord. As they become bolder and more explorative, adolescent dogs get into all kinds of scrapes, just as boys and girls do. By the time they reach maturity, however, all of them will have learned to recognize their physical limitations, and experience will have taught them to beware of certain common dangers.

In spite of their worldly wisdom, human adults are still victims of food poisoning and automobile accidents, just as intelligent adult dogs can still be run down by cars, struck by stray bullets, or cut by broken bottles and barbed wire. There are simply too many hazards in modern life for dog or man to remain completely immune from accidental injuries.

A few notions of first aid may save your dog's life. They may even save your own life, because the principles of human and canine emergency care are practically the same. More often than not, an accident occurs at a most inconvenient time and place, far from a veterinary clinic, on a Sunday, holiday, or after office hours. During the delay while seeking professional attention, you can often administer effective first aid. Remember, though, that first aid is not a cure and is seldom a complete treatment for injuries, most of which require veterinary care as well.

When dealing with an injured dog, remain as cool and calm as possible. First of all, size up the situation. Decide what needs to be done, and proceed gently but efficiently. Talk to your dog constantly in a reassuring tone of voice. He will know instinctively that you are trying to help him; he will be grateful and, usually co-operative. But if your intervention is apt to cause him pain, take the precaution of muzzling him. A dog's automatic reaction to pain is to bite, even against his will. It would only complicate matters if there were two injured patients to treat instead of one.

WOUNDS

If you notice your dog limping when he comes home from a romp, if he persistently licks a spot on his limbs or body, if he leaves a bloodstain where he has walked or lain, or if you witness an accident in which he is wounded, you should fetch your first-aid kit and go to work.

The gravity of a wound depends on its location, its type, and its importance. Minor, superficial cuts usually heal rapidly with first-aid care and the dog's own licking. Body wounds may require stitching by a veterinary surgeon, as do head wounds of any importance, if only to prevent their leaving a disfiguring scar on your dog's face. Any wound involving the eye should be touched only by the vet. Wounds involving an artery require urgent veterinary attention, and immediate first aid in order to control the bleeding in the meantime. Never give aspirin to a wounded dog, because of its anticoagulant effect.

BLEEDING from a wound comes either from a *vein* (in which case the blood flows dark red in a steady flow and can be stopped by applying pressure with a tight bandage or your fingers); or it can come from the *capillary blood vessels* near the skin surface, generally the result of a bruise (in which case a sufficiently large gauze pad, dampened to prevent it from sticking, will be needed to apply pressure over this wide area); or it can come from an *artery* (in which case the blood is bright red, spurts out in rhythm with the heartbeat, and can be stopped by direct pressure on the bleeding area with a clean cloth or an ice pack).

Bleeding from an artery can also be stopped by placing *a tourniquet* between the wound and the heart, but this should be considered a last resort, when pressure has proven insufficient, because its entails a certain risk. You will need a soft, strong strip of cloth. A necktie or a handkerchief will do. You must tie it tightly enough to stop the bleeding, and release it for one minute every 10 minutes, or as soon as the skin beyond the tourniquet feels cold, in order to prevent damage to the tissues, while you rush your dog to the vet. You can also tie it loosely and slip a stick through the loop, twisting it to tighten the tourniquet, and untwisting it to release the pressure.

In all of these cases, you should try to keep the dog still, because movements tends to increase the flow of blood.

ALL ORDINARY WOUNDS should first of all be examined and any foreign matter removed. If the wound is dirty, you may let it bleed for a moment, then wash it thoroughly with mild soap and water. Wipe or sponge it dry and apply an antiseptic, such as:

—mercurochrome (good for bruises and minor cuts), or

—3 per cent hydrogen peroxide (recommended for deep cuts, since it foams on contact with flesh and helps to clean the wound).

The majority of minor cuts need no more treatment than this, not even a bandage. Your dog will lick it, which will keep it clean, and it will heal rapidly. You must simply check it morning and night, cleaning it if necessary. If there is redness or swelling, the wound is infected and you should take your dog to the vet for an antibiotic or penicillin injection.

There are four types of wounds:

PUNCTURE WOUNDS, most often made by an object such as a nail, thorn or splinter, or another animal's tooth. They are deep and narrow, and you must wash them and pour antiseptic into them to reach the bottom of the puncture, where the risk of infection is greatest. No other treatment is necessary.

In the case of a *dog bite*, you should take precautions against rabies if the attacking dog is unknown to you. In the case of a cat bite or a nail puncture, you might ask your vet if he considers an anti-tetanus injection worthwhile. He will probably reply "No," unless your dog lives on a farm or plays in a fertilized garden, because tetanus infection is rare in dogs.

PORCUPINE QUILLS cause the most painful of all punctures, especially if your dog has received them in his head or face. Because of their barbed tips, they are difficult to remove, the short black quills being more strongly barbed than the long white body quills. Speed is important, as is immobility, for the quills travel whenever the dog moves, and quills in the underbelly or around the ears are a menace to vital internal organs. Whenever possible, give your dog a sedative or a painkiller and rush him to the vet, who will anesthetize him and remove the quills with dexterity, since he has undoubtedly had more experience than you in performing this delicate task.

If you have no choice and must do it yourself, you should first muzzle and immobilize your dog, for it will be very painful for him. With sharp scissors, snip off the ends of the quills, to deflate the barb. Then with a pair of tweezers or small pliers, pull on each quill gently but steadily to remove it from the flesh. Where the skin is thin, between the toes and around the mouth, it may be easier to pull the quill straight through, barb and all. Each wound must be treated with antiseptic.

FISH HOOKS pose a similar problem because of the barbed tip. Never try to remove one by pulling backward which can cause dreadful lacerations. Instead, cut off the hook eye with cutting pliers, and push the barb through, then thoroughly disinfect the wound.

GUNSHOT WOUNDS are an occupational hazard of Hunting dogs. Furthermore, farmers and ranchers have the right to shoot a dog that attacks or molests their livestock. All gunshot wounds require medical attention because of the risk of blood poisoning. First aid starts by stopping the bleeding.

Sometimes the experience will send a dog into a state of *shock* (see page 222), in which case his gums will be pale and gray, his heartbeat weak and rapid, his breathing difficult, and his body cold. Wrap him in a blanket to keep him warm. If he can swallow, give him an oral stimulant such as a little warm coffee, a few drops of whiskey or brandy, or strong tea. But never attempt to force a liquid into an unconscious dog. Instead, give him a whiff of ammonia or smelling salts. Rush him to the vet, who can administer more effective stimulants such as adrenalin and glucose, and treat the injury.

INCISED WOUNDS are clean-cut. Normal wound treatment is sufficient for minor ones. But when the incision is fairly long or over a joint, it is advisable to have your vet stitch it, if only to ensure the finest possible scar, and hair regrowth. After disinfecting the wound with hydrogen peroxide, bring the edges closely together and hold them in place with a bandage, if possible, until the vet can treat it.

LACERATED WOUNDS are jagged tears that may be just a torn triangle of skin, or a long mangled cut—as, for example, when a dog has been caught on barbed wire and pulled himself free. Even minor tears can leave ugly scars, so it is best to let your vet treat and stitch them. You will have to be very thorough in cleaning these wounds, due to their irregularity, which makes it difficult to remove foreign matter.

Long-eared, smooth-haired dogs may emerge from a dogfight with lacerated ears, which are irresistible gripping points for their assailants. If the ear is also swollen, you should follow the cleaning process with the application of cold-water compresses or ice packs in order to reduce the swelling and relieve the pain. Then bandage the ears up over the dog's head.

BRUISES AND SCRATCHES are superficial wounds that usually respond to first-aid treatment and the dog's licking. A dog's pads may be bruised from running over rough terrain. Heavy dogs are more vulnerable to this kind of injury than light breeds.

Treat the bruise in the normal way, and finish off with a softening healing ointment. Eliminate long walks until the pads have completely healed.

Hunting dogs often return from a day in the field with scratches on their underbellies from prickly underbrush. These will clear up rapidly, but you should disinfect them, just to be on the safe side.

Claw scratches are more serious because they are generally caused by an attacking feline, whose instinct is to aim for a dog's eyes. Any injury to the eye, or even near to it, must be treated with the utmost skill. Do not attempt to do it yourself. Instead, prevent your dog from touching the injured eye by covering it with a gauze pad soaked in cold water, and take him to the vet at once.

BITES

DOG AND CAT BITES should be treated like puncture wounds (which they are): washing them with soap and water, pouring in antiseptic, and checking for signs of infection which would warrant an antibiotic or penicillin injection by the vet. If the biter was a stray, wild, or unknown animal, take your dog to the vet at once for precautionary protection against rabies, if he considers it necessary.

FLEA AND FLY BITES can drive a dog crazy. They can also lead to infection if he scratches them a lot, and even infect him with certain diseases carried by these insects. The only permanent solution is a regular program of insecticide with powders or dips, and insect-repellent measures in the dog's kennel and run. Until the insecticide has done its work, you can relieve the itching with an antihistamine ointment which your veterinarian will prescribe as a permanent element of your first aid kit, especially in warm regions.

BEE, WASP, AND HORNET STINGS cause pain and swelling which can reach almost intolerable intensities, depending on your dog's sensitivity to the venom they inject along with the stinger. If the bite is accessible and the barb visible, try to extract it with tweezers. You can then treat the spot with warm compresses of a bicarbonate of soda solution or diluted ammonia and give him an oral dose of antihistamine.

Some dogs, like some humans, have a violent allergic reaction that can cause a state of shock or even death. The symptoms are dizziness, shortness of breath, and choking. If you have the slightest doubt, rush your dog to the vet. He can give him an injection that will neutralize the venom.

SNAKE BITES require immediate first aid as well as veterinary treatment in order to save the dog. If you have not observed the incident, you should know that the symptoms of snake bite are: a visible mark of one or two punctures, swelling, intense pain, impaired vision, weakness, shortness of breath, vomiting, and paralysis. First aid for dogs is the same as for humans: Place a tourniquet between the bite and the heart, remembering to release it for one minute every ten minutes, or as soon as the part of the body beyond the tourniquet feels cold. If, on the contrary, it becomes hot and swollen, you must move the tourniquet higher toward the heart.

If necessary, cut away the coat around the bite. Sterilize a knife and make a cut in the form of an X at the point of the puncture in order to open up the wound. Encourage bleeding by pressing around the cut, always away from the heart. It is risky to suck the venom by mouth if you have never done it before. Snake-bite kits contain a suction apparatus for this purpose. After the venom has been removed, wash the wound thoroughly with soap and water and rush the dog to the vet or nearest doctor, since speed is vital. During the entire process, try to keep the dog quiet, for any movement will facilitate the progress of the venom toward the heart. Cold in any form tends to slow it down and is the only safe kind of first aid when a dog has been bitten by a poisonous snake in the neck or head, where it is impossible to apply a tourniquet.

If you walk or hunt with your dog in regions where poisonous snakes abound, you should always carry a snake-bite kit. Study the instructions carefully, or, better still, get an experienced person to show you how to use it before it actually becomes necessary.

BURNS

Treating burns in dogs is no different from treating burns in humans, except that you may sometimes need to trim the dog's coat in order to apply medication to the burn.

Burn treatment has changed completely in recent decades. The old-fashioned method of greasing a burn with oil or butter has been discarded. Now it is recommended to cool the burn with cold-water compresses or ice packs, and then apply a tannic-acid ointment. In an emergency, you can apply compresses of strong cold tea, damp tea bags, a baking soda solution, or damp gauze compresses. But never use an antiseptic or absorbent cotton on burns, and never rub them. Human burn ointments are just as effective for dogs. Unless the burn is a minor one, take your dog to the vet for antiseptic or antishock treatment.

SHOCK

Characterized by pale, grayish gums, weak, rapid heartbeat, short, difficult breathing, and a subnormal body temperature, shock often accompanies or follow burns, accidents, poisoning, internal bleeding, gunshot wounds, bloat—in fact, any particularly traumatizing experience.

Immediate first aid consists of trying to raise the body temperature and keep the dog warm with blankets, hot-water bottles, and stimulants. Try to keep his head lower than his body, to ensure a blood supply to the brain. If the dog is conscious and able to swallow, you can give him warm coffee or strong tea, perhaps spiked with a few drops of whiskey or brandy, or a syrup of brandy and honey (half and half). But it is best, whenever possible, to keep him warm and take him to the vet, who will be able to administer more immediately effective stimulants and, if necessary, oxygen or a blood transfusion.

HEAT STROKE

This cause of many canine fatalities every summer could practically be eliminated if dog owners always remembered to:
—Never shut up a dog in a parked car in the summer.
—Never take a dog on a long trip in a car that is not air conditioned in the summer.

—Never leave a dog tied up in a shadeless area, or even in a shady one, during sultry weather.

—Always provide an accessible supply of fresh cool water, even during car rides and long walks.

—Never exercise a dog during the heat of the day.

—During the hot summer months, give a dog his main meal after sunset and add a pinch of salt to it.

If you observe these simple rules, you should never have the distressing experience of seeing a dog in the throes of a heat stroke: panting, staggering, finally too weak to stand, with starey, blank eyes, and perhaps a purplish tongue. Short-nosed breeds like Pekingese, Bulldogs and their derivatives including Boxers, all heavy-coated dogs and obese ones, are particularly vulnerable.

As soon as you notice the first sign of discomfort, you should immediately make an effort to lower the dog's body temperature. The quickest way is to plunge him into a tub of cool water, pouring cool water over his head or placing an ice bag on it. Install an electric fan nearby, if possible. If no tub is available, douse the dog with cool water from a pitcher, pail, or the garden hose (but make sure that the water is flowing cool before spraying your dog). Cold-water enemas have an immediate cooling effect. Cool drinking water is essential.

When you can feel that the dog's body is cool, let him rest. But if the dog was already in a state of prostration when you cooled him off, you should take him to the vet, for he will probably need oxygen, glucose and saline injections, and perhaps adrenalin to help him recover completely from the horrible, unnecessary shock that he has experienced.

ELECTROCUTION

Puppies during their chewing stage often discover that a plastic-covered electric cord is a delightful chewing toy—until they chew through to the live wire and receive a violent shock, possibly a fatal one. The only means of prevention is to keep your puppy under supervision until he has outgrown this period, to remove temptations from his play area, and to be suspicious when a normal puppy is suddenly as quiet as a lamb. If you do not see him sleeping in his bed, he is probably up to some mischief.

First aid in the case of an electric shock involves first of all switching off the electric current in order to avoid electrocution to yourself when you touch your dog. The shock may have provoked urination, so be careful not to step in it; liquid and metal contacts would transmit the current to you. Then, and only then, remove the wire from your dog's mouth—for perfect safety, with a dry wooden broomstick or a cane. Verify that his heart is still beating. If so, there is hope of reviving him by artificial respiration (see page 200). When he has regained consciousness, he may be in a state of shock and shiver violently. Keep him quiet and warm with blankets. Give him a whiff of aromatic spirits of ammonia. Call your vet for further instructions. If there are burns on his paws or body, give them normal first-aid treatment.

Do not expect your dog to have learned anything from the experience. It all happens so quickly that he may never associate the shock with the electric cord. So until he has acquired adult forms of play, keep all household wiring beyond his reach, especially when you leave him alone.

FOREIGN OBJECTS

If your veterinarian ever has a moment free for idle conversation, ask him what were some of the unusual objects he has removed from a dog's stomach. His answer will astound you. It may also convince you that the dog is definitely an omnivorous animal.

Adult dogs as well as puppies swallow an amazing variety of objects by accident or during play. Since it is practically impossible to keep all swallowable objects out of reach, the best prevention is to give your dog plenty of harmless toys of an appropriate size. No matter how attached your dog is to his favorite puppy ball, replace it with a larger one as he grows bigger. When there are young children in the home, they should be sternly warned never to push any object into the puppy's ears, nose, or other orifices.

If you actually see your dog swallow a button, marble, coin, or whatever, try to remove it with your fingers, if it is accessible. If not, induce him to regurgitate it. Dogs can vomit at will. Should he refuse, you can give him an *emetic*, such as:

   —a solution of slightly soapy water
   —a solution of 2 tablespoons of salt in a cup of warm water, or 2 teaspoons of salt placed on the back of his tongue
   —a solution of 1 tablespoon of dry mustard in a cup of warm water
   —a mixture of 1 part water and 1 part of 3 per cent hydrogen peroxide, in a dose of 1½ or 2 tablespoons for every 10 pounds of the dog's weight (the best of all).

When he has swallowed a small object, you might feed him a little milk-soaked bread before administering one of these emetics. He will certainly vomit the bread, and the object may be expelled with it.

An old wives' remedy for a dog who has swallowed glass or some sharp object is to feed him asparagus, on the theory that the fibers will surround the cutting edges and prevent injury when the object is eliminated naturally.

Sometimes a foreign object has not been swallowed, but is *wedged between the teeth* or caught *in the dog's throat or the roof of his mouth.* This is often the case of bone slivers, fish bones, pins and needles. Hold the dog's mouth open (see page 199), or get somebody to do it for you while you seek the object and remove it with your fingers or with sterilized tweezers. If it is too deep in the throat for you to reach, you will have to take the dog to the vet, who has the necessary instruments for removing it.

Dust, cinders, sand, and blades of cut grass are among the things that get *into a dog's eyes* and cause irritation when they are not flushed out by the natural watering of the tear ducts. The dog can aggravate the condition and cause infection by scratching the eye. Bathing the eye with ordinary boric acid eyewash can do no harm and may flood out the irritating object. If not, do not tamper with it. Cover the eye with a pad of gauze wrung out in cold water, tied on as securely as possible to prevent scratching, and take your dog to the vet.

Foreign objects *in the nose* are very painful. If the object is visible and accessible, remove it with tweezers or your fingers, when you are sure that you can extract it entirely. Otherwise, it is a job for the vet, who may have to administer a local anesthetic.

Foreign objects *in the ears* should be removed as soon as possible, because the dog's reaction is to shake his head, which forces the object deeper into the ear canal. So lose no time in removing visible burrs, awns, and seeds from the outer earflaps and from the insides of the ears. If the object is deeper down inside the ear, take your dog at once to the vet, who will be able to remove it by using an auriscope and special tweezers.

Limping and licking may indicate that a foreign object has been picked up *in the paws.* Put on your glasses, take your dog into a good light, lift the afflicted paw and examine it carefully, separating each toe, and running your finger gently over each pad. Thorns, burrs, pine needles, and prickly seeds can cause great pain when they are wedged in these tender spots. Remove the object and apply an antiseptic.

A foreign object that has reached *the stomach or intestines* definitely needs veterinary attention, but the degree of danger depends on the size and nature of the object, and this is not always immediately determinable. For that matter, you cannot assume that your dog has a foreign object in his stomach until he has manifested one or more of the following symptoms:

—He whines and cries in pain.

—He continually stretches his body and legs, as this is the most comfortable position for him when he has some intestinal obstruction.

—He sits a lot, in preference to lying down or walking.

—His movements are stiff and stilted, especially the hindquarters.

—He seems confused and miserable.

If you cannot identify the object from circumstantial evidence, such as a missing shoelace or bottle cap with which your puppy had been playing, the veterinarian may be able to do so by palpation or X-ray. If not, your dog will have to be given barium on an empty stomach, which should make the mysterious object show up on the X-ray.

Subsequent treatment depends on the nature of the object. If it is digestible, time and your dog's gastric juices will dispose of it. If it is sharp or poisonous (golf balls, for example, contain a liquid core that is poisonous to dogs), if it cannot disintegrate and is too large to be eliminated normally or with the aid of an enema through the rectum, your vet will have to resort to surgery. This is an obvious instance in which prevention is infinitely simpler than the cure.

POISONING

While there are numerous poisonous substances fatal to dogs, there are two general categories of canine poisoning: accidental, and (sad to say) deliberate. The latter is a despicable crime and its perpetrators usually administer the poison in such a large dose that nothing can be done to save the dog. It is kinder to put him out of his misery.

Accidental poisoning, on the other hand, can be avoided. It is inconvenient and troublesome, considering the many household products in daily use that are potential pet-killers. But remember that the life of your beloved dog may be at stake, and take the trouble to:

—Keep such poisonous articles as detergents, cleaning products, deodorant soap, wax-soaked rags, paint, polishing cloths, sponges, and plastic bags on a high shelf or in a closed cupboard.

—Keep garbage pails out of reach and tightly closed.

—Abstain from using poisonous products such as weed killers, slug and rat poison, in areas accessible to your dog.

—Never give a puppy painted toys or painted pieces of wood to play with.

—Eliminate from the garden poisonous plants such as laurel, oleander, rhododendron, azalea, hemlock, locoweed, castor bean, and deadly nightshade.

—Do not permit your dog to become a nuisance to an irascible neighbor, or destructive of his property.

—Carefully supervise puppies and small dogs, who are most likely to swallow poisonous substances through playfulness, and for whom the effect of poison is quicker and more often fatal.

—Never attempt to worm a dog without veterinary instructions. In fact, never give your dog any potent remedy without professional advice. Keep your medicine chest cleared of all products more than one year old, since most of them concentrate with age and can cause violent intoxications.

—Learn to recognize the *symptoms of poisoning,* in order to act as swiftly as possible:
  —acute abdominal pain
  —crying and whimpering
  —vomiting or retching
  —panting
  —curling up in a dark corner

As soon as you suspect that your dog has been poisoned, you must lose no time. But first, take a few seconds to retrace your dog's movements and try to detect the nature of the poison. Most poisonous commercial products specify the antidote on the label, and the more precise your suspicions, the more effectively your vet can select the proper antidote. Then try to induce vomiting by administering an emetic (see page 224), and save a sample of vomit for your vet to examine.

There are, however, two rare cases in which an emetic would do more harm than good: when a dog has swallowed an acid or an alkali (such as drain cleaner). The acid must be neutralized as quickly as possible by milk of magnesia or a baking soda solution (4 teaspoons to a glass of water) and the alkali by administering a mild acid such as lemon juice or vinegar. Follow both with milk, raw beaten egg yolk, or olive oil.

Call the vet at once, while you wait for your dog to vomit (which he should do almost immediately). If the vet is not available, call your doctor, pharmacist, your local Red Cross, hospital, or the poison information service of the Department of Health, if there is one in your locality. (Most cities have them, with 24-hour telephone information service.) These authorities will indicate the antidote for any poison.

Among the readily available common antidotes are:

for lead poisoning (paint): Epsom salts (1 teaspoon in water), char-
coal

for rat poison (phosphorus): hydrogen peroxide solution

for food poisoning: hydrogen peroxide solution, followed by an enema

for acids: no emetic, but milk of magnesia, or 4 teaspoons of baking
soda in a glass of water

for strychnine (severe cramps, contortions, howling): an emetic by
force-feeding salt, strong tea

for worm medicine: sugar and sweet syrups

for household products: Read the label to find the antidote.

for arsenic (heavy flow of saliva, vomiting, swollen tongue): an eme-
tic, then strong tea, or milk and egg whites

Afterward, give the dog as much milk as he will drink. Slightly beaten
raw egg white is also recommended. Wrap him in a blanket and take him
to the vet, as he may need an enema, a stomach pumping, and perhaps
shock treatment as well.

DROWNING

Dogs are instinctive swimmers, and drowning is fortunately rare. How-
ever, if you take your dog sailing, there is a risk of his falling overboard.
And if you have a swimming pool, he may slip and fall in, or even jump
in voluntarily, and then find that he is unable to climb out. Dogs cannot
scale vertical ladders as a rule, nor can they get a grip on the smooth
tiles that often border modern swimming pools. If you own a dog as well
as a pool, you should install a nonskid ramp or staircase for him at the
shallow end.

First aid for a drowning dog starts by removing as much water as pos-
sible from his insides. Take off his collar, hold him upside down by the
hindlegs, and let the water drain out through his mouth and nose. But be
quick about it, for the essential lifesaving operation is to get him to
breathe. Pull his tongue out of his mouth as far as possible, clean off any
mud, sand, or grass, and apply artificial respiration (see page 200).
When natural breathing has resumed, you should treat him for shock
(see page 222). Even though he may seem to have recovered completely
from his frightening experience, wrap him in a blanket and take him to
the vet for a checkup, in order to avoid complications, such as pneumo-
nia.

DISLOCATIONS

Dislocations occur when a hip or shoulder is displaced from its socket. They may be caused by a blow, an automobile accident, or some violent movement. All too frequently they are caused by thoughtless children and adults (who should know better) pulling or even carrying a puppy by one of his legs.

Hip-joint dislocations are the most frequent as well as the most difficult to replace. It is best not to tamper with it, but to get your dog to the vet as soon as possible.

In the case of a dislocated shoulder, you may be able to replace the ball in the socket yourself. You can try, at least—but only once. If you do not succeed the first time, ask the vet to do it. You will need another person to hold the dog. Grasp the leg above the elbow on the affected side and give it a quick forward pull.

If you have the misfortune to own a dog afflicted with hip or shoulder dysplasia, dislocations are apt to recur, and your vet may be able to teach you how to deal with them.

AUTOMOBILE ACCIDENTS

These are one of the principal causes of premature death in pet dogs. First aid must be given immediately and with great discretion because of the multiple internal and external injuries that may be involved.

As a general rule, you should not move an injured dog until and unless you must. But when you see a dog hit by a car, you obviously have to get him out of the traffic, to the side of the road, and this is often easier said than done.

A dog suffering from shock and pain is apt to bite, so prepare the loop of a bandage muzzle (see page 201), approach the dog calmly, speaking to him in a reassuring tone of voice and, from behind, swiftly slip the muzzle over his jaws and tie it behind his ears. Slide him onto a blanket or coat, then slide or carry him to the side of the road. If you can find a rigid board, it would be even better, especially if there are spinal or internal injuries. Try to get someone to telephone to a veterinarian or an animal welfare society, while you see if there is something you can do until help arrives. Do not touch the dog unnecessarily, however, not even to caress him. You should look for:

1) BLEEDING. Identify the type of bleeding (see page 217), and

apply pressure bandages or a tourniquet if necessary. If blood oozes from the mouth and nose, the bleeding is internal and there is nothing you can do except to avoid moving the dog and keep him warmly covered.

2) BROKEN BONES. If a limb is broken, be very careful that your handling does not aggravate the injury. Keep the dog warm and immobilized, apply a splint (see page 203), and get the dog to the vet as soon as possible.

If it is *a simple fracture,* he will simply immobilize the limb with a splint or plaster cast (to be removed 4 weeks later, during which time the dog should be given convalescent care).

If it is *a compound fracture,* it will probably require surgery in order to set the bones and to secure them internally with pins or plates, and the dog will probably have to be hospitalized before he can be taken home.

There is nothing you can do about *other fractures,* aside from exercising care in handling and moving the injured dog. Pelvic fractures are frequent when a dog is hit by a car. Spinal injuries are often fatal. If the dog can move his tail, you know at least that his back isn't broken. Generally speaking, stopping bleeding and treating for shock are more urgent than doctoring broken bones.

3) INTERNAL INJURIES, which are beyond the scope of first aid and are aggravated by movement. Try to enlist the help of another person to carry the dog to the car and transport him to the nearest veterinary clinic without delay.

It is safer *to carry an injured dog* on a stretcher than in your arms. You may be able to improvise one from something in your car, or from one of your personal garments. Best of all is a rigid board. You can also use a folded blanket. A jacket or coat make good emergency stretchers if you can find two poles, and another person to help you carry it. You turn the coat sleeves inside out, slip the poles through the sleeve openings, and button the coat or jacket over the poles.

When no material of any kind is available, you should carry a small dog *not* curled up in your arms like a baby, but *flat* on his side on your outstretched palms. In an emergency, a large dog can be carried around your neck, like a lamb, with his forelegs held in your right hand and the hindlegs grasped on the other side by your left hand.

Never give an injured dog water, food, or stimulants. They could make internal injuries worse. Let the vet handle it, and save your brandy for yourself while he is treating the dog.

Should you remain with your dog while he is being treated? Probably not. In his state of pain and shock, or under anesthetics, your presence will mean little to him and is apt to distract the veterinarian from his work. Stay in the waiting room, where he can send for you if he needs your assistance. In the meantime, if the injured dog is not your own, you can try to identify and notify the owner from the information on his collar.

CANINE EPIDEMIC DISEASES

There are six of them. All are serious, highly contagious, capable of reaching epidemic proportions, and frequently fatal. All have been the subject of intense research, with such success that all of them can be prevented by vaccines and serums, and some can be cured by prompt veterinary attention.

If your dog was healthy when you bought him, and if you give him normal care including regular immunization shots, the chances are that you will never have to deal personally with any of these dread diseases. Still, every dog owner should know something about their nature, treatment, and possible consequences, if only to stress the importance of specific preventive measures and to aid in early recognition.

RABIES

This ancient and horrible virus disease, transmitted by the saliva of afflicted animals (which may include horses, wolves, squirrels, raccoons, bats, goats, pigs, cattle, skunks, rabbits, cats, rats, and other species as well as dogs), has been brought under control in most civilized countries by compulsory protective vaccinations, destruction of afflicted animals, and strict quarantine laws.

The virus affects the nervous system, resulting in two possible kinds of reactions: the "mad dog" type, with foaming mouth, a change of voice, biting, snapping, and roaming; and the "dumb" type, in which the dog seems to be in a state of shock, his jaw hanging open, his throat muscles paralyzed (a symptom responsible for the old-fashioned term of "hydrophobia," fear of water, due to his inability to swallow).

The incubation period after infection ranges from two weeks to several months. Only a microscopic examination of the brain tissues can determine that an animal is rabid, which is why the body or head of a dog suspected of having died of rabies must be immediately turned over to local health authorities for analysis.

There is no cure for rabies. An afflicted dog must be destroyed. In doubtful cases, the dog is isolated and observed for 10 to 14 days, during which death is certain if he is rabid. If he survives, this fact alone proves that he did not have rabies.

Prevention is sure and simple, consisting of a vaccination when the puppy is at least 5 or 6 months old, followed by a booster shot every 1 or 4 years (depending on the type of vaccine used). In many areas this is wisely obligatory, and a plaque must be attached to the dog's collar as proof of vaccination.

If you are bitten by a dog suspected of rabies, you should wash the wound thoroughly with soap and water and see your doctor at once in order to undergo the Pasteur treatment, consisting of daily injections for 14 days. This is an effective preventative if undertaken at once, before the end of the incubation period. Once contracted, rabies is incurable in humans as in dogs. Your doctor will notify the health authorities. You should also notify the dog's owner, if you know the dog, and warn all of your neighbors, if it was a stray dog that bit you.

Rabies has made a reappearance in Europe, but it is fortunately rare in the United States. Nevertheless, it would be criminal to neglect or economize on the cost of regular vaccinations or to smuggle an unvaccinated dog into a state where this is required. These laws protect you as well as your dog, and they are the only means of controlling and eventually suppressing this dreadful plague.

DISTEMPER

Unlike rabies, which seldom strikes puppies, distemper (also called "Carré's disease") is more apt to affect puppies than adult dogs. They are believed to be protected from it during the first 6 weeks of life thanks to the colostrum in their mother's milk, but at that point "puppy shots" are essential for continued protection from this serious malady. Older dogs have usually built up a natural resistance to it, although there is no age limit. Human beings cannot contract distemper, but they can transmit the virus, which is spread by contaminated articles, even by airborne particles, as well as by direct contact. It can cause ravages in a kennel.

The earliest symptoms resemble those of a cold: runny nose and eyes, coughing, diarrhea, lack of appetite, and fever. Later, nervous disorders appear, including fits and convulsions. Since there is no specific cure, treatment consists of dealing with the symptoms as well as with the secondary infections that frequently occur. Dogs who contract and recover from distemper often bear traces of it throughout their lives, in the form of partial paralysis or spasmodic tics, called "chorea."

Immunization is therefore vital: temporary "puppy shots" at 4 to 6 weeks of age, follow-up shots, and regular booster shots thereafter. There are several different immunization methods. Let your vet apply the one he considers móst effective, and do not carelessly permit the protection to lapse even a single day.

Because of the highly contagious nature of the disease, when you have the misfortune to lose a puppy to distemper, you should burn all of his belongings, disinfect everything he has come in contact with, and refrain from getting a new puppy for at least a month. Even then, make sure that your new puppy has already received protection from this very serious disease.

INFECTIOUS HEPATITIS

Not the same as human hepatitis, this virus disease affects the dog's liver and is transmitted through saliva and urine. It starts with symptoms such as high fever, immoderate thirst, vomiting, sore throat, abdominal pain, diarrhea, loss of weight, and a humped posture, which relieves the pain caused by the inflamed liver. It may accompany or follow distemper. Its evolution is rapid and the mortality rate high, especially in puppies.

Treatment includes antibiotics, suppression of symptoms, and assiduous nursing care. An infected dog can continue to spread the virus in his urine, saliva, and nasal discharge for months after he has recovered.

Prevention is much simpler than treatment. The modern method is to give a triple vaccination against hepatitis in combination with distemper and leptospirosis vaccines, which offers almost total protection if it is renewed annually.

Since canine hepatitis is spread through the excretions of afflicted dogs, show dogs, who share sanitary facilities with hundreds of other dogs from all over the country, are particularly vulnerable to this disease, and hepatitis vaccination is indispensable for them.

LEPTOSPIROSIS

This highly contagious bacterial disease is not restricted to dogs. Cattle, man, horses, and other mammals can contract it too. The bacteria settle in the kidneys, and the most obvious symptom is dark or orange-colored, odorous urine, accompanied by fever and chills, vomiting of bile, stiffness in the hindlegs, and abdominal pain. Prompt treatment is necessary in order to avoid permanent damage to the kidneys and liver. The disease is particularly prevalent in unsanitary conditions and rat infested areas, and it can assume epidemic proportions.

Treatment consists of antibiotics and nursing care. But even if a dog recovers, he is apt to suffer from chronic uremia for the rest of his life, which is apt to be short.

The importance of preventive vaccination is obvious. It is usually given in a triple shot, combined with vaccines against hepatitis and distemper, and must be renewed every year. Some veterinarians believe that the leptospirosis vaccine should be administered every 6 months, in order to give absolute protection. This is probably advisable for show dogs and city dogs, who are most exposed to the disease.

HARD PAD

This highly contagious, very serious virus disease may be related to distemper or to hepatitis. Its symptoms include runny eyes and nose, a very high fever and, most peculiarly, a thickening of the pads of the feet and of the nose, which crack and form crusts as the disease develops.

There is no specific cure, and at the present time no preventive vaccine, although the triple vaccine probably offers some protection. Treatment is therefore difficult. The most that can be done is to administer antibiotics, provide solicitous nursing care, and hope for the best.

ENCEPHALITIS

This very grave virus disease may also be associated in some way with distemper, hepatitis, leptospirosis, or hard pad. At any rate, it is one of the dire complications, causing inflammation of the brain, that may follow infection by the other viruses. Fortunately, the triple vaccine gives effective protection from it.

It is impossible to summarize in a few pages all of the canine diseases and disorders (although it would take fewer pages than to enumerate all of our human ailments). We have seen the most common cases in which an owner can intervene to protect his dog's health. There is no point in discouraging dog owners with descriptions of all the viral, bacteriological, and functional menaces to their pets. Many of them are the same as human ailments and require professional diagnosis and treatment: pneumonia, tonsillitis, rheumatism, diabetes, epilepsy, skin troubles, organic disorders, tumors, and venereal infections such as metritis (see page 360) and canine brucellosis (see page 330).

Remember that dogs are more resistant to disease than we are—

although they are more exposed to infection too. If you provide your dog with protection against the principal contagious diseases, and if you give him a wholesome environment and a well-balanced diet, he should lead a long and healthy life.

YOUR DOG'S MEDICINE CHEST

Nevertheless, it is always wise to be prepared for an emergency. So, when you acquire a dog, you should also prepare a special medicine cabinet for him, composed of remedies for the most common emergencies. For example:

—a paper with the name, address, and telephone number of your regular vet and of the nearest animal clinic
—absorbent cotton
—cotton swabs
—adhesive tape
—gauze bandage (2 or 3 inches wide)
—elastic self-adhesive bandage of the same width
—nail clippers
—rectal thermometer
—blunt-nosed scissors
—alcohol
—aromatic spirits of ammonia
—mercurochrome
—3 per cent hydrogen peroxide
—styptic pencil or powder
—boric acid eyewash
—1 per cent yellow mercuric oxide ophthalmic ointment
—a healing salve or powder
—an antihistamine (ointment and oral)
—a tannic-acid burn ointment
—aspirin
—flea powder
—bicarbonate of soda
—a canine tranquilizer
—vaseline
—germicidal soap
—milk of magnesia
—witch hazel

11.

Your Dog's Psychology

Dog lovers tend to attribute human characteristics to their pets. Dog haters consider them unfeeling beasts. The truth, of course, is somewhere in between. Dogs are dogs. Their mental and physical capacities are different from ours, inferior in most ways, superior in some. Although a pet dog brought up as a member of the family is often similar to a child in his behavior and reactions, it is a mistake to try to promote him on the biological scale and place him on a level with humanity. Instead, we should accept him for what he is and make an effort to understand his canine mentality.

Scientific experiments have taught us quite a lot about canine psychology. Observation and conjecture provide us with many further suppositions.

Dogs, like children, are influenced by environment as well as by heredity. The argument as to which of these is stronger still rages among child psychologists, but canine authorities agree that while environment certainly affects a dog's behavior and character, heredity is even more important. He inherits not only physical characteristics and working instincts, but also certain temperamental attributes, a certain intellectual capacity, and a certain amount of "inherited knowledge" which ensures his survival and procreation.

The dog is a less complex creature than man, and his psychology is less sophisticated. All dogs share certain basic psychological patterns which vary in detail, just as ours do. An understanding of the instincts and aptitudes that are common to all dogs will therefore help you to know your own dog better, to train him more effectively, and to live with him more happily. Furthermore, you will recognize the limits of his physical and mental capacities and be able to exploit them to the fullest without asking too much of him, or being satisfied with too little.

A DOG'S FIVE SENSES

The dog receives impressions from the outside world through his five senses, which are the same as man's, but of a different quality. He sees, smells, and hears the world around him quite differently from the way we do.

His EYESIGHT, for example, is not as keen as ours, with the exception of Sight Hounds, which have been selectively bred for long-distance vision. Other breeds are myopic and tend to become increasingly shortsighted as they age. The eyesight of the average dog has been aptly compared to that of a shortsighted person who has lost his glasses. The range of vision of small and medium breeds is also restricted by the fact that they are so close to the ground. Peripheral vision varies according to the breed, depending on the way the dog's eyes are set in his skull. The close-set eyes of Terriers obviously encompass less than those of Collies or Greyhounds, which are placed more to the sides of the head, like a horse's. Most dogs, however, possess as great a scope of vision (or greater) as our own modest one of some 180 degrees. On the other hand, their binocular vision (the area they see with both eyes at the same time) is generally inferior to ours.

Despite the skepticism of most owners, scientists maintain that dogs, like all four-footed mammals, are color-blind, distinguishing only various degrees of color intensity, and thus seeing everything in different shades of gray. At the same time, the canine eye is particularly keen to detect movement. A Greyhound can spot a moving object half a mile away. The dog's night vision is also better than ours, since he can dilate his pupil more in the dark and is aided by the acuity of his other senses, perhaps too by his whiskers. Animals whose eyes shine in the dark possess the keenest night vision.

Dogs probably cannot see quite as clearly as we do, because their focusing element, the forea, is very rudimentary compared to ours, causing an inferior sense of depth and distance, and only a vague discrimination of patterns and forms. However, some dogs are more observant of detail than others. One dog will cock his head or howl in approval or protestation when his owner appears with a new haircut, or moves an object from its usual place, whereas another will never notice the change. Some authorities claim that dogs are unable to focus on details at all, and that their unfailing ability to distinguish between adults and children, even between a small adult and a large child, or a large puppy and an adult Toy dog, is due to scent and intuition rather than to observation. But it is a fact that dogs are very interested in the faces of animals and people, and certainly notice changes of facial expression. Performing dogs who seem to have learned to count, add, and subtract are usually responding to eye-blinking signals from the handler.

Some dogs even develop visual phobias, manifesting fear or hostility whenever they encounter a person wearing boots, for example, or a long black garment. Many dogs are suspicious of anything black.

Their reaction to reflected images, such as mirrors and television screens, as well as to photographs and portraits, is unlike ours. It seems that only man and chimpanzees are fascinated by their own reflections. Dogs seem to recognize the species, but not themselves. They generally investigate by sniffing, discover at once that the image is inanimate, and lose all interest in it.

The dog's SENSE OF SMELL is infinitely stronger than ours. Hunting dogs and Scent Hounds have developed extraordinary olfactory powers, with the Bloodhound the undisputed champion of them all, capable of performing incredible exploits of scent detection. There is a simple explanation for this marked superiority. The dog possesses in his nasal and throat passages millions of tiny air cavities receptive to odors, which are countless times more numerous than ours. His olfactory lobes (the part of the brain receiving the olfactory nerve messages) are also more highly developed. Tests have proven that he can smell a drop of blood in 5 gallons of water, a bone that is buried 2 feet deep, a bird 200 feet away, and a teaspoon of salt (an almost odorless substance) in 13 gallons of water. Long-nosed breeds with large nostrils, which have a wider area of scent cells, naturally possess greater scenting ability than short-nosed breeds.

The dog's memory for scent is absolutely fantastic, precise enough to be his principal means of identification. Sometimes a dog will fail to recognize a person by sight, even by the sound of his voice, but as soon as he is within sniffing distance, recognition is immediate. Dogs are also capable of analyzing scents, distinguishing a familiar odor in a mass of different ones, as when a Bloodhound designates the culprit he is seeking from a group of suspects, or when an obedience-trained dog selects an object his owner has handled from an assortment of identical articles.

The dog's highly developed sense of smell is a valuable asset in hunting, guarding, tracking, mountain lifesaving, and many other activities. Dogs have been trained to detect a wide variety of things, including explosives, drugs, and truffles. Bomb-detecting dogs patrol 24 major American airports, and have proven to be quicker and more accurate than human searchers after bombing threats on ocean liners, in warehouses, skyscrapers, trucks, and mailbags. Incidentally, in most breeds the sense of scent or sight seems to predominate, the German Shepherd being the outstanding exception to this general rule, for his sight is as keen as his scenting ability.

The dog's SENSE OF HEARING is also better than ours. In addition to what the human ear can capture, he can detect fainter sounds from greater distances and on higher frequencies: at least 25,000 cycles, and as high as 50,000—compared to our maximum of 15,000 or 20,000, beyond which everything is inaudible to us. Dogs are able to determine the direction from which a sound is emitted much more accurately than we can, except when the source of sound is higher than they are. They can also differentiate better than we can between similar sounds. For example, if one dog is called "Tom" and another "Ron," each will quite clearly distinguish his name. Breeds with erect ears have keener hearing than those with floppy, pendulous ones, for their ears act as trumpets, capturing and intensifying sounds. This, of course, was the original purpose of cropping the ears of Dobermans, Great Danes, and Boxers, as an aid to their guarding aptitudes.

The dog's ultrasensitive hearing has been exploited in many ways. Some hunters use "soundless" high-frequency whistles to guide their dogs in the field. All dog-training methods start with voice commands. Because dogs clearly distinguish different pitches, the tone of your commands is as significant to him as the words that you pronounce. Since he responds most quickly to sharp sounds, you will find it easier to get a puppy to come when called if you reinforce your voice command with whistling or hand-clapping at first. Emergency instructions such as "STOP" should always be sharper in tone than ordinary communications. Dogs love being talked to in a very soft voice, almost a whisper.

Any unexpected or unusual voice will alert a dog. His immediate reaction is to twitch his mobile ears, cock his head, or face the direction of the sound and then approach the spot, warily or aggressively, as his intuition dictates. Familiar sounds like the rattling of his food bowl, his owner's footsteps, and the motor of the family car, are identified at once, even from a distance.

Nevertheless, dogs seldom recognize voices over the telephone or radio, perhaps because it does not occur to them to focus their attention on these inanimate objects; perhaps also, due to the voice distortion and to extraneous sound vibrations imperceptible to the human ear. On the other hand, they recognize words and commands they have been taught even when they are pronounced by different voices and in different tones.

Dogs perceive sound by feeling as well as through their auditive equipment. They react to the vibrations of airplanes and earthquakes long before we are aware of them. Continued strident or percussive noises can cause them real suffering. A dog may seem to have a pathological fear of thunderstorms or explosions, when the real reason for his cringing behavior or attempt to hide is simply physical pain.

Oddly enough, considering their aural sensitivity, dogs seldom suffer from vertigo, which is commanded from the inner ear. Curious and bold dogs can follow their owners over narrow ramps, look through the railings of high balconies, into deep holes and over cliffs, without any apparent dizziness (although they prefer ground level).

The dog's SENSE OF TASTE is very weak compared to ours. He gulps his food without really tasting it at all, and accepts or rejects a meal or tidbit on the basis of odor rather than flavor. It is useless to try to tempt a fussy eater with gourmet recipes. Instead, try to bring out the aroma of his regular meals by quickly grilling or searing his meat, or by soaking his dry food in warm water for a few minutes. The various "flavors" prepared by commercial dog food manufacturers are more often the result of scent additives than of different basic ingredients.

Taste is a highly conditional sense in dogs. A puppy will often refuse a lump of sugar, which has little or no odor. But after he has been encouraged to eat it, he will find it to his liking and afterward accept it readily, even beg for it. Many dogs like candy and cake only because their owners do. Their personal preference is for stronger flavors, even some that are disgusting to us. However, a dog who suddenly develops an interest in garbage or manure is probably seeking to complete a diet deficient in cereals, salt, or minerals, rather than to satisfy his gourmandise.

Unlike humans, dogs do not require variety in their diets in order to stimulate their appetites. They eye a new food with suspicion, and are quite satisfied with the same familiar menu day after day.

This lack of taste would be of no importance if it did not comport a serious danger: the ease with which a dog can be poisoned. Many poisons are odorless, and he will unsuspectingly swallow them without realizing it until it is too late. Since you cannot depend on his own taste discrimination, you must try to protect him by training him from puppyhood to eat only what you give him at mealtimes or from your hand, by keeping poisonous substances out of reach, by preventing him from investigating garbage pails, which often contain caustic waste, and by stopping him from picking up stray bits of edible material he may find around the house or in the street.

The dog's SENSE OF TOUCH differs from ours mainly in that he lacks our sensitive fingertips. On the other hand, we do not have his whiskers, which grow out of wart-like lumps that contain nerve endings, but seem to be of little practical sensory significance.

Dogs can distinguish different textures through the pads of their paws as well as the nose, and this ability is utilized in certain housebreaking methods. A dog who has been trained to paper, cement, grass, or sand, will often automatically lift his leg or squat whenever he feels a similar surface under his feet.

Most dogs are sensitive to heat, but more for respiratory reasons than because of discomfort. They tolerate the cold much better than we do, and are more apt to catch cold from drafts than from low temperatures. They are fussier where food is concerned, preferring water cool and food at room temperature.

Dogs probably feel pain to the same degree that we do, with the same individual variations, some being more stoical than others. Roughhousing puppies are more gentle than they seem. When one of them becomes overexcited enough to inflict real pain, an indignant yelp from his playmate reminds him that he is breaking the rules. Dogs weaned and sold at an early age are far more likely to become biters than are those who have remained long enough with their littermates to develop this natural social inhibition. During dogfights, the flow of adrenalin acts as a temporary anesthetic, and the dog's apparent insensitivity is merely an illusion. Dense coats and thick skins (such as those of St. Bernards and Terriers) naturally offer more protection from pain, heat, and cold than do smooth coats and fine skins (such as those of Greyhounds and Whippets). Some dogs are squeamish about injections, eye- and eardrops, and even simple grooming procedures. But this is probably more mental than physical, like children who make a scene over being bathed or vaccinated.

If you remember that the dog's most sensitive points are the same as ours (the genitalia, nose, inside the thighs, and under the forearms), and that his reaction to pain is similar, you should be able to give him any normal handling without ever hurting him. But you may have to be very strict with children and prohibit sadistic games such as pulling tails, poking with sticks, or picking up puppies by their ears, all of which cause pain and may elicit a perfectly justified reaction of self-defense.

It is never necessary to inflict pain during training, even in order to administer a deserved correction. Your own clearly expressed displeasure is the most effective punishment for your dog. Electric training devices which cause mild pain in order to establish certain automatic reflexes may live up to their claims. But the robot-like reactions they produce cannot compare to the obedience of a dog who has been educated to use his brain rather than his nerve endings in responding to your commands.

SIXTH, SEVENTH, AND EIGHTH SENSES

Does the dog possess a sixth sense? Yes, indeed. In fact, not only does he possess a sixth (a sense of orientation), but also a seventh (a sense of time) and an eighth (intuition).

The dog's uncanny SENSE OF ORIENTATION has never been fully explained, although it is documented by countless cases of lost or abandoned dogs finding their way home again, sometimes from enormous distances. Even more mysterious is the ability of some dogs to rejoin their owners who have moved to some faraway place, completely unknown to the dogs, to which memory or scent could not possibly have guided them. They obviously cannot steer their course according to the sun or to star patterns, as migrating birds are believed to do. Perhaps it is a question of magnetic fields, as "supernaturalists" propose. For the moment, it remains one of Nature's mysteries. We know, however, that the dog's homing instinct tends to diminish with civilized life and urban residence, as do many atavistic behavior patterns. So if you love your dog, give him a collar with your name and address on it and do not count on his own ability to find his way home.

The dog's SENSE OF TIME may be merely a combination of observation, memory, and habit. In any case, he seems to know to the minute when it is mealtime, when school is over, and when the mail arrives. But many dogs also know which day is Sunday, the date and hour inscribed on your return plane ticket, and the day the children are due to arrive home from summer camp. This too may be due to sharp observation and nothing else. But could there be a psychic element as well?

All dogs enjoy adhering to a regular schedule. If you establish a time-table for meals, exercise, training, and grooming sessions, your dog will appreciate the sense of security it gives him. It will save you time and trouble too, because when the hour arrives, he will already be in the mood or resigned to the next activity, as the case may be.

Canine INTUITION is another faculty we are unable to explain or understand very well, although there is massive evidence of its existence. Dogs obviously possess a perception that does not depend on conscious application of their senses. Do you know a single dog owner whose pet has not, at one time or another, performed a feat of extrasensory perception?

Countless incidents attest to the dog's uncanny foresight in warning of impending danger. It is true that many of them can be explained by his sense of smell and hearing—in detecting the rumbles that precede an earthquake, for example, or the scent of smoldering before a fire breaks out. But what about the "scent" of death? Dogs often howl, a weird and wailing cry, when death is imminent in a home, even when a member of the family is ill or dying many miles away. (Do not be alarmed, though, whenever a dog howls. He howls for many other reasons too.)

Dogs certainly sense changes in the weather, changes in our moods, impending departures and arrivals, our illnesses and pains, even our secret intentions. They also sense and share our attractions and antipathies. Many of these apparent feats of intuition (perhaps most of them) are due to the acuity of other senses. But some of them defy any logical explanation and must be accepted as genuine psychic phenomena. These generally fall into one of two categories: clairvoyance of some future event, most frequently of danger to himself or those he loves; and telepathy, which enables a dog to remain attuned to his owner's thoughts and activities, and especially to his state of health and safety, even when he is very far away.

INTELLIGENCE

The intelligence of the dog is among the highest of the animal kingdom, perhaps higher than we give him credit for. Although his brain is proportionately only half as large as ours, he is certainly the most intelligent of domestic animals.

As with humans, individual intelligence varies greatly according to inherited genes. While no one breed can be said to be more intelligent than another, some strains that have been selectively bred for intelligence and working ability are often brighter and more receptive than those bred primarily for specific physical attributes. Intelligence may be affected to a certain degree by skull shape. There is obviously less brain room in dogs with exaggeratedly narrow and elongated heads, and perhaps in those with excessively foreshortened ones. Intelligence is also influenced by environment and experience.

Mongrels are no more intelligent than purebred dogs—probably less so. They have had to use and therefore develop the intelligence they were born with, whereas too many modern pet dogs are obliged to lead an overprotected, confined, and stultifying life. You do not have to turn your dog onto the streets in order to develop his intelligence. Simply give him an opportunity to investigate and manipulate all sorts of objects, to explore all sorts of places, to share all sorts of experiences with you, and to learn to obey simple commands. Aside from getting a lot more out of life, your dog will be eager to learn more, and he will learn with increasing ease and rapidity. Nothing is sadder and more wasteful than an intelligent dog who is confined in a kennel and deprived of mental stimulation.

The dog's INTELLECTUAL CAPACITY is limited by his inability to think abstractly, his meager means of communication, and his absence of logical foresight. He can distinguish between different sounds and associate them with different objects and actions. But it is impossible for him to go beyond the concrete universe into the realm of abstract thought.

"If you do not eat now, you will have to wait until tomorrow," is far too abstract an idea—moreover, involving foresight, which he lacks—for him to understand. "Eat your dinner," in the form of a command, is well within his grasp. But do not expect him to be grateful to you for sparing him midnight hunger pangs. That sort of imagination is beyond his means.

He is not completely lacking in IMAGINATION. But it is more a remembrance of past experience than creative fantasy, as you can easily observe in sleeping dogs who drool when they presumably dream of food, twitch their legs when probably dreaming of hunting, and react appropriately to erotic dreams and nightmares.

Despite opinions to the contrary, dogs are endowed with an elementary REASONING POWER, as has been proven by many experiments in which problems of mazes and mechanical devices had to be solved in order to attain an edible reward. Anyone who has ever owned a dog has often seen him size up a situation and then take some logical action. Guide Dogs for the blind, as well as Working and Hunting dogs of many breeds, constantly have to use their own judgment and make decisions. When faced with alternatives, a dog, like a young child, is apt to choose the one that offers the most immediate satisfaction. But he obviously gives the matter some thought, which indicates an attempt, at least, to reason.

MEMORY is an important component of intelligence. The dog's memory for scents is extraordinary. His visual memory is only fair. His memory for sounds is very good, since he can remember and identify familiar footsteps and voices even after an absence of many years. While he builds up a large store of identifiable sounds without the slightest effort, remembering different words requires greater concentration. Some dogs are quicker than others to develop a vocabulary. The record-holder is probably a famous German Shepherd, "Fellow," who was studied by Columbia University psychologists. He could recognize 400 different words, no matter who pronounced them. But all dogs, even those of only ordinary intelligence, can learn many names and words if they are repeated often enough. The more you talk to your dog, the more words he will learn and retain.

The dog's *capacity for learning* is more a matter of memory than of true understanding. He will remember the sequence of cause and effect in his actions, but he is unable to draw broad conclusions from his experiences. For example, you can scold a puppy for chewing up a shoe, and he will be impressed by the fact that if he chews a shoe he will be punished. But he will never grasp the basic principle that articles of clothing should not be used as playthings.

HOW DOES A DOG LEARN? First of all, by imitation. The puppy's first teacher is his mother, who simply performs some act and encourages her offspring to follow her example. Then, dogs learn (as we do) from experience, and the more different experiences they have, the more they learn. They also manage to solve problems by trial and error. Thanks to their excellent memory, dogs seldom make exactly the same mistake twice. The knowledge acquired in these ways can only be of a practical kind. Advanced education, including the meaning of words, obedience to commands, good manners, and more sophisticated behavior patterns, requires training with a human instructor.

In short, dogs are bound by nature to remain intellectually inferior to man. And a lucky thing it is for us, for otherwise we might lose much of the esteem that permits us to be so willingly accepted as their masters. However, in assuming this flattering role, we should also accept the responsibilities that go with it, and one of these is to give our dogs a chance to develop their native intelligence.

EMOTIONS

Dogs are much more similar to human beings in their emotions than they are in their mentality. Some of their emotional reactions are so much like ours that we tend to humanize them, which is almost as great a mistake as going to the opposite extreme and considering them unfeeling beasts.

The dog's emotions are visibly expressed in his eyes and face, his ear and tail carriage, his posture, movements, and general behavior. Sometimes they are vocally expressed as well. He can feel and express the same emotions we do: love, hate, joy, sorrow, grief, anxiety, jealousy, remorse, fear, anger, and even more subtle ones such as distrust and resignation. Pet dogs have an endearing tendency to imitate their owners' emotional reactions, which may not weigh much in an argument, but certainly offers moral support.

Dogs are no more individual in expressing their emotions than we are. Just as all human beings laugh or cry in appropriate circumstances, all dogs wag their tails and wriggle their bodies to express happiness, friendliness, and enthusiasm. Fear, hostility, and aggressiveness are visible in the bristling ridge of hair along the spine, an extended tail, bared teeth, and a wrinkled nose, with or without accompanying sound effects. Dogs approach and seek contact with objects and beings that inspire friendly feelings, and avoid or shy away from those they fear or find repugnant. Often a dog will simply pretend not to see a person or animal he dislikes. A crouching position and a watchful eye mean that he has not yet made up his mind about trusting or distrusting an approaching stranger. Intense fear can cause defecation, and terror sets off the emptying of the anal glands with their horrid odor. Dogs can also be literally paralyzed by fear.

Some canine facial expressions are very much like ours. They too can produce adoring gazes, worried frowns, angry glares, suspicious squints, twinkling humor, questioning looks, seductive glances, and even genuine smiles. Guilt feelings are so evident in a dog's face that human beings who are ashamed or remorseful are said to have a "hangdog" look. Teeth-baring by pulling the corners of the lips back is friendly, like a smile; but baring the incisors and canine teeth by raising the upper lip is hostile and threatening. A smile accompanied by half-closed eyes and ears held low signifies intense pleasure.

Body language is used extensively by dogs to express their feelings, especially when establishing social relationships. A wagging tail and

Expressions and postures of dogs as recorded in *Le Livre de la Chasse* of Gaston Phébus (c. 1405). (*Courtesy of the Bibliothèque Nationale*)

friendly grin are invitations to approach and perhaps make friends, while a snarl, a fixed stare, stiff, straight legs and tail, are warnings to keep one's distance.

This question of distance, incidentally, is of great importance to dogs, undoubtedly for reasons of self-preservation. An observant owner who notes the distance at which his dog keeps other dogs and people will have an accurate idea of their social relationship to him. Family and intimate friends can come as close as they like, and the closer the better. A canine or human neighbor may be accepted as a friend only beyond a certain radius. If they overstep the limit, they will be chased away, or at least chased back to the distance which the dog considers fitting. A strange dog or an enemy will be chased to an even greater distance, probably beyond the boundaries of the territory where, no longer a threat, it is no longer of interest.

Dogs often give voice to their emotions, and their meaning is generally clear. A happy dog gurgles or squeals with pleasure. A gentle whine can often be translated as "Please." Snarling is definitely hostile, either fearful or aggressive (but sometimes a reaction to pain). Growling, on the other hand, can be a menace (much more than barking), an invitation to play, or a sign of impatience. It may also be a bad habit the dog has acquired from a playmate. Dogs yelp from pain or fright, whine from frustration or discomfort, and sigh for the same reasons we do. Puppy cries are easy to interpret. They scream when they are too hot, whimper when they are cold, and protest loudly when they are hungry. Whining bitches and howling dogs who have scented or heard them are expressing respectively their availability and their interest.

COMMUNICATION

What about *barking?* Is it a form of language among dogs, with precise significance?

Almost certainly not. When a dog goes to his owner and deliberately barks, it is merely to attract his attention. You must try to guess what he wishes to communicate from the circumstances and his general demeanor, rather than from the particular form of yip, yap, or yelp that he emits. Dogs who bark for no apparent reason, like kennel dogs who bark at night, are probably simply working off excess energy or manifesting their presence, and this is undoubtedly the only message conveyed to other dogs within earshot. The baying of Hounds is an instinctive hunting cry informing the pack that the dog is on a trail. Pet Beagles who bay are probably expressing the same instinct, even though the normal stimulus for it may be absent.

Barking at strange noises is a warning as well as a threat display. A lonely dog who howls may be sending out an atavistic gathering cry, for it is what the wolf does when he has lost contact with the pack. Wild dogs, in fact, never bark. They only howl. Could the barking of domesticated dogs be a sort of refinement, a step toward some more precise form of communication more closely resembling human speech? A pet dog who shares a close relationship with his owner and has been taught to understand many words of human speech obviously makes an effort, sometimes quite successfully, to impart meaning to his own utterances, which are far more varied than those of kennel dogs.

Dogs are more advanced than man in agreeing on an international language, if we can judge by our phonetic transcription of barking in different lands. In English-speaking countries they say "Bow wow" or "Woof woof"; in France, "Ouah-ouah"; in Germany, "Vow vow"; in Sweden, "Vov vov." The Spanish spell it "Guao guao" and pronounce it "Wow wow" too. In an ancient Greek comedy by Aristophanes there is a speaking part for a dog who says "Ow-wow." In China, however, your dog would need an interpreter, for there, it seems, they say "Wang-wang."

Dogs exchange information among themselves less by voice than by a wide range of *facial expressions, body postures and gestures,* as well as by *various scents.* A dog who wishes to assert his importance and boldness instinctively employs all of the effects that make him look bigger and more frightening: rising hackles on his neck and back in order to increase his height, and a peculiar gait as if he were walking on stilts. A dog who wishes to express submission does just the contrary. He makes himself as small as possible by crouching low with his tail between his legs and his ears laid back flat, his head close to the ground. Both of these messages are perfectly clear to other dogs.

A dog who wishes to assert his dominance will take a perpendicular position with his head over the other dog's shoulders, perhaps nudging or pushing, his neck arched, head and tail raised and tense. Merely shoving another dog with his hip or shoulder, or placing the forepaws on his back, may also be an act of dominance—when it is not an invitation to play or to mate. The conventional play invitation is a posture with the forehand crouched, the hindquarters high, a gaily wagging tail, a bright eye, and perhaps a little yip. A rigid stance with a steady gaze and a high, trembling tail is hostile, or at least self-assertive. A high, steady tail signifies self-confidence. Held low, it indicates inferiority, fatigue, ill health, or a bad mood. Held between the legs, it is an expression of fear, shame, or an inferiority complex.

Licking is a sign of friendship and affection, a request for pardon, or a sexual gesture. Nipping may have sexual implications too, but it can also express a desire for attention or be a part of play. Pawing at the neck is an expression of affection; puppies do it to adults, and males to females. Nose-nudging is another invitation to play. Paw-giving is a conventional canine gesture with two possible meanings. When a dog spontaneously gives his paw to his owner, it is either a sign of contrition or an attention-getter, as if to say, "I'm sorry, please forgive me" (in which case he usually avoids eye contact in an exaggerated fashion), or "I'm here, please don't forget me." When he offers his paw to another dog, it is a symbol of submission, the lower-ranking dog or puppy presenting his paw as a sort of homage to his superior. You will most often see this gesture among breeds that have a strong sense of social rank, such as German Shepherds and Collies. The most abject form of submission is, of course, the voluntary exposure of vulnerable areas by lying on the back.

As for scent communication, dogs are equipped to produce a variety of odors that transmit to other dogs sexual messages, alarms, territorial and trail information, as well as clues to social behavior.

An owner who takes the trouble to observe his dog and pay him the courtesy of listening to him, can establish a simple two-way communications system with his pet. Canine messages are generally very elementary, as he asks much less of us than we do of him. "I'm hungry," "I'm thirsty," "I need to go out," or "Come with me, I think something is wrong," are among the messages he manages to convey remarkably well, considering his limited means. His most eloquent utterance is perhaps the emotion-strangled gurgle or arpeggio of barks that means to say, "It's about time you came home. I've missed you!"

CHARACTER

The traits of character we find in dogs are also very similar to those found in human beings: courage, timidity, selfishness, altruism, patience, nervousness, loyalty, generosity, laziness, tenacity, jealousy, determination, sensitivity, even a sense of humor. Dogs of the same breed tend to share the same general traits, as we have seen. But individuals vary widely in their temperamental composition, and consequently in their reactions to the same conditions.

A puppy starts to develop his personality after his eyes have opened. You can help to form it by encouraging a timid puppy, for example, and by teaching self-discipline to an aggressive one. But the most we can hope for is to teach a dog to control his behavior, not to alter his basic character. We can train a jealous dog to tolerate another dog in the house, but he will remain a jealous dog who behaves correctly (perhaps a jealous dog who sulks). Shyness and pugnacity are the most difficult traits to deal with. If they are due to genetic weakness, they are practically incurable.

Nevertheless, dogs are generally more malleable than children, because of their adaptability and their innate desire to please. Some breeds with a long history of human companionship are capable of developing very refined personalities. Others, like some of the Sight Hounds and very large breeds, are apt to remain more elementary in character, perhaps because of the practical difficulties involved in sharing as many experiences with them.

What is the ideal character of a dog? It all depends on the role you wish him to play in your life. For a pet dog, one might say that he should be self-confident without being too bold; devoted and loyal without being overprotective; pleasant with strangers without being overfriendly; alert but not nervous; inquisitive and eager to learn but not a wanderer.

Theoretically, such a pet, if he has ever existed, would be temperamentally perfect. In actual practice, the perfect character of a dog is that of the dog you love. We have all met egotistical dogs, belligerent dogs, stupid dogs, slovenly dogs, and quite odious dogs, who have so endeared themselves to their owners that the owners have become blind to their faults. If you happen to own such a dog and if you really love him, you should, of course, attempt to reform his character. But if the dog belongs to one of your friends or relatives, you would be well advised to refrain from pointing out his obvious deficiencies. They may be just what his owner most admires in him.

INSTINCTS

In addition to his physiological equipment and his inherited traits, the dog's behavior is influenced by certain basic instincts of which you should be aware if you wish to understand your dog. Some of them have been attenuated by the protected life led by modern pets. In fact, the dog as a species seems to be undergoing an important period in his evolution, since never before in history have so many of them been bred exclusively as pets.

The INSTINCT FOR SURVIVAL is common to all living creatures. No acquired behavior pattern is strong enough to dominate entirely this powerful drive. When it is aroused, the only effective means of controlling it is constraint.

The INSTINCT FOR PROCREATION—in other words, the mating

instinct—involves numerous behavior patterns. It is normally very strong, although it varies among dogs to the same degree that it varies among human beings, and for the same reasons of health condition, hormonal balance, opportunity and, more rarely, psychological inhibitions. But we will come to that in Chapter 15, "Your Dog's Sex Life."

Another instinct common to man and dog is the NEED FOR COM-PANIONSHIP. Many canine personality disturbances have no other cause than the solitary confinement that is imposed on them by people who expect dogs to accept conditions which human society reserves for hardened criminals. The dog's preference for human attachments over those with other animals, which probably originated for practical reasons of survival, seems to have since become instinctive in many breeds. It is certainly dormant in most of them and can be aroused by early human handling. Dr. Konrad Lorenz, the Austrian Nobel Prize-winning expert on animal behavior, was one of the first to study the subject, and his conclusions have been confirmed by the research of illustrious colleagues, including Clarence Pfaffenberger and Dr. Michael Fox, who have written enlightening books on dog psychology. It seems that the critical period when a puppy forms his primary attachment to either canine or human society is between the ages of 3 and 10 weeks. If he is "imprinted" by sufficient pleasurable human relations during this time, he is apt to remain forever attached to humanity. But if he is confined in a kennel with other dogs and deprived of human love and companionship, he will prefer animal to human society throughout his life.

As an extension of their instinct for companionship, most dogs are gregarious. They are attracted to other dogs. All puppies are attracted to children. They are also attracted by movement and excitement. They want to be where the action is.

Once there, dogs like to conform. This is one of the reasons why group obedience classes are so successful, and also why an older, well-trained dog is the best professor for a puppy, since the puppy will instinctively imitate the older dog's behavior. Housebreaking poses no problem if a puppy is brought into a home where there is already a housebroken adult dog.

Like human beings, dogs are vulnerable to mob psychology. The PACK INSTINCT is a more accurate term, or even "the call of the wild," because it usually awakens the most savage side of their nature. It may take no more than one other dog for this psychological phenomenon to occur. (Even wolf packs consist of only 6 to 10 family members, and not of a hundred or so, as is popularly believed.) For example, most dogs learn to live in harmony with a cat, when there are only the two of them in the home. But if you bring a cat-chasing dog onto the scene, his example will arouse the cat-chasing instinct that is dormant in your own pet, and once awakened, it is very difficult to suppress again. Likewise, most dogs desire to please the owner they respect. But once they become a member of a pack, atavism takes over and the owner is forgotten. It is therefore important never to let your dog run loose and unaccompanied where he can get into bad company.

We should also realize that most dogs retain an atavistic NEED FOR A PACK LEADER, and that this is the role we play in our pet's life. Dogs in whom this instinct is strongest are also the most trainable, such as German Shepherds, Doberman Pinschers, and many Working and Hunting breeds. They are the ones who follow you around as puppies, who never want to leave your side as adults, who listen to you, study your facial expressions, and enjoy being handled and caressed. Without the slightest servility, they seek the approval of their pack leader and will do for free, so to speak, what other dogs need to be bribed to do.

Most owners provide protection, food, and shelter, as do wildlife pack leaders. But in order to fill all of the latter's functions, they must also offer leadership, enforce discipline, and maintain their prestige and authority. In this regard, psychological superiority is more important than greater physical strength, even in the animal kingdom. In a home where there are several dogs, it is not always the biggest and strongest who is the leader. Moreover, the modern dog's dependence on his owner is as much emotional as it is physical.

Your dog will love and respect you more if you live up to his leader image of you. Be dependable and consistent so that he can trust you. Be reasonable and fair in order to avoid offending his innate sense of justice. But above all, do not think it is a kindness to let your dog always have his way. In their wild state, dogs instinctively seek and accept leadership as well as a strict social code. In fact, discipline and obedience are probably more natural to them than indulgence, which they have experienced only as modern pets.

The TERRITORIAL INSTINCT has a profound influence on a dog's behavior, as it has on ours, if we are to believe modern ethologists who have done much research on the subject. It is obviously related to the instinct for self-preservation and is therefore powerful, since the acquisition and defense of a territory by an individual, a pack of animals, or a nation of citizens, is vital to its subsistence as well as to its safety.

Puppies as young as 2 or 3 weeks old display their sense of territory by refusing to soil a certain area, and by annexing a certain corner of the nest, a bed, cushion, or chair, as their personal domain. Their territory grows bigger as they do. Adult pets transfer their territorial instinct to their owner's home, just as they transfer their pack instinct to their human family.

While dogs spontaneously respect man-made boundaries such as fences, walls, and gates, they also establish markers of their own, such as certain trees, stones, and bushes, which they conscientiously mark with urine and visit regularly, sniffing and refreshing them as necessary.

If you live in a neighborhood where there are many dogs, you can make an interesting experiment. As you walk down the street with your dog, notice at which point one canine neighbor barks and runs to the fence or gate with a defensive attitude, at which point he ceases his display, and at which point the next dog takes over. You will be aware of the mutually accepted, invisible barriers where each dog's territory begins and ends. If you observe your own dog's behavior when he is putting on a territory-defending show for a passer-by, you may find that your property is much larger or smaller than you thought it was.

Domesticated dogs are as respectful of their neighbors' territory as they are jealous of their own, and seldom engage in territorial warfare, as do certain wild animals and most civilized nations. In the animal kingdom, an intruder is always psychologically inferior to an individual who is on his home territory. A tiny Terrier, in these conditions, can chase away a Great Dane. This is also why breeders recommend sending a bitch to a stud dog, instead of the other way around. The male animal, whatever his size and strength, is always braver and bolder in his own domain.

Generally speaking, dogs are most aggressive on their own territory, most submissive on another dog's territory, and most sociable on neutral ground. Experienced dog owners say that an old family dog will make friends more easily with a new puppy if the two are introduced on neutral ground before the newcomer is taken home. The idea seems sound in theory, if seldom practical, so why not try it when you can?

Some breeds and dogs, like some human races and individuals, require more territory than others in order to feel secure. It is more a question of temperament than of size. Pack hunting dogs such as Beagles and Foxhounds, who instinctively crowd together at rest and even at work and play, may be compared to those human races and individuals who happily cluster together in tribal villages, suburban communities, and modern apartment buildings, surrounded by large unpopulated areas. At the same time, other breeds and civilizations achieve a feeling of security only within a vast expanse of private territory, and are ill at ease when they have to live in crowded conditions.

The territorial instinct thus varies in intensity and quality from one breed and individual to another. In dogs, it may also be related to working aptitudes. It is clearly stronger in Herd and Guard dogs than in Hounds and Hunters, who are consequently apt to accept a change of ownership and residence with far greater equanimity than the former.

Still, in all dogs, as in all humanity, there is a territorial instinct. Both species will defend their territory from foreign aggression in one way or another. Oddly enough, both will accept with tolerance, and sometimes even welcome, intrusions by innocent infants, unthreatening inferiors, and attractive members of the opposite sex.

The ROAMING INSTINCT is present in some breeds, but is by no means common to all of them. Some, in fact, have just as strong a compulsion to remain at home, or at least within their territorial boundaries. Neither of these may be basic instincts, but rather behavior patterns related to working aptitudes, to environmental conditions, and especially to sexuality, since non-hunting bitches outside of their heat periods, preadolescent puppies, and castrated males are practically devoid of wanderlust.

An INSTINCT FOR CLEANLINESS is common to all dogs. They are averse to soiling their living quarters, unless forced to do so when they are enclosed there for too long a time. They also instinctively groom themselves and often their canine companions too. Not as well as you can do it, of course, but their efforts at least demonstrate a desire to be clean.

What about the canine INSTINCT FOR DISTINGUISHING BETWEEN GOOD AND EVIL? It is probably nothing but a myth. Too many dogs have enthusiastically greeted robbers and assassins, and too many kindly dog lovers have been attacked and bitten by dogs, for anyone to maintain the contrary. As a judge of human nature, the dog is no more infallible than we are—perhaps because his basic instinct is to distinguish simply between family, friends, and enemies, whereas we ask him to form much more subtle relationships, which are unnatural to him.

Finally, dogs possess an INSTINCTIVE LOYALTY that is much stronger than ours. Once a dog has accepted someone as his master, it is very difficult for him to switch his devotion to another. Better food, greater comfort, kindness, and understanding may not succeed in swaying his allegiance even from an unworthy owner. How cruel it is to respond to such fidelity with indifference and neglect! On the other hand, if you adopt a dog who has been happy in his previous home, give him plenty of time to transfer his loyalty to you. His reluctance to do so right away is to his credit, and you should not be offended by it.

All dogs respect a number of INSTINCTIVE BEHAVIOR PATTERNS. Imitation may be a factor in some of them, but in others a dog could not possibly have observed the act that he has compulsively performed. Many of them must have originated for practical reasons which no longer exist, although the behavior pattern remains. How often dog owners exchange anecdotes of the curious inventions of their pets, only to learn that all of their dogs indulge in the same rituals!

One of these is the dog's peculiar *attachment to bones*. Whenever you give a dog a bone, you are triggering an entire series of primeval rites. He carries off the bone with a stiff tail and a triumphant air, and then must bury it in some secret place. If he suspects that he is being observed, he must dig it up and bury it again somewhere else. A city dog who has no garden for bone-burying will go through the same performance, the only difference being that the bone will turn up underneath a sofa cushion, behind a curtain, or in the toe of a shoe. All of this is most amusing. But do not underestimate the compulsive nature of these acts, which have survived domestication even in well-fed pet dogs. Never take a bone away from a dog unless he has discarded it. Never let children tease a dog by offering him food and then snatching it away. Either action can incite the most docile animal to bare his teeth, or worse, and it would be unfair to blame him under the circumstances.

Never underestimate the dog's primeval instinct to defend his bone! (*Lacz-Lemoine*)

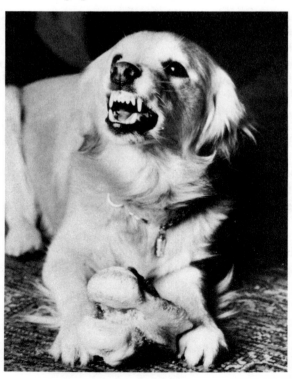

Why do dogs *turn around in circles* before lying down? It has been suggested that this is a pantomime of making a nest in grass or underbrush. According to other theories, the rotation is designed to curve the dog's spine in the most relaxed position, to make sure that no snakes are present, or to place his nose in the direction of the wind in order to capture the scent of approaching enemies. A more modern idea is that he turns in order to place his own magnetic field in harmony with the earth's magnetic lines. Whatever the explanation, the behavior is common to all dogs, as well as to wolves.

One of the dog's most time-consuming rites is the act of *urination.* Male dogs mark their territory with urine and cover (and recover) the urine of other dogs. They leave "calling cards" at communal marking posts. They conscientiously mark their trails as well as their territory. New territory requires a lot of work, while well marked boundaries need only regular maintenance. One of the reasons why a new pet is easily lost is because he has not yet marked his territory or learned to recognize the scent of his neighbors.

Dogs begin to lift their legs at adolescence in an instinctive, untaught gesture, apparently dependent on hormonal development. Females who have been given male hormones as a medical treatment defy convention by lifting their legs too, while male dogs who have been castrated early in life never learn to do it.

Canine greetings are primarily anal, perhaps because the highly individual anal gland secretion is a factor of recognition, and obviously because of the more interesting question of sex identity. When sympathy has been aroused, the next step is to sniff or lick around the muzzle, and sometimes the ears. While this is universal canine behavior and very difficult to prevent, you should try to at least encourage restraint, especially during encounters with strange dogs, if only because so many contagious diseases are transmitted through urine and saliva.

Another atavistic act is *eating grass,* the purpose presumably being to cause regurgitation or to act as a purgative. Dogs are very fussy about the grass they choose, some instinct seeming to guide them to the proper variety.

Turning over on the back is an instinctive canine gesture of varying significance. Performed at the feet of the dog's owner, it is a sign of confidence, recognition of mastery (or, perhaps more often, simply an invitation to scratch his stomach). An adult dog who rolls over on his back in front of a puppy is inviting the infant to play and assuring him that he has nothing to fear. A male dog who does the same with a female is also inviting her to play, undoubtedly less innocent games. A small dog who

Canine greetings are primarily anal. (*Claus Ohm*)

turns over on his back in front of a larger one is recognizing the latter's superiority and suggesting that a confrontation of strength would be unnecessary. At the end of a fight or a tiring game, the dog who lies on his back is conceding victory to his adversary.

Maternity sets off an entire series of canine behavior patterns, as it does in all mammals except for human beings. From the nest-building ritual of a bitch about to whelp, to her regurgitation of partially digested food as an introduction to the weaning process, there are countless instinctive actions, some of them very complicated (see Chapter 17).

A dog can alarm and embarrass his owner by *scratching* himself. It is always a good idea to verify that the dog is not suffering from parasites or some skin disease. But sometimes scratching seems to be a ritual gesture. If one dog scratches for some logical reason, all the other dogs present invariably scratch themselves too. Why? Simply the instinct for imitation? Could scratching be "contagious" like the human yawn? Or is it the observance of some canine rite? *Sniffing* is another act that is compulsively imitated by other dogs, but it is more understandable.

Why do dogs *scratch the ground with their hind feet* after defecation? If it is in order to conceal their waste from prowling enemies, they are

A dog may scratch himself because he has fleas, but he may also be performing some mysterious atavistic canine ritual. (*H. Armstrong Roberts*)

not very efficient about it. It has been suggested that the scraping action transfers scent from the dog's pads to the ground, and is thus another means of marking his territory. It may be merely a nonfunctional display action. Whatever the explanation, the gesture is common among adult male dogs, especially when other dogs are present. But it is rare in females, who are, however, generally more fastidious about such matters.

Chasing is an instinctive activity of all dogs. Puppies love to run after a ball and to play tag with their brothers and sisters as well as with children. It is obviously a vestige of the essential wildlife activities of chasing away marauders and hunting smaller animals for food. While the chasing instinct has remained strong, the ensuing killing has been practically forgotten. We can observe a trace of it in the way dogs vigorously shake pillows, rags, or some retrieved object. Just as often, however, a puppy who is not of a natural retrieving breed will run after a ball or some thrown object and then not quite know what to do with it. Even in the wild, young dogs chase prey instinctively, but have to acquire the skill to catch and kill it.

Finally, certain *working instincts and behavior patterns* have been fixed in certain breeds by selective breeding, so that bird dogs are excited by anything feathered and anything that flies, water dogs are natural swimmers, sheepdogs are instinctively attracted to sheep and cattle, terriers instinctively hunt vermin and investigate holes, guard dogs are instinctively protective of their homes and suspicious of strangers, retrievers instinctively retrieve without having been trained to do so. We should try to offer our pet dogs some substitute activity for their unused working instincts. Above all, we should try to avoid acquiring a dog whose physical appearance may please us, but whose innate instincts are designed for a life entirely different from the one we are able to offer him.

PSYCHOLOGICAL DISTURBANCES

Canine psychology is simpler than human psychology because the dog's mentality is more rudimentary and his imagination less developed. Nevertheless, dogs can suffer from psychological disturbances just as we can, including complexes, phobias, and nervous breakdowns. There even exist canine psychiatrists, whose methods of treatment are similar to those of human specialists: attempts at analysis and rehabilitation, and, increasingly, narcotic and chemical therapy. Sometimes abnormal canine behavior can be traced to a traumatic incident during the patient's puppyhood, often to some emotional deficiency in his home environment. Even more often, it is the owner who needs analysis rather than the dog.

The emotional requirements of a well-balanced dog are virtually the same as those of a well-adjusted child:

A SENSE OF SECURITY. In order to create and maintain it, you should never amuse yourself by inspiring fear in a puppy, tossing him in the air, pretending to drop him, or making terrifying sounds and gestures. Give him a cozy bed in a quiet place and meals at regular hours. Announce your departures whenever possible, and never leave him all alone for long periods of time.

A SENSE OF BEING LOVED AND NEEDED. Be generous with your affection to your dog. Pay attention to him. Try to include him in your plans whenever possible. Give him a sense of individual dignity. Make him feel that he is part of the family.

PHYSICAL AND MENTAL ACTIVITY. Provide your puppy with toys and games and teach him his ABCs. Adult dogs should be given responsibility as well as suitable training. All of them need regular daily exercise.

EDUCATION

The education of dogs and children depends on the effective communication of information and instructions. Children develop by leaps and bounds once they have acquired sufficient vocabulary to understand the meaning of spoken and written words and to ask pertinent questions. But how can we establish the necessary communications with a dog, who lacks the power of speech and cannot learn to read?

The keenest of the canine senses, the sense of smell, is practically unexploitable as a means of communication. We can, however, utilize his sense of hearing. Voice commands and whistles offer many possibilities, thanks to his retentive memory for sounds. We can also utilize his eyesight to teach him visual commands. But it is through his sense of feeling, combined with memory, that results are most quickly achieved, by administering pleasurable feelings (a caress or satisfaction of hunger) or painful ones (mild corporal punishment), in order to communicate simple lessons to him. This is the basis of all conventional training methods.

With a dog of your own, however, pleasure and displeasure are just as effective teaching tools and far less dangerous than pleasure and pain. The pleasure may still take the form of a caress or an edible reward, or merely an expression of praise. But the displeasure need be no more than a scolding tone of voice, a wagging finger, a withdrawal of freedom or attention. "Fellow," the dog with the 400-word vocabulary, was trained by using "Good dog!" as a reward, and "What a shame!" as a punishment, and nothing more. While it is only natural to be impressed by the effectiveness of more severe training methods, you should remember that the relationship between a dog and a professional trainer is very different from the one you wish to establish.

There is another form of communication between a dog and his owner that is quite unique, based on his observation, memory, intuition, but most of all on his devotion. When you have really become friends with your dog, you will find that he understands many of your meanings without the need of audible, visible, or tactile aids.

If you take the trouble to observe your dog as attentively as he studies you, you will be amazed by the depth of mutual understanding that develops between you. You will also be surprised to find how much canine psychology and basic human psychology have in common. Learning to understand your dog will improve your understanding of human nature too.

12.
Playing with Your Dog

Play is an essential activity for the young of most animal species, including man and dogs. We say, "as playful as a puppy," because puppies always seem to be in the mood for fun and games.

Bitches encourage their young to play, realizing instinctively that it is the first step in their education. From their puppy games they learn the rudiments of chasing, preying, and retrieving. They learn to be leaders and followers, and to make many social adjustments. In their rough-and-tumble romps, they learn that male and female bodies are different, and they are better prepared for mating when the time comes than are dogs who have been deprived of the company of the opposite sex during infancy. Most important of all, puppies learn from mock battles that nipping and biting are acceptable only to the point where they cause real pain. This social inhibition, as you know, is practically instinctive with litter-bred puppies, but must be taught to those who have been brought up all alone.

Even after they have outgrown the puppy play stage, the desire to play may be triggered by the sight of a favorite toy; or, on the contrary, a mood for play may set a dog off in search of his ball, which he hopefully deposits at his owner's feet.

Toy dogs are apt to remain playful all their lives. Hunting and Working breeds generally outgrow this stage, if they can apply their energy and sporting instincts to the practical purposes for which they were bred and which they really prefer. Nevertheless, even the most dignified, arthritic old fellow may one day roll over on his back and make a touching attempt to play with a puppy, a child, or a bitch in an interesting condition.

Like children, animals learn much from games, so do not think that playing with your dog is a waste of time. It is not only the first step in his education and useful physical exercise; it is also a bond-forming ritual. Dogs form a stronger attachment to the person who plays with them, works with them, and trains them, than to the person who feeds them and does nothing more. Playing with your dog can be fun for you too. It is certainly a refreshing change from the sophisticated, competitive games that human beings play together.

TOYS

Until he has been weaned, a puppy plays with his littermates, and playthings are unnecessary, uninteresting to him, and possibly dangerous.

From the age of 6 to 8 weeks, he starts to take an interest in toys. Almost anything will do, if you exclude articles that can be swallowed or cause injury. Bits of wood that cannot be splintered or swallowed, pieces of rope, empty plastic milk bottles, three old neckties or stockings braided tightly and securely knotted at the ends, your own fingers and toes, are all delightful playthings to him. Puppies enjoy pulling things, shaking things, carrying things around in their mouths; and, as soon as they are able to run without toppling over, they enjoy chasing things. This is the moment to buy your pet a rubber ball.

Not just any kind of a ball, and certainly not the soft foam-rubber type (which can be chewed to bits and swallowed), nor the inflatable child's ball (which he will soon pierce with his sharp baby teeth, tear to shreds, and perhaps also swallow). Buy him a hard rubber ball that is too large to be swallowed, but small enough for him to hold comfortably in his mouth. Buy it, like all of his toys, in a pet shop rather than a toy shop, and select it with care. Large puppies can be given a worn tennis ball— but never a used golf ball, which contains a poisonous liquid core. Never give a puppy a stuffed animal either, or an object of painted wood or flimsy plastic. Avoid toys resembling actual objects like gloves and slippers, unless you are prepared to face the inevitable consequences. Remember that while children can be warned against putting potentially harmful objects in their mouths, dogs are obliged to pick up everything in their mouths, since they have to use their jaws and teeth to do many of the things for which we use our hands and fingers.

When a puppy is separated from his littermates, he misses them intensely at first. The best substitutes for his regretted playmates are a few toys (one is not enough) with which he can play alone, children (who have been carefully instructed and are supervised if necessary), and you. Try to schedule a regular daily playtime. Never right after a meal, because he needs quiet for proper digestion. And never after a long period of confinement, because the excitement of play will make him want to urinate. Before mealtimes is a good moment. Before bedtime too, but only if he is given an opportunity to empty his bladder before retiring for the night. Whatever the time, the 10 or 15 minutes you devote to playing with your puppy will be the high spot of his day.

During the puppy's teething period (from 3 to 7 months, more or less), you should provide him with chewing toys of digestible rawhide or, even better, a harmless nylon bone of suitable size. They will keep him occupied for hours on end. They will also prevent a lot of destruction. When you spot him gnawing on a chair or table leg, it is much more effective to say "NO" and immediately offer him the alternative of a chew-

Very young puppies enjoy playing together, and toys are unnecessary. (*Terence A. Gil/FPG*)

able bone or ball, than it is to try to suppress by scolding this perfectly natural canine activity which, at teething time, is not only obsessive but also of practical value in dislodging baby teeth to make way for permanent ones.

Like a child, your puppy will become attached to his old toys—to those, at least, which he has not destroyed or lost. But as he grows bigger, you should think of replacing them with others more suitable to his size and strength.

WALKS

When your puppy has completed his protective inoculations, he may be taken for walks. Put on his collar and leash, even if you intend to walk him merely around the yard. It will establish a pleasant association in his mind, and you will never have a problem with leash training.

The first walks are a puppy's introduction to the outside world. They need not be long, certainly not so long as to tire him, but long enough to satisfy his curiosity. Everything will seem wondrous and a bit intimidating to him at first, with all the noise and activity, the strange scents and, in the city, the dense forest of human legs. Keep him close to you, but give him leeway to investigate the things that interest him whenever possible. If he is frightened, take him in your arms, or stop and give him a reassuring caress. Show him that there is no reason to be afraid (if this is so), and do not turn for home immediately, but continue your walk until his fear has been forgotten.

Your own attitude can have a profound effect on the future behavior of your dog. Some owners innocently plant the seeds of shyness or aggressiveness. One of the most common errors is committed by overprotective owners who jerk their puppies away from every friendly dog who prepares to greet them. While it is obviously advisable to avoid contact with diseased or dirty animals, you are merely training your pet to be distrustful and fearful if you prevent him from exchanging a greeting with another healthy dog. (You can usually tell at once from the dog's appearance; if in doubt, size up the owner.) In any case, you can safely let him stretch his neck to sniff the stranger from a distance. You should, of course, remain in control of these casual encounters, although a friendly, confident puppy is rarely attacked. On the other hand, never be indulgent to the point of letting two leashed puppies play together. The result is certain to be an inextricable tangle, maybe a lost or injured pup, or a furious, fallen owner.

Meetings with admiring adults and impulsive children can be handled in the same way: by permitting a restrained exchange of greetings which preserves the friendliness and confidence of both parties.

As your puppy grows older, the daily walk can be longer and brisker. Half an hour to an hour is adequate for most dogs—although Hunting dogs and Hounds would not agree. Even less active breeds living in the city benefit from a weekly outing in an open space where they can run at liberty. It is during adolescence that they need it most. Adult dogs are content with shorter regular exercise sessions. However, overexertion can be as harmful as an insufficient amount of exercise for puppies of large and heavy breeds such as Great Danes, Boxers, and St. Bernards. Too much running and jumping before their bones and joints have become hardened enough to support their considerable weight can cause lifelong infirmities. Care must also be taken with breeds such as Salukis and Deerhounds, whose long legs are very fragile before (and even after) maturity has hardened them. Exercise requirements, as you see, vary from one breed to another.

You may try to diversify your walking itineraries for your own interest. But your dog will be quite satisfied with the same old walk, which for him is always different due to the continually changing scents he meets along the way. In fact, new scents encountered in strange territory are less informative and probably less exciting to him than those he finds at his usual sniffing posts.

Walking with your dog provides many opportunities for teaching him words and commands. He will learn them effortlessly because they are of immediate practical interest to him. So develop the habit of giving him useful instructions as you stroll along. Tell him to STOP at every street crossing, to WAIT for the traffic light to change, to JUMP over a puddle or onto a high curb, to be CAREFUL or SLOW or, on the contrary, to be QUICK, to see the DOG (a word that is very quickly learned), to greet the FRIEND, and so forth. Constant repetition will fix many useful words in his brain.

During your outings, you will discover that some breeds retain atavistic attractions for their original environments. Hounds are apt to take off at a tear in wide-open spaces. Setters scour open terrain in circles or zig-

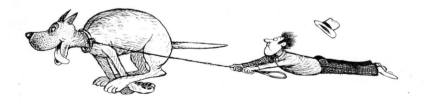

zags rather than a beeline, but with the same spontaneity. Terriers can not resist diving into underbrush and investigating holes. Shepherds tend to gravitate to pastures, and if there are cattle or sheep in them, so much the better. Hunting instincts are aroused by fields and forests. The mere sight of a pond or lake inspires in Water Retrievers, Spaniels, and many Poodles an irresistible urge to go for a swim. If you wish to give your dog a special treat, take him into the kind of country that was the natural habitat of his forefathers. But when you unexpectedly encounter natural conditions that arouse his primeval instincts, recognize the need for reinforced control.

What is the best time to take your dog for a walk? Your dog would say, "Any hour of the day or night." As a matter of fact, most dogs love walking at night, perhaps because the cool evening moisture, which evaporates slowly, is an excellent scent retainer. Nevertheless, since sunshine is healthy for dogs and indispensable for growing puppies, the daily walk should take place during daylight and sunshine whenever possible, later in the afternoon or earlier in the morning during the hot summer months. When you walk your dog on an unlit country road after dark, you might stick some fluorescent tape on his collar and leash. You should certainly carry a strong flashlight.

Dog walking can be a revelation to a novice owner, especially in the city and the suburbs. Admittedly, it is often a bore and an inconvenience. But it is also an introduction to another universe, a world inhabited by other dog owners, which is certainly one of the most democratic, varied, and colorful societies in existence. Even the shyest introvert will not feel lonely when he has become a faithful dog walker. Animal and human contacts are almost unavoidable. Friendships are formed, news and information exchanged, opinions compared. Human as well as canine matings have resulted from the sidewalk encounters of two friendly dogs.

CITY WALKS are the principal form of exercise for urban pets. Try to find a nearby park or enclosed area where you can let your dog stretch his legs for a few minutes, off the lead. If this is impossible, buy an extralong leash and seek a safe spot where he can roam within its limits.

This is unfortunately easier said than done, since more and more cities are banning dogs from wider areas. It is a criminal offense to take a dog into a Chicago park, and the entire Icelandic capital city of Reykjavik is out of bounds for dogs. Before the antidog lobby scores further victories, dog owners can strengthen their position by respecting a few rules when walking their pets on city streets:

—Since most dogs feel the urge to relieve themselves shortly after they are taken out of doors, plan your walk to start with suitable comfort stations. In other words, business first, pleasure later.

—Train your dog to relieve himself in the gutter, and walk him on the curb side of the sidewalk so that you can pull him into the gutter if necessary.

—Always carry a few plastic bags with you. If your dog should make "a mistake" on the sidewalk (or even in the gutter in New York City and in a number of other cities), slip your hand into the bag as if it were a glove, scoop up the feces, then pull the bag inside out in order to enclose it. Twist or tie it shut, and drop it in a waste container. A law requiring owners to clean up their dogs' defecation is being adopted increasingly throughout the United States.

—Never cross the street against a traffic light. Even if the light is green, it is better to wait for the beginning of the next green phase in order to have the full period of time for crossing the street with your dog.

—Try to avoid rush hours and crowded places. When you are unavoidably caught in a crowd, keep your dog close at heel on a short lead or, if he is small enough, carry him in your arms.

—Never let your pet greet a passing dog if the encounter would cause a pedestrian traffic jam.

—Do not let him make advances to strangers either. Some people, believe it or not, do not like dogs.

SUBURBAN WALKS differ little from those in the city. The vehicle traffic may be less dense, but it is even more dangerous because it moves faster. Always keep your dog on the lead and under control.

When he is well-trained, you can run the risk of unleashing him in selected safe spots from time to time. But be prepared to snap on the lead if necessary, and always leash him to cross the street.

WALKING IN THE COUNTRY, your dog can be unleashed most of the time, except when walking along busy roads. Try to keep him always in sight, however. Let him discover for himself the wonders of nature, and point out things of interest too, such as holes and tracks that may escape his notice. Be sure to respect "No Trespassing" signs, and to avoid hunting terrain during the season.

A big, fast dog will get a good run if he follows you as you ride a bicycle down a country road. But never ask a dog to run alongside or behind an automobile. The exhaust fumes can cause great harm, and the psychological effect is almost as bad.

ON ROADS, it is a good idea to walk always on the side, never in the middle, and to stop until an oncoming car has passed. This will soon become an automatic reflex in your dog and will be doubly useful: first, because he cannot chase a car when he is standing still; and second, because although it will not teach him to avoid cars, it will at least give the driver a chance to spot him and steer clear of him. This isn't orthodox training, but it is easily accomplished. Pet owners, you will find, must often be satisfied with such expedients.

The WOODS are full of fascinating sights and scents for a dog. Let him roam on his own, but call him back when he gets out of sight. In dense woods, it may be practical to train your dog to come to whistled signals, your own or a mechanical one, both of which carry much further out of doors than does the human voice.

In MOUNTAINS OR ROCKY TERRAIN, your dog will be more sure-footed if he is unleashed. Small Terriers are in their element in rocky places and find footholds that would never support your own weight, so be wary when you follow them. At the same time, many dogs have an instinct for finding passages through apparently impenetrable country, and are excellent guides.

A SANDY BEACH is a marvelous place for giving your dog a good long run. Unfortunately, many beaches are out of bounds for dogs during the swimming season, sometimes all year round. Find out at what times dogs are admitted (and try to find out at what times the beach is patrolled).

Shingle beaches and pebbly ones are hard on a dog's pads. Even more dangerous is the risk of cuts from broken bottles and picnic litter. Small dogs are light enough to scamper over such débris unharmed, but it represents a real danger to heavy breeds. Steer your dog clear of it when you can, and check his paws when you get home.

SWIMMING

Swimming is an ideal recreation for dogs on hot days, as it is the best way to cool them off. Harsh-coated dogs and oily-coated ones can swim in either fresh or salt water, after which they simply shake themselves dry. Silkycoated, sparsely coated, and softcoated breeds should be rinsed off with fresh water after an ocean bath, because the sea salt (the chlorine in swimming-pool water too) reaches their skin and causes irritation.

Dogs are natural swimmers almost from birth. Experiments have shown that puppies make swimming movements with their legs when held over a stretch of water even before their eyes have opened. Usually you need only supervise the first swimming experience to make sure it is a pleasant one.

You can start by wading into shallow water with your puppy (fresh water, if possible, because he may swallow some). Play with him. Throw

The Labrador Retriever is one of the breeds that loves to swim. (*H. Armstrong Roberts*)

a stick or a floating ball, first at the shoreline, then into increasingly deep water, so that he finally has to swim to reach it. Swim along with him at first.

Small dogs can also be held in your arms and released for a few seconds, then for increasingly longer periods. All dogs instinctively make running movements with their feet which keep them afloat and advancing. Their reactions usually progress from anxiety to surprise, pride, self-confidence, and pleasure—which is the result you seek.

Some dogs develop a veritable passion for swimming. Those who are afraid of water were probably introduced to it ineptly, or were frightened by teasing water games. In such cases, never force the dog into the water against his will. He will struggle frantically, get a dunking, and end up with a greater water phobia than before. Instead, wait a while.

Reintroduce him to it gradually, supporting him firmly at first, encouraging him, praising him for the slightest effort, and above all, trying to persuade him that swimming is fun.

GAMES

While a certain discipline is expected of your dog when going for a walk, his playtime should be unrestricted pleasure. Well, not entirely unrestricted. For safety reasons, you need to find an enclosed area. Even a very intelligent dog, carried away by the spirit of his game, will chase a ball right under the wheels of a passing car if that is where the ball rolls. So if you cannot find a safe outdoor space, play with your dog only in your own home. He will enjoy it almost as much.

The earliest games of very young puppies are based on fighting, boxing, wrestling, biting, chasing, and tug of war. At 8 or 9 weeks they develop an interest in retrieving-ball games, even all by themselves. Between 8 and 12 weeks they enjoy playing with people as much as, or more than, with their littermates.

Playing with your puppy provides an excellent opportunity to observe his actions and reactions and to become acquainted with his innate character. Games develop alertness and intelligence and can also satisfy instincts for hunting, retrieving, and tracking. Terriers like to dig, wrestle, and fight, generally going for their mock adversary's throat. Greyhounds chase. Corgis nip heels. Gun dogs retrieve and carry things around in their mouths. Many Working dogs prefer practical exercises to playful games.

Play is one of the best forms of exercise for a puppy. Fifteen minutes of vigorous play can be the equivalent of an hour's walk. Many owners do not realize that games are also good vocabulary builders. When it is all part of a game that he enjoys, your puppy will very quickly learn the meaning of many words long before he is ready for formal training.

You can help or handicap your dog's future training by the choice of games you play with him. If you eventually wish to train your dog for Obedience Trials, Hunting, Tracking, or whatever, you should learn enough about them to be able to apply the same rules to your playtime version of these activities. For example, when you throw a stick for your Retriever puppy, you should make correct retrieving form the rule of the game. If not, his later training will be complicated by having to unlearn bad habits. Tug of war, to take another example, is the worst possible game for a Retriever—in fact, not a very good one for any breed.

The resources of your playground, your own ingenuity and your dog's, will suggest many simple, harmless games, such as:

RETRIEVING STICKS AND STONES. All dogs enjoy this. Do not, however, throw stones so small that they can be swallowed in excitement, or so large that they can break a tooth. Green sticks are better than dry ones. Never throw a painted stick because of the danger of lead poisoning, or a piece of construction rubble because of the danger of nails. Your dog will soon learn to watch your throwing motion in order to get a head start in the right direction, and it is tempting to make a false movement and then throw elsewhere or not at all. Unless you integrate your deception into an exercise for training your dog to retrieve only on command, don't do it. In fact, never cheat when playing games with your dog. Instead, invent a harder game.

PLAYING BALL. You can roll or toss it long or short distances, on a surface where it remains visible, or in grass or bushes where your dog has to use his nose to find it. You can teach your dog to roll the ball along a stretch of pavement or down a short flight of stairs and catch it in his mouth when you toss it back to him. Buy a ball that is the right size for your dog's mouth. Heavy balls roll best, but if your dog enjoys catching it, buy a light one, throw it from short distances and toss it gently. Another indoor ball game that small dogs enjoy is simply rolling the ball back and forth between the two of you.

PLAYING TAG. Puppies love to play tag with children and with each other, but it is not a good game for adult dogs. Nervous individuals become overexcited, and it is apt to bring out the attacking instinct in Guard breeds, with the risk that the mood of playfulness may change to one of genuine aggression. It is just as bad to chase your dog. He should be trained to come to you, not to run away from you. Let your dog play tag with other friendly dogs, or run after a ball—but not after you.

HIDE AND SEEK. Tracking Hounds and Hunting dogs understandably delight in this. It can be played indoors or out. The first few times, you can have another person hold your dog while you hide behind a tree or in another room. Once the dog has caught onto the point of the game, you can simply tell him to SIT, STAY until you release him by calling, SEEK! When he has become clever at finding you, the more ingenious and surprising your hiding place, the more he will enjoy it.

FIND THE OBJECT. This is one of the best indoor games for all dogs. The object which is hidden while the dog is told to SIT, STAY should be a toy or glove or some other small article that bears a scent the dog knows well. If you guide your dog verbally, he will learn many words: SIT, STAY, NOW, SEEK THE BALL! NO, NOT THERE. THAT'S RIGHT! GOOD DOG!

RACING. All dogs need to stretch their legs from time to time in an all-out run. Hound breeds, as well as many Hunting dogs (especially Pointers and Setters) absolutely require it. For their own safety, release them only in an enclosed area or one far removed from road traffic. They will generally run in circles, but do not count on it. Let your dog race with other dogs, if he likes, or all alone. But do not compete with him yourself, especially if he can run faster than you can.

WRESTLING. One of the earliest forms of puppy play, wrestling can be a harmless outlet for aggression in small breeds, but is potentially dangerous in large ones. Social inhibitions are usually retained during play, but they can be forgotten in excitement or when one dog inadvertently causes pain to the other. Never let children wrestle with a dog, and resist your own impulse to get down on all fours and behave like a puppy. You are the pack leader, remember? There are lots of games that you can play together and still maintain your standing in your dog's eyes.

Whatever games you play with your dog (and you will find that he is very inventive in this domain), try to observe a few sensible rules:

—Do not become involved in a game in which the dog is superior and risks discovering the fact.

Do not expect your pet to join you in a game of checkers like this Boxer. There are a lot of simpler games that you can play together. (*Photoworld/FPG*)

—Never let violent play become prolonged to the point of fatigue or overexcitement.

—Never play "anxiety games," by pretending to be hurt, to cry, or to attack another member of the family.

—Always follow active playtime with the opportunity for a drink and a rest. (You may need them too.)

Finally, do not think there must be something wrong with your dog when he loses interest in games and playthings. And do not expect him to get the same pleasure you do from watching television. Only very large screens attract his attention anyway. He may be intrigued at first, sniff around and behind the set, and prick his ears when he hears a barking dog. But he soon loses interest. In fact, most adult dogs get the greatest pleasure simply from following you around, keeping you company, or lying quietly at your feet.

GOING FOR A DRIVE

Riding in a car is a treat for most dogs, especially if they are driven to an enjoyable destination. Even if you only take your dog to the local shopping center, the outing will add a little variety to his daily life and widen his horizons.

All pet dogs should be car-trained as puppies. Many of them ride in a car the first time when they are taken to their new home, which leaves an ambiguous impression that is partly pleasant and partly disquieting, since it involves an upheaval in their lives. So make your puppy's next drive reassuring, like a short trip to some pleasant playground, or simply a 5- or 10-minute spin around the neighborhood before returning to the security of home.

Always wait several hours after a full meal before taking your dog for a drive. Make him ride in the back seat, never on your lap when you are driving. You might cover the seat with an old blanket, well tucked in. Plastic is good protection for the upholstery, but offers too slippery a footing for a dog. Many dogs enjoy looking out of the window, and if you lower it a few inches they can also enjoy the passing scents. But do not open it far enough for them to stick their head out. While they like the feeling of the wind in their faces, it can seriously irritate their eyes. Foreign particles can also be blown into their ears.

Small dogs get less pleasure from drives because they seldom see anything but the interior of the car. Many of them simply curl up and go to sleep. Small dogs are also most prone to carsickness, perhaps because they haven't the visual distractions of larger ones. Some owners find that trailing an antistatic grounding strip prevents carsickness in their dogs. It also helps if you set off with enthusiasm—and a supply of tissues for cleaning up, just in case.

If you have to leave your dog alone in the car, even for a few minutes, be sure to:

—Lock the car doors and leave two windows open a few inches. (But the safest way to leave a dog in a car is locked in a wire crate on the back seat, with the windows open.)

—Park your car in a shady spot, remembering that the sun moves and that your shady spot may be a furnace an hour later.

—Never leave your dog in the car in an underground parking place or in a closed garage, and never anywhere for a long time.

Old dogs who have trouble moving around, like elderly people, benefit the most from going for a drive, as it helps to keep them alert and interested in the outside world when their daily lives have become more restricted.

If your dog is one of the youngsters who gets a thrill from riding in the car, dashes to your side as soon as he hears the tinkle of the car keys, and sometimes even tries to stow away, try to give him this simple treat whenever possible. But remember that it is a passive diversion, and not a substitute for active exercise and play.

13.
Training Your Dog

Most dogs enjoy learning and are proud of the knowledge and skills they acquire. Untrained dogs are seldom as happy as trained ones, and lead much less interesting lives. Many dogs, generally the most intelligent ones, also derive a sense of security from obedience and discipline. Every observant dog owner can see for himself that his dog gets greater satisfaction from the praise rewarding a well-executed command or good behavior than he does from the momentary exhilaration of disobedience, which is generally followed by evident guilt feelings, even when he has not been punished.

Owners vary in their pedagogic talent just as dogs vary in their trainability. Some people are born animal trainers and accomplish remarkable results with little effort, although a trainer is seldom equally successful with every breed of dog. A basic mental affinity, even a certain type of personality, seems to be necessary, quite aside from the fact that training procedures that are highly successful with one type of dog may be totally ineffective with another.

All good dog trainers possess authority, patience, and self-control. Brilliant ones possess in addition an indefinable "X" quality. Nevertheless, dog-training techniques have been so well systematized in recent years that the least gifted owner can achieve reasonably good results with effort, persistence, and the guidance of an experienced Obedience Class instructor. In fact, all modern pet dogs should be given basic obedience training as a matter of course, and not only when their behavior causes problems. Training cannot completely compensate for poor breeding, a bad environment, or inept upbringing—but it can help.

Specialized training is quite another matter, requiring certain aptitudes on the part of the dog, specific skills on the part of the trainer, and in many cases special equipment and facilities that are beyond the means of most pet owners. Professional trainers are responsible for the preparation of most Field Trial and many advanced Obedience Champions. But a surprising number of amateurs also excel in these competitions. What they lack in time, skill, and equipment is compensated for by their dog's desire to please the person he loves and lives with, which is one of his strongest motivations.

REWARD

The basis of all animal training is reward and punishment, and repetition leading to the establishment of reflex actions. Pleasure and displeasure are sufficient rewards and punishments for dogs, as they are for children, although dogs never become capable of understanding the moral distinctions between right and wrong, as children eventually do. They seldom evolve beyond the childish stage of doing something because "it makes Mother happy and Father proud," or, in less permissive homes, "because you will get a spanking if you don't."

The most effective canine rewards are:

—a word of praise, such as "GOOD DOG!" in an affectionate, enthusiastic tone of voice.

—a caress, such as stroking the back, rubbing behind the ears, along the muzzle, stroking the head, or gently taking his nose in your palm.

—edible ones, such as a piece of cooked liver, a biscuit, a canine candy drop, a sliver of cheese, or whatever the dog particularly relishes. (These are most useful with puppies. Adult dogs generally prefer praise. Food motivation is also stronger in Hunting breeds and, to a lesser extent, in Hounds, than it is in Working dogs.)

—for many Hunting and Working dogs, the activity itself and the satisfaction of a job well done—a retrieved bird, a safely penned lamb, his owner's glove at the end of a trail.

PUNISHMENT

Expressions of praise can never be overdone. But punishment requires great discretion. The most effective methods are:
—absence of praise.
—"NO, BAD DOG," firm but not necessarily loud. (However, try to say NO as seldom as possible. Emphasize the positive instead.)
—a sharp tug on a slip chain collar, which causes a moment of discomfort and alerts the dog to the fact that he is committing an error.
—constraint, such as obliging a dog to sit or to lie down after some misbehavior, being sent to bed, or returned to the leash when he has taken advantage of his freedom to misbehave.
—a whack on the rump with a folded newspaper or the end of his leash in an emergency. (Never strike a dog on any other part of the body, and never strike him with your hand.)
—the most severe punishment of all, the one that is meted out by the pack leader of wild dogs and mothers of disobedient puppies, when a cuff of the paw or a warning growl have been ignored: being picked up by the scruff of the neck and shaken. It is humiliating, traumatizing, and should be resorted to only in the case of deliberate and violent disobedience, or to punish a crime such as biting people or killing fowl.

In dog training, punishments and rewards are really an elementary form of communication, a means of getting the dog to understand what you wish him to do. You will get the best results from the mildest punishment and the most extravagant praise at first. Later on, an affectionate word or an imperceptible pat will suffice. Shy and sensitive dogs respond to gentle admonishment and lavish praise. They can be terrorized by severe handling. In spite of their reputation for toughness, most Terriers require gentle handling too, since they tend to associate pain with fighting, and painful punishments can trigger instinctive resistance or aggression. Sheepdogs and Hounds also react to the gentlest measures. Many dogs learn from rewards alone. In fact, due perhaps to the dog's rapid evolution toward a more civilized, sensitive mentality, old-fashioned punishment is not as effective as it used to be, and may often have a negative effect.

When you have to use it, punishment should always be brief, never given in anger, and only when you are sure that the disobedience was deliberate and not due to incomprehension. Never bear a grudge either, but return at once to the lesson or to some other activity. In short, resort to punishment only in cases of willful disobedience when all positive methods have failed.

TRAINING PROCESS

Canine training is the same as for all animals:
1) You communicate to your dog what you wish him to do.
2) When the dog has performed as desired, you reward him.
3) You immediately repeat the exercise a few times.
4) You review it frequently until the dog's response to the command is practically automatic.

That is all there is to it. But, of course it isn't quite as simple as it sounds.

In the first place, COMMUNICATIONS WITH YOUR DOG, as we have seen, are limited. Sometimes you can demonstrate the action you wish him to perform. Sometimes you have to force or inveigle him into doing it. In certain cases (SIT or COME, for example), you can, if you are alert, give your dog the appropriate command every time you see that he is about to perform these actions anyway, then praise him. The first few times he will be mystified. Eventually, he will connect the cause and the effect.

Try to be calm, distinct, brief, patient, and perfectly clear in repeating your commands. Above all, be consistent. If your dog just sits there, cocking his ears with a bewildered air, it is obvious that you are not getting your message across and that you need to improve your communications system. Start over again, not only trying to clarify your command, but also increasing the concentration and will power behind it. One-word commands are best at first. Later on, you can use the key word in a sentence, pronouncing it gradually less emphatically.

When your dog has grasped your meaning and performed correctly, and after he has been rewarded, repeat the performance at once in order to fix it in his memory. Three or four times are sufficient for the first lesson, because you do not want to bore him with it. You can repeat it an hour or two later, again the next day, and thereafter at the beginning of each training session. You will see that your dog really enjoys showing off what he has learned to do.

Certain CONDITIONS are necessary for successful dog training. Try to schedule the lessons at the same time and in the same place, one that is as secluded as possible and free from distractions such as arriving cars, playing children, and the presence of other animals. Needless to add, it is a waste of time trying to train a bitch in heat or a male who is within scenting distance of her. Do not attempt to school a tired dog either, an ailing one, or one that has just eaten. And do not school your dog when you are nervous, irritable, or in a bad mood.

There are more or less FAVORABLE AGES FOR TRAINING a dog. Young puppies are too preoccupied with discovering their environment to concentrate on formal lessons, and you should be satisfied if your pet simply acquires an understanding of your expressions of pleasure and displeasure and the elementary social graces that most puppies pick up naturally in the course of daily life. Most training schools and classes will not accept canine students under 6 months of age, after the teething process has been completed. During adolescence, dogs, like children, tend to resist authority. Even those experts who believe in starting training as young as possible interrupt it during this rebellious stage.

Generally speaking, you can start to give a dog formal training with the best chances of success between the ages of 12 and 18 months. Small breeds and females, who mature earlier, can start sooner than large male dogs. Army dogs and Guide dogs for the blind are never trained before the age of 1 or 1½ years. Many Hunting dogs and Sheepdogs, on the other hand, are taken out with well-trained older dogs when they are only 4 or 5 months old, and frequently start formal training at 8 months. It is not unheard of for a 9-month-old puppy to win laurels in Field Trials and Obedience competitions. But they are exceptions to the rule.

There is no maximum age for starting to train a dog. You *can* teach an old dog new tricks as long as he lives. One of the best Obedience competitors in history was a Dalmatian who started training at the age of twelve. The principal handicaps in training unschooled adult dogs are the need for unlearning bad habits, and the greater length of time it usually takes to establish the basic learning process in his undisciplined brain.

The LEARNING PROCESS, from the dog's point of view, involves listening attentively and watching you as you give a command, realizing that each sound and gesture signifies something he is being asked to do, and finally performing the corresponding action. Once this sequence has been established in his mind, there is no limit to what he can learn. It is rather like our study of foreign languages. The first one is terribly difficult and confusing, the second more easily acquired, and linguists who have already mastered several foreign tongues learn additional ones with enviable ease.

Canine TRAINING EQUIPMENT for ordinary purposes is neither complicated nor expensive. You merely need:

—a quiet, secluded spot, indoors or out
—10 or 15 minutes a day

—a slip chain collar of the proper size
—an ordinary leash
—a training leash 6 feet long (or as long as you are tall)
—a length of clothesline rope 25 feet long or more
—a few tidbits in your pocket
—calm, self-control, patience, clarity in your commands, promptness in
   your rewards and corrections.

It is useful to bear in mind A FEW TRAINING TIPS of proven effec-
tiveness:
—Schedule your dog's lesson every day at the same time and in the
   same place.
—Be enthusiastic. Make training seem fun.
—But be authoritative too. Insist on a higher standard of obedience
   during lessons than at ordinary times. Don't, for example, ask your
   dog to do something. *Tell* him to do it, and to do it at once.
—Use your tone of voice to help get your messages across: a clear,
   firm one for commands; an enthusiastic one for encouragement; a
   cheerful one for approval; and a minor, low tone for disapproval. Lit-
   tle is accomplished by loud or strident tones, which dogs dislike. Bar-
   bara Woodhouse, the extraordinarily gifted English dog authority and
   author, performs training miracles using what she calls a "wee voice,"
   which is hardly more than a whisper.
—Start each lesson by reviewing what your dog already knows, and
   praise him for his good performance, even for his well-meaning
   efforts. Praise him, in fact, for the slightest thing that he does right.
—Be as concentrated and observant during training sessions as you ex-
   pect your dog to be. You will then be able to anticipate his moves, to
   encourage him when he is on the right track, and to discourage mis-
   takes before he makes them.
—Never proceed to difficult tasks until your dog has mastered the
   more elementary ones. It is much more useful for you to be certain
   that he will obey three or four simple commands than it is to hope
   that he will obey ten or twenty if he happens to feel like it.
—Follow each lesson with a moment of play.
—Persuade the other members of your family to give the identical
   commands and to use the same terms of encouragement and dis-
   pleasure.
—Do not let your dog forget what he has learned, nor confine his obe-
   dience to lesson times. Use the commands he has been trained to
   obey whenever suitable circumstances arise. That is what training is
   all about, after all: to facilitate your dog's integration into civilized
   daily life, and not to give a circus performance.

BASIC COMMANDS

By the time your puppy is ready for training, he will already have learned quite a lot of things, perhaps more than you realize. He will certainly know his name, the meaning of the word NO and of GOOD DOG (or whatever praise expression you use), since these are the words that have been most often addressed to him.

Now you can teach him the basic commands which every educated dog should understand and obey.

COME. Like all commands, this should be preceded by your dog's name: "FIDO, COME!" in order to alert his attention. From the day you acquire your puppy, you can start implanting the meaning of the word in his mind by calling him to COME for his dinner, to COME for a walk, to COME to receive a toy or tidbit, and to COME whenever that is what he obviously intends to do anyway. Puppies will often come to you instinctively if you drop into a crouching position, which is a more friendly posture than standing.

The traditional training technique is to attach a long piece of rope to the dog's lead or collar, then let him roam for a few minutes. When you give the command "ROVER, COME!" accompany it with a sharp tug on the rope, pull it in to you, and reward your dog. The exercise is repeated many times, then without tugging or pulling, and finally without the rope. Eventually, the correct response will be practically automatic—if you do not spoil everything by asking your dog to COME for something disagreeable.

Many trainers prefer to teach the COME command after the dog has already learned the SIT-STAY, because when he is in a SIT-STAY position what he most wants to do is to COME to you.

SIT. This is one of the most useful commands of all, since when your dog obeys it consistently, you will be in control of him in most circumstances. For example, when he rushes to the door to greet a friend, you can ask him to SIT and he will be unable to jump up on the visitor. On many occasions SIT is equivalent to STOP, which is harder to teach.

The training method is to put your dog on the lead and some edible rewards in your pocket. As you pull upward on the lead, push the dog's hindquarters down with the other hand, saying, "ROVER, SIT!" Reward and repeat.

Informally, every time you see that your dog is about to sit down of his own accord (as he often does when you hold a tidbit, his leash, or a

To teach your dog to sit, push down gently on the rump with your left hand and raise the head with your lead in the right hand. (*Sue Maynard*)

toy in your hand), tell him to SIT as he does so. He will soon associate the action with the word.

When your dog has learned to sit on command, it should not be difficult to teach him to

STAY. First ask him to SIT. Then place your palm in front of his nose, like a policeman stopping traffic, and say in your most authoritative tone, "STAY," as you back up a few steps. Your dog will want to follow you, and you must immediately return him to a sitting position and repeat the STAY command and gesture. Repeat as often as necessary. When he has grasped the idea and has performed correctly, release him after a few seconds with another command, such as OKAY or ALL RIGHT. Then go to him and make a big fuss over him.

Repeat and repeat, rewarding every good performance. The first week you should withdraw only a few steps and for just a few seconds. Afterward, you can move further and further away, then turn your back on him, and finally move completely out of sight. In Novice Obedience tests, the SIT-STAY lasts for one minute, with the handlers at the opposite side of the ring, and a dog is penalized for standing up, lying down, or shifting his position before receiving the release command. Open Classes have stiffer requirements: three minutes for the "Long Stay" while the handlers are completely out of sight.

Teaching a dog to stay. (*Sue Maynard*)

STAND. This command is most important for show dogs, who must learn to stand quietly for examination by the judge and to show themselves to best advantage throughout their appearance in the ring. But it is also useful in daily life, especially when you have to take your dog to the vet.

It is simple to teach if you start early enough. Leash your puppy and place him on a table. Tell him to STAND, as you support him in an upright position with one hand under his loins and the other under his chest or chin. Whenever he starts to sit down, as he will undoubtedly do at first, prop him up again, repeating the command. You can gradually remove your manual support, then the leash, and finally back up a step or two. Use your release command (OKAY, or whatever) to let him know that the exercise is over, and reward him.

Show dogs are trained to stand not merely erect but posed in a stance that emphasizes desirable features of conformation such as a sloping topline, a long neck, or a beautiful tail. In some breeds, show poses have become exaggerated to a rather ridiculous degree, but handlers are obliged to conform if they wish to win, and the dogs don't seem to mind it. So while you're at it, why not train your dog to pose as Show Champions do? Since these fashions change from time to time and vary according to breed, you should observe carefully how dogs of your breed are posed during important dog shows and study the photographs of show dogs in magazines. Then try to "stack" your dog in the same way (see Chapter 22 for further tips). But do not be dismayed if your dog cannot reproduce some of the photographed poses without your help. Retouching has probably removed the telltale hand that grasps the jowls on the far side of the camera, the one that holds the tail at the ideal angle, and the lead that stretches the neck—not to mention the piece of liver or other "bait" that is the real reason why the dog is looking so alert.

DOWN. Although this is one of the basic commands in the training of Hunting dogs and in Obedience Trails, it makes little difference in daily life whether your dog is sitting down or lying down, as long as he remains in the same spot. However, the DOWN is the logical command to teach your dog after he has learned to SIT and STAY. Moreover, it may be of psychological value, since lying down implies submission, and therefore total obedience.

Teaching a dog to go down. (*Sue Maynard*)

The standard training method is to place your dog in the SIT position, then give the command "DOWN" as you pull his front legs gently forward, forcing him into a lying-down position. Praise, reward, and repeat. He may not like this as much as his previous lessons, and many repetitions may be necessary before he complies without reluctance.

If your dog refuses to lie down when you pull his forelegs forward, you can try a stronger method. Have him SIT, and as you say "DOWN," grasp his leash close to the collar under his neck and pull it firmly downward. Another way, which avoids the use of direct force, is to step on his leash fairly close to him as he is sitting, and pull firmly upward on it, letting it slide under your foot, as you say "DOWN!" The same downward pressure is exerted indirectly.

If your dog has already mastered the SIT-STAY, he will quickly add the DOWN-STAY to his repertory. This is taught in exactly the same way and presents no special problem. The difficulty of the exercises in Open classes of Obedience Trials is that the dog is required to stay down, with his handler out of sight, for 5 full minutes.

STOP (or WAIT or HALT, if you prefer), to make your dog stop short in his tracks, or stop whatever he is doing. This is easily demonstrated during your daily walk, by giving the example of coming to a full stop, if necessary pulling your dog up close to you with a short tug on the leash. Repeat as often as possible—at every street crossing, for example, and whenever you wish him to stop so that you can remove his leash or snap it on again. If you ask him to STOP for pleasant reasons, he will do so willingly.

When he has become proficient in obeying the STOP command while he is at your side, you can train him to obey it from a distance. Let him rove or run ahead of you on a long lead or your even longer rope, and when he is several feet away, tell him to STOP, as you give a sharp little tug on the lead. You must then try to prevent him from returning to you by using your policeman's STAY gesture. This is hard. But if your dog already responds correctly to STOP and STAY, you should eventually succeed.

Of all the commands your dog learns to obey, this one is most likely to save his life. Remember that your eyesight is keener than your dog's in some ways and that you can often anticipate impending dangers before he can. There is seldom time to point out the peril of a speeding car, for example. But if you have trained him to stop short on command, you may avoid a tragic accident.

HEEL. This is an important part of Obedience training. It is the correct way for a dog to walk with his owner on or off the lead. He should be on your left side, his head level with your left knee, and he should

Teaching a dog to heel. (*Sue Maynard*)

neither run ahead nor lag behind, never pull, cross in front of you, or deviate from a straight line.

Obedience dogs are required to drop into a sitting position without command whenever you stop. Show dogs are trained to heel on a looser lead, on both the left and right sides, and not so close to the handler, remaining standing still whenever they stop. You might think that these two different styles of heeling would be confusing to dogs who compete in show classes as well as in Obedience Trials. However, they usually associate the different kinds of handling and the different kinds of lead (a show lead and an Obedience slip chain collar) with the different behavior expected of them. Furthermore, most handlers employ two distinct commands: "HEEL" for Obedience, and "LET'S GO!" (or some such phrase) for showing.

Obedience heeling is taught with the aid of a slip chain collar and an ordinary leash. Put your dog in the SIT position on your left side, hold-ing the leash in your right hand, and grasping it at the halfway mark with your left hand. As you step determinedly forward with your left foot, give the command to HEEL. Your dog will probably follow, and now you need only keep him in position by giving short jerks on the lead whenever necessary to bring him back into line, repeating the command to HEEL every time you do so. If you walk along a fence or wall, with your dog between you and the wall, he will be obliged to advance in a straight line at your side.

In order to train your dog to sit automatically when you stop, you should start by giving him the verbal command to SIT, accompanied by an upward pull on the lead, whenever you come to a halt. Praise him, then advance again, saying "HEEL." After a certain number of repeti-tions, you can eliminate the voice command (but not the praise). When your dog continues to perform correctly, you can discontinue the leash signal. Theoretically, the series of actions should now be automatic. Even if you are not interested in formal Obedience training, you will find it surprisingly practical in everyday life to have your dog sit every time you stop.

At this point your dog will know the obedience ABCs, which will ena-ble you to control him in most ordinary circumstances. The process of giving him this basic instruction will also have furnished you with a clue as to his TRAINING APTITUDE.

If it has all been a terrible strain on his intellect and self-control, there is no need to insist further, as he is already sufficiently educated for the role of a pet companion, unless, of course, you really enjoy the challenge. Some Terrier and Hound breeds are so independent by nature that you can feel proud of yourself if you succeed in teaching them no more than these seven basic commands. But if your dog has enjoyed his training sessions (as many of them do, especially Hunting breeds, Sheepdogs, and Poodles), you might consider preparing him for competitive Obedi-ence Trials. You can certainly teach him some or all of the following.

ADDITIONAL COMMANDS

GO ON or GO AHEAD (or some other term of encouragement). This is slightly different from your word of approval (OKAY, GOOD DOG or, whatever), because you are spurring your dog into action of some kind, such as jumping over a ditch, or doing something that is normally forbid-den, like mounting a bitch, running ahead of you, or accepting food from a stranger. In order to teach it, you simply take advantage of the occasions as they arise, trying to make your meaning clear by tone and gesture, encouraging and praising a correct response.

QUICK, indicating to your dog that you want him to hurry up. Use the word whenever you wish him to come to you at once, to jump into the car without dawdling, or simply to walk faster. As a matter of fact, the easiest time to demonstrate the meaning of the word is during your daily walk, when you can say "QUICK" each time you accelerate your pace. An urgent tone of voice along with your own example will soon get the idea across. Repetition will do the rest.

SLOW. Pronounce it with a long, dragged-out vowel: "SLOOOOOW." Your own example in slowing your pace during a walk is again the clearest way to demonstrate its meaning. You can also use the word to stop your dog from snatching at a tidbit or gobbling down a meal. There are so many daily occasions when it is of practical value for your dog to be either quick or slow that he will learn these words very rapidly, if you remember to use them.

UP or HUP is a useful command, asking your dog to jump over some obstacle, into the car, onto a grooming table or a chair. You can demonstrate it during your walks by giving an upward pull on the leash as you pronounce the command whenever you come upon a high curb, a fallen tree, a ditch, or a water-filled gutter. At home, you can make your meaning clear by patting the chair or table onto which you wish him to jump, as you encourage him to "HUP!" A word of warning, though: Do not teach this to a Gun dog or Retriever, for whom the command "HUP," as we shall see, has a special significance.

CAREFUL or ATTENTION!, to signal some impending danger or difficulty. Use the word to put your dog on his guard whenever you encounter treacherous terrain, unknown animals, hazardous traffic conditions, and so forth. Your tone of voice and behavior, along with sufficient repetition, will soon make your dog alert and cautious whenever you pronounce it.

DO YOUR BUSINESS! No dog will defecate on command, of course, if he does not feel the urge to do so. However, if you repeat these words (or others of your choice) whenever your dog is obviously about to relieve himself, he will eventually associate them with the act and you will be able to exert a certain influence on the choice of the spot he soils. It can be useful when traveling, during bad weather, or whenever you want your dog to know that he is being let outdoors for a specific purpose. In any case, city dog owners have one or two opportunities each day to implant this association of word and action, so why not try it?

SPEAK! Although most owners are more interested in stopping their dog from barking, it can be useful to train him to bark on command. While it is a popular parlor trick, it may also save your dog's life if he has been lost or injured, has fallen into a ravine or hole, or is trapped in some enclosed place where you would otherwise be unable to find him. You can teach a dog to speak by encouraging him to bark as you say, "REX, SPEAK!," giving the best imitation of it that you can, and rewarding his efforts.

QUIET! can be demonstrated by tapping your dog on the muzzle with a finger when he barks incessantly for no valid reason. If he persists, you can hold his jaws shut for an instant, repeating the command, "QUIET!" But if he has barked for some good reason, be sure to praise him first: "GOOD DOG! That's right! Now, QUIET."

TRICKS

Any dog can be taught to perform simple tricks, and most of them love it. Some dogs are born entertainers and enjoy showing off for company. Sometimes they will do a trick for visitors without even being asked, simply because an audience is present. Generally speaking, large breeds have a greater sense of dignity and perhaps less sense of humor than small breeds. They are usually happier doing practical work such as guarding and hunting than performing parlor tricks. As a matter of fact, if you love and respect dogs, you will refrain from teaching your pet to do anything that is humiliating, including the time-honored begging routine. Make trick-performing fun and not embarrassing.

Your dog's individual temperament and any special aptitudes, such as unusual agility, or adroitness with his forepaws, will suggest original tricks to you. In the meantime, you can start by teaching him some of the traditional ones, such as:

SHAKING HANDS. Put your dog in a sitting position, grasp his right paw and raise it, saying, "SHAKE HANDS." After several repetitions, simply tap the paw, and praise him when he extends it. Finally, use only the verbal command.

For some strange reason, some of your friends to whom he holds out his paw like a perfect gentleman will try to confuse him by asking for "the other one," although they would never dream of doing so with a human acquaintance. So you might as well prepare your dog for it by teaching him this variation too.

LEARNING NAMES. In a home with several pets, dogs quickly learn their names by simple observation, especially if you call each one by name as you distribute their food bowls.

It is just as easy to teach them the names of the different members of the family. Put your dog on the leash. Lead him to the selected person, saying, "This is MARY." Then take him a short distance away, say "Go to MARY," and lead him to her. After several repetitions, try it without the leash, then without accompanying your dog, then when Mary is in another room, and finally when she is with a group of people. Both you and Mary should, of course, praise your dog when he goes to her. He may very well surprise you by dashing over to Mary the first time you ask him to because he has known her name all along.

FETCH. This is really a basic command rather than a trick, especially for Retrievers. Retrieving balls is a natural form of play for all young puppies, who can be taught to fetch from the age of 3 months or even earlier.

The traditional teaching method is to select an object such as a stick or ball, offer it to your dog, and when he takes it in his mouth, say, "FETCH." The exercise is repeated, with the object held farther and farther away from him. Then it is placed on the floor, at gradually increased distances, and the dog is praised when he takes it in his mouth.

The hardest part is teaching him to bring it to you and to release it. When he has picked up the object, give him the command to COME. If you are not sure that he will do so, put him on the lead and pull him to you. Then say, "GIVE" or "DROP," and gently remove the object from his mouth. If he does not want to yield it, you can force him to open his mouth by grasping his lower jaw with your right hand and the object in your left. Then slide your right thumb into his mouth, pressing the lower lip against his teeth. This will make him open his mouth and you can withdraw the object, reward him with a caress and a hearty, "GOOD DOG!" Repeat, praise, repeat, ad infinitum. (This is the eternal refrain in dog training, but there is no escaping it.)

Once your dog has learned this basic routine of fetching, you can easily teach him to fetch your slippers, the evening paper, and many other objects too, simply by teaching him the name of the object and combining the two tricks. One clever Retriever was trained to "answer the phone" by bringing the receiver to his owner whenever the telephone rang.

SELECTING AN OBJECT. From early puppyhood your dog has been told to "GO TO BED," so he already knows the word that designates his basket or blanket. If you have told him every time you take him for a drive that you are going "in the CAR," he associates that word with that particular vehicle. It is not difficult to extend his vocabulary by teaching him the names of other objects.

A simple way to start is with his playthings. Show him his ball and say,

"This is your BALL." Then place it next to some other object—his bone, for example—and say, "FETCH your BALL." If he sniffs the bone first, say, "NO, The BALL." And when he noses the ball, praise him: "YES! GOOD DOG! That's your BALL. Now FETCH the BALL!"

When the association between the sound of the word and the idea of the object is imprinted in his mind (which may be sooner than you think), you can teach him the meaning of "BONE," "MOUSE," "SLIPPER," "BLANKET," and so forth. Finally, you can line up an assortment of objects and impress your friends by asking him to fetch a particular one.

PLAYING DEAD is distasteful to many dogs, because lying flat on the side or back is an act of submission in the animal kingdom. While this is often a spontaneous gesture with pet dogs, it is not the same when they are ordered to do it. If your dog obviously resents it, do not insist. There are many other tricks that you can teach him. But if he doesn't seem to mind, all you need to do is to repeat the command at the same time that you gently force him into a supine position. The traditional signal is "Dead Dog," a rather unpleasant expression. A loyal Yale graduate used to ask his dog, "What would you rather do than go to Harvard?"— whereupon his dog "dropped dead." Perhaps you can invent a variation on this theme which will amuse your guests as well as your dog.

ROLL OVER. This is a rather pointless trick, but some dogs love to do it. Besides, it is simple to teach, since you can easily place your dog in the DOWN position and roll him over gently as you pronounce the command. Praise, reward, and repeat, until he rolls over unaided.

OPENING AND CLOSING DOORS. Dogs cannot open locked doors or turn a doorknob, but many of them learn to unfasten latches, and all of them can be taught to shut an open door by either pushing it closed with their nose (large dogs), or by pushing at it with their forepaws (small ones). Dogs can also open (with their nose or body) a door that is ajar. In order to teach your pet to do it on command, you simply select a signal, demonstrate the action simultaneously, persuade your dog to do it unassisted, praise and repeat. Your friends will be astonished when he has learned the lesson so well that you can say in a conversational tone, "Rex, would you please shut the kitchen door?"—whereupon Rex dashes over to slam it shut.

THE HANDKERCHIEF TRICK consists of gently removing a handkerchief from a man's breast pocket with his teeth, then sitting and offering it to his owner. The teaching method is the standard one: demonstration, praise, reward, and repetition. Insist on gentleness, even a certain daintiness, when the dog grasps the handkerchief in his teeth.

Most dogs enjoy this immensely, perhaps because it satisfies some re-pressed instinct for stealing. Once a dog has learned to do the handker-chief trick, it is easy to teach him to "steal" other objects too.

JUMPING THROUGH A HOOP must be the oldest dog trick in the world, for it is pictured on an Athenian jug that was made in 500 B.C. Since hoops are seldom found in modern homes, small dogs can be taught to jump through a circle made by your arms, and large dogs to jump over your outstretched leg as you say "HUP," or whatever you like. It takes two people to demonstrate the action to your dog: one to create the barrier to be cleared, and the other to stand with the barrier between him and the dog in order to urge the dog to jump through or over it and attain a suitable reward. This trick is such fun for an agile animal that edible rewards, advisable at first, are soon unnecessary.

CORRECTING CANINE VICES

Teaching your dog to do practical and amusing things is the most en-joyable part of training. But it is just as important, if not more so, to teach him what *not* to do and to correct bad habits. Because canine vices are usually the result of environment, temperament, breeding, the bad example of other dogs, or some atavistic behavior pattern, negative train-ing is more difficult and less fun than the constructive kind. But it has to be done, and drastic measures may be necessary. The solution will be more easily found if you start by trying to see the situation from the dog's point of view.

Some of the canine vices you may have to deal with are:

BARKING. Barking is the dog's instinctive means of giving a warning, and it would be against your interest to discourage it. However, once you have been alerted, your dog should realize that his job is done. So select a word of praise, such as GOOD DOG or OKAY, or a command such as QUIET, and give your dog a pat to indicate that he must now be still. If necessary, you can make your meaning clear by holding his mouth closed. He may gurgle or growl, but he can no longer bark.

Hysterical barking, such as during a thunderstorm, can be treated by reassurance, companionship, distraction, by tossing a glass of water in the dog's face, or, if all else fails, by tranquilizers. Barking at a strange object can be quickly stopped by showing him there is nothing to fear.

Barking from boredom or in order to attract attention is best treated by eliminating the cause. If you give your dog ample attention and ex-ercise every day, you can insist on quiet behavior the rest of the time.

Obedience training is of great indirect benefit due to the self-discipline it imposes and the mental and physical activity it provides.

Whining, barking, or howling when left alone should not be tolerated. It is easier to prevent in a puppy (if you follow the advice in Chapter 5) than it is to correct in an adult dog. However, even an inveterate lonely barker can be cured in an afternoon or evening if you arm yourself with patience and whatever acting talent you possess. If you normally leave your home by car, you will need a motorized assistant too.

You must pretend to leave your dog alone, telling him to "Guard the house" and that you will be "Back soon." Close the door and move away, but not very far. If you live in an apartment, you can wait down the hall or in the stairway. If you live in a house, your assistant should drive off in the car, while you remain near the door but beyond scenting distance. In both cases, as soon as your dog starts to bark or howl, you must burst furiously into your home, saying "BAD DOG! NO!" If you whack a folded newspaper against your palm as you enter, the scene will be even more impressive. But it need not be violent or long. A single experience may suffice to make it clear to your dog that his barking displeases you.

When he is duly impressed by your dissatisfaction, you should forgive him, caress him, settle him down on his blanket or in his favorite chair, tell him to "Guard the house," and leave once more. You will probably have to move further away this time, because a smart dog will suspect that you are lurking nearby. This is where patience is required. If your dog has not barked within 5 or 10 minutes, you can be almost certain that he has learned the lesson. But if he resumes his barking, you must repeat the entire scenario, and repeat it as often as necessary.

As a final scene, stay away for so brief a time that you are sure he will not bark. Return, greet him fondly, caress and praise him. Then reward him with a tidbit or a walk, whichever he prefers.

The next day you can test him by making a point of leaving him alone for a short period of time. The chances are that he will pass the test. In the future, if you take the trouble to give him plenty of exercise beforehand, an opportunity to relieve himself, a diverting toy or bone, water and food, whenever you have to leave your dog at home alone for an evening, he will never howl or bark without some justifiable reason.

A simple trick will stop your dog from barking with joy when you come home in the middle of the night. Immediately give him his ball or bone or favorite toy. He cannot hold something in his mouth and bark at the same time. He may gurgle with delight, but this will not disturb the neighbors.

JUMPING UP ON PEOPLE should be discouraged from puppyhood, especially with puppies of large breeds, since the habit can be dangerous when they have attained their adult size and weight. The traditional remedies are:

—placing your hand flat on top of his head and pushing down sharply.
—grasping and squeezing the dog's front paws as he jumps up.
—raising your knee against his chest and toppling him over backward.
—stepping lightly on his hindpaws as he jumps.

All of these maneuvers should be accompanied by a firm "NO," and the suggestion of an alternative action, such as sitting down and giving his paw.

If your dog is small, it may never occur to him to jump up on people if you take the preventive measure of kneeling down to his level to greet him with an affectionate caress whenever you come home. In any case, when a dog jumps up on you, you should always take a step forward, never back away.

ROAMING is a dangerous habit that is practically incurable in certain breeds and individuals. Highly sexed male dogs and bitches during the critical days of their heat periods will rove for miles in search of a mate. Confinement is the only preventive measure, and castration or spaying the only definitive cure. In milder cases, lots of curiosity-satisfying accompanied walks may suppress the roving urge.

Some dogs are born explorers. Until they settle down in old age, the only way to contain their wanderlust is to keep them in an enclosed area as large as possible, to try to satisfy their curiosity with varied daily walks, and to exercise their intellect by training. Even so, you may have to choose between offering your dog a happy life that may be cruelly abbreviated, or a longer one that is more restricted and undoubtedly less exciting for him. It is a difficult choice that only you can make—in the country, at least. In the city and suburbs you have no choice, because roaming dogs are considered outlaws and can be impounded and destroyed.

Often a dog will wander away from home in search of companionship, or because he feels bored and neglected. A canine companion of a home-loving breed can work wonders, especially a female companion for a male dog. A congenial cat or a turtle would be better than nothing.

Whatever the cause of his wandering, it is unwise to punish your dog when he finally returns home, even if his absence has caused you untold anguish. He will think he is being punished for coming home, and will be even more reluctant to return the next time. Instead, welcome him back with open arms like the prodigal son. Give him a good meal. Show him that you have missed him and are happy to have him back. It will not cure him of the vice, but it is sounder psychology than punishment.

INCONTINENCE is a common infirmity of old dogs which your vet can usually cure in a day or two with proper medication. It may also be a sign of genetic weakness in nervous dogs, in which case the poor dogs simply cannot help it. All you can do is protect your furniture, store your valuable rugs, and arrange a corner where your dog can relieve himself when he cannot wait to be taken out of doors.

Deliberate soiling is another matter, although it is often just as pathetic. The most frequent case is that of a neglected dog who knows he will be punished for his error but who prefers punishment to no attention at all. The obvious remedy is to give him the companionship he craves, or to get another dog who doesn't mind being left alone.

Except for aged and ailing individuals, you should scold a dog whenever he makes a mistake, deliberate or not, if only mildly. You can be very firm with spoiled pets who use this as a form of blackmail whenever they are left alone. If you do not insist on cleanliness, they will not even make an effort to control themselves.

DESTRUCTIVENESS. All young puppies are destructive because everything is a plaything to them until they have been taught otherwise. Destructiveness in an adult dog may be a means of relieving solitude and boredom, of attracting attention, of working off excess energy or relieving nervousness, or of punishing a neglectful owner. It is a favorite form of blackmail by spoiled pets.

Dogs are seldom destructive in the presence of their owners, a fact which tends to confirm this diagnosis. When they are, it is probably an expression of an atavistic killing instinct that has been aroused by boisterous games, for example when they tear to shreds a toy or garment they have been given to play with.

Willful destruction should be punished and prevented when possible. If you have to leave your dog at home alone for a long period of time, give him sufficient exercise beforehand so that he will be tired and content to rest quietly until you return. You can provide an illusion of company for him by turning on the radio or television. You can suggest a pastime by leaving him a bone or toy. As a last resort, you can confine him in an enclosed area where he can do no damage.

Some owners take no chances and give their dog a tranquilizer before they leave him alone for an evening. But this is an artificial, potentially harmful solution. The only sound one is to make it clear to your dog that destructiveness is a vice, and to offer him a daily schedule that provides him with normal amounts of exercise and rest, companionship, and solitude.

PULLING ON THE LEASH can cause embarrassment, discomfort, even a slipped disc or a dislocated shoulder to the owners of dogs who are addicted to this vice. Dogs who have been leash-trained as puppies seldom become pullers. They may be a bit headstrong during adolescence, but a few training sessions with a slip chain collar properly fitted and used should bring them into line again before pulling has become a habit. Professional trainers can cure a puller quickly, often in a single lesson. Obedience Classes are also effective, since an unruly dog usually conforms to the behavior pattern of the majority, and with sufficient repetition, the good behavior becomes habitual.

You can buy harnesses, spiked collars, and various patented gadgets designed to prevent a dog from pulling. But none are a substitute for proper training.

CHASING CARS should be vigorously discouraged. It is one of the most dangerous of all canine vices, certainly the one most likely to shorten your dog's life or to cause him serious injury. As in all corrective training, the only effective treatment is to associate car chasing in your dog's mind with unpleasant consequences.

You will need the help of one or two friends, a borrowed car (because your dog will recognize your own), and some kind of a dissuader, which may be a bucket of water, a water pistol filled with a weak but stinging solution of ammonia, several tin cans filled with pebbles, or whatever your ingenuity suggests.

Your friend drives the car where the dog will be tempted to chase it—in front of your own home, or out of your driveway and down the street. As soon as the dog starts to chase, you (or the passenger in the car) squirt the water in his face or bombard him with the cans (the rattling of the pebbles making the noise more terrifying). Sometimes this works, sometimes it doesn't. When it does, one treatment is usually sufficient. But do not hesitate to repeat it if your dog seems tempted to recommence.

If your dog chases your own car, it is because he wants to accompany you. The simplest solution is to confine him when you leave, telling him to "Guard the house" and that you will be "Back soon." He will eventually become accustomed to the procedure, confident that you will indeed return soon, and need no longer be confined. You can also try an entirely opposite technique. Stop the car when he runs after it, open the door, let him jump in, and take him with you. He may learn that some of your errands are very tedious, and that he would have been better off if he had stayed at home.

CHASING CATS. For many friendly dogs and cats, this is a natural form of play.

Terriers and Hounds are the most confirmed cat-chasers, but even they can learn to live in harmony with felines. Obedience training develops self-discipline and makes it easier for a dog to control his cat-chasing instincts—until another cat-chaser appears on the scene to arouse them again. Since dogs generally respect the young of other species, your pet should tolerate a kitten, and by the time the kitten has become a cat they will be old friends.

Fortunately for them, cats can climb trees and jump onto high places beyond the reach of dogs. They can also outrun and outmaneuver most dogs, except for running Hounds. Sometimes the cat enjoys the chase, perhaps because the odds are strongly in its favor.

Nevertheless, you should never fail to express your displeasure when your dog goes after a cat. Even if you personally dislike cats, your next door neighbor may love them. Besides, bringing up a dog in civilized society includes teaching him to live and let live.

CHASING LIVESTOCK. All dogs, some breeds more than others, instinctively run after moving things, either to investigate or to chase them. In the country, where there are chickens, sheep, cows, and horses, it can be dangerous for the dog as well as for his owner, who is responsible for any damage. A dog who molests livestock may be shot by the farmer and condemned to death by the dog warden.

By all means teach your dog that he can run after balls and sticks, even after rodents, but not after other living creatures.

The simplest training method is to put your puppy on a leash with a slip chain collar and lead him around the livestock he is apt to meet. Whenever he makes a move to chase or even approach them, jerk sharply on the leash and tell him firmly, "NO!" Farmers say that if a young puppy is taken around a mother hen who is with her brood, the hen will give him a scare he will never forget. It is vital to start this training as early as possible, because a dog that has "tasted blood" is practically incurable. Until you are absolutely sure of him, do not let him roam among livestock unleashed or unaccompanied.

There are several country methods for curing chicken-killers, the most repulsive of which is to tie the dead chicken around the dog's neck and make him drag it around for several days. Another is to give him a beating with the dead body. A less severe means of making chickens unpleasant to the dog is to take him around fowl and, as soon as he starts to go after one of them, squirt him in the face with a water pistol or douse him with a pail of water.

DIGGING is an instinctive canine activity that is of practical value in wild life. Terriers and Dachshunds are the most incorrigible diggers because they were bred to hunt burrowing animals. Dogs also dig holes in order to bury bones and to prepare a cool resting place during hot weather. Pregnant bitches dig holes in which to make a nest for their puppies. It is therefore impossible to suppress this instinct completely. Besides, it is generally harmless. All you can do is teach your dog that gardens and lawns are forbidden digging territory, protect your precious beds with wire fencing or harmless repellent sprays, and provide some innocent outlet for the digging drive: a sandpile, for instance, or even bedding that can be rumpled to his heart's content, thus sparing the sofa cushions and the rose garden.

STEALING FOOD is not a universal instinct among dogs. It is far more often encountered in adopted mongrels who have had to fend for themselves than in pet dogs who have never worried about where their next meal was coming from. A gluttonous pet may steal a liver canapé from a coffee table, and if the theft is greeted with amusement, he will be encouraged to repeat it. The next time it may be the Sunday roast. So scold your dog when you catch him stealing food. Once is generally enough. You can tell from his furtive manner during the act and his guilty demeanor afterward that he knows very well that he is doing wrong.

JEALOUSY is present in all animal temperaments. Some dogs, like some people, are more jealous than others. You cannot eliminate entirely this natural ingredient of your dog's personality. You can only train him to control his behavior.

Be scrupulously fair in giving a jealous dog his rightful share of attention and affection, but insist that he tolerate the attention and affection you give to the other members of the household. Even jealous dogs possess a sense of justice. In the rare cases of unreasoning jealousy that makes a dog literally sick, you should consult a sophisticated veterinarian.

A jealous dog goes through a painful adjustment when a new baby arrives in the home where he was previously the center of attention. It is wise to take precautions and never leave the two alone until your dog has accepted the new situation. If it is too much for him, you have no choice but to find another home for him.

Another delicate situation arises when the owner of a jealous dog gets married. Even if the dog has already accepted the bride or groom as a friend, he may be outraged by the cohabitation, and particularly by the new sleeping arrangements. Don't take chances. Move your dog's bed into another room. Although human sexual odors do not arouse canine libido, there is the possibility that the dog will interpret amorous gestures as aggression and try to protect his beloved master or mistress by attacking the "assailant." Or, on the contrary, the dog may think this is some new kind of a game and try to join the fun. It is obviously advisable for newlyweds to sleep behind closed doors, with the dog on the other side. He may sulk at first, but he will soon get used to it.

SPOILED DOGS are like spoiled children. The vice might be described as habitual, deliberate disobedience. Dogs and children are often spoiled by owners and parents who try to compensate for something in their own past by overprotecting and overindulging their children and pets. In the best of cases, the spoiled dog or child corrects himself as he grows up and learns that selfish caprice does not make life any easier; quite the contrary. In the worst of cases, the spoiled individual dominates the household, refuses to obey the simplest command, and insists on always having his way. Sometimes he goes on a hunger strike, refusing to eat unless he is given special dishes or is fed by hand. Sometimes he goes on a sit-down strike in the middle of the sidewalk. Sometimes he indulges in a destructive rampage, confident that he will not be punished for it.

Owners should realize that dogs require domination and appreciate authority, for this is the law of wildlife society. If you own a spoiled dog, try being firmly but fondly dictatorial with him during 24 hours. You will be surprised by the increased respect and devotion that your show of strength inspires in him.

Is there such a thing as a hopelessly spoiled dog? Alas, yes. At least, it can be hopeless for a particular owner. Professional trainers can teach obedience to almost any dog, even to the point of winning competitions. But they can never guarantee that a dog will obey his owner, especially if the owner needs to change his own behavior first.

Most owners who cannot control their dogs have selected the wrong breed. The best solution is to find a good home for the intractable dog and get another of a more congenial variety. Or perhaps another member of the family possesses the necessary authority to train and discipline the dog. Many parents have found this solution to problems of child discipline. It may work with your dog too. Enrollment in an Obedience Class is excellent therapy for many dog problems. In desperation, you might seek the aid of a canine psychiatrist, who specializes in straightening out neurotic dogs.

One thing is certain. Life is too short to make any portion of it miserable by trying to cope unsuccessfully with a badly spoiled dog. Recognize your errors and your limitations. Above all, recognize that it is not the dog's fault or your own, but merely a matter of incompatability

GROWLING AND SNARLING in a chronic way are symptoms of fear, often preliminary to fear-biting. This ugly habit should be corrected by your obvious displeasure and a disgusted, "NO! BAD DOG!"

If the dog is so pathologically fearful that growling is his principal form of expression, and if your admonishments do not discourage him, there is little you can do. Never delude yourself into thinking that your dog is simply being protective. He is behaving abnormally. Obedience training, which often gives confidence to shy dogs, may help. If it doesn't, you can try to calm his nerves with mild regular doses of a canine tranquilizer. You will have a nongrowling but perpetually groggy pet, which is not much fun either. Whatever you do, you should never breed from him.

NIPPING AND BITING PEOPLE. Nipping is generally a demand for attention, an invitation to play, or a sexual gesture, sometimes the result of erotic play or dreams. Say "NO" and give the dog a light tap on the nose. Offer him the distraction of a moment of innocent play, a walk, or a chewing toy.

Biting, on the other hand, is a cardinal sin and should be severely punished. Oddly enough, big, fierce-looking dogs are less apt to bite than are many small breeds, probably because they do not feel the need for this form of self-defense. Statistics show that Working breeds bite more than others, Hunting dogs bite more than might be expected, females more than males, young dogs more than adults, and Hounds far less than other categories.

Since the consequences of biting are so grave, you should forget your principles of justice for once and punish your dog even when he bites for some legitimate reason. He must learn that biting is a crime in any circumstance. It is, in fact, quite abnormal in the domesticated dog, as proven by the fact that even Guard breeds must be trained to attack.

Never keep a dog that is a biter in a home where there are elderly people or children. If you own a dog who has bitten more than once, never take him into a crowd or a public place without a muzzle, and only if you are well-insured.

There is no truth in the saying, "A barking dog never bites." Barking and growling often precede an attack. If a strange dog barks at you in an unfriendly way and assumes a threatening posture, with tail stiff and high, eyes starey, and hackles raised, and if these signs increase as you move closer, beware! If the dog shifts his weight onto his hindlegs and drops his tail a bit as you approach, he may be putting on an act. If he wags his tail in a friendly way, with his hackles raised and his facial expression one of aggression, these ambivalent signs reflect his own inner conflict between aggression and submission, fearfulness and curiosity. Your behavior will determine the outcome of the encounter.

Try not to be afraid. Fear produces adrenalin, which dogs can scent and which arouses their aggressive instincts. Never let a hostile dog get behind you. Pivot slowly so that you are always facing him. Don't throw anything at him, try to kick him, or make menacing gestures, unless he is very small. A big dog would merely be aroused to battle. Instead, try to give an impression of confidence and disinterest.

If you are on neutral territory, continue casually on your way in an oblique line rather than a direct approach. If you are on the hostile dog's territory, it is wiser to retire discreetly, without panic or haste, and without turning your back on him. If the incident occurs on your own property, you can stand your ground and firmly order the dog to GO AWAY, then pretend to interest yourself in something else. The chances are that he will stop in his tracks, seek the nearest post or tree and lift a leg (urination being the canine solution to many social dilemmas), and finally wander off.

Nobody can guarantee that he will do so. But these tactics often work, probably because they take into account the dog's sense of territory as well as his so-called "Flight Distance," which is a factor in the behavior of all wild animals and many domesticated ones. Experiments and observation have shown that there is a critical distance within which an animal will chase or attack a stranger, and beyond which he will retreat or remain indifferent.

Generally speaking, dogs attack human beings only if they have been provoked (perhaps unwittingly), have been trained to do so, or are mentally disturbed. Some dogs have phobias about such things as bearded men, long black garments, and walking sticks. Dogs have also been known to attack menstruating women. Some even seem to be racially prejudiced. Many dogs with a strong guarding instinct are hostile to visitors who remove something (like garbage collectors), but accept those who deliver goods—although mailmen may have a different theory. It is true that mailmen are bitten by dogs more often than any other category of humanity, but this is probably due to the frequency of their visits.

Fear-biting may be a symptom of genetic degeneration, in which case the behavior is chronic and the infirmity incurable. Tranquilizers calm aggressive instincts and consequently the impulse to bite. But far better than drugs, whose effect is temporary, is obedience training, which develops the more civilized part of the dog's nature. When this does not succeed in reforming a biter, a professional trainer may be willing to tackle the case. If even he considers it hopeless, the only solution left is retirement in confinement, like a wild animal in a zoo, or euthanasia. This may sound heartless. But you should realize that chronic biting is abnormal. A vicious dog has no place in human or animal society.

Isolated instances of biting, on the other hand, are a reflex action, often caused by pain or by some thoughtless or cruel human act. Most of them are easily avoided if you:

—*Never* disturb a sleeping dog, even with a caress, without first waking him by speaking to him.

—*Never* attempt to give a painful treatment to a dog without first muzzling him.

—*Never* take a bone or food away from a dog or even pat a dog while he is eating.

—*Never* offer a dog a tidbit and then snatch it away.

—*Never* keep a dog chained where he can be teased by other dogs or children. If he has to bite in order to defend himself, he may remain overaggressive forever after.

—*Never* handle a dog roughly, especially around the genitalia.

—*Never* let your dog become overexcited at play.

—*Never* touch an injured dog who is in pain or coming out of anesthesia. He is even more apt to bite than is the sleeping dog who is disturbed.

—*Never* caress or make advances to a strange dog. Present the back of your hand for him to sniff and leave the next move up to him.

—*Never* open the door of a house that is guarded by a dog. Let the owner do it. It may seem all the same to you, but to the dog there is an enormous difference.

—*Never* stare a dog straight in the eye. This is an unfriendly act among animals, and most dogs hate it.

—*Learn to recognize the signs of hostility in a dog:* ears laid back, hair bristling along the spine, a crouched position, tail stiff, and teeth bared. When you see one or more of these, beware.

If, in spite of all of this advice, you are actually attacked by a dog, it is time to cease pretending to be friends and to think of defending yourself. Protect your face with folded arms, and if the dog jumps up on you, turn aside so that he will strike a glancing blow. Remain facing him, as you call for help and curse his owner. You can also shout "NO!," hoping that he has been trained to understand this word. When the dog ceases his attack, keep on standing still and do not move away until he does. If you are attacked by a small dog, you can use your legs to keep him at a distance and try to throw him off balance. But these tactics would only excite a big dog.

If you are bitten by a dog, do not ignore the injury. When you know the dog and are sure that he is healthy, you can treat the wound as an ordinary puncture wound, washing it thoroughly and applying antiseptic. The sad fact is that people are far more often bitten by their own dogs than by strange ones, usually when they are trying to stop a dogfight. This alone should prove that dogs do not bite only ill-meaning persons, but sometimes their best friends, in certain circumstances.

If you know the dog's owner or can find out his name from the dog's collar tag, you should notify him of the incident. If the dog is insured, you should be able to recuperate the cost of your treatment.

When you are bitten by a strange dog or a stray, greater precautions are advisable. Have the wound treated by your doctor, even if it is a minor one. He is required by law to report the incident to the local health authorities, because of the danger of rabies. He is also the best judge of the subsequent steps that should be taken.

AGGRESSIVENESS toward other dogs and people can be caused by some congenital defect, by an ailment, by pain, by jealousy, by insufficient attention or exercise, by a traumatic early experience, by the bad influence of another dog and, perhaps most often, by excessive confinement. Wild animals kept in old-fashioned zoo cages used to be in a permanent state of aggression. But do not believe the old wives' tale that raw meat or too much meat makes dogs vicious, because it is not true.

Obedience training is always a help, if not a sure cure, in canine behavior problems. A change of environment, which probably means a change of ownership, can completely transform the personality of an aggressive dog. Castration of males certainly diminishes aggressiveness— sometimes too much, to the point of apathy. Oddly enough, spaying females does not seem to have the same effect, although specific hormone treatment may help. When aggressiveness has been deliberately bred into a breed, as in the case of some Guard breeds and show Terriers, little can be done aside from keeping the dog muzzled and leashed in society, and in a kennel the rest of the time, where his belligerency can do no harm.

If your own dog suddenly becomes aggressive, you should try to analyze the cause and then remove or correct it. If you do not succeed in curing the vice or in controlling your dog, you should seek another home for him and get another dog.

We have already seen how to deal with a dog who is aggressive toward people. But what about those who are aggressive toward other dogs? If you are walking peacefully down the street with your dog and a strange one attacks him, what can you do to prevent or stop a *dogfight?*

Normally, a dog will not attack another dog who is on a leash or tied up. Even wild dogs and wolves will not bite a dog who is down in a submissive position. Male dogs seldom attack females or very young puppies. On the contrary, they will defend them, if necessary, by attacking an aggressive strange dog. But an unaccompanied male dog of aggressive character or in a bad mood may attack another dog because he thinks the other dog has offended him in some way, has shown insufficient respect for him, has violated his territory, or simply because he does not like the other dog's scent or tail carriage.

The most immediately effective means of separating two battling dogs is to turn a water hose on them or to douse them with a pail of cold water. Unfortunately, this is not always possible.

You can also try to separate the dogs by wielding a broomstick or some long-handled garden tool, even a long stick. But never try to separate them with your hands. The strange dog will probably turn on you. Even your own dog may bite you if you touch him while he is trying to defend himself. It is practically impossible to stop a dogfight between two big dogs without the aid of another person—preferably the owner of the attacking dog. If you are brave and strong and enjoy taking risks, you can pull or lift the aggressor by the tail or hindlegs and throw him aside. If you are afraid of nothing, you can grab his testicles, which will cause him to release his grip immediately—after which anything can happen. When the dogs have been separated by one means or another, you must then stand between them, with the weaker one behind you, facing the aggressor, scolding him and shouting for help. If both owners are present, they should shout "NO!" and "STOP!" But hysterical screaming will only excite the dogs to fight more fiercely.

Your principal goal should be to avoid making things worse by getting injured yourself, to produce some distraction that will cause the attacking dog to loosen his hold, and to get the separated dogs rapidly under control by putting them on the lead and dragging them away.

If you try to snatch away a small dog or to get him out of danger by holding him in your arms, the attacker will probably turn on you. Instead, urge the owner of the attacking dog to force his pet to release his grip by pulling his tail or hindlegs. When his hindlegs are lifted off the ground, a dog loses much of his force and belligerence.

Once your dog is safe, you can vent your justifiable anger on the owner of the other dog, who is indirectly responsible for the distressing incident—as you would be, if the attacking dog were yours.

SHYNESS AND FEARFULNESS become vices rather than merely traits of personality when they are so extreme that a dog is afraid of strangers, afraid to leave his home or even his bed, afraid of any unusual object or noise, panics for no apparent reason, cowers when you reach out to caress him, and prefers to curl up in a corner rather than lead a normal social life. Such pathological shyness often leads to fear-biting and incontinence.

Sometimes it is due to a miserable infancy, to too much confinement and solitude and not enough love. Many puppies raised in commercial breeding establishments where they are deprived of human contacts and caresses, suffer from "kennel shyness" forever after. It may also be a reflection of the owner's character. An overprotective owner who refuses to let his dog satisfy his natural curiosity about people and things can unwillingly plant the seeds of shyness. All too often nowadays, shyness is the result of inept breeding, therefore genetic and incurable.

The experience of motherhood may give self-confidence to a shy bitch, although her mate should be carefully selected in order to counteract her temperamental weakness and avoid its reproduction in her offspring. Breeding a male can make a shy dog bolder too, but there is the same danger of reproducing undesirable characteristics if his mate is not chosen with care. Training of any kind instills confidence, and a regular daily schedule is always reassuring to insecure individuals. Until the age of 3 or 4 months, a shy puppy can usually be transformed into a confident one merely by understanding handling. Beyond that age, the problem is much more difficult to solve.

A pathologically shy dog is a particularly endearing creature, who looks up at you timidly, begging for love and protection. He is apt to remain forever excessively dependent on his owner, as well as extremely devoted, which may be just what some owners find most satisfying. Even so, neither the overshy dog nor the overdependent relationship can be considered entirely normal.

14.

Your Dog's Social Life

Dogs are highly sociable creatures. Given the choice between solitude and companionship, almost all of them would vote for companionship—preferably of human beings or of other dogs, but also of cats, cattle, horses, turtles, sheep, even of birds in a cage or fish in an aquarium. Your dog will probably be unhappy if you shut him up in his kennel or in a separate room when you are entertaining guests, and he may mope if you leave him at home when you spend an evening with friends. On most occasions, it would be inconsiderate to impose your dog on your guests or hosts. But there are other times when a dog can be a welcome and popular member of society if he is taught to observe a few elementary rules of courtesy.

Young puppies, like young children, should be seen and not heard. In fact, they should be seen only by doting parents and relatives and for brief periods of time until they have learned to behave themselves. But small and medium-sized adult dogs are socially acceptable almost anywhere if they (and you) observe the following

RULES OF CANINE ETIQUETTE

"Never jump up on people."

You can suppress this natural instinct most easily during puppy training (see page 294).

"Never force your attentions on people or try to attract attention to yourself."

Unless your dog has been invited as an honored guest, his presence should hardly be noticed. Keep him close to you, leashed if necessary, and train him to lie quietly at your feet or under your chair.

"Never beg for food from the dining table."

He will not want to if you feed him beforehand.

"Never be a four-footed gate-crasher."

Even if you know your friends love your dog, ask for permission to bring him with you.

"Never leave traces of your visit in the form of pawmarks on the furniture or hair on the carpets."

Brush your dog before you take him on a visit. Wash his face and paws. Make sure that his behind is clean. When it rains, carry him in your arms from the car to your friends' home in order to avoid mud stains on the rug—or leave him at home.

"When your owner visits friends who have a dog, be content to stay at home and guard the house."

The danger is not so much of a dogfight as of a leg-lifting contest between the host dog, who wants to mark his territory, and the guest dog, who wants to leave his visiting card.

Most dog owners know that two male dogs or two females are apt to be less friendly than two animals of opposite sexes. Dog of the same general type, such as Hounds, Terriers, Spaniels, and so forth, are apt to get along better than breeds of very different temperaments, who may have different rules of play. Very large dogs are apt to be amazingly tolerant of small ones. All adult dogs are indulgent with young puppies. Nevertheless, compatibility between two dogs is as much a matter of temperament as of sex, age, or breed. As with human friends, it is impossible to foresee whether or not two individuals will get along well.

Obviously, you should never take your Hunting dog with you when you visit friends who own birds, nor a Hound or Terrier to the home of cat owners, nor any dog to a house where there are pet mice, hamsters, or rabbits. Even if these creatures are safely confined and out of sight, your dog will scent them and perhaps spoil the entire evening by his persistent attempts to ferret them out of their hideaways.

"Never make indecent gestures toward your hosts or guests."

Owners of bitches in heat, and women at certain times of the month, carry odors that excite male dogs. The best solution is to leave your dog at home. When you are unable to anticipate the situation, at least keep him leashed and under control.

"If you find the party dull, be patient and catch up on your sleep. If you feel the urge of nature, control yourself."

When your dog is restless and starts tugging at your sleeve or pawing your knee with an imploring look, take him outside to do his business, or take him home.

As unfair as it may seem, some dogs are unacceptable in other people's homes, even though they observe all of these rules to the letter: large or cumbersome dogs, bitches in heat, any dog who is ill or shedding, any dog who is not perfectly housebroken, any dog who is teething, dogs who drool excessively, and puppies under 6 months of age.

VISITS

A well-behaved city dog makes many friends and often receives invitations, especially if the dog and his owner are known to be inseparable. A little foresight on your part can do much to maintain his popularity.

—If you and your dog are invited to spend A DAY OR A WEEKEND IN THE COUNTRY, pack a kit bag with his water bowl, feed bowl, sufficient dog food, a towel, a chewing toy or ball (but not his squeak toy), his brush and comb. Try to respect his normal schedule for meals and walks, as long as they do not conflict with your hostess' program. If they do, don't worry. Your dog will happily adjust to the change of program as long as he is a member of the party.

—If your dog is INVITED TO GO FOR A DRIVE, you should either hold him in your lap or bring along a blanket or towel to protect the back seat of your friend's car. Needless to say, you should not accept the invitation if your dog is prone to carsickness.

WHEN YOUR DOG IS HOST TO A CANINE VISITOR, it will come as a surprise to him, and the moment of introduction is a critical one. Your own attitude will set the tone. If you are friendly and enthusiastic, your dog is apt to imitate you. But if you fearfully keep him at a distance from the four-footed guest, he too will be suspicious and hostile, and you may spoil what might have been a beautiful friendship.

When two dogs take an instant dislike to each other, the only courteous solution is to shut your own dog up in his run or in another room. When the visitor has left, praise him for his sacrifice and take him for a walk to cheer him up—and to change his ideas too, so that he does not urinate wherever there remains a trace of the intruder's scent.

If, on the other hand, your dog and his visitor make friends, you can let them play together, indoors or out. But keep an eye on them. Do not let them romp for very long, and do not give them a toy or bone to play with, for it is likely to become an object of dispute.

WHEN YOU ENTERTAIN FRIENDS, your dog will become excited as soon as he hears the car in the driveway or the sound of the doorbell. Let him bark, as a good guard should. The say "GOOD DOG. Now, QUIET. They are FRIENDS." Make him SIT before you open the door, so that he cannot jump up on your visitors. Then introduce your dog: "This is ZORRO." A guest who understands dogs will respond by saying, "Hello, Zorro," in a friendly tone, without attempting to caress him. He may hold out the back of his hand for Zorro to sniff, but he will leave the next move up to the dog.

If your guests are allergic or afraid of dogs, as some unfortunate people are, your pet should be confined and out of sight during their visit.

If your guests arrive with their children in tow, it might again be wise to whisk your dog away—not so much to protect the children as to protect your dog.

Some pet dogs, in the presence of guests, seem to think it is their duty to be the life of the party. Discourage this idea at once. Train your pet to lie quietly at your feet or in his favorite corner.

TRAVEL

IN PUBLIC PLACES, your dog should always be completely under control. A good rule is never to take into a public place a dog that has not been obedience-trained, or is not small enough to be carried in your arms if necessary.

RESTAURANTS generally admit dogs (other than Guide dogs for the blind) only as far as the cloakroom. It is a city health ordinance in most cases, and has nothing to do with the restaurant owner's opinion of dogs. Since a dog in a cloakroom is an inconvenience for everyone and no fun for the dog, it is better to leave him at home or in the car.

If your dog is permitted to enter with you, do not abuse this rare privilege. Keep him leashed, with the hand loop around your foot or wrist, underneath the table—or, better still, a banquette or booth, whenever possible. Never let him put his paws on the table. In fact, never let him put his head above the table. Never feed him from any of the tableware (he should have been fed beforehand anyway). If the restaurant is overheated, as so many of them are, he will probably become thirsty. Ask the waiter for a bowl of water, or fill a clean ashtray with water, but never a cup or even a saucer. At the end of the meal, a lump of sugar can reward your dog's good behavior. When you leave, hold him close to you on the leash or carry him in your arms, if he is small.

SHOPPING TRIPS are not an ideal form of fun for dogs and certainly do not replace the daily walk. But every experience widens your dog's horizons and develops his intelligence and manners. You might take him with you to buy a newspaper, a package of cigarettes, or a bottle of wine, even in an uncrowded suburban department store, if dogs are admitted. But shops where food is sold are forbidden territory. Shoestores and china shops should be excluded for obvious reasons.

If you take your dog with you into PUBLIC BUILDINGS (not the post office, where dogs are prohibited), or into an APARTMENT BUILDING, you will face the problem of acquainting him with various means of entrance and escalation.

Revolving doors were designed for two-footed features, not four-footed ones, but most dogs can manage them very handily if you keep them close to you. You can also carry a small dog in your arms. But it is more educational to let him stand on his own feet whenever possible.

Elevators present no problem if you hold your dog in your arms or keep him on a tight leash, entering and leaving rapidly, with your dog preceding you in order to be sure that the door does not close on his nose or tail. But never enter a crowded elevator with a dog. Wait until you have it to yourselves. This is, incidentally, a good opportunity to teach your dog several useful words of immediate practical significance to him: "WAIT for the elevator. NO. There are too many people, we will have to WAIT longer. NOW you can COME. Be QUICK! NOW we can get out. Be QUICK! GOOD DOG!"

Escalators are hazardous because your dog's paws or nails can get caught in the joints, causing him untold agony and possibly permanent injury. Take a small dog in your arms. If he is too big or heavy, use the staircase or the elevator.

Since TAXICABS are not obliged to accept canine passengers, it is only common courtesy to ask the driver for permission to get into the cab with your dog. It would be unreasonable to ask him to take a very large dog or a wet or muddy one. A small dog who can be carried in your arms or on your lap is seldom refused, but do not be offended if he is. And when a cabbie offers you this special service, reward him with a word of thanks and a generous tip. (A generous tip offered beforehand may even persuade him to accept a big dog.)

SUBWAYS AND BUSES in some cities permit four-footed passengers if they are enclosed in a carrying case, which means that some other means of transport must be found for medium-sized and large dogs.

It is evident, that the only universal transportation available to dogs is a private car or their own four legs, accompanied by your two.

You know all about car training (page 274) and the rules of sidewalk safety (page 265). But what about SIDEWALK ETIQUETTE? For example, should you speak to strangers on the street who admire your dog?

Why not? Dog fanciers are democratic and generally discreet. Their compliments are usually sincere and their curiosity genuine. These casual contacts can brighten the lives of lonely people and are easily avoided by busy ones.

Should you let Fido greet strange dogs? Again, why not? If it will not cause a traffic jam and if the other dog and his owner seem clean and healthy. But never let the greeting go beyond a sniff and a tail wag. The sidewalk is not the place for play, even less for sexual advances.

When you meet a friend on the street, your dog will probably be delighted by the surprise encounter, and you should hold him tightly on the lead to prevent him from literally jumping with joy.

Conscientious dog walkers who make their daily rounds at regular hours soon recognize one another, and there is nothing compromising in exchanging a friendly greeting. Many people who have lived for years in the same block or even in the same apartment building without ever having spoken to each other have formed lasting friendships through their dogs.

SOCIAL EVENTS

In addition to these fortuitous friendships, there are other ways in which a dog can enlarge his owner's social life.

First of all, there is your LOCAL DOG CLUB, which provides an opportunity to meet other dog lovers as well as to learn about dog care and training and to participate in Match shows, Obedience classes, and other activities. Any town that is large enough to have a newspaper probably has a dog club too.

Joining an OBEDIENCE CLASS is fun for dogs and owners alike, and particularly beneficial to recalcitrant dogs and inexperienced owners. You are sure to meet people who have the same dog problems as you do (perhaps worse), and you can exchange ideas or simply sympathize. If your local dog club does not sponsor an Obedience class, why not organize a group, hire a good instructor, and start one yourself? The National Association of Dog Obedience Instructors, Inc. (Secretary: Olive Point 5407 Coxson Road, Richmond, Virginia 23231) should be able to help you.

If you own a purebred dog, by all means join the NATIONAL BREED CLUB, if only in order to receive the club magazine or bulletin with news and information of special interest to you. The names and addresses of breed clubs can be found in the *AKC Gazette* and other dog magazines.

Animal welfare organizations are always grateful for volunteer help. There may be in your town or vicinity a branch of the ASPCA, the Humane Society, of PAWS, or some other group to which you can offer your services.

If you are politically minded, you should be especially interested in the activities of the American Dog Owners' Association (1628 Columbia Turnpike, Castleton, New York 12033), whose 900 member clubs protect and further the interests of animals and their owners legislatively, on a state and national level. Their legal prosecution and investigation have been successful in combating inhumane pet store chains, dogfighting, and other forms of cruelty to animals.

A particularly lively group that combines social events with informative seminars and luncheons with guest speakers, even chartered overseas trips at bargain rates to visit foreign dog shows and breeders, is the Dog Fanciers' Club.

If you read carefully one of the national all-breed magazines, you will find news of these canine organizations as well as many others. With over one hundred national breed clubs in the country, more than 3,000 specialty clubs, and perhaps two or three thousand all-breed dog clubs, your problem will be to choose among them.

DOG SHOWS used to be important social events which were even reported in the Society section of the New York *Times*. The current emphasis may be less on socializing and more on churning out Champions, but a dog show is still a very good place for meeting fellow breed fanciers and for participating in social events and informative meetings.

Some dog shows are so famous and spectacular that you should try to attend at least one of them during your lifetime, even if you are not interested in showing. While dog shows are held every year in most large cities, the one that most often makes the front page and attracts dog lovers from all over the world is the Westminster Kennel Club show, which has been held in New York City at the beginning of February without interruption for over a century. The five-star outdoor dog event of the year in the East is the fashionable Westchester Kennel Club show in early September. The Trenton (New Jersey) Kennel Club show in May is becoming increasingly important too. For Midwesterners, there is the two-day spring show of the International Kennel Club of Chicago, which registers even more entries than Westminster. On the West Coast, the California circuit has been breaking records for entries and attendance, and setting new standards of organization and presentation, with such major events as the June show of the Kennel Club of Beverly Hills in Los Angeles, the Santa Barbara Kennel Club show at the end of July, the Ventura County Dog Fanciers' Association show the same weekend, the Sun Maid Kennel Club of Fresno show in the spring, the Santa Clara Valley Kennel Club show in San José at the end of February, the Kern County Kennel Club show in Bakersfield in April, and the very elegant annual San Francisco show.

Try also to attend the National Specialty of your particular breed. One of the oldest is the Spaniel Specialty at the Roosevelt Hotel in New York just after Westminster. Most of them, however, are held in rotation in different parts of the country. The American Kennel Club and the all-breed dog magazines are your best sources of information about Specialty Shows, as they are for dates and places of major Obedience Trials.

National Championship Field Trials generally take place between the end of October and the beginning of December, except for the National Amateur Retriever Championship, which is held in June. The American Kennel Club, the American Field, and individual national breed clubs can give you information about dates and sites.

Unfortunately, your dog will be admitted to all of these events only as a qualified competitor. But he will surely benefit indirectly from your attendance, if only because of the increased admiration and respect for dogs that the experience is bound to give you.

15.
Your Dog's Sex Life

The dog's sex life is surprisingly elementary, considering his advanced stage of social evolution. Canine sex is limited to the goal of reproduction, devoid of sentiment and imagination, and sadly lacking in gallantry.

Love does not enter into canine sexual relations. At least, not our idea of love, nor even that of wild dogs and wolves, who practice courtship and monogamy and share family responsibilities. How strange that these refinements should be present in wildlife and absent in domestication, instead of the other way round!

While a few dogs and many more bitches show a sexual preference for a particular mate, sometimes to the exclusion of all others, attractions and aversions between a bitch and a dog at mating time are usually due to the timing of the bitch's cycle, or to some purely physical compatibility or incompatibility. Most often it is the bitch who rejects a suitor, while a healthy stud dog literally jumps at every mating opportunity that comes along. The bitch's greater discrimination does not seem to be based on sentimental considerations. Could it be that Nature has given her the responsibility for thus effecting some kind of instinctive natural selection in order to improve the species?

Females are interested in sex only during the few days, usually twice a year, when they are in heat and capable of conceiving. The rest of the time, they regard male dogs as playmates, friends, or enemies, but never as potential lovers.

Male dogs are interested in sex almost all of the time, but they are interested in a particular female only during her heat periods. Unmoved by beauty, charm, or intelligence, indifferent to fame and fortune, many dogs are, oddly enough, aware of social position when they select their sexual partners. A dominant or socially superior bitch may not permit a socially inferior male to mount her, while male dogs invariably perform with greater skill and confidence when they are socially dominant over the female. At the same time, a male is apt to lose interest in an over-submissive female. Moreover, although a flirtatious bitch who coyly eludes his advances will arouse his male ardor, he is quickly put off by one who is genuinely shy or fearful.

Normal male dogs will sniff any bitch they meet, but will woo her only if she happens to be in heat. When they find her receptive, they do not bother to dress up in fancy plumage or perform ritual dances, as do many lower-ranking creatures. Neither do they present her with gifts and compliments, as do higher ones. Their only idea is to get down to business right away. The dog's sexual instinct is thus designed simply to propagate the species and to improve it when possible by permitting the strongest dogs to mate with a maximum number of bitches.

Sexual fidelity, common in many wildlife species, is not the rule among domesticated dogs. When it exists, it is more often due to lack of extra-marital opportunity rather than to sentimental conviction. A male who has been bred to a neighborhood bitch may continue to pay her regular visits in order to check on her condition. But he is undoubtedly checking on all the other bitches in the area too. The female is no less libertine. The sire of her puppies is just another male, and the fact that she may never see him again does not bother her a bit. Even immediately after intercourse, male and female are perfectly content to go their separate ways and, if possible, repeat the act with other partners.

Furthermore, while females have so highly developed a maternal instinct that they are among the most exemplary mothers of the animal kingdom, male dogs are not only faithless husbands but also terrible fathers. They may not actually deny paternity of the puppies they have sired, but they certainly take little interest in them. This too seems to be an effect of domestication. Wild dogs and wolves help to prepare the nest. They bring back food to the nursing bitch, help to wean the litter by regurgitating partially digested food for the puppies, and even, on occasion, baby sit. Most domesticated dogs, on the other hand, may be induced to sniff their newborn offspring once or twice, but they generally prefer to ignore and avoid them. Instead of being shocked by this behavior, we should accept it as further evidence that canine sexuality and its consequences are not the same as ours.

The sex drive is powerful in a normal healthy dog, male and female. However, in some breeds, lines, and individuals, the instinct seems to have become attenuated, possibly due to hormonal insufficiency, to the effect of civilized life, to loss of vigor through indiscriminate breeding, or to some psychological factor. A male dog may be inept or confused by the mating procedure, and a female may be reticent, hostile, or terrified. So, ridiculous as it may seem, human intervention is sometimes necessary in order to effect a successful canine mating.

To breed or not to breed? The question should be carefully considered, especially by the owner of the bitch, because whelping and raising a litter of puppies requires a considerable investment of time, money, and loving care, as we shall see. But even if you decide not to breed your bitch or dog, you will understand them better physically and psychologically if you learn a few of the basic facts of canine sexuality. Above all, you will realize that the dog's attitude toward sex is nothing like ours, and that it would be unfair to judge his sexual behavior by our standards.

THE MALE DOG

The male dog's SEXUAL ORGANS consist, firstly, of a pair of *testicles* in which the sperm is produced, descending from the abdominal cavity into the *scrotum,* a bag of skin with two compartments hanging underneath the abdomen.

Normally, the testicles have descended into the scrotum at birth and can be felt with the fingers as two small swellings. Sometimes, however, only one testicle had descended properly, a physical malformation called *monorchidism.* The dog can still reproduce, thanks to his remaining testicle, but his sperm is only half the normal quantity. It is unwise (although permissible) to breed him, since the condition is believed to be hereditary. When both testicles remain within the body cavity, the condition is known as *cryptorchidism* and is far more serious, since the dog will be sterile, the testicles either atrophying inside the body or the sperm produced there being killed by body heat. In both cases, the dog's sexual behavior is quite normal, even though his reproductive ability is limited or nonexistent. These conditions seem to be most prevalent among Bulldogs and certain Toy breeds. Hormone therapy or surgery may sometimes correct monorchidism, but nothing can be done in the case of cryptorchidism. Both conditions disqualify a dog from the show ring.

The sperm that is formed in the testicles passes through a pair of fine tubes, the *epididymis,* which act as a sort of storehouse; then into a pair of 'ducts, the *vas deferens,* which carry it into the *urethra,* the tube through which urine flows and from which the sperm is ejaculated during copulation. Dogs also have a *prostate gland* inside the pelvis, which secretes a fluid that is combined with the sperm during the mating act.

The dog's most prominent male organ is, of course, the *penis.* Placed visibly in front of the testicles, it also runs back inside the body, curving up under the anus and through the pelvis to meet the urethra. One of the reasons why dogs love to have the base of their tail rubbed may be the pleasurable pressure the action exerts on the internal portion of this sensitive organ.

The penis is protected by a sheath of skin which is retracted during mating. Sexual excitement causes it to become engorged with blood, to swell and stiffen. Petting and erotic dreams can cause erections too.

So far, you see, the male dog's sexual equipment is similar to the human male's. But wait. In addition to the muscles, nerves, lymph ducts and blood vessels in the penis, there is an ingenious *penis bone* which helps to maintain it rigid during copulation. Another marvelous peculiarity of the canine penis is the *bulb,* a globular swelling that occurs near the base of the shaft after penetration. When it is gripped by the sphincter muscles of the bitch's vagina, it produces the *tie* or *lock* that ensures fertilization by maintaining the penis inside the bitch until all the sperm has been discharged—a much longer process than human ejaculation. Only afterward does the swelling subside and can the penis be removed.

Sensitive to touch, these male organs are also very sensitive to heat and cold. You can see for yourself that dogs carry their penises and testicles close to the body for warmth during cold weather, and hanging free for keeping cool on hot days. Excessive temperatures destroy the sperm, which may account for a certain number of otherwise inexplicable missed breedings.

Like females, male dogs have five pairs of *mammary glands* with nipples, symmetrically placed on the underside of the body. They are, however, underdeveloped and, of course, never lactate.

The dog's sexual equipment is immediately aroused to action by the scent of a bitch in heat, particularly by her vaginal secretions, but even by her urine. His eye becomes bright, his tail erect and trembling with excitement, his stance bold. Dogs can also be excited by the memory of a bitch's scent. They can have erotic dreams that terminate in erection and ejaculation, often aided by penis-licking *masturbation*. An aroused or highly sexed dog will also masturbate with such objects as pillows, chair or table legs, cats, and human limbs. It is certainly wise to discourage these practices before they become obsessive. But they are not sufficient cause for considering your dog a sex maniac. Within reason, masturbation may offer a beneficial relief from the celibacy that most pet dogs are obliged to endure.

Is VIRGINITY harmful to your dog's health? Probably not. His sex life, or rather lack of it, undoubtedly causes more concern to his owner than it does to him. In natural wildlife, many males of many species never have a chance to mate throughout their lives. Even Thoroughbred racing stallions are used for stud only during four or five months of the year and remain celibate the rest of the time. Among the millions of pet dogs in America, only a tiny percentage of them—mostly professional stud dogs—have any kind of regular sex life, the vast majority remaining virgins. A mating may give confidence to a shy dog. It may also make him less friendly with other males, whom he henceforth considers rivals. This is certainly true of stud dogs, who for this reason are separated from other males in breeding kennels. But sexual experience, or absence of it, does not alter a dog's basic character.

Puppies become vaguely aware of sex as early as the age of 4 weeks, when they often mount their littermates, male or female, but without erection or penetration. Puberty occurs around the age of 7 months, when innocent sex play, including nipping, is frequent. Male puppies become more masculine in appearance and behavior. Like little boys, their voices deepen, their chests fill out, and their hair grows in masculine patterns, forming beards, mustaches, and neck ruffs. However, male puberty is not signaled by any physiological event as unmistakable as a bitch's first heat. Civilization seems to hasten puberty. Domesticated dogs attain sexual maturity much sooner than wild dogs and wolves, who become adult only at the age of 2 or 3 years.

A dog is capable of breeding between approximately the ages of 1 and

12 years. The older dog is apt to be less fertile, although many exceptional litters have been sired by aged dogs who were bred to vigorous young bitches. The American Kennel Club will not normally accept a litter for registration if the sire is under 7 months of age or over 12 years old, undoubtedly due more to skepticism than to moral considerations.

The usual practice is to breed a stud dog for the first time during his second year, as a sort of virility test, engaging him in regular stud service only after his second birthday. In the best-run kennels, this involves no more than one or two matings a week during the "high season" for dog breeding, which corresponds to the heat periods of most bitches: during the winter, early spring, and late summer.

The pet owner often feels guilty (which is nonsense) for depriving his pet of normal sexual relations. More justifiable is concern for perils the dog may encounter in trying to satisfy his urge. He will wander far afield in order to track down a bitch in heat, exposing himself to the risk of traffic accidents as well as to the possibility that he will be unable to find his way home again. Once he has reached his destination, there is the danger of a dogfight, because he is unlikely to be the only suitor. It is not first come, first served in the canine world, but the prize to the victor and survival of the fittest. Small, weak animals haven't a chance, and the greater a little fellow's courage, the greater the risk of his being injured by stronger rivals. The only solution is to keep your dog under control or in confinement at all times, give him plenty of exercise and attention every day, and be particularly careful when a neighborhood bitch is in heat. You might even try to persuade the bitch's owner to give her deodorant pills and to be doubly careful about confining her.

When a male dog is so highly sexed as to be practically uncontrollable, CASTRATION may be considered. It is much more frequently practiced in England than in the United States, in order to reform the temperament of wandering and over-aggressive dogs as well as oversexed ones. The surgical removal of a dog's testicles completely eliminates his interest in females and changes his behavior and character to a certain extent, making him more home-loving, more obedient, less aggressive, and more affectionate. It may also make him more lethargic. Furthermore, the hormonal change can lead to obesity if the dog is not given an adjusted diet and perhaps a compensating hormone treatment. The operation is not dangerous if performed early enough, between the ages of 3 and 10 months—which is, however, usually too early to detect an abnormal degree of sexuality or aggressiveness in a dog. There is a recovery period of 2 or 3 days, and a month or so of recuperation. Although horsemen consider it perfectly normal to geld their riding mounts for identical reasons, the idea of castrating a pet dog is understandably repugnant to most dog lovers as well as to many veterinarians. On the other hand, many vets contribute their services to "neutering clinics" which exist in some cities, and where the operation is much less costly than in a private animal hospital. Castration is, of course, an extreme and definitive measure which should be carefully considered, taking into account the fact that a castrated dog is not only useless for breeding, but also ineligible for show.

Since dogs are uninhibited by moral or emotional considerations where sex is concerned, they seldom develop SEXUAL ABNORMALITIES OR DEVIATIONS. The most common are monorchidism and cryptorchidism, as we have seen, which are purely physiological and cause a diminution of the sexual drive along with a lessening or absence of fertility, and nothing more.

Homosexuality in the human sense does not exist in dogs. Sometimes a hormonal imbalance will cause a dog to be rather feminine in temperament and appearance, or a female to be tomboyish, while all young puppies indulge in explorative sex play with littermates of either sex. A bitch in heat may mount other bitches as the fertile part of her cycle approaches. This is, in fact, one of the signs that she will soon be ready to be bred. Even spayed bitches mount other females, perhaps during the periods when they would have been fertile had they not been spayed. These activities, as well as masturbation (if it is not overdone) are perfectly normal. Never punish your dog or become upset. Instead, offer him some distraction by taking him for a walk or playing a vigorous nonerotic game that he enjoys.

When a dog is disinterested or unable to copulate with a willing bitch, it is due to *impotence* rather than to homosexuality. The condition can generally be cured by hormone treatment and especially by diet, since impotent dogs are often obese.

When males mount males and females mount females, it is generally an expression of *nymphomania*. If it occurs during puberty, it should not last for long. But if it is habitual in an adult dog, the only way to remedy the embarrassing situation is to try to distract the dog's attention toward more innocent activities, such as obedience training or active sport, which at the same time develop self-control. The extreme cure is castration or spaying. Saltpeter in the dog's food has no effect. Mild tranquilizers are not much better and cause undesirable side effects. A thorough veterinary examination may, however, reveal some minor physical malformation or malfunction that might account for the dog's abnormally frequent sexual arousal and could be treated successfully.

What is the best policy for a fond owner to follow concerning his dog's sex life?

If your dog is purebred and an outstanding example of his breed, there is no reason why you should not breed him to a suitable purebred bitch if the opportunity arises. But do not let him become a promiscuous vagabond, no matter how fine a sire he would be. Above all, do not feel guilty about obliging your dog to live and die a virgin. Given a sufficient amount of affection, physical and mental activity, he can lead a perfectly happy life without a regret for an experience that he has never known.

THE BITCH

The canine female SEXUAL ORGANS consist of a *clitoris, vulva, vagina,* and *uterus,* similar to the female human organs, except that the canine uterus is Y-shaped instead of oval. Likewise, the essential female canine sex glands are two *ovaries,* which produce the *ova,* or eggs, that combine with the male sperm to create the fetus of a new organism. When a bitch is in heat, the ova ripen and burst through the membranous covering of the ovaries, to make their way into the *Fallopian tubes,* and from there into the horns of the uterus. In these *uterine horns,* the eggs are fertilized by the male sperm, attach themselves to the walls of the horns, and there grow into mature fetuses. The lower part of the uterus ends in the *cervix,* which leads into the vagina.

The *mammary glands,* or breasts, are arranged in two rows of five (occasionally only four) on each side of the underbelly, with perforated nipples, larger than the male variety, for milking. The breasts nearest the groin are usually the most developed and secrete the most milk during lactation. Breasts and nipples become enlarged during the final days of a bitch's pregnancy, although no milk is produced until whelping time approaches. In maiden bitches bearing their first litter, it may not be present until whelping is actually in progress. Unmated bitches may also have "false" pregnancies and secrete milk at the time that puppies would have been born had the bitches been mated. This is quite a common occurrence and is no cause for alarm, as it can be treated successfully by a veterinarian.

Like pregnant women, pregnant bitches develop other reproductive organs: the *placenta,* or afterbirth, which is a flat organ composed mostly of blood vessels, by which the embryo is attached to the uterine wall and in which the exchange between the maternal and fetal circulations takes place. By way of the *umbilical cord,* which joins the fetus to the placenta, the bitch supplies oxygen and nutrition to the fetus and also carries away waste matter.

All of the female sex organs are modified during the bitch's heat period, and even more during pregnancy.

Like their little brothers, female puppies indulge in innocent sex play, including mimicry of the sex act. But once they have had their first HEAT PERIOD, or OESTRUS, around the age of 7 or 8 months, they are interested in sex only during the first fertile days of this biannual event. The first heat may occur as early as 6 months in small breeds, and at 10 months or even later in large breeds that are slower to develop. Some bitches, like wild dogs and wolves, have only one heat period a year instead of two. With age, the periods normally become less frequent and less intense. Nevertheless, a female dog can become pregnant as long as she lives, for there is no such thing as canine menopause.

The female dog's sex life is thus, in a way, less troublesome to her owner than is the sex life of a male. It may be easier to keep her confined or boarded during 3 weeks twice a year, than it is to control a sex-minded male dog all year round.

As with human females, the bitch's behavior during her period varies from one individual to another. Some of them are apathetic and go off their feed, while others are ravenous. Some refuse to go outdoors, become restless or irritable. In others, the heat period is practically imperceptible.

The onset of the period is signaled by a discharge of bright red blood from the vagina.

During the first 5 to 7 days, there is also a visible swelling of the vulva, often accompanied by a change of appetite, irritability toward other females, and frequent urination in normally inviolable spots including her own front doorstep, as if to advertise her imminent receptivity to male dogs in the neighborhood. Although she does what she can to keep herself clean by licking (which may be sufficient if she bleeds very little), a bitch who bleeds profusely will stain carpets and furniture if protective measures are not taken. You can keep her in the kitchen, or in a room where the floor is covered with newspapers and the furniture shrouded in old sheets or plastic. Or you can buy canine hygenic pads, which are horribly unesthetic, but do avoid soiling. Or you can board her, and let somebody else worry about it all.

From the 5th to the 9th day, the discharge gradually pales to pink or colorless. This is the moment when males will start arriving from miles around. Since some of your bitch's scent will probably cling to your clothing, even you will become an object of interest to them. Instead of nipping and snarling at her admirers, as she did the week before, the bitch will be playful and flirtatious with them, coy and affectionate with you.

You can try to throw unwanted suitors off her scent by carrying her in your arms from the house to the car and driving some distance away to do her business, if possible at some odd hour when no other dogs are apt to be around. Never let her off the lead. She will not feel much like exercise anyway, and it is your only means of preventing an amorous escapade.

Around the 10th day, the discharge is quite pale, the bitch actively solicits male attention of a specific kind by switching her tail aside and presenting her rump in a most shameless fashion. Although she has not yet entered her maximum fertility period, there is a risk of conception from the ninth day on if she is permitted to mate, as she is obviously eager to do.

Around the 11th day, the discharge ceases and ovulation begins. From now until the 15th day, conception is very likely and the bitch is most anxious to mate. It is certainly the most difficult and frustrating period for everyone concerned. If a breeding is not desired, the bitch must be constantly supervised. If you do want to breed her, the best days are usually the 12th and the 13th. Many breeders schedule a mating on the 11th day, with a repeat on the 13th. Others prefer to take a chance on the 9th to 11th days, believing that fertilization early in the cycle produces bigger, better litters. Some hedge by recommending the 10th day, with a repeat on the 11th. As you see, there is no hard-and-fast rule. The breeder of your bitch can probably advise you better than anybody else.

On the 16th day, the honeymoon (if there was one) is over. The bitch rejects her suitors, including her mate. Nevertheless, conception may still be possible. A good rule at this point is to beware of possible fertility if you do not want a breeding, but not to count on it if you do.

On the 17th day, there is seldom any doubt. The bitch strongly rejects males and will resume her interest in sex only six months later.

On the 20th or 21st day, copulation as well as conception is impossible. The heat period is over. Male dogs turn their attention to other females and other activities. However, some interesting odor may still cling to the bitch's coat. Spare her unwanted male attention by giving her a good bath.

Broadly speaking, you can think of the oestrus cycle as beginning with one week of preparation, followed by one week of ovulation, and terminating with a week of decline. With such a precise scenario, why should there be so many missed breedings?

The answer is that, in actual practice, the procedure is not always so predictable. It varies from one bitch to another, even from one heat period to another of the same bitch. Unusually cold weather, a chill, or some minor ailment can retard or interrupt a bitch's heat. It doesn't really matter if you do not want to breed her. But if you do, the proper timing of the mating can mean the difference between success and failure.

The most common error is to breed too soon. This may be avoided by buying a chemically treated strip called "Tes-Tape," which was originally devised for diabetic urinalysis but has also proven useful as a canine fertility test. It is inserted in the bitch's vagina, and if it turns bright green, it indicates that the bitch will be ready for mating 24 hours later. Since the fertile phase usually lasts for several days, breeders often schedule a breeding 24 hours after the bitch first displays her willingness to be bred, with a repeat breeding, just to be sure, the next day or, preferably, the day after that so the male's sperm will be fresh. Experienced owners also take into account the condition of the bitch's vulva. Hard and swollen during the first phase of the period, it becomes soft again when her fertility is at its height. The least scientific method may be as good as any. It is so simple that it works even if you lose track of the days: Breed your bitch when she is most eager for it. If in doubt, repeat the breeding the following day.

A bitch should never be bred during her first heat period. She is still a puppy herself, and even if conception is possible, she is much too immature for the physiological demands or to be a solicitous mother. Wait until the second, or preferably the third heat. Large breeds that are slow to mature should have attained their adult size before being bred, which may mean an even longer delay. The only exception to the rule is the Bulldog and other abnormally large-headed breeds, which are often mated young in the belief that the delivery of large-headed puppies is facilitated when the mother's bones are still soft and pliable.

The American Kennel Club will not accept a litter for registration if the bitch is under 8 months of age or over 12 years. As in the case of stud dogs, the ruling is inspired less by humanitarian considerations than by skepticism that a bitch so young or old could have whelped a healthy litter. Serious breeders retire their brood bitches at the age of 7 or 8. They never permit more than one breeding every 18 or 24 months, in order to leave time for recuperation. They generally undertake the first breeding no earlier than the third heat, no later than the age of 3 years, and permit not more than 3 litters during the bitch's lifetime.

A bitch can be fertilized by more than one dog during the same heat period. Roving bitches indulge in many matings during their fertile phase. The result may be a SPLIT LITTER, with some of the puppies sired by one dog, some by another. Even if all of the puppies appear to be purebred, a litter of mixed parentage is ineligible for registration.

A repeat breeding with the same stud dog can result in a TWO-PART LITTER, if both matings were successful. In this case, all of the puppies are genetic littermates and the litter can be registered, although some puppies will be more mature at birth than others. In order to avoid too great a disparity, a repeat breeding should therefore take place no later than 48 hours after the first one.

There is no truth to the old wives' tale that a bitch who has been bred to a mongrel will never be able to bear a purebred litter. This superstition, called TELEGONY or IMPREGNATION, nevertheless persists. Perhaps it started and survives simply because a bitch who is sufficiently unsupervised to mate with a mongrel once is apt to repeat the adventure. Or perhaps it is because owners who have successfully bred their bitch to a selected sire then relax their supervision, enabling the bitch to mate again with a mongrel of her own choice. In any case, it is scientifically impossible for a breeding to be influenced by a previous one. Disappointing litters may occur, due to some throwback on one side or the other, or to some genetic incompatibility. But never are they caused by an earlier mismating.

When an UNDESIRED MATING has occurred, pregnancy can be interrupted if the bitch is taken to the veterinarian within 4 to 5 days (the sooner the better) for a series of hormone injections. Later than that, abortion is much more dangerous and seldom advisable.

Human CONTRACEPTION measures do not work on dogs. A special canine contraceptive pill is widely used in Europe, and a similar method, called "Ovaban," is now available in America on veterinary prescription. It is, however, seldom prescribed, partly due to possible undesirable side effects, and also because there are so many restrictions to its use that it is not very practical anyway. Experiments are being made with intrauterine devices and implants as well as male contraceptives, but these are still in the laboratory stage. You can buy a canine chasity belt: a hideous contraption that offers an obstacle to male advances, but no real security. At the present time, solicitous bitch owners must face the fact that the only sure and safe means of temporary canine contraception are human vigilance and confinement.

SPAYING is the most common form of permanent contraception, involving the surgical removal of the bitch's ovaries, thus eliminating further heat periods as well as the risk of contraception. The operation is simple and safe for a puppy 6 months old, but it becomes more delicate as she grows older, especially older than 18 months. There is a difference of opinion as to whether it is better to spay a bitch before her first heat period, or to wait until 2 or 3 months later. If her ovaries are removed before she has developed all of her feminine characteristics, she is apt to remain forever tomboyish in appearance and behavior. Besides, many pet owners, advised by their vet to wait until after the first heat, find that the 3-week period is not as troublesome as they thought it would be, and decide to keep their bitch unspayed.

A spayed bitch is ineligible for showing, although she can compete in Obedience Trials. Like castrated males, she tends to put on weight, to become quieter, more home-loving, and more affectionate. She will never be bothered by false pregnancies, uterine infections, or breast tumors, and will remain more youthful in appearance and spirit than bitches that have been bred. Seeing Eye dogs and Army dogs are systematically spayed, as are many trained Guards. Canine welfare societies encourage the spaying of all mongrel bitches, in order to control the canine population explosion, and many of them sponsor neutering clinics. Many communities, for the same reason, charge a higher license fee for breedable bitches than for spayed ones.

If you own a mongrel, it is probably wise to have her spayed. There is little point in breeding her, because you cannot tell what her puppies will be like anyway. But if you own a fine purebred bitch, be very sure of your decision before having her spayed. You may regret it.

TUBAL LIGATION is a means of preventing pregnancy by tying the bitch's ovarian tubes. Her heat periods continue, as does her interest in mating. The intervention is therefore seldom worthwhile.

Virginity is no more harmful to a bitch's health and temperament than it is to a male dog's, although some unbred bitches cause their owners great distress by indulging in FALSE PREGNANCIES. They go through all the stages of true pregnancy, complete with increased weight and appetite, milk production, nest-making, and the various instinctive rituals of actual motherhood. The condition is due to a hormonal disturbance which causes obvious physical and mental anguish to the bitch. Some veterinarians recommend breeding as a cure, although many bitches resume false pregnancies even after having whelped a litter. Suitable hormone treatment and a diet eliminating milk and cutting down on meat can frequently ease, if not completely cure, the condition. Veterinary care during these difficult days can at least avert the principal physical risk, which is the formation of mammary abscesses due to the bitch's unrelieved milk supply. Most owners learn to understand and live with bitches prone to this pathetic condition. As a matter of fact, a bitch who has had one false pregnancy is apt to make a habit of it if she remains unbred and unspayed.

THE MATING ACT

The canine sexual act is preceded by a certain amount of foreplay. If the timing is right and the bitch has entered her receptive phase, she will coyly tease the male, who will be immediately aroused by her odor. He will sniff her vulva, become increasingly excited, and then will lick it, preparing it for penetration.

Even before his penis has become fully erect, he will mount the bitch, encircling her body with his forelegs and making rhythmic pumping movements. The female has, in the meantime, taken a stance in front of him with her hindlegs braced and her tail switched aside, exposing the enlarged entrance to the vagina.

Once the dog has penetrated, a portion of his penis near the base enlarges like a "bulb," and the bitch's sphincter muscle surrounding the vagina tightens, causing the "tie" as the male starts to ejaculate. Because this process takes some time, from 5 to 10 minutes to half an hour or more, and because the mounted position would be too tiring for both animals, the male instinctively turns aside without breaking the tie, and swings a foreleg over the bitch's back so that both of his forelegs are on the same side. And so they remain, rump to rump or side by side, until the ejaculation has been completed and the penis swelling has subsided. At this point the penis can be withdrawn. The act is over. Male and female go their separate ways without so much as a goodbye kiss.

It seems absurd to have to help a pet perform so simple and instinctive an act. When two normal, healthy dogs of opposite sex are brought together at the right moment and in favorable conditions, the mating does indeed generally take place quite spontaneously. In the case of an inexperienced couple, however, the male may need encouragement and the female reassurance. The male may even need help in guiding his penis into the correct orifice, or in placing both forelegs on the same side of the bitch during the tie. The bitch may need to be supported in her stance or prevented from sitting down during the tie, which could fracture the male's penis bone, causing him excruciating pain, rendering him useless for breeding, and perhaps causing uterine injuries to the bitch as well. This is why you should never, never attempt to break a tie. The best way of supporting the bitch is to place your hands under her belly and her head between your knees.

Obviously, it is desirable for one or both owners to be present during a mating in order to intervene if necessary. The owner of a maiden bitch or

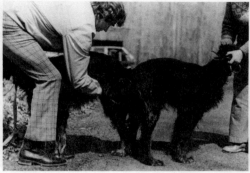

A male Gordon Setter mounts female. The owner helps the male turn around for the "back-to-back" position.

The "tie." (*Photos by Lee Whitney*)

of a shy or nervous one should always insist on being present. Even if the bitch is experienced and co-operative, it is a good idea to keep her leashed, but to leave the male free to operate unencumbered. The bitch's owner can sit on a stool or chair, holding and caressing her head. If an overexcited male has difficulty in penetrating, it may help to hold the bitch's hindquarters steady and slightly raised.

Most of the owners' contributions are, however, preliminary to the act. First of all, the selection of a suitable mating site, preferably a quiet, enclosed place, indoors or out, free from distracting sights and sounds and possible interruptions. For practical reasons as well as because a stud dog is apt to be more confident in his home territory, the bitch is customarily taken or shipped to the male. Pet owners, of course, can make any arrangement that suits them best. It is certainly better to take a pet bitch to the male rather than to ship her, which means selecting a stud dog within driving distance. It is also customary for the owner of the bitch to pay the owner of the male a stud fee in the form of a sum of money, the choice of a puppy from the resulting litter, or both; while the owner of the stud dog often promises a free return breeding at the next heat if this one proves unfruitful. Whatever the agreement, it should be put in writing, including provisions for the case where there is only one living puppy, and a time limit for selecting the free puppy so that the rest of the litter can be sold.

Before breeding, both owners should make sure that their dogs are in healthy condition, free from worms and contagious disease, well-groomed and clean, especially around the genitalia. The long hair around the vulva of a very shaggy bitch is often trimmed. The choice of a mating hour may be important too. The morning is perhaps the best time, when both dogs are relaxed and fresh. In any case, both dogs should have a full meal not less than 3 or 4 hours before the great moment.

Stud dogs are generally given a sperm test at regular intervals to make sure that their sperm count is sufficient for successful breeding. There is no equivalent fertility test for females, but both dogs should be given a simple test to make certain they are not infected with CANINE BRUCELLOSIS, a sort of venereal disease that causes abortion in the female and infertility in the male and is usually transmitted by infected vaginal discharges and seminal fluids during mating. This world-wide plague seems to affect Beagles more than any other American breed, and stray dogs more often than pets. Although there is no specific cure, antibiotics and blood culture are usually prescribed, while research laboratories seek a means of controlling the disease.

The owners' attitude during a mating can influence their dogs' behavior and consequently the outcome of the project. Owners improve with experience too. If it is your first time, try to suppress any feeling of anxiety or embarrassment. Above all, be patient. Canine copulation takes a long time. And remember the guiding rule: Manipulate the bitch only when necessary, and leave the male dog free to work things out for himself.

He is usually quite capable of doing so. In fact, a healthy male and female of the same breed or of harmonious size will normally mate without the slightest difficulty. When one or the other is stubbornly reticent or hostile, it is unwise to force them. Nature often knows best. Perhaps there is some mechanical or genetic disharmony, or perhaps the timing is wrong. Some experienced stud dogs have an unerring instinct for sensing the right moment for mounting a bitch. Let the matter drop and try again the next day.

After a successful mating, you should praise the male (who will be feeling very proud of himself anyway) and take him outdoors to relieve himself. Also praise the bitch (who will be feeling satisfied but tired). Be sure to continue supervising her, because she may remain receptive for several more days during which there is still a risk of fertilization. After the mating, the two owners (or two witnesses) should sign a stud-service certificate, attesting to the act.

Sometimes the sexual act is expertly performed, yet pregnancy does not ensue. Human beings experience the same disappointment. Most often the female's failure to conceive is due to the mistiming of her cycle. But it can also be caused by the STERILITY of either partner, in other words, the inability to produce live sperm or ova. The condition may be temporary or permanent. In pet dogs, it may be congenital or the result of infection, but even more often it is caused by dietary or hormonal deficiencies, and especially by obesity, all of which can be remedied by veterinary treatment. Theoretically, healthy dogs and bitches are capable of procreation as long as they live.

Professional dog breeders occasionally resort to ARTIFICIAL IN-SEMINATION in order to effect a breeding when a natural mating is impossible for one reason or another. This technique, which replaces the mating act, is widely practiced by cattle breeders, but is very seldom used with dogs, and practically never with pet dogs.

The procedure is simple. The male sperm is produced by manipulation leading to erection and ejaculation. It is collected in a sterile container and immediately injected into the bitch's uterus. Both animals are present at the artificial mating, although it is also possible to impregnate a bitch with sperm that has been frozen (in which case the resulting litter is unacceptable for registration).

While experienced breeders may use artificial insemination in exceptional circumstances, pet owners should be wary. If your bitch or dog is unwilling or unable to breed naturally, there may be some good reason for it: a malformation, incompatibility, or insufficiency of some kind that would make the breeding undesirable. There are too many well-bred and willing dogs of both sexes available to make such a risk worth taking.

Furthermore, mating is a pleasurable event for dogs, who, we can reasonably suppose, experience some form of ORGASM during the sexual act. At least, male dogs during intercourse proceed from a state of excitement to increased tension, then ejaculation, and finally relaxation; while the female's visible enjoyment of clitoral stimulation during the foreplay and her blissful expression and submissive behavior during the ensuing stages of the act would seem to indicate some kind of ecstasy. This is, of course, only conjecture. All that we know for certain is that in dogs, as well as in all other mammals except for human beings, it is propagation of the species rather than romance that provides the inspiration for sexual intercourse.

You now know just about all there is to know about your dog's sex life. Sexuality is certainly an important element of his existence as well as a vital factor in the survival of his species. But it is by no means the dominant influence on his behavior and personality. Other instincts are just as strong and may be stronger. The late Charles Morgan, an eminent authority on Hunting dogs and trainer of three National Retriever Champions, told of the time a pheasant escaped from its cage not far from the spot where his Champion Retriever had started to mate with an eager bitch. The Retriever immediately abandoned the bitch, dashed off to seek the pheasant, retrieved the bird, presented it to his owner in perfect style, and only then resumed and completed the mating act. What do you suppose Dr. Freud would have said about that?

16.
Breeding Your Dog

Preventing pregnancy is not always easy, but breeding your bitch successfully to a suitable male in order to produce a litter of sound puppies that is up to standard presents another set of problems.

PRELIMINARY CONSIDERATIONS

The actual mating generally takes place quite smoothly, if it is intelligently planned and supervised. But there are a number of preliminary questions to consider and decisions to be made.

First of all, *are you quite sure that you want to breed your bitch?* Do you have a suitable whelping place and the necessary time and funds to devote to raising a litter of puppies? If your principal purpose is to earn a little pocket money from the profit on a litter of purebred puppies of some fashionable breed, disillusion awaits you. It has never been easy to raise a healthy litter, and it has become quite expensive, when you add up the cost of prenatal and postnatal care, of whelping and raising the puppies and then trying to sell them. Unless you already have firm orders for the unbred puppies, and unless you can give them a happy home yourself if they remain unsold, do not breed your bitch.

Do not breed her if she is a mongrel, even a most beautiful and intelligent one. There is no certainty that her puppies will resemble her. Far too many mongrel puppies are born in proportion to the homes that can be found for them—ask any animal welfare society. It is sheer thoughtlessness to breed a mongrel bitch. Have her spayed instead. At the same time, the mere fact that your bitch is purebred with an impressive pedigree is not sufficient reason for breeding her either.

If, in spite of these dissuasions, you are still determined to breed your bitch, there are other decisions to be made.

To start with, you must decide *when to breed her*. The first heat is highly inadvisable; the second hardly more recommendable. The third heat is generally selected for a first mating by experienced breeders, since by then the bitch is about 2 years old and has attained maturity. But do not delay too long. A first breeding beyond the age of 3 or 4 is apt to cause physical and psychological problems, especially if the bitch has become obese or spoiled. The precise breeding date depends, of course, on the bitch's heat cycle (see the previous chapter). One month before the breeding date, which is to say about a week before the expected heat period, she should be given a veterinary checkup, tested for intestinal parasites and, if necessary, wormed. Worms are very debilitating to a newborn litter, and it is dangerous to administer the poisonous remedies to a pregnant bitch. So precautions must be taken before the mating occurs.

The next important decision is the *choice of a mate*. No true dog lover would dream of mating two dogs simply because the bitch is in heat and the male dog lives next door. Both owners should be discriminating, no matter how anxious they are for their dogs to have the experience. The male's merits as a stud will be judged by the results of his first breeding. If he sires a really good puppy in his first litter, his future as a stud dog is practically assured; but if he is permitted to breed to a mediocre bitch who produces a nondescript litter, his breeding career will be seriously compromised. The female, as fine as she may be, should be given a chance to improve her line by selecting a male whose genetic characteristics, combined with hers, will produce even better puppies. In order to do so, you must know something about

THE SCIENCE OF GENETICS

Genetics, or the study of heredity, is so young a science that it is composed of a few established laws, but also of many unproven theories, many mysteries, and many empiric principles that are more often true than not, although we do not know exactly why. It is largely based on the work of Gregor Mendel (1822–84), an Austrian monk and botanist who experimented with the hybridization of plants, particularly of pea plants, and who formulated the principles which bear his name: *the Mendelian Laws*. The account of his experiments was first published in 1866, but it was only after the turn of the century that scientists throughout the world took serious notice of his work and engaged in research along the same lines.

Mendel discovered that the characteristics of an organism that reproduces sexually are determined by chemical factors now called *genes*, which are carried in the *chromosomes* that are components of the cell structure of all plant and animal life. The genes are always present in pairs, one of them transmitted by the father's sperm and the other by the mother's ova. When sperm and ova combine to form the embryo of a new individual, these countless genes are also combined in a new pattern and determine the characteristics of the new organism. Since dogs possess 78 chromosomes, thus 39 pairs, each carrying as many as a thousand genes (human beings having 46, or 23 pairs), the possible combinations are practically unlimited. This is why Mendel used the simple pea plant for his studies, and why genetic research has made much use of the fruit fly known as *Drosophila*, which possesses only 4 pairs of chromosomes.

Every characteristic, or "factor," is governed by different genes which regroup into myriad patterns. Each individual inherits genes not only from his parents, but also from all the preceding generations, and when one genetic pattern is combined with that of another individual by mating, what was recessive in one of the parent's patterns may become dominant, therefore "expressed" or evident in the offspring, as when two brown-eyed human parents give birth to a blue-eyed child. When an attribute present in neither parent appears in the progeny, it is always traceable to some more distant ancestor. This is what is called a *throwback*. The explanation, of course, is that the genes for the attribute that has been recessive during a certain number of generations are reinforced by another set of recessive genes, thereby becoming dominant and expressing the attribute in the resulting offspring.

Sometimes a descending gene may, for reasons we do not fully understand, express some totally different factor from that of the parent gene, and continue to breed true to its new form. This phenomenon is called *mutation*. It is the process responsible for the evolution of all species.

An individual is said to be "pure," or *homozygous,* for a characteristic when it has inherited identical genes for it, and hybrid, or *heterozygous,* for that characteristic if it carries contrasting genes. In the latter case, even though the individual may display only one aspect of the hybrid characteristic, he can still pass on the opposite aspect to his offspring.

Prepotent dogs, male or female, bear so concentrated a gene pattern, homozygous (or pure or dominant) for so many characteristics, that they can produce offspring which resemble them no matter what they are bred to. These are the dogs that have impressed their individual stamp on famous breeding lines, even on entire breeds. The foundation sires and bitches of all modern breeds obviously possessed great prepotency.

Modern breeders are becoming increasingly skilled in manipulating dominant and recessive genes. Since it requires a pair of recessive genes to express a recessive factor, the breeder can, by selective breeding and a thorough knowledge of the two mates' genetic inheritance, either concentrate and perpetuate a previously recessive trait, or gradually eliminate it. But in order to do so, he must also take into account Mendel's *Law of Dominance.*

This is based on Mendel's discovery that when a pure strain of one factor is crossed with a pure strain of its opposite, one of these factors consistently prevails. In his experiments, it was red pea flowers that dominated white flowers in the first generation, although these first-generation red flowers, when bred to white, could produce a mathematically predictable number of white flowers as well as red ones. Dog-breeding experience has shown that pigmented eyes are thus dominant over walleyes; normal sight is dominant over blindness; normal hearing is dominant over congenital deafness; solid coats are dominant over particolored ones; black noses are dominant over Dudley noses; short hair is dominant over long; black is dominant over red and white in many breeds; and erect ears are probably dominant over lop ears. Shyness may unfortunately be a dominant characteristic. It has certainly spread like wildfire from time to time in certain lines. One the other hand, almost all so-called "lethal genes," which are incompatible with life, are recessive.

Because color is one of the genetic factors most clearly conforming to the Mendelian Laws—as well as one of the least complex, since it is believed to be determined by only 10 pairs of genes—let's take it as an example of how genetic transmission functions.

Let's suppose that you have a black male dog whose parents were both black, and whose ancestry was so predominantly black that both of his color genes can be presumed to be pure or homozygous for black. You mate him to a female with the same genetic pattern. Since both pairs of genes are pure for black, all of the puppies are bound to be black.

If, on the other hand, you breed the same dog (who is pure for black) to a bitch who is pure for white, the puppies will inherit genes for both colors, one of which will dominate the other. Since it is black that dominates white, all of the puppies will be black, but they will carry recessive white genes which will enable them, when mated to a dog who also bears white genes, to breed pure white puppies.

If you breed a dog who is pure for black to a hybrid black bitch (one who bears one gene for black and one for white), half of the resulting litter will be pure for black and the other half hybrid black.

Finally, if you breed together two dogs who each bear hybrid, or heterozygous, genes for black and white, the result is predictable over a sufficient number of litters: one out of four puppies will be pure white; one of four will be pure black; and the remaining two will be heterozygous or hybrid black (not hybrid white, since black is dominant over white)—in other words, they themselves will be black, but they will carry white as well as black genes, permitting them to produce white puppies when they are bred to a dog (even to a black dog) who also carries white genes.

This classic illustration should make the process perfectly clear:

Dominant genes, as you can see, manifest a characteristic when present in a single dose, inherited from only one parent. Recessive genes are masked by their dominant opposites unless they are present in a double dose—that is, inherited from both parents. Consequently, not all gene patterns are visible or "expressed." A dog may have a lovely *phenotype* (physical appearance, in genetic jargon), and a perfectly terrible *genotype* (genetic makeup). When undesirable recessive genes are combined with similar recessive genes, the result is a very disappointing litter, such as can occur when two dogs of unknown or unstudied background are bred together simply because each of them is an attractive individual. Succeeding generations are apt to be even more disappointing.

Another Mendelian study showed that when two hybrids, both the progeny of hybrid parents, were mated, the two sets of genes could combine in 16 ways, producing 9 different genotypes, but only 4 different phenotypes. In other words, while there are only 4 possible manifested variations, the invisible genetic patterns are much more varied, so much so as to produce increasing disparity in succeeding generations, if inbreeding is not practiced. In fact, the principal cause of degeneration is not inbreeding, but the combination of double recessive genes for some weakness that is thereby expressed, for example, when a normal dog car-

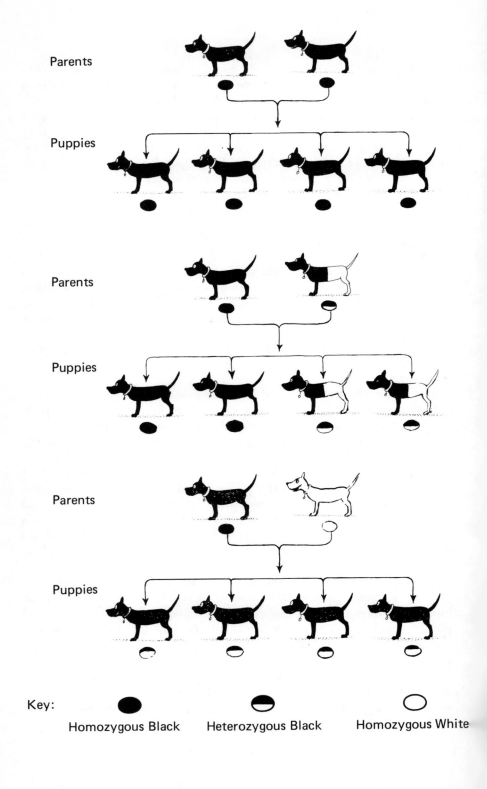

Parents

Puppies

Parents

Puppies

Parents

Puppies

Key: Homozygous Black   Heterozygous Black   Homozygous White

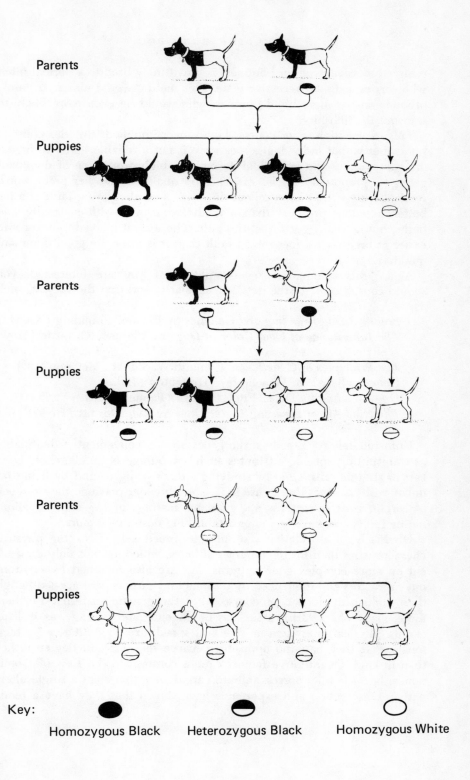

Parents		
Puppies		
Parents		
Puppies		
Parents		
Puppies		

Key: ⬤ Homozygous Black   ⬬ Heterozygous Black   ◯ Homozygous White

rying a recessive gene for blindness is unwittingly bred to a normal bitch who carries a similar recessive gene. This mating would almost certainly produce one or more blind puppies, who would be even more likely to transmit the infirmity.

This explanation is, of course, highly oversimplified. But the point to remember is that individual appearance is not a reliable guide to breeding value, unless the individual possesses a high proportion of dominant genes (is prepotent) for his or her good qualities. Another point worth remembering is that an excellent dog with a single glaring fault is a far better breeding prospect than a mediocre animal with no really bad faults, but no really good qualities either, because it is much quicker and easier to breed out a recognized fault than it is to create good dominant qualities.

Again, this summary is oversimplified. If you are interested, you should consult some of the detailed, scholarly works on the subject, such as:

> Practical Dog Breeding and Genetics by Eleanor Frankling (Arco)
> The Inheritance of Coat Color in Dogs by Clarence C. Little (Howell)
> The Principles of Genetics by Edmund W. Sinnot (McGraw Hill)
> Genetics by A. M. Winchester (Houghton Mifflin)
> Dog Breeding by Dr. E. Fitch Daglish (Palmetto Pub.)
> The New Art of Breeding Better Dogs by Kyle Onstott (Howell)

Unfortunately for breeders, the genes are not conveniently identifiable as transmitting specific attributes such as courage or intelligence, good ears or straight tails. Only by studying a dog's pedigree and by being familiar with the dogs that figure in it, can a breeder presume the presence of certain genetic patterns and plan his matings in the hope of eliminating faults and introducing or establishing desirable factors.

Obviously, it is relatively simpler to breed selectively for physical characteristics than for temperamental ones, which are not only dependent on more complex gene patterns, but are also modified by environmental factors and influenced by training and early experience (although these influences do not, of course, alter the genetic pattern). Furthermore, many characteristics such as intelligence and courage, as well as certain physical ones such as size and speed, are "quantitative," which means that they have no opposites because they vary in degree rather than in kind. Quantitative factors cannot conform to the Law of Dominance, because they possess infinite variations rather than a single alternative. Observation and experience have shown that they have a tendency to gravitate toward the average, with extremes becoming increasingly rare. In other words, Nature, if left to itself, tends to produce creatures of increasingly average size, average intelligence, and average speed.

Since the breeder can match only two sets of genes at a time, a selective breeding program cannot be accomplished in a single mating, but over many generations. For example, if his own line has a poor color and imperfect ears, he will breed to a dog that is prepotent for a good color. He will then select the best-colored individual from the resulting litter to breed to a dog who will introduce genes prepotent for correct ears. Frequently problems arise because the dog with the good color has some weakness that now crops up and must be eliminated by the selective breeding of another generation before returning to the project of establishing good ears.

Because of the number of generations involved, scientific selective breeding is feasible only for professional or amateur breeders who are equipped to undertake a continuous, long-range breeding program. Just think of Parson Jack Russell, who devoted 60 years to breeding the famous little Terrier that bears his name! Yet, oddly enough, small breeders often produce dogs of equal or superior quality to those of larger establishments, perhaps because they have to be more careful in planning each mating. Perhaps too, the small amateur breeder is more sincerely devoted to his particular breed and interested in improving it.

BREEDING METHODS

There are several different kinds of breeding:

INBREEDING is the mating together of close relatives, such as brother to sister, parents to progeny, uncle to niece, or nephew to aunt, which involve considerable duplication of inherited gene patterns. Therein lies the value as well as the danger of inbreeding. If the gene patterns control desirable qualities, these will be reinforced. But if they control weaknesses, the faults will be just as strongly established and passed on to future generations. It is certainly the most rapid way to achieve a desired physical conformation, sometimes to the detriment of temperament.

Perhaps it would be more accurate to define inbreeding as the combination of similar gene patterns, for it is the genetic similarity rather than the family relationship that counts. A mating between a brother and sister with very different gene patterns may practically amount to outcrossing, whereas mating two cousins with almost identical genes would be extreme inbreeding. We see the results of this in human families, when two brothers may be very dissimilar in appearance and character, and two distant cousins as alike as identical twins.

There is nothing unnatural about inbreeding. Animals in their wild state often mate with close relations. The idea of incest was invented by man, and fairly recently at that. Inbreeding was widely practiced by the ancient Greeks and Romans, the Inca Indians, the royal families of Egypt and Hawaii. It persists in many Asiatic lands even today. Nor is it true that inbreeding necessarily leads to degeneration. All of our pure breeds have been established by inbreeding, and in most lines the serious weaknesses have been completely bred out, so that there is less danger of degeneration from inbreeding than from outcrossing.

Nevertheless, successful inbreeding requires careful selection of the parents and systematic culling of the offspring. When the process is repeated by breeding the best offspring together, the desirable characteristics should be evident. A second culling and inbreeding should produce a consistent type and quality, with prepotency for transmitting them.

Six generations of poodles. The matriarch is the gray in the center, aged sixteen and a half, and the youngest is the eight-week-old puppy at the bottom. (*Bruce Baum*)

This, at least, is the theory of inbreeding. In actual practice, the project may be complicated by the appearance of reinforced faults along with the reinforced virtues. The emergence of recessive undesirable characteristics is actually helpful in the long run, because once their presence is revealed, the breeder can take steps to eliminate them. But, of course, precious time is lost and severe selection is essential. In order to minimize his risk, the inbreeder must be thoroughly familiar with each of the individuals involved in a mating as well as with their ancestors for several generations, which is possible only if he has bred, whelped, and raised them. For this reason, intense inbreeding is best left to the experts with a long-range breeding program.

LINE BREEDING is the breeding together of more distantly related dogs who trace back to the same ancestor, but who have no other duplication in their pedigree. When the ancestor is a superior example of the breed, prepotent for a maximum number of desirable characteristics, this method is the safest way to produce a litter of puppies that is consistent in type and quality and bears a strong resemblance to the outstanding forebear.

First-cousin matings (common grandparents) are a popular example of this breeding method. As a matter of fact, geneticists have remarked that first-cousin human matings within illustrious families, which were perfectly acceptable in earlier eras, produced an unusually high percentage of exceptional individuals. The formula of grandparent to grandchild is another that is widely used. The mating, for example, of a Champion grandsire to his best granddaughter, or of a Champion grandmother to her best grandson, also complies with many breeders' predilection for breeding a young bitch to an experienced male, and a mature bitch to a vigorous young stud dog. In dog show Brace Classes, grandparent-grandchild entries are often more closely matched than littermates.

The results of line breeding are less immediate than those of closer inbreeding, which generally produces an effect on the first generation. But the risks are also lessened.

Line breeding is thus merely a mild form of inbreeding, completed by selection of the offspring. It is undoubtedly the method of purebred dog breeding that is most favored by professional breeders at the present time.

You will sometimes see puppies advertised in dog magazines as being "line bred" to a certain dog. The value of these puppies obviously depends on the quality of the founder of the line, not on the mere fact of being line bred to something. Certain exceptional, prepotent dogs have engendered an astonishing number of superior offspring, like Lochinvar

of Ladypark, a famous English Collie who produced during his lifetime
some fifty International Show Champions and himself was Best of Breed
at Cruft's at the age of 3 and again at the age of ten; or the English Set-
ter Field Champion Sports Peerless, whose life record was 16–168–608,
meaning that he won 16 Field Trials and that 168 of his offspring won
608 Field Trials! On the other hand, a carelessly supervised program of
line breeding (as of inbreeding) can yield a consistent production of in-
creasingly mediocre dogs, or dogs of similar attractive superficial appear-
ance, but all of them congenitally cow-hocked, shy, or nervous.

OUTCROSSING is the breeding together of two unrelated dogs of the
same breed. (*Crossbreeding* is the mating of two purebred dogs of
different breeds.)

Complete outcrossing is theoretically impossible within any purebred
variety, because all dogs of the same breed share common ancestors if
you trace back far enough. A normal pedigree records just four genera-
tions, including 30 names, usually with a certain number of duplications.
But if you trace back to the tenth generation you would have 2,046
names, and to the twelfth generation 8,190, certainly with numerous du-
plications. So when we speak of outcrossing, we imply that there is no
duplication in a normal pedigree, in other words, no common ancestor
during the previous three or four generations.

Since outcrossing is the combination of two dissimilar sets of genes,
the results are highly unpredictable, unless the breeder is thoroughly
acquainted with the antecedents of both partners, or unless one of the
mates is very prepotent. You would always get a Cocker Spaniel from
outcrossing two Cocker Spaniels, of course, because the established
varieties have been sufficiently inbred to breed true to type. But you
might get a nondescript litter of puppies, none of which resembles either
parent very closely.

Nevertheless, outcrossing is a valuable tool for experienced breeders.
Not so much because of the stamina and vigor it produces in the
offspring (since these qualities are transmitted only to the immediate
progeny and not to succeeding generations), but because outcrossing can
introduce virtues that were lacking and can be fixed by subsequent
inbreeding. However, at the same time it can destroy established values.
Experienced breeders therefore outcross infrequently, and only with very
carefully selected mates.

Most modern breeds were created by an original outcross or series of
outcrosses, followed by many generations of inbreeding. These programs
were closely controlled by knowledgeable breeders who exercised great
skill, ruthless selection, and infinite patience in accomplishing their task.

All purebred dogs are thus the result of controlled inbreeding, while mongrels are the result of uncontrolled outcrossing. It is interesting to know that indiscriminate outcrossing between different breeds eventually results in an animal that is very similar to the original wild dog. Breeders have also noticed that indiscriminate outcrossing within the same breed, when it does not reinforce some degeneracy, tends toward the average.

INSTINCTIVE BREEDING, although unrecognized as a breeding method, has been responsible for the birth of many superlative dogs. Call it instinct, intuition, breeding talent, or what you will. It is as inexplicable as a gift for music or painting, but it just as certainly exists in some people who possess the ability to mate two dogs together and produce superior progeny.

The British dog breeders of the nineteenth century, who created many of our modern Sporting breeds, are fine examples of this form of breeding art. They had never heard of genes or chromosomes. They used their instinct, their "eye for a dog," in breeding what they considered to be "the best to the best," weeding out what they considered undesirable.

The breeder's "eye for a dog" is not quite the same as the pet owner's. The breeder appreciates and seeks not so much outstanding beauty in the individual dog, as the ability to pass on desirable qualities to his offspring. He thus applies the Mendelian Laws in an instinctive way. The ideal of many breeders is a brood bitch who is free from major faults and perfectly sound, although perhaps not a beauty; and a stud dog who is prepotent for a maximum number of good qualities. It is then the stamp of the male that is impressed on all the puppies, resulting in a consistent type, an instantly recognizable family resemblance, you might say, which incarnates the breeder's idea of the perfect dog of his chosen variety.

Breeding therefore remains an art in which science and inspiration both play a part, since even the most intuitive breeders, whether they realize it or not, are guided by the laws of genetics; and even the most scientific ones are obliged at times to rely on instinct.

BREEDING A PET DOG

All of this may be fascinating, but it is of little immediate practical interest to a pet owner who decides to breed his bitch simply because he wants a puppy from her, or because his vet has told him that the experience of motherhood would be beneficial. Nevertheless, some basic notions of breeding science will at least help a pet owner to avoid such naive errors as believing that breeding a black dog to a white bitch will result in a litter of gray puppies (for you know that some of the puppies may be black and some white); or that mating a big dog to a tiny bitch will produce a litter of uniformly medium-sized puppies (you are likely to get an assortment from large to small). Nor could you possibly make the foolish mistake of breeding a prick-eared Collie bitch to a lop-eared male in hopes of getting puppies with perfect ears. (You know that all of them would have bad ears, and that the only way to breed for good ones is to mate your prick-eared bitch to a male who is prepotent for perfect ears; there is a good chance that at least one puppy will have correct ears, and you can breed from that.) In short, the important point for the pet owner to understand is that when you breed, you are not merely mating a pretty bitch to a handsome dog. You are bringing together two different sets of genes. And it is the combination of these gene patterns, not the appearance of the parents, that determines what the puppies will look like and also, to a certain extent, how they will behave. Even though your ambition may be merely to breed a healthy, normal litter rather than to found a Championship line, you should try to make a constructive contribution to the improvement of your chosen breed when you seek a mate for your bitch. You will not only have better puppies, easier to place in better homes, but also an indescribable sense of pride and accomplishment.

If you have wisely purchased your bitch from a serious breeder, you should seek his (or her) advice before selecting a mate for your pet. The breeder can probably recommend a stud dog of his own, or perhaps one that he has used successfully himself and knows to be compatible with his line. The repetition of a successful breeding formula is called "nicking." You will be line-breeding in the best of conditions.

It should be added that when you arrange a marriage of this kind, you are expected to provide your bitch with a dowry in the form of a stud fee, which can range from a choice of a puppy from the litter and no cash at all, to a fee of $100 for a male with a good pedigree, up to $200 or more. But $300 is likely to be a maximum for a top Champion stud dog. If he is really tops, his owner will also want to make sure that your bitch is worthy of being bred to him, which is understandable.

This is the best way to find a mate for your bitch. However, since most pet owners have neither the contacts nor the time that serious breeders devote to the project, outcrossing is by far the most widely practiced breeding method. In some cases, it is the only one available. The risks can at least be limited by observing these old-fashioned rules:

—*Breed like to like.*

If you breed like-to-like phenotypes (physical appearances), you will probably be outcrossing. You may produce a nice litter of puppies, but there is no telling what future generations will resemble unless you fix their good qualities by subsequent inbreeding. If you breed like-to-like genotypes (genetic patterns), you will, of course, be inbreeding, with the risks and advantages that this incurs. The first method is a short-term policy that can improve the immediate litter, but will decrease the breeding value of the line. Inbreeding, as we have seen, is more suitable for long-term breeding programs and should be associated with rigorous culling of the resulting litter.

It is always advisable to avoid great disparity of size, which is bound to cause pregnancy and whelping difficulties. The Toy breeds established from larger varieties were gradually miniaturized by breeding small male dogs of small stock to bitches also from small stock but who were themselves large enough to whelp normally.

—*Breed to the best and hope for the best.*

Never breed your bitch to an inferior dog. It is better not to breed her at all. Try to find a mate who possesses the same good qualities to an even higher degree, and whose weak points are different from hers. You may thus be able to reinforce her virtues and eliminate her faults in the offspring. Above all, avoid selecting a male with any of the same faults.

DOG BREEDING AS A PROFESSION

is a most uncertain means of earning a living.

If you do not have a private source of income and if your heart is set on a career with dogs, it would be far more sensible to make your business a shop for dog supplies and grooming services, and do your breeding as a hobby. You might also learn to be a professional show handler who breeds on the side. Various jobs with canine associations, dog magazines, pharmaceutical and food companies with canine divisions, veterinary clinics, and research laboratories provide steadier income and enough free time to run a small breeding program at home.

If you possess sufficient capital and unswerving determination to become a professional dog breeder, you will save a lot of time and money and avoid many mistakes by first serving an apprenticeship in one or several established kennels before launching an operation of your own. A course in business management would be useful if you have had no previous business experience. Kennel management is a commercial enterprise, and you need to have commercial aptitudes and sound business methods in order to run it profitably. A love of dogs and an interest in breeding are indispensable. But they alone are not a guarantee of success in this demanding, increasingly competitive field.

DOG BREEDING AS A HOBBY

is such an absorbing interest that it risks becoming a full-time occupation.

It is also a luxury activity, requiring a considerable amount of time, space, money, and equipment. The fact that you are dealing with living creatures increases the fascination as well as the responsibility. This is also what makes dog breeding a genuine creative endeavor, an enriching scientific and psychological experience, and, at its best, an art.

17.

Whelping Your Bitch

About 62 days after a successful mating, you can expect your bitch to give birth to a litter of puppies. The happy event may occur a day or two sooner with small breeds or large litters. It may also be a day or two later. In both cases, the chances are that you have miscalculated and the whelping will be normal. But if the litter is really premature or overdue, the puppies and their mother may need special care. So it is wise to mark your calendar and to follow the progress of the bitch's pregnancy with solicitude.

SIGNS OF PREGNANCY

But first—are you sure she is pregnant? The signs are highly variable. Some bitches hardly show their condition, while others display every textbook symptom without being pregnant at all. If you take your bitch to the vet 3 or 4 weeks after the mating, he can generally make an accurate diagnosis. At 6 weeks, even you should be able to feel little globular forms and hear faint heartbeats.

The most noticeable sign of pregnancy is, of course, the enlargement of the abdomen, which becomes apparent around the fourth, fifth, or sixth weeks, large litters naturally showing sooner than small ones. There is often a change of behavior too. The bitch may become more quiet and less playful. She may be fussy about her food at first, and then develop a ravenous appetite. The teats of maiden bitches will develop, although this detail cannot help diagnose pregnancy in an experienced one whose teats have already been enlarged by previous pregnancies. The most reliable sign appears only a week or so before the whelping date, when movements of the unborn puppies can be felt and seen, especially when the bitch is lying on her side. An X-ray examination at this time can even determine the number of puppies, although veterinarians prefer not to perform one without some special reason because of the possible harmful effect on the unborn litter.

A pregnant bitch is not an invalid, but she requires special care during her 8- or 9-week gestation period. A sensible program is to take her to the vet 28 days after breeding, so that he can confirm her pregnancy and give you instructions for her care and diet. Then take her back to him 3 or 4 weeks later for a checkup and in order to make whelping arrangements.

DIET

Her diet is most important, for she must supply from her own substance all of the elements to create several (sometimes many) puppies, at the same time retaining sufficient strength and condition to face the strain of whelping and the task of nursing and caring for her offspring. She obviously needs more than her usual rations, a high proportion of body and bone-building proteins, as well as supplementary vitamins and minerals, especially Vitamins A, D, B Complex, and calcium. Your vet will undoubtedly recommend a special diet. It will probably include a generous quantity of meat, whole-grain cereals, bone-meal biscuits, an occasional egg, cod-liver oil, perhaps a yeast preparation for the B Complex vitamins, possibly calcium lactate, and plenty of fresh water. When her appetite becomes gargantuan, you can increase the protein content, but not the "filler" elements, as you did before she was pregnant. She will put on weight, of course, but do not let her get fat. It would make whelping more difficult.

At the same time, certain things should be eliminated from her diet: appetite cutting snacks, low-calorie, high-bulk preparations like canned dog food, and bones, because of their constipating effect. You should supervise her bowel movements daily. If she strains, add a little olive oil or mineral oil to her next meal, or insert a canine or baby laxative suppository. Bitches often become constipated during the last week of pregnancy, and you should treat the first sign of it.

As the puppies develop and distend the uterus, the bitch's stomach is compressed, and she will need smaller, nourishing meals at greater frequencies—for example, 5 or 6 meals a day instead of two large ones. One of these extra meals might be an evening snack consisting of an egg yolk beaten up in a bowl of milk. It provides valuable vitamins and minerals, and pregnant bitches love it.

EXERCISE

What about exercise? It is still essential. She is not sick, after all, simply pregnant. In the country, you can let her exercise according to her needs and moods. In the city, you can maintain your normal program of daily walks and outings, but at a more leisurely pace as pregnancy advances, curtailing them whenever she obviously has had enough and wants to go home.

Aside from these sensible adjustments, all your bitch needs is lots of understanding and affection, especially if this is her first pregnancy and she is disturbed and mystified by the wondrous things that are going on inside her.

WHELPING PREPARATIONS

As soon as you are sure that your bitch is pregnant, you should start to make arrangements for whelping—in other words, for delivering the puppies. You know that the red-letter day will arrive in approximately 2 months' time, and you must decide where and how to whelp her.

Animals in their wild state have no help in giving birth to their young, but who knows how many infants and mothers have died because there was no aid in an emergency? Besides, human beings place a greater value on life, and we want every infant to survive, not only the strongest. Certain preparations and precautions are therefore necessary.

If the bitch's pregnancy has progressed normally, whelping is likely to be normal too, and you need only prepare a suitable whelping room in your own home and arrange to stand by in case your assistance is needed. The vast majority of pet dogs give birth to their puppies at home, unaided.

On the other hand, if the pregnancy has not been normal, whelping difficulties can be expected. If this is your first experience, you may be nervous. A maiden bitch may also be alarmed and inefficient during her first whelping, which is apt to be more difficult and take longer than those of experienced matrons. It is advisable to invite or hire an experienced person to be present, and certainly to make sure that a veterinarian will be available if needed. If you are terrified by the event, it might be better to have her whelped at a veterinary clinic. But you would deprive yourself of an interesting and satisfying experience, and you would deprive your bitch of the comfort of your presence and of her home environment at this important moment of her life.

The WHELPING ROOM should be an enclosed place that can be kept quiet, warm, and dimly lit, safely secluded from people, other animals, and the bustle of household activity. It may be a corner of the kitchen, a well-heated spare room, or a bathroom that can be appropriated for this purpose during several weeks. Warmth is vital, especially in the winter. Newborn puppies are unable to provide their own body heat during the first few days, and they are expelled from the comfortable temperature of their mother's womb (at least 101 degrees) into a much cooler atmosphere. The whelping room should therefore be heated to at least 75 or 80 degrees the first week or two, then gradually reduced, but never to lower than 70 degrees. Place a thermometer near the whelping box and keep a constant check on it. You may need to put insulating strips around the doors and windows in order to prevent drafts, or install a supplementary heating element such as an infrared lamp suspended over the whelping box. You can see the importance of making plans ahead of time.

One week or so before the estimated birthday, you will also need to prepare a WHELPING BOX large enough for your bitch to lie comfortably stretched out, with plenty of room for the puppies too. A square or oblong wooden packing case of suitable size is fine, if you remove the top and reduce the sides to a suitable height. They should be high enough to confine the puppies and to offer protection from drafts. Fixing a narrow ledge around the inside, 5 inches wide and 5 inches above the floor, is a good safety measure that will prevent a puppy from being crushed against the side of the box by a clumsy or agitated bitch. One side may be lowered to within a few inches of the floor, in anticipation of the time when the puppies can be permitted to leave the nest at will. But devise some means of barring the opening in the meanwhile. You may need to block it even when the puppies are older and you want to be sure that they are in their bed and not wandering around getting into mischief.

Many kinds of material make good BEDDING, as long as it is warm and disposable: shredded newspapers or straw, piled high around the edges like a real nest, covered with pieces of old rugs, blankets, flannel or woolen garments, bath mats or towels. Since the puppies must be kept dry as well as warm, the bedding will need to be changed at least once a day. Beware of slippery surfaces, like smooth newsprint, which provides no traction for the puppies during nursing and when they start to walk. It can cause delay and perhaps permanent harm to their normal locomotion.

As the whelping date approaches, it would be a good idea to refrain from making any appointments for the crucial days between the 60th and the 65th, since it is impossible to calculate the exact date and hour of the impatiently awaited event.

On the 60th day, it may help to calm your nerves if you install the whelping box and give your bitch a little PRENATAL BODY CARE:

—Wash her genital area and abdomen with warm water and soap, then dry her thoroughly.
—Soften her teats by rubbing them with baby oil. If there are already drops of milk, you can take her to the vet to have it tested.
—If she is heavy-coated, you should trim the long hair around the teats and genital region. (Most bitches start losing the hair around the nipples 2 weeks before the puppies are due.)
—Make sure that she is free from fleas. Her efforts to scratch or bite could cause injury to the newborn pups.

You can also prepare your WHELPING EQUIPMENT. You may not need all of it, but it will save precious time if you are ready for any eventuality.

—sterilized blunt-edged scissors
—a mild antiseptic
—a stack of towels, and means of warming them
—plenty of clean bedding
—a rectal thermometer
—a package of absorbent cotton
—a small-sized baby bottle with a tiny nipple
—an eyedropper
—the telephone numbers where your vet can be reached at any hour
—a notebook and pen for keeping a written record of the whelping, including the time labor starts, the time each puppy appears, and any unusual symptoms or behavior of the bitch. If something goes wrong, it will help the vet to make a rapid diagnosis and take appropriate action without delay.

PRESENCE OF A VETERINARIAN. Veterinarians are too over-worked and too shorthanded nowadays to assist at every normal whelping. But when the delivery seems likely to be difficult, try to persuade your vet to be present or at least to pay you a house call during the process, especially if:
—the bitch is old.
—it is your first whelping and you are panicky.
—the sire of the litter was much larger than the bitch, in which case one or more of the puppies may be too large to slip unaided through the bitch's pelvis. (In this case, you should already have discussed with your vet the advisability of a Caesarean section.)
—the bitch has had difficulty in whelping before.
—she has had a pelvic injury, or rickets.
—she has had a difficult pregnancy and is in a weakened condition.
—she is a Bulldog, Boston Terrier, Scottish Terrier, Chihuahua, or one of the other breeds that are notoriously difficult to whelp.

If your vet cannot be present even for a few minutes, perhaps he can recommend an experienced person who will lend assistance if necessary. In any case, it is always a good idea to alert a competent friend or an adult member of the family to be on call to help you in your vigil if the whelping turns out to be an all-night production. Let the children watch, if they insist, but do not allow them to participate or even to touch the bitch or her puppies.

SIGNS OF APPROACHING LABOR. From the 60th day on, you should keep a watchful eye on your bitch, alert for any sign of approaching labor. Many bitches refuse to go outdoors during the last two or three days, although this is by no means a general rule. Some hide food around the house. Most of them start thinking of nest-building, and this is the moment to show your pet the whelping box you have lovingly prepared. If she prefers your bed, or the bottom shelf of the linen closet, you can humor her for now, but move her to the box when actual labor starts. The only infallible sign of imminent whelping is a drop in her body temperature, which occurs 24 to 48 hours before whelping. So the best means of avoiding surprise is to take her temperature twice a day. It may be even more convenient to know that if her temperature remains at its normal level, the bitch is unlikely to go into labor for at least 24 hours.

Twelve hours before whelping, maybe less, she will refuse to eat. A few hours later, there will be a ropy mucus discharge from the vagina, and perhaps (but not always) milk in her teats. The upper part of her eyes may be bloodshot. She will be restless and uncomfortable, perhaps even in pain from the invisible internal contractions of the uterine muscle as it begins the process of softening and dilating the uterus and vagina in order to permit the passage of the newborn puppies. This phase can last for a few hours, or for an entire day and night.

THE BIRTH PROCESS

When the spasmodic contractions become regular and are perceptible to touch and sight, and when the bitch strains and pants, you can be sure that the first puppy is about to arrive. At this point, the bitch helps force the puppy to emerge from the uterus and through the softened, lubricated vagina by pushing with voluntary contractions, exactly like the human technique of natural childbirth.

As you know, each puppy is connected by an umbilical cord to a placenta, which is attached to the uterine wall and has been responsible for the exchange of nourishment, oxygen, and waste matter between mother and offspring during pregnancy. The entire placenta, cord, and puppy are enclosed in a membranous bag (the "fetal envelope" or "amniotic membrane") which is filled with fluid and acts as a cushion to prevent injury to the puppy during its passage from the uterus into the outside world.

The first visible sign of the emerging puppy is a rounded swelling at the opening of the vagina, which is the fetal envelope. It may require several contractions to expel it, and during the process the bitch usually licks and bursts the bag, dispersing the amniotic fluid. Now the first puppy is visible, normally arriving head first, the shoulders and hind quarters following. However, it is not unusual for a puppy to be born tail first, known as a "breech birth." In breeds of normal conformation, this should cause no problem.

Immediately after the puppy has emerged, another contraction expels the placenta, or afterbirth, which the bitch proceeds to eat, snipping off the umbilical cord close to the navel with her teeth. Watch carefully to make sure that a placenta follows each puppy. If the cord is broken with the placenta still inside the bitch, it can interfere with the birth of the next puppy. In this event, you will generally see the end of the broken cord hanging out of the vagina. Grasp it with a clean cloth, withdraw it gently, and give it to the bitch to eat.

Sometimes the fetal envelope does not burst open spontaneously, in which case the bitch instinctively opens it with her teeth and liberates the puppy. If she doesn't, it must be done for her at once or the puppy will die from lack of oxygen, which is no longer being supplied through the umbilical cord. You simply break the membrane gently at the puppy's mouth with your fingers and give the puppy to the bitch to be licked clean. The little creature will gasp for breath and for the first time fill its lungs with air.

Sometimes the bitch fails to bite off the umbilical cord, and this too must be done for her. Some bitches, particularly those with a faulty bite or an undershot jaw, tend to snip it off too close, and in these cases it is also better to do it for her. You simply squeeze the cord between the fingers toward the puppy's body in order to press the blood back, then snip it off (or, better, crush it) with sterilized blunt scissors, about 1 or 2 inches from the navel. It is unnecessary to tie the cord before cutting it, as it will dry up and drop off in a few days. When you have time, you can apply a little antiseptic to the stub, although this is not really necessary either.

Sometimes a bitch is too tired or preoccupied to clean and stimulate the newborn puppy by licking, and you can again supply this indispensable care. At least you can approximate the same effect by cleaning the puppy with a soft cloth moistened with warm, antiseptized water, rubbing it briskly but gently against the lie of the hair. It will squirm, cry out, expelling any fluid remaining in the respiratory tract, and begin to breathe. You can then place it at one of the teats, where it will soon start to nurse.

In a small litter, the puppies are usually born at intervals of 15 to 30 minutes. In a large one, it is quite common for several puppies to be born close together, with a much longer wait before the next batch appears. This is perfectly normal if the bitch rests and regains her strength during the interval, which tends to be longer as she tires from her efforts. But if she strains and pants instead of resting quietly, and if the condition persists for as long as an hour, there may be some obstruction to the next birth, such as a puppy placed transversely, thus blocking the passage from the uterus into the vagina. This situation requires expert, rapid veterinary intervention, very possibly a Caesarean section. Do not try to handle it yourself.

On the other hand, if a puppy is only partially expelled and seems to be stuck, as may occur during a breech birth, you can help. With scrupulously clean hands, grasp the puppy's slippery body very gently, remembering that the slightest pressure can injure its fragile flesh and bones. When the bitch makes her next contraction, pull the puppy outward, stopping as soon as the bitch's contraction stops. It seldom takes more than one or two contractions to release the puppy. Never use force.

Never attempt to use an instrument of any kind. And never intervene unless the puppy is within easy reach.

The newborn puppy's first move is to seek its mother's teats and start to nurse. Animal instinct usually guides it to the right spot, but you may have to make sure that a weak or inept puppy is not left out. Remember too that the breasts nearest the groin provide the most milk. You might place the weakest puppies at these to start with, and then rotate them so that each one gets its fair share. According to some observers, the puppy who monopolizes the best teat not only gets more milk, but also establishes itself as first in the "pecking order" (the social status) of the litter forever after.

If a bitch is particularly agitated and thrashes about a lot, it is advisable to remove each puppy to a separate warm box in order to avoid in-

Newborn Rhodesian Ridgeback puppies nursing. (*Jeffrey Hanna*)

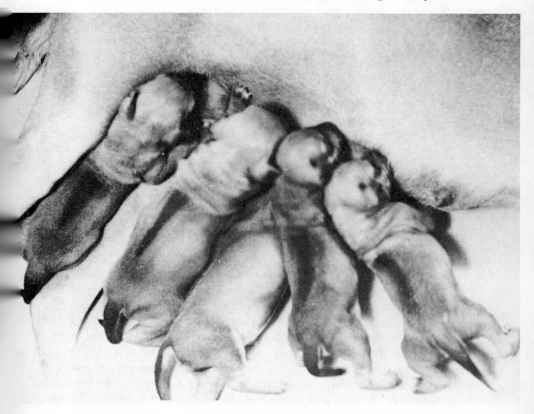

jury by the following birth. Some breeders do this systematically, although the disappearance of her puppies may worry and distract the bitch. It is probably better to adopt the same policy that guided you when you mated your bitch: Interfere as little as possible, and only when necessary. But be prepared to supervise the bitch and her puppies constantly during the first 24 hours, especially in the case of big breeds and large litters.

The entire process generally takes from 5 to 12 hours. If labor starts late in the evening, as it frequently does, you will spend a sleepless night. When the last puppy has been born, the bitch will relax and her uterus will contract. You can usually tell by feeling her abdomen that there are no remaining puppies waiting to be born. Are you sure that all of the afterbirths have been expelled? If there is any doubt, notify your vet. The unexpelled membrane can poison the bitch and, through her milk, the entire litter. The vet can give her an injection of pituitrin, which will expel any remaining placentas from the uterus.

When the last puppy has been born, when the bitch is lying quietly on her side, tired but satisfied, and the puppies are greedily nursing, you can give the happy mother a drink of warm milk, laced with a few drops of brandy if she seems exhausted. Then leave the entire brood alone to rest quietly for a few hours. And get a little well merited sleep yourself.

The great majority of puppy births take place without drama or even incident, more or less as described. When complications arise, there has usually been some reason to expect them, as in the case of mismating a large dog to a small bitch, or of whelping large-headed breeds. In the latter case, your vet will probably have recommended a:

CAESAREAN SECTION

This, as you probably know, is an operation permitting delivery of offspring through an incision in the mother's abdomen. It is called "Caesarean" because Julius Caesar is supposed to have been delivered that way. It is certainly a very ancient technique, nowadays virtually risk-free. But it should be performed no more than twice on the same bitch. It requires anesthesia beforehand and a rather long convalescent period afterward, during which the litter may have to be fed by hand. For this reason alone, it is better to rely on natural whelping whenever possible, although Caesarean puppies are just as healthy and strong as normally whelped ones. There is also much less risk of injury than with a forceps delivery. In fact, with some breeds Caesarean births are the rule rather than the exception: those of abnormal conformation like Bulldogs, Boston Terriers, and Pekingese, and some of the miniaturized Toys who simply are not strong enough to whelp themselves.

WHELPING PROBLEMS

Even during a normal whelping, emergencies may arise, and it is better to be forewarned than to be taken by surprise. For example:

—If signs of labor do not appear within 48 hours of your Estimated Time of Arrival, you may have simply miscalculated. But then again, something may be wrong. Take your bitch to the vet. The longer the delay, the greater the risk.

—If the bitch is exhausted by her whelping efforts and ceases her contractions when there obviously remain puppies to be born, call the vet. She may be suffering from UTERINE INERTIA, which is not uncommon in old bitches, in weak ones who have been debilitated by their pregnancy, and in certain breeds, including the Dachshund, Yorkshire, Boston Terriers, and the Chihuahua. The vet can give her an injection which will stimulate the uterine contractions. If this fails, he can perform a Caesarean section.

—If a puppy appears to be STILLBORN, it may be possible to revive it. First of all, make sure that the membrane covering the mouth is broken. You may have to open the puppy's mouth with your fingers and wipe off any fluid. Take it in your arms to share your body warmth with it, and rub it briskly against the lie of the hair. This stimulation usually suffices to start it breathing and thus make a transition from the watery element in which it lived before into the open air that will be its environment from now on. If not, you can try breathing into its mouth as you gently massage its chest. You can also hold the puppy by the hindlegs and swing it gently to and fro a few times. Or you can try artificial respiration, but with the greatest of care because of the fragility of the puppy's soft little bones. Another method of stimulation is to dip the puppy alternately in warm (not hot) and cold water. Another is to pass a wad of cotton with a drop of aromatic spirits of ammonia on it in front of the puppy's nose, hoping that the ammonia will cause the puppy to gasp and fill its lungs with air. Once it has started to breathe, you should place it at its mother's breast and let Nature take over.

—Previously undetected infections and insufficiencies may cause complications during and after whelping, such as:

METRITIS, an infected inflammation of the uterus, resulting from contamination during whelping in unsterile conditions or from a retained placenta. The bitch runs a high temperature, strains, suffers abdominal pains, and may produce a bloody or foul uterine discharge. This is a serious ailment requiring immediate veterinary treatment with appropriate antibiotics and possibly pituitrin injections to empty the uterus. Needless to add, the puppies must be removed from her at once and reared by hand. Some bitches seem to suffer from chronic metritis. The infection must be treated, and until it is completely cured, the bitch should not be bred.

ECLAMPSIA or MILK FEVER, a condition caused by a serious calcium deficiency due to pregnancy and lactation, which usually occurs during the first 3 weeks after whelping. The first noticeable symptoms are nervousness and rapid breathing, followed by spasms, staggering, and a high fever when the critical stage is reached. Fortunately, the cure is almost immediate, for an intravenous calcium injection can stop the distressing symptoms in a matter of minutes. But do not delay.

Eclampsia can usually be avoided by giving the bitch suitable vitamin and mineral supplements during pregnancy, and plenty of whole milk and bone meal while she is nursing her puppies.

A FADING LITTER is a tragic occurrence. A litter is born apparently sound and then, almost immediately, the puppies die one by one, despite all efforts to save them. One theory is that it may be due to a lack of Vitamin C in the bitch's organism. Another puts the blame on antibiotic treatment. A herpes virus has been found to cause weak or stillborn puppies as well as fading litters. But as yet very little is known about this unhappy phenomenon.

Extremely rare but worth mentioning, if only to point out its infrequency, is canine CANNIBALISM, when a bitch kills and even eats her offspring. This is believed to be caused by some nutritional deficiency leading to temporary mental aberration. The best prevention is obviously a sound prenatal diet with vitamin and mineral supplements. Perhaps it is a deviation of the placenta eating instinct. In any case, you should remove the puppies from their hostile mother as soon as they are born. They can be returned to her for feeding every 2 hours, if she is muzzled and supervised. But it may be simpler to find a foster-mother for the litter or to raise it by hand. You should certainly consult your veterinarian, because the bitch needs treatment for her most abnormal condition.

CULLING THE LITTER

There are circumstances in which the only humane course of action is to destroy a puppy at birth, when the process is swift and painless. The infant may be malformed; it may have been unwittingly injured by the bitch or by careless handling during delivery; or it may be so undersized and weakly that it has no chance of survival anyway. A puppy who is very wrinkled, cold and clammy, crying, or, on the contrary, completely motionless, generally has little chance of survival under normal conditions. In very large litters, some puppies may have to be eliminated in order to ensure the welfare of the others. Some breed clubs have established a "Breeder's Code of Ethics," including a list of malformations and degeneracies that should not be permitted to survive. Breed authorities in West Germany not only require official approval of all proposed German Shepherd matings, but also permit the bitch to keep and raise only 5 puppies.

Most often, a bitch will give birth to no more puppies than she can handle. Small breeds average 3 or 4 puppies; large ones, 9 or more. Toy breeds frequently produce just 1, and seldom more than 2. But some large breeds whelp huge litters, as many as 10 or 12 puppies with Bloodhounds, and up to 15 with Greyhounds and some Setters, which is far more than Nature would permit to survive. Only 8 of the bitch's 10 teats provide an adequate milk supply anyway. Some bitches cull their litters themselves by refusing to nurse or even by destroying sick or dying puppies.

If you act swiftly and discreetly, the bitch will never notice the removal of 1 or 2 puppies. Choose a moment when she is busily occupied with another, and remove it stealthily to another room, far enough away so that the bitch can neither smell nor hear it. You can also caress her, then quickly cover her eyes for a few seconds, while another person removes the puppy.

Experienced breeders consider drowning (in a bucket of warm water) or chloroform the most humane methods of disposing of unwanted newborn puppies. If the idea understandably upsets you, you can ask your veterinarian to administer a painless lethal injection, or ask your local animal welfare society to do this disagreeable deed for you. Remind yourself that it is far kinder than permitting a sickly puppy to die in suffering, or a malformed one to survive, permanently handicapped. Then do as the bitch does. Keep yourself so busy looking after the remaining members of the litter that you do not have time to think of this particularly painful but sometimes necessary phase of dog breeding.

You will, in fact, be even busier than the bitch, because you have to look after her too, and she requires a certain amount of:

POSTNATAL CARE

After her puppies are born, the bitch will be very occupied caring for them and feeding them. She may refuse to leave them during the first few days, and you will have to leash her and take her outdoors to do her business after each meal, which you may have to bring to her in the nest. She herself will take care of the puppies' waste matter by licking them clean.

During the first day or two after whelping, do not give her solid food, but a bland, milky diet, such as milk with an egg beaten into it, a milky cooked cereal, or a nourishing broth. Then you can feed her a rich diet of two meat meals and two milk feeds a day. She needed twice her normal amount of food during pregnancy, but during lactation she may need three times as much, which means that you can feed her practically all that she will eat. Check her milk supply regularly by gently squeezing

The bitch keeps her newborn puppies clean by licking them, which stimulates evacuation and also removes it. (*Claus Ohm*)

her teats. If the milk seems insufficient, the vet can give her an injection that will stimulate her production. Liver mixed with her normal feed is said to promote milk production. The third or fourth day, you can return to an almost normal diet, rich in meat and protein, supplemented by cod-liver oil and a special postnatal vitamin complex which your vet may prescribe, since extra calcium and phosphorus are often recommended at this point. It is important to pay special attention to the bitch's diet now, for deficiencies can cause lasting harm to her puppies as well as to herself.

She will have quite a lot of bloody vaginal discharge during the first week or so, and you will have to change the bedding every day, if not more often, so that it is always dry and clean. If the discharge is foul in odor or greenish in color, notify your vet at once. It may indicate a uterine infection, dangerous to her as well as to the nursing litter. There is no need for alarm, however, if her feces are voluminous and black during a few days. This is quite normal and is due to the placentas she has eaten.

As for the puppies, they will be spending all of their time feeding, sleeping, and growing at a phenomenal rate. The greatest growth takes place during the last week in the womb and the first 3 or 4 weeks after birth. An ample, healthy milk supply is of utmost importance, since it is their only source of nourishment. You must therefore continue to feed the bitch an enriched diet until the puppies have been weaned—that is, for at least 5 or 6 weeks.

The highest puppy mortality rate occurs at birth and within the first week of life. So keep a close watch on the litter to make sure that all the puppies are developing normally and are free from injuries and infection. Navel irritation, for example, often caused by insufficient or improper bedding, can cause fatal infection in the tiny creatures.

Even if the whelping has been uneventful, as it usually is, try to persuade your vet to visit the puppies and examine them when they are 2 or 3 days old. At the same time he can examine the bitch, test her milk, and check for worms again. This is also the moment for removing dewclaws if necessary (see page 174). The operation at this age is relatively painless, since the brain cells receptive to pain messages are not fully developed at birth, and healing is rapid. As you know, dewclaws are appendages believed to be vestiges of a sixth toe, but set higher on the legs where they are useless, unesthetic, and possibly harmful if they become ingrown or cause injury to other dogs. If the operation is delayed, it may require stitching, there is more copious bleeding, and the entire process is much more delicate. So do not put it off.

TAIL DOCKING (see page 173) is also preferably done when the puppies are only 2 or 3 days old, ensuring painlessness without the need for anesthesia, as well as rapid healing. The skin is pulled back toward the body in order to leave coverage for the stub. The tail is cut with sterilized scissors to the proper length (which varies according to the breed). And the slight bleeding is easily controlled with pressure bandages and a styptic dressing. The litter must be supervised afterward to make sure that the bitch does not remove the dressings and lick the wounds.

Be sure to check your state laws first, because some states prohibit tail docking, and the American Kennel Club standards that used to require it for certain breeds, including Poodles, Schnauzers, Weimaraners, some Spaniels, some Toys, Boxers, and Dobermans, now declare it optional for some of them. Seek the advice of an experienced, active breeder, especially if you wish to show.

You have presumably selected a vet who is thoroughly familiar with your breed. Otherwise, it would be worth the risk of offending his pride by showing him the breed standard as well as photographs of Champions of the breed before he performs this simple but definitive operation. If you still have qualms, persuade him to leave the tail a bit long (which can be corrected later, if necessary) rather than too short (which is irremediable).

Is the dog handicapped by his abbreviated tail? The tail protects the anus, of course, and is an important element of canine body language. It can act as a rudder when swimming. Bitches indicate the state of their sexual cycle by the way they hold their tail, while Gun dogs use it in various ways as signals during hunting. It may also be an aid to balance, although dogs with docked tails seem to balance themselves just as well as those with natural ones. However, it has been noted that Greyhounds cannot run as fast without a tail as they can when their streamlined shape is perfectly intact.

NAIL CLIPPING is a part of early puppy care that you can do yourself. A puppy's nails are sharp little pinpoints that grow rapidly. During nursing, they can scratch or cause pain to the bitch, and during play they can injure littermates. The sharp tips must be snipped off with nail clippers once a week until the puppies are running around on a hard surface and wearing them down naturally. If they run on carpets and lawns, you will have to continue clipping them indefinitely. As with adult dogs, the important point is to avoid cutting into the quick, which bleeds profusely. When this occurs, you can apply alum powder, cornstarch, or a styptic pencil to the nail tip and press it with a gauze pad until the bleeding has stopped.

HAND-REARING A LITTER

Do you remember the advice to cancel all of your appointments during and after your bitch's estimated whelping date? You will be glad you followed it if you ever have to raise a litter by hand—for example, when a bitch has died during whelping (which is rare), is convalescing from a Caesarean section, has a deficient or poisoned milk supply, or when some temperamental or physical defect makes her unfit to nurse and raise her puppies herself.

The ideal solution would be to find a FOSTER MOTHER for the litter, a sort of canine wet nurse, generally a bitch who is producing milk due to a false pregnancy, or one that is nursing a very small litter of her own and whose condition and milk supply permit her to add two or three adopted infants to her brood. Female dogs with strong maternal instincts are amazingly generous in accepting strange offspring, even if they are not of the same species. They have been known to nurse kittens, lambs, mice, rabbits, even baby skunks. At the Budapest Zoo, a Puli bitch named Bogancs has raised 3 black panthers, 1 Canadian puma, and a Bengal tiger. In England, specialized agencies provide foster mothers for orphaned puppy litters. In America, however, such services do not exist. Large breeding kennels may keep a motherly bitch to be bred every year, not for her puppies, but for her milk. More often, the foster mother is a female in the same kennel who has whelped at about the same time. If the breeder simply wants to spare his prize bitch the strain of raising a large litter, he may leave the best puppies with her and entrust the rest to the foster mother, either in supplement or substitution for her own puppies. This sleight of hand must be performed when the bitch is away from the nest. The foster puppies are rubbed with a little of the bitch's milk or vaginal secretions in order to impregnate them with her scent and prevent her from discovering the subterfuge. Supervision is essential when she returns to the nest. You can tell at once if she is going to accept or reject the strangers. Should she display the slightest sign of hostility, the project must be abandoned. The breeder then has to fall back on the only method available to the average pet owner: be a foster mother yourself and replace the bitch in all of her maternal duties.

First of all, you must provide SOME SUBSTITUTE FOR THE WARMTH OF THE MOTHER'S BODY, because the brain cells controlling body metabolism and temperature regulation do not become fully developed before the age of 2 or 3 weeks. Until then, the newborn puppies are very susceptible to chills. The whelping box should be lined with warm blankets and preferably covered, for example by an overturned chair with a blanket draped over it. The room should be well-heated, even overheated, as much as 85 or 90 degrees during the first five days, then gradually reduced to 80 or 75 degrees. You can also place in the bed a heating pad (some are specially designed for this purpose) or a hot-water bottle (actually, a warm one) filled with water heated to the temperature of a bitch's body (101 degrees) and wrapped in several thicknesses of flannel or blanketing. Newborn puppies are as sensitive to heat as they are to cold, so take care not to burn them.

Of course, you must also provide MILK, with feedings every 2 hours around the clock for the first week at least. Your vet can give you a formula for supplementing cow's milk so that it approximates the nutritional value of bitch's milk, which is 3 times richer in fat and protein. You can also buy a commercial formula especially devised for this purpose, such as Esbilac, made by the Borden Company and sold in drugstores. One of many homemade formulas is: 30 ounces of cow's milk, 1 egg yolk, 1 pinch of bone meal, 1 pinch of citric acid powder. Another recipe requires one can of unsweetened evaporated milk, ½ can of water, 1 beaten egg yolk, and 1 teaspoon of honey. All of these should be mixed well, warmed to 101 degrees before feeding, and the temperature maintained by wrapping the nursing bottle in a warm cloth.

The best kind of bottle is a tiny premature baby's bottle, with a small nipple, sterilized before each use. You may have to enlarge the hole in the nipple, if you see that the puppies are having trouble sucking it. As with babies, it is important to prevent air from being sucked from the bottle, and the simplest way to avoid it is to make sure that the neck of the bottle is always filled with milk during feeding. You can give the puppies all the milk they will drink. It won't be much at a time. As a rule of thumb, a 4-ounce puppy will suck about a teaspoonful of milk every 2 hours. If a puppy is reluctant to nurse from a bottle, you will have to nourish it by patiently placing drops of milk in its mouth from an eyedropper or a syringe, until it eventually accepts a bottle. Tube-feeding is also resorted to by some experienced, adroit breeders and many vets.

Finally, there is the problem of EVACUATING WASTE MATTER. The bitch normally does this by licking the puppies' tiny excretory organs, thus stimulating evacuation and at the same time removing it. So it is not enough to clean the puppies' behinds. They must be induced to evacuate after each feeding by rubbing the genital area gently with a piece of warm moist cotton. Within a week or two at the most, they will

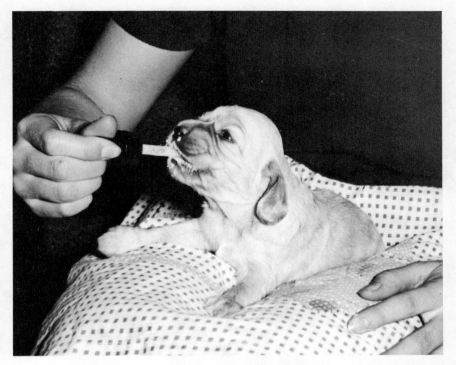

Feeding a puppy from a dropper. (*FPG*)

perform these natural functions unaided, but you must check up daily to make sure they do. You must also change the soiled, damp bedding several times a day so that the nest is always dry and clean.

Hand-rearing a litter obviously requires considerable stamina and devotion. You must be watchful during the first week or two for signs of distention, constipation, or diarrhea, as well as runny eyes or noses. Remain in close contact with your vet so that he can advise you and intervene if necessary. At the age of 2 weeks, it is advisable for him to give the hand-reared puppies an injection to prevent distemper, since they have by then lost the immunity they received from their mother's colostrum in the womb, and there is no other means of supplying this protection artificially.

Needless to say, the first few weeks of life are difficult for puppies and owners alike in these conditions. The puppies may not develop quite as fast as a bitch-nursed litter, but they will soon catch up and be just as sturdy and healthy as if they had been normally reared. Moreover, they are apt to forever remain particularly attached to the person who was literally "like a mother" to them.

18.
Raising a Litter

DURING THE FIRST 10 DAYS OF LIFE

Newborn puppies do little but sleep and nurse at their mother's side. They cannot see yet because their eyelids are closed. They cannot hear very much either because their ears are closed too during the first week or so. They are presumably guided to their mother's teats by their senses of smell and touch, but they can reach their goal only by tumbling and slithering along with swimming-like movements, because their legs are still too weak to support their weight. In a sense, all puppies (human babies too) are born prematurely, when you compare them to horses or sheep, for example, which are able to gambol on all four legs, however wobbly, as soon as they leave their mother's womb. Moreover, puppies, like babies, are born with a "soft spot" on top of their heads, which is protected by the skull bone only from the age of 2 or 3 months. Until then, they are particularly vulnerable to brain injury (or worse) from rough handling, bumps, and falls.

Some newborn puppies will be male and some female, which you can tell by observing or feeling their tiny genitalia. Litters born during the winter and early spring tend to have a higher proportion of males than those whelped in the summer and fall. Some puppies, not necessarily the males, will be larger than others. They may have different colors and markings, but these give only a faint clue to their color and markings as adults. Their soft baby coat is also bound to change in texture. And yet they will already have an individual aspect and personality, which you will soon be able to distinguish if you handle each of them gently twice a day, examining them for cuts, lumps, fleas, distended bellies, navel irritation or infection, runny eyes or nose—in fact, for anything abnormal that should be reported to the vet. If one or two of the puppies grow much faster than the others, it may be because they are monopolizing the best teats (the rear ones), and you might intervene to effect a more equitable milk distribution. By the end of the first week, all of the puppies should weigh twice as much as they did at birth.

Give lavish praise, affection, nourishing meals, and hygienic care to the bitch. There is not much more that you can do at this stage.

FROM THE AGE OF 10 DAYS TO 2 WEEKS

The puppies' eyes will open over a period of 2 or 3 days, starting at the inside corner. Eyes that seem to be stubbornly stuck shut or gummy can be gently bathed with slightly salted water, but do not tamper with them more than this. And do not be surprised that all the puppies have blue eyes. They will darken and lose their opacity within 5 weeks or so. Until they have been open for a week, you should keep the litter away from bright lights and sunshine, because these pale eyes are very sensitive.

There are two minor malformations of the eyelids that you may notice: *entropion* (inverted eyelids) and *ectropion* (everted eyelids). Both conditions can be corrected by simple surgery (see page 172). You should arrange for this with your veterinary surgeon while the puppy is young and no harm has been done to the eyeball.

Once the puppies' eyes are open, their hearing as well as their brain functions begin to operate normally. The nest will soon be too small to contain their wakening interest in the outside world, so one side of the box should be removed to permit them to enter and leave at will. At 2 weeks, they will try to walk. You must then provide a larger enclosure in which to confine and protect them, but one that will provide enough space for them to wander around. If you can sacrifice an entire room, you need only remove the carpet and install a folding gate in the doorway for easy supervision. Another solution is a heated porch, also with a folding gate, or a baby's playpen. You can place the puppies there in the daytime, returning them to the whelping box for feeding and during the night.

The flooring of this first play area is important, for it should offer some grip to the puppies' feeble paws in their first efforts to walk and run. Cover slippery, smooth surfaces with old rugs or carpets, rubber matting, or ordinary newspaper, not the glossy kind.

When you find a free moment during this busy period, think of officially legitimizing the puppies by registering them with the American Kennel Club, the American Field Stud Book, or other agency, if they are eligible. Upon request, you will be sent a form for Litter Registration, which must be filled in and signed by the owner of the sire as well as by the owner of the bitch, if they are not the same person. When it has been returned to the AKC, you will receive an Individual Registration form for each puppy. Keep these in a safe place until the day you find permanent owners for them. If you intend to retain ownership of the entire litter yourself, you can complete the forms and return them immediately with the required fee. Within a few weeks, you will be sent their individual registration numbers and certificates.

In the meantime, if the puppies are nursing normally, they should be growing at a steady rate. If not, the weaker ones may need your help at nursing time, or perhaps supplementary hand feeding.

THE THIRD AND FOURTH WEEKS

The puppies' feeding program starts to change. Although they are still nursing, they can now be taught to lap. The bitch herself often gives the signal for this great step by regurgitating partially digested food from her own meals and offering it to her puppies. Take the cue from her and give the infants a saucer of tepid fortified milk as a starter. Most puppies learn to lap immediately. The others catch on quickly if you gently dip the tips of their noses in the milk. They will lick it off their muzzles, think it over, then go back for more. A good formula for these first feedings is 1 cup of whole cow's milk mixed with 1 tablespoon of whole dried milk. Another popular recipe is diluted evaporated milk mixed with baby cereal or Wheatena to form a liquid gruel. There also exist commercially prepared puppy weaning formulas, including one under the Borden label.

Perhaps one of the reasons why the bitch is encouraging her offspring to feed themselves is that she is starting to feel their sharp little *milk teeth,* which begin to appear at about 3 weeks and have usually emerged completely at 5 weeks. There are 28 of them, softer but sharper and more

Rhodesian Ridgeback puppies lapping from a special dish that makes it a little harder for them to wade in the milk. (*Jeffrey Hanna*)

widely spaced than the permanent teeth which will start to replace them at the age of 4 or 5 months.

These baby milk teeth, being temporary, do not always determine the bite of the adult dog, so do not worry yet if the bite does not seem perfectly correct. A more accurate indication of the adult bite is the set of the puppy's jaws. If this is as it should be, the bite will probably be right as well, once the permanent teeth have emerged. Even if the puppy's jaws seem overshot or undershot when the breed standard requires a "scissors bite," do not despair. There is always a ray of hope until the permanent teeth have come in, and even then, in breeds with long muzzles, the lower (moving) jaw may continue to grow.

At the age of 4 weeks or so, when the puppies are lapping the milk formula from a saucer as well as nursing, you can give them one meal a day of finely minced beef, raw or cooked, free from fat and gristle. Cottage cheese is also an excellent weaning food and protein provider. One tablespoon per puppy is a beginning ration, which should be gradually increased.

Boxer puppies learning to lap under the solicitous eye of their mother. (*H. Armstrong Roberts*)

This first real food will give you an opportunity to introduce the system of feeding each puppy from his own dish, as well as to teach each one his name, as you call him to COME for his dinner. He will quickly learn this basic command at the same time.

Now that you are offering solid food, you should also provide a permanent supply of fresh drinking water. You may have to change it often, as the puppies will be sloppy at first. You can also continue one fortified-milk feed per day, adding a beaten raw egg yolk.

The bitch, you will notice, is grateful for this supplementary feeding, because she is getting rather tired of the nursing business and her maternal devotion may not be as intense as it was a week ago. She increasingly urges the puppies to leave the nest and to explore the world around them. They are becoming more independent too, for example, by seeking their own sleeping places, whereas until now they all slept together in a heap—perhaps because the heat-regulating function of their metabolism is now operating normally. Moreover, with their first solid meals, the puppies will instinctively prefer to leave the nest in order to defecate, and you should cover a portion of the surrounding area with newspapers, replacing them with clean ones as necessary. You can also give them their first toys: harmless articles such as an old sock, or a small plastic bottle they can roll along the floor. Toys will encourage them to play outside the nest. You can even let them play in the garden, if you have one and if the weather is fine.

This stage of development is critical psychologically as well as physically. Eminent biologists have pinpointed the age of 3 weeks as the moment when a puppy starts to form its basic attitude toward humanity. The period of maximum receptivity to "imprinting" or "socialization" continues until the pups are 5 to 6 months old. If human handling is frequent and is associated with pleasant feelings such as comfort, security, love, and fun, the puppies' attitude will be trustful and loving. But if human contacts are associated with unpleasant things like discomfort, loud noises, and rough handling, it can plant the seeds of shyness, anxiety, distrust, and even fear of human beings. A traumatic experience now, such as being dropped, shouted at, frightened, or isolated for a long time, can mark a puppy for life. Human contacts, however, are only part

Rhodesian Ridgeback puppies in a heap. (*Jeffrey Hanna*)

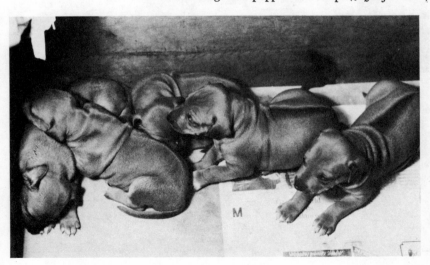

of socialization. Puppies also need to learn to adjust to the society of adult dogs (their mother) and of their peers (their littermates). A puppy who has exclusively human contacts during his early life may become too "people oriented," aggressive, or indifferent toward other dogs, and even sexually frigid.

The puppies will start to recognize people, probably more by voice and scent than by visual recognition. They also start to wag their tails, to react to sounds by pricking their ears, and to bark (yap, rather) in a high little puppy voice.

THE FIFTH AND SIXTH WEEKS

This is the full weaning period, which will be completed when the puppies are 6 to 8 weeks old, large litters usually being weaned sooner than small ones, in order to spare the bitch unnecessary fatigue. Then it

A litter of Afghan puppies who have graduated to eating solid food. (*H. Armstrong Roberts*)

is time to collect fecal samples and take them to the vet for a worm analysis. Internal parasite infestation at this age is particularly debilitating.

The bitch will continue her natural weaning method of regurgitating food for her offspring. You can add a little starch to the puppies' minced meat in the form of crumbled wholewheat toast, puppy biscuit, or meal soaked in water. They should now be getting 4 meals a day: milk and egg the first thing in the morning; meat and biscuit at noon; milk and biscuit around 5 P.M.; and a final meat meal at night, with plenty of fresh water always available. There are other good schedules too. It is the total daily quantity that is most important. Since the puppy's stomach is tiny, considering his needs, small meals at frequent intervals are better than a few large ones. Your goal is to maintain a steady increase in size and weight.

From the time the puppies are 6 weeks old, they should all be given supplements of codliver oil, and perhaps calcium as well. Your vet will prescribe the proper amounts. The codliver oil is particularly beneficial to winter litters, who cannot be taken out of doors, since it compensates for the lacking Vitamin D from natural sunshine. In summer and spring, you should let the puppies spend as much time as possible out of doors when the weather is warm and sunny. Arrange an enclosed area with sun and shade, where you can leave them safely during the mildest part of the day. It is a good idea to feed them outdoors too, because they usually defecate right after eating, and this will help form clean habits. They already dislike soiling their nest. If they must be kept indoors all of the time, you should arrange a paper-covered official toilet spot. They are, of course, far too young to control their bodily functions, but you should still encourage every effort in the right direction.

This is a very busy period, as you can see. But do not neglect one of the most important things of all: the litter's *puppy shots*. While they are nursing, the puppies are protected from disease by the colostrum in their mother's milk, which is rich in antibodies. But this lasts only for a few weeks, after which the puppies must develop their own immunity, especially to distemper. It is customary to take the entire litter to the vet's for protective injections as soon as the maternal protection is no longer effective. Some puppy shots are given as early as 4 weeks, other as late as 10. But the most popular method at the present time is a multiple vaccine given at the age of 6 weeks, which offers protection from three diseases: distemper, leptospirosis, and hepatitis. During the week following the shots, the puppies need to be protected from fatigue and chills. Most of them show no reaction. Be sure to ask your vet how soon the immunity will be effective, because they should not be taken for outside walks until it is, especially not on city streets or suburban sidewalks. And note on your calendar that the puppies will need a second, longer-lasting vaccination at the age of 12 weeks.

In the meantime, you can start training the puppies to walk with a collar and leash inside the house, around the apartment, or in the garden. This is only practice. They will get their real exercise from playing together. They will also be consuming a surprising amount of food, following their mother around, following you around too, investigating every sight and sound, but still sleeping much of the time.

If the bitch is shedding profusely, or has done so, do not worry, for it is normal. Your vet can prescribe dietary supplements that will hasten her return to condition.

THE SEVENTH AND EIGHTH WEEKS

The bitch's milk is practically depleted, and she is increasingly irritated by the puppies' insistent sucking in addition to slurping down their four daily prepared meals. If, however, she enjoys her maternal role and clings to it, there is no harm in letting her continue for as long as she likes, although the puppies are now getting almost all of their nourishment from their own meals. This is the natural age, physically and psychologically, for completing the weaning process.

When the puppies no longer nurse, the mother's supply of milk dries up spontaneously. It is not normal for a bitch to produce a large amount of milk beyond the seventh week. You can try to discourage it by giving her less liquid, no meat or milk, a mild laxative, gentle breast massages to decongest them, limiting the time she spends with her puppies, and resuming her normal program of exercise. Some breeders withhold all food and water during 24 hours in order to "dry up" the bitch.

The puppies will be getting bolder and stronger every day. Both testicles of male puppies will generally have descended into the scrotum by now. If not, do not lose hope. They may descend as late as 3 or 4 months, and in rare cases, six.

You should try to broaden the puppies' experience by letting them explore the house under your supervision, and by taking them for walks, one or two puppies at a time. Introduce them to nice friends, but do not let young children handle them until they are older and stronger. You can also start to teach them simple words, but particularly good behavior patterns. Their little brains are very receptive, and if you don't guide them, they will learn on their own and perhaps develop bad habits that will be very difficult to correct later on.

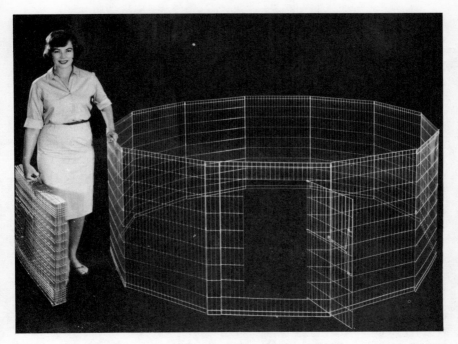

A portable, folding wire pen is ideal for safely enclosing a small dog, a puppy, or even an entire litter of puppies out of doors when the weather is fine. (*Courtesy of Kennel-Aire Mfg. Co., St. Paul, Minn.*)

If your puppies are Boxers, Doberman Pinschers, Great Danes, Schnauzers, Bouviers des Flandres, Boston Terriers, or one of the other breeds whose standard permits or requires *ear cropping*, this is the most favorable moment to have the operation performed by your veterinary surgeon (see page 174). Some vets do it as early as 6 weeks, but most agree that the danger is slightest and healing quickest between the ages of 7 and 10 weeks. None of them really approve of this stupid fashion. In fact, the anti-ear-cropping lobby has succeeded in making it optional for many of the breeds that previously required it. Even so, if you want to show the puppies in the United States, and if you want your friends to accept them as genuine purebred members of their breed, you will have to crop. Be sure to select a vet who is experienced in performing the operation and is familiar with the show standard of your breed, since it involves not only lopping off the overhanging tip of the ear, but also cutting it at the proper angle, which varies according to the breed and even according to the individual dog. The puppies' appearance for the rest of their lives depends on the vet's judgment at this crucial moment, so select him carefully.

Healing cropped ears takes much longer and is more troublesome than healing a docked tail. The scabs must be removed daily and the incisions dusted with an antiseptic healing powder. The ears must be kept taped tightly enough for the two outer layers of skin to seal together. Until the edges have closed, the puppies should be leashed during walks and separated the rest of the time so that they cannot play together and perhaps ruin everything. In order to train the cropped ears into an erect position, they are bandaged around an upright form of plastic, cardboard, or aluminum, and usually taped together at the tips. If they heal in a lopsided position, they will never stand up straight without further plastic surgery.

THE NINTH AND TENTH WEEKS

The same program continues. The puppies' meals should be more plentiful as they gain in size and weight. They need a lot of sunshine too, and perhaps calcium supplements as well as cod-liver oil. Cottage cheese, milk, and bone meal are good natural sources of calcium, which is particularly important at this stage because the puppies' permanent teeth are developing inside the gums.

THE ELEVENTH AND TWELFTH WEEKS

The litter will be 3 months old at the end of this period—the perfect age for moving to their permanent homes.

Twelve weeks is also the moment for completing one type of puppy shots with a permanent injection that will continue their immunity to distemper, leptospirosis, and hepatitis for a full year. Do not postpone it. Even a few days' delay can expose them to the danger of infection. Heartworm protection, if advisable, can be started at the same time.

You can prepare your puppies for adoption by taking them for walks alone, by letting them meet strangers, by teaching them basic commands, by getting them used to being groomed, by housebreaking, and by encouraging them to face new experiences and strange environments with confidence and enthusiasm. You can take a different puppy with you each time you go to the mailbox, in the car to buy a newspaper, or merely into the living room to watch the news on television. Give them lots of affectionate handling, but lots of peace and quiet too. They still need frequent daytime naps. You can already start to teach simple com-

mands such as COME, SIT, and NO, by using the words and gently co-
ercive gestures. But it is far too early to do any real training or to expect
real obedience. At this age, the most effective method is to try to make
good behavior seem like fun.

SELLING A LITTER

If you breed your bitch primarily in order to have one of her offspring
to succeed her, you will naturally want to keep a puppy for yourself,
probably the one that most resembles her. Depending on your breeding
arrangements with the owner of the stud dog, the latter may have first
choice of a puppy from the litter. We have already seen how to choose a
puppy. It is much easier when you have whelped and raised the litter
and are familiar with all of them. Perhaps you have already become par-
ticularly attached to one. In any case, after you and the other owner
have made your choices, there will probably remain several puppies for
whom you will want to find a happy home. How do you go about it?

Your first principle should be: Always sell a puppy, never give one
away. Human nature being as it is, the new owner will appreciate his ac-
quisition much more and care for it much better if he has invested
money in it. If the buyer is a person of modest means, and if you are sure
that he can offer your puppy a happy home, you can arrange for pay-
ment in monthly installments. In setting a monetary value on the pup-
pies, the basic rule is that each puppy is considered to be worth the stud
fee paid for the services of the sire, or somewhat more or less according
to individual quality.

Conscientious breeders size up prospective buyers just as carefully,
though more discreetly, as the latter examine the puppies for sale. They
do not hesitate to refuse to sell a puppy to an unsuitable home, while
they will make concessions in order to place him in a good one. Nowa-
days, they even have to beware of buyers who seek puppies of certain
large and reputedly pugnacious breeds in order to train them for illegal
dogfighting or as professional attack dogs.

The most usual way of finding a buyer is simply by word of mouth,
through friends, acquaintances, and neighbors; then by advertising in the
classified section of the local newspaper; and if that does not bring re-
sults, in the Sunday paper of the nearest large city. Another way is to
spread the news of your litter among the members of your dog club, and
especially of your breed club. A fellow fancier may be seeking just the
bloodlines that your puppies bear. You can also contact the breeder of

your bitch, if only to announce the happy event. Serious breeders are always interested in learning about the offspring of their stock. The breeder might even have puppy requests that he is unable to satisfy, and yours, being of the same line, may fill the bill.

Although pedigreed puppies of attractive and popular breeds can always be sold without difficulty to a pet shop, *never do it!* You will have no say in the choice of a home for your puppies, and the conditions in which they will live while waiting for a buyer are nothing like their happy home environment in the best of cases. In the worst, they are quite shocking.

Does this sound excessively sentimental and unbusinesslike? It isn't, really. All successful small breeders operate this way. Of course, they do not expect to get rich from breeding dogs (and neither should you). Even the large commercial breeders probably earn more from stud fees, boarding charges, and an occasional big price for an adult show Champion, than they do from selling puppies.

Selling a puppy successfully depends on many factors: on the time of year, on the economic situation, on current fad and fashion for various breeds. If your prime interest is to make a profit, sell encyclopedias, sell antiques, sell home-baked cakes—but don't sell puppies.

Let's suppose that you have found a suitable buyer for one of your puppies, most likely a neighbor, a friend who knows and admires your bitch, or a friend of a friend. Don't let the social relationship lead you into a casual agreement. Selling a puppy is a commercial transaction, and misunderstandings can be avoided only when it is made in a businesslike manner. You should furnish the buyer with a detailed bill of sale, a receipt for the sum paid, an AKC (or other) application for registration of the puppy, a pedigree, a health certificate, a certificate of past vaccinations and a reminder of those that should be given next, a diet sheet, and a few days' supply of the puppy's customary food. You might add a sheet of grooming instructions, and recommend a good breed book. If the buyer lives nearby, you can also give him a list of recommended veterinarians, boarding kennels, food suppliers, and so forth. These thoughtful details can help to ensure the future happiness of the puppy you have raised and loved.

19.
Traveling with Your Dog

Small adaptable, curious, obedient dogs are delightful traveling companions: Dogs who are large, unruly, fearful, or unreliable can turn even a short trip into a costly ordeal. Small Terriers and Toys such as Miniature Schnauzers, Poodles, and Pugs, make excellent globe-trotters. Most Working dogs, Hunting dogs, and Hounds, on the other hand, prefer to guard the house during your absence and to give you a delirious welcome when you return.

Big dogs of any breed considerably complicate travel not only because of their size, but also due to their need for a generous amount of daily exercise, food, and space, and the problem of disposing of their voluminous waste matter. They are seldom accepted in planes, trains, or buses (unless they are guiding the blind), and must be shipped as freight in public carriers, causing discomfort to the dog and anxiety to his owner. It is also much more difficult to find a place to spend the night with a big dog than a small one. When travel by private car is out of the question, there is little pleasure for either of you, only complications, concern, and expense, which may spoil your trip.

Dogs of all sizes and shapes are shipped as freight to a new home or owner, to be bred or shown, with increasing frequency and over increasing distances, and they usually recover from the experience—large dogs more quickly than small ones, and adult dogs more easily than puppies, who may never get over it. But pleasure travel involving planes or trains is difficult with animals weighing more than 10 or 12 pounds, which is the limit most airlines set for dogs accompanying their owners in the passenger cabin. If you cannot bear to be separated from a larger dog, the best policy is to restrict your holiday travel to destinations within driving distance—and even then, prepare your trip with care.

TRAVEL DOCUMENTS

First of all, you must provide your dog with certain travel documents, which he will need for crossing most interstate and foreign borders as well as for re-entering the United States:

1) A rabies vaccination tag attached to the dog's collar, or the certificate carried in his document case. Even if this is not obligatory in your own state, most states and almost all foreign countries require it.

2) A certificate from your veterinarian, declaring that your dog is in good health and free from contagious disease. This, too, is required for almost all interstate and international travel. The more official looking the paper, the more it will impress border officials. So ask your vet to adorn the document with all the rubber stamps and Latin terms he has at his command.

3) Your dog's insurance policy, or at least the essential references. Although this is obligatory only for freight shipment, it is advisable to insure all canine travelers for theft and loss as well as for any damage they may cause.

4) If you intend to cross state lines or foreign borders, you might also take along your dog's registration papers or his bill of sale, in case you are asked to show proof of ownership. It seems an unlikely occurrence, but it has happened. You might also pack his pedigree, Obedience certificate, and anything else you can think of. The sheer volume will impress foreign Customs officers.

LUGGAGE

Your dog's personal luggage will vary, as yours does, according to your travel plans. Everything he needs should fit into an airlines kit bag:
—his brush and comb
—a packet of disposable tissues
—his water and food bowls
—flea powder
—an emergency supply of dog food, biscuits, and treats
—his favorite toy
—his blanket or cushion
—a thermos bottle filled with water
—vitamin tablets, travel sickness pills, and any usual medication
—a 6-foot-long leash or rope to give more leeway for exercise than his normal leash
—a canine travel guide. Two concise and practical booklets that can be ordered by mail are:

Touring with Towser, published by the Gaines Company, P. O. Box 1007, Kankakee, Illinois 60901 (enclose check or money order for one dollar).

Traveling With Your Pet, published by the ASPCA, 441 East Ninety-second Street, New York, New York 10028.

You should also prepare your dog for the trip by:
—feeding a light meal 6 hours before leaving home.
—giving nothing or little to drink within 2 hours of departure.
—taking him for a walk one hour before you leave and making sure that he relieves himself.

Depending on your means of travel and your destination, you will encounter different conditions and problems. For example:

TRAVELING BY PLANE

Policy concerning canine passengers varies from one airline to another and from time to time, so you should seek the advice of your travel agent or the airline representative when you make your reservation. You will need to make a reservation for your dog as well, even though he will not be permitted to occupy a seat, but only to travel at your feet in a closed carrying case.

Rusty, an American-bred Cairn Terrier, traveled in the radio room of the plane that delivered him in Paris to his new owner, the Duchess of Windsor. For less VIP canine passengers, plane travel is far less comfortable and many precautions are necessary. (*Wide World Photos*)

CARRYING CASES are sold by pet supply shops and luxury luggage stores. The best kind is made of heavy canvas or plasticized fabric with a rigid frame, double handles securely attached, a washable plastic lining, air holes at one end, a screened window at the other end that can be covered by a flap, and a zipper closing at the top. The best way to select the proper dimensions is to try it on for size. Your dog should be able to curl up comfortably inside, but not necessarily stand up. Wicker baskets, less expensive as well as more fragile, are adequate for very small breeds. Some airlines provide cardboard carrying cases, but these are sturdy enough only for a single flight. While maximum dimensions are no longer specified for hand baggage, the case should, of course, be able to fit into the ridiculously cramped space that plane designers consider sufficient leg room.

When you carry your dog in his case, he will probably enjoy the free ride if you think of holding the case level, putting it down gently, never placing it near a source of heat or in a draft, and being careful not to catch your dog's hair in the zipper when you open or close it. Inside the plane, select a window seat and place the case lengthwise at your feet, with the closed end against the side of the plane and the screened end facing the aisle. You can reassure your dog by speaking to him from time to time and by keeping your feet close to the case so that he can scent your presence.

Most airlines impose a weight limit of 10 or 12 pounds and calculate the dog's fare at the rate of excess baggage which is 1 per cent of the First Class fare for each kilogram (2.2 pounds) on international flights. Most companies also limit to one or two the number of dogs transported in each plane, sometimes in each class. The captain, who is master on board just like the captain of a ship, may accept a supplementary dog if the quota has been filled. In any case, his permission must be sought before your dog will be allowed to travel with you. So make your reservation well ahead of time and hope for a dog-loving captain.

When you have the choice, select a flight that is least likely to be full. If you can manage to keep the seat next to you unoccupied, you and your dog will travel in greater comfort, even if it means traveling at a less convenient hour. Try to avoid crowds by traveling several days earlier or later than the holiday hordes.

Plan to check in early. Your dog will be weighed in his case, you will be asked to pay the excess baggage charge, and you can then board the plane together. Theoretically, your dog must remain enclosed in his case throughout the flight. In actual practice, you can hold a small, well-behaved, leashed dog on your lap, let him sleep under your seat or on the empty seat next to you, if the flight personnel is indulgent and other passengers do not object. Certainly nobody will mind if you open the top of his case, in which he may be perfectly content to remain curled up throughout the flight. Most dogs are better plane travelers than restless children and apprehensive adults. The faint drone of the engines seem to have a soporific effect on them.

Nevertheless, dogs become dehydrated in a plane, just as we do, since the conditioned atmosphere is much drier than normal air. If you haven't brought a small plastic water bottle and drinking container with you, do not hesitate to ask the hostess for a cup of water for your dog. When a meal is served, you can share your beefsteak with him or give him a cracker, if he begs for it. But do not attempt to feed him a normal meal until you have reached your destination. He will probably not be interested in food until then anyway.

The first time you travel by plane with your dog, you may be more nervous than he is. Even so, try not to leave your seat during this maiden flight. The next time, your dog will be accustomed to the routine. He may even leap joyously into his case in anticipation of another magical change of scene. Sedatives and tranquilizers are seldom necessary, since your own presence is the best tranquilizer of all. Even a new puppy who does not know you yet will cling to you, and the protection and comfort you give him can be an excellent first step in forming a lasting bond between you.

When the landing announcement is made, enclose your dog in his case and carry him in it until you are outside of the air terminal building. As soon as he steps on solid ground again, his first impulse will be to urinate. So give him a chance to relieve himself immediately and completely by taking him for a stroll.

Dogs who are too large or heavy for admittance to the passenger cabin may still travel in the same plane with you, crated and in the luggage compartment, as ACCOMPANIED LIVE CARGO. This space is also limited and must be reserved ahead of time. Furthermore, not all types of aircraft have baggage compartments that are properly pressurized and heat controlled for live animals. Even in the heated ones of large jetliners, the temperature may be maintained no higher than 40 or 50 degrees and may drop to 35 degrees. Be sure to check this point at the time you make your reservation. Your dog's life may depend on it.

SHIPPING CRATES are much larger than carrying cases, because your dog should be able to stand up and turn around in it with ease. Most airlines sell fiberglass, heavy-duty plastic, or wooden dog crates made to their specifications for a reasonable price—$10 to $30 or so, depending on the size. These are in such demand that your dog must be an airlines passenger in order to purchase one of them, and it must be ordered well in advance of your travel date. After the flight, the crate remains your property. Show kennels and professional handlers, who do a lot of traveling, prefer to invest in aluminum travel crates, which are lightweight, expensive, but practically indestructible.

You may equip your dog's crate with various useful accessories such as a floor mat and a water container. If it is a nonspillable model, you can fill it before you crate your dog. Otherwise, the water would spill and wet his bed. It would be better to install the bowl in a spot accessible from outside the crate and attach instructions for filling it at regular times, in the slender hope that some kind-hearted employee will do so.

While wire crates are perfect for car travel and for conversion into a den where your dog can safely be enclosed in a hotel room, they are not always acceptable for shipping him as freight, since they are seldom strong enough to stand being banged around and perhaps having other crates and baggage piled on top of them. Incidentally, it is a good idea to attach a thick wooden strip all around the outsides of solid crates in order to ensure a minimum amount of breathing space around them in crowded cargo compartments.

Whether freight or excess baggage, the dog's crate should be firmly fastened shut so that he cannot possibly escape—for example, with twisted heavy wire. Padlock it only if the key is attached to the crate and if you have a duplicate in your pocket. You want your dog to be safely confined, but also to be liberated rapidly in an emergency.

Try to abbreviate the time your dog has to spend in his crate by putting him in it at the last possible moment. If it is very large, have it delivered ahead of time and take your dog to the airport in the car, crating him just before departure.

You will probably have to register your dog an hour or two before the scheduled flight time. But place him in his crate at the last possible moment, along with some object or garment that bears your scent. Do not bother with food or water if the flight will last no longer than a few hours. It is also better not to muzzle him (which might interfere with his breathing), or to give him a tranquilizer (which might interfere with his natural adjustment to changes of temperature). The airlines personnel will attach the proper labels, but you might take the precaution of previously stapling or gluing two additional ones, one on a side and the other on the top, bearing your name, home address, and phone number, the flight number, date and destination and, for extra security, the address and phone number where you can be reached at your destination. (This same security measure is essential when you ship your dog by train.)

When you reach your destination, your crated dog will be delivered with the rest of the passenger baggage. If there are Customs and Health inspection formalities, you must keep him crated until these have been completed. Otherwise, you can remove him from his crate at once. However, since his first impulse will be to make an enormous puddle, it is better to release him only when you are outside of the terminal building —if you can control your joy at seeing him again for a few minutes more.

It is also possible to ship a dog under 70 pounds in weight as UNACCOMPANIED AIR FREIGHT, in which case the procedure is slightly different and the entire enterprise more risky. The charge is based on the dog's weight plus the distance traveled, and amounts to about $150 for shipping a medium-sized dog from coast to coast. Although thousands of dogs are shipped by plane successfully every year, there have also been many deplorable accidents, most often due to inept arrangements and missed connections. Small dogs and puppies suffer most from the experience. In fact, the Animal Welfare Act, enforced by the Department of Agriculture, prohibits shipping by any form of transport a puppy who is under 8 weeks of age and has not been weaned for at least 5 days previously. It specifies further that the shipper must deliver animals within 4 hours of departure time, notify the consignee no later than 6 hours after arrival, and provide ventilation, temperature control, food, and water during the trip—which is still a harrowing experience for a puppy.

If you cannot possibly avoid shipping your dog as air freight, at least contact a shipping agent who is experienced in animal transport and knows how to select the best airline, flight, plane, and route for the particular destination.

In some fortunate areas, there exist professional pet travel agents. Perhaps your classified telephone directory contains listings such as:

Cosmopolitan Canine Carriers: 5 Brook Street, Darien, Connecticut 06820 (Tel. 800-243-9105).

Pet Transports: 68–77 Selfridge Street, Forest Hills, New York 11375 (Tel. 212-544-8518).

Flying Fur Travel Service: 310 South Michigan Avenue, Chicago, Illinois 60604 (Tel. 800-621-4155); 4800 Melrose Avenue, Los Angeles, California (Tel. 213-988-4947); and other major cities.

Animal Air Transport: Cincinnati, Ohio (owned and run by veterinarian Richard Burns, who flies his canine clients to their destinations on weekends in his private plane).

TRAVELING BY TRAIN

The only satisfactory way to travel with your dog by train is to reserve a private compartment, in which case a small dog may be permitted to travel with you if you bring him aboard in a carrying case. The catch is that private compartments have practically disappeared from modern railways. Moreover, AMTRAK bars dogs (except for Guide dogs) from all passenger areas, even from private compartments. Crated dogs are accepted in the baggage cars of passenger trains as excess baggage, the owners having access to their pets for feeding and exercise, and the baggage master providing water. But baggage cars have also practically disappeared from passenger trains, except for a few long-distance ones. Can you remember when you last saw one?

If you have the opportunity and the choice, prefer an overnight train trip, which is least disruptive to your dog's normal daily schedule. During a longer trip, you must take advantage of every stop to give your dog a chance to stretch his legs and to relieve himself, which is not a simple matter in modern railway terminals. The best policy is to ask a station attendant to suggest a suitable spot for this inevitable necessity.

If you are the Queen of England, shown here with her Pembroke Corgis, you can confidently travel by train with a dog. But in the United States and for ordinary citizens, canine railroad transportation poses many problems. (*Wide World Photo*)

You can also ship your dog by Railway Express as unaccompanied freight, crated and in a freight train. Freight train cars are generally dirty, drafty, dark, either too hot or too cold, and seldom disinfected, which makes the voyage an unhealthy, uncomfortable enterprise. Even if you deal with a reliable express firm, there is always the danger that your dog may sit around for hours, miserable and shivering (or, on the contrary, sweltering and thirsty) in some dreary railroad freight room or even on the station platform, if he is unloaded during the lunch hour, a holiday, or a weekend, when freight offices are understaffed, if they are open at all. If you absolutely must ship your dog by freight train, do it during the week, and at night during hot weather. Attach a full pail of water inside his crate and a supply of food. Plaster the outside of his crate with instructions, which may or may not be heeded. But before accepting this solution, try to arrange a better form of travel for your dog: by car, a rented one if necessary, if you are traveling a reasonable distance; or with you as a passenger or as accompanied live cargo in a plane, if your destination is more remote.

TRAVELING BY BOAT

Luxury ocean travel, like luxury train travel, has become almost obsolete. It is, furthermore, just about the slowest form of long-distance travel there is, which means a long period of discomfort for your dog. You can take your dog with you on one of the few remaining liners that have a shipboard kennel, which is generally situated on the top deck, with an adjoining exercise and bathroom area and a full or part-time kennel attendant. Of course, you pay for these accommodations, but relatively little compared to the cost of your cabin. You should give the attendant instructions for feeding and care when you hand your dog over to him. You can visit your dog during specified hours, but you cannot take him to your stateroom or to other parts of the ship.

In general, the newer the ship, the better the kennels; and the more prosperous and prestigious the line, the better the personnel. A tip at the beginning of the voyage, followed by frequent visits, may ensure better care. If you are traveling in First Class and your dog is small and well-behaved, you might ask the captain or the purser for permission to let him sleep in your cabin with you. It is always worth trying. If your request is granted, it is up to you to see that your dog does not abuse the privilege. You will still have to take him to the kennel deck several times a day for exercise and elimination.

Customs, quarantine, and import regulations are more strictly enforced at seaports than at any other point of the frontier, so you must make sure that your dog's travel documents are in perfect order.

TRAMP STEAMERS never accept dogs. Very few CRUISE SHIPS are equipped with kennels. When they are, the dogs are not permitted to leave the kennel area, nor can they accompany their owners on sight-seeing trips ashore.

In short, nowadays there is little possibility and less reason for travel-ing with your dog on an ocean liner.

However, boats, like dogs, come in all shapes and sizes. Barge dogs know no other home. Many fishing boats count among the crew a canine guard or mascot. And countless owners take their dogs aboard their per-sonal PLEASURE CRAFT for an afternoon's sail or even for a holiday cruise.

Generally speaking, dogs of breeds with an innate attraction to the water, such as Labradors, Poodles, Water Retrievers, and Schipperkes, take readily to nautical life, as do puppies of almost any breed who have been born at sea or on a seacoast. Most pet dogs who are introduced to boats at a sufficiently early age can adapt to ocean life and learn to like it if only because of the varied experiences they share with their owners during port calls.

If you love sailing and love your dog as well, you can try to persuade him to share your enthusiasm by taking him for a short introductory out-ing on your boat when he is 6 months old or so. If he loathes the experi-ence, there is no point in going further. Arrange to leave him at a good boarding kennel during your sailing holidays. But if it has intrigued him, and if you are willing to devote the necessary time and attention in order to ensure his comfort and safety, you can take him for increasingly longer sails, and eventually for an overnight cruise or longer.

If you are the skipper of your boat, you might assign the responsibility to a member of the crew, because supervising a dog at sea is practically a full-time job. You should always:

—Know where your dog is at every moment, keeping him constantly in sight, or else shut in an airy cabin. Never tie him up on deck during rough weather, but never let him loose on deck either, if it is not sufficiently enclosed so that he cannot possibly slide or fall over-board.

—Make your dog wear a canine lifejacket (or a child's) whenever you are navigating. But do not think that this absolves you from constant supervision. A tiny yellow or orange dot is quickly lost from sight at sea, almost at once if the sea is rough, which is when he is most likely to fall overboard.

—Protect your dog from sunshine and heat by arranging a safe, cool, shady spot for him and giving him a constant supply of water, refreshed with ice cubes if necessary.

—Bring aboard an ample supply of his usual food, serve him normal meals at normal hours, but let him eat as little or as much as he likes. He knows better than you do how to adjust his diet to these new conditions.

—At least twice a day, and whenever possible, take your dog ashore for a leg-stretching run and in order to relieve himself. Never fail to give him a morning and evening constitutional, even if it means making a special trip ashore in a dinghy. Most dogs consider the entire boat an annex of their home and refuse to soil any part of it. Some may be persuaded to do their business in a litter pan, like a cat. But most would rather burst than soil their territory. Fortunately, even large dogs produce less urine, less often, during hot weather, and can thus contain themselves without distress for longer periods of time. But do not ask your dog to perform miracles of self-control.

—Never take your dog with you in a fast open motorboat, even if you hold him in your arms. Move at a moderate or slow speed, and keep your arm around him. If the sea is rough, put on his lifejacket, slow down as much as possible, and hold onto him firmly.

—Never take your dog in an open boat after dark, nor leave him unleashed and unsupervised on an open deck after nightfall.

—Let him share the fun whenever possible. His pleasure will add to yours. That is why you wanted to bring him along in the first place, wasn't it?

TRAVELING BY CAR

All dogs should be car-trained as puppies, since this is by far the most practical means of transportation for them, as well as the most agreeable form of travel.

If you follow the advice on puppy handling, you should have no problem. But if you are dealing with an adult dog who is unaccustomed or afraid of car travel, you may have to make a regular training project out of it.

Many adult dogs who have never been car-trained, as well as some puppies, may balk at entering a car. You can often trick them in by getting into the back seat yourself. Your dog will follow you willingly. You then get out by the other door, leaving the dog inside.

In the beginning, leave him in your parked car in the driveway for 15 or 30 minutes from time to time. Then take him for short drives, at first holding him in your lap or seated beside you with your arm around him, while someone else drives. You can then graduate to the next step, with your dog sitting on the back seat or lying down, as he prefers.

All dogs should also be taught to jump in and out of the car on their own. If you start by lifting your puppy into it, you may end up trying to heave and push a 50-pound animal who has never learned to make this simple maneuver by himself.

Big dogs usually prefer to travel standing up or seated on the back seat. Small ones often curl up and go to sleep either on the seat or on the floor. But never let your dog stand with his hindlegs on the back seat and his forepaws behind the driver. It is too easy for him to lose his balance during a sharp turn or a sudden stop, with possibly tragic consequences.

When your dog is used to riding in the car and seems to enjoy it, you can take him with you for longer car trips, even for touring holidays. These, however, require certain preparations.

The best way for your dog to travel by car is on the back seat or on the deck of a station wagon, enclosed in a folding wire crate. Show dogs,

One of the best ways for a dog to travel by car is enclosed in a folding wire crate. These are installed on the deck of a station wagon, but crates suitable for small and medium-sized dogs can easily fit on the back seat of a family car. (*Courtesy of Kennel-Aire Mfg. Co., St. Paul, Minn.*)

who cover almost as much mileage as a political candidate during a campaign, always travel this way. The crate can also be used as a private bedroom for your dog in a corner of your hotel or motel room. If you haven't a wire crate and are afraid that your dog will be unmanageable loose in the car, never tie him up inside it. Instead, install a wire partition to fence off the driver's seat from the rear, or fence off the back section of a station wagon. You can also install "window gates" which permit you to leave them partially open for ventilation, but barred for safety. These accessories are made to fit most makes of cars and are advertised in dog magazines. Needless to add, station wagons or cars in which the back seat can be transformed into a flat deck are the best choice of a car for dog owners.

Whatever you do, never put your dog in the trunk, even if it has been specially equipped for this purpose. Many dogs have died from heat prostration, dehydration, and asphyxiation in a car trunk, even in supposedly ventilated ones. Many have been injured by jolts and accidents.

A wire partition like this one is a simple and reasonable means of letting your dog (or dogs) ride unattached in the rear part of the car, but still safely separated from the driver. (*Courtesy of Kennel-Aire Mfg. Co., St. Paul, Minn.*)

Before setting out on a long automobile trip with your dog, pack his kit bag and place in the glove compartment a roll of disposable towels or tissues, a few dog biscuits, a thermos bottle of fresh water and a container for serving it. Be sure that your own travel gear includes a pair of boots, a raincoat, and hat, because you will have to walk your dog whatever the weather. You will be prepared for cleaning up after him if necessary by packing in the trunk a small shovel or litter-scoop and a roll of plastic bags.

Plan your itinerary to include a brief stop every 3 hours in order to give your dog a drink, to let him stretch his legs and relieve himself. Car travel seems to stimulate the kidneys. The long hours of inactivity and the change of diet also tend to constipate. Do not worry about this. Everything will get back to normal when the trip is over—perhaps aided by a mild laxative or a meal of liver, which has a laxative effect. Always keep your dog on a leash or a longer length of rope during your wayside halts. When you stop for a picnic lunch, you might attach his long lead to a swivel stake driven into the ground. But don't neglect to take him for a walk before resuming your route.

When you have to leave your dog IN A PARKED CAR, be very careful in your choice of a parking place. Select a shady spot that is certain to remain in the shade as the sun moves. Lock the car doors as well as your dog's crate, if he has one. Even if there is no risk of theft, some curious child may open the car to pet your dog and he may escape. If you leave him for more than an hour or two, place a bowl of water on the floor and pay him a visit, if possible, in order to reassure him (and yourself as well). Never leave your dog in the car when you have to park it in an enclosed garage or an underground parking lot. The darkness, isolation, and pollution make it a most unhealthy experience for him, physically and psychologically.

DURING HOT WEATHER you must take special pains to see that your dog does not become overheated or dehydrated. Give him frequent opportunities to drink a little cool water, and keep the rear windows open far enough for ventilation, but not so far that he can jump out or even stick his head out. Fresh air is vital to dogs, but they are even more vulnerable to drafts than we are. When the temperature soars and the air conditioning doesn't work, you can protect your dog from heatstroke by giving him a damp towel to lie on, by draping a damp towel over his back, or by moistening his coat with cool water.

Even IN COLD WEATHER, you should always leave two windows slightly open. If your dog has to remain in an unheated car for more than an hour, put on his sweater, or pin a blanket over his back.

TRAVEL SICKNESS

is as miserable for dogs as it is for people, and the cause is generally the same: partly physical and partly psychological, due to apprehension. A dog who is carsick during his first drive is apt to suffer a self-induced spell of nausea every time he gets into a car.

Drooling, swallowing, and chop-licking are the usual warning signals of travel sickness. When the saliva streams, get out your roll of paper towels and prepare to clean up, because the next step will be retching. Panting is also a sign of imminent vomiting.

Sailors nibble biscuits and snacks all day long, claiming that travel on an empty stomach is sure to bring on nausea. A more sensible rule for dogs is to refrain from feeding or watering them less than 2 hours before a trip, to give them an easily digested meal 5 or 6 hours beforehand, and another one an hour after arrival. When a normal mealtime is delayed, give your dog a few dry biscuits and a drink of water.

Canine versions of antihistamine travel-sickness remedies require a veterinary prescription, and it is useful to have a supply on hand. Be sure to ask your vet to specify the proper dose and the proper timing for a preventive effect. Usually it must be given at least half an hour before departure. Like the human pills, they have a soporific effect and cause great thirst, so be prepared to give your dog all the water he wants and to make the necessary comfort stops afterward. Some vets prefer to prescribe a tranquilizer with an antinausea ingredient, but these are soporific and dehydrating too. Both remedies are effective during a limited period of time, generally no more than 8 hours. When a dog has passed this danger period, he is unlikely to feel sick again. But be prepared to repeat the dose if he still seems queasy.

Experienced owners recommend various nonmedical preventive measures such as abstaining from smoking in the car, attaching an antistatic strip to the rear axle, placing the dog's crate (or inducing him to stand) facing forward instead of sideways, covering his crate or installing him on the floor in order to avoid "sight sickness," and keeping the rear window of station wagons closed in order to avoid drawing exhaust fumes into the interior.

When preventive measures fail, do not scold your dog for being sick. He is more unhappy about it than you are. Instead, comfort and reassure him. Remember that anxiety is one of the causes of his sickness, and scolding will only make it worse. Try to take his mind off his misery by offering him a biscuit or a lump of sugar, by encouraging him to look out of the window, and by talking to him. At the end of the trip, make a big fuss over him. If his final impression is pleasant, he may forget the rest.

MEALS

When you travel with your dog you must usually provide his meals. The simplest method is to start off with a supply of his regular dog food, replenish it when you can, and replace it with fresh food whenever possible.

During a trip that lasts no more than 8 or 10 hours, it is better for your dog and more convenient for you if you do not feed him at all, or at least no more than an occasional snack. Even a 24-hour period of fasting will do him no harm.

ON AIRPLANES, a portion of your own meal or a few biscuits that you have brought with you should keep him satisfied, since he is unlikely to be very interested in food during the flight.

ON TRAINS, dogs are not permitted in the dining car. During an overnight trip, this will pose no problem. But during an all-day train ride or a longer one, you will have to bring sufficient dog food with you, which you can supplement with table scraps from your dining-car meal. If you serve your dog a full meal during a train trip, time it carefully. Remember that he will feel the urge to eliminate some 6 or 8 hours later.

ON SHIPS equipped with kennels, meals are included in the price you pay for your dog's passage. You can even request a special diet. Although mealtimes are outside of the regular kennel visiting hours, you might try to drop in then just to check up on what your dog is being fed. You may find it is better than what he gets at home.

DURING A LONG AUTOMOBILE TRIP, try to feed your dog at his normal mealtimes, but less than usual. It is not difficult to keep a supply of dry or canned prepared dog food in the car. You can feed your dog in the car while you are enjoying a restaurant meal. You can feed him beforehand in order to keep him company. Or you can feed him afterward, adding your own table scraps to his dog food. Always carry a plastic bag for this purpose, or a square of aluminum foil. If your dog food supplies suddenly run out, a practical though costly solution is to give your dog hamburger without the bun, purchased from a highway drive-in. It is a meal your dog will relish and one that is available night and day along American highways.

HOTELS AND MOTELS

Before you set off on a trip with your dog, you should gather all the information you can about possible lodging places and plan your itinerary accordingly. The Gaines Dog Research Center publishes a handy booklet with a list of hotels and motels which accept dogs. Automobile clubs also provide this information. Many ordinary guidebooks indicate by some special symbol the hotels that open their doors to four-footed guests. You will find that not many of them do: luxury hotels (the Hilton, Sheraton, and Holiday Inn chains, for example) more often than commercial establishments, and motels (such as Howard Johnson, Quality Inns, Ramada Inns, and Days Inns of America) more often than hotels. Even if you intend to camp in your own tent in a National Park, you should check the park regulations (your automobile club can help you), because they vary from one to another, some of them requiring dogs to be muzzled, and others restricting their presence to certain areas of the park.

As a rule, motels are the best choice if only because their locations usually offer more possibilities for dogwalking than do centrally situated hotels. In all cases, you should mention your dog at the time you reserve your room and not attempt to smuggle him in.

Reluctant hotel managers can most easily be persuaded to accept a small dog who is used to city apartment life, or a large dog who is Obedience-trained and sleeps in a wire crate. Some hotels require the owner to sign an agreement to respect certain conditions, such as keeping the dog leashed whenever he is outside of the room, and paying for any damage he may cause. Some experienced dog owners spontaneously offer a deposit to cover possible damage and say that no hotel or motel manager has ever refused either the deposit or the dog. Incidentally, a modest daily rate is usually charged for canine guests.

You can do much to make your dog popular with the management. Inquire at the time you register where you can take him for a walk. You should, of course, never walk him in a garden, around a swimming pool, or in a children's play area. If he forgets his manners in a forbidden spot, remove the evidence with tissues, a plastic bag, or the scoop in the car trunk, and dump it in a waste container. When you take your dog back and forth to the room, use the service elevator.

As soon as you are shown to your room, install your dog's crate or cushion in a corner, his water bowl in the bathroom, order a bottle of soda water or seltzer, and ring for the maid. If by miracle there is one

and she answers the call, introduce your dog to her and give her a tip for
the extra work that he may cause, if only by shedding hair on the carpet.
Why the soda water? It is an excellent antidote for urine stains on car-
pets (see page 111). If you treat the spot at once, nobody will ever sus-
pect your dog's little lapse.

When you have to leave your dog alone in the room, take no chances.
Shut him in the bathroom with his cushion, a toy, and an article bearing
your scent. Or shut him in his crate. Hang the DO NOT DISTURB sign on
the door and double-lock it. You might leave the radio or television
turned on low to keep him company during your absence, and give him a
dog biscuit to nibble on. You might also test him by leaving him for only
a few minutes the first time, and observe his reaction. Even if you can
trust your dog to remain loose in the room, make sure there is no window
open wide enough for him to escape and try to rejoin you. Never remove
his collar. Some owners add a slip chain collar with a duplicate identity
disc to the dog's regular collar for extra security during travel.

If your dog is used to sleeping on your bed, he need not change his
habits, nor will anyone be the wiser if you have packed a blanket cover
or sheet for protecting the hotel bedding. If he is used to sleeping on the
floor, place his cushion or blanket in its usual position in relation to the
bed. Adhere as far as possible to his normal daily schedule of meals and
walks. Above all, remember that hotels are not obliged to accept dogs, so
do not abuse the privilege.

Most dogs are excellent travelers, better behaved than most children.
The strange environments and experiences will make your pet feel more
dependent on you. He will stick closer to you and obey you more
promptly than he does at home. So the responsibility for his good behav-
ior rests on your shoulders. You will have no problem if you simply antic-
ipate your dog's needs and provide for them.

Many hotel managers say that dogs are better guests than most adults.
One of them placed a notice on the reception desk, reading:

> "We are happy to accept the dogs because
>   they do not wipe their shoes on the curtains;
>   they do not steal silverware;
>   they do not swipe ashtrays;
>   they do not come in late at night drunk and disturb the neighbors;
>   they do not burn cigarette holes in blankets or
>   stop up the toilet and washbasin;
>   they do not pay their bills with bad checks;
>   they bring nice people with them."

FOREIGN TRAVEL

Traveling abroad with your dog is no different from traveling with him in the United States, except for Customs and Quarantine regulations. Since these vary from one country to another and also change from time to time according to the animal epidemic-disease situation, it is essential to check the current regulations with the Consulate of the foreign country you intend to visit.

Some countries have passed stringent laws that practically prohibit the temporary importation of canine visitors. Among them:

Australia, whose frontiers are closed to all foreign dogs. Smuggled dogs are automatically destroyed.

Great Britain and *Ireland,* which enforce a 6-month quarantine in an official kennel at normal boarding rates, thus virtually banning transient dogs and even pets of homecoming British citizens. English breeders who wish to introduce foreign bloodlines in their stock circumvent the law in a way by importing a pregnant bitch. The puppies, born on British soil, are free from quarantine, although the bitch must serve the full term.

Sweden, Norway, Finland, and *Hawaii* are slightly more lenient, imposing a quarantine, at the owner's expense, of 4 months.

In *Denmark* it is 6 weeks. But some Scandinavian nations also require a permit from the Ministry of Agriculture.

Communist countries are risky destinations when you travel with your dog. Even if you comply with all of the instructions the Consulate has given you, local Customs officials will always find some pretext for barring entry to a capitalistic dog.

Most European countries, including *France, Spain, Italy, Belgium, Holland,* and *West Germany,* along with *Canada, Mexico, Puerto Rico,* and *Cuba,* welcome canine tourists as long as they arrive at the frontier with an up-to-date rabies vaccination certificate (at least 1 month old, but less than 1 year), and a veterinary certificate of good health (dated no more than 10 days previously). The same is true of most South and Central American nations. If you wish to keep your dog's papers in order, you will therefore have to procure a new veterinary health certificate every 10 days, even though these papers are seldom examined carefully.

Once you and your dog have crossed the border, and especially if you have crossed the Atlantic Ocean, you will find that he is more welcome in foreign hotels, restaurants, public places, trains, and buses than he is in their American counterparts. Germans and Austrians are extremely fond of dogs. The Swiss are also great admirers of well-bred, well-behaved dogs who respect the Swiss obsession for cleanliness. The Latin attitude toward dogs seems to be either passionate love or violent dislike. In France, Spain, and Italy you are apt to meet the most outrageously pampered pets as well as the most cruelly neglected ones.

Still, it is wise to mention your dog at the time you make your foreign travel reservations, and to carry with you a guidebook that lists the establishments that accept dogs. The Michelin Guides include a canine symbol in their hotel and restaurant lists for most European countries. In France you can also buy a canine travel guide, the *Guide Mi-Chien* (a pun on the Michelin title, since "chein" means "dog" in French). Automobile clubs, official tourist offices, and travel agencies can also advise you.

Does it sound terribly complicated to travel with your dog? Obviously, it involves additional preparation and extra expense. It may also entail delays, perhaps lengthy discussions and arguments.

IS IT WORTH IT?

Definitely yes, if you are establishing residence in another part of this country or abroad, even if you are planning a long stay in a place where your dog can lead a normal life with you.

Yes, if you intend to show your dog at home or abroad in the hope of earning a National or International Championship. Your dog's show entry papers will facilitate his temporary admittance to foreign countries.

Yes, if your dog is small and weighs no more than 10 pounds or so, if he is a perfectly housebroken, well-trained adult who is used to accompanying you everywhere.

Maybe, if your dog is large but well-trained, if your itinerary is suitable, if you have a generous travel budget, if he is devoted to you, and if you love him enough to adjust your plans to suit his needs and to accept the restrictions that his presence will impose.

Definitely no, if your trip is designed as a short holiday, a sightseeing tour, a rest cure, or a honeymoon.

No, if you are traveling Economy Class on a strict budget. (Haven't you noticed that the dogs most often photographed debarking from ships and planes are held in the arms of the Duchess of Windsor or Elizabeth Taylor?)

No, if you expect to lead an active social life during your trip. (Even the Queen of England leaves her Corgis at the Palace during her official travels.)

No, if your dog suffers from confinement, solitude, constraint, and a change of routine.

Instead of taking him with you in these cases, pay a dependable friend to look after your dog during your absence, or board him in a good kennel which you have visited personally. You will be more carefree during your trip and he will be happier too, even though he misses you.

You do not need to send your dog a postcard announcing your return. He will know the date of your arrival without being told. But please, don't forget to bring him back a present.

20.
Boarding Your Dog

The first time you leave your dog in a boarding kennel, he will seem pathetically helpless and innocent, even if he is a bold little Terrier or a powerful Great Dane. How you wish you could explain to him that you are leaving him just for a week or two and not abandoning him forever! Try to reassure him as best you can, but resist the impulse to turn around for one last glimpse before you leave. His expression of pained bewilderment will haunt you for days.

You should realize, however, that dogs, like children, adjust quite rapidly to new circumstances. Moreover, there are times when the only sensible thing to do is to board your dog—for example, during a business trip or a holiday when you cannot take him with you and there is nobody trustworthy available to look after him; when illness prevents you from giving your dog his daily care and exercise and there is no one else to do it for you; during the hectic period of moving to a new home, or even a redecoration or building project in your house, when it is impossible to keep your dog safely out of the way; when your bitch is in heat and you are unable to supervise her constantly, or when her condition is apt to cause havoc among male canine members of the household.

If a dog is given adequate care, sufficient exercise, and a normal standard of comfort, he can be quite happy in a boarding kennel, surrounded by activity and other dogs. But if he is ill-fed, ill-housed, or neglected, he will not be able to write you a tear-stained letter, like a child who is miserable in summer camp. So it is up to you to select the best possible kennel for him, and if you cannot find a suitable one, to seek some other solution. In any case, you should never consider boarding in a commercial boarding kennel an aged or ailing dog, or a puppy under one year of age.

The ideal solution would be to board your dog at the kennel where he was born and raised (yet another advantage of buying your dog from a private breeder who lives within driving distance of your home). If the breeder is unable to accept your dog as a paying guest, he may be able to recommend a commercial breeding kennel with which he has had satisfactory personal experiences.

You can also ask for recommendations from dog-owning friends, from your veterinarian, and from the secretary of your local dog club. Perhaps your local Obedience-class instructor has a kennel with room for boarders, in which case you might enroll your dog in a course of private training lessons during his boarding period and thus offer him a constructive occupation during your absence.

Many veterinarians run boarding kennels too, although this is viewed askance by the profession. Obviously, unless the boarding establishment is completely separated from the clinic, it would be a foolish risk to introduce a healthy dog into an environment populated by ailing animals.

You should also think twice before leaving your dog with friends or relatives, no matter how much they love him. You will find that nobody knows how to look after your dog as well as you do, and that a normal professional standard of canine care if often more dependable than well-intentioned amateur efforts. If, however, you have a friend or relative who is free to move into your home during your absence and look after your dog as well as your house, this might solve all of your problems.

When you are unable to obtain any personal recommendations, you will have to do your own field work. Boarding kennels advertise in newspapers (often among the classified ads), in dog magazines, and are listed in the classified section of the telephone directory. The Gaines Dog

Research Center publishes a useful booklet: *Where to Buy, Board, or Train a Dog*. Select a few kennels that are within driving distance, telephone to arrange for an appointment, and visit them personally. If your dog enjoys riding in the car, you can take him with you.

WHAT SHOULD YOU LOOK FOR IN A BOARDING KENNEL?

1) *Security.* Above all, you want to be sure of finding your dog again when you return for him. Kennel security involves well-constructed fences, dogproof gates and latches, and around-the-clock supervision.

2) *A satisfactory standard of comfort and hygiene,* which means: sufficiently spacious individual kennels and runs for each dog; both sunshine and shade in the exercise area; draft-free, insulated indoor sleeping quarters; regularly changed bedding; and regularly cleaned runs. In order to judge the cleanliness of a kennel, do as your dog does: use your nose as well as your eyes. A well-run kennel should not have a doggy odor, and on no account should it smell like a latrine. On the other hand, an overpowering odor of disinfectant should be considered suspect too.

3) *Constantly available fresh water and well-balanced meals.* Inquire about the normal boarding diet before you make any special requests. It will give you a clue to the quality of the services provided. You can leave a supply of your dog's customary food if you like. But if the kennel diet is suitable, this might be just the opportunity your dog needs to shed a few excess pounds.

4) *Sufficient personnel* to care for the number of dogs accommodated.

5) *Good kennel management,* businesswise as well as dogwise. Cross off your list at once a kennel that refuses to let you visit its installations— unless, of course, you have not telephoned for an appointment but have simply dropped in at an inconvenient hour. Be wary of an establishment that desperately seeks your patronage, proposes unrealistically low rates, is run down and gives the impression of having a hard time making both ends meet.

Boarding fees in good kennels are quite expensive. They vary according to the size of the dog, the location and luxury of the kennel, and sometimes the time of year (holiday periods being more costly because of the greater demand). In general, you should be prepared to pay:

For a large dog $5 or $6 a day.

For a small dog or a Toy: $3.50 to $5.00.

In a luxury canine hotel: $9 and up.

6) *The supervision and collaboration of a good veterinarian.* You should consider it a favorable sign if the kennel refuses to accept your dog unless he has been inoculated against distemper, hepatitis, and leptospirosis (the "triple shots"), as well as vaccinated against rabies.

7) *A pleasant atmosphere.* Observe the current boarders. Do they greet your approach with wagging tails, or do they slink into corners or bark hysterically? Are their runs clean or soiled with excrement? Does the personnel seem competent, confident, and kindly, or harassed and irritable? Again, do as your dog does: sniff the air and let your intuition be your guide.

HOW TO FACILITATE HIS ADAPTATION

Since badly run boarding kennels do not remain in business for long, the chances are that one of the first on your list will meet your requirements, and you can make a reservation for your dog. You will probably be asked to leave a deposit.

Some pet owners recommend a trial boarding period before the actual date, on the theory that if you leave your dog first for an afternoon, then for a weekend or overnight, he will be confident of your return when you leave him for a longer period of time. Another suggestion is to board your dog a few days ahead of your departure date and telephone or pay him a visit 24 hours later to see how he is getting along. Both ideas are fine in theory, but hardly practical. Usually, you must exercise your best judgment ahead of time, and then simply hope for the best.

It is seldom a good idea to pay your dog a visit while he is boarded. He will be even more forlorn when you disappear, leaving him behind. Let him make his adjustment as best he can, without complicating the situation for him.

On the contrary, you should do everything possible to facilitate his adaptation. For example, you can:

—Leave with him his favorite toy, his blanket, cushion, or even his bed, and an article that bears your scent. You will naturally leave his collar and leash.

—In order to have a choice of the best accommodations in the best boarding kennels, make your reservation well in advance, especially during holidays and over weekends.

—The night before you deliver your dog, take a few minutes to draw up a list of special instructions. You will undoubtedly be given a detailed questionnaire to fill in at the time you register your pet, but at the poignant moment, you may forget the very items that are most important. You should make a note of your dog's daily feeding program, including quantities and time schedule; any regular medication or vitamin supplements, along with an adequate supply of them; the name, address, and telephone number of your veterinarian, and also of a friend who can be contacted in an emergency. This is generally more practical than leaving a copy of your travel itinerary. If your dog is ill or injured while you are on a business trip to Paris or London, what can you possibly do to help? Instead, ask a close friend to assume the responsibility of coping with the emergency and of judging whether or not it is advisable to inform you of it before your return.

—Deliver your dog in perfect condition: clean, well-groomed, free from fleas and worms. The kennel staff is apt to take better care of him if he gives the impression of being used to a high standard of living. If the kennel has a grooming service, as many of them do, you can also order a bath or clipping for him the day before you plan to take him home.

When the boarding period comes to an end, your dog will be overjoyed to see you again, but he will express his delight in various ways. He may practically jump out of his skin and slobber all over you. Or he may pretend not to recognize you at first, even to sulk for a while, which is his way of punishing you. Do not worry or feel hurt. He will not be able to keep it up for long.

His boarding experience will probably have influenced him for better or for worse—generally the latter. He may have become a sloppy eater or a gobbler, when he was most fastidious before. He may have picked up a flea or two, or have become unhousebroken. If he has a dull eye or coat, a runny nose, or a listless attitude, have him checked by your veterinarian on the way home. If he has a "kennel smell," give him a thorough grooming, including an insecticide bath, as soon as possible.

During the first few days you may have to be stricter than usual with your dog, because he may have forgotten some of his good manners too. Kennel-boarded dogs often pick up the habit of barking, which is highly contagious. If you refuse to tolerate the slightest lapse of good behavior, your dog will resume his former habits at once. But if you fail to correct his newly acquired "kennel vices" immediately, they will be very difficult to eliminate.

The first experience with a boarding kennel is the hardest, for you as well as for your dog. Next time, both of you will know what to expect: the pain of parting, the ache of absence, and the joy of being reunited. In fact, you may never realize how much your dog means to you until you have had to board him.

21.

Your Dog and the Law

The long arm of the law reaches even into the lives of our dogs, limiting the freedom of dogs and their owners and imposing certain responsibilities.

Legally, your dog is considered an object of personal property and nothing more. As such, all transactions concerning him are governed by federal commercial law. If he is injured or stolen, you can seek indemnity as for any other piece of property. If he causes damage or injury to property or people, you can be held responsible. Dogs are neither bound by criminal law nor protected by it. Nevertheless, the law implicitly recognizes that dogs are a special kind of property, since courts have upheld an owner's right to name a dog in his will as beneficiary of a trust fund.

(But if you want to disinherit all your relatives in favor of your dog, be sure to have your will drawn up by an expert lawyer who is prepared to prove your mental capacity.)

Federal laws virtually ignore dogs. The only nationwide legislation specifically concerning them deals with interstate shipment of livestock (in order to control epidemic disease) and live animal experimentation (in order to prevent inhumane treatment). Consequently, canine legislation consists almost entirely of state laws, county regulations, city and town ordinances, even building lease agreements and prohibitions, which vary according to local conditions. Many lawsuits involving dogs are decided simply by referring to the common law of the locality, to previous court decisions, or the prejudices of the judge or jury.

It is impossible to summarize the canine statutes of every state, although this would be an interesting and useful subject for one of your dog club meetings, particularly since the trend seems to be toward stricter laws and higher fines. However, bearing in mind the fact that laws can be amended and repealed, and that canine lobbyists, pro and con, are more active than ever before in proposing new legislation, these are some of the most widely recognized legal rights and responsibilities of dogs and their owners:

OWNERSHIP

In the absence of a special contract, a dog becomes the property of a new owner when the dog has been delivered to him, or when the buyer, by spoken or written agreement, accepts the seller's offer of the dog. TITLE passes to the new owner on delivery even if the dog has not been paid for, and even if he has been paid for with a bad check. Payment is an entirely separate legal matter from transfer of ownership.

The clearest PROOF OF OWNERSHIP is a bill of sale, which may be no more than a handwritten, dated statement to the effect that a particular dog is sold by a specified seller to a specified buyer. It is not necessary to specify the price. Ownership may also be presumed by the payment of an annual dog license fee, inscription by the tax assessor, registration in a tattoo registry (see page 419), or even by common knowledge.

A kindly person who shelters a stray dog does not automatically become the legal owner, unless it can be proven that the original owner abandoned the dog or willfully permitted it to run away. In order to avoid having a good deed misconstrued as theft, you must make every effort to locate the stray dog's owner by notifying the police, the dog pound, the local animal shelter, by advertising in the newspaper, and by making personal inquiries. Even so, the original owner can claim his pet many years later, although he would be responsible for the expenses you incurred in caring for his dog. In the meantime, you are responsible for the dog's welfare as well as for any damage he may cause, as long as he is harbored in your home.

Ownership disputes may arise even between the best of friends when BREEDING OR LEASING AGREEMENTS are vague or verbal. Try to anticipate every eventuality, be as specific as possible, and put everything in a written contract, signed by both parties. In the case of a stud dog owner's choice of a puppy from the litter resulting from his service, you should specify the sex, what happens if there is only one living puppy (it is customarily accorded to the owner of the stud dog), and a date limit for selecting the puppy (generally at 8 weeks of age). In specifying breeding terms, be sure to mention whether or not there will be a free mating at the bitch's next heat if the first one proves fruitless. Otherwise, the male dog is expected to provide a single mating with a "tie" and nothing more.

Remember that the American Kennel Club and similar agencies are primarily studbook registries, not law courts. They accept in good faith the owners' names that are submitted to them in due form for registration and show purposes. But they cannot and will not attempt to solve ownership disputes.

LICENSES AND TAXES

The ANNUAL DOG LICENSE you must buy for your dog is a form of tax, a payment for the privilege of keeping a dog, and a source of revenue for local canine-control operations. It is obligatory and nontransferable. If you move to another town, you will have to get your dog a new license. If you sell your dog, the new owner will have to get a new license even if the dog remains in the same town and the old one has not yet expired.

Dog license regulations vary from one place to another: in age, from 3 to 6 months; in cost, from $3 to $5 or so, generally with a supplement for unspayed females and un-neutered males, and a wholesale price for kennels. Proof of an antirabies inoculation may be required as a prerequisite for licenses, which are usually issued by the town or city clerk and must be renewed annually, generally in January or June. Do not neglect this obligation. Not only is a dog license the best form of identification for your dog, but it also may avoid his being picked up and possibly disposed of as a stray. Aside from which, you risk a fine.

Many states impose a SALES TAX, and it may be useful to know that this does not apply to canine grooming or boarding services, to the sale of puppies from an occasional litter by an amateur breeder, or to sales of dogs exported to another state. However, if the breeder owns an established kennel, advertises, and publicly offers dogs for sale on a regular basis, a tax must be paid on every transaction, even though selling dogs may not be his principal means of livelihood.

In some communities, a PERSONAL PROPERTY TAX is also levied on dogs, since they are considered property just like automobiles, pianos, or (more aptly) works of art.

Even pet owners are legally obliged to report revenue from stud services and puppy sales on their INCOME TAX returns. If dog breeding or showing is a business, they can also deduct the business loss, if any, from other income. For this reason, tax consultants sometimes advise clients in high tax brackets with expensive private kennels to convert them into commercial operations in order to benefit from loss deductions. However, in order to qualify as a genuine commercial operation, the kennel must make a profit during at least 2 years out of 5 and fulfill other commercial obligations.

Not exactly a tax, but an obligatory expense for every dog owner, is the annual ANTIRABIES VACCINATION, which is now compulsory in almost every state. The dog must wear his vaccination tag attached to his collar at all times when he is outside of his own home. In areas where the danger of rabies is great, loose dogs without antirabies tags can be impounded, and in some cases destroyed.

RIGHTS AND RESTRICTIONS

In addition to license and tax payments, the dog owner has other legal obligations, most of them designed to ensure that his dog does not become a public nuisance or menace the public welfare in any way.

Most local ordinances require a dog to be under his owner's control whenever he is in a public place, including public parks and even his own apartment hallway. He is usually permitted to patrol the public highway adjacent to his home, but if he annoys or chases another dog, a person, or a vehicle, the owner may be fined or even jailed. Almost everywhere, it is against the law to permit a bitch in heat to run at large. Some laws specify that a dog must be leashed in public places and that the leash must be no longer than 6 feet long. It is understood that you must hold the other end of it. If you let your dog roam in the park, dragging his leash behind him, do not be surprised if you are fined for failing to leash your dog. And do not waste time trying to convince the park patrolman that your dog just happened to pull the lead from your hand. He knows the scenario by heart.

When a dog is permitted to run loose contrary to a specific local or state law, he can be impounded, whether or not he is wearing a collar and a license tag. The length of time he must be held in the DOG POUND before being disposed of varies from as little as 24 hours to as long as 7 days. The pound is obliged to make an effort to contact the owner, and the owner is responsible for the cost involved in the dog's arrest and, for his board, and he probably will be fined as well.

Nobody has the right to maintain a PUBLIC NUISANCE—an epithet frequently applied to dogs by neighbors who are bothered by persistent or untimely barking. If a legal complaint is filed, the case will come to court. The plaintiff will have to prove that the dog is a genuine public nuisance, and not simply an alert and loving pet who yelps with joy when greeting his owner and who barks a warning as a good guard should. The law respects the dog's right to bark for some logical reason, but not to bark continually. If the owner loses the case, he may be ordered to pay damages to the plaintiff and to observe certain restrictions where his dog is concerned. But he cannot normally be obliged to get rid of his noisy pet.

Your very RIGHT TO KEEP A DOG may be subject to restrictions. If you own your home, you can bring into it any dog you like. But municipal zoning laws may prevent a home owner from establishing a commercial kennel, and you can be prevented by a court order from maintaining so many dogs or such turbulent ones that they constitute a public nuisance, or such unsanitary conditions that public health is endangered.

It may be claimed that you operate a commercial kennel if you post a sign on or near your property and if you advertise your kennel in newspapers and magazines. Boarding and grooming are always commercial enterprises, and they can pose problems if established in a residential zone. On the other hand, it is generally permitted to maintain a noncommercial kennel on residentially zoned property if the kennel is on the same land as the owner's dwelling and the dogs are kept for the owner's pleasure, including the pleasure of hunting, exhibition in dog shows,

Field Trials, and Obedience competitions and, of course, for guarding and protecting the owner's property. The occasional sale of a litter of puppies does not alter the noncommercial character of the kennel. Nevertheless, it is advisable to check with your local zoning board before deciding to keep more than two or three dogs.

If you rent your home, your landlord has the right to prohibit keeping dogs on his property by specifically stipulating it in the lease. If he suddenly changes his mind about dogs, he cannot force you to get rid of the pet he originally accepted. But he can add a prohibition clause when your current lease expires.

Many co-operative apartment buildings, condominiums, and housing developments limit or prohibit dogs. These rules may not always be strictly enforced, however. Small, well-behaved pets are frequently tolerated where large, unruly, or noisy ones are banned.

The RIGHT OF ADMITTANCE of dogs in hotels and motels is generally left to the discretion of the management. But state and local laws increasingly bar dogs from public places, including the post office, department stores, theaters, and, almost always, from any place where food is served, prepared, or sold. Local public transport also generally prohibits dogs unless they are small enough to be carried in a case on the owner's lap. On the other hand, federal law obliges interstate and international public carriers, such as trains, ships, and trucks, to transport your dog as long as he is in good health, free from infectious disease, inoculated against rabies, and crated according to the company's requirements.

In most cities and many towns, it is a misdemeanor to permit a dog to "COMMIT A NUISANCE" on the sidewalk (translation: to urinate or defecate), and the owner can be fined. This particular fine, by the way, is one that has inflated most in recent years. In some cities and states the law obliges an owner to remove his dog's feces even from the gutter. In West German cities where this same law is in effect, there are sidewalk vending machines providing paper bags and cardboard shovels and scrapers.

A dog owner is also obliged to exercise normal care in order to prevent his dog from doing DAMAGE TO OTHER PERSONS OR PROPERTY, and he can be held responsible for reparations. In France, he can even be required to pay the cost of a car wash to the owner of a car whose tires or fenders have been splashed by his puppy's *pipi*. Of course, it is only fair to try to repair the damage done by your dog—for example, by replacing a child's chewed-up toy or someone's glove, or by paying for an object swept off a table or a store counter by your dog's gaily wagging tail. An owner is also responsible for damages indirectly caused by his dog, and these can be far more onerous: for example, if your dog frightens a passing pedestrian who then stumbles and breaks a leg; or if your dog suddenly darts across the street and a driver, swerving to avoid him, is involved in an automobile accident. So do not think it is unnecessary to take out an insurance policy for your dog (or to make sure that he is covered by your personal or household liability insurance), simply because he is so small and gentle. Indirectly and inadvertently, he can cause grave and costly accidents.

Strangely enough, there is no law (except in Kentucky) that penalizes canine TRESPASSING if the dog does no harm—although a trespassing dog may be considered to be "roaming at large," which is forbidden by law in many places.

It is also surprising, in view of the severity of most canine legislation, that the law in many states is relatively indulgent concerning one of the most common causes of lawsuits against dog owners: BITING A PERSON or another dog. On this issue, many state laws recognize that it may not always be the dog's fault.

In general, if a dog has never bitten anybody before, and if it can be proven that he was provoked by teasing, by abuse, or by a trespasser, the dog is given the benefit of the doubt. The owner must then take every precaution to prevent a recurrence, such as enclosing the dog in a run or fencing his property, and posting a prominent "Beware of the Dog" sign, because if his dog bites again, statutory provocation must be clearly proven in order to avoid a damage award.

The legal principle is that a person cannot be held responsible for acts beyond his knowledge or presumption—which is not quite the same as the widespread belief that every dog is legally entitled to one bite! Obviously, an owner can no longer claim that he never imagined his dog capable of biting if the dog has already done so. As a matter of fact, if you keep a trained guard dog, a dog of one of the reputedly aggressive breeds, or simply a great big ferocious-looking animal, the court will assume that you should have realized from the start the potential danger involved, and unless you have posted a warning and confined the dog, he will not even be permitted the famous first bite.

If your dog was trespassing at the time he bit somebody, you will probably be held liable for damages. If your dog bites somebody on your own property, his guilt or innocence will depend on the nature of the victim, a distinction being made between trespassers and visitors with a legitimate reason for entering your grounds, such as milkmen, mailmen, and even traveling salesmen. Your dog is most likely to be absolved if you can prove that his victim was bitten through his own negligence or misbehavior; by teasing, abusing or provoking your dog; or by entering your property with the intention to commit some unlawful act.

While the right to one bite is merely a myth, the "three bite" theory is incorporated in many state laws: after three reported biting incidents, a court may declare that a dog is vicious and order him destroyed. It is not an automatic procedure, however. You have the right to argue in your dog's defense.

Law courts no longer accept the posting of a "Beware of the Dog" sign as sufficient warning to uninvited visitors that they are entering at their own risk. Consequently, as you may have noticed, increasingly terrifying signs are appearing on dog owners' gateposts, such as: "A vicious dog is at large on the premises. Enter at your own peril!" This might be considered ridiculously exaggerated by the owner of a tiny Chihuahua or an affectionate Yorkshire Terrier. But perhaps it is not as foolish as it seems, considering the current fad for filing damage suits. Of course, you should complete this protection by normal control measures over your dog, and above all by full insurance coverage.

WHEN A DOG BITES ANOTHER DOG, the owner of the injured dog can sue for damages, and the case will be judged according to the circumstances, taking into account the reputation and past record of both dogs, the property on which the incident took place, and whether negligence or infraction of the law was involved.

The most stringent antidog laws in the country are found in states with important livestock industries, where every year countless POULTRY AND LIVESTOCK are injured or killed by dogs—very rarely by pet dogs, it should be added, but usually by abandoned or semiwild animals. Proven sheep killers can be shot on sight in certain states. In others, it is a misdemeanor to keep a dog who is known to have killed livestock. In a few, there is a cruel "sunset law," providing that dogs found off their owner's premises between sunset and sunrise may be summarily destroyed. Most farmers and ranchers have the legal right to shoot stray dogs who are molesting their stock. And in some areas, a dog seen running deer may be killed.

However, these are special laws for special situations. In most states, even a police officer hasn't the right to kill a dog without a special warrant, unless the dog is actually threatening the life of persons or livestock. Nor can a policeman remove a dog from his owner's premises without a special court order, or without the owner's consent. Legally, your dog is your private property, and the Constitution guarantees that property cannot be confiscated without due process of the law, the only exceptions being when public welfare is endangered, as, for example, when a rabid dog is impounded and destroyed.

What about THE DOG'S RIGHTS? With all of these restrictive laws, American dogs do not seem to share many of their owners' historic rights to life, liberty, and the pursuit of happiness, do they? Perhaps not. But the situation is improving.

Thanks to the tireless efforts of animal welfare societies and devoted dog lovers, often in the face of derision and hostility, there are at last a few "humane laws" which guarantee our dogs some care and protection and punish those who treat them cruelly. All dogs now have the legal right to adequate food, water, shelter, and freedom from malicious abuse. It is a misdemeanor to fail to offer one's pet these vital necessities, and it is a misdemeanor to abandon him. Abuse or cruelty includes: leaving an injured dog at the scene of an accident: keeping a dog chained short day and night: setting traps or poison for stray dogs: beating, torturing, inhumanely killing; taking part in organized dogfighting; and mutilation, which in some states includes docking tails and cropping ears except by a veterinarian and under anesthesia. Violators can be denounced, investigated, brought to trial, and possibly fined or even jailed.

As we have seen, you have the right to own a dog, in the absence of some specific prohibition. You also have the right to defend him, as you can defend any other item of property. (But if you rush to his defense in a dogfight, you do so at your own risk and peril.) If your dog is injured by a car, you can file a claim for damages from the offending or negligent driver. You have the right to walk with your dog along the public highway, if he is under your control.

The best way to protect your rights and your dogs is to defend them vigorously. Do not be intimidated by overzealous police officers and dog wardens, or by irate neighbors. Learn about the laws concerning dogs in your locality, report instances of cruelty you may observe to the competent authorities (preferably a humane society), and support the animal welfare associations, which need all the help that they can get.

INSURANCE

As soon as you acquire a dog, you should contact your insurance agent. The *personal liability* clause of your comprehensive household policy probably includes coverage for damage caused by your dog. If not, you should take out a separate liability policy for him. The cost is modest, and the protection is indispensable nowadays.

You may be offered a canine *health and hospital insurance* policy. This is apt to be expensive, but it is certainly worth examining.

Canine life insurance policies (often combined with liability and accident insurance in a single policy) provide an indemnity to the owner in the case of natural or accidental death. No matter how highly you value your pet, the reimbursement will be the actual market price of your dog. These policies are therefore generally reserved for valuable stud and show dogs.

It is obligatory to insure your dog during *shipping,* and it is advisable to insure him when he is *traveling* with you. Make sure that the travel policy covers damage to hotel furnishings, if this is not covered in a separate liability policy. The cost of these policies is slight, and they can usually be issued by the airline, express or travel agency at the time you make your shipping or travel arrangements.

Needless to add, you should take the trouble to read the fine print so that you will know exactly what protection you are getting and exactly what your obligations are. If not, you may find that your canine insurance is invalid just when you need it most.

LOSS AND THEFT

One fine day, you are walking with your unleashed dog along a country lane when he suddenly takes off after a rabbit, or is attracted by the distant howl of a bitch in heat. You shout, "Rover, Come!" with increasing desperation. But he does not even seem to hear you.

Perhaps you are taking your pet for his usual walk in the city or suburbs, without bothering to attach his leash because he is so perfectly trained and obedient. Suddenly a car backfires, your dog panics and flees despite your frantic attempts to call him back.

Or perhaps you have left your dog enclosed as usual in the yard or locked in your parked car while you spend an evening at the movies. When you return, he is no longer there.

A person who has never lost a dog cannot imagine the feelings it inspires: terrible apprehension mingled with outrage, sorrow, guilt, and helplessness. What can you do in order to recover your beloved friend?

For once, you can be grateful for the laws permitting stray dogs to be captured and impounded. But first of all, you should take immediate steps to try to find your dog yourself.

There are three possible courses of action:

1) In the case of a runaway, remain where your dog left you, hoping that he will remember the spot and eventually return to it. You can also leave an article of personal clothing on the spot, hoping that he will return to it and perhaps stay there until you come for him. This is seldom effective in strange surroundings, where the dog has not established reference points and signposts, and where memory cannot aid him. If your dog has not returned within a reasonable length of time, it is probably better to try the next method:

2) Scour the general area, calling him, asking everyone you meet if a dog resembling yours has passed, and if so, in what direction he was headed. You may be given a clue as to his destination and his present whereabouts. More often, you will be sent on an exhausting wild-goose chase. You should follow up every lead, of course, but bear in mind that children in particular are apt to be imaginative in their response to such inquiries. It may be more helpful to know that lost dogs instinctively tend to follow paths and roads, and are attracted by children at play and by other dogs. In the country, you can cover more ground by car, stopping at every house. If it is your lucky day, you may even spot your dog trotting proudly down the road, headed for home. Or, returning home distraught and empty-handed, you may find him there waiting to greet you.

3) Return home after a reasonable waiting period (timed by your watch, because every minute will seem like an eternity), and pray that he will find his own way back, or that some kind person or efficient public officer will take him in charge, note your name, address, and phone number on his collar tag, and contact you. In the country, there is a good chance that your dog will return on his own when it is time for his next meal. If that crucial moment passes without a sign of him, he may return at nightfall, especially if he has been hunting. In the city, however, if he has not managed to find his way home within an hour or so, he is unlikely ever to do so. You must therefore take other steps at once:

—Notify every shopkeeper and doorman in the neighborhood, leaving your name, phone number, and address, a description of your dog, and the promise of a generous reward for finding him.

—Call the local police, the dog pound, the dog warden, the ASPCA, the Humane Society, and every other animal welfare association in the city, leaving a detailed description of your dog as well as your name, address, and phone number. Do not be afraid to make a nuisance of yourself. Call every day if necessary.

—If your local radio station broadcasts news of lost and found pets, phone or deliver a bulletin with all the pertinent details.
—Enlist the help of neighborhood children in looking for your dog.
—Ask your postman, milkman, newspaper delivery boy, and garbage collector to keep an eye open for your dog as they make their daily rounds.
—Post a "Reward for Lost Dog" sign on neighborhood bulletin boards, at schools, in supermarkets, and other public places.
—Place an advertisement in the newspaper offering a reward for your dog. (Do not, however, mention your dog's name in your ad or elsewhere. If he has been stolen, it will only give the thief easier control over him.)

Do not delay advertising your dog, especially if you suspect that he was stolen. There are people who deliberately capture roaming dogs in order to claim the reward. Even more shocking is the increasing number of dognappings, the dog being stolen and held for ransom. At least the owner has more chance of recovering his dog than in the days when unscrupulous gangs would round up all the dogs they could lay their hands on in order to sell them to experimental laboratories. This heartless racket seems to be on the wane, perhaps because dognapping is more profitable, and also because laboratories have become wary about accepting stolen dogs, particularly if the dog is purebred and obviously a pet. Moreover, they will not accept dogs who have been tattooed.

Thieves can easily remove collars and license tags, but they cannot efface tattoo numbers, which makes this identification system one of the best means of protection for your dog. *Tattoo registries* are cropping up throughout the country. You will see their advertisements in dog magazines. It is obviously advisable to select a well-established firm, such as the National Dog Registry (227 Stebbins Road, Carmel, New York 10512; telephone: 914-277-4485). Fees vary, generally consisting of a registration fee of $25, to which must be added the $10 or so that your vet will charge for tattooing your Social Security number inside your dog's thigh or on his stomach. This obviously represents an undeniable proof of ownership.

When you recover a pet who was stolen or dognapped, there is little you can do to prosecute his unknown thieves or abductors. You should report the incident to your local police, just for the record, if you can find an officer who is willing to listen to your tale. Try to be brief, precise, and unemotional, and to remember that policemen are already overwhelmed by the alarming increase of more serious crimes.

When your dog returns home voluntarily after an escapade, it is unwise to punish him, for this might merely discourage him from returning another time. Besides, he may have been so terrified and miserable during his adventure that he will never want to repeat it. On the other hand, he may have thoroughly enjoyed his moment of independence and be totally unaware of the perils that he risked. So take no chances. Keep him confined, leashed, or under your control and supervison at all times.

SOME REALISTIC RULES

Since laws are made for and by men, without considering the needs and nature of the dog, it is practically impossible to prevent your dog from ever committing some minor legal infraction. Experienced owners try to respect the following realistic rules:

1) INSURE YOUR DOG against loss and theft, but above all insure yourself against personal liability for any damage he may cause. Insure also any stray dog you may harbor for more than a week or so, since you can be held responsible for his behavior too.

2) If you are accused of permitting your dog to commit some minor offense, such as soiling the sidewalk, being unleashed in a public park, or unmuzzled where muzzles are obligatory, first OFFER AN APOLOGY AND CORRECT THE INFRACTION (by leashing or muzzling your dog, or by cleaning up the mess). You may get off with only a warning. But if the policeman or guard is of the antidog school (which is most unusual), do not attempt to argue or make a scene. Pay the fine.

3) If you are persecuted by the complaints of a dog-hating neighbor, DEFEND YOUR RIGHTS and those of your dog to the limit, but BE CONSIDERATE AND REASONABLE too. For example, if you cannot stop your dog from barking at the moon, you can at least bring him indoors at night, where his barking will bother nobody but you.

4) Do all you can to AVOID LITIGATION. Lawyers' fees and court costs are expensive. Lawsuits are nerve-wracking and time-consuming. If you remain calm and co-operative, and if you are as tolerant of your neighbors' dogs as you would like them to be of yours, you will find that most incidents can be settled amicably without recourse to the law.

In the case of dog bites, it is always advisable to take the initiative. Human nature being as it is (and damage awards having reached astronomical levels), there are people who will stoop down to pat your dog in the street and, if your dog responds with a nip, will immediately envision generous indemnities. One wonders how they would react if a perfect stranger passing by reached out to ruffle their hair or pat them on the rump. In any case, you should examine the wound at once. You will usually find that it is merely a scratch, a warning nip rather than a real bite. But if there is any bleeding, insist on accompanying the person to a doctor. If you don't, the superficial scratch may develop overnight into some incapacitating injury.

5) Realize that when an adult dog continually causes damage, there must be something basically wrong with the life he leads, or perhaps with him. A normal, happy dog will never cause willful harm. If your pet is always getting into trouble with the law, perhaps you should consider seeking a more suitable home for him. Not one where his new owner doesn't mind destruction or prefers aggressive dogs, but one where your dog will find normal, harmless, legal outlets for his energy.

22.

Showing Your Dog

Dog shows have evolved a great deal since the first British show was held at Newcastle-on-Tyne in 1859, and the first really important American one, sponsored by the Westminster Kennel Club, was held in New York City in 1877. Like the early horse shows, they were designed to recognize breeding achievements and to provide a meeting place where breeders from far and wide could exchange ideas, evaluate each other's stock, and plan future breedings, while prospective buyers could compare different breeds and breeding lines.

Although dog shows still fulfill these original functions, the emphasis has become less and less on breeding and more and more on show and competition. Instead of being restricted to a few wealthy fanciers interested mainly in Sporting breeds, dog shows have become a leisure activity for men, women, and children from all walks of life, and for some 65,000 show dogs. It has also become a flourishing business. Throughout the year, all over the country, more than 1,500 licensed dog shows are held (and countless unlicensed ones), mostly on weekends. Many of them attract 1,000 entries, and some exceed 2,000.

It is difficult to define a dog show exactly. It is undeniably a show, since anyone can buy a ticket, visit a display of dogs, and witness the spectacle of classes being judged—although, to tell the truth, this is even less spectacular and more incomprehensible to the noninitiated than are horse show conformation classes, to which they might be compared. Dog shows have also become a popular competitive sport. Perhaps not exactly a sport (because athletic ability is not involved), but certainly more than a beauty contest (which is the favorite disparagement of critics).

Competition is gradually shifting from the dogs to their owners, as preparation, presentation, and handling have become increasingly important in determining awards. Dog show judges are no longer expected to select the dog who is intrinsically the best example of his breed in each class, nor the most desirable one to breed from, nor even necessarily the dog who comes closest to the official breed standard (as they are theoretically obliged to do). They designate as winners the dogs who on a particular day, at a particular moment (during the few minutes in the judging ring), make the best impression, put on the best show, and outshine the competition, whether by innate excellence or skillful showmanship. Furthermore, the ultimate goal of an exhibitor is no longer to compare his breeding stock to that of other fanciers, nor even to win a Blue ribbon by placing first in a class. It is to make his dog or bitch a Champion —which, as we shall see, cannot be achieved in a single show but during a campaign that involves numerous ring appearances (although a superior dog can do it in three).

Since showmanship has become so important, professionalism is threatening to dominate the dog show ring, as it has so many other arenas. In the major dog shows, only a skilled amateur can hope to compete successfully with the best professional handlers, unless he owns an outstanding dog, preferably of a breed that is presented in a natural condition and in which show-ring fad and fashion have not deviated from the official standard. Unfortunately, the number of these breeds is diminishing. Even in the Working and Sporting Groups, where you would think that soundness and utility would be the criteria of excellence, the trend is toward a double standard: one for elegant show dogs, and another for Working and Field Trialers.

An indoor dog show. (*William P. Gilbert*)

DOG SHOWS

Most of the MAJOR DOG SHOWS in America are governed by the American Kennel Club, restricted to AKC-registered purebred dogs, sponsored by an affiliated dog club, and managed by a professional AKC-licensed dog show superintendent, such as the Foley Dog Show Organization, Onafrio, Moss-Bow, Thomsen, Webb, and Jones, whose personnel and equipment you will meet time and again during your dog-showing career.

Dog shows are listed in the AKC *Gazette* calendar and are advertised in dog magazines, including the names of the judges as well as any special features such as Obedience Trials and nonregular classes.

A show may be an all-breed show or a "Specialty" for a single breed or group. It may be held indoors or out. It may be "benched" (where the dogs are obliged to remain on exhibition all day long), or "unbenched" (where the dogs are obliged only to appear in the ring for judging, after

An outdoor dog show. (*William P. Gilbert*)

which, if not competing further in Group classes, they may be taken home). It may be a one-day show, or it may—more rarely—span two or three days, with different Groups judged each day. The majority by far are one-day and unbenched, since longer shows are inconvenient for exhibitors, and benched ones are increasingly expensive for the organizers.

This explains the present trend of holding multiple shows on a single site. In 1976, the Colorado Centennial Canine Circuit organized 6 different dog shows during a 9-day period in one Denver building. More common is the practice of organizing dog show circuits, scheduling three or more shows within easy traveling distance on successive days, generally over a weekend. In Texas, where things are done in a big way, the circuit includes some 8 shows, numerous Specialties and Obedience Trials, during a period of 15 days. The Florida circuit, among others, offers the opportunity to win a Championship in a minimum period of time.

Another popular trend is to cover the outdoor circuit in a motor-home, parked as close as possible to the show ring, equipped with awnings,

bathroom, and a refrigerator stocked with beverages suitable for cele-
brating Blue ribbons. There were thousands of such mobile homes at
a recent Santa Barbara show, which is the biggest in the country. And
this underlines another trend in dog showing: the importance of West
Coast shows, particularly in California, whereas the big shows used to
be in the East. Incidentally, another trend should give satisfaction to
the feminists: in a field originally dominated by the men, 40 per cent of
dog show judges and 60 per cent of the exhibitors now are women.

Every licensed show may offer Championship points, varying from one
to five according to the number of entries in a class and to the region in
which the show is held. It also varies according to breed. A show may
offer no points at all for some breeds, one or two for breeds with few en-
tries, and three, four, or five for others. If it incorporates a Specialty for a
certain breed, it will automatically be a five-point show for that breed. A
show's point values are not announced but must be calculated from the
number of entries listed in the judging program that is mailed to exhibi-
tors before the show.

In addition to licensed or "point" shows in which Championship points
are earned, there are M A T C H S H O W S , which are usually sponsored by
a local dog club, observe the same rules and procedures in less formal
fashion, and are held as practice sessions and social occasions on Satur-
day or Sundays or in the evening. Match shows sanctioned by the AKC
are restricted to registered dogs. But local kennel clubs also organize
nonsanctioned Match shows that are open to all dogs, purebred or not,
just for fun. In addition to the standard classes, there may be competi-
tions for "The Best Tail Wagger," "The Most Comical Dog," "The Best
Costume," or "The Dog Presented in the Best Condition," and so forth,
and the club makes its own show rules.

DOG SHOW JUDGES

Judges are licensed by the American Kennel Club after meeting
certain qualifications to guarantee their competence in judging one or
several specific breeds or groups. Very few of the 1,500 or so licensed
judges have qualified as "all-rounders," authorized to judge all breeds.
For their efforts, they are usually paid a fee in addition to traveling ex-
pense. They also have the opportunity to visit attractive places where

they receive a VIP welcome, and reign over the tiny area of their ring with the power of a monarch—more accurately, of a constitutional monarch, since they are bound to respect the AKC Show Rules and the official breed standard.

Conscientious judges work hard for these rewards. They may examine as many as 25 dogs an hour, and 175 dogs during a day. They must at the same time attempt to evade the scenes of disgruntled losers as well as the seductions of hopeful owners, and to pronounce sound judgments.

THE JUDGING PROCEDURE

This varies little. As each class is called, the dogs assemble in the ring (which is no more than a fenced in area, varying in size according to the size of the breed), where they circle in a counterclockwise direction while the judge stands in the center, getting his first overall impression. The dogs are then lined up along one side of the ring and the judge gives each one an individual examination. While the dog is posed standing still (small dogs and Toys are often placed on a table), he checks the teeth and bite, the structural conformation by going over the dog's body with his hands (including the scrotum, to make sure of the presence of both testicles); he feels the texture and condition of the coat, and tests the dog's responsiveness when alerted by a sound or gesture. He then studies the dog's gait when trotting in a straight line away from him and back again and over an L or T-shaped or triangular course. The dog is then sent to another side of the ring to wait until all of the others have been examined in the same way.

Now the judge has them all circle the ring again, perhaps varying the pace or changing the direction. Already he has probably mentally separated the contestants into possible winners and discards. If the class is large, the latter may be dismissed at this point. A dog possessing some disqualifying fault, who is lame, sickly, or vicious, is sent out of the ring at once.

The dogs are lined up again, the judge often indicating by a gesture that his tentative top choices take the first places at the left of the line-up. He then proceeds to make his final placements by elimination, shifting dogs around, studying and comparing them more closely, asking some to gait again, perhaps gaiting two close rivals at the same time for a sharper comparison, or posing them side by side. When he has selected his four top dogs, he dictates his decision to the ring steward, distributes the ribbons and prize money, and quickly clears the ring to make way for the next class.

Nobody can predict how long it will take a judge to come to a decision —least of all the judge. But any judge will tell you, in a confidential mood, that it is relatively easy to select the four best dogs from a group of good ones, much more difficult to pick the best of a mediocre lot. Although dog-show judges, like baseball umpires, inspire criticism, most of them know and love dogs. They are thrilled to discover a future Champion in a Puppy class, proud and satisfied if their choice of Best of Breed is so good that he ends up Best in Show. Some owners would be surprised, to say the least, to hear their breed judge boast that "his" dog went Best in Show.

If show judges are competent and honest, then *why doesn't an outstanding dog win First Prize every time he is shown?*

Some exceptional individuals have done so. But dogs, like people, can have an off day. A dog may be tired from a long trip to the show. He may be out of coat. He may just be in a bad mood. Furthermore, judging a dog is like judging a beautiful woman, in that there may be a basic standard but there is always room for personal taste. Perhaps the judge happens to prefer a slightly different type of appearance or personality. It might be added, in a whisper, that since many judges earn a large part of their income from dog shows, they naturally wish to fill their calendars with as many judging assignments as possible, including return engagements. They therefore, consciously or unconsciously, hope that their decisions will meet the approval of the sponsoring club and show authorities, and of the major exhibitors and handlers whose entries are vital to the success of a show. Although they are not allowed to see the show catalogue until their judging assignments have been completed, they naturally cannot fail to recognize professional handlers, consistent exhibitors, and dogs who have been widely campaigned and advertised. The popularity of a judge is measured not by ringside applause, but by the number of entries filed when it is announced that he is to officiate at a show. On the whole, this situation probably leads to better judging. Politics and self-interest are undoubtedly less widespread than critics claim. At least, it would be impossible under present show rules to repeat the results of that early British show at Newcastle-on-Tyne, where the Pointer class was won by a dog owned by the Setter judge, and the Setter class was won by a dog owned by the Pointer judge.

DO DOGS ENJOY SHOWING?

What do the dogs think of all this?

Some of them obviously enjoy it—especially those who have never known any other kind of life. Dogs tend to enjoy what is familiar to them, even if it involves being popped into a crate, trundled to a noisy exhibition hall, brushed, combed, plucked, and powdered for hours on end, then paraded before a crowd of strangers among other dogs whom they are not allowed to sniff or play with, much less seduce (bitches in heat being permitted in the show ring). In spite of the discomfort and boredom involved, even a pampered family pet may find the experience diverting the first few times, if only because he is the center of his owner's attention.

THE OWNER'S POINT OF VIEW

The atmosphere of intense competition that is present in major dog shows may discourage some owners, but it may provide a stimulating challenge to others. It is an undeniable achievement to win a big class in an important dog show, even to win a ribbon.

Unfortunately, dog showing has become an expensive hobby when you add up the cost of conditioning, grooming, perhaps handling, travel expenses (including hotel and restaurant bills), plus the cost of show entries (from $8 to $15 a class). For this reason alone, many small breeders and pet owners have abandoned showing, or are not tempted by it in the first place. Countless dogs, including potential Champions, have never put a paw inside a show ring because their owners appreciate their companionship above all and couldn't care less about a Championship title. To be perfectly realistic, however, even a small amateur breeder will find better homes for his puppies, better studs for his bitches, and better bitches for his stud dogs, if he can boast of owning a Champion. Breeders, whether they enjoy it or not, are practically obliged to show.

SHOULD YOU SHOW YOUR PET?

The answer depends on personal considerations, of course. But first of all, you should determine whether or not your dog is really of show quality. This is not the same as being eligible for show, which requires no more than registration by the AKC and freedom from disqualifying faults that are described in the breed standards. Most private breeders are perfectly honest when they sell a puppy as a show prospect. They have to be. Dog show catalogues list the breeder's name as well as the owner's, and it would not enhance the breeder's reputation to advertise inferior stock. However, nobody is infallible, and it is difficult to foresee how a puppy will develop. Ugly ducklings practically never turn into swans, but a plain individual can grow into a raving beauty, while a lovely youngster may be far less attractive as an adult. Moreover, a dog who is rather conceited or a tireless showoff makes a better show dog than a superior specimen who simply isn't an "actor." When a breeder produces an outstanding puppy, he generally keeps it in order to improve his breeding program. Sometimes he will sell it on condition that the new owner agree to show it, retaining certain breeding rights; or on a co-ownership basis, undertaking the management of his show career himself. On the other hand, if you have purchased a so-called "show puppy" from a pet shop or a mail-order firm, have no illusions. Well-bred puppies of superior quality practically never end up in these commercial outlets.

If you own a nice, well-bred dog at least 6 months old, and if you are intrigued by the idea of showing him, you should study his breed standard and compare him to it. If he does not comply with the limitations concerning size, weight, color, and markings, there is no point in going further—unless he is simply overweight, in which case you can put him on a diet, which would be good for him anyway. If his ear and tail carriage are not ideal, you will probably never make a Champion out of him. But if his flaws are minor and not too glaring, and if they are offset by other good points, he will not disgrace you and may even win some ribbons. Try to confirm your opinion by seeking the objective advice of experts. You can meet them by joining the specialty club of your dog's breed, your local kennel club, by attending shows as a spectator, and by entering your dog in Match shows under competent judges.

Actually, 8 or 9 months is quite young enough to submit a puppy to the upsetting routine of regular showing—10 or 12 months for a puppy of a large, heavy breed. Showing takes a lot out of a young dog. Some of them sleep an entire day after a benched show or a long car trip. Regular meals, rest, and exercise, which are indispensable at this stage, are impossible to provide during a dog show. So in order to ensure your puppy's proper development, it is advisable to limit these early show appearances to twice a month at the most.

If you have not done so already, you should write to the American Kennel Club to make sure that your dog's registration is in order; subscribe to *Purebred Dogs—The AKC Gazette*, which contains the dog show calendar; and request the AKC brochure *Dog Show Rules and Regulations*.

The next step is to spend a day at an important show. The experience of seeing with your own eyes top dogs, top grooming, top handling, and top judging can teach you more than any book. Arrive early, buy a catalogue, select a ringside seat where your breed is to be judged, and follow the proceedings attentively. You will have to pay attention, because the ring procedure at a big show is generally swift and silent (except for a stray yap and occasional applause). You may not always be sure which class is being judged, or which dogs are the winners. Do not hesitate to ask for explanations from the experienced fanciers around you. After the judging, visit the dogs on their benches if possible, to study them more closely. Visit the commercial stands too. You will probably find the appropriate show lead for your dog (a one-piece nylon or leather slip lead is best for most breeds), various show-grooming products, as well as books on grooming and handling from which you can pick up many practical tips.

When you return home, you may still think that your dog is the most beautiful in the world. On closer inspection, however, he may seem more or less unkempt and unsophisticated compared to the sleek show beauties you have seen. If you have decided to show him, you must start:

PREPARING YOUR DOG FOR THE SHOW RING

1) The longest but most vital project is CONDITIONING, which is no more than super health. No grooming technique can replace the glow of good health or completely camouflage poor condition. Conditioning is accomplished by a long range program of sensible diet, perhaps enriched by vitamins and minerals and linseed or wheat germ oil to promote a glossy coat; by regular exercise; regular care of teeth, nails, and ears; vigilance against internal and external parasites; and a well-balanced life that will bring out the best in your dog's character and personality.

You can buy various conditioning products that claim to give an instant shine to a coat or brightness to the eye. But these have a temporary, cosmetic effect at best and are no substitute for the "bloom" (to use the popular show-ring expression) that is the result of good health and good humor.

2) GET YOUR DOG USED TO NOISE AND CROWDS AND THE PRESENCE OF OTHER DOGS by taking him with you frequently into shops, on crowded streets, and in the park on Sunday afternoons, letting strangers pet him. Join a Handling or Obedience class if possible.

3) TAKE YOUR DOG FOR FREQUENT AUTOMOBILE RIDES if he is not already a calm and confident passenger. How can he shine at a show if he has been carsick en route?

4) TRAIN YOUR DOG TO STAND STILL IN A SHOW POSE while a friend runs his hands over him, as the judge will do during his examination in the show ring.

Posing a dog to his best advantage is one of the techniques in which professional handlers surpass most amateurs, mainly because they have given the matter far more thought and practice. The way you pose your dog can do much to enhance his good spirits and conceal his weaknesses. It can also ensure that your dog does not appear to possess a weakness where none exists.

As you will notice when you attend dog shows and study photographs of Champion dogs, each breed is posed in a particular stance, which you should learn to reproduce.

In all breeds, *the head* is held high and forward. Practice lifting your dog's head by pulling the show lead up behind his ears, but without choking the poor fellow or letting him hold his nose in the air, which would spoil his neckline. With some breeds, handlers point out desirable length of neck by bringing the dog's ears forward on the sides of the head while grasping the muzzle with both hands, pulling it forward and upward into the desirable position. If the dog has too much jowl (as many Spaniels do), they grasp the excess skin with the hand on the side opposite the judge, in order to produce a clean jawline; or they pull up the loose skin at the back of the neck behind the slip collar to create a clean throat line.

You must also accustom your dog to having his *mouth* examined while he is posed. In the show ring, you usually are expected to display his bite by pulling his upper lip up with one hand as you put the lower lip down with the other, both sides simultaneously, while keeping his jaws closed. It is easier than it sounds. Afterward, make sure that an upper lip is not caught on a tooth. Since some judges prefer to examine the mouth without assistance, you should also prepare your dog for this by asking a friend to play the role of the examining judge.

In almost all breeds, *the front legs* are placed directly beneath the shoulders, straight and parallel, with the toes pointing straight forward and the elbows well tucked into the sides. In breeds requiring a broad

A Springer Spaniel. (*William P. Gilbert*)

An Old English Sheepdog. (*William P. Gilbert*)

front, the elbows are set slightly out from the body. If a dog has splayed feet (a serious fault), professional handlers pinch them together while they are setting the legs.

If you try to position your dog's legs by shifting his paws, you will only throw him off balance. Instead, run your hand down the leg until you reach the elbow or hock and gently lift or slide it into position. The best way to pose a small dog is to lift the entire forehand, then the hindquarters, setting the legs in position as you let the dog down. In order to separate the hindlegs, place an appropriate number of fingers between them as you set the dog down.

In almost all breeds, *the hindlegs* are placed slightly wider apart than the front ones. "Angulation" is the point to watch, making sure that the hindlegs are posed in a straight line from the hock to the ground. As you set up the rear, you must be vigilant to see that the dog does not alter the position of his forehand. If he does, you will have to start all over again from the beginning. When the four legs have been set correctly, you should check:

The topline. A weak or sagging topline is bad in any breed, and one way to avoid it is to tickle or prod your dog under the abdomen to make him tuck up. Most breeds require a level or sloping topline, but Bedlington Terriers and many running Hounds are posed with more or less roached backs, which you can accentuate by tucking up the loins with one hand and by placing the forelegs closer to the hindlegs. If a dog of other breeds humps his back, you can make him flatten it by rubbing him gently along the spine.

The German Shepherd has a unique stance that has spread to other Sheepdog breeds. Because a pronounced sloping topline is specified in the standard, his left rear leg is extended far behind the body with the hock vertical, while the right rear leg is placed under the right hip with the hock sharply angled. This threepoint stance produces a topline that slopes more steeply as the hindlegs are more separated. Twelve or fifteen inches is generally the best distance.

Tail carriage varies from one breed to another and is simple to adjust. Even during the judge's examination it is permissible to hold your dog's head with one hand and his tail with the other ("top and tail" in showring parlance). Beagles, Foxhounds, and Terriers are posed with a vertically upright tail. Sporting breeds carry their tail horizontally, or with only a slight upward angle. The tail of Basenjis, Malamutes, and others should curl over one hip, while the curly plume of Pekingese and Pomeranians should fall over the back. Check your breed standard, study photographs, and try to reproduce the same effect in front of a mirror, viewing it from every angle.

Ear carriage varies too. A dog whose ears should be erect when alerted can be urged to put them up by some discreet gesture or sound, or if these fail, by tossing a toy or coin to the ground, or by holding out a sliver of liver. Some handlers simply hold a dog's ears in an erect position by pinching them gently at the base, or else tickle the base of the ears to make the dog bring them up himself.

During your practice sessions at home, always pose your dog from his right side, for this is the side from which you will usually have to set him up in the show ring. Since the dogs generally circle the ring in a counterclockwise direction, you thus avoid placing yourself between your dog and the judge. Most of the time you will use your right hand for setting the dog's head and holding it in position, and your left hand for "stacking up" the body, positioning the legs, and holding the tail.

You can steady a nervous puppy by firmly grasping his muzzle with one hand while you pose him with the other. Pulling the tail backward

Jane Forsyth poses a winning Irish Setter, Ch. Powderhorn Yankee Rifleman. (*William P. Gilbert*)

Damarra Bolte shows a Basenji, Absinthes Sazerac. (*William P. Gilbert*)

encourages a dog to brace his hindlegs, and pressing down on the shoulders firms the forehand. Pushing back the muzzle gently will also tighten and firm the hindquarters.

During a show, you will have to pose your dog for his individual examination and also when the judge examines the entire lineup or is moving about the ring. Experienced handlers continually reset their dogs so that the judge, whenever he glances at them from wherever he may be, will see only their most attractive aspect.

When you have found the pose that shows your dog to best advantage, train him to remain in that position. Select a command such as "HOLD IT" or "POSE," and a release command such as "OKAY." Follow your usual training methods, rewarding your dog for every effort and gradually prolonging the posing time. But do not overdo it to the point of fatigue or boredom. Oddly enough, many dogs actually seem to enjoy holding a pose, if they have been trained early enough.

5) TRAIN YOUR DOG TO GAIT PROPERLY on a loose lead, on both sides and in both directions, around a circle, along a straight line and a diagonal, over a T-shaped course, an L-shaped course and a triangular course. These patterns have become customary because they permit a view of the dog's gait from every angle.

Practice gaiting your dog indoors and out, over different surfaces. Enlist the help of a knowledgeable friend who can criticize your gaiting technique and then take over the lead so that you can judge your dog's movement for yourself. Some professional handlers are wizards in making bad movers look good. Watch them in action during dog shows, try to analyze and later copy their technique.

The lead is held tightly in your left hand, with the surplus neatly folded in your fist and your arm outstretched sufficiently so that you do not crowd your dog. Your main job is to keep his head up, never let him sniff the ground, keep him moving in a straight line with his body straight, and follow the judge's instructions. It is usually best to let your dog pick his own speed and to follow it, playing the leash in and out as necessary. The longer your strides (or lopes, in the case of large dogs), the livelier your dog's action will appear to be. Some handlers lighten the forehand by holding the leash shorter and higher than normal, in order to accentuate the driving action of the hindquarters. But as a general rule, if your dog has good natural movement, it is better simply to follow him on a loose lead. If he tends to deviate from the course, walk more

A Chow Chow. (*William P. Gilbert*)

briskly and stay slightly in front of him. If he breaks into an amble or a gallop, stop dead and start again. Breaking gait is not as serious a fault in the dog show ring as it is at the trotting track, but it may give a slight edge to a rival dog when the contest is very close, so avoid it if you can. The best way to do so is to practice gaiting your dog at home. You too may need practice in smoothly transferring the lead from one hand to another when making a half-turn so that you are never placed between your dog and the judge.

6) HAVE YOUR DOG GROOMED BY A PROFESSIONAL SHOW GROOMER. You may be able to learn to groom your dog yourself, but pay an expert to do it at least once so that you can observe the procedure and see what your dog should look like when he is groomed for show. Show grooming (see page 170) includes refinements that the average pet owner would never dream of, and professionals devote more time to grooming their show dogs than most amateurs would have the patience to do. At a recent Westminster show, the owner of a white Poodle admitted to spending 10 hours grooming her dog; a handler who brought 15 dogs to the show also brought 3 assistants who did nothing but groom all day long; and an Old English Sheepdog exhibitor said that it took 6 to 8 hours just to add the finishing show touches to his normally groomed dog. (Needless to add, when you visit a dog show as a spectator, you should never touch a groomed dog or disturb a single hair on his head!)

AKC rules forbid the use of any substance that alters a dog's appearance, such as hair dye. Cosmetic surgery of any kind is grounds for disqualification. On the other hand, it is permissible to whiten a coat by rubbing chalk into it if every trace of chalk is brushed out afterward. There are also numerous borderline practices which are not specifically forbidden but can give a false impression, such as sandpapering a rough coat to make it look and feel smooth; teasing, spraying, and using cornstarch on a long coat like that of the Old English Sheepdog to make it seem more voluminous than it is. Recent AKC regulations, however, place limits on such artificial measures. Be sure to check the Rule Book.

Some breed clubs discourage overgrooming, but with little success, even among their own memberships. At the moment, if you want to succeed in the show ring, you must present your dog in the same style as the competition. Moreover, once your dog is in top show condition, every precaution must be taken to preserve the results of all these efforts. No more hunting or rambles in the country for Setters or Spaniels. No more rabbit- or rat-chasing for Terriers. Even bright sunshine must be avoided by solid-colored dogs, especially black ones, because it can "rust" their coats.

A top Wire-haired Fox Terrier, Ch. Harwire Hetman of Whinletter. (*William P. Gilbert*)

FIRST PUBLIC APPEARANCE—AT A MATCH SHOW

In the meantime, you have been perusing the Dog Show Calendar, seeking a suitable occasion for your pet's debut.

By all means choose an *AKC sanctioned Match Show*. These events were created specially for the purpose of introducing novice dogs and owners to the show ring. Since most dog clubs hold several Match Shows a year, you should be able to find one in your locality. Entries need not be filed in advance, the fee is very modest (2 or 3 dollars), and the atmosphere is relatively relaxed and friendly. If you have a choice, select the Match Show with the most renowned judge. You may have a chance to seek his opinion about your dog's future in the show ring. His advice could be invaluable.

Your first Match Show should make it clear whether or not you and your dog have a chance of success in showing, and, far more important, whether or not you are going to like it.

   —If you have both enjoyed the experience, and if you have the time and means to pursue it, why not?

—If you have enjoyed it but your dog has loathed it, or if he is obviously not up to show standard, you can let him resume his happy life as a companion dog and look around for another dog whose temperament or quality is more compatible with showing.

—If your dog has taken it in his stride but you have found it unrewarding, he will not blame you for forgetting the whole thing. If he is exceptionally promising, you might consider turning him over to a professional handler, provided that you can stand the separation and the expense, and that a Championship title means that much to you. Your dog couldn't care less.

—If both of you dislike the entire business, write it off as experience. If you seek an outlet for your competitive spirit, perhaps Obedience Trials would be more in your line.

CHAMPIONSHIP POINT SHOWS

Let's suppose that your match show was a success and that you have caught the dog-show fever. What next?

Preferably another Match show or two, in order to perfect your showing technique and your dog's.

If all goes well, the moment has come to select a Licensed Championship Point Show in which to enter your dog. When you have found one with a convenient date and site, write to the Show Superintendent for a Premium List and entry form. From then on, you will be placed on the mailing list and will receive the Premium Lists of all the dog shows in your area.

Premium Lists are issued 5 or 6 weeks before the date of the show. There is a strict deadline for filing entries: generally 3 weeks before the show. Sometimes the entry list is closed as soon as a certain number of entries has been received, so it is wise to file yours promptly. You simply return the filled-in entry form along with a check or money order to cover the cost of entry fees. If it is a distant show, do not delay reserving a room for yourself and your dog in one of the recommended hotels or motels. Study the Premium List carefully in order to select the class or classes for which your dog is eligible. Fill in the form with care. Oddly enough, the only error that will not disqualify your dog is entering him under the wrong sex.

CLASSES. All AKC licensed shows offer the following regular classes, which are also judged in this order—first the dogs, and then the bitches:

Puppy Class: For puppies at least 6 months and less than 1 year old,

OFFICIAL AMERICAN KENNEL CLUB ENTRY FORM

1	2	3	4	5	6	7	8	9	10	11	12	13	14	15	16	17	18	19	20	21
			REG. NO.						BREED		SEX	CLASS		DIV	CLASS		DIV	CLASS		DIV

FOR OFFICE USE ONLY

53rd ALL-BREED DOG SHOW AND OBEDIENCE TRIAL
SPRINGFIELD KENNEL CLUB
BETTER LIVING CENTER BUILDING, EASTERN STATES EXPOSITION GROUNDS
WEST SPRINGFIELD, MASSACHUSETTS
SATURDAY, MAY 13, 1978

ENTRY FEE $8.50 for the first entry of a dog and $8.50 for each additional entry of the same dog except PUPPY and BRED BY EXHIBITOR CLASSES in which the entry fee is $6.50. Junior Showmanship fee $3.00. All fees include 25 cents recording fee.

ENTRIES CLOSE at the Secretary's office, Thomas W. Baldwin, P.O. Box 2462, Springfield, MA 01101, 12: NOON, WEDNESDAY, APRIL 26, 1978 after which time entries positively will not be accepted, cancelled or substituted.

ENTRY FORM must be signed on the bottom line by the owner or duly authorized agent.

MAKE CHECKS and Money Orders payable to the Springfield Kennel Club.

MAIL ENTRIES with FEES to Thomas W. Baldwin, Show Secretary, P.O. Box 2462, Springfield, MA 01101. Phone (413) 583-3128.

— PLEASE TYPEWRITE OR PRINT CLEARLY —

I ENCLOSE $ **8.50** for entry fees.
- **IMPORTANT**—Read Carefully Instructions on Reverse Side Before Filling Out

Breed	Variety See Instruction #1, reverse side (if any)	Sex
RHODESIAN RIDGEBACK		M

DOG SHOW Class	See Instruction #2, reverse side (Give age, color or weight if class divided)	Obedience Trial Class
BRED BY EXHIBITOR		

If dog is entered for Best of Breed (Variety) Competition—see Instruction #3 reverse side —CHECK THIS BOX ☐   Additional Classes

If entry of dog is to be made in Jr. Showmanship as well as in one of the above competitions, check this box, and fill the data on reverse side. ☐

If for Jr. Showmanship only then check THIS box, and fill in date on reverse side. ☐

Name of Actual Owner(s)	See Instruction #4, reverse side
	ELLIN K. & RICHARD E. ROBERTS

Name of Handler (if any) [handler] •

Full Name of Dog   INDODAKAZI'S BONGOZA •

Insert one of the following:	Date of Birth	Place of Birth
AKC Reg. # HC403622	6/5/77	☑ U.S.A. ☐ Canada ☐ Foreign Do not print the above in catalog
AKC Litter #		Breeder
I.L.P. #		
Foreign Reg. # & Country		OWNER

Sire CH. KWETU KOYA'S JACOB

Dam CH. JABULISA'S INDODAKAZI

Owner's Name ELLIN K. & RICHARD E. ROBERTS
(Please print)

Owner's Address BOX 391A RD 1

City WOODSTOCK State N Y Zip Code 12498

I CERTIFY that I am the actual owner of this dog, or that I am the duly authorized agent of the actual owner whose name I have entered above. In consideration of the acceptance of this entry, I (we) agree to abide by the rules and regulations of The American Kennel Club in effect at the time of this show or obedience trial, and by any additional rules and regulations appearing in the premium list for this show or obedience trial or both, and further agree to be bound by the "Agreement" printed on the reverse side of this entry form. I (we) certify and represent that the dog entered is not a hazard to persons or other dogs. This entry is submitted for acceptance on the foregoing representation and agreement.

SIGNATURE of owner or his agent • duly authorized to make this entry   _Ellin K Roberts_

PHONE NO. 914-679-6893

sometimes divided into puppies 6 to 9 months, and 9 to 12 months, all of them whelped in the United States or Canada.

Novice Class: For dogs over 6 months old, whelped in the United States or Canada, which have not already won 3 First Prizes in a Novice Class or a First Prize in an Open Class, or any Championship points.

Bred-by Exhibitor Class: For dogs, excluding Champions, 6 months of age or over, whelped in the United States or Canada, owned and shown by the breeder or by a member of his immediate family.

American-bred Class: For dogs, excluding Champions, 6 months of age or over, whelped in the United States as a result of a mating in the United States.

Open Class: For dogs 6 months or over. This is where the keenest competition is often found, including dogs that have already won Championship points. It is the only regular class in which foreign-bred dogs are accepted.

These five regular classes may be subdivided in order to separate different Varieties of the same breed, such as Longhaired, Smooth and

A Siberian Husky. (*William P. Gilbert*)

A Basset Hound. (*William P. Gilbert*)

Wirehaired Dachshunds; Black, ASCOB (any Solid Color Other than Black as well as Black and Tan), and Particolored Cocker Spaniels; Yellow, Black, and Chocolate Labradors; Smooth and Long-coated Chihuahuas. Beagles are divided according to height. Some breeds, including Boston Terriers and Pekingese, may be divided according to weight.

Many shows, including all Specialty shows, offer additional "*nonregular*" classes, such as Locally-bred or Locally-owned, Champions Only, Brace (2 matched dogs of either sex), Group (4 matched dogs of either sex), Stud Dogs (a sire accompanied by 2 or more of his offspring), Brood Bitch (a bitch with 2 or more of her progeny, not necessarily by the same sire), Veteran (over 7 years old), and a range of extremely popular Junior Showmanship Classes for boys and girls over 10 and under 17 years of age, in which the handler, not the dog, is judged. The ribbons awarded in these classes, as well as in the Miscellaneous Class (where dogs of certain unregistered but partially recognized purebred breeds are judged together), are different from the regular class ribbons: Rose for first, Brown for second, Light Green for third, and Gray for fourth.

Most Specialty shows also include two competitions which provide a chance to recover the cost of show entries and perhaps to make a profit: the Futurity Stakes and Sweepstake. The Futurity is invariably restricted to members of the sponsoring club, who must nominate their Puppies (6 to 12 months old) and Junior dogs (12 to 18 months old) prior to birth. The puppy must also be entered in one of the regular show classes in order to be eligible for the Futurity. The breeder as well as the owner of the winners is awarded a percentage of the entry fees as prize money. The Sweepstake classes, like the Futurity, are judged before the regular classes and are open to dogs and puppies entered in a regular class. They are divided into several age groups, and the money prizes are on a percentage basis too.

An American-bred dog at least 6 months old who is not a Champion is thus eligible for all of the five regular classes. As a rule, however, a dog is seldom entered in more than one of them, because if the dog wins one class but loses another, he is ineligible for the all-important Winners' competition, since he is not undefeated. However, this does not necessarily mean that he will make only a single appearance in the ring. If he wins his class, he is eligible for further competition. Even if he is second, he may be called back into the ring, as we shall see.

A MONTH BEFORE THE SHOW

You should start seriously conditioning your dog by paying special attention to his diet, grooming, and general health. Make sure that he is free from internal and external parasites, and have him wormed if necessary. You will see an improvement in his coat at once.

Several times a week, practice gaiting and standing for examination. Working and Hunting breeds need lots of road work. Brisk walks on hard surfaces improve the feet, while uphill work develops the hindquarters. Slow, steady trotting is the best pace for large breeds, as it is for show horses. If this is too fast for you to follow, you can ride a bicycle. One mile out and one mile back are ample for most breeds, and far too much for small ones. Avoid violent exercise that could cause sprains or injuries, even rambles in the woods that could spoil the coat of long-haired breeds. Your dog should be left uncollared as much as possible, in order to avoid breaking the hair of long coats or leaving a mark on short ones.

Check your dog's vaccination certificates to make sure they will be valid on the date of the show, and give him a booster shot if necessary.

The exercise area of dog shows is a hotbed of bacteria, and you cannot be too careful. Many exhibitors try to avoid contaminating their kennels by keeping their show dogs separated from their kennelmates several days after a show, and by washing their feet with antiseptic before bringing them home.

It is not too early to make an appointment with a first-class professional show groomer, if you have not become sufficiently expert yourself. Tell him the date of the show. He should know whether it is best to groom your dog a day or two beforehand or sometime earlier.

A WEEK BEFORE THE SHOW

Take your dog to the vet to have his nails clipped (if you have not learned to do it yourself), to clean his teeth, and to empty his anal glands. You can make his daily grooming more thorough than usual, and

Peter Green and the famous Sealyham Terrier, Ch. Dersade Bobby's Girl. (*William P. Gilbert*)

even bathe him if he needs it. Wirehaired and roughcoated breeds should not be bathed less than one week before the show because of the softening effect on their coats.

This is the moment when you will probably receive an envelope from the show superintendent, including a receipt for your entry fees, your gate pass, an identification card bearing the entry number of your dog (which is also his bench number if it is a benched show), and a judging program listing the number of dogs entered in each breed (so that you can calculate the number of Championship points to be awarded), and a time schedule.

THE DAY BEFORE THE SHOW

This will be largely devoted to your dog, especially if he is of a breed that requires extensive last-minute grooming.

Feed him a nourishing but not necessarily copious meal, because he will not get much to eat the following day. Put him to bed early, for he needs all the rest that he can get.

When he is comfortably tucked away, you can pack his show kit with:

—a show lead—plus an extra one, just in case

—a water bowl and feed bowl

—a thermos bottle of fresh water

—a thermos container for dog food, including cooked liver (Most dog shows provide free dog food and disposable bowls, but it is usually better to feed your dog in the manner to which he is accustomed.)

—grooming equipment

—a box of disposable tissues or a roll of paper towels

—a towel (many towels if it is an outdoor show and there is a risk of rain or excessive heat)

—a toy

—a simple first-aid kit

—a pen for marking your catalogue

—your identification card and gate pass

—if it is a benched show: a blanket for the floor of the bench stall; a bench chain about 30 inches long with a swivel at each end; a leather collar for attaching the bench chain

—a folding chair (even when provided by the show, there are never enough chairs to go around)

—a picnic lunch, or at least a supply of snacks and beverages (Dog show catering is far from gastronomic.)

Having prepared your dog's equipment, it is time to think of yourself. You will be appearing in the ring too, and you do not want to detract from your dog's appearance.

Men make a better impression if they wear a jacket and necktie, unless the weather is torried. The judges do, and it is only courteous to do the same. But never wear a hat in the show ring. Although flashy colors and patterns seem to be the current vogue, conservative sports clothes are still the best choice.

Women should also dress relatively conservatively, avoiding extreme styles, jangly jewelry, and floppy ornaments that would distract attention from their dog. Color is important. Select a dark shade if your dog's coat is pale, and a light one if his coat is dark. Solid colors are better than prints, unless the dog is solid-colored and of a contrasting shade. Grass-green and sky-blue show up most canine colors to advantage. Never wear a dress of the same color as your dog unless it is definitely lighter or darker in tone. Avoid materials that are easily rumpled or soiled, skirts that are very full or, on the contrary, very tight. Pantsuits and culottes are practical, since they ensure both decency and freedom of movement when gaiting. Whatever the garment, choose one with pockets large enough to hold the various articles you need to take into the show ring with you. Above all, wear comfortable, nonskid shoes.

When you set the alarm clock before you go to bed, leave plenty of time for getting to the show, including leeway for traffic jams and unforeseeable delays. If you arrive later than the time limit for a benched show, your dog will not be admitted. At an unbenched show, you only need to be present when your dog is due in the ring, but experienced exhibitors arrange to arrive at least 2 hours earlier (knowing that they will waste at least half an hour in the portable restroom waiting line).

ON THE DAY OF THE SHOW

Everything should go smoothly, thanks to your preparations the night before, no matter how excited and nervous you are.

Professional handlers usually fast their dogs for 36 hours before a show, but many owners feed a light meal in the morning if the dog is scheduled to be judged in the afternoon, and otherwise feed him nothing on the day of the show until he has been judged. When in doubt, do not feed. But make sure that your dog has emptied his bladder and bowels before leaving the show. (A professional handler's trick to make a

A Long-haired Dachshund. (*William P. Gilbert*)

dig evacuate quickly is to lick the tip of a paper match and insert it half-way in the rectum. The effort to expel the match will empty the bowels.)

WHEN YOU ARRIVE AT THE SHOW GROUNDS, look for the Exhibitors' Entrance. If the show has been announced as an "examined show" (which is increasingly rare), there will be a veterinarian in attendance to check each dog and stamp his card before permitting him to go further.

Then check in at the Show Secretary's office and buy a catalogue, which includes the names of the entries in each class (and for the first time tells you the competition your dog will face) and the numbers of the rings assigned to the different breeds.

Look for your bench (if it is a benched show), locate the ring in which your dog will be judged, and figure out the shortest route between these vital points. Find out where the exercise area is situated and at what times you can take your dog there to relieve himself. Do not fail to do this half an hour before he is to be judged. It is unforgivable to soil the show ring (and grounds for disqualification in Obedience Trials).

Then settle your dog on his bench, making sure that the bench chain is neither too short for comfort nor too long for safety. You may place his wire crate on the bench and keep him in it. This is certainly the best arrangement. At an unbenched show, you merely need to locate the ring and then stake out a spot nearby (seeking a shady place at an outdoor show) where you can wait until your dog is due to be judged. In both cases, never leave your dog alone if you can help it, and never let him play with another dog. Try to persuade a friend or a member of the family to accompany you so that you can spell each other off in keeping an eye on your dog and your belongings.

DURING THE SHOW, the time schedule is seldom adhered to exactly, because it is impossible to predict how long it will take to judge each class. Exhibitors must therefore be alert in order to be at the entrance to the ring a few minutes before their class is called. It is among the duties of the Ring Stewards to give out the numbered armbands and to herd the handlers into the ring for the correct class. But they obviously cannot leave their posts to hunt for absent exhibitors. At your first show, when you are apt to be a bit confused, it is a good idea to spot one of the dogs who is entered in the same class as yours and follow his example.

A Collie (Rough). (*William P. Gilbert*)

Although you will see tables set up, clippers at work, fur flying, and clouds of powder in the grooming area, it is not advisable to attempt a complete grooming at the show, but only last-minute touch-ups, such as spot-cleaning travel stains, brushing and combing, cleaning eyes and nose, and trimming the stray hairs that have mysteriously sprouted since your grooming session only the day before.

If possible, try to watch your judge in action during an earlier class. Most judges adhere to a personal routine in examining a group of dogs, and you will be better prepared to follow his directions in the ring if you already know what to expect.

JUST BEFORE ENTERING THE RING, fluff up your dog's coat or smooth it down, carry him in your arms if he is small, or keep him close to you on a tight lead, all the while trying to put him in an enthusiastic mood. Get your armband from the ring steward and attach it securely to your upper left arm. Then make your ring entrance as calmly, confi-

A Komondor. (William P. Gilbert)

dently, and cheerfully as possible. From now on, keep one eye on your dog and the other on the judge. Start showing at once.

Experienced handlers try to be first or last to enter the ring, especially in a large class. While there may be an advantage to these positions, you are far more likely to find yourself placed somewhere in the middle. Do not worry about it. Instead, concentrate on trying to give the judge a good view of your dog by keeping him not too close to you and uncrowded by the dogs and handlers who precede and follow him.

IN THE SHOW RING, handling technique depends on the merit and temperament of the dog who is being shown.

Some dogs are natural showers: animated, gay, extrovert, and probably a bit conceited. They only need to be guided to follow the judge's instructions. They even pose themselves better than you could do it. If you own such a dog, intervene as little as possible. Merely make sure that he is never hidden from view, thrown off stride, or provoked into a change

A Shetland Sheepdog. (*William P. Gilbert*)

of mood by an envious rival. On the other hand, if your dog is a shrinking violet, you will have to make a real effort to show him to advantage.

The basic rule is never to get between your dog and the judge. When gaiting, keep him always on the inside of the ring. When standing for examination, move to the dog's rear when the judge is examining his forehand, move to the head when he is examining the hindquarters, and stand well back from your dog if you can trust him to remain still. You can prevent him from sitting or lying down while the judge is examining or observing him (which may be at any moment after all of the individual examinations have been completed) by leading him forward a few steps whenever he starts to sit, or, if necessary, by placing your hand between his legs and hoisting up his hindquarters.

You do not have to keep your dog posed throughout the entire class, of course. You will set him up for his individual examination, and again when the judge is moving down the line-up and is about two dogs away. If he then backs up or moves around for an overall view, experienced handlers may slightly shift their dog's pose in order to keep his best angle in the judge's line of vision. They may also subtly try to draw attention to a feature in which their dog excels by smoothing a perfect topline or stroking a lovely head. When the judge is comparing two close competitors, the professionals are quick to be the first to set up their dog or to position him for gaiting, selecting the side on which the dog looks and gaits the best, leaving the rival handler no choice.

Because many breeds must show their ears erect as well as relaxed, and because all dogs look more attractive when they are alert, "baiting" has become an accepted show ring practice. This is simply alerting a dog by tempting him with a tidbit (generally a piece of cooked liver), a toy (but squeaky toys are considered unprofessional and unsporting), a cluck, or whatever will make him put his ears up. Baiting by a person outside of the ring is strictly forbidden, since it amounts to "double handling," which is illegal (although visibly practiced around certain breed rings). It is important to hold the bait low enough and far enough away so that the dog's head remains in a normal position, not tilted back unattractively with his nose in the air. Many dogs can be kept alert and interested in the show ring simply by talking quietly to them.

Showmanship is made up of countless such details. But it is also practiced long before the dog enters the show ring, by grooming artifices as we have seen, but also by campaign strategy. For example, if a dog is an excellent mover, he will be shown in outdoor shows where the ring is large enough to display his excellent action. If, on the contrary, gaiting is his weak point, he will be entered only in indoor shows where his better-

Ch. Cede Higgens, a Yorkshire Terrier, goes Best in Show in the Westminster Kennel Club show at Madison Square Garden, 1978. (*William P. Gilbert*)

moving rivals will be handicapped by the restricted ring area and the judge may not notice his deficiency. Or if a dog's strong point is his sound general conformation, he will be shown under all-breed or multiple-breed judges. If he possesses to perfection some typical breed characteristic such as coat color or texture, but is weak in some other point, he will be shown only under judges who are specialists in his breed and are more apt to appreciate the details in which he excels.

It even seems to pay to advertise successful show dogs, preferably with a magnificent photograph in a leading dog magazine, accompanied by an enumeration of the dog's previous show triumphs. Perhaps it is true that judges are influenced by such publicity, recognize an entry in the ring as having appeared on a recent dog magazine cover, and hesitate to "put down" a dog who has been highly esteemed by eminent colleagues. They may also be influenced by the fact that a knowledgeable owner thinks enough of his dog to invest a considerable sum of money in his Championship campaign. Needless to add, you would only cover yourself with ridicule by publicizing a mediocre animal. But well-planned, dignified advertising of a superior dog's virtues and achievements may give him just that extra advantage needed to win against keen competition. At least, this is one of the current show-ring practices, and there must be a reason for it.

AT THE CONCLUSION OF EACH CLASS the prizes are distributed: a Blue ribbon for first place, a Red ribbon for second, a Yellow ribbon for third, and a White one for fourth. There may be other prizes too: silver trophies, books, money—anything, in fact, except liquor. If you are awarded a White ribbon when you were expecting a Blue, accompanied by some hideous ceramic object, you should still conform to show ring etiquette and thank the judge.

If your dog wins a Blue ribbon in a regular class, or even a Red, do not dash off to celebrate. His win makes him eligible to compete in the Winner's Class, perhaps beyond. So stay close to the ring. The second-place dog or bitch will be eligible to compete for the title of Reserve Winner if the entry that beat him (or her) is selected Winner's Dog (or Bitch).

AFTER THE FIVE REGULAR CLASSES HAVE BEEN JUDGED, the show is by no means over. Up to this point, the judges have measured the competing dogs against the breed standard and against each other. From now on, the competition becomes an elimination contest.

First, the unbeaten First place dogs of each breed return to their respective rings for the Winner's Class, and one of them is selected as "Winner's Dog," earning a Purple ribbon and, far more important, championship points. A dog who has been beaten only by the Winner's Dog can now join the other Blue ribbon winners to compete for the title of "Reserve Winner" and a Purple and White ribbon. The identical procedure is followed for females after the judging of the bitch classes.

The Winner's Dog and Winner's Bitch are now eligible to compete against the male and female Champions entered in the "Best of Breed," or "Specials Only" Class for the title "Best of Breed," which is rewarded by a Purple and Gold rosette and trophy, and for the "Best of Winners" title, which yields a Blue and White Ribbon. The dog or bitch who wins "Best of Winners" receives the maximum number of Championship points available to the breed at this particular show. There is then another, rather curiously named award: "Best of Opposite Sex" (the sex opposite to that of the Best of Breed winner). If the Best of Breed winner is a male, all of the females in the Best of Breed class, joined by the Winner's Bitch, compete for this award with its Red and White ribbon.

Considerable elimination has already taken place, but there is more to come. From the Best of Breeds in each of the six Groups, an individual is selected as "Best of Group" (Blue rosette and trophy): second, third, and fourth placings are also awarded. This decision is often made by a new judge.

The dog show has now reached its climax. Six finalists, the winners of the Groups, parade before a special judge to decide which is "Best in Show." Winning this award (Red, White and Blue rosette and trophy) is the greatest honor for a show dog.

Here is a graphic illustration of how a dog show proceeds by elimination from the hundreds of entries in the five regular classes to an individual dog or bitch who is crowned Best in Show.

This, in brief, is the scenario and countdown of a dog show. As you see, there has been no ceremony for awarding:

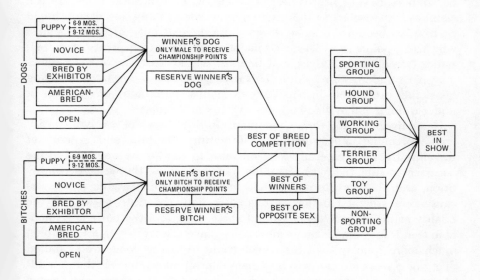

CHAMPIONSHIPS

The dream of most exhibitors is to make their dog a Champion, to place the magic letters "Ch." before his name, to inscribe it in red ink on his pedigree, and hang his framed AKC Championship Certificate in a conspicuous spot. Yet, as we have seen, a dog may win every class in which he is entered, go Best of Breed and even Best in Show, and still not be a Champion.

In order to earn a Championship title, a dog must win 15 Championship points in dog shows. These points can be won only by being selected Winner's Dog or Bitch in an AKC licensed point show. The number of points awarded at a particular show is determined by a scale drawn up by the American Kennel Club, taking into account the number of breed registrations in different parts of the country, and the number of competing dogs in the qualifying show class. The minimum is 1 point; the maximum, 5. Specialty shows are always worth 5 points to the Winner's Dogs and Bitches. If you own one of the popular show breeds, such as a German Shepherd or an Irish Setter, you will have to meet and beat 60 or more rivals in order to earn the maximum 5 points, while a Puli or a Smooth Collie may win the same number of points for beating only 6 or 7 competing dogs. An exception is made for a dog who wins the Best of Winners, Best of Breed, Best of Group, or Best in Show titles. He can claim as many points as the maximum awarded to any dog of any breed that he has beaten. To make things more difficult but fairer, a dog must win his 15 points in at least two major shows (worth 3 points or more), under two different judges, and he must win at least one of the remaining points under a third judge. This ruling prevents a dog from amassing his points exclusively in small shows against minimum competition, or under a single judge who happens to think he is great.

Campaigning a dog for a Championship title therefore involves considerable planning and strategy, not forgetting the time and expense of traveling from one carefully selected show to another in order to find the necessary points, the most favorably inclined judges, the weakest competition, and above all to avoid confrontation with unbeatable rivals. Because professional handlers are familiar with the taste of judges, the quality of the current generation of show dogs, and the current fashionable trends in a breed, they can usually make a worthy dog a Champion much more quickly than his owner could. A really good, well-handled dog 3 or 4 years old can win his Championship more quickly than an adolescent, although most owners who have caught the show bug are too impatient to wait. The more popular the breed, and the more numerous the entries, the harder and longer it takes to make a Champion. The greatest-winning bitch of all time is a Sealyham Terrier, Ch. Dersade Bobby's Girl, whose breed ranks 110th with only 98 registered dogs. On the other hand, a leading professional handler estimates that it takes an investment of at least $2,500 and 15 show ring appearances to "finish" a good German Shepherd, which is one of the leading breeds, and even more time and money to make a Champion of an average one.

Many ambitious owners who can afford it turn their dogs over to professional handlers, especially for campaigning after the Championship title has been won. The goal then is to build up a collection of Best of Breed, Best of Group, and Best in Show wins. Show Dog of the Year awards are offered annually by the leading dog-food companies to the show dogs who have won the most of these titles throughout the year. And there are "Top Ten" ratings in the breeds as well. Since the top-scoring dogs usually have won 40 or more titles during the previous 12 months, this obviously involves a fulltime show schedule. A male dog may have a better chance than a female, for although more bitches than dogs compete at shows, males win more Best of Breed and higher honors.

A Canadian Championship is easier to win, due to lesser competition and less stringent qualifications: 10 points won under 3 different judges, but without the major point show requirement as in the United States.

Incidentally, there is no officially recognized title of "International Champion" in America. A dog so described is undoubtedly imported from abroad, where this distinction is awarded to dogs who have won a qualifying certificate (a "CACIB") in 3 official International Dog Shows in 3 different countries, under the rules of the FCI (Fédération Cynologique Internationale), an international organization that governs dog shows in most of Europe and South America.

THE PROFESSION OF DOG SHOW HANDLING

is less exclusive than it was before 1978, when only about 2,000 qualified handlers were licensed by the American Kennel Club. Since the AKC abandoned this responsibility, anybody who is paid for showing a dog is considered a professional handler. Many of the more experienced are members of the Professional Handlers' Association or the Professional Handlers' Guild. Some of them specialize in a single breed or group; many are all-rounders; and the best of them, such as Bob and Jane Forsyth, Peter Green, Ric Chashoudian, and William Trainer, are in great demand. They usually take prospective Champions as boarders throughout the show campaign, starting at least a month ahead of time in order to provide conditioning, grooming, and show training.

Handler's fees vary from about $25 to $50 per show, plus a bonus for an important win, to which is added the cost of boarding, transportation, and entry fees. The handler keeps any prize money won, but the owner gets the ribbons and trophies. He also gets the thrill of owning a Champion, since the top handlers seldom accept a dog they do not consider capable of earning a title. In fact, the top handlers may be better judges than the licensed ones, if only because they see what goes on outside the show ring as well as inside it.

Nevertheless, many of the 9,000 or 10,000 dogs who win a Championship title every year are handled by their owners. If you own a really good dog, and if you possess moderate skill in handling him, it would be regrettable to deprive yourself of the experience. The dog show world is a universe apart, entirely revolving around dogs, where you can meet people from all walks of life who share a common interest, where you can learn much, make many friends, and achieve a feeling of accomplishment when you win, without the risk of developing an inferiority complex when you lose—because it is your dog who is being judged, not you. Dog showing can be a sport for the entire family, most fun of all when each member of the family has a dog to handle. Junior Handling classes are increasingly important in many shows (for information write to Junior Handlers Division, 1763 West Thirteenth Street, Brooklyn, New York 11223). So by all means show your dog and handle him yourself if what you seek is a pleasant activity rather than an unbroken string of victories. After all, riders do not consider horse shows a waste of time, even though most of them are often out of the ribbons and haven't a ghost of a chance of winning an Olympic medal.

The constant increase in the number of dog shows and the number of entries must prove that they fill some basic need and give satisfaction to a great many dog owners. But what about the original objective: to improve the quality of purebred dogs?

A Junior Handling Class. (*William P. Gilbert*)

Judging the finalists for Best in Show. (*William P. Gilbert*)

One of the principal criticisms of contemporary dog shows is that they tend to have the opposite effect by overemphasizing superficial appearance and showmanship to the detriment of soundness, thus permitting the propagation of weaknesses which eventually lead to the deterioration of a breed.

It must be admitted that there is a grain of truth in these accusations. In some Sporting breeds, the show type has become so unfunctional as to be incapable of doing the work for which it was originally bred, while the field type is too often remarkably unbeautiful. Nevertheless, the number of Dual Champions (field and show) proves that beauty and brains are not incompatible, although the combination is certainly rare. It is also infinitely more difficult to breed in a consistent way.

One day there may be a reaction to the present double standard. We will then have fewer Champions every year, but more worthy ones. We will certainly see less popeyed, woolly-coated Cocker Spaniels; unsound, unreliable German Shepherds; hysterical Toy Poodles; and idiotic examples of breeds it would be too unkind to mention by name.

In the meantime, there is consolation in the fact that many breeds, especially the less fashionable ones, have remained perfectly sound and normal, and have even shown continual improvement, partly due to the standardization required by showing.

As a final argument in favor of dog shows, even the most violent critic must admit that some wonderful breeds, endowed with unique qualities and glorious pasts, would have become extinct if dog shows did not provide an incentive for their preservation. All things considered, dog shows have certainly done more good than harm.

23.
Obedience Trials

Obedience Trials may be the best things invented for dogs since kibbled biscuits. Like many sporting events involving animals, they originated in England, where the largest crowd at a dog show is often gathered around the Obedience ring. Since the first official American Obedience Trial was held at the North Westchester Kennel Club Show in 1934, it has become the fastest-growing form of canine competition in the United States.

The purpose of Obedience Trials is to demonstrate the usefulness of the purebred dog as a companion of man, not merely the dog's ability to follow specified routine in the Obedience ring. And it is true that the basic elements of many Obedience exercises, particularly the Novice ones, are also very practical in the daily life of a companion dog.

All sorts of owners (and members of their immediate family) and all sorts of dogs are eligible, as long as the dog is of a recognized or qualified breed (for an AKC Trial), and is not totally blind, deaf, lame, vicious, or in heat. A dog may compete in an Obedience Trial no matter what he looks like, even if he possesses some defect of color or conformation that would disqualify him from the show ring. Spayed bitches, cryptorchid, monorchid, or castrated dogs are all eligible, although bitches cannot compete during their heat periods. If you own a purebred dog who has no papers, you may qualify for a special type of registration that will enable your dog to compete in AKC Obedience Trials and to earn Obedience titles (but not breed competitions). This is called ILP (Indefinite Listing Privilege). The AKC will send you detailed information on request.

Obedience Trials are an increasingly frequent feature of All-breed dog shows and of many Specialty shows, particularly Specialties for breeds that take well to training, like The Golden Retriever, Shetland Sheepdog, and German Shepherd—in fact, most Working and many Hunting breeds. Obedience Trials may also be run as a separate event. They are governed by the American Kennel Club, with many of the same regulations and formalities that apply to dog shows, such as approved judges, ribbon awards, precise rules for filing entries, judging, and scoring, and Sanctioned Trials for practice as well as regular licensed ones where points toward a title can be earned. The Obedience ring itself, however, is quite unlike a show ring. In fact, is isn't a ring at all, but a rectangular roped-off space 35 feet wide and 50 feet long at an indoor Trial, and 40 by 50 feet out of doors.

TITLES AND CLASSES

In Obedience Trials, proper performance of the prescribed exercises is all that matters. Even the competition is a secondary factor. A dog can earn an Obedience title without ever having won a Blue ribbon.

There are FIVE OBEDIENCE TITLES:

C.D. (Companion Dog), awarded in the Novice Class
C.D.X. (Companion Dog Excellent), awarded in the Open Class
U.D. (Utility Dog), awarded in the Utility Class
T.D. (Tracking Dog), awarded in a Tracking Test
U.D.T. (Utility Dog Tracker), the supreme achievement.

The AKC has recently created a sixth title: OTCH (Obedience Trail Champion), which can be earned by dogs who have already won their

UD. Points are awarded to the First and Second-placed UD dogs, according to the number of dogs defeated in the class. When a dog has amassed 100 points, he is awarded the Obedience Trial Championship Certificate. In addition, there are various nonofficial titles, generally offered by dog food companies, such as "Super Dog of the Year," which is awarded at the United States Obedience Classic held in St. Louis, Missouri.

The first three titles must be earned in progression. In other words, a dog must have won his C.D. before competing for his C.D.X., and his C.D.X. before being eligible to try for his U.D. In order to earn the U.D.T., he must have won all three other titles and also passed the Tracking Test.

Most Obedience Trials offer FIVE REGULAR CLASSES, all of them open to eligible dogs of both sexes, of any registered breed, and of any age 6 months or over:

Novice A (for amateur owner-handlers and dogs that have not yet won their C.D. title)

Novice B (for professional handlers or amateurs who have previously shown a dog to an Obedience degree and dogs that have not won a C.D. title)

Open A (for amateur owner-handlers and dogs that have won a C.D. but not a C.D.X. title)

Open B (for amateur or professional handlers and dogs that have won a C.D. or a C.D.X. title, even a U.D. This is the class in which the best performances are generally seen.)

Utility (for amateur or professional handlers and dogs that have won a C.D.X. or a U.D. title)

An Obedience Trial may also offer NONREGULAR CLASSES, such as:

Graduate Novice (for dogs that have won their C.D. but have not received any qualifying score toward a C.D.X.)

Brace Class (for a pair of dogs, unattached or coupled, not necessarily owned by the same person, but with a single handler. The Novice test is performed.)

Team Class (for 4 dogs and 4 handlers, scored by two judges in a performance of the Novice test plus a Drop on Recall)

Veterans Class (for dogs 8 years old or over who have already earned an Obedience title, performing the Novice class test)

Versatility Class (for dogs capable of performing the Utility exercises. The test compromises the first 2 exercises from the Novice, Open, and Utility classes.)

PERFORMANCE

The exercises performed in every class are described in detail in the AKC Obedience Regulations, which the AKC will send you on request. Most of them are performed off the leash, but the dogs are always collared. The only kinds of collar permitted are a single slip collar made of leather, fabric, or chain; or a simple, unadorned, well-fitted buckled collar. The leash may be of fabric or leather, long enough to provide sufficient slack when heeling on leash.

Show grooming is unnecessary, even for Poodles. A judge may refuse to judge a dog who has been dyed, powdered, chalked, or adorned—except for Maltese, Poodles, Shih Tzu, and Yorkshire Terriers, who may have their topknot tied back from their eyes.

Performance is scored by points, with a certain number of points allotted to each exercise. A perfect score for the lot is 200 points, and a passing score 170, on condition that at least 50 per cent of the allotted points has been scored for each exercise. In order to earn a passing, qualifying score, a dog must therefore perform all of the exercises moderately well, and several of them almost perfectly. A single exercise scored under the 50 per cent point will disqualify the entire performance, even if the rest of it is flawless.

A dog may perform the routine correctly and still be penalized for certain faults, such as snapping, barking, relieving himself in the ring, displaying fear, resentment, or nervousness, and for anticipating a command (which is a common result of overtraining). The handler can also incur penalties for such things as excessively loud commands, allowing his dog to get out of control, disciplining his dog in the ring, repeating a command or signal, being rough or peremptory in his commands, and for touching his dog in the ring—although petting and praise are permitted between and after the exercises. On the other hand, a dog can win bonus points for steadiness, precision, and displayed willingness and enjoyment, while the handler will get plus marks for naturalness, gentleness, and smoothness.

In most exercises, the handler must instruct the dog either by voice command or hand signal. The only time he is permitted to command and signal simultaneously is when the dog is left alone, as in the "Long Sit" and "Long Down." Moreover, the dog's name may be used only with a voice command, never with a signal.

After all of the dogs in a class have performed, first individually, then in the group exercises, the judge calls back into the ring those who have scored passing marks and awards the ribbons: Blue, Red, Yellow, and White for the first four places (the four top scores), plus a Dark Green "Qualifying Prize" ribbon for each dog who has earned a passing score. All of these prizewinners have also gained a leg toward the title that they seek. At the end of the Trial, a Blue and Gold ribbon is awarded to the "Highest-scoring Dog in the Regular Classes."

In order to win an Obedience title, a dog must earn three qualifying scores under three different judges at three licensed Obedience Trials where no less than 6 dogs competed for a C.D. or C.D.X., 3 dogs for a U.D.

NOVICE CLASSES

In the Novice Classes (A and B), the dogs are required to:

1) HEEL ON LEASH (40 POINTS). The dog must accompany his handler around the ring, at his left side, on a loose lead, to move "Forward," "Halt," make a "Right Turn," a "Left Turn," an "About Turn," to go "Slow," at a "Normal" pace, or "Fast." At every halt, the dog must sit straight and promptly in the heel position without command. These orders can be mixed up and repeated, but the same pattern is given to

At heel position. (*Sue Maynard*)

each dog. To conclude, the dog must follow at heel over a figure-eight course, making a loop around 2 ring stewards, during which the judge can order a halt at any point.

2) STAND FOR EXAMINATION (30 POINTS). The handler must pose his dog off leash, then command him to STAY, walk about 6 feet in front of the dog, turn around and face him, while the judge touches the dog's head, body, and hindquarters and then orders the handler, "Return to your dog." The handler must then walk around behind his dog, returning to the heel position, where they remain until the judge announces, "Exercise finished." (This is the required finish for every exercise.)

Sitting down during the examination, as well as cringing, growling, snapping, or moving away, are penalized by a score of zero. This apparently simple test is therefore harder and more important than it may seem to be.

3) HEEL FREE (40 POINTS). This is exactly the same as the Heel on Leash, except that the dog is unleashed, and there is no figure eight.

4) RECALL (30 POINTS). The dog must stay on command in a sitting position where the handler leaves him when the judge orders, "Leave your dog." The handler then goes to the other side of the ring, about 35 feet away, turns and faces his dog. When the judge says, "Call your dog," the handler commands or signals his dog to COME, which the dog must do briskly, and sit straight, centered immediately in front of the handler's feet. On the judge's order to "Finish," the handler commands or signals his dog to go smartly to the heel position and sit again.

This exercise is strictly scored, zero points going to a dog who does not respond to the first STAY or COME command, who moves from the designated staying-place, or who does not come close enough to the handler for the latter to touch his head without stretching. In addition, a dog is penalized for lagging, for standing or lying down instead of remaining seated, and for failing to sit or to move into the heel position at the finish.

5) LONG SIT (30 POINTS) and

6) LONG DOWN (30 POINTS). These two final exercises are performed in a group of not less than 6 dogs or more than 15, which means that the class may be divided into several groups, or that the A and B sections may be combined. The unleashed dogs are lined up along one side of the ring, and each handler placed his armband on the ground behind his dog, giving him the command or signal (or both) to SIT, then

The long sit. (*Sue Maynard*)

The long down. (*Sue Maynard*)

to STAY. The handlers then go to the opposite side of the ring, turn to face their dogs, and wait for the longest minute of their lives, hoping their dogs will not move until the judge orders them to return to their dogs. They must do this at a normal pace, walk around and behind their dog, and into the heel position. The dogs must not move from their sitting position until the judge has announced that the exercise is "Finished."

The Long Down is exactly the same as the Long Sit, except that the dogs must remain lying down for 3 minutes, and are not required to sit at the end.

A dog is scored zero if he changes position, moves from the appointed spot, barks, whines, or goes over to another dog. He is only slightly penalized for changing his position when the handler returns to heel—which must prove that the AKC Rules Committee is not completely ignorant of the instinctive reactions of a loving pet.

As you can see, these exercises are not extremely difficult—which is not to say that it is easy to win a C.D. title. Many dogs perform the routine perfectly in their own back yard and go to pieces in the Obedience ring. A moment of inattention can lead to some disqualifying fault. Or a dog may simply not be in the mood to obey with such precision at a particular moment on a particular day. While the scoring of faults is described in the Rules, there is still a lot of leeway for the judge's personal appreciation, which is reflected in the scores. Nevertheless, there is certainly less subjectivity in Obedience judging than in the show ring, which may be one of the reasons for the popularity of the sport.

OPEN CLASSES

The open classes (A and B), for dogs who have already won their C.D. title, are harder, since the dogs are required to:

1) HEEL FREE (40 POINTS). This is the same as the Novice Heel on Leash, including the figure eight, except that the dog is unleashed.

2) DROP ON RECALL (30 POINTS). This is the same as the Novice Recall, except that the dog is required to *drop* to a *down* position on his way back to the handler. The handler can either command or signal his dog to *Drop,* and then to *Come* when the judge orders, "Call your dog," even adding the dog's name if he uses a voice command. The judge

may designate in advance the point at which he wishes the dog to drop, or he may give the order while the dog is on his way to the handler.

3) RETRIEVE ON THE FLAT (20 POINTS). The handler stands with his dog sitting in the heel position. When the judge orders, "Throw it," he gives his dog the *Stay* command or signal (or both), and throws a wooden dumbbell of appropriate size. At the next order, he commands or signals his dog to retrieve, and the dog must take off in a direct line at a fast trot or gallop and deliver the dumbbell, sitting straight and centered in front of the handler's feet, close enough for the handler to easily take the dumbbell when the judge orders, "Take it." This is followed by the usual order to "Finish" in the heel position. As always, the dog will be penalized for lack of obedience or precision, but also for dropping the dumbbell, for playing with it, or for releasing it reluctantly.

4) RETRIEVE OVER HIGH JUMP (30 POINTS). This is the same as the Retrieve on the Flat, except that the dumbbell is thrown over a jump which the dog must clear both going and coming back. For most breeds, the jump is set at a height one and a half times the height of the dog at the withers. However, for certain big, heavy dogs like Great Danes, St. Bernards, and Newfoundlands, it is set at the height of the dog or 36 inches, whichever is less; and for a number of small, short-legged dogs like Dachshunds, Corgis, Pekingese, Bulldogs, and certain Terriers, the jump is set at the height of the dog or 8 inches, whichever is greater. Not only must the dog obey the handler's commands or signals promptly and correctly, he must also clear the obstacle like a Champion Show Jumper, without touching the jump, climbing it, or using it for aid in getting over.

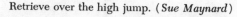

Retrieve over the high jump. (*Sue Maynard*)

5) BROAD JUMP (20 POINTS). This exercise requires the dog to sit until directed to jump over a set of four sloping wooden hurdles, but without having to retrieve anything. The handler, on the judge's orders, first commands or signals (or both) his dog to STAY, while he takes up a position anywhere along the right side of the jump, about 2 feet away from it. He then commands or signals the dog to clear the entire jump, without touching it, after which the dog, without any further signal or command, must return to his handler and sit immediately in front of him. It should be added that the handler makes a 90-degree turn in place while the dog is jumping, and so is facing the returning dog.

A dog who refuses to jump on the first command or signal, or who fails to clear the full distance with his forelegs, is scored zero. So is one who walks over any part of the jump (although he may very possibly have the highest I.Q. of all).

6) LONG SIT (30 POINTS) and

7) LONG DOWN (30 POINTS). The last two Open exercises are performed and scored as in the Novice Class, with two important differences that make them infinitely harder: First of all, the handlers not only leave their dogs and cross to the other side of the ring; they must then file out of the ring and remain out of sight until the judge orders them to return. Secondly, the staying time is longer: 3 minutes for the Long Sit, and 5 minutes (which can seem like an eternity to a deserted dog) for the Long Down.

The broad jump. (*Sue Maynard*)

UTILITY CLASS

The main distinction of the utility class is the Scent Discrimination tests that are added to the usual Obedience exercises. While practically any willing dog of average intelligence and with competent schooling can win a C.D. or even a C.D.X., a dog who qualifies for the U.D. title must possess in addition an innate scenting ability, which cannot be acquired from Obedience lessons. This is the most spectacular class for the onlookers, and perhaps the most fun for dogs of suitable aptitudes. But everything they are asked to do is difficult, starting with:

1) SIGNAL EXERCISE (40 POINTS). The orders are the same as for Heeling on Leash and Figure Eight, with the additions of "Stand your dog," "Leave your dog," and the incorporation of the Long Sit and the Long Down with Drop on Return. Throughout the entire exercise the handler must remain absolutely silent, using only signals to communicate the judge's instructions to his dog. A dog who earns a good score in this part of the test must be a well-trained dog indeed, with a highly proficient handler besides.

2) SCENT DISCRIMINATION, ARTICLE 1 (30 POINTS) and

3) SCENT DISCRIMINATION, ARTICLE 2 (30 POINTS). In these exercises, the dog must select an article bearing the handler's scent

Scent discrimination. (*Sue Maynard*)

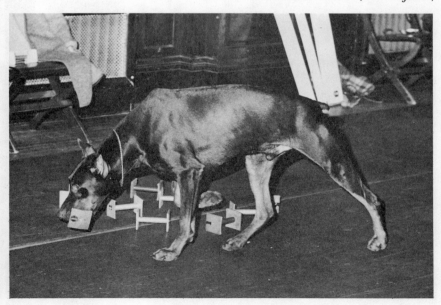

from an assortment of articles, and deliver it to his handler. The handler provides two sets of five identical small numbered objects, one set of rigid metal and the other of leather, from which the judge selects one from each set and gives them to the handler to handle, while he or the ring steward handles all the others. These articles, including the first selected one, are strewn on the ground while the dog and handler are standing at the opposite end of the ring with their backs turned. When the judge says, "Send your dog," they make a right-about turn, with the dog in the heel position, and the handler orders his dog to retrieve. The dog must go briskly to the articles and select the right one, delivering it correctly as in the Retrieve on the Flat.

The second article is then added to the assortment, and the procedure is repeated. If the dog retrieves the wrong article the first time, both this and the correct one are removed before the second test, and his score is zero. However, because natural scenting aptitude is stronger in some breeds than in others, a dog is not penalized for taking more time than his better-nosed rivals, as long as he works continuously and eventually succeeds in retrieving the correct article.

4) DIRECTED RETRIEVE (30 POINTS). Three white gloves, provided by the handler, are placed in the corners and center of one end

Sending the dog in a directed retrieve. (*Sue Maynard*)

Over the bar jump. (*Sue Maynard*)

of the ring while the handler and his dog stand at the other end, with their backs turned. The judge orders which glove should be retrieved: One, Two, or Three, from left to right. The handler then gives the command to heel and turns in place, facing the designated glove. With a single motion of his left hand and arm along the right side of the dog, he indicates the selected glove, which the dog must retrieve briskly, as in the Retrieve on the Flat. The handler is permitted to bend his knees and body when indicating the proper glove, as is obviously necessary when working with a small dog.

5) DIRECTED JUMPING (40 POINTS). Two jumps are set up midway in the ring at right angles to the sides of the ring and 18 or 20 feet apart—the bar jump on one side, the high jump on the other. The handler stands in the center of the ring with his dog in the heel position. On the judge's order, "Send your dog," he commands or signals (or

both) his dog to go at a brisk pace to a point between the two jumps and about 20 feet beyond them, at which point he commands his dog to SIT. The judge then tells the handler which jump is to be taken first, and the handler must command or signal (or both) his dog to return to him over the designated jump, sitting and finishing as in the Recall. After the dog has returned to the heel position, the judge inquires, "Are you ready?" and then follows the same procedure for the second jump. In addition to all the obvious difficulties, the dog must clear both jumps without touching them in order to earn a perfect score.

6) GROUP EXAMINATION (30 POINTS). The competing dogs perform this exercise together in groups of not less than 6 or more than 15. The handlers and dogs line up in the heel position down the center of the ring, each handler placing his armband behind his dog. When the judge orders, "Stand your dogs," the handlers pose their dogs. When the judge says, "Leave your dogs," they command or signal (or both) their dogs to STAY, walk across the ring, turn and face their dogs. Now the judge approaches each dog in turn and examines him as in show judging, but without touching the mouth or testicles. When all the dogs have been examined and the handlers have been away for at least 3 minutes, the judge orders, "Return to your dogs." The handlers return and walk around and in back of their dogs to resume the heel position, whereupon the judge says, "Exercise finished." The scoring is similar to that for Stand for Examination in the Novice Classes.

OBEDIENCE TRAINING

There are no secret formulas or professional tricks for excelling in these Obedience tests, although, of course, some individuals are more gifted dog trainers than others. The best way for the average owner to train his dog for Obedience Trials is to join an Obedience class with a really good instructor, and to practice at home. Remember that too much practice can be as bad as an insufficient amount, since the dog's anticipation of commands or an overdisciplined, military style are considered serious faults and are penalized.

An Obedience course of preparation for the Novice Class usually consists of one lesson a week for 6 to 12 weeks, and costs from $25 to $50 or so. The *AKC Gazette* lists affiliated training clubs throughout the country. Many local kennel clubs, branches of the ASPCA and the Humane Society, as well as professional trainers, organize classes too. If none is available in your area and you are unable to organize one with other interested friends, you can always attempt to train your dog alone, with the help of an excellent training book such as:

The Complete Book of Dog Obedience and Obedience Training Course by Blanche Saunders (Howell Books)

The Koehler Method of Dog Training by Bill Koehler (Howell Books)

Your dog may learn his lessons even more quickly this way. The principal disadvantage is that individual training does not reproduce the conditions of the Obedience ring, and particularly the distracting presence of other dogs and handlers. The only way to compensate for this is to enter your dog in several practice Sanctioned Trials before his first Licensed one. Like Sanction Matches for show dogs, the atmosphere is more relaxed, and the entry fees are modest: perhaps one dollar, compared to the entry fee of about $8 for a licensed Obedience Trial.

THE FIRST TRIAL

Before you go to your first Trial, study the official rules carefully and ask your Obedience class instructor to clarify any points of confusion. For example, you should know the faults in each exercise which automatically disqualify, and those which are merely penalized. Sometimes it may be worthwhile to repeat a command, thus incurring a penalty, in order to ensure the completion of an exercise and avoid a score of zero.

Make sure that your dog gets a good night's rest and that he empties his bowels and bladder before leaving for the Trial. You will not really need to take anything with you but your dog, his collar and leash, and perhaps a water bowl, since food is prohibited in the ring; grooming is unnecessary (although he should, of course, be neat and clean), and Obedience Trial dogs are seldom benched.

When you arrive at the Trial grounds, the first thing to do is purchase a catalogue and see where your dog is listed in his class, since the dogs are usually tested in catalogue order. If your dog is among the first, you should report at once to the ring steward. You can then take your dog for a stroll, offer him a drink of water, and give him a light going over with a brush or comb so that he will look his best. But do not romp with him or fuss over him. You want him to remain calm and collected.

If you have time, try to watch some of the preceding dogs. You will be able to observe the patterns the judge prescribes, and this may help you to follow his orders when it is your turn to perform.

In the Obedience Ring, try to remain as calm as possible. Nothing is more contagious than nervousness. If you concentrate, but without tension, your dog may catch that mood too. Give your commands clearly and distinctly, loud enough for your dog to hear them but without shouting. Make your signals distinct too, and only when you are certain that your dog is watching you. During the heeling exercises, walk briskly and in a straight line, make sharp 90-degree turns at the corners, and clear changes of pace when ordered. During the figure eight you are supposed to maintain an even pace, which means that your dog must be trained to go faster on the outside of the loops and slower on the inside. Remember that your left foot and leg guide your dog and keep him in the proper heel position. Always start off with the left foot when your dog is to accompany you, and with the right foot when he is to STAY. Always halt on the right foot and then bring the left foot up even with it. And don't forget that you are permitted to pat and praise your dog at the end of each exercise.

After the Trial, make a note of the exercises and details of ring behavior that could be improved. Try to criticize your own performance objectively, so that you can correct your faults too. A knowledgeable friend at the ringside is an invaluable aid in spotting deficiencies, in you or your dog, of which you may be completely unaware.

If your dog has earned a qualifying score, you can be proud of him, as well as certain that he is capable of winning an Obedience title. It is a good idea to enter another Trial a week or two later, without too many training sessions in between, so that he can qualify for his title before becoming bored with the routine. On the other hand, if he fails two or three Trials in succession, it may be advisable to give him a vacation for a few months before resuming his Obedience training.

TRACKING TESTS

are entirely different from Obedience Trials. In fact, obedience hardly enters into them at all. It is tracking ability only that counts, and this must be inherited, then developed by practice. The best instructor for a novice Tracking dog is probably another dog who is an expert in the field. Tracking cannot be taught in a back yard or in the living room. To some dogs, it cannot be taught at all.

The official Tracking test is held as an event of its own, on a tract of land sufficiently large to permit the laying of a separate track for each competing dog. Even the date cannot be set definitively in advance, because of varying weather and scent conditions. Any purebred dog over 6 months of age is theoretically eligible. But each entry form for a licensed Tracking test must be accompanied by a written statement from an approved Tracking judge, certifying that the dog is ready to take the test —a condition that considerably limits the field.

Two Tracking judges preside. Their work starts a day or two before the test, when they plot the tracks, which must be between 440 and 500 yards long and include at least 2 right-angle turns, preferably more, so that the dogs are obliged to work in different wind directions. The tracks are marked by flags, and the judges draw up a duplicate chart of each track. They must also approve of the articles to be left at the end of the trails (generally a dark wallet or glove, well impregnated with the tracklayer's scent), and of the tracklayer's shoes (leather, or fabric with leather soles), in order to ensure leaving an adequate trail. Not more than 2 hours nor less than half an hour before the test, the tracklayer follows the track the judges have stalked out, collecting the flags, except for the first two. The first one is the starting line for each dog; the second gives the direction of the track. He deposits an article at the end of the track, and leaves the course.

Soon after these preparations have been made, it is time for the dogs to go into action. They must wear a harness and a leash, 20 to 40 feet long. The handler may restrain his dog, but never guide him, and must follow the dog at a distance of not less than 20 feet. If a dog fails to capture the scent between the first two flags, he may be given a second chance, as long as he did not pass the second flag. There is no time limit. A dog who is working may take as long as necessary. On the other hand, a dog who is not only off the track but also obviously not tracking, fails the test, even though he may eventually find the article by luck. When a dog is unfairly handicapped by poor scenting conditions, the judges can give him a second chance on a new track.

There are only two scores in a Tracking test: Passed or Failed.

The judges mark their charts of the tracks by tracing the tracks actually followed, noting the starting and finishing times, and describing the ground, wind, and weather conditions. These are forwarded to the American Kennel Club, which then mails to the proud owners of the "Passed" dogs a Tracking Dog Certificate, entitling them to add the letters "T.D." after their names. When a dog has already earned his U.D. title, his new one will be "U.D.T."

If you ever meet a dog who has earned his U.D.T., the most prestigious title in dogdom, be sure to show him the respect and admiration he deserves.

24.
Field Trials

Field Trials are almost as old as dog shows, the first American one having been held in Memphis, Tennessee, in 1874, with an entry list of nine Setters and Pointers. Today, the sport is far more important than most city and suburban dog owners probably imagine. Almost one thousand Field Trials are held every year in the United States (about half of them for Beagles). Still, it has remained a predominantly masculine activity, in which the participants' interest in dogs is inseparable from their passion for hunting. It is also a rather exclusive activity, mainly because of the time, expense, and problems involved in organizing and competing in them. In bird-dog Trials, for example, the participants must be skilled not only in training and handling techniques, but also in bird raising, bird behavior, and in horsemanship.

PURPOSE, RULES AND REGULATIONS

The purpose of a Field Trial is to measure a Hunting dog's aptitude and ability in a series of judged tests under natural hunting conditions. A Trial is obviously more difficult to run and judge than a dog show, for it requires a vast expanse of hunting terrain, suitable live game (natural or planted), at least two judges, one or more marshals to assist the judges and control the gallery, and sometimes one or more official "guns" to do the shooting.

Rules and regulations have been formulated by the American Field (the specialist organization for bird dogs), the United Kennel Club (specializing in Hunting Hounds), the American Kennel Club, and by individual breed clubs, providing tests for various kinds of canine hunt-

A general view of a Field Trial in Connecticut, with two mounted judges, one handler and his dog setting out into the "bird field" upper left, and the rival handler lower left, with his dog already beyond the camera range. (*John Falk*)

ing skill. A Field Trial may be open to one or several breeds. It may be a recognized event where Field Trial Championship points and certificates are awarded; it may be a "Sanctioned Trial," for practice; or an informal one, just for fun.

KINDS OF TRIALS

POINTER TRIALS (for all of the pointing breeds, including English Pointers, the various kinds of Setters, Brittany Spaniels, Vizslas, and Weimaraners) test the dogs on upland game such as pheasant, quail, partridge, and grouse. The dogs must quarter the terrain (which consists of a "back course" and a "bird field" 5 to 10 acres large, in which two birds are released for each brace of competing dogs), find a bird by air scent, indicate the spot by pointing, and remain staunch until it has been flushed and shot. Field Trial Pointers cover so much ground so fast that the handlers, judges, marshals, and even the public are usually mounted on horseback.

RETRIEVER TRIALS (for all of the retrieving breeds, including Labradors, Chesapeake Bays, Goldens, the Continental breeds, and Irish Water Spaniels) consist of a series of marked and unmarked retrieves of pheasant and duck in or over water as well as on land.

SPANIEL TRIALS (for all of the Spaniels except for the Brittany, who points, and the Irish Water Spaniel, who retrieves) require the dogs to flush small game birds within gun range, mark the fall and retrieve on command, the different Spaniel breeds competing separately. The game varies, but is usually pheasant, partridge, duck, or pigeons.

BEAGLE TRIALS are run on rabbit or hare, without guns, but in natural hunting conditions. There are competitions for single dogs, couples, small packs (under 13 inches high), and for large packs (over 13 inches high), working hare.

When the hounds are "cast" (sent to seek the game), the handler remains with the dogs in Brace and Small Pack Trials, but with the rival handlers in Large Pack Trials. The Hounds are judged on ability to search, pursue, and trail accurately, to use voice ("bay") when on scent, as well as for endurance, adaptability, patience, determination, independence, and intelligence. They are penalized for quitting a scent, for

An English Pointer on point. (*John Falk*)

A Labrador Retriever retrieving a training "bumper" from the water. (*John Falk*)

"back-trailing," "ghost-trailing" (pretending to follow a nonexistent trail), "pottering," "babbling" (giving voice excessively or unnecessarily), for "swinging" (casting too far, too wide, or too soon), for "skirting" (intercepting other trailmates), for running mute (failing to give "tongue" or "voice"), and for abandoning a "check" (the point where scent is lost).

FOXHOUND TRIALS are similar, except that the larger Hounds may be run on fox as well as hare and rabbits.

In DACHSHUND FIELD TRIALS organized by the Dachshund Club of America under AKC rules, the dogs are run on rabbit, usually over Beagle hunting grounds. Once the competing dogs have been released in braces (two at a time), their handlers are not permitted to guide or influence them in their work. German Dachshund Trials are very popular and slightly different. There, the dogs are required to detect and enter artificial "earths" (burrowed tunnels), which have been baited with caged vermin.

BASSET HOUND TRIALS are unique in that there are generally as many women handlers as men competing. The gallery flushes a rabbit and the competing dogs are then released in braces, followed by the mounted judges, then the handlers, and finally the gallery. The dogs are required to trail by scent and are judged on their performance as well as for such qualities as independence, nose, and intelligence. As a matter of fact, Basset Trials are quite different from normal Basset pack hunting, being faster, truer to the line, and more like trailing than hunting.

COONHOUND TRIALS are held at night under special rules of the United Kennel Club.

TERRIER TRIALS are organized under rules formulated by the various Terrier breed clubs, and generally require the dogs to work an artificial earth 30 feet long with caged rats at the end. These are informal events, unrecognized by the AKC, and successful competitors are awarded a "Certificate of Gameness" rather than Field Trial Championship points. They are just one example of the current trend to revive or invent Trials for various Working and Sporting breeds, as dog owners become increasingly interested in promoting the activities for which their dogs were originally bred. Among them are Water Trials for Newfoundlands, which include underwater retrieving, towing a small boat, rescuing a person fallen from a boat, delivering a life preserver to a person hanging onto a capsized boat, and the directed retrieve of two articles floating far offshore, in addition to less spectacular tests. Various breed clubs also organize Sheepdog Trials, racing and hauling competitions for sled dogs, and carting races and demonstrations for harness dogs.

PROCEDURES

Most Field Trials are run along the same general lines. The dogs are not tested individually, but in "braces," two at a time, each with his own handler; and in "heats," from 15 to 40 minutes long—or longer—depending on the event. They proceed by elimination, the winners of the first series of tests being called back for a second, and the winners of these for a third, and so forth. Instead of offering different "classes," like dog shows, Field Trials are divided into "Stakes" according to age and past winnings, with dogs and bitches competing together in some Trials, separately in others. There are usually Puppy Stakes (for dogs over 6 months and under 2 years old), Derby Stakes (for dogs 6 months or over), Gun Dog Stakes, and All-Age Stakes. The more advanced Stakes are divided into Amateur and Open divisions. For Field Trial purposes, an amateur is a person who has not accepted remuneration for training or handling a Hunting dog during the previous 2 years.

The Stakes are scored on a point system. Each heat is given a score, and the four dogs with the highest total scores at the end of the Trial are awarded the top four ribbons (Blue, Red, Yellow and White), as well as trophies and prize money (which can be quite a lot in an important Trial). The dogs who have passed all of the tests but have not been placed receive a Dark Green ribbon, symbolizing the "Judges' Award of Merit" in Retriever Trials, and most of the others offer some similar recognition of aptitude.

Field Trialers are scored on hunting ability and style rather than on the number of birds they find, and the different Stakes are judged according to slightly different standards. Puppies and Derby dogs are evaluated mostly on natural hunting aptitude and training capacity. Gun dogs are measured against an ideal hunting dog, while the dogs in All-Age Stakes are expected to display greater range and initiative. Certain faults can disqualify a competitor, such as being out of control, breaking a point, failing to retrieve or deliver properly, retrieving a decoy, interfering with the work of a brace mate, damaging game, failing to find a bird when possible, and misconduct on the part of the handler.

While superior hunting aptitude, skillful training, and expert handling are the keys to success in Field Trials, there is still a certain amount of luck involved. Weather conditions, the varying quality of the game, or interference by another dog, can handicap a competitor. One of the advantages most professional handlers have over most amateurs is that they are usually more experienced in anticipating and avoiding trouble, and more apt to remain cool when something goes wrong. Even the pros recognize the part luck plays, however, and many respect the Field Trial tradition of carrying a rabbit's foot in the left-hand pocket. Another indication that chance is involved is the lively side-betting that sometimes goes on.

Although there is only one National Field Champion each year for each breed (or two, if there are Amateur and Open divisions), there are many new Field Trial Champions, since this title, like the Championship title of show dogs, is earned by accumulating a certain number of qualifying points in official competitions. In general, the more important the event and the higher the number of entries, the greater the number of points that can be won. The AKC, The American Field, and the UKC award Field Championship titles for the breeds and dogs that are registered with them. A dog that wins a Field Trial Championship as well as a show Championship is a "Dual Champion," which is a fine achievement indeed. For some breeds, it is practically impossible, due to the diver-

A Springer Spaniel retrieving a bird through underbrush, where he excels, with evident enjoyment. (*John Falk*)

A Labrador Retriever delivering a bird. (*John Falk, courtesy of Mr. & Mrs. Tom Prior, Hamden, Conn.*)

gence that has arisen between the show and field types, as in the case of the Cocker and Springer Spaniels, English and Irish Setters, and the English Pointer. But an impressive number of Brittany Spaniels and German Short-haired Pointers have been Dual Champions.

Champion Field Trialers nowadays must be specialists in their sport— their sport being competitive Trials rather than natural hunting. Because of the different conditions and standards, the two are not quite the same. A dog who is an ideal companion for pleasure hunting would probably have trouble placing in a Field Trial, while a Field Trial Champion might well be too keen and fast for a weekend hunter. There is, however, less difference between pleasure and Trial work for Retrievers than there is for Pointers.

So much time, effort, and expense are involved that Field Trials are not an activity for dilletantes, nor for the average dog owner. To start with, a suitable dog, sired or whelped by a successful Trialer, preferably from a well-known line of Trialers, is one of the most expensive puppy purchases you can make. Training, which requires a lot of land, equipment, live birds or suitable game, and a helper or two, entails further investment, as does traveling to Field Trials, which are often at considerable distances. Unless an owner possesses a property with suitable hunting terrain, he will have to pay a fee to work his dog on a commercial shooting preserve. Professional coaching is advisable for the handler as well as for his dog, in order to develop the polish and style and the high standard of obedience that is needed to win. As dogs and trainers become increasingly skilled, Field Trial tests have been made more difficult. Some critics claim that they have also become more artificial, and that innate aptitude, while still crucial, is less important than expert training. Obviously, few amateurs possess the equipment, skill, and leisure time necessary for preparing and handling a prospective Field Trial Champion.

On the other hand, Field Trials on the local club level can be great sport. If you love to hunt, love your Hunting dog, and enjoy competition, by all means give it a try.

FIELD TRIAL TRAINING

The best way to start is to contact and join your appropriate breed club (listed in the *AKC Gazette*), since most clubs organize training classes and seminars in addition to Field Trials and other events.

You can write for information, official rules, and calendars of Field Trial events to:

The American Field (Pointers and Setters)—222 West Adams Street, Chicago, Illinois 60606

The American Kennel Club—51 Madison Avenue, New York, New York 10010

The United Kennel Club—321 West Cedar Street, Kalamazoo, Michigan 49007

The Amateur Field Trial Clubs of America (Miss Leslie Anderson, Secretary), Hernando, Mississippi 38632

The American Coonhunters' Association—Wickliffe, Kentucky 42087

The Chase (Hounds)—152 Walnut Street, Lexington, Kentucky 40507

You will also find much information in the specialized Hunting dog magazines, such as:

The American Field (Pointers and Setters)—222 West Adams Street, Chicago, Illinois 60606

The Retriever Field Trial News—Grange Building, 435 East Lincoln Avenue, Milwaukee, Wisconsin 53207

Bloodlines (the UKC magazine)—321 West Cedar Street, Kalamazoo, Michigan 49007

Hunting Dog—215 South Washington Street, Greenfield, Ohio 45123
The Springer Bark—San Leandro, California
Full Cry (Coonhounds)—Box 190, Sedalia, Missouri 65301
Mountain Music (Hounds)—Sapulpa, Oklahoma 74066
Hounds and Hunting—Bradford, Pennsylvania 16701

Finally, one of the best ways to acquire information, instruction, and inspiration is to observe some important Field Trial events, including, if possible, the National Championship of your breed.

The season opens in the spring and ends in the fall. While some Trials are limited to certain regions, others follow an annual circuit that covers most parts of the country. The most important bird-dog Trials, for example, start in Canada in the spring and move around to the Southwest, the Deep South, and up the Eastern Seaboard to finish in the Northeast in the fall, when the English Setter Club of America holds its annual Championship event at Medford, New Jersey. The famous and historic National Championship Stake of the National Retriever Club is held in Tennessee.

For most of the Hunting breeds, in fact, there is an annual National Championship event to climax the Trial season, after which the dogs and their owners enjoy a long winter's rest, both of them probably dreaming of past pleasures and of the exciting season to come.

25.

Canine Careers

Most dogs are born and bred for some kind of work. Even the Toy breeds provide love and pleasure, which is one of the oldest human professions. Still, few owners think of their pets as working dogs, and even fewer think of offering them some useful job to do.

Canine careers have changed radically during the past 50 years, just as ours have. Men and dogs have been replaced by machines in many of the roles they used to fill in agriculture and transportation. However, no mechanized substitute has completely usurped the dog's role as a shepherd, guard, and hunter, and new fields have opened up for dogs in crime prevention, the entertainment industry, advertising, medical and scientific research. Don't forget that the first living being to explore outer space was a Russian Spitz called "Laika."

Our dogs' working aptitudes are largely a matter of breeding. You may come across a rare Spaniel who dislikes hunting, a Greyhound who hates to run, or a Beagle who takes no notice of a fresh rabbit trail. But most dogs have inherited a vocation from their ancestors and have no other professional ambition than to follow in their forefathers' footsteps.

The outstanding examples are Sheepdogs, Hunting dogs, and Guards. You might say they are the doctors, lawyers, and bankers of dogdom: trained professionals who sometimes specialize in a single area of their field, who have had to study long and hard before being admitted to practice. Superior instruction and determination may sometimes compensate for lesser aptitudes, but basic talent is essential to a really successful career. (It also helps to have a father or uncle who has already made a name for himself in the field.)

SHEEP HERDING

dogs guide, protect, and supervise their flocks, moving them from one grazing ground to another. They also herd them back to the fold at night, separate selected individuals for sale, medical treatment, and for shearing. A good sheepdog can handle as many as 1,000 sheep, and he may cover as many as 10,000 miles a year in tending such a large flock. Yet he senses immediately when a single lamb is missing. He is ready to defend his charges from the attacks of other animals, to report to the shepherd lost or injured sheep. He controls his flock not only by superior speed, intelligence, and agility, but even more by psychological domination. No electronic device can do the work of the sheepdog's "eye."

There is no systematic training method. The usual way for a young sheepdog to learn his trade is by accompanying an older, experienced one. Instinct, intuition, and inherited aptitudes are more important than acquired techniques, although practical experience is essential, and the dogs must also learn to respond in a specific way to whistled or shouted commands and crook signals from the shepherd.

The number of working sheepdogs in the world has never been officially estimated, but there are certainly hundreds of thousands of them. Many pastoral countries hold national Sheepdog Trials, the most important of which are governed by the International Sheepdog Society (Southport, Lancashire, England). The most famous is the International Championship held annually in rotation in England, Wales, and Scotland, in which actual working sheepdogs perform fantastic feats of gathering, herding, driving through gates and over a long triangular course, into a ring, separating marked sheep and driving them into a special pen, all within a time limit. At the end of the day, you will see these same remarkable dogs (most often Border and Welsh Collies) happily sleeping at their owners' feet at the local pub or underneath the banquet table, just as content and devoted as your own pet, if not more so.

Efforts are being made by the American Sheepdog Society to organize Sheepdog Trials in the United States. The W.D.A. (Working Dogs of America, 1164 Wall Road, Webster, New York 14580) promotes Trials and training for sheepdogs as well as for other working breeds, as does the North American Working Dog Association, Inc. (1677 North Alisar Avenue, Monterey Park, California 91754). Try to attend one of these fascinating events, especially if you own a Sheepdog.

HUNTING

is a natural activity of all dogs and one of their most ancient careers. The instinct and aptitude for hunting certain game in certain conditions has been concentrated in different breeds. No longer an essential means of providing food for survival, hunting is now practiced almost exclusively as a sport, and nonhunters seldom realize what a very widespread sport it is.

Hunting dog owners who are more interested in hunting than in dogs usually buy a trained adult dog at least one and a half years old. Those who hunt as much for the pleasure it gives their dog as for the pleasure it gives them, enjoy it even more when they train their dog themselves. Almost anyone is capable of training a dog for ordinary hunting. Competitive Field Trials are a different matter, and professional training is practically mandatory. Even for a family pet who also hunts, the instruction of a professional trainer during a dog club seminar or clinic is invaluable, as is the expert advice found in specialized books on hunting training, such as:

The Practical Hunter's Dog Book and
The Complete Guide to Bird Dog Training both by John R. Falk (Winchester Press)
Hunting Dog Know-How, Bird Hunting Know-How, and Hunting Hounds, all by David Michael Duffey (Winchester Press)
Charles Morgan on Retrievers, edited by Ann Flower and D. L. Walters (October House)
Training Your Retriever by James Lamb Free (Coward)
Wing and Shot by Robert G. Wehle (Country Press)

Every professional trainer has his personal secrets, the result of years of experience. All of them agree that there is no point in wasting time on an insufficiently gifted hunting dog, and that it is inadvisable to push a talented one too fast. Pointers and Setters are usually started in basic training between the ages of 9 and 14 months, field-trained from 16 to 22 months, and fully trained only at the age of 3 years or more. Retrievers usually start at the same age, but finish sooner. Spaniels are the most precocious, and often are the easiest to train.

Play-training at home is the best foundation for formal lessons when the time comes. It is no different from the early training of a pet dog: learning his name, learning to ride in the car, becoming accustomed to loud noises, to obeying simple commands, developing self-confidence, being encouraged to explore and investigate strange places and objects, to enter water and to swim.

Puppies invent *retrieving* games instinctively, and all you have to do is to avoid forming bad habits by encouraging the puppy to deliver the retrieved object to you without shaking or playing with it en route, and to release it willingly.

The *pointing* instinct is so strong in some breeds that puppies point a bird or chicken when they are only a few weeks old. It is never too soon to encourage a dog to hold his point by caressing him when he stiffens, saying "WHOA" (which is the standard command for holding a point).

During early walks in the country, you can plant the habit of *quartering* (which is instinctive in Spaniels, just as pointing is instinctive in the Pointing breeds). Instead of following a straight line, walk with your dog diagonally, alternately right and left, but always moving forward. Call him back to you when he gets too far out of range, that is, beyond gunshot range, about 35 yards to each side.

Most Hunting dogs start formal training at the age of 8 or 9 months. The basic principles are the same as those that govern all training (see Chapter 13). Start by attempting to explain or demonstrate what you wish your dog to do, first in simulated conditions ("yard training"), then in natural ones ("field training"): first using simulated game (a bird wing, a dummy, or a sawdust bag impregnated with artificial scent for Trailing Hounds); then using planted pigeons or other game; and finally letting the dog find natural game for himself.

Hunting dogs are first taught to obey spoken commands to HEEL, WHOA (to remain immobile), SIT, STAY, COME, FETCH, HUP (to sit when another dog has flushed a bird or when a shot is fired). These are then reinforced by hand and whistle signals. Other useful commands are QUIET, GO ON, GIVE, DOWN, and BED (designating the wire

Working Sheepdogs penning sheep on a Montana ranch. (*John C. Haberstroh /FPG*)

crate in which most hunting dogs are transported to the hunting terrain or Field Trial grounds).

Advanced training includes such refinements as following the hunter's whistle or arm signals from a distance when seeking game ("casting"), or making "blind retrieves" (when the Retriever has not seen where the shot game has fallen), honoring another dog's point or retrieve, working within practical gun range instead of roaming far afield, and finally polishing the dog's style by training him to work with speed and precision. Corrective training may be necessary at some point too: correcting gun-shyness, teaching a dog to be "soft-mouthed" with the game he retrieves (the traditional method is to have him retrieve a scrubbing brush or a fresh egg), to ignore decoys in retrieving duck, and so forth. But most important of all is practical field work, which is the only way to familiarize a dog with the behavior of his prey, whatever it may be. In short, training a Hunting dog consists mainly of controlling and directing his natural instincts, and providing him with opportunities to learn for himself from practical experience.

Comparatively few dogs make a professional career of hunting: Field Trialers; a few well-trained dogs attached to commercial hunting preserves; and those used as helpers by professional trainers. By far the vast majority are, like their owners, genuine amateurs. The proof is seen in the special relationship that exists between a hunter and his dog, which has nothing in common with that of an employer and an employee. It is one of the most intimate relationships of all, composed of mutual respect and confidence, unconditional devotion, and the sense of complicity that develops when two individuals understand each other perfectly, form an effective team, and have a lot of fun together.

GUARDING

is also a natural aptitude of all dogs, but stronger in some breeds than in others. Any dog is a good enough guard for normal purposes, thanks to his innate protective and territorial instincts, and the fact that defense is far more important than attack in ordinary circumstances.

Trained guard dogs are in greater demand than ever before, due to the worldwide rise of crime. You should know, however, that a trained guard dog, especially one that has been trained to attack, is like a loaded gun. He needs a trained owner. He also needs a really qualified trainer, and there are very few of them. An improperly trained guard dog can be dangerous even to his owner. Because of the considerable fees involved (from $500 to as much as $2,500), the field has attracted a certain number of profiteers as well as perfectly honest people whose experience and knowledge are totally inadequate. If you are considering buying a trained guard dog, be very careful in selecting his breeder and trainer. If

This specially trained German Shepherd patrols a Chicago department store warehouse for signs of prowlers, fire, and water leakage. At regular intervals on his rounds, he pushes a pedal device which rings a bell to signal that all is well. In order to sound an alarm to the human watchman, he barks. (*Wide World Photos*)

you are thinking of having your own dog trained for guard work or attack, think again. You will probably ruin him as a pet.

Trained guard dogs are professionals, and their place is not in a home but in professional employment. Commercial protection services use them for patrolling department stores, warehouses, airports, office buildings, and factories. Most but not all of these dogs are German Shepherds who have been bred for guard work and have been schooled for 3 or 4 months in a training center. The headquarters for training Federal Aviation Administration (airport) and Law Enforcement Assistance Administration (police) dogs is at Lackland Air Force Base in Texas. After the training period, the dogs live with their individual handlers.

POLICE WORK

involves more than defense and attack, although these are the basic elements of the dogs' training and activity. In England, where ordinary policemen are unarmed, dogs have been used for years as law-enforcement aides, and they are increasingly in demand by American policemen as patrol companions. Again, German Shepherds are the favored breed, although Dobermans also have their supporters. Bloodhounds are used by the police as trackers, but more often to find missing persons and lost children than to trail escaped criminals.

THE CUSTOMS SERVICE

employs canine detectives to ferret out contraband explosives, and especially drugs nowadays. Dogs are said to be far more feared by dope peddlers than are human agents. Thanks to their extraordinary sense of smell, millions of dollars' worth of drugs have been confiscated at border Customs posts. Trained canine detectives have also intercepted letter bombs, and have detected plastic bombs concealed in public buildings and in airplanes.

FRONTIER GUARD

One of the dog's oldest roles, as a frontier guard, has been revived in certain Communist countries, particularly those in Eastern Europe, where closely sealed national borders are maintained. The dog's keen senses complete the radar installations, since dogs can detect moving objects and persons close to the ground beyond the range of radar.

Rico, a German Shepherd, is inspecting the mail at the International Customs in Oakland, California, in search of smuggled hashish and marijuana. Canine drug detectors have proven to be quicker and sharper than human specialists. (*Wide World Photos*)

WAR WORK

Dogs have a long history of valiant service in wartime. In ancient times, they were even active combatants, armored and sometimes armed. During World War I, the German and French Armies each employed over 50,000 dogs as sentries.

It was the German Army Dog School, founded in 1848, that first trained dogs for modern warfare. In World War II, an American civilian effort called "Dogs for Defense" led to the formation of the famous K9 Corps, in which some 10,000 dogs were trained to serve with American troops on every battle front. These dogs were mostly German Shepherds, but also included Doberman Pinschers, Boxers, Airedales, Alaskan Malamutes, Huskies, Briards, Great Danes, and Retrievers. Before accepting a recruit, the Army measured his aptitudes by grading him in five qualities: sensitivity, energy, aggressiveness, intelligence, and willingness. They learned to perform many kinds of jobs in addition to defense, sen-

try, and patrol work. They carried messages, munitions, stretchers, and
food supplies. They detected mines, located wounded soldiers, and laid
cables.

In peacetime, the American Army uses dogs mainly for guarding and
patrolling Army installations, and suspends its breeding operations. But
it maintains an important training center at Lackland Air Force Base
(Dog Center Detachment 37, HQ SAA MA [AFLC], Texas 78236), and
another at Loring Air Force Base in Maine. The dogs selected for Air
Force training are taught to respond to hand and voice signals on and off
leash, and to obey different handlers. Their official title is "Patrol Dog,"
but they are actually a sort of combination sentry, tracker, army scout,
and civilian police dog, once they have followed the curriculum that con-
sists of such courses as Steadiness to Gunfire, Military Drill, Confidence,
Controlled Aggressiveness, Tracking, Vehicle Patrol, and Building Search
—and, for advanced students, Drug and Explosive Detection. German

Kim, a German Shepherd, with his Marine Corps handler and a member of the
native Popular Forces troops, on patrol at Tom Ky during the War in Vietnam.
(*Wide World Photos*)

An American soldier and his war dog in a foxhole on Leyte Island during World War II. A Coast Guard combat photographer took this unusual picture under fire from an adjoining foxhole. (*Wide World Photos*)

Shepherds, male or female, are used almost exclusively, although smaller breeds like the Cairn Terrier have been trained in Drug Detection because of their good nose and small size, which permits them to investigate areas inaccessible to larger breeds.

Incidentally, many canine military skills are the basis of "*Schutzhund Trials,*" a sport which was recently brought from Germany (Schutzhund means "protection dog" in German) to the United States, where it is gaining popularity, especially in the West. This rigorous test of aptitude and training which is governed by the rules of the FCS (Fédération Cynologique Internationale) can take 2 full days to complete. For example, a Championship Schutzhund Trial may consist of: an Endurance test over 12½ miles, with the owners jogging or bicycling alongside their dogs—which is followed by a veterinary examination (rather like the first day of a three-day equestrian competition); an Obedience exercise, including a 40-inch high jump; a Tracking test; a Protection test; and a "G.A." (Guarding Aptitude) test. The Schutzhund Club offers prizes, Championship points, and Awards of Achievement and Recognition to the well-trained, well-conditioned dogs that earn a passing grade—most of which are German Shepherds, Doberman Pinschers, Tervurens (Belgian Shepherds), Briards, and Malamutes.

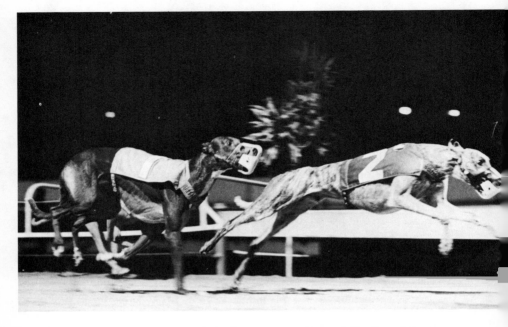

Racing Greyhounds. (*Mike Serlick Photo, courtesy National Greyhound Racing Association*)

DOG RACING

is the oldest example of transforming a practical canine activity (hunting running game) into a spectator sport.

GREYHOUND RACING is big business in England, and is popular in Germany, Italy, Spain, and Latin America. In America, meetings are held under the rules of the National Greyhound Association (P. O. Box 543, Abilene, Kansas 67410) at tracks in Florida and a few other places, but its progress has been hindered by the fact that dog racing is banned in many states. Nevertheless, there are reported to be some 6,000 active racing Greyhounds and 400 active racing kennels in the United States.

These dogs are bred and raised as professional athletes and have little in common with pet dogs. They run, muzzled, over an oval course 330 to 770 yards long (depending on the event) in pursuit of a mechanical rabbit, and they attain speeds as high as 40 miles per hour. The Saluki, it is claimed, is even faster as a sprinter, capable of running at a speed of 45 miles an hour over a short distance; while the Eskimo Husky is unsurpassed in producing consistent speed over very long distances.

WHIPPET RACING is also popular in some parts of England and is said to be an even more ancient sport than Greyhound racing. It is practiced, however, only in an amateur form (called lure coursing) and a most amusing one. The dogs seem to love it. The owners post themselves at one end of a straight 200-yard course, with the dogs at the other end. As the dogs are released, their handlers wave a rag or handkerchief to urge them to the finish line, which they reach in an average of merely 12 seconds. There are very few competitions in America. The most famous is run in connection with the annual American Whippet Club Specialty Show.

Specialty breed clubs of other coursing Hounds are also trying to revive racing or to invent some form of Hunting Trial for Borzois, Afghans, and Salukis.

One of the entries in a sled dog race in Quebec, Canada. (*Herbert Lanig/FPG*)

SLED DOGS

used to provide the only means of transportation in ice-bound areas which were otherwise inaccessible before the invention of the airplane and, later, of the skimobile. Sledding has since become an exciting sport, although it is still a useful means of transportation in some Arctic areas.

The dogs work in teams of 8 to 12 and are harnessed in various ways, the most common being single file or in a fan shape. Famous races are held in Alaska every year, such as the Canadian Dog Derby; the All-Alaska Sweepstakes held at Fairbanks, a 5-day, 420-mile test of speed, stamina, and weight-pulling ability; and the World Championship Sled Dog Race in Anchorage, which has taken place without interruption since 1936, a 3-day event in heats over a 12-mile track. The New England Sled Dog Club also sponsors races in Lake Placid, New York, and in New Hampshire.

Sled dogs have rendered vital services to Arctic exploration. There is fascinating literature on the subject which is bound to inspire immense respect for the courage and devotion of these northern breeds. Even today, explorers utilize sled dogs in areas where it is impossible to land a plane. The Siberian Husky is generally considered to be most expert and reliable on an Arctic expedition.

MOUNTAIN RESCUE

In other snowbound regions of the world, dogs have won renown for their skill and bravery in discovering and rescuing lost and injured persons.

The rescue exploits of the St. Bernard are legendary. In fact, there may be more legend than truth in some of the accounts of his deeds since A.D. 962, when the Great St. Bernard Hospice was founded in Switzerland. His original job was to guide the monks through the St. Bernard Pass, situated between Switzerland and Italy at an altitude of 8,000 feet, and snowbound most of the year, rather than to rescue fallen skiers and lost mountain climbers. But it is a fact that many persons owe their lives to these remarkably altruistic dogs.

The most famous of them all, Barry, was responsible for saving 40 persons until he was killed by the forty-first, who mistook his offer of aid for

Sled dogs are still indispensable as a means of transport in snowbound areas of the world. This team of Huskies is bringing a sledge loaded with equipment down Ross Barrier to the Bay of Whales during one of Admiral Byrd's Antarctic expeditions. (*FPG*)

an attack. Nor is it merely legend that these dogs are able to scent a human being buried under many inches of snow, release him from his prison, and warm his frozen body by lying on top of him and licking his face. Dog owners have reported that their pet St. Bernards have done this when playing with children in the snow.

Nowadays, German Shepherds are used for Alpine rescue work as much as St. Bernards. They are trained to disregard all people except those in a prone position, and to report them to their handler, who then attaches a harness to the dog and is led to the injured person. They are also trained to work in pairs.

GUIDE DOGS FOR THE BLIND

Without minimizing the rescue work of these valiant saviors, the modern "saints" of dogdom are certainly the GUIDE DOGS FOR THE BLIND.

The idea of training dogs to guide the blind originated in Germany during World War I in order to aid wounded veterans. The project captured the interest of an American expatriate living in Switzerland, Mrs. Dorothy Harrison Eustis of Philadelphia, who owned a kennel of German Shepherds. She started by establishing a school in Vevey; then, in 1929, the first American Seeing Eye training center, in Nashville, Tennessee, which was moved 2 years later to Morristown, New Jersey, its present headquarters. There are now a number of other training centers for guide dogs for the blind, including the Master Eye Foundation in Minneapolis; International Guiding Eyes in North Hollywood; Leader Dogs for the Blind in Rochester, Michigan; Guiding Eyes for the Blind in Yorktown Heights, New York; Guide Dogs for the Blind in San Rafael, California; and Second Sight Guide Dogs in Forest Hills, New York. But only the Seeing Eye Foundation-trained dogs can be described as "Seeing Eye Dogs."

All of these organizations follow the Seeing Eye methods, however— first of all, in selecting the dogs. Only spayed bitches and castrated males are used, since they are less easily distracted from the task, less liable to quarrel with other dogs, and seem to have a greater sense of responsibility, in addition to the obvious advantage of eliminating sexual adventures and inconveniences. The majority are German Shepherds, although other breeds have been trained successfully too: Border Collies (who possess great intelligence and initiative, but whose movement is too quick for most blind people); Collies (of whom the same is true); Keeshonds (who are too small for most blind owners and require too much grooming); Boxers (who are often too phlegmatic); Labrador Retrievers (who, like most Gun dogs, often lack sufficient initiative for the work); and Doberman Pinschers (but only from lines that are not aggressive).

The Seeing Eye runs its own breeding farm for German Shepherds and Labradors, and also, like the other associations, accepts donated dogs. Puppies are often farmed out to foster homes until they are ready for training at the age of 14 to 18 months. The 4-H Clubs also have a program for raising future Guide Dogs. It takes 3 or 4 months to train the dog, then one month more to train the dog and the blind person as a team at the training center. The dogs are taught to obey commands such as "right," "left," and "forward," but also to disobey commands that could lead to danger. Incidentally, during their training the only reward used is verbal praise in the form of "That's a good girl (or boy)!"

Guide dogs are given to their blind owners or sold for a token price that represents only a fraction of their value, and for this reason contributions are vital to these charitable organizations as they attempt to satisfy a demand that is relatively limited but that still exceeds the supply.

When you meet a blind person with a Guide dog, do not let your own dog sniff or distract him, or try to play with him. He may be terribly tempted, but he has a job to do. How many people do you know who would be capable of displaying such abnegation? Would you?

Inspired by the success of Guide Dogs for the Blind, the American Humane Society, in collaboration with the National Association for the Deaf, has recently started a program of training dogs as "Hearing Ears." The training center is at AHA headquarters in Golden, Colorado, and various breeds of dogs are being tried in these first experiments, mostly animals recovered from Humane Society shelters. The initial results are most encouraging.

ENTERTAINMENT

Dogs have contributed to the entertainment of humanity from the time they first wagged their way into our ancestors' caves.

The *theater* has assigned roles to dogs in pageants and plays since the days of the Ancient Greeks, and in later eras even in *operas* and *ballets*. Performing dogs have starred in *circuses* and *fairs* for centuries as acrobats, comedians, even as mind-readers and mathematicians. More recently, they have won fame and fortune as movie stars, television personalities, and nightclub attractions.

Some of these canine performers have become international celebrities, like Strongheart and Rin-Tin-Tin, the German Shepherd movie heroes of the twenties; Lassie, the valiant Collie (who was really three different dogs, owned and trained by Rudd Weatherwax); Asta, the Wire-haired Fox Terrier of *The Thin Man* film series (who was also trained by Weatherwax); Meatball, the white Bull Terrier television star who is, in private life, an expert tracker, often called upon by the Los Angeles

Police and by the Federal Aviation Administration; not to forget Nipper, the Smooth-haired Fox Terrier who became the trademark of "His Master's Voice."

Canine film acting is very much like that of their human co-stars. They have agents to negotiate their contracts, coaches (usually their owner-handler) to work with them at home on the difficult scenes that need rehearsal, and stand-ins. They are required to appear on the set on time, in good form, and to follow the instructions of the director. As with human stars, physical beauty is less important than personality. Histrionic ability can be contrived to a certain extent in the cutting room. Type-casting exists with dogs as it does with human actors and has followed the same trend. Handsome males, who used to be the heroes, are now more often villains, while the homely but appealing personality is given the sympathetic role. Canine film actors are sometimes required to perform scenes for which a human movie star would need a stunt man. This is one reason it is a specialized profession, open mainly to dogs belonging to professional animal trainers.

Circus dogs also owe their career to their owners' training ability, although they must collaborate with all their skill and wits. They lead a very special life and seem to enjoy it immensely, as you can see for yourself if you ever have the chance to visit behind the scenes of circus life.

Among the most famous and clever animal trainers in the world are certainly the Popovs of the Moscow Circus, who train dogs to perform entire playlets unaided. In one of their most amusing numbers, an entire troupe of dogs enacts the drama of a burning house. To the sound of sirens and the desperate cries of the four-footed inhabitants trapped upstairs, the canine fire brigade arrives, the fire wagon drawn by a trained pig. At breakneck speed, each dog proceeds to do his duty: one unrolls the fire hose, another pumps water, another sets up the fire ladder, while another rescues the inhabitants and saves their belongings, not forgetting the laundry that is hanging on the line. Their mission accomplished without the slightest human prompting, the proud firemen remove the ladder, roll up the hose, pile the rescued victims into the wagon, and triumphantly leave the circus ring to deafening applause.

MODELING

Next to babies, dogs have proven to be the best salesmen in the world, and so are often featured in television and magazine advertisments.

Commercial photographers and television casting directors seldom deal directly with dog owners, but through established animal talent agencies (among the most famous of which is Animal Talent Scouts, 331 West Eighteenth Street, New York City, which is owned and managed by Patricia Poleski). In order to be accepted for listing in an agency's files, a dog must meet certain requirements, including Obedience training at least to the C.D. level. He must also, of course, be photogenic, which excludes all-black dogs, who are practically impossible to light and photograph. A purebred dog should be an excellent example of his breed, but appealing mutts are also in demand. Beagles and Cocker Spaniels are always popular with advertisers, since so many dog owners can personally "relate" to them, as is not the case of rare breeds of strange appearance, which few people can even recognize as dogs.

There is no canine model's union and no established rate of pay, each job being negotiated on a flat fee basis, out of which a commission is paid to the agency. You should not expect to make a fortune from managing your dog's modeling career. Neither should you let your ambition for him lead you to become the victim of unscrupulous photographers and so-called animal talent agencies which demand costly listing fees or expensive sets of photographs in return for modeling and television assignments that never materialize. Legitimate agencies never demand a listing fee. While they are highly selective of the dogs and owners they accept, they are also constantly in search of new talent, as appealing puppies become gawky adolescents, and adult dogs, alas, age far too quickly.

Although there are, as you can see, quite a few canine career opportunities, very few dogs are capable of earning their own beefsteak.

However, all dogs, even modern pet dogs if they are normal and healthy, dislike idleness. They would much rather be active, preferably in collaboration with their owners. If you don't believe this, just try assigning a few simple daily tasks to your dog. (If you haven't done so already, he has probably invented chores of his own.) Encourage him to warn you when visitors approach, and then to greet them amiably; to keep your home free from rats, mice, and other unwelcome intruders; to bring you the newspaper as soon as the delivery boy has tossed it on the front lawn; to let you know when the postman passes; to guard the house during your absence. He will accept these responsibilities with enthusiasm, fulfill them with pride. He may even become less restless, more alert and self-confident, simply because he has the satisfying feeling that he is doing a useful job.

26.

Canine Hobbies and Collections

When you have a dog in your life, it is surprising how often other interests and activities will relate to your canine ones. Whatever your profession, whatever your present or previous hobbies, your interest in dogs will open up new vistas. You may also be surprised to find that you still have time for a hobby, after all of the walking, feeding, grooming, and training sessions with your dog. But you will.

BREEDING, TRAINING, AND RESEARCH

Many dog owners are irresistibly drawn into certain areas of research or recreation. Active hunters, for example, often develop an absorbing interest in *breeding or training,* since the results of both are so evident in their field work. Show dog owners, particularly of breeds that are prized above all for esthetic attributes, cannot fail to become intrigued by *the science of genetics,* and especially by the genetic transmission of qualities such as color and details of conformation.

You do not have to be a professional psychiatrist to take an interest in *the study of animal behavior.* Ethology, as it is called, provides clues to the more complicated mysteries of human behavior, and nobody can deny that an understanding of psychology is an asset in many professions as well as in daily life. Even amateur research, if conducted properly, can contribute to our growing fund of knowledge in this relatively new science. Simple observation, carefully and consistently recorded, provided the foundation for the Nobel Prize-winning work of Dr. Konrad Lorenz, one of the outstanding pioneers in this field. Many psychological studies are more valid when undertaken in a natural environment than in a laboratory, which means that amateur researchers are not necessarily handicapped. If the subject interests you, you should start by reading all of the available pertinent literature, which is fascinating. You might then select for study some specific aspect of canine behavior, such as "Seniority Among Animals of the Same Species" (or of different species, if you have a household full of different pets to observe) or "The Social Relationship Between the Young and the Aged"; or "Canine Courtship Rituals"; or "The Comparative Behavior of Adolescents, Human and Canine." These are only random ideas. The possibilities are endless.

DRAWING, PAINTING, AND SCULPTURE

Dog owners whose gifts are artistic rather than scientific are apt to reach for a sketchbook rather than a notebook as they observe their pets. The dog's incredible range of facial and body expressions has provided inspiration for drawing, painting, and sculpture during thousands of years. In fact, many of our suppositions about the early history of the dog are based on pictorial records.

The very first representations of dogs appeared in prehistoric cave paintings and drawings—although, to tell the truth, it takes a certain amount of imagination to recognize some of these four-legged creatures as dogs. You can also see them on Egyptian, Assyrian, and Babylonian tablets, in Egyptian tomb paintings and sculpture, in Oriental and Mayan religious art. The ancient Greeks and Romans portrayed a variety of canine types on vases, friezes, mosaics, and coins.

Among the earliest examples of dogs in European art are the war dogs in the Bayeux Tapestry which Queen Matilda, wife of William the Conqueror, is reputed to have embroidered while her illustrious spouse was away at war; the recognizable Whippets and Bichons in the exquisite tapestry of "The Lady and the Unicorn"; and the boar-hunting dogs in the illuminated manuscript "Les Très Riches Heures du Duc de Berry." Dogs also figured frequently in medieval heraldic coats of arms, in wood carvings on furniture, and in stone carvings and stained-glass windows as architectural decoration.

Many great masters of the Italian Renaissance painted dogs. Among the earliest were the Sheepdogs and Hounds in religious paintings, such as the rather naive works of Giotto (1266–1336), and the "Adoration of

the Magi" by Filippo Lippi (1406–69). One of the first portraits of a dog
was the work of a master animal painter, Vittore Pisanello (1380–1456).
Judging from its appearance, it must also have been one of the first dogs
to sport a Poodle clip.

The great painters of the Venetian school, including Titian
(1477–1576) and Tintoretto (1518–94), portrayed dogs in mythological
and allegorical scenes as well as in portraits of their masters. Jacopo Bas-
sano (1510–92) used a little Spaniel as his signature in many of his
religious and genre paintings. Paolo Veronese (1528–88), the favorite
portrait painter of the Venetian aristocracy, often included the pet dog of
his illustrious clients in their portraits, including some beautifully ren-
dered Salukis, Italian Greyhounds, and Toy Spaniels. A later Venetian
artist, Tiepolo (1696–1770), most renowned for his Baroque frescoes
lavishly adorned with clouds and cupids, did a painting of performing
dogs.

If you ever have the chance to visit the Prado Museum in Madrid, you
can see the original paintings of many familiar Spanish masterworks and

Stained-glass window of "Tobias and Sara." (Obviously, neither bedroom slippers nor
canine sleeping habits have changed much since this work was created in the
Twelfth-century.) (*Courtesy of the Victoria and Albert Museum*)

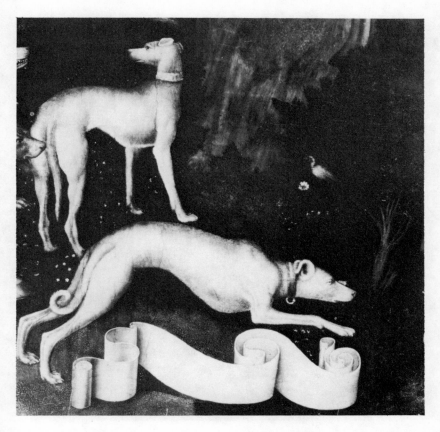

A detail from a painting of "The Legend of St. Hubert," the patron saint of hunters, by Pisanello (1380–1456). (*Courtesy of the National Gallery*)

many different types of dogs: the Sheepdogs in early religious paintings; the Spaniels and Terriers of Murillo (1617–82); the Mastiffs, Great Danes, King Charles Spaniels, and a Hunting dog rather resembling a Labrador in a number of the royal portraits by Velasquez (1599–1660).

In northern Europe at the same time, Van Dyck (1599–1641), the Flemish master, was painting portraits at the English court, many of which depict a dog in some royal lap or at some noble feet. Peter Paul Rubens (1577–1640) excelled in painting dogs as well as corpulent ladies and dramatic battle scenes. His canvas of "Diana and Her Nymphs" portrays the hunting goddess surrounded by the entire hunting pack of the Archduchess Elizabeth, each dog bearing an individual expression and personality.

Portrait of "Miss Bowles" by Sir Joshua Reynolds (1723-92). (*Courtesy of the Wallace Collection*)

While royal pets were generally Hunting dogs, huge Mastiffs, or small Spaniels, the so-called "genre" painters portrayed many other breeds of dogs as well as mongrels in their scenes of village and country life. Griffon Terriers can be distinguished in early Flemish, Dutch, and German paintings, including those of Dürer, Holbein, Memling, and Cranach. Jan Steen painted a clipped Poodle. In works by Kuyp and Brouwers there are Schipperkes, and in those of other northern artists one can see Dachshund-like Terriers, Pugs, Spaniels, Pomeranians, coursing Greyhounds, and Retrievers. All of these paintings showed dogs taking part in daily village life, working, playing, eating, even relieving themselves.

When pictorial art began to flourish in England in the seventeenth century, the dog was a favorite model, either as an accessory to the principal subject, or as the principal subject himself. Francis Barlow (1626–1765), the father of British sporting painting, best known for his marvelous pictures of birds, also painted dogs, particularly the Hound breeds. John Wooton (1678–1765) excelled in equestrian portraiture, but he too sometimes selected dogs as subjects, particularly Salukis. Sir Joshua Reynolds (1723–92) included pet dogs in many of his portraits of fashionable ladies, among them a black Cocker Spaniel and a Maltese Terrier. Some of the most famous society portraits of Thomas Gainsborough (1727–88) show lovely Setters, Collies, and Pomeranians. George Romney and Sir Thomas Lawrence were also highly skilled in painting beautiful women accompanied by charming dogs.

Other English artists, no less renowned, painted ordinary people and ordinary dogs in typical poses and natural settings. Hogarth (1697–1764) expressed his earthy sense of humor by showing two dogs in the process of mating in a corner of his famous satirical work "Marriage à la Mode." In his self-portrait, he is accompanied by his adored mongrel "Trump." Thomas Rowlandson (1736–1827) also portrayed many mongrels in his caricatural drawings.

The eighteenth century and the first half of the nineteenth was the Golden Age of sporting art in England. Most of the great sporting painters specialized in coaching, hunting, and racing scenes and in equestrian portraits, but many of them also painted dogs. You will find

"A Hound and Bitch" by George Stubbs (1724–1806). (*Courtesy of the Tate Gallery*)

Painting of a Newfoundland by Sir Edwin Landseer, entitled "A Distinguished Member of the Humane Society." (*Courtesy of the Tate Gallery*)

excellent canine portraits in the sporting paintings of George Stubbs (the master of them all), of Gilpin, George Seymour, Sartorius, Ben Marshall, Ferneley, Henry Alken, and Herring (who did a famous portrait of a Greyhound, and another of a Bulldog). Sir Edwin Landseer (1802–73) was so fond of painting Newfoundlands and was so prolific in his production that a black-and-white Newfoundland has been called a "Landseer" ever since. He was also the most sentimental of the canine painters, dressing his dogs as human beings, placing them in pathetic situations, and giving descriptive titles to his works, such as "A Distinguished Member of the Humane Society" (a Newfoundland), "The Larder Invaded," "The Old Shepherd's Chief Mourner," "There Is Life in the Old Dog Yet," and "A Random Shot," over which many a Victorian tear must have been shed.

In France, one of the first great animal painters was Alexandre-François Desportes (1661–1743), who has left masterful canine portraits of

"Dog and Pheasants" by Jean-Baptiste Oudry (1686–1755). (*Courtesy of the Wallace Collection*)

hunting dogs and of entire hunting packs. Some of his most impressive works are the life-size portraits of Louis XIV's favorite hunting Hounds designed as wall panels for the royal château at Marly. Jean-Baptiste Oudry (1686–1755) is another French name which every art-minded dog fancier should know. Artistic director of the royal Beauvais tapestry works, he was also an outstanding animal painter, particularly of hunting dogs. The still-life paintings of Chardin (1668–1755) sometimes included Hunting dogs too. Later French animal painters, such as Carle Vernet (1758–1836) and Alfred de Dreux (1810–60), worked more in the British style. Both of them produced fox-hunting scenes of the same fine technical and artistic quality as those of their English contemporaries.

After the French Impressionists arrived to revolutionize the entire art world, animal portraiture, like the human kind, became somewhat outmoded. The dog was not entirely forgotten, since Gauguin, Toulouse-Lautrec, Renoir, Bonnard, Le Douanier Rousseau, and others painted dogs. But each artist painted them in his own style, and few of them were concerned with achieving the realistic, detailed perfection of preceding figure painters.

The Victorian Era saw a revival of sporting painting and animal portraiture, typified by the realistic Sheepdogs in the pastoral scenes of Rosa Bonheur (1822–99), the lifelike Whippets of Augustus Edwin John (1878–1961), and the works of Francis Barraud (1856–1924), whose painting of a Fox Terrier entitled "His Master's Voice" became a world-famous commercial trademark. On the American side of the Atlantic, superior canine art was being produced by John Sargeant Noble (1848–96), Arthur Wardle, Gilman Low, and Martin T. Ward. Other prestigious signatures are those of Emms, Duke, Binks, Daws, and German-born Muss-Arnolt (the only fine artist who was also a licensed dog show judge).

Although a few more recent artists have specialized in painting dogs—such as Marguerite and Persis Kirmse, Enno Meyer, Edwin Megargee, and Morgan Dennis—most modern painters seem to have neglected them, perhaps because they have become an increasingly popular subject with illustrators. Many fine artists famous for their dog pictures also illustrated books: Cecil Aldin, whose drawings, prints, and books are highly prized (*The Cecil Aldin Book, Dog Days, Dogs of Character, Sleeping Partners, Just Among Friends, Ten Little Puppy Dogs,* and many others); Lucy Dawson (*Dogs as I See Them, Dogs Rough and Smooth, Neighbors,* and *Lucy Dawson's Dog Book*); Diana Thorne (*Your Dogs and Mine, Dogs, Paintings and Stories, Drawing Dogs, Puppies, Paintings*); and those too numerous to detail of Maud Earl and of her father, George Earl.

On a more popular level, modern cartoonists seem to be particularly enamored of dogs. Even though you may not consider it art with a capital *A,* you must admit that Walt Disney, James Thurber, Eric Gurney, Charles Schultz (who invented Snoopy), even Harold Gray (who created Orphan Annie's faithful Sandy), have drawn dogs with great humor, understanding, and skilled draftsmanship.

What does a capsule history of the dog in art have to do with modern dog owners and their hobbies? Everyone knows that only richly endowed museums can afford to buy fine paintings nowadays, on the rare occasions when one appears for sale or auction. Even anonymous, minor works are priced for millionaires (unless, it seems, they contain cows, which tend to have a devaluating effect). However, photographic reproductions exist and can usually be purchased from the museums or art galleries that house the original works. If not, you may be permitted to take your own photographs of those that interest you. If you are excited only by originals, why not try to collect drawings and paintings of dog cartoons and illustrations for magazines and books? This field has not yet been exploited by art dealers, and who knows? Some of today's commercial artists may be tomorrow's masters. It has happened in the past.

In any case, if you pay them a visit, you will find that museums and art galleries are not the exclusive domain of schoolchildren and esthetes, but treasure houses of fascinating material, even for dog lovers.

PHOTOGRAPHY

Dogs have provided a challenge and an inspiration to great photographers, such as Ylla and Chandoha, as they have to famous artists.

Anybody who possesses a photogenic dog, a simple, reliable camera, a sharp eye, and a quick finger on the shutter button, can produce good candid dog pictures. A dog owner may even have an advantage over a professional photographer, because he knows how to persuade his pet to hold a pose and how to elicit his most amusing or attractive expression.

Action photographs require a fast lens and fast film. The super cameras for action shots are the Robot and its successors, which take a series of rapid exposures during movement, such as jumping, running, or performing tricks.

Closeups are more difficult because care must be taken to avoid distortion of the dog's features, especially with long-nosed breeds which it is best to photograph from a distance with a telephoto lens. In order to avoid body distortion, you must get down to the dog's level, whatever it may be—or raise him up to yours. If you have a helper who can hold your dog on a nylon show lead while you pose him, you will have a better, steadier pose for a formal portrait, and the lead can easily be removed from the final print.

Needless to say, you should photograph your dog when he is at his best, after you have groomed him, cleaned his eyes, nose, and mouth, trimmed stray hairs around his muzzle and ears, and tidied his paws. You might even, show-style, snip off his whiskers (unless he is a Terrier).

The best dog photographs are taken out of doors in natural lighting, since flash bulbs are reflected in the eyes and give an eerie look that alters the expression. Natural backgrounds are also most attractive for animal shots. Keep it uncluttered if your dog has a spotted or particolored coat. Choose a dark background if he is pale-colored, and a light one if he is dark-coated. Green lawns, blue skies, fields and forests provide flattering settings for most dogs. The scale of the background is important too. Try to avoid too wide a divergence between the background and the size of your dog, unless you are seeking some special effect. For example, it is more effective to pose a small dog with children or small objects, or to hold him in your arms, than to snap him standing insignificantly next to a tall adult or beside the family car.

It can be fun to take contrived pictures of your dog, if you select a moment when he is relaxed and anxious to please you. Dogs with other animals, dogs with children, dogs in human situations are popular subjects

A fine portrait. (*William P. Gilbert*)

with unlimited variations. You can pose a puppy in an unusual container or introduce him to some strange object and try to capture his reaction on film. One of the most difficult pictures of all to take successfully is a pretty girl with a beautiful dog. Seldom are both of them at their best at the same instant. You usually have to choose between flattering (or offending) one or the other.

There are many books, brochures, and articles in dog and photography magazines that deal with the technical details of animal photography which is considered a specialty in the profession. Camera manufac-

turers, magazines, and commercial enterprises of various kinds regularly
announce photography contests. Although nudity has edged out dogs
and babies as the favorite subject of calendar and advertising art, a re-
ally good dog photograph is always in demand. Your canine hobby may
even turn out to be an unexpected source of income.

PHOTO COLLECTIONS

If you are untalented or distinterested in taking pictures of your own,
you might enjoy collecting photographs by others. You can clip them
from magazines and newspapers, buy them from photo agencies and
news services and, now that photocopying machines are installed in most
public libraries, you can make your own copies of curious old photo-
graphs in dog books and encyclopedias. You can also buy reproductions
and slides from museums and art galleries.

Your photo collection will be more interesting if it expresses a theme:
a single breed and its evolution; or simply beautiful, humorous, or dra-
matic dog pictures. If you are a *theater* fan, the subject of "Theatrical
Dogs" could lead to interesting research in collecting pictures of per-
forming dogs in the circus, theater, movies, and television, perhaps of
dogs belonging to famous actors and actresses.

If *history* is more your field, you might fill an album with photographs
or reproductions of paintings depicting famous historical personages
with their dogs. Many great statesmen, including Bismarck and Glad-
stone, were practically inseparable from beloved pets. In earlier eras,
Alexander the Great named a city "Perites" after his favorite dog, and
Plutarch described how the Emperor Vespasian taught his dog Zoppicus
to "play dead" and come to life again, to his great amusement.

European royalty has always been associated with dogs. For instance,
there was King Charles II of England and the Spaniel variety that bears
his name; William and Mary and the Pugs they brought from Holland
when they assumed the throne of England (and acquired Spaniels);
Queen Alexandra and her Dalmatians and Collies; Queen Victoria and
her pet Pomeranian; Queen Elizabeth II and her Welsh Pembroke Corgis
and less publicized Labradors; the Duke and Duchess of Windsor and
their Pugs (but it was a faithful Cairn Terrier bitch who accompanied
the Duke into exile after his abdication from the British throne). Em-
press Josephine also owned a Pug, called "Fortune," who slept at the foot
of the imperial bed even on her wedding night with Napoleon (which
may be why he preferred his Poodle named "Mustache").

From the English Foxhounds of George Washington (his favorites were "Tippler," "Mopsey," and "Sweetlips"), to the mongrel pets of the Carter family, many American Presidents have kept dogs in the White House—providing another theme for a canine photo album.

Thomas Jefferson owned Sheepdogs, and Samuel Adams a Newfoundland. Calvin Coolidge owned no less than 12 dogs in addition to a donkey, a bobcat, a series of lion cubs, and a pigmy hippopotamus. (But his Wire-haired Fox Terrier, "Peter Pan," was exiled from the White House for nipping distinguished visitors.)

Herbert Hoover fancied large breeds, particularly his German Shepherd, "King Tut," and his English Setter, "Eaglehurst Gilette." President Roosevelt's famous Scottish Terrier, "Fala," probably heard more state secrets than any contemporary dog—including Mrs. Roosevelt's two Pekingese.

President Eisenhower was given a Weimaraner whom he named "Heidi," and Margaret Truman romped on the White House lawn with her Irish Setter, "Mike." The Kennedy family was always surrounded by four-footed friends, including the President's personal pet, a Welsh Terrier called "Charley." Lyndon Johnson outraged dog lovers when he picked up his pair of Beagles by the ears. (Incidentally, both of them died prematurely: "Him" by being run over by a car in the White House driveway, and "Her" as the result of swallowing a stone.) Although Richard Nixon's most famous pet was a Cocker Spaniel, he also kept in the White House a Yorkshire Terrier, a Miniature Poodle, and an Irish Setter. During his brief presidency, Gerald Ford owned two Golden Retrievers—"Misty" and her mother, "Liberty." These were succeeded by Amy Carter's Springer Spaniel-type mongrel called "Grits," and another mixed breed dubbed "Jet Black" (or "J.B." for short).

It seems, in fact, that a dog has become an indispensable political accessory for a presidential candidate nowadays, although no study has been made of the role dogs play in political campaigns. Do you suppose that Johnson's Beagles attracted more votes than Goldwater's Bloodhound? Be this as it may, you could probably fill a very thick album with pictures of "Dogs in American Politics."

Is your field ADVERTISING OR SALES? With no offense meant, dogs have probably sold more products than you could ever dream of doing. A scrapbook of advertisements featuring dogs could make an amusing and original canine collection requiring more ingenuity than investment.

If you are a devout person, you do not need to be told that dogs have figured in the RELIGION of many cultures, although less in Christianity than in many others. Canine demigods were respected and sometimes worshiped by the Mayan Indians, the ancient Egyptians, Greeks, and Romans, and are still revered by many oriental cults, including Buddhism. Even in Christianity, St. Anthony's blessing of dogs is a part of Catholic ritual, and St. Francis of Assisi is the most famous, but only one, of many saints who loved and owned dogs. St. Hubert was the first patron saint of dogs, and St. Roch is never depicted without his faithful canine companion. You should have no trouble finding material for an album of interesting texts and pictures illustrating the theme of "Dogs and Religion."

Any of these projects, or others you invent yourself, can give you many hours of pleasure and result in a unique collection, perhaps interesting enough to provide an evening's entertainment for your local kennel club.

HANDCRAFTS

If you are good at handcrafts and you own a suitable breed, you can carefully gather your dog's shed hair and combings, spin it into yarn, and make either knitted garments or woven cloth from it. Pekingese hair has been considered a luxury fabric for centuries in Asia, rather like vicuña, which it resembles. Keeshond and Collie hair furnish a yarn that is somewhat like cashmere. Poodle and Old English Sheepdog hair can also be spun and woven successfully. But the best dog hair of all for this purpose is said to be that of the Samoyed, which is soft and luxurious, dyes well, and will not shrink.

STAMP AND COIN COLLECTING

If you have *a stamp or coin collection,* you know that dogs have been depicted on coins since antiquity, and occasionally on postage stamps. The first American stamp to feature a dog was issued in 1959 in commemoration of Admiral Peary's conquest of the North Pole half a century earlier. Czechoslovakia has a set of dog stamps with head and body profiles of several breeds, including a Cocker Spaniel, a Dachshund, an Irish Setter, and a short-haired German Pointer. Romania issues head studies of an English Setter, Cocker Spaniel, Poodle, German Shepherd, Bulldog, and a Wire-haired Fox Terrier. The Principality of Monaco honors a different breed each year, while Yugoslavia pays tribute postally to its native breeds, including the Dalmatian. If you own a dog but haven't yet thought of collecting stamps or coins, one of these classic hobbies (which are also, it seems, good investments) might be a pleasant way to spend your idle hours, rainy days, and pocket money.

ART OBJECTS

Collecting figurines of dogs in metal, wood, or ceramics is less rewarding, because so few modern ones are attractive. Have you ever seen a pottery dog that really conformed to the official standard of his breed? The best porcelain is probably old Staffordshire, if you can find it; Royal Doulton, at least 10 years old; and old Royal Copenhagen. The most impressive signature on postwar American porcelain is "Boehm," but this too is scarce and expensive.

There have been great animal sculptors in the past, starting with the anonymous ancient Egyptians, Greeks, and Romans, and including the Florentine master Benvenuto Cellini (1500–71); the Frenchman Antoine-Louis Barye (1796–1875), who sculpted wild as well as domesticated animals; Bonheur, Fratin, Meme, and the late American sculptor Herbert Haseltine, who specialized in horses. But all of their works have become museum pieces.

MUSIC

It may surprise you to learn that dogs and music are not worlds apart. Dogs have served as companions, but also as inspiration for some of the world's great composers. Some works are dedicated to dogs; others use dogs as a theme, sometimes even incorporating barking sounds into the music. A musical dog lover could have great fun creating a canine record or tape collection, although he would probably have to record some of these works himself. As a start, he could try to find recorded performances of:

—Vivaldi's *Spring Concerto* (The second movement is a musical description of a shepherd with his dogs.)

—Banchieri's *Contrapunto Bestiale* (a fifteenth-century madrigal that is full of "Bow-wows")

—César Franck's *Le Chasseur Maudit* (a musical version of the St. Hubert hunting-dog legend)

—Chopin's *Waltz in D Flat* (inspired by a dog chasing his tail)

—Eric Satie's piano pieces entitled *Flasques pour un Chien*

—Elgar's *Enigma Variations* (one of which musically describes the dog "Dan" falling into the water)

—Mozart's *German Dances* (which are dedicated to his dog, "Goukerl")

—Gluck's opera *Orpheus and Eurydice* (In the Furies Scene of Act II, there is a role for the dog Cerberus.)

—Schubert's *Im Dorfe* (a musical piece describing watchdogs)

—Haydn's round on the theme of "Old Dog Tray"

—Purcell's song "I'll Sail Upon the Dog Star"

—John Alden Carpenter's *Adventures in a Perambulator* (The Fifth movement is entitled "Dogs.")

—Haydn's Oratorio *The Seasons* (The bass aria in the Autumn movement mentions Spaniels barking at night.)

—Many Elizabethan rounds and songs include barking dogs among the street cries.

COLLECTING BOOKS

A dog owner can hardly avoid collecting books, if only a few essential reference books. Why not go a step further and add a second shelf of fiction, and perhaps a third of collector's items?

It should be simple enough to buy the *reference books* you need from your local bookstore or by mail order. Every dog owner should possess:

1) *The Complete Dog Book,* (Howell) which includes the official American Kennel Club standard for every recognized breed.

2) A comprehensive book on canine health care, written by a competent veterinarian, such as:

> *The Complete Book of Dog Care* (Doubleday) by Leon F. Whitney, DVM
>
> *Your Dog, His Health and Happiness* (Arco) by Louis L. Vine, DVM
>
> *The Well Dog Book* (Random House) by Terri McGinnis, DVM

3) A book devoted to your dog's breed. The *Complete Dog,* the *Popular Dog,* and *This is The . . .* series all publish volumes, written by experts, on most of the leading breeds. Howell Book House (730 Fifth Avenue, New York, New York 10019), the leading publisher of dog books in the United States, lists in its catalogue books on almost every breed.

You may also want to acquire practical works dealing with some field of canine activity that particularly interests you, such as hunting, show-ing, grooming, obedience training, or breeding. Excellent books exist, and more are continually being published.

You will have no trouble filling your *fiction* shelf either, because dogs have figured in literature throughout the ages and throughout the world, frequently as incidental characters, occasionally as villains, and quite often as heroes and heroines—so often, in fact, that you may want to re-strict your collection to stories featuring a certain breed or type of dog, such as Hunting dogs, Sled dogs, Sheep dogs, or War dogs.

Dogs were often mentioned by Greek and Roman military historians and authors, some of whom had strange ideas about their origin. Xenophon, for example, seemed to think dogs were related to foxes, and Aristotle believed that hounds were a cross between a cat and a tiger.

Since then, many famous authors have loved dogs and written about them, including La Fontaine, Tolstoy, Sir Walter Scott (especially in *Guy Mannering*), Horace Walpole, Lord Byron, Charles Dickens (who preferred big dogs, and owned an Irish Wolfhound, a Bloodhound, a Newfoundland, and a St. Bernard), Émile Zola, Alexandre Dumas (*Black, The Story of a Dog*), George Sand, Anatole France, John Gals-worthy (*Memories,* the story of a Cocker Spaniel), Maurice Maeterlinck, Christopher Morley, Alfred Ollivant (*Bob, Son of Battle*), Virginia Woolf (*Flush,* the biography of Elizabeth Barrett Browning's Cocker Spaniel), and Rudyard Kipling.

Dogs are featured in many of the novels of Jack London, whose *The Call of the Wild* is still one of the best dog stories ever written. Among his many memorable canine heroes are the Irish Terriers in *Jerry of the Islands,* and *Michael, Brother of Jerry,* which describe their adventures among the cannibals of the Solomon Islands. Albert Payson Terhune's numerous books about Collies, such as *Lad, a Dog* and *The Way of a Dog,* did much to popularize the breed long before Lassie appeared on the screen.

A famous best-selling mystery writer, S. S. Van Dine, wrote a book called *The Kennel Murder Case.* Among contemporary authors who have been inspired by dogs are John Steinbeck (*Travels with Charley*), Jacqueline Susann (*Every Night, Josephine*), MacKinlay Kantor (*The Voice of Bugle Ann*), Gladys Taber (*Especially Dogs*), and many others.

You can look up these works and others in your public library, read them, and try to buy a copy of those you like. You will surely reread them with pleasure many times.

Collecting *rare books* on any subject has become a costly hobby, since merchandise is scarce and the competition for it is keen. The best source is one of the few canine rare-book dealers, such as Nigel Aubrey-Jones (4170 Decarie Boulevard, Montréal, Québec, Canada). With luck, you may occasionally run across a choice volume in a secondhand bookstore or at a book auction.

The first books about dogs were treatises on the art of hunting, which started to appear in the thirteenth century in France, Germany, Italy, and England, dealing with the selection, breeding, care, and training of hunting dogs of various types. As in equestrian literature, many of the precepts these early authors expounded are just as valid today.

In 1570, Dr. Caius, a famous British physician and anatomist, mentioned dogs in his medical studies. In 1576, John Kaye, the royal physician to Edward VI and Elizabeth I compiled a descriptive breed list, *De Canibus Anglicis,* which was later translated from the original Latin into English under the title *Of English Dogges.*

The first book dealing with dogs to be published in America was *The Sportsman's Companion* (1783). During the succeeding years, there has been a continual production of dog books, some of which have become classics because of their text, and others collector's items because of their superb illustrations by the leading artists of the day. Individual breed books began to appear around 1850.

Some of the most famous titles in this rare canine literature are:

The General Character of the Dog by Joseph Taylor (1807)

The Dog by Lamb (1836)

The Dog and the Sportsman by John Stuart Skinner (1845)

The Dog by William Youatt (1846)

Dogs, Their Origins and Varieties by H. D. Richardson

The Sportsman's Vade Mecum by Jonathan Peak ("Dinks") (1850)
—highly prized by Hunting dog fanciers

Dog-graphy by Francis Butler (1856)

The Dog by "Dinks" (1864)—a big, superbly illustrated American publication

The Dogs of the British Isles (1872), edited by Stonehenge and written by various contributors

Dogs, Their Points, Whims, Instincts, and Peculiarities by Henry Webb (1872)—one of the first dog books to include photographic illustrations rather than engravings

British Dogs by Hugh Dalziel

The American Book of the Dog (1891), edited by G. O. Shields

Twentieth-Century Dogs by Herbert Compton (1904), illustrated with photographs of winning show dogs of the day

The Dog Book by James Watson (1906)

Dogs of All Nations by Count Henry de Bylandt (1905)

The New Book of the Dog by Robert Leighton (1907), with color plates by outstanding artists, including Maud Earl, Arthur Wardle, and Vernon Stokes

Dogs, Their History and Development by Edward C. Ash (1927)

Hutchinson's Popular Dog Encyclopedia (1934)—three fascinating illustrated volumes, packed with information

The Book of the Dog (1948), edited by Brian Vesey-Fitzgerald

Needless to add, these works, if you can find them, are expensive, but they are of lasting, probably increasing value. For that matter, new dog books are expensive too, especially such lavish albums as *The Encyclopedia of the Dog* published by T. Y. Crowell, which contains detailed descriptions and marvelous color photographs of 308 purebreeds throughout the world. If you have more time than money, you may be able to find some of these more recent volumes at reduced prices in "remainder" or secondhand bookstores, or through a book club.

Perhaps you have time only for reading the morning newspaper. Does it occur to you to clip out the *news items* about dogs that interest or amuse you? It could become a hobby or collection too. You might concentrate on some aspect of canine behavior that particularly intrigues you, such as the homing instinct, extrasensory perception, lifesaving, or examples of humor and ingenuity in dogs. If you are alert to spot such reports, you will be amazed by how many you will collect—perhaps enough to entertain your kennel club another evening, or to provide material for a dog magazine article.

This is by no means an exhaustive survey of the ways in which your dog can help to broaden your horizons and enrich your leisure hours—when you are not grooming, training, walking, or playing with him. Remember, though, that no skill is mastered, and no collection created overnight. Research, persistence, and resourcefulness are more important than money in many of these canine hobbies. But even your dog would tell you, if he could, that the greatest fun is the pursuit.

27.

Another Dog of Your Own

The incomparable joy of having a dog of your own is marred by the fact that his lifespan is so much shorter than ours. Almost every dog owner experiences the tragedy of losing his beloved pet, by accident or illness, or simply because his dog has reached the end of his allotted days.

The inevitability of this painful occurrence has dissuaded many animal lovers from acquiring a dog. Others, once bereaved, swear, "Never again! The sorrow is too great." Most often, they find after a while that life without a dog is even more unbearable, and they renew the experience. To their astonishment, they soon become as emotionally involved with their new dog as they were with his adored predecessor, without the slightest feeling of disloyalty. They love each dog, perhaps for different reasons, but neither more nor less. Sometimes they may have the impression that they are selecting better, brighter dogs. But the truth is that they are simply becoming better owners.

Because our higher intellect enables us to philosophize, the discrepancy between our dogs' lifespan and our own may be less cruel than it seems. Human beings are able to cope with sorrow and to accept the inevitability of death (if not always the vicissitudes of life) more easily than dogs. It would be too distressing to recall instances when dogs who have survived beloved masters have literally died of grief. There have been many of them.

Some owners attempt to soften the blow of their inevitable loss by breeding their dog or bitch, and keeping one of the offspring. This is an excellent idea whenever practical. Perhaps the breeder of your dog can provide you with a puppy bred along the same lines who will bear a physical and temperamental resemblance to the dog you loved and lost. Another school of thought recommends selecting a successor from a different breed, but of the same group, in order to avoid comparisons as well as constant reminders of your previous pet. For example, instead of adopting another Scottish Terrier, you might get a West Highland White or a Cairn; instead of a second Cocker, you might consider an English Cocker, a Brittany, or a Springer Spaniel.

Owners of Hunting dogs often seek a successor to their field companion about 3 years before their present dog's normal retirement age, so that the puppy will be ready to take over the older dog's role when he is no longer up to it. This is also the custom among shepherds. Far from resenting the newcomer, the older dog usually takes pride and interest in training him. It is, after all, one of the traditions of animal wildlife.

When dealing with pet dogs, the situation may be more complicated. Most family dogs will accept the arrival of a puppy. They will even teach it good manners, housebreaking, and (undoubtedly with some self-interest) respect for elders. You can help by meticulously respecting the older dog's seniority too, laying down his food bowl first, giving him the first morning caress, the first and warmest greeting when you return home. The new puppy will not resent it. He knows instinctively that one day he will be promoted to Number One Dog, and he is perfectly willing to wait. This too is a law of Nature. On the other hand, many "one man" dogs and those who have established an intimate personal relationship with a single owner, can be terribly upset by the arrival of a new puppy in their master's life. It may take the form of jealous hostility toward the younger rival, or of self-pitying withdrawal. So you must consider very carefully the advisability of acquiring a successor to your faithful old dog during the latter's lifetime and take into account his individual character and his probable reaction to the change.

CARING FOR YOUR OLD DOG

In any event, you should realize that older dogs, like older people, are hypersensitive. As your pet ages, you should multiply reassuring gestures of affection. Take care to disturb as little as possible the normal pattern of his life. Never board an old dog if you can possibly avoid it, and only in a familiar environment. Do not hospitalize him either, unless it is absolutely impossible to care for him at home. Adhere to a rigid schedule of regular meals (less copious, because he is exercising less, and softer, because his teeth and digestive apparatus are not what they used to be), regular walks (slower and shorter, because he tires more quickly), perhaps an earlier bedtime and a softer bed. Never let an old dog sleep outdoors, even if he has done so all his life.

Old dogs need and merit greater patience, understanding, and protective measures as they become less alert, less resistant, and more vulnerable. Even if your dog has never been sick in his life, you should start taking him to the vet for regular checkups. The field of canine geriatrics has made immense strides in recent years. Your veterinarian now has the knowledge and the means to help your old dog live out his life free from pain and from most incapacitating dysfunctions.

The aches and ailments of old dogs are similar to those of human senior citizens. They include rheumatism and arthritis, diminished sight and hearing, constipation, loss of teeth, kidney and liver disorders, tumors, and heart trouble (particularly with overweight individuals). After a thorough examination, your veterinarian will prepare a health program for your aging dog, including an adjusted diet. Regular visits will permit him to treat insufficiencies before they develop into graver maladies.

Dogs learn to live with the infirmities of old age just as we do. They manage to cope with failing eyesight so well that many old dogs have become almost totally blind before their owners have suspected anything was wrong. As a matter of fact, a blind dog can get along quite well as long as he remains in familiar surroundings. His senses of hearing and smell seem to become even keener as his eyesight declines. Nevertheless, you should never take a blind dog out of doors unleashed. You should also remove any possibly dangerous objects from your home, and avoid shifting the furniture from its usual place.

Loss of hearing is probably a greater handicap, and also more upsetting to the dog. It is very unusual for a dog to lose his sense of smell. But loss of mobility may occur as a result of injury, disease, or degeneration; and this is most unfortunate, for it poses serious problems. To his owner, first of all, because of the practical complications involved in helping the dog to perform his natural functions. Immobilization also frequently leads to pneumonia or organic disorders. The dog suffers terribly, mentally and physically. In fact, this is one of the cases in which an old dog's infirmities may be of such a nature and pose such unsurmountable problems that his owner should muster the courage to discuss with his veterinarian the possibility of euthanasia.

LOSING YOUR DOG

Modern canine euthanasia is rapid and painless. It may consist of an overdose of anesthetic, or of a first injection to put the dog to sleep, and another that stops the heartbeat. Death follows swiftly and gently, in less than a minute. In hopeless circumstances, this is the only humane course of action. It would be sheer cruelty to refuse to release a dog from needless suffering, and stupid selfishness to refuse to face the fact that he is in agony and getting no pleasure out of life. Ask your vet for his professional opinion. But have the courage to make the final decision yourself.

Breaking the news to children is another painful responsibility. Child psychologists recommend telling the truth, as gently as possible, avoiding the old-fashioned euphemism of having the dog "put to sleep," which, it seems, can cause bedtime anxiety and make a child afraid of going to bed for fear that he will never wake up again. Whatever terms you use, do not lie to your children. They are bound to learn the truth one day, and it will be doubly upsetting because they will be hurt by your deception too.

Accepting the loss of loved ones is a very personal matter which each individual must face in his own way as best as he can. Advice is generally useless and importunate. Some inconsolable owners have built costly monuments to their dogs. The growing number of commercial dog cemetaries (over 500 at a recent count), which provides funeral ceremonies and marked graves for prices ranging from $100 to $200 and up, would seem to indicate that there is some solace in this form of extravagance. If you insist on spending a lot of money to honor the memory of your dog, why not consider making a donation in his name to a Humane Society, or to a fund for animal health research? Your deceased dog may even help to further veterinary science if you permit his body to be used for autopsy.

Country-living dog owners often arrange a canine burial plot in a corner of their garden, or bury a beloved dog on the spot that was his usual sentinel post, or from which he used to enjoy the view (although it is against the law in many places to bury an animal on residential property, even your own). City-dwellers, who haven't such possibilities, can turn to their veterinarian, municipal health authorities, and Humane Societies, which are equipped to dispose of the body, usually by cremation.

Do dogs rejoin their masters in some afterlife? Who knows? Christianity is one of the few religions to close the portals of Paradise to dogs, at least in official doctrine. Most dog lovers feel otherwise—including dog-loving ministers and priests. Dogs can certainly achieve immortality to the same extent that we do—through their descendants, in works of art and literature, and above all in human memory. One of the best ways to honor the dogs we have loved and outlived is to try to emulate some of the qualities they possess in such abundance and which so enrich and brighten our lives: honesty, fidelity, devotion, simplicity, spontaneity, a sense of fun and justice.

Lord Byron, the British romantic poet, came very close to expressing this thought when he composed the moving epitaph that is inscribed on a gravestone in the garden of his home at Newstead Abbey:

Near this spot
Are deposited the Remains of One
Who possessed Beauty without Vanity,
Strength without Insolence,
Courage without Ferocity,
And all the Virtues of Man without his Vices.
This Praise, which would be unmeaning Flattery
If inscribed over human ashes,
Is but a just Tribute to the Memory of
BOATSWAIN, a Dog,
Who was born at Newfoundland, May 1803
And died at Newstead Abbey, Nov. 18, 1808.

ANOTHER DOG OF YOUR OWN

The chances are that you too will one day lose a beloved pet. When your tears have dried, when time has dulled the pain, when coming home is not the same if there is no dog impatiently waiting behind the door to greet you, when your eyes avoid the spot where your dog's bed and food bowl used to be, and when you find that no human relationship gives you quite the same emotional satisfaction that your dog did—in short, when you realize that your life is not complete without a dog—you will get another.

If you take the trouble to select a really worthy successor and then give your new dog comfortable living conditions, sensible care, adequate exercise, and, above all, understanding, companionship, and love, it will be the finest tribute you can pay to the unforgettable friend who was the very first dog of your own.

Index

Spaying, 14, 326–27
Spinning dog hair, 519
Spitz, xx, 52
Splints, emergency, 203
Spoiled dogs, 300
Sporting dogs, 27–34
  drawbacks, 28
  ideal owner, 28
  virtues, 28
Spot cleaning, 156
Springer Bark, The, 487
Springer Spaniels, 9, 29, 86, 433,
    484, 526
  grooming, 168
Staffordshire Bull Terriers, 56
Stamps, dogs depicted on, 519–20
Stealing food, 299
Sterility, 14, 331
Stillborn puppies, 359
Stings, 221
Stray dogs, 81–82
Stripping, 164–65
Strongwilled owners, best breeds for,
    73
Stubbs, George, 511
Suburban dogs, 4, 268
Sussex Spaniels, 33
Sweaters, knitted, 184–85
Sweden, 400
Swelling up, 206–7
Swimming, 269–71
  grooming after, 156
Switzerland, 401

Tags
  identity, 178–79
  municipal, 179
  rabies vaccination, 382
Tail docking, 117, 173, 363–64
Tapeworms, 215
Tar removal, 149
Taste, sense of, 240–41
Tattoo registries, 419
Taxes, 410–11
Teen-agers, best breeds for, 6, 72
Television, 503–5
Temperament, 11–12, 74
Temperature taking, 197
Terriers, 3, 5, 8, 10, 27, 52–58, 84,
    403, 526
  bathing, 158

clipping, 165–68
collars for, 177
drawbacks, 52
grooming, 11, 168–69, 172
ideal owner, 52
sexual characteristics of, 14
stripping, 164–65
temperament of, 11, 87
traveling with, 381
trimming, 163
virtues, 52
See also types of Terriers
Territorial instinct, 253–55
Tes-Tape, 325
Theft of your dog, 417–20
Thirst, excessive, 211
Tibetan Spaniels, 69
Tibetan Terriers, 68, 86
Ticks, 153–54
Tie, the, in mating act, 328, 329
Ties, 183–84
Time, sense of, 242–43
"Tobias and Sara" (stained-glass
    window), 508
Tomarctus, xxii
Touch, sense of, 241–42
Touring with Towser, 383
Toy dogs, 3, 6, 27, 58–63, 94
  drawbacks, 58
  food requirements, 10
  ideal owner, 58
  temperament of, 12
  virtues, 58
  See also types of Toy dogs
Toy Manchester Terriers, 61
Toy Poodles, 5, 16, 59, 60, 63, 86
  deterioration of breeds, 459
  housebreaking and, 113
  temperamental qualities of, 87
Toys (for dogs), 263–65
Toy Terriers, 113
Tracking Dog (T.D.), 462, 463
Tracking tests, 476–77
Trainer, William, 457
Training, 276–307, 506–7
  basic commands, 282–90
  breeds difficult for, 74
  communications, 279
  conditions for, 279–80
  correcting vices, 293–306
  equipment for, 280–81

favorable ages for, 280
first night in new home, 110
housebreaking, 111–14
introducing oneself, 108
learning new name, 105–6, 111
learning word "no," 111
leash training, 114–15
praise and encouragement, 111
process of, 279–81
punishment during, 278–79
rewards during, 277
staying alone, 115–16
tips for, 281
tricks, 290–93
Training Your Retriever (Free), 490
Train travel, 388–90, 397
Tranquilizers, 396
Travel agents, pet, 388
Travel documents required, 382
Traveling, 310–12, 380–402
  documents required, 382
  foreign, 400–1
  hotels and motels, 398–99
  luggage required, 383
  meals during, 397
  preparation for trip, 383
  pros and cons, 401–2
  See also Airplane travel;
    Automobile travel; Boat travel;
    Train travel
Traveling With Your Pet, 383
Travel sickness, 396–97
Tree Hounds, 35
Trembling, 209–10
Tricks, 290–93
  learning, best breeds for, 73
Trimming, 163–64
Tubal ligation, 327
Turning over on the back, 257–58
Tweedsmouth, Lord, 33
Twitching, 142

Unbenched shows, 424–25
Underweight, 140–41
Undesired matings, 326
Union Cynologique Saint-Hubert, 70
United Kennel Club, 35, 69, 479, 484
United States
  canine population of, xxvi, 26
  hunting breeds in, 33–34

most popular breeds in, 47–48, 68
  purebreds in, 26
United States Obedience Classic, 463
Urination, act of, 257
Uterine inertia, 359
Utility Dog (U.D.), 462–65, 471, 477
Utility Dog Tracker (U.D.T.), 462, 477

Vaccination records, 89
Vertebral malformation, 86
Veterinarians, 79, 193–96
  annual visit to, 196
  selection of breed and, 74
  symptoms warranting visit to, 196–97
  whelping bitches and, 354
Veterinary certificates, 89
Vices, correcting, 293–306
  aggressiveness, 304–5
  barking, 293–94
  biting people, 301–4
  chasing cats, 297–98
  chasing livestock, 298
  destructiveness, 296
  digging, 298–99
  fearfulness, 305–6
  growling, 300–1
  incontinence, 295–96
  jealousy, 299–300
  jumping up on people, 294–95
  nipping at people, 301
  pulling on leash, 296–97
  roaming, 295
  shyness, 305–6
  snarling, 300–1
  spoiled dogs, 300
  stealing food, 299
Virginity, 319, 327
Visiting, 309–10
Vitamin requirements, 129
Vizslas, 34
Vomiting, 142–43, 211

Walks, 265–69
Walters, D. L., 490
War work, 495–97
Water requirements, 129, 137
Water Spaniels, 33
Weaning period, 119

Wehle, Robert G., 490
Weight loss, 212
Weimaraners, 24, 33
Welsh Cardigans, 42
Welsh Corgis, 15, 41, 42
Welsh Spaniels, 168
Welsh Springer Spaniels, 30
Welsh Terriers, 24, 55, 164
Western Kennel World, 77
West Germany, 71, 361, 400
West Highland White Terriers, 18,
  53–54, 526
Westminster Kennel Club, 422, 453
Whelping bitches, 349–67
  birth process, 355–58
  Caesarean sections, 356, 358–59,
    365
  culling the litter, 361–62
  diet, 350–51
  exercise, 351
  preparations for, 351–55
    bedding, 353
    prenatal body care, 353
    signs of labor, 354–55
    whelping box, 352–53
    whelping equipment, 353
    whelping room, 352
  problems with, 359–60

signs of pregnancy, 349–50
veterinarian in attendance, 354
Where to Buy, Board or Train a Dog,
  77, 405
Whining, 208
Whippet racing, 499
Whippets, 8, 10, 15, 18, 24, 34, 38,
  54
  clothing, 184
Whipworms, 215–16
White Bull Terriers, 85
White Collies, 17, 85
White German Shepherds, 17
White Poodles, 156
Winchester, A. M., 340
Wing and Shot (Wehle), 490
Wire-haired Fox Terriers, 11, 19,
  164–65
Wire-haired Pointing Griffons, 34
Working dogs, 3, 27, 41–52
Working Dogs of America (W.D.A.),
  490
Working instincts, 259–60
Wounds, 217–20

Yorkshire Terriers, 16, 60, 61, 415,
  453